THE COMPLETE CORRESPONDENCE OF
# SIGMUND FREUD
AND
# KARL ABRAHAM

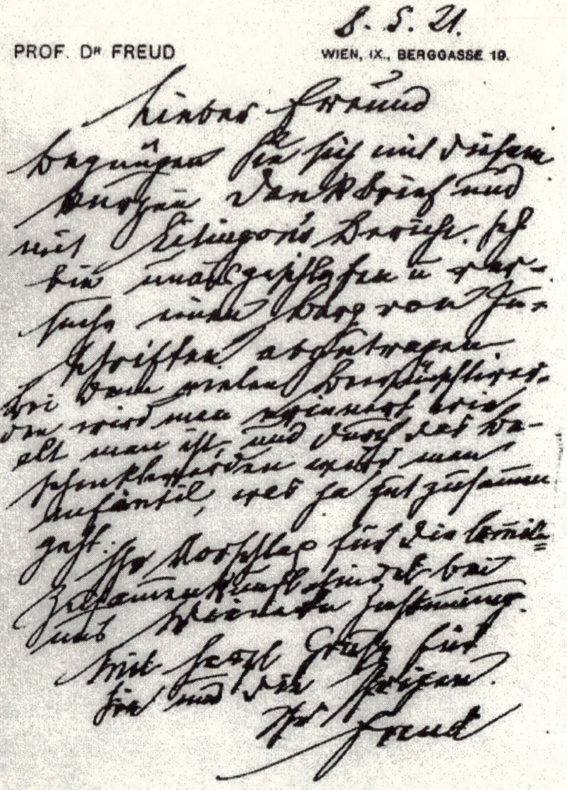
8. 5. 21.
PROF. Dr FREUD
WIEN, IX., BERGGASSE 19.

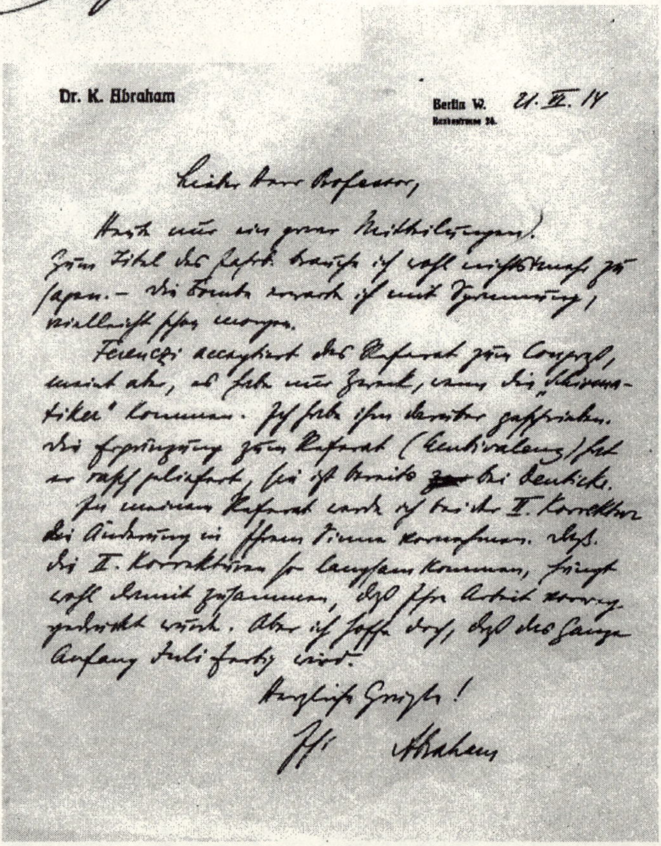
Dr. K. Abraham
Berlin W.
21. VI. 14

# THE COMPLETE CORRESPONDENCE OF
# SIGMUND FREUD
## AND
# KARL ABRAHAM

### 1907–1925
### Completed Edition

transcribed and edited by
*Ernst Falzeder*

translated by
*Caroline Schwarzacher*

with the collaboration of
*Christine Trollope & Klara Majthényi King*

Introduction by
*André Haynal & Ernst Falzeder*

LONDON       NEW YORK

First published in 2002 by
H. Karnac (Books) Ltd.
6 Pembroke Buildings, London NW10 6RE

A subsidiary of Other Press LLC, New York

Freud material copyright © 1965, 2002 by A. W. Freud et al.
Abraham material copyright © 1965, 2002 by the Estate of Grant Allan
Editorial material and annotations copyright © 2002 by Ernst Falzeder
Introduction copyright © 2002 by André Haynal
Translation copyright © 2002 by Caroline Schwarzacher

Facsimiles of letters on pp. ii, 442, and 495 and photographs on pp. xxii, xxv, and 453 reproduced by courtesy of the Freud Museum by agreement with Sigmund Freud Coprights Ltd.

*A Psycho-Analytic Dialogue. The Letters of Sigmund Freud and Karl Abraham 1907–1926* (ed. Hilda C. Abraham and Ernst Freud). London: The Hogarth Press and The Institute of Psycho-Analysis, 1965.

The rights of the authors, editor, and translator to be identified as the authors of this work have been asserted in accordance with §§ 77 and 78 of the Copyright Design and Patents Act 1988.

All rights reserved. No part of this publication may be reproduced, stored in a retrieval system, or transmitted, in any form or by any means, electronic, mechanical, photocopying, recording, or otherwise, without the prior written permission of the publisher.

**British Library Cataloguing in Publication Data**

A C.I.P. for this book is available from the British Library

ISBN 1 85575 051 1

10 9 8 7 6 5 4 3 2 1

Edited, designed, and produced by Communication Crafts

Printed in Great Britain

www.karnacbooks.com

# CONTENTS

ACKNOWLEDGEMENTS vii
PREFACE ix
INTRODUCTION
   André Haynal & Ernst Falzeder xix
EDITORIAL NOTE xxxi
TRANSLATOR'S NOTE xxxiii
ABBREVIATIONS xxxv

**Correspondence**

| | | |
|---|---|---|
| **1907** | Letters 1–13 | 1 |
| **1908** | Letters 14–57 | 16 |
| **1909** | Letters 58–80 | 74 |
| **1910** | Letters 81–98 | 101 |
| **1911** | Letters 99–118 | 124 |
| **1912** | Letters 119–147 | 145 |
| **1913** | Letters 148–189 | 173 |
| **1914** | Letters 190–262 | 214 |
| **1915** | Letters 263–285 | 295 |
| **1916** | Letters 286–305 | 322 |
| **1917** | Letters 306–330 | 341 |
| **1918** | Letters 331–348 | 368 |

| **1919** | Letters 349–367 | 390 |
| **1920** | Letters 368–385 | 415 |
| **1921** | Letters 386–406 | 437 |
| **1922** | Letters 407–415 | 452 |
| **1923** | Letters 416–427 | 463 |
| **1924** | Letters 428–469 | 479 |
| **1925** | Letters 470–500 | 533 |
| **1926** | Letter 501 | 568 |

*REFERENCES* 569
*INDEX* 609

# ACKNOWLEDGEMENTS

The *spiritus rector* of this work has been Cesare Sacerdoti, formerly of Karnac Books, who initiated this project and, despite serious difficulties, supported it throughout. I am deeply indebted to André Haynal in too many ways to be mentioned here; suffice it to say that without his help this project would not have been realized. My special thanks go to Caroline Schwarzacher, and for much more than the translation—in many respects this volume is a joint work by her and myself. Klara Majthényi King has been indefatigable and conscientious. I gratefully acknowledge the support and assistance of my friends and colleagues Carlo Bonomi, Florence Borner, Eva Brabant, Bettina Decke, Judith Dupont, Norman Elrod, Michael Good, Bernhard Handlbauer, the late Peter Heller, Axel Hoffer, Peter Hoffer, Robert Kramer, Marina Leitner, Patrick Mahony, William McGuire, Mark Paterson, the late Helene Rank Veltfort, Alvaro Rey de Castro, Paul Ries, Paul Roazen, Thomas Roberts, Elisabeth Roudinesco, Sonu Shamdasani, Giorgio Simonetto, Maud Struchen, and Urban Zerfaß.

E.F.

# PREFACE

In 1965, a selection of the letters of Sigmund Freud and Karl Abraham was published by The Hogarth Press and The Institute of Psycho-Analysis under the title, *A Psycho-Analytic Dialogue*. It was edited by Abraham's daughter Hilda, who also translated her father's letters, and Freud's son Ernst; Freud's letters were translated by Eric Mosbacher.[1] Following the letters to Wilhelm Fliess (Freud, 1950a), the correspondence with Oskar Pfister (Freud & Pfister, 1963), and a selection of letters to various correspondents (Freud, 1960a), it was the fourth volume of Freud letters to be published. There followed, before the end of the decade, the exchanges with Lou Andreas-Salomé (Freud & Andreas-Salomé, 1966), with Arnold Zweig (Freud & A. Zweig, 1968), with Georg Groddeck (Freud & Groddeck, 1970), and with Edoardo Weiss (Freud & Weiss, 1970).

None of these was a complete, unabridged edition: whole letters were left out, and passages that were considered unimportant, repetitive, indiscreet, offensive, or not fit for print for whatever other reason were deleted. Sometimes the place where something had been omitted was marked, sometimes not; in no case was it indicated how many words, phrases, or paragraphs had been omitted. There were occasions when the original wording was changed in order to cover up the omissions. Patients' names—and in some instances the names of analysts and colleagues—were made anonymous through the use either of their surname initial or of arbitrary letters or combinations of letters; in addition, the various editors did not use the same pseudonyms for the same analysands. The transcriptions of the originals on which these publications were based contained a number of errors, some of which altered or inverted the meaning. The editorial notes, where they existed at all, were sparse and sometimes misleading or wrong. The English translations generally added a further distortion. They often suffered from a poor command either of German—in particular of Freud's

Jewish–Viennese variety of it—or of English, as well as of the theory and history of psychoanalysis, psychiatry, neurology, arts, or literature. In addition, there was a tendency to water down or even to launder Freud's emphatic, often indiscreet, offensive, pejorative remarks about third persons. As a result, until the mid-1970s, what the reader—the English-speaking reader in particular—took to be Freud's letters was not Freud but a censored and distorted version of what he had actually written.

In the introduction of the 1965 edition of the Freud–Abraham letters, Hilda Abraham and Ernst Freud state:

> Omissions and cuts have been made for reasons of discretion where names and facts might lead to recognition of patients or their families, or where the people discussed would not be of any interest nowadays; furthermore to avoid repetition or details about the various psycho-analytical organisations which were of purely local interest and, finally, to avoid unimportant personal details about the writers and their families, which do not contribute to the knowledge and understanding of their personalities and of their scientific work. [p. vii]

When these abridged editions appeared, many of those involved were still alive, and the editors—not scholars, but children, friends, or disciples of the correspondents—had an understandable interest in preserving a modicum of privacy and discretion. Although Anna Freud did not edit any of her father's correspondence herself, she was the "grey eminence" behind most of those editions—such as being chiefly responsible for the selection of letters. Despite their shortcomings, these early editions were a valuable addition to the literature and served a purpose. Let us only remind ourselves, for example, of the first edition of the Fliess letters—saved by Marie Bonaparte, in contravention of Freud's intention to buy and destroy them—which instigated a large number of investigations on the origins of psychoanalysis.

In 1974, the nearly unabridged Freud–Jung letters appeared, meticulously edited by William McGuire (Freud & Jung, 1974). For the first time, there was a reliable and almost complete text[2] of a Freud correspondence, substantially enriched with generous and accurate notes. McGuire's editorial apparatus was used for years to come as one of the most important reference works on the background of psychoanalytic history. There followed the letters to Fliess (Freud, 1985c), Silberstein (Freud, 1989a), and Binswanger (Freud & Binswanger, 1992), all of them unabridged but still using pseudonyms. The three-volume Freud–Ferenczi correspondence (Freud & Ferenczi, 1992, 1996, 2000) and the letters exchanged with Ernest Jones (1993) were the first to include the full names of analysands. The present edition is, after the Fliess letters, the second to have been published first abridged and then in complete form, and the first completed edition to give all the names mentioned by the letter writers.

PREFACE xi

Why a complete new edition? Apart from making the whole story, not just a version *in usum delphini*, available to the public, such an unabridged version allows the reader to *compare* it with the expurgated one. Both volumes are not only highly important source material for the history of psychoanalysis but, at the same time, a reflection of changing attitudes towards how this material should be presented—so that they themselves represent a part of the making and construction of the history of psychoanalysis.

The omissions, alterations, and misunderstandings in the cut versions affect at times major and at times minor issues. But even these "minor" points are significant and may give us surprising insights. They are more than *lacunae* and unimportant trifles. Moreover:

> In its implications the distortion of a text resembles a murder: the difficulty is not in perpetrating the deed, but in getting rid of its traces. We might well lend the word *"Entstellung* [distortion]" the double meaning to which it has a claim but of which to-day it makes no use. It should mean not only "to change the appearance of something" but also "to put something in another place, to displace". [Freud, 1939a (1934–1938), p. 43]

But such a distortion—like repression—not only changes the appearance of the text and places the suppressed into a hidden place, it simultaneously preserves the concealed. Secrets do not evaporate in their well-guarded hiding places, and the traces leading to them stand out as fresh as when they were made.

While preparing this volume for publication, I had at my disposal both a microfilm of the original letters (which are held by the Library of Congress, Washington, DC) and a copy of an old typescript, on which the editors of *Dialogue* had obviously based their edition. In the typescript, the passages that were eventually not printed are struck out by hand, and it contains hand-written footnotes that were more or less taken over into the publication. It soon became clear that the printed version was not only a censored one but also full of errors, due partly to oversight—every now and then a word, half a sentence, or more is inadvertently missing—and partly to misreading by the transcriber(s). Let me give an example of each.

In *Dialogue*, in Freud's letter of 21 October 1907, the words *"der das Wesentliche ist"* [which is the essential characteristic of it] are missing after *"den Mechanismus, der ihn [den Traum] dement macht"* [the mechanism that makes the dream demented]. This is not only the essential characteristic of the dream mechanism, but also the essential statement in this sentence.

A misreading that at first seems minor occurred in an often-quoted line in Freud's letter of 23 July 1908. In *Dialogue*, this reads: "May I say that it is consanguineous, Jewish traits that attract me to you [*in Ihnen*]?" (p. 46). What Freud had actually written was *"in ihnen"* [in them]—referring to

Abraham's writings and, subtly, to a comment Abraham had made on 11 May 1908:

> I freely admit that I find it easier than Jung does to go along with you.[3] I, too, have always felt this intellectual kinship. After all, the Talmudic way of thinking cannot disappear in us just like that. Some days ago a small paragraph in *Jokes* strangely attracted me. When I looked at it more closely, I found that, in the technique of apposition and in its whole structure, it was completely Talmudic.

It was to this that Freud must have been referring when he wrote in July:

> I value the resolute tone and clarity of your writings so highly that I must ask you not to think that I overlook their beauty. May I say that it is consanguineous, Jewish traits that attract me to them [*in ihnen*]? We understand each other, don't we?

Thus, he refers not to an unspecific "Jewishness" that would attract him to Abraham, but to a particular point raised by the latter, implicitly acknowledging Abraham's view of Freud's "Talmudic" way of writing and returning the compliment. A difference that seemed negligible at first sight suddenly opens new perspectives.

As far as the deliberate omissions are concerned, we can look to the letters of the years 1924 and 1925 for examples. These years mark the climax of a serious conflict within the Secret Committee, with—to various degrees of involvement—Rank and Ferenczi on the one side and the Berliners (Abraham, Eitingon, Sachs) and Jones on the other. This conflict threatened to destroy the existence not only of this "old guard" but also of the psychoanalytic movement itself and of its journals. At the same time, a heated theoretical discussion was carried on, the outcome of which would influence for decades the intellectual history of psychoanalysis (cf. Falzeder, 1992; Leitner, 1998). It is to the credit of the editors of *Dialogue* that they did publish some of this material and also included two *Rundbriefe* [circular letters] of Freud's. Nevertheless, there is also much that was left out of the 1924 letters: remarks about the meeting of the Committee on the occasion of the 1924 Congress in Salzburg; a detailed account of this Congress—the first that Freud did not attend—by Abraham; various remarks about Rank and Ferenczi and about plans to re-establish the Committee and the *Rundbriefe* without Rank. In addition, most of what was written about preparations for a meeting of German analysts in Würzburg and the meeting itself was omitted, as were Freud's warning to Abraham not to go to America at the invitation of an American analysand of Freud's, Asch, "a pathological fool"; details about Abraham's and Freud's interest in the symbolic meaning of the number seven; a passage in which Abraham half defended Dr Felix Deutsch for not having disclosed to Freud the truth about his cancer; some commentaries on Alix Strachey's analysis with Abraham;

## PREFACE

remarks about Urbantschitsch, Federn, Helene Deutsch, Hitschmann, and others; as well as family news, holiday plans, and so on.

Most of Freud's and Abraham's emphases, such as exclamation marks and underlining, though they were in the transcript, were not carried through into print. In his letters of 1924 and 1925, Abraham usually refers to the other members of the Committee by their *first* names. In the publication, the *family* names were printed instead, and so the reader cannot appreciate the subtle change in Abraham's attitude when, in his letter of 12 November 1924, he reverts to the family name when speaking of the "divorce from Rank".

As for the 1925 letters, the most interesting among those that were left out concern, again, Rank and Ferenczi, but above all the "film affair" (cf. Ries, 1995). The correspondence ends on a bitter note. In his very last letter of 27 October 1925, the terminally ill Abraham stands up to Freud, defending his own opinions and decisions in a way that he had never done before. In a cut passage that runs over several pages, he reaffirms that nothing he—and Sachs—had done would justify Freud's "unpleasant aftertaste" (Freud to Abraham, 11 September 1925), that he had informed Freud, "even though I was already ill in bed", that "Sachs and I have not done the slightest thing that would have been open to ethical objections", that in contrast to Freud, he had a completely different (negative) opinion of Bernfeld and Storfer, that he rejected Freud's accusing him of "harshness", concluding with: "This whole affair is to me a bagatelle that I should have liked to pass over long ago, to return to the order of the day". Freud, in his rejoinder of 5 November 1925, maintains his position and directly accuses Abraham of not telling the truth: "I turned directly to Eitingon for information and from him I learned the *contrary*". The controversy could not be resolved—a few weeks later Abraham died.

One can divide the omissions as falling into three categories: (1) unimportant details; (2) references to third persons, to psychoanalytic politics, and to inner conflicts; and (3) intimate data about the letter-writers and their family members, colleagues, and patients.

Many of the omissions do, indeed, seem to be trifles at first sight. It could be argued that, on the whole, the reader of the abridged edition does not miss a great deal. Why should one not leave out references to "people of no interest nowadays", "repetitions", "details of purely local interest", and "unimportant personal details"? But, then, why should one? Unimportant in themselves, some might prove to be key pieces in a larger puzzle—and which these pieces may be, it is impossible to say in advance. To further complicate matters, sometimes these details were published, sometimes not. Why is an influenza not mentioned, but Freud's self-diagnosis—in connection with the dream of Irma's injection—of "sexual megalomania" (9 January 1908; *Dialogue*, p. 20) included? Why can we read about plans for one scientific project, but not about another? Or why do we learn about

Freud's general reaction to a work of Abraham's (7 June 1908; *Dialogue*, pp. 39–40), but not about his detailed discussion of it (17 July 1908)?

Often when a decision had been made not to print a question, a statement, some advice, an expression of thanks, and so on, the consequences of this were not systematically followed through. Thus, sometimes we find questions but not the answers, at other times we read answers to questions we have to reconstruct. While the correspondents themselves did conduct a very careful dialogue, meticulously referring and alluding to, expanding on, and answering each other's questions and statements—as in the case of the above-quoted remarks about Jewish traits in both their writings—the overall effect on the reader of *A Psycho-Analytic Dialogue* is rather the opposite of this title: the correspondence as published is not a real dialogue, let alone a psychoanalytic one.

More glaring are the omissions concerning third persons and conflicts within the psychoanalytic movement. Many of the passages that were left out refer to two areas of conflict and controversy—the Rank and the film affairs—that overshadowed the relationship between Freud and Abraham during the last years of the latter's life. Obviously, the editors of *Dialogue* tried to take the edge off the whole story by printing conciliatory remarks made by Freud and Abraham rather than acerbic ones, by omitting their more hostile remarks to each other and about third persons, and by deleting indiscretions. But theirs was essentially a thankless job, because they did have to include many other references to the mentioned conflicts; had they omitted these, the remaining torso would have made no sense. The effect is that the reader learns that there were serious controversies, but without being given many of the details, so that it is impossible to follow the events as they really developed.

The most delicate issues, however, are without doubt the passages dealing with intimate personal details and with patients. Oskar Pfister's letters of 1912 to Freud did not survive, for instance, because they were destroyed by Freud at Pfister's own request. The editors tried to omit references to why he wanted them destroyed, but the "secret" leaks through every now and then, and one need not be a Sherlock Holmes to make a good guess—reading, for instance, that some letters were not of "impersonal content" and that Pfister had been in danger of committing "stupidities" (Freud & Pfister, 1963, pp. 108–109). Freud's report of 1 June 1927 that he fulfilled the "hangman's job" of destroying these letters is duly reprinted, but not a paragraph in the same letter in which he assured Pfister:

> I have accommodated to your wish, although I have the intention to prevent a literary utilization of my correspondence through a certain expression of my will. I want to bother the folks [*Leutchen*] as little as possible with my person. To tell the very truth: the present generation really sickens me too much, and I have no reason to believe that the future generations will be different. [Library of Congress]

PREFACE

Freud's heirs were in the uncomfortable position of making "literary utilization" of his letters by publishing them while feeling forced to delete the paragraph in which Freud said that he wanted to prevent this. Freud's son Ernst was well aware of this, writing to co-editor Heinrich Meng on 26 October 1961: "I would rather not justify the publication [in the preface]. This is a delicate issue, and had we taken into account the wishes of my father, a publication would not have been possible at all" (Sigmund Freud Copyrights; Wivenhoe).

As for medical discretion, while we would all agree that confidentiality is a great good—perhaps the quintessence of discretion—the problem lies in the particulars. In view of the significance of the matter, some general remarks might be in order. Should one omit *all* references to *all* patients? Or just those to certain patients? Or include only those details that one considers not to be offensive? Or not abridge comments on cases, but keep the patients' names anonymous? After how long a period would it be possible to publish these names? Obviously, opinions diverge.

Some 70 years after the "Rat Man's" death, for example, Patrick Mahony published his name—Dr Ernst Lanzer—as well as those of his siblings (Mahony, 1986, pp. 2–3); nevertheless, in the following year, 1987, in the *Nachtragsband* to the German *Gesammelte Werke*, which included the original notes on this case (Freud, 1955a) in a new transcription, the pseudonyms originally chosen by James Strachey were kept. Curiously enough, this very edition also shows a facsimile of one page of the manuscript, in which a couple of names are clearly legible, even though they are still kept anonymous in the transcribed text on the facing page. While this was due to oversight, it nicely illustrates Freud's point that "the difficulty is not in perpetrating the deed, but in getting rid of its traces" (Freud, 1939a [1934–1938], p. 43). The same holds true for the policy of the Sigmund Freud Archives at the Library of Congress—namely, to make accessible only photocopies of the originals in which patients' names had been blotted out. Inevitably, sometimes those names were overlooked and were included, and we also know of at least one instance when the name of a literary figure was mistaken for that of a patient—and obscured.

Some editors provide even more information than did the correspondents themselves. In the 1986 edition of the letters between James and Alix Strachey from 1924 and 1925, not only are references to analysands not cut out, but abbreviations by the letter-writers are completed in brackets; thus we read, for instance: "It does seem horribly difficult to see what's best to be done. Perhaps fresh data will turn up—Mrs. D[isher] will solve all, or Mr. W[innicott] will die or f–ck his wife all of a sudden, & Mr. H[artsilver] likewise" (Meisel & Kendrick, 1986, p. 166).

And what about analyses between colleagues? Would it be acceptable to make public the fact of a training analysis, as opposed to the analysis of a patient? But is there a clear dividing line between a "training" analysis and a psychoanalytic "cure", and if so, where can it be drawn? Actually, "training" and "treatment" were inseparably linked from the beginning (cf. Falzeder, 1994b), and it would be a distortion of history if one were, in retrospect, to treat the two as separate issues.

There is also at least one instance in Freud's writings when the name of an *analyst* was omitted by the editors. In the posthumously published paper, "Psycho-analysis and Telepathy" (Freud, 1941d), we read: "The girl . . . behaved more and more in a contradictory manner, and it was decided that she should be analysed" (p. 192); the original manuscript includes: ". . . by Dr. Deutsch".[4]

The editors of the abridged editions were clearly guided by the assumption that what should be published were primarily theoretical ideas and discussions, and to some extent also personal affairs and opinions, where they shed a humane or humorous light on the correspondents. They felt that more intimate details about them and their analysands, as well as outright aggressive remarks made by them, should be left out. As a result we find, in the remaining text, very little undiluted love and hate, but much sublimation. Such a policy has at least two side effects: First, it tends to backfire: this is the soil on which phantasies and speculations flourish out of proportion, often far exceeding the all-too-human reality. Second, it has an important consequence—a distinct, if implicit, dividing line is drawn between theory on the one hand and personal experience on the other. The former is seen as fit for the public, the latter as in need of discretion. But just as sexuality does not enter "into children at the age of puberty in the way in which, in the Gospel, the devil entered into the swine" (cf. Matthew, 8, 28–34; Mark, 5, 11–17; Luke, 8, 32–33; Freud, 1910a [1909], p. 42), so psychoanalytic theory does not enter into analysts' heads like a demon from nowhere—it springs precisely from their personal and intimate experiences. In cutting these out, the missing links between the theoreticians and their theories—psychoanalytic epistemology and the "context of discovery"—are obscured.

One final reflection might be appropriate. In the Freud–Ferenczi correspondence, the analysand about whose intimate life and troubles we learn most, in a very indiscreet way indeed, is Sándor Ferenczi himself. This also holds true, to a somewhat lesser extent, for the analyst, Sigmund Freud. Their whole correspondence revolves around their quasi-analytical and analytical relationship, and its publication, however abridged, would have been impossible had one opted to treat that with discretion.[5] Or should one have published it as the "Freud/X letters" (Shamdasani, 1996, p. 231)? Or even—given the fact that there are numerous details about Freud as a patient (although not an analytic one)—as the "X/Y letters"?![6] As far as I know, no one has so far objected to the publication of these letters as such; on the contrary, they were generally greeted enthusiastically by the scientific community and the public, although there were a few objections against the publication of patients' names—but not those of Freud and

Ferenczi (Eissler, 1995; Fichtner, 1994; cf. Haynal, 1995). This is a double standard: one has to decide to publish the correspondence as it is, or not at all.

It is noteworthy that Freud himself, shortly before his death, took a very liberal stance on this question: "When . . . an individual whose life and works are of significance to the present and future has died, he becomes by common consent a proper subject for biography and previous limitations no longer exist" (Freud, 1966b [1938], p. xiv). It is my conviction that the best way to deal with the situation today, more than a century after the birth of psychoanalysis, is to make accessible and publish primary material. Although the situation is still far from being satisfactory, there are undeniable signs that archival restrictions have been loosened. Moreover, important writings and letters, such as Freud's neuroscientific papers, his correspondence with various family members, with Max Eitingon and Otto Rank, as well as the circular letters of the Secret Committee, are now being prepared for publication. The final goal is, naturally, a complete, unabridged, annotated edition of Freud's writings and letters—although there is still a long way to go if we consider estimates that Freud wrote, and received, more than 20,000 letters during his lifetime.

*Ernst Falzeder*

## Notes

1. Freud & Abraham (1965), cited hereafter as *Dialogue*. Mosbacher appeared under the pseudonym Bernard Marsh (cf. Roazen, 1975, p. 552).
2. Some rude remarks in Jung's letters about Eugen Bleuler were omitted at the request of the Jung family, out of consideration for Bleuler's son, Manfred, then living. In accordance with the heirs' wishes, patients' names were made anonymous (A, B, C, etc.). There are plans for a new edition, filling in the few suppressed passages and giving the full names of the analysands (McGuire, letter to the editor, 4 March 1996).
3. Wrongly translated in *Dialogue* as: "I find it easier to go along with you rather than with Jung".
4. This manuscript (Library of Congress) further contains unpublished passages about this and another case (cf. Falzeder, 1994a).
5. This is, in fact, one reason for the delay in publication. Although the heirs had already agreed decades earlier to the publication of a selection of the letters, nothing came of it because of the impossibility of such a selection (cf. Haynal, 1993).
6. To the best of my knowledge, no one has protested against the publication of intimate details in Freud's medical record (e.g. Jones, 1957; Romm, 1983; Schur, 1972). Schur discusses the question of discretion at length, concluding that it would not be in keeping with Freud's spirit to withhold any details of his suffering and dying.

# INTRODUCTION

*André Haynal & Ernst Falzeder*

Karl Abraham was a central figure in the early history of psychoanalysis. He succeeded in making his own views the prevalent ones, sometimes even against those of Freud, leaving his imprint on the development of psychoanalysis for decades to come. He prevailed over all his opponents and competitors within the movement: Alfred Adler, Wilhelm Stekel, Carl Gustav Jung, Otto Rank, Sándor Ferenczi, Ernest Jones. He succeeded Jung as president of the International Psychoanalytic Association and as editor of its official journal. He contributed important elaborations of Freud's ideas, and he systematized and formulated them in a way that seemed more exact and could more easily be taught to others. He actively sought to establish relations with other disciplines and institutions—sexology, academia, psychiatry, pedagogy, general medicine—or public opinion in general, and in Berlin he developed and implemented, with Max Eitingon and Ernst Simmel, the so-called tripartite model of psychoanalytic training (personal analysis, seminars, supervision) that is still in existence today. Among his pupils and analysands one can mention Helene Deutsch, Edward Glover, James Glover, Melanie Klein, Sándor Radó, and Theodor Reik.

Nevertheless, Abraham's life has aroused relatively little interest so far, and there is no full-scale biography of him.[1] Abraham may not have the appeal of the enigmatic Max Eitingon, the charming, original, generous character of Sándor Ferenczi, Otto Rank's deep humanistic culture and immense dedication to the chores of "the Cause", or the masterful proficiency in institutional matters of Ernest Jones. But he impressed his colleagues with his rigour, his earnestness, his precision in scientific matters, his unrelenting work, and his deep conviction of the truth and the importance of the Freudian theory and Cause [*die Sache*]—of all of which this correspondence gives a faithful image.

For his excellent knowledge in the fields mentioned, he needed a profound psychiatric training, and he found it at the Burghölzli, the Cantonal Sanatorium and Psychiatric University Clinic in Zurich, Switzerland. "Abraham was first assistant physician [at the Burghölzli] from 1 Jan. to 11 Nov. 1907, under Jung as senior staff physician" (ed. note, Freud & Jung, 1974, p. 76) and Eugen Bleuler as director. The Burghölzli was founded in 1870, based on the plans of Wilhelm Griesinger (1817–1868) and Heinrich Hoffmann (1809–1894, author of the well-known children's book, *Der Struwwelpeter*). Following Bernhard Aloys von Gudden[2] (director 1870–1872), Gustav Huguenin (1873–1874), Eduard Hitzig (1875–1879), and August Forel (1879–1898), Eugen Bleuler [born 1857, died 1939] was its fifth director (1898–1927). Abraham had come to Zurich, because "[n]o clinic in Germany could have offered [him] even a fraction of what I have found here" (7A, 13 October 1907). In him, as in Eugen Bleuler and Carl Gustav Jung, Freud found the collaborators he needed—collaborators who were well versed in psychiatry, which he himself, as a trained neurologist, was not. Freud wrote his book on Schreber (on schizophrenia) under the influence of and in response to Jung. Bleuler, Jung, and Abraham not only opened the psychiatric world to psychoanalysis, they also provided an academic setting and background with its scientific prestige.

Contrary to widespread belief, it was Bleuler, not Jung, who had introduced psychoanalysis at his clinic. "It was me, after all, who called Jung's attention to [psychoanalysis]"—as Bleuler himself later pointed out to Freud (20 November 1912, Library of Congress). Bleuler recruited staff open to dynamic psychiatry in general and to this new discipline in particular, among them C. G. Jung, to whom Bleuler offered a position as assistant physician [*Assistenzarzt*] even before the latter had finished his studies (15 July 1900, ETH Zürich, Archives Sonu Shamdasani).

The Burghölzli quickly attracted a large number of young physicians and psychiatrists as interns or members of staff. In the German-speaking countries, the only clinic and name rivalling that of Bleuler and the Burghölzli was that of Kraepelin in Munich, but Kraepelin's classifying approach to psychiatry was clearly losing out among the younger generation to the dynamic views endorsed by those at the Burghölzli. In short, for any ambitious, open-minded young psychiatrist, the Burghölzli was *the* place to go. Indeed, Zurich—that liberal, metropolitan city, then also Albert Einstein's refuge—became one of the main recruiting centres for the nascent psychoanalytic movement. Most among the first generation of those who practised psychoanalysis as a profession came to Freud via Jung and Bleuler—among them Roberto Greco Assagioli, Ludwig Binswanger, Trigant Burrow, Abraham Arden Brill, Charles Macfie Campbell, Imre Décsi, Max Eitingon, Sándor Ferenczi, Johann Jakob Honegger, Smith Ely Jelliffe, Ernest Jones, Alphonse Maeder, Herman Nunberg, Johan H. W. van Ophuijsen, Nikolai J. Ossipow, Franz Riklin, Hermann Rorschach, Tatiana Rosenthal, Leonhard

Seif, Eugenie Sokolnicka, Sabina Spielrein, Philipp Stein, Wolf Stockmayer, Johannes Irgens Stromme, Jaroslaw Stuchlík, G. Alexander Young—and Karl Abraham.

The beginning of the relationship between Sigmund Freud and Karl Abraham cannot be understood without taking into account these factors, the complexity of their environment, the rivalries within it, and especially their respective relationship to a third party, Carl Gustav Jung. In the end, as we know, Abraham became one of Freud's staunchest supporters and closest collaborators, whereas Freud had not one good word left for "the brutal saintly Jung" (235F, 26 July 1914). In the beginning, however, Freud was enamoured by Jung and deliberately seduced him to become his crown prince. Although he valued Abraham's early contributions and his courage to defend in public Freud's views, particularly his libido theory, there is no doubt that Jung was much more important to him and closer to his heart. Jung could give Freud something that Abraham evidently could not.

One great advantage Jung had over Abraham in Freud's eyes was his not being Jewish. Freud was gratified by the support of his first powerful psychiatric followers, Bleuler, Jung, and Ludwig Binswanger, allaying his fears that psychoanalysis might become "a Jewish national affair" (28F, 3 May 1908). He went to great lengths to secure their staying within the fold, and he had great plans as to their roles in a psychoanalytic movement.

All this was not without ambivalence, and it was also soon subject to change. Freud stressed the common background that linked him to Abraham. Perhaps more than in any other correspondence Freud conducted with a follower, the repeated evocation of their Jewishness plays a central role. Abraham felt that he could make a career neither in a German nor in a Swiss institution, because "as a Jew in Germany and as a foreigner in Switzerland, I have not advanced beyond a junior position in the past seven years" (5A, 6 October 1907). The strained relationship with Jung, with undertones of a conflict between Jung's emphatically Christian background (he was a Protestant pastor's son) and Abraham's Jewish one, probably contributed to this. The situation was complicated by the fact that Jung was Abraham's superior in the clinic's hierarchy. In short, they did not get along well at all with each other—and this from the very start.

When Freud, who had not yet met Abraham in person, asked Jung: "What is he like?" (10 July 1907; Freud & Jung, 1974, p. 75), it took Jung more than a month to respond that Abraham was not ". . . quite [his] type, . . . intelligent but not original, highly adaptable, but totally lacking in psychological empathy, . . . very unpopular with the patients. I would ask you to subtract a personal touch of venom from this judgment." Very early, Jung was also concerned about matters of priority: "[H]e pricks up his ears whenever Bleuler and I talk about what we are investigating, etc. He then comes up with a publication" (19 August 1907; p. 78).

*Karl Abraham (1912)*

For the time being, Freud accepted Jung's unflattering description of Abraham but already pointed out two factors that would continue to strengthen his relationship with the latter and put a strain on that with Jung: "I was predisposed in Abraham's favour by the fact that he attacks the sexual problem head on", and "By the way, is he a descendant of his eponym?" (27 August 1907; Freud & Jung, 1974, pp. 79–80).[3] Jung assured Freud that Abraham was indeed "what his name implie[d]" and again complained about the missing "emotional rapport" with him. Although Jung apologized for having "painted Abraham . . . in too dark colours", two sentences later he used some black paint again, speaking of Abraham's "mild ideas of persecution about [Jung]" (29 August 1907; p. 81).

In the following months Freud manoeuvred between Jung and Abraham, confiding to one about the other while assuring each of his affection. There is no question, however, that at that time he still preferred Jung over Abraham.

In November 1907 Abraham moved to Berlin to set up in private practice as a psychoanalyst and psychiatrist. Freud encouraged him: "[T]hat as a Jew you will encounter more difficulties will have the effect, as it has with all of us, of bringing out all your productive capabilities" (6F, 8 October 1907). Freud would have to welcome Abraham's move: it would mean the implantation of psychoanalysis in the capital of the German *Reich* and probably also in the non-Jewish bourgeoisie outside Vienna. It is true that when this mission was accomplished and Abraham showed himself not so much the obedient pupil as the president of the Berlin Psychoanalytic Society, who expressed his own point of view—also in the name of his group, such as in the "film affair" (see Preface)—their relationship deteriorated. Freud did not appreciate pupils who would not work for the Cause in the manner he conceived it. . . .

Shortly after his move, Abraham visited Freud in Vienna. Abraham was overwhelmed by being "surrounded by so much kindliness and at the same time so much culture" and by Freud's parting presents, two Egyptian figures from his collection (13A, 21 December 1907). Freud reported to Jung that he found Abraham "[m]ore congenial than [Jung's] account of him, but there is something inhibited about him, no dash. At the crucial moment he can't find the right word" (21 December 1907; Freud & Jung, 1974, p. 105). Even so, Jung was jealous that Abraham seemed "to have been more forthcoming with [Freud] than with" himself, and he sarcastically attributed this to "the 'self-preservation complex' of our colleague" (2 January 1908; p. 106). Freud countered that he did find Abraham "very nice" and that he could "understand only too well" the source of the latter's inhibition: "the fact of being a Jew . . ." (14 January 1908; p. 109).

The conflict between Abraham and Jung came fully to the fore at the first international meeting of psychoanalysts, in April 1908, in Salzburg, Austria. It is worth while to take a closer look at that controversy, which occurred barely a year after the start of the correspondence between Freud and Abraham and just a few months after their first meeting. It set much of the tone of their future relationship and already showed a pattern and certain characteristics that were to repeat themselves in other conflicts to come.

Not surprisingly, Abraham and Jung—both of them psychiatrists—spoke on what Bleuler had termed "schizophrenia" (until then generally called "dementia præcox"), the central research topic at the Burghölzli. Abraham's paper was on "Psychosexual Differences between Dementia Praecox and Hysteria" (Abraham, 1908[11]), Jung's "On Dementia praecox". Abraham's "main idea", in Jones's succinct summary,

> was the suggestion that disturbances of the ego functions could be purely secondary to disturbances in the sphere of the libido, in which event it might be possible to apply Freud's libido theory to the elucidation of dementia præcox. . . . In it the libido is withdrawn from objects—the opposite of hysteria, where there is an exaggerated object cathexis—and applied to the

self. To this he traced the delusions of persecution and megalomania. . . . In contradistinction from hysteria, the psycho-sexual peculiarity of dementia præcox lies in an inhibited development at the auto-erotic level, with consequently a tendency to regress to this level. [Jones, 1926, pp. 22–23]

In Abraham's own words, "The psychosexual characteristic of dementia præcox is the return of the patient to auto-erotism, and the symptoms of his illness are a form of auto-erotic activity" (Abraham, 1908[11], pp. 73–74). And "Auto-erotism is . . . the feature which distinguishes dementia præcox from hysteria" (p. 77).

If Abraham's paper sought to colonize schizophrenia for the Freudian libido theory, Jung's was an attempt to come to terms with the tricky question of a physiological versus psychic ætiology of this illness. Although Jung's lecture has not been published, it is possible to deduce much of its content from his own abstract (Jung, 1910) and from the Freud–Jung and Freud–Abraham correspondences. Like Abraham, Jung dealt with the differences between neurosis (such as hysteria) and psychosis (such as schizophrenia), but he arrived at a different conclusion. While stating that Freud's theory was important for a psychological understanding of schizophrenia and that it could explain and give meaning to its symptoms, he pointed to the similarity of, in Janet's (Jung's teacher) words, the "*abaissement du niveau mental*" [lowering of the level of mental functioning] in both schizophrenia and states induced by intoxication or poisoning. Thus Jung ventured that a still unknown "toxin" could be an ætiological factor in dementia præcox. In schizophrenia, however, this *abaissement* was not generalized, as it was in the analogous cases of intoxication or diseases of the brain, but it affected mostly "complex"-related areas, and it could also be exacerbated or improved by psychic and environmental factors. Jung left open the question of which of the two factors—the psychological or physiological—was the primary ætiological one.

In essence, Jung restated the position taken in his previously published book on the subject, *The Psychology of Dementia Præcox* (1907)—that landmark in the psychological understanding of the illness which as late as 1936 was called by the Freudian Abraham A. Brill, its translator, "the cornerstone of modern interpretative psychiatry" (Brill, 1936, p. ix[4]). There Jung stated:

> [T]he mechanisms of Freud are not comprehensive enough to explain why a dementia præcox originates rather than a hysteria; we must therefore postulate that in the case of dementia præcox there is a specific resultant of the affects (*toxine*?), which causes the definite fixation of the complex by injuring the sum total of the psychic functions. But one cannot, however, dispute the possibility that the "intoxication" might appear also as primary as a result of "somatic" causes and then seize the last complex which happened to be there and change it pathologically. [Jung, 1907, p. 32]

*Sigmund Freud (1918)*

It should be noted that Jung's position is more sophisticated than has usually been attributed to him: although he did leave open the possibility that such a "toxin" could in fact be the main ætiological factor, he favoured the idea that an intoxication was the secondary *result* of the affects involved, influencing, in turn, the development of the disease by a "fixation of the complex". In that sense, Jung's is a very "modern" view, grappling with a question not satisfactorily solved even today, and it clearly shows him as one of the leading experts in the field.

Both Abraham's and Jung's papers, however, are conspicuously lacking in certain respects. Jung did not pay more than lip service to Freud and, above all, did not draw the obvious conclusion that his and Freud's—and Abraham's—views could be easily reconciled if the "toxin" in question were somehow connected to, or even identical with, the "libido"—a strange omission indeed, in a paper delivered by the heir apparent at the first congress in honour of Freud.

As for Abraham, in his paper he did not mention Jung's and Bleuler's, that is, his former superiors', pioneering work in the field at all. Only in the printed version, and only at Freud's insistence, did he insert two footnotes on the subject—one a reference to Jung's book, the other an acknowledgement of Abraham's great debt to Freud, adding: "I have *also* been able to formulate many points more clearly through discussion with Prof. Bleuler and Dr. Jung in the course of my work at the Zürich Psychiatric Clinic" (Abraham, 1908[11], p. 65; italics added). The only other reference to Jung is indirect: if Abraham's—and Freud's—view of an "abnormal psychosexual constitution in the direction of auto-erotism" as the explanation for the manifestations of schizophrenia were correct, Abraham wrote, this "would render the recently discussed toxin theory unnecessary" (p. 78).

Jung was furious, although the reason he gave is confusing. He accused Abraham of *plagiarism*. "In Salzburg", Jung wrote to Freud, "I was able to prevent a scandal only by imploring a certain gentleman, who wanted to shed light on the sources of A.[braham]'s lecture, to abandon his plan" (7 May 1908; Freud & Jung, 1974, p. 149). Abraham was plagiarizing him and Bleuler, Jung implied, by presenting as his own views that he had learned at the Burghölzli. Abraham's paper did *not*, in fact, espouse the Burghölzli view; it presented, for the first time in public, *Freud's* competing theory on the ætiology of schizophrenia. According to Jones, "the main idea of the paper . . . as Abraham himself avowed, emanated from a conversation with Freud (his first one)" (Jones, 1926, pp. 22–23). But Abraham may well have heard about Freud's idea first from Jung, to whom Freud had spoken of it already in early 1907. "I threw out the suggestion", Freud wrote to Jung, "*he heard it from you* and corresponded with me about it as well" (10 May 1908; Freud & Jung, 1974, p. 150; italics added). In any case, Abraham was not plagiarizing Jung, but Freud—either in Jung's version, or in Freud's own.

Jung, on the other hand, played down or even questioned the very ideas he accused Abraham of plagiarizing. Perhaps Jung's anger and disappointment also stemmed from the fact that his former student not only failed completely to mention his teacher's previous work in the field (in which he had participated) but even suggested that his—that is, Freud's—new view would make Jung's theory obsolete. What Jung may have felt to be Abraham's aggression was not that Abraham failed to acknowledge the strong influence Jung had had on him, but that Abraham had already freed himself from that influence and no longer bothered to mention it at all.

As a matter of fact, the controversy between Abraham and Jung amounted to a "war by proxies". Both spoke not only for themselves, but also for

Freud and Bleuler, respectively—and let us repeat that Abraham had himself been a member of the Burghölzli team. Abraham acted in Freud's stead and Jung, to a somewhat lesser extent, in Bleuler's. Bleuler had not spoken at all at the meeting; he left it to Jung to represent the Burghölzli. Freud had actively encouraged Abraham to present his paper and even assured him that it would not bring him into conflict with Jung. "Actually I became involved in the conflict quite innocently", Abraham wrote to Freud. "In December I asked you whether there was any risk of my colliding with Jung on this subject, as you had communicated your ideas to him as well. You dispelled my doubts at the time" (30A, 11 May 1908).

Thus it seems as if Freud himself had brought about the very conflict he then deplored. He then tried to obfuscate that fact and to put the blame on Abraham and Jung. In the aftermath of the Congress, Freud reinterpreted the conflict as a *priority dispute between Abraham and Jung*, a conflict over who had been the first to solve the riddle of schizophrenia with the help of psychoanalysis. Simultaneously, however, Freud made it perfectly clear that the actual question of priority was with *himself*, thus ridiculing the alleged priority conflict between his followers. It was his own idea, which he had given to both men as a gift: "I gave the same suggestion to each of you" (44F, 23 July 1908). But obviously Freud would have preferred Jung, not Abraham, to espouse that suggestion in public. In fact, Freud criticized Abraham for making use of the idea while chiding Jung for *not* using it. To Jung, Freud wrote that Abraham would have been completely within his rights to use it: "I only regret that *you* didn't appropriate it" (10 May 1908; Freud & Jung, 1974, p. 150). To Abraham: "[I]t would have shown greater delicacy of feeling not to have made use of [my idea]. . . . In picking it up, you are to an extent forcing [Jung] to the other side" (44F, 23 July 1908). Freud wanted to conquer psychiatry with the help of a brilliant and ebullient Gentile with excellent connections, not with a young Jewish doctor, dedicated but without "dash"—at the difficult beginnings of his own practice.[5]

As far as Abraham is concerned, it is interesting to see how quickly and wholeheartedly he took over an idea of Freud's, how he put it into an apparently precise, almost formulaic form, and how he then used it to counter, or attack, Freud's crown prince. We can find a similar pattern in Abraham's later conflicts. In any case, these early rivalries, with Jung and, later, with Rank and with Ferenczi, had a great influence on the subsequent history of psychoanalysis as a movement and a theory.

\* \* \*

Abraham's early work already shows him a master in the field. Psychoanalytic understanding of, and research into, psychoses is what Freud entrusted him with as a mission, and this is what came to be central to his life's work. It also paved the way for others, particularly for his pupil, Melanie Klein, whose theories cannot be understood without the basis laid down by Abraham—incidentally, with the approval of and in agreement with Freud.

Naturally, Abraham did it in his own style. It may be characteristic that Freud, at the beginning of their collaboration, recommended that he change "the sober scientific form" of his work on *Dreams and Myths* (Abraham, 1909, 14) "to the style of a lecture or essay" (26F, 29 April 1908); Abraham replied that first the whole "must rest on a scientific basis before it is ready to be dealt with in an essay" (33A, 27 May 1908). In fact, this correspondence does show him as a precise and rather dry writer. The portrayal of him as an "uninspired plodder" (*trockener Schleicher*—see note 2) may have been inspired by animosity, but we can also understand how one could arrive at such a description. Without doubt, Abraham's work is characterized by a striving for exactitude and precision, even if, with the passing of the years, his style acquires somewhat more freedom. The ideas and hypotheses he permits himself to put forward are, in any case, supplements to a doctrine and rather dogmatic themselves.

Ever so often Abraham asks Freud whether the latter has any experience with one or another illness or whether he knows of data in the scientific literature about it—much as in the traditional relationship between the clinical medical teacher and his pupil. Abraham's way of thinking and describing is based on the *nosographic* tradition in psychiatry and medicine. He gives us much information about the behaviour of the patient and about his or her "complexes" but little about what today we would consider specifically "psychoanalytic"—how the analyst experiences the patient and how the interplay of images and phantasies of one about the other develops.

This should not diminish our appreciation of Abraham's important contributions. He fulfilled the hopes vested in him through his research and publications on psychiatric disorders, starting with his work "On the Significance of Sexual Trauma in Childhood for the Symptomatology of Dementia Praecox" (1907[9]), followed by "The Psycho-Sexual Differences between Hysteria and Dementia Praecox" (1908[11]), his paper on manic-depressive psychosis (1911[26]), and the one on ejaculatio praecox (1917[54]), among others. After the loss of Bleuler and Jung, Abraham remained for some time Freud's only important specialist in psychiatry.

He does not centre, as for instance Ferenczi did, on the actual *clinical* situation but tries to come to a *theoretical* understanding, be it of depression, schizophrenia, or of obsessional neurosis. He repeatedly reverts to his interest in manic-depressive states and the stages of libidinal organization. He searches for the links between grief, mourning, depression, and obsession, stressing the notion of ambivalence, a concept that originated with Eugen Bleuler and the Burghölzli. In this, he precedes Freud, as hardly any others of his followers had done. Freud's "Mourning and Melancholia" (1917e [1915]) takes up Abraham's main concerns, and Abraham, in turn, refers to Freud's work in his studies of the years 1922[81], 1923[87], and 1924[105].

If depression is linked to the loss of an object, obsession tries to avoid loss by anal control. In his work of 1917, Freud took over Ferenczi's important concept of *introjection* (Ferenczi, 1909[67]), whereas as late as 1924, Abraham still had reservations about using this concept for the explanation of melancholia. Could this be the reason why he seems to ignore Freud's paper of 1923 on the second topic (1923b), introducing what later came to be called the structural model (superego, ego, id)?

All this led Abraham to publish his ideas on psychosexual development—for example, "The First Pregenital Stage of the Libido" (1916[52]), "Contributions to the Theory of the Anal Character" (1921[70]), culminating in his synthesis of 1924, *A Short Study of the Development of the Libido, Viewed in the Light of Mental Disorders* [105]. He tried to establish a causal connection between certain pathologies and developmental stages of the libido. This "scientific" and appealing view has had a great influence on psychoanalytic theory, even as late as the work of Erik H. Erikson (1950). During recent decades, however, research on direct infant and caretaker–child observation has radically put into question Abraham's position, and clinical psychoanalysts, too, find it not always sufficiently flexible to make use of it in their own practice. Yet many find it still worth while to discuss the classical sequence of libidinal stages as laid out by Freud and rigidified by Abraham, who further divided them into sub-stages. The inspiring force of Abraham's ideas on later generations of psychoanalysts should, however, not be underestimated.

Abraham, despite certain frictions and conflicts a true and faithful follower to the end, died in 1925, at the age of 48 years [1877–1925]. Paradoxically, during his terminal illness Abraham was assisted by Freud's one-time friend, with whom he had completely fallen out and against whom he had warned Abraham: Wilhelm Fliess (cf. 102F, 13 February 1911; 106F, 3 March 1911). The cause of Abraham's death remains a mystery: whether it was a septic broncho-pneumonia and a terminal subphrenic abscess caused by injury to the pharynx from a fish-bone, as the traditional view has it, or perhaps an undiagnosed lung cancer remains an open question.

## Notes

1. Although his daughter, Hilda, wanted to write one, it remained a sketch (H. Abraham, 1974).
2. He drowned trying to rescue his patient, King Ludwig II of Bavaria.
3. Freud summed up Jung's description of Abraham: "You make him out to be something of an 'uninspired plodder'" [*trockener Schleicher*] (Freud & Jung, 1974, p. 79; with

reference to Goethe's *Faust I*, 521). Although Anna Freud wanted this remark to be omitted in the publication of the Jung letters *"under all circumstances"* (in Shamdasani, 1997, p. 362), it was kept (as was most of the often satirical and vituperative rhetoric) by William McGuire despite her protests.

4. This is unusual praise coming from Brill, who usually did not mince his words when dealing with other "dissidents"—as in the cases of Rank or Ferenczi, for instance.

5. Freud's vacillating and ambivalent attitude may also be linked to the fact that the whole question of schizophrenia/paranoia was connected, for him, to his troubled relationship with Wilhelm Fliess, to whose behaviour Freud attributed his theory of paranoia (Freud & Jung, 1974, pp. 120–121).

# EDITORIAL NOTE

The present edition is as complete as possible. All letters, postcards, telegrams, notes, and enclosures that have been preserved and could be found are reprinted without omissions or pseudonyms. It is a new edition in that the transcription, translation, and footnotes that appeared in the abbreviated publication of 1965 have all been replaced (see Preface).

The project was accomplished in several stages. First, I made a transcription, based on a microfilm of the German originals. Second, a translation into English was made (see Translator's Note). Third, editorial footnotes were added. My guiding line was to give the contemporary reader information about anything with which she or he might not be familiar: persons, events, literary and scientific works, quotations, cryptoquotations, allusions, and so on. Such annotation can only be an approximation: the specialist, on the one hand, might find some notes superfluous or redundant, where another reader, on the other, might want more information on some points.

Some minor changes were made to facilitate readability and understanding: titles of books and journals, abbreviated expressions, and words—like Freud's "u" and Abraham's "&" for "and"—were usually spelled out. Some characteristic abbreviations, however, such as the Greek letters $\Psi\alpha$ for psychoanalysis, or *Ucs.* for unconscious, have been left intact. Dates at the head of letters and the letterheads have been standardized. Words that the writers of the letters had underlined have been reproduced in italics, as have terms that remain in German or in other foreign languages. Anything added to the original text appears in square brackets.

*Ernst Falzeder*

# TRANSLATOR'S NOTE

In 1965, a selection of the Freud–Abraham correspondence appeared under the title, *A Psychoanalytic Dialogue,* translated by Hilda Abraham and Eric Mosbacher (under the pseudonym Bernard Marsh). In preparation of a completed edition, the remaining letters were translated by Christine Trollope. Originally, my task had been to put these two translations together and to smooth out any inconsistencies or to correct occasional errors. More and more, however, this developed into a new translation of its own. Nevertheless, Christine Trollope's preliminary work provided an excellent basis to proceed from. From the beginning, Klara King's help far exceeded her role as a copy editor. It goes without saying that I assume sole responsibility for the version as printed.

I have tried to keep as close as possible to the style and meaning of the original. In cases of doubt I opted for a translation close to the German original rather than for fluency in idiomatic English. For technical terms, I generally used those chosen by James Strachey et al. for *The Standard Edition of the Complete Psychological Works of Sigmund Freud*; in some instances, however, I preferred the terms chosen by Peter Hoffer in his translation of the Freud–Ferenczi letters (1992, 1996, 2000) and made a note to that effect.

I gratefully acknowledge the support and assistance of Ernst Falzeder, William McGuire, Mary Schwarzacher, and Gail Polacsek.

*Caroline Schwarzacher*

# ABBREVIATIONS

| | |
|---|---|
| BL | Butler Library, Columbia University, New York, NY |
| Cs. | the Conscious |
| FM | Freud Museum, London |
| G.W. | Sigmund Freud, *Gesammelte Werke, Chronologisch geordnet*. London, Frankfurt/M.: Imago Publishing Co., S. Fischer |
| *Imago* | *Imago, Zeitschrift für Anwendung der Psychoanalyse auf die Geisteswissenschaften* |
| IPA | International Psychoanalytic Association |
| LOC | Manuscript Division, Library of Congress, Washington, DC |
| Pcs. | the Preconscious |
| Ψ | psyche |
| ψ | psychic |
| Ψα | psychoanalysis |
| ψα | psychoanalytic |
| S.E. | *The Standard Edition of the Complete Psychological Works of Sigmund Freud*. London: Hogarth Press and The Institute of Psycho-Analysis |
| SFC | Sigmund Freud Copyrights Ltd., Wivenhoe |
| Ucs. | the Unconscious |
| Verlag | Internationaler Psychoanalytischer Verlag |
| *Zeitschrift* | *Internationale Zeitschrift für (ärztliche) Psychoanalyse* |
| *Zentralblatt* | *Zentralblatt für Psychoanalyse: Medizinische Monatsschrift für Seelenkunde* |

THE COMPLETE CORRESPONDENCE OF
# SIGMUND FREUD
AND
# KARL ABRAHAM

# 1907

## 1 F

Prof. Dr Freud
Vienna IX, Berggasse 19
25 June 1907

Dear Colleague,

I already knew about your paper,[1] which I have now read with great interest. The complete analogy in the pre-history of these neuroses[2] is really very peculiar. I have the impression that there is less difficulty in uncovering these experiences in the case of dementia praecox than there is in hysteria, just as paranoia in general is the more transparent so far as the first part of the correlation is concerned.

I eagerly await your communications. If I can offer you something of use through my remarks on your new findings, I shall gladly do so. I particularly like that you have tackled the sexual side of the problem, the side that hardly anybody is willing to approach.

Collegially and respectfully yours,

*Dr Freud*

1. Abraham, 1907[9]. The paper is based on a lecture at the annual meeting of the *Deutscher Verein für Psychiatrie* in Frankfurt/Main on 27 April; the article had just appeared, and Abraham had sent an offprint to Freud.
2. Dementia praecox and hysteria. At that time the group of illnesses now combined under Bleuler's term "schizophrenia" was generally called "dementia praecox" (A. Morel; E. Kraepelin).

    In his paper, Abraham had tried to show that "the infantile sexuality of the individual is expressed in the symptoms of a subsequent outbreak of dementia praecox in the same way as Freud has demonstrated in cases of hysteria" (1907[9]: p. 13).

## 2 F

Prof. Dr Freud
Vienna IX, Berggasse 19
7 July 1907

My dear Colleague,

I have read your acute and, what is more important, conclusive remarks[1] with quite special interest. Before I deal with them, there is just one possibility that I should like to clear out of the way, namely that you should not regard remarks of mine such as "That we knew already" or "I came to a similar conclusion" as making any claim, in whatever direction. Please also consider yourself at liberty to make use of my observations in any way you wish. You have, of course, been spared the mistake, through which I had to pass, of considering sexual traumas to be the specific aetiology of neurosis.[2] At that time I did not yet know that these experiences are very common, and when I discovered this, I was still fortunately able to turn to the psycho-sexual constitution. But it is really salutary that work on these sexual traumas should be undertaken by someone who, unlike me, has not been made uncertain by that first great error. For you, as for me, the compelling thing is that these traumas become the *form-giving factor* in the symptomatology of neurosis.

There is one consideration that I must not withhold from you that is certainly valid in the case of hysteria—I do not know whether it also applies to dementia praecox. The hysteric later moves very far away from infantile auto-erotism, he exaggerates his object-cathexis (in this he is the counterpart of the fully demented case, who, in our assumption, reverts to auto-eroticism). He accordingly fantasizes his need of objects back into his childhood and clothes his auto-erotic childhood in phantasies of love and seduction. Rather like lovers who can no longer imagine that there was ever a time when they did not know each other and construct earlier meetings and relations on a flimsy basis, i.e. a part of the sexual traumas reported by patients are or may be phantasies; distinguishing them from the very frequent genuine ones is not easy, and the complication of these circumstances and the relationship of sexual traumas to forgetting and remembering is one of the chief reasons why I cannot persuade myself to a definitive presentation.

My impression is that the age of from three to five is that to which the determination of symptoms dates back. Later traumas are mostly genuine, earlier ones or those falling within this period are *prima facie* doubtful. So here is a gap to be filled in by observation.

I am also aware of the multiplicity of traumas, in part from glaring examples. This multiplicity is partly a result of phantasy, but partly seems to be also a consequence of the circumstance that in a certain milieu the conditions for such experiences are very favourable, while in another they are meagre. In my cases of recent years, which come from very good social circles, sexual traumas before the age of five have definitely come second to auto-eroticism. From eight years onwards the opportunities, of course, abound in all social classes.

The question why children do not report sexual traumas has forced itself on our attention here too, and has been answered by us just as it has been by you: children keep silent when they have experienced a pleasure gain. That was how we explained the puzzle of why abuse by nurses and governesses is heard of only a long time after their dismissal, even though the child could have been sure of the protection of its affectionate parents. Masochism kept the secret. The behaviour of grown-up girls, incidentally, is analogous in most cases and may have the same motives. Your remark about the displacement of the sense of guilt is unquestionably absolutely correct.[3] But why do some children talk all the same? It is hard to ascribe an abnormal organization to the others, because this abnormal constitution is the general infantile constitution. Perhaps here we are once again faced with a more-or-less rather than with a sharp dividing line, and the sexual trauma would then develop its pathogenic effect, release pleasure and sense of guilt, where it encounters a basis of strong auto-erotic foundation.

I find the two main points of your exposition, the unconscious intention in the experience of sexual traumas and the abnormal constitution,[4] very convincing, only to me everything becomes more indistinct, i.e. it dissolves into a number of series. In one sense this constitution is, as I said, peculiar to all children, and the same infantile perversities, anal erotism, etc., can be found in the mentally healthy. However, in hysteria in particular the perverse talents can be assumed to be greater than in the basically healthy. A conclusion is confused and made more difficult to draw because later life events so often become the decisive factor and force back infantile experiences to play the role of dispositions of which use has fortunately not been made. As for the unconscious purpose—and I think that your view, in all its stringency, is valid even for a number of infantile personalities—this should be modified to the extent that the dividing line between consciousness and unconsciousness has not yet been established in early childhood. The child reacts as if compulsively to sexual impulses, as if unconsciously in fact, but without an inner conflict arising in the process.

I think it was in a passage in the *Interpretation of Dreams* (or in another work? Aetiology?[5]) that I hinted at the idea that theory could find the fundamental prerequisite for the possibility of neurosis in the phenomenon of the sexual latency period. The child is not equipped to cope mentally with stronger sexual impressions, and hence reacts to them compulsively, as if unconsciously—that is the first deficiency in the mechanism; as a consequence of the somatic intensification of the releasing of sexuality, these impressions later exercise more powerful effects as a retrospective reaction [*nachträglich*][6] and as *memories* than they did when they were real impressions, and that is the second psychological deficiency, because this constellation of retrospectively strengthened *unpleasure released by memories* [*Erinnerungsunlust*] makes repression possible, which would not succeed against *perceptions*. Even today, I have not got any further than that, and yet I feel that a thorough examination of the whole question is still necessary. In spite of these reservations, or rather uncertainties, of mine, I can grant you that whole large parts of your exposition make a fascinating, even convincing impression; I am thinking in particular of what refers to traumas experienced at a somewhat later age. So do not let yourself be dissuaded from telling me more about your experiences. I shall gladly tell you all I know or can think of, and I honestly ask you to excuse that my present reactions have turned out to be so meagre.

In any case, you have tackled the problem at the right end and, moreover, at the point where most people are unwilling to touch it. Also I am particularly glad that the approach to dementia praecox by way of auto-eroticism seems hopeful to you. This, however, should be weighed against the normal auto-eroticism of childhood, and merely a return to auto-eroticism be postulated in dementia. I am very glad to know that all of you in Zurich are taking this heavy labour out of my hands. Your youth and fresh vigour, and the fact that you can spare yourselves the wrong turnings that I took, all promise the best.

With heartfelt thanks and in expectation of further friendly news from you, I am,
your devoted
*Dr Freud*

1. The reference is to a lost letter of Abraham's. The ideas to which Freud goes on to refer appear in Abraham, 1907[10], published in November 1907.
2. Between 1895 and 1897, Freud had developed what was later called "seduction theory", claiming that the memory of sexual seductions or assaults in early childhood was the primary factor in the aetiology of neuroses. His renunciation of this theory is generally regarded as the decisive step towards psychoanalysis proper, which stresses the importance of phantasy, inner reality, and infantile sexuality.
3. Abraham, 1907[10]: p. 52.
4. In his article, Abraham stated "that in a great number of cases the trauma was desired by the child unconsciously, and that we have to recognize it as a form of infantile sexual activity" (1907[10]: p. 48), but that "[i]nfantile sexual traumas play no ætiological rôle in hysteria and dementia præcox. . . . Instead of an *ætiological* significance, the infantile sexual trauma now receives a *formative* one" (ibid.: p. 62).
5. The following ideas had been discussed by Freud at length (1950c [1895]: pp. 352–359; 1896b: p. 167; 1896c: p. 212; cf. the editor's comments in *S.E. 1*: p. 356, and *S.E. 3*: p. 167).
6. James Strachey's translation of *Nachträglichkeit* as "deferred action" in the *Standard Edition* has been the subject of recent criticism. We take over the term used by Peter Hoffer in his translation of the Freud/Ferenczi letters. [Trans.]

## 3 F

Hôtel du Lac
Lavarone (South Tyrol)

Lavarone[1]
26 July 1907

My dear Colleague,

Your letter[2] is the first of scientific content that has followed me here into the holidays. It only increased my enjoyment, because it again bears witness to the advance of knowledge in the matter of dementia praecox and revives the prospect of the realization of long-restrained hopes. I reply to your rich offerings with only two remarks, which I have had in store for a long time, and which coincide so perfectly with what you say that I can let them merge with them.

1. It has struck me that patients, when they finally turn towards dementia and lose the resemblance to hysteria, hand over their (sexually infantile) phantasies without resistance, as if these had now lost their value, rather the way a person who has renounced marriage throws away the devalued keepsakes, ribbons, locks of hair, etc. The context in which I should like to place this behaviour also is that the essence of this turn [to dementia] lies in the withdrawal of the libido from the sexual object.

2. I have always assumed that in individuals formerly usually described as "idiopathic" [*Originäre*], and who later become obviously paranoid, the necessary development from auto-eroticism to object-love has only inadequately been achieved. With a proportion of cases of dementia this factor would supply the *looked-for predisposition* for the later illness, and that would fit in admirably with the general pathological view that illness always means regression in development. (The *evolution and involution* of English authors.[3])

This is nearly the same as what you report, and this correspondence may strengthen anew your being forced to look at things in this way.

So allow me to thank you cordially for your communications, to the continuation of which I wish to encourage you because of the most lively interest I take in what you are working on.

Moreover, let us neither forget the mostly *partial* nature of the withdrawal of libido, nor that the development of sexual life permits a similar predisposition to be indicated in the case of hysteria. With regard to the obsessional neurosis I do not yet see clearly.

Your cordially devoted

Dr Freud

---

1. South Tyrolian (then Austrian) resort. From there, towards the end of August, Freud and his family moved to Wolkenstein in the Dolomites, and then to Annenheim in Carinthia.

On 12 September, Freud went to Bolzano, and then to Rome via Florence and Orvieto. He left Rome on 26 September and started work on 30 September. (Cf. Jones, 1955: pp. 35–38.)
2. Missing.
3. Italicized words in English in original.

4A

Zurich
9 August 1907

Dear Professor Freud,

Today, once again, I have to ask for your understanding for not having replied to your letter any sooner. As both my superiors, Bleuler and Jung,[1] were away at the same time, I have had no opportunity for anything but hospital duties during the last fortnight. I was very glad indeed to hear that you identify with the views I expressed in the last letter. However, I would add some comments regarding the two main points of your last letter.

The communication of phantasies, delusional ideas, etc., happens without resistance in certain phases of dementia praecox. Right at this moment I am treating a lady who reels off her most intimate affairs, including her religious delusion of grandeur, as an outsider would speak of some commonly known incident. Many mental patients behave like this in a particular phase. At other times, however, it is impossible to elicit even a single word about these matters. On yet other occasions, one easily obtains information about the delusional constructions, but not the least about the "voices". This alternating behaviour is not clear to me. I would be ready to admit that the revelation of the most intimate secrets is a sign of the onset of dementia, if the concept of dementia had been clarified; so far, however, this is not the case. I believe what *in cases of chronic mental illness* is called dementia is nothing but the patient shutting himself away from the world, the withdrawal of libido from persons and objects. In organic psychoses and in epilepsy, one also speaks of dementia. This is unfortunate, since we are dealing with two completely different things. The epileptic becomes demented in a completely different way: in his case the mental impoverishment is progressive. Yet he retains the capacity to react emotionally, which is lost in the patient suffering from dementia praecox. *In spite of all the dementia*, even in deepest imbecility, the epileptic shows definite object-love. He is full of exaggerated praise for the members of his family; his handshake with the doctor cannot be cordial enough; he cannot find words enough to express his emotions; he clings tenaciously to his possessions—in everything the complete opposite of dementia praecox. Thus, we are faced with a strange fact: epileptics become "demented" and *keep* their object-libido, the chronic mental patients become demented and *lose* their object-libido. Therefore, the concept of dementia urgently needs clarification. In psychiatry, they literally play around with this concept! Some regard paranoia (or dementia praecox, or whatever one may call it) as a partial mental disturbance involving only certain psychic capacities; others call every absurd delusion "demented" or imbecile. One might just as well regard the thousand apparently meaningless and yet meaningful absurdities of the dream as demented, and every person as imbecile when dreaming. What is called dementia in the chronic mental patient seems to me something dissoluble, in contrast to epileptic, paralytic or senile imbecility, which is irreversible. As for dementia praecox, ideas and emotions are temporarily *barred* (though often for a very long time). Whether or not this can be cleared up seems to me to depend on the severity and depth of the "complex".[2]

In connection with the second point in your letter, I would like to try to substitute another term for that of dementia in cases of chronic mental illness. Apparently, the insufficient development towards object-love is due to an inhibition in the unfolding of the personality. Personality is, after all, nothing but the individual's way of reacting to the stimuli emanating from his environment. It has become clear to me from your works that the reaction to the environment is very closely connected with sexuality. Every acute episode of dementia praecox is an obstacle to the development of the personality, and, in severe cases, it may stop this development *for good*. I therefore believe that in cases of chronic mental illness one ought to speak of a standstill in personality development rather than of dementia.

To conclude, I should like to express to you, dear Professor Freud, my warmest thanks for your interest. It was more than I deserved that you should have concerned yourself with my letter even during your holidays. I am sending this letter to your address in Vienna, since this might be the surest way for it to reach you, should you still be travelling. Much as I am anxious to hear from you further, I do ask you to postpone your answer until your return.

Your gratefully devoted

Dr Abraham

1. Eugen Bleuler [1857–1939], famous Swiss psychiatrist, professor in Zurich, director of the Cantonal Sanatorium and Psychiatric University Clinic Burghölzli in Zurich. He coined the terms schizophrenia, autism and ambivalence. He was a champion of the temperance movement.

    Carl Gustav Jung [1875–1961] was then senior staff physician [*Oberarzt*] at the Burghölzli and thus Abraham's direct superior.

    Bleuler had introduced psychoanalysis at the Burghölzli, which gradually became the international centre of "dynamic psychiatry" and one of the most important and progressive institutions of Europe. It was through Bleuler and Jung that nearly all important psychiatric disciples of Freud's first came into contact with him—among them Abraham, who had joined the staff at the end of the year 1904.

2. The notion of "complex", a repressed group of ideas and associations, is usually ascribed to the Zurich School, especially to Jung (see 1906, 1909b), but earlier it had already been used by Breuer (Breuer & Freud, 1895d: p. 231) and by Freud (e.g. 1950c [1895]: p. 355) in this sense. Abraham published these ideas on dementia in condensed form (1908[11]: pp. 75–76).

## 5A

Zurich, Burghölzli
6 October 1907

Dear Professor,

Please forgive me for approaching you today without waiting for your reply to my last letter. This time I am not writing about scientific matters but about something personal. I intend to leave Zurich in about a month. In doing so, I am giving up my present work as a doctor in a psychiatric hospital. The reasons are not far to find: as a Jew in Germany and as a foreigner in Switzerland, I have not advanced beyond a junior position in the past seven years. I shall therefore try to set up in practice in Berlin as a specialist for nervous and mental diseases. To be sure, there is no shortage of neurologists in Berlin, but I am building my hopes on two factors: first, the use of psychoanalysis; and, second, my psychiatric training, which all Berlin doctors lack completely. You will already have guessed why I am writing to you. I should like to ask for your recommendation, should you ever be in a position to have to recommend a doctor for psychological treatment in Berlin. I am fully aware of the difficulties I shall encounter, and I should therefore also like to ask your permission, to turn to you for advice if the occasion arises. I should be most beholden to you for your kind support in both these respects.

I have unfortunately not yet been able to publish my paper on the sexual trauma in childhood,[1] since the preparations for the move to Berlin and other matters have kept me too busy. I hope, however, to be able to finish it still within this month. After that I shall perhaps allow myself to submit something new to you again.

Your respectfully devoted

*Dr K. Abraham*

1. Abraham, 1907[10].

## 6F

Prof. Dr Freud
Vienna IX, Berggasse 19
8 October 1907

Dear Colleague,

I soon suppressed the first impulse of regret I felt on reading your letter. No harm can come to a youthful man like you from being forced into open life *"au grand air"*, and that as a Jew you will encounter more difficulties will have the effect, as it has with all of us, of bringing out all your productive capabilities. That my sympathy and best wishes are with you on your new path goes without saying; and more than that, whenever possible. If my intimate friendship with Dr W. Fliess[1] from Berlin still existed, the way would be levelled for you; but now unfortunately that road is completely blocked. During the past year I have repeatedly been in the position of having to tell patients from Germany I was sorry I knew no confidant in the *Reich* to whom I could recommend them. If such cases recur this year, however, I shall know what to do. If my reputation in Germany increases, it will certainly be advantageous for you, and if I may forthrightly refer to you as my pupil and follower—you do not seem to me to be a man to be ashamed of that—I shall be able to back you energetically. On the other hand, you yourself know the hostility with which I still have to struggle in Germany. I hope you will make no attempt whatever to win the favour of your new colleagues, who first of all are like those everywhere else, and then a whole lot more brutal on top of it, but will instead turn directly to the public. At the time when the fight against hypnosis was at its most violent in Berlin, a very disagreeable hypnotist named Grossmann quickly built himself up a big practice on the basis of that therapy. So one should rather expect that with the aid of psychoanalysis you should do even better.

You indicate that there is still something you would like to submit to me, and I hope you know that I am at your disposal to the best of my ability. Does not the journey from Zurich to Berlin conveniently take in Vienna?

I shall look for your last letter in order to answer it as soon as you have enough peace again to discuss scientific matters.

With my most intense good wishes,

your devoted

*Dr Freud*

1. Wilhelm Fliess [1858–1928], Berlin physician and otorhinolaryngologist; Freud's closest friend between 1887 and 1900 (cf. Freud, 1985c [1887–1904]).

## 7A

Zurich, Burghölzli
13 October 1907

Dear Professor,

Your letter gave me great pleasure and was, at the same time, the best encouragement I could receive. Many thanks for your warm interest, which is apparent in every line of your letter. If you want to call me your pupil, I see no reason why I should object. On the contrary, I see in this a recognition on your part and assure you that for the past three years—that is how long I have studied your works—I have regarded you as my teacher. I shall accept your invitation to come to Vienna as soon as I can. I hope to be settled in Berlin by the beginning of December. If at all possible, I should then like to come to Vienna for a few days.

The Berlin colleagues I know well. I was a physician at the Berlin mental hospital Dalldorf[1] for more than three years, until I could bear it no longer. I know how difficult it is in medical Berlin to stand up against an established doctrine. In Zurich I could breathe freely again. No clinic in Germany could have offered me even a fraction of what I have found here. That is also why I do not find it easy to leave. But I have to think of the future, especially since I am married.[2]

I hope before long to be able to report personally on my scientific plans. I fear I claimed enough of your attention for the time being with my letter about the problem of dementia, and so I would rather not put anything more before you today. Incidentally, in spite of the impending move, I am quite in the mood for a discussion.

No fewer than twenty doctors appeared at the second meeting of our "Freud Society"[3] here; some came quite a long distance, from hospitals in the country. So there is no lack of interest here. The next time I shall talk about the question of the infantile sexual trauma. I secretly hope that I can gradually make some propaganda in Berlin.

With kind regards,
your gratefully devoted

*Dr K. Abraham*

1. This name was later changed to Wittenau.
2. To Hedwig Marie, née Bürgner [1878–1969].
3. An open and informal forum for discussions, founded in 1907.

1907 October

## 8F

Prof. Dr Freud
Vienna IX, Berggasse 19
21 October 1907

My dear Colleague,

Seeing that you are in a humour for disputation, I will gladly answer your letter of 9 August.

I am in full agreement with what you say about dementia, that is to say, I have explained things to myself in a similar way without being able to find the confirmation in the material. I see dementia praecox only very rarely, and other cases of imbecility practically never. I can repeat in your own words that the dementia of dementia praecox must have a different mechanism than that of the senile, epileptics, etc. After all, it does not matter what tricks the psychiatrists play with the word. The dementia in dementia praecox must therefore be dissoluble (*virtute*!), a functional one, so to speak. Its prototype would be the unbelievable momentary stupidity that we observe in analyses when the insight we are looking for has to work against great resistances. The intellectual cathexis simply does not want to go where we wish to direct it. Given the reluctance to cathect the object that we assume in dementia praecox, the phenomenon must, naturally, turn out to be a much more impressive one. Another prototype—scientifically not usable—would be the highly remarkable stupidity that we are accustomed to finding in the arguments of our opponents, even of otherwise rather intelligent ones. Also just resistance.

But you now want to launch an inquisition into the term "dementia" itself and replace it, in the case of dementia praecox, by another, that of "inhibition of the personality". Unimportant as such questions of definition are, in this matter I would rather not go along with you. Why? Who expects "dementia" to stand for anything other than a symptom that may occur under the most varied conditions (mechanisms)? It just means that the intellectual cathexis is not available for the necessary tasks. The term dementia is not meant to specify whether this is so because the intellectual cathexis is not there, or because it is needed elsewhere, or because this activity is forbidden it. I do not care if anyone wants to call the dream demented; but with such scolding he does not touch at all on the mechanism that makes the dream demented, and which is the essential characteristic of it. It is like the case of a son in need who asks his father for support. If the father gives nothing, the reason may be that he himself has nothing, or that he no longer likes the son and does not want to give him anything. To the son this is to a certain extent of no importance, he can starve or go under just as well in one case as in the other.

"Personality", analogous to your superior's[1] notion of the ego, is a rather vague term from surface psychology that does nothing in particular for the understanding of the actual processes, that is to say, does nothing in particular *metapsychologically*.[2] One easily believes, however, that one is saying something meaningful in using it.

Collegially and respectfully,
your very devoted

*Dr Freud*

1. Eugen Bleuler.
2. The term "metapsychology" was introduced by Freud and first used in his correspondence with Fliess (13 February 1896, Freud, 1985c [1887–1904]: p. 172), in an analogy with metaphysics, for a "psychology that leads behind consciousness" (10 March 1898, ibid.: pp. 301–302). Metapsychology supposes models of the "psychic apparatus"—e.g. id, ego, superego; unconscious, preconscious, conscious; distribution of drive energy—at a high level of abstraction. Freud later defined a metapsychological presentation as one that describes "a psychical process in its dynamic, topographical and economic aspects" (1915e: p. 181).

## 9A

Zurich
31 October 1907

Dear Professor,

Heartfelt thanks for your letter. Our move is now taking place earlier than we intended at first after all, so that I will not have another chance to reply in Zurich. As soon as I am settled in Berlin, I hope to be able to come to Vienna, and I am already looking forward very much to talking with you. Would it be inconvenient for you if I came in the second half of November? My address from 7 November onwards is: Berlin W., Schöneberger Ufer 22.

Your gratefully devoted

*Dr K. Abraham*

## 10A

Berlin W., Schöneberger Ufer 22
24 November 1907

Dear Professor,

Having been in Berlin for a fortnight, I have settled in to some extent and would soon like to start my practice. Before doing so, as I wrote to you from Zurich, I would like to talk to you about various things, both scientific and practical. So I am now taking the liberty of asking whether a visit in about a week's time would be convenient for you. I would, of course, like to fit in entirely with your arrangements; I should especially like to know whether you would prefer my visit on a weekday or on a Sunday. I am looking forward to your kind reply and I thank you very much in advance.

At the same time, I am taking the liberty of sending you my paper on the sexual trauma in childhood, which has just appeared.[1]

Your respectfully devoted

Dr K. Abraham

1. Abraham, 1907[10].


11 F

Vienna IX, Berggasse 19
26 November 1907[1]

Dear Colleague,

I have read your excellent paper[2] with satisfaction, and, having already previously acknowledged the justification of your basic idea, I can now praise the clarity with which you describe the differences in the concepts of infantile traumas, the relationship between pleasure, silence, and guilt feelings, and the like. To your description of the abnormality of subsequently neurotic children (quantitative increase of libido, precocity, rampant growth of phantasies) I should like to add as an essential feature the existence of a strong tendency to repression, otherwise we should get, not neurotics, but scoundrels. The proof of this pair of opposites, to an extremely high degree and in split form, seems to me to be the latest result of analysis to date.

I would like to get as much as possible from your visit to Vienna and therefore ask you to include in your programme a *whole* Sunday on which you would be my guest. On weekdays I have hardly a free hour in the evening, and then of course I am not very good company. I would appreciate to know a few days in advance on which Sunday I may expect you.

Yours with sincere regards,

Dr Freud

1. The translation is based on the text as in the German edition of Freud & Abraham, 1965; the letter is missing in the holdings of the Library of Congress [= LOC].
2. On the following day Freud mentioned Abraham's article at the meeting of the Wednesday Society (see letter 13A, 21 December 1907, n. 1; Nunberg & Federn, 1962: p. 233).

## 12A

## Dr med. K. Abraham

Specialarzt für nervöse und psychische Krankheiten
Berlin W. 35. Schöneberger Ufer 22
Tel. Amt VI, 13245
Sprechst. 9–10, 4–6. Sonntags 9–10

6 December 1907

Dear Professor Freud,

Your appreciative words, as well as your kind invitation, have given me much pleasure. I now intend to come to Vienna at the end of next week, so that I can spend Sunday, the 15th, with you. I would be very grateful for a short note from you informing me whether this date is convenient for you and at what time you expect me.

With respectful greetings,
Yours,

*Dr K. Abraham*

## 13A

Berlin
21 December 1907

Dear Professor,

Late on Wednesday night,[1] when I got back to the hotel, I found the little box[2] in my briefcase. The contents and the accompanying words gave me much pleasure. With this so charmingly chosen courtesy you topped all the preceding ones. Let me thank you cordially once again for all your hospitality and for all the instruction and stimulation. I do very much hope that the number of the followers of your science may increase. But if they were all to come and make as much claim on your hospitality and time as I did, then perhaps you might one day prefer your enemies to your friends! The days that I was allowed to spend in your company and in the midst of your family were most gratifying to me. To be surrounded by so much kindliness and at the same so much culture is a rare joy. I left with the feeling of staying deeply indebted to you. Maybe I shall be able to pay off, step by step, a part of this debt by scientific collaboration.

I shall soon present to you something on the question of the withdrawal of libido in dementia praecox. I was consulted today about a young patient whom you examined some time ago in Görlitz.[3] He now has a severe hallucinatory psychosis; the obsessional symptoms persist.

1907 December

This case, in conjunction with two others I observed previously, seems to me of great importance for our views.

I shall conclude for today with kindest regards, also from my wife, and I also ask you to remember me to the Wednesday Society.

Your cordially devoted

*Karl Abraham*

1. In 1902, Freud's followers had begun meeting in Freud's waiting-room on Wednesday evenings, forming the so-called "Wednesday (Psychological) Society", which in 1908 became the Vienna Psychoanalytic Society [= Vienna Society]. On 18 December, Abraham had attended such a meeting as guest (Nunberg & Federn, 1962: p. 254). Abraham described his stay in Vienna in a letter to his friend and colleague Max Eitingon (1 January 1908, LOC; also in H. Abraham, 1974: pp. 72–74), who had been the first from the Burghölzli staff to visit Freud.
2. Containing two small Egyptian figures from Freud's collection.
3. Freud described this case in his letter to Jung of 14 April 1907 (Freud & Jung, 1974 [1906–13]: pp. 33–34).

# 1908

### 14F

Vienna IX, Berggasse 19
1 January 1908

Dear Colleague,

I wish you the best of luck for this year, in which you will begin to build yourself a position in Berlin, and I am delighted to conclude from all the signs that you have the right companion at your side.

As for the Görlitz patient. His parents, good souls, did, however, induce me to make the journey to the institution only by concealing something. Only once there did I find out that he also hallucinates voices, and thus exceeds the frame of hysteria/obsessional neurosis. I observed one attack myself, it is immensely instructive in that it represents a coitus or, rather, his rage at such an act of coitus observed by him [obviously between the parents].[1] His spitting is sperm-ejaculation. The whole thing is very transparent; tragic for his fate, and of extreme interest for our views, is the organic accompaniment of and reason for his repudiation of sexuality—the infantility of his genitals. It was because of the latter that I held out so little hope of recovery to his parents; but then they will be very content with improvements. There is surely no doubt that the case must be regarded as dementia praecox; but the relationship of the latter to hysteria and obsessional neurosis undeniably also comes to the fore.

I am very eager for your further communications, whether the young woman came to you, and many other things.

My family thank you for your greetings, and your wife's in particular.

A happy 1908,
your very devoted

*Dr Freud*

---

1. Square brackets in original.

## 15A

Berlin
8 January 1908[1]

Dear Professor Freud,

First of all, many thanks for your letter. It is good that you are keen to hear "much" from me, for I have a great deal on my mind. I am quite pleased with the beginnings of my practice. I have two cases of obsessional neurosis in treatment, which were recommended by Oppenheim.[2] In one of them, where all other means had been applied in vain, Oppenheim has in fact asked me straight out to try your method! It is exactly this case, a severe form of obsessional thinking, that worries me a great deal.[3] The patient suffers, (1.) from obsessional praying, (2.) he has to look at every object carefully and to brood over its origin, and, in so doing, he passes over to cosmic problems in the way we know so well. The patient spontaneously produced a very nice screen memory: as a boy of seven, he once chanced to see a woman during a quarrel with neighbours pull up her skirts and show the opposing party her bare buttocks. The patient told the maid at home about this, and she said that he was very naughty and threatened that a policeman would come and fetch him, etc. Thereupon he became very frightened and began to pray, and soon he could not free himself from the compulsion to pray, would cover scraps of paper with all kinds of prayer formulae so as to omit nothing, etc.—I then gradually succeeded in recovering a number of analogous incidents from repression: how as a boy of four he slept with his former wet nurse and pulled her night-dress up over her bottom (here he probably equates breasts and *nates*[4]); how he, later on, when his mother once took him into her bed, did the same thing *with her*, whereupon she scolded him for being indecent. The incident with the woman next-door happened at around the same time! Here the patient was only a *witness* of an exposure, in the other cases he *actively* brought it about. That is why this scene is remembered and covers the more embarrassing ones. Then repressed memories followed of how he later shared a bed with his eldest brother and touched his genitals, and also of several other incidents, such as locking himself in with a girl of his own age and touching her bottom. In short, up to his 18th year—*always analogous experiences*. The praying has persisted up to the present, apart from temporary remissions, and is easily explained by self-reproaches for his sexual activities. There is no doubt that the looking at female buttocks plays a part in the compulsive looking at indifferent objects. I have noticed that the patient always turns objects around when looking at them, so that their reverse side is facing him. This is as far as I got in two sessions without resistances that were too great. But now I am stuck. I am searching in vain for analogous events *in his later life*. For years, the patient has repeatedly been almost entirely free from his obsessional symptoms. Five years ago, however, and again one year ago, the old symptoms reappeared in very acute form. Can one make any general inferences as to the cause of this deterioration? Furthermore, I am certain that I have uncovered only a part of the repressed material, but up to now I have found no way of access. Perhaps you know from similar cases how to find a way to these deeper layers. Finally, I should like to know whether one can draw any conclusions from the *thematic content* of the brooding. My patient racks his brain over the *origins* of objects, the material they have been made of, etc. Is there any known determination for this? The general explanation of brooding is well known to me, but can one draw any conclusions from the types of problems the patient sets himself?

The case of Grabower seems very important to me for our concept of dementia praecox—that is, its differentiation from neurosis.[5] There is a far-reaching similarity with obsessional neurosis. I consider the following points to be diagnostically decisive (leaving aside those crude psychotic symptoms supervening during the last few years): (1.) the patient transfers strongly onto his mother in early childhood, wants to have her all for himself, is jealous of his father and brother, idolizes his mother, and is effusively affectionate. All this lasts up to the moment when she places him in a boarding-school. In a neurotic, a strong emotional reaction would set in now; his longing would become unbearable, etc. In G. there follows a brusque withdrawal of libido. From this moment on he cuts his mother, does not mention her in his letters any more, treats her with cold formality. Now, he pays no attention to her visits and destroys the presents she brings him. (2.) The early negativism = sexual rejection, which is characteristic of dementia praecox. The mother says: at the age of two he was already the spirit that continually denies.[6] (3.) The early automatisms, for instance, screaming fits. As a very small boy he was once taken to task for this and replied: "Oh, Daddy, *it screams on its own.*" The case coincides in every detail with the two cases of obsessional symptoms in dementia praecox in early adolescence of which I told you. In one of these cases it is also the *grandmother* who plays this strange role. In Grabower's case I have made the following conjecture, about which I should like to have your opinion: according to your analysis, the patient was present during the parents' coitus. Might he not have displaced this experience from his at that time much-loved and jealously guarded mother onto the great-grandmother, whom he barely knew? After all, he also has a compulsion to utter obscene words, especially those referring to the female genitals. I assume that he wants to separate these painfully embarrassing ideas from his mother and link them with another female person, whom he has only seen once or twice.—I could say much more about this case, but would rather like to get on to some other matters today, too.

I should like to know whether the interpretation of the paradigm dream in the *Interpretation of Dreams* is incomplete on purpose ("Irma's injection").[7] I think that trimethylamin leads to the most important part, to sexual allusions that become more and more distinct in the last lines. Surely everything does point to the suspicion of syphilitic infection in the patient? The *spot* in her mouth = plaque, the *infection*, the injection of trimethylamin, which has been carelessly given, the dirty syringe (!!). Is not this the organic illness for whose continued existence one cannot make you responsible, because syphilis or a nervous disease originating from it cannot be influenced by psychological treatment?

I have still not finished! You see, I am just reading the *Interpretation of Dreams* once again and find that I have all kinds of questions to ask. I will confine myself today to the *flying dreams*. The infantile source seems clear to me, but I believe I have found an actual one as well, occasioned by the following dream of an acquaintance. The lady dreams that she is floating in the sky as a small pink cloud. Then a large hand appears, follows her, comes nearer and nearer, and finally grasps her. I find the following interpretation for this aesthetically very beautiful dream. Two sisters of the dreamer have been married for some considerable time. A third became engaged shortly before the dream. She alone is left, is no longer young, has been getting very stout for some time, and is obviously afraid of being left on the shelf. In the dream she is as light as air instead of plump, and a male hand finds her desirable. Might not the flying in the dream, for others too, mean: I should like to be lighter? Perhaps you have had some experience with regard to this.

In the *Interpretation of Dreams* you regret that concerning the dreams of healthy persons you are completely restricted to self-analysis.[8] In case you should like to have some nice examples of analysed dreams of healthy people for the new edition, I could tell you several of mine and of my wife's.—The psychiatrists' congress in Berlin is on 24–25 April. Bleuler's paper is now officially announced.[9] I hope that Salzburg[10] will not clash with it. Egotistical as I am, I want to be present at both. You will surely have heard from Jung already about the change for the better in Jena.[11] So things are on the move. I have recently heard of several physicians who study your work thoroughly. Maeder in Zurich has published a short paper on the psychopathology of everyday life.[12] It does, after all, become a pleasure to live.

Finally, my wife and I wish to thank you for the honourable attribute you bestowed on her. But how could you arrive at this opinion?? With kindest regards from house to house, and please kindly remember me to the Wednesday Society.

Your gratefully devoted

*Karl Abraham*

The young woman you asked about has not yet turned up.

1. In original: "07".
2. Hermann Oppenheim [1858–1919], German neurologist, founder of a famous private clinic in Berlin [1891], 1893 professor. His wife Martha was Abraham's cousin.
3. Abraham described this case (1909[14]: p. 199, 1913[38], passim).
4. Latin: "buttocks".
5. Abraham described this case briefly in a paper dealing with this differentiation (1908[11]: pp. 70, 77–78).
6. *Der Geist, der stets verneint*: self-characterization by Mephistopheles in Goethe's *Faust* (part I, ii, verse 1338).
7. Freud, 1900a: pp. 106–121.
8. Freud, 1900a: p. xxiii.
9. Annual meeting of the German Society for Psychiatry; Bleuler read a paper on dementia praecox—see *Berliner Klinische Wochenschrift*, 45, No. 22, 1 June 1908: 1078–1079.
10. The first international meeting of psychoanalysts in Salzburg, which took place on 27 April 1908.
11. Referring to the rising prospects of psychoanalysis at the Psychiatric University Clinic in Jena, headed by Prof. Otto Binswanger [1852–1929]. His nephew Ludwig Binswanger (see letter 47F, 24 August 1908) stayed there between April 1907 and June 1908, conducting psychoanalytic treatments. On 2 January 1908, he reported to Jung on "the progress of Freud's cause in Jena" (Jung to Abraham, 3 January 1908, LOC). In late February 1908, Jung went to Jena and "got a gorgeous reception" (3 March 1908, Freud & Jung, 1974 [1906–13]: p. 127). Evidently, Freud and Abraham hoped to get a foothold in German psychiatry and academia through Otto Binswanger's university chair and clinic.
12. Maeder, 1906–07. Alphonse E. Maeder [1882–1971], Swiss psychotherapist, for a time chairman of the Zurich Psychoanalytic Society. He followed Jung after the latter's separation from Freud. Maeder later developed a method of brief analysis and became associated with the Oxford Movement. At that time, he was director of the hospital for epileptics at Zurich.

## 16F

Vienna IX, Berggasse 19
9 January 1908

Dear Colleague,

I write to you hurriedly, formlessly, impersonally, to enable you to make use of my technical information as soon as possible.

Sorry you are afraid of getting stuck. Doesn't happen to me all year round. I must get those technical rules of mine out soon.[1]

Your compulsive case is bound to be very instructive. The technique is somewhat more complicated than in hysteria, the means of repression a bit different, different dialect, but no more.

You will soon find confirmation of the activity: from the start, with your patient, one has to reckon with a great sense of guilt and with masochistic and homosexual tendencies (beating, buttocks). The brooding is the direct continuation of the earlier sexual curiosity, which is certainly still struggling with problems, even today.

## 1908 January

The periods of obsession correspond, of course, to times of increased libido, that is, whenever the patient falls in love or his specific condition for loving (jealousy) is touched on in life. Origin of things = Where do babies come from? Anthropogeny.[2] The cosmic, celestial bodies are to be associated with the anatomical. In the case of a young person, a great deal can be done by giving sexual enlightenment as soon as it is asked for.

The chief rules are: [(1.)] Take your time, in the words of the Salzburg motto.[3] Mental changes are never quick, except in revolutions (psychoses). Dissatisfied after only two sessions. At not knowing everything! (2.) A problem like: How do I go on? must not exist. The patient shows the way, in that by strictly following the basic rule (saying everything that comes into his mind) he displays his prevailing $\psi^4$ surface.

In the paradigm dream there is *no* mentioning of syphilis. Sexual megalomania is hidden behind it, the three women, Mathilde, Sophie and Anna, are the three godmothers of my daughters,[5] and I have them all! There would be one simple therapy for widowhood, of course. All sorts of intimate things, naturally.

The actual meanings of flying dreams are of course very varied. Yours is a very fine case, I should like it for the second edition.[5] But other things can equally well be made of the material, as I shall show from examples.

I gladly accept your offer of your own dreams. Your optimistic view of the situation cheers me greatly. We must still expect to have hard work before us. My opinion of your wife is based on a so-called instinctive knowledge of mankind. I shall write to you about other things another time. I am posting this at the main post office.

Your cordially devoted

*Freud*

1. A first hint of Freud's plan to write a "General Methodology of Psychoanalysis". He continued on this project until 1910, but then he gave it up in this form and instead wrote six short papers on technique between 1911 and 1914 (see the "Editor's Introduction" in *S.E.* 12: pp. 85–88).
2. Abraham took Freud's hint (1909[14]: p. 199).
3. Probably referring to the upcoming meeting there. "In our Alpine regions", Freud wrote later, "there is a customary greeting, when two acquaintances meet or part: 'Take your time' [*Zeit lassen*]. We have often made fun of it, but have come to realize, in light of the way Americans hurry, how much wisdom lies in this formulation" (unpublished part of the postscript to *The Question of Lay Analysis*, LOC).
3. $\Psi$ = psyche; $\psi$ = psychic, in accordance with German usage.
4. The godmothers are Josef Breuer's wife Mathilde [1887–1978], Sophie Schwab-Paneth [1893–1920], and Anna Lichtheim [1895–1982]—the latter two Freud's patients and both widows. Lichtheim was a sister of Breuer's son-in-law. (Cf. Bonomi, 1996: p. 32, and Swales, 1983: pp. 24–25.)
5. Freud did not include this dream in the forthcoming editions, however.

## 17A

Berlin
15 January 1908

Dear Professor Freud,

Heartfelt thanks for your prompt reply, which was most welcome. I now feel a little ashamed that I turned to you for help instead of digging on by myself for a few more sessions. It can, however, be explained by the circumstances. I wanted a quick analytic triumph, and precisely in a case that was referred to me by Oppenheim, and I was therefore annoyed when I could make no headway, especially as the first session went so well. It is true, though, that I am dealing with a very difficult case, 47 years old and full of strong repressions. The following incident serves to show how good he is at hiding his secrets. In one of the next sessions after I had written to you, I went in greater detail into the hypnotic treatment that the patient had previously had. He told me that hypnosis had harmed him. On further questioning: something had occurred to him in the first hypnotic session, something painfully embarrassing, he had not spoken about it, and he had not remembered it on waking up. On his way home in the tram the thought returned, and he immediately had to say certain obsessional formulae in an undertone, became excited about this, was afraid of being noticed by the other people in the tram, got out, and ran through the streets for a long time, repeating the formulae, before going to his apartment. So far I have not succeeded in getting at this thought, in spite of sincere efforts. What these efforts led to, already in that session, was that the patient did not really respond to my instructions any more. He obviously transferred onto me the grudge he had then felt against the hypnotist. He was late for the next session and in a completely negative emotional state. The typical superficial talking and jumping from one theme to another were all he produced; at the same time, he showed a false euphoria, described his obsessional symptoms as not very important, and said that he would overcome them by energetic efforts. Very clearly: I do not need your treatment! In the following session his superficial talk gradually subsided, and I had little difficulty in confirming my assumption that his investigations into the origin of all things really arise from sexual curiosity. I hope that I shall now get even further, although the case is unfavourable in several respects.—I hope to gain greater confidence with practice. It consoled me today to find, in a note at the end of the analysis of the case of hysteria (Dora), that you yourself were not always better off at first in similar situations.[1] I have yet to acquire the technique and am therefore very grateful for the hints that you gave me in your letter.

I am so glad that you can use the flying dream I sent you. Today I am sending you one of my dreams* and two of my wife's.[2] Please use them as you wish, or also alter them. We do not, of course, want to be mentioned by name. The dreams are written in direct speech, the interpretations are given impersonally, as if the dreams had come from a stranger. The first long dream of my wife's does not seem to me to be interpreted as fully as it should be. Possibly a shared complex has prevented it. The Godiva[3] dream seems to be useful as a paradigmatic example, since it is so condensed.

My letter was interrupted at this point by my obsessional patient. Today I made good progress and found various sources, from which, after quite a long remission, compulsive praying and brooding have reappeared. I shall report to you later on this. My enclosures today will give you enough reading matter. Just one more request. Would you let me know *occasionally* how you explain the change-over from compulsive praying to compulsive denial of God's existence (followed again by increased praying)? I have a suspicion concerning my patient in this respect.

But now I must keep a promise I made to your wife when I was there [in Vienna]. I made enquiries at the Park Hotel, which is close to the Zoological Gardens station. The cost of a room with two beds on the 1st–3rd floor is 10 M (or more). Naturally, I shall be very glad to make enquiries in guest-houses etc. as well. It goes without saying that we should be pleased to know when your wife and daughter are coming. Please pass this request on to the ladies, with my wife's compliments and mine.

With kind regards,
your gratefully devoted
    Karl Abraham

\* marked no. III

P.S.: With regard to my wife's two dreams, I have another request to make to you. I should prefer to have the personal circumstances somewhat less recognizable if the two dreams should be printed. I should be grateful if I might see this section of the manuscript or proof, so as to disguise a few points without harming the value of the dreams. I wanted to tell *you personally* about the dreams and their interpretation without changing them in any way.

1. Cf. Freud, 1905e [1901]: p. 120, n. 1, where he speaks of "the fault in my technique".
2. Missing.
3. Legend has it that Lady Godiva, wife of Leofric, Earl of Mercia, rode naked on horseback through Coventry, to fulfil her husband's condition for freeing the citizens from paying tax. Nobody watched except "Peeping Tom", who was punished with blindness.

## 18F

Vienna IX, Berggasse 19
19 January 1908

My dear Colleague,

I am answering your letter today especially with the purpose of thanking you for the suggestions you made for my wife and daughter's visit to Berlin. They had to give up this visit, as my daughter became ill on the day before the one fixed for it: feverish with peritoneal symptoms.[1] Our doctors concluded that there is an abscess round a stitch that had been left in after her bad appendix operation two years ago. They say her condition is not serious. However, she will probably need an operation.

If, as an experienced senior, I may give you some advice, conduct the psychoanalysis of the O.[ppenheim] patient without a great deal of "sexual displacement" [*Sexualverlegung*] and without any ambition to impress O. by rapid success. For in the first place it will go better like that, and in the second the case is not suitable for being developed into a show-piece. Such a long-standing obsession in a man nearing the 50s is technically very difficult and therapeutically rather unfavourable. Obsession must be treated early, in persons who are still young, and then the treatment is a triumph and a pleasure. But do not allow [yourself] to be discouraged, and keep the man as long as possible; such patients generally become easily attached and are often satisfied when the physician is not. So far as details are concerned, I shall always tell you what I can divine from a distance, and thus try to compensate for the lack occasioned by the technique not yet having been published in detail. The switch from prayer to atheism is characteristic (typical) of these obsessional neuroses. From the beginning they have to express both contradictory voices, generally in immediate juxtaposition. Hence also their inability to make decisions, because of the equal weight of both sides of the motivation. A patient, for instance,[2] sees a stone lying in the roadway and has compulsively to remove it; then it leaves him no peace, and he has to put it back again. The explanation is that the girl he is in love with is going away that day and will be passing along that street in a cab. The cab might jolt over just that stone; so, away with it. And then: no, just let the cab overturn, with her inside it; so, back with it. In his unconscious he simultaneously has excessive affection for his beloved and a hatred of her!

Thank you very much for the three fine dreams. Your wife's dreams, the Seal and Godiva, are enchanting. But I should rather not use them, as you obviously dislike publicity because of the Zurich readers. I have no lack of material, and should like to avoid distortion as far as possible.

Again, to technique! You are right, that was the most taxing to acquire, and that is just why I want to spare those who follow in my footsteps part of the grind and—part of the cost.

Your cordially devoted

*Freud*

1. Mathilde, Freud's eldest daughter, was suffering from an abdominal irritation after an appendectomy.
2. The "Rat Man", in the session of 28 December 1907 (cf. Freud, 1955a [1907–8]: pp. 306–307).

## 19A

Berlin
29 January 1908

Dear Professor Freud,

I hope you did not take it as a lack of interest that I have not written up to now, and especially that I have not asked after the progress of your patient. The influenza that is raging in Berlin has not spared me, and so I had to postpone writing. I should very much like to ask you to tell me in your next letter how your daughter is. But if you do not feel like writing at present, I beg you *not* to bother for the time being about the following things that I want to ask you and tell you. Your last letter has once again given me some very important insights. It always seems to fit in so incredibly well with my patients! Recently I had yet another opportunity of confirming the fact that I would be totally unable to understand most cases of neurosis without knowledge of your concepts. I saw two cases of anxiety neurosis on the same day, both men, as if they had conspired together to give me a demonstration of the main aetiological factors of their illness. In one case *coitus interruptus,* in the *other* it can be proved that frustrated sexual excitement is the main factor in the illness. In both cases a few questions led me to the root of the matter, and my own confidence quickly gained me theirs. In both, treatment is progressing very satisfactorily. I may perhaps report to you at a later date on the very interesting symptoms of one of them. Just one small detail, incidentally, about the other one. I spoke to his wife privately and reassured her with regard to her husband's impotence. Hardly had I said to her that potency could be restored, when the lady, who had hitherto held her handbag quietly by its chain, began opening and shutting it.—The patient with obsessional symptoms, about whom I asked your advice the other day, improved a little and then lost patience. I had to break off the analysis, which had been very uphill work.

I have received an invitation to Salzburg from Jung. As I hope to be able to take part in the meeting, I have announced a talk on "Psycho-Sexual Differences between Hysteria and Dementia Praecox."[1] Some new points of view on this subject have occurred to me, which fit in well with the theory of auto-eroticism. I hope you like the subject. Since you have previously acknowledged that in the early work I had tackled the problem from the most important angle, that of sexuality, I thought it important to stress at this, our first congress, that sexuality forms the nucleus of the problem.

I have just received from Juliusburger a review of his paper, "Contribution to the Theory of Psycho-Analysis".[2] If you have not also received it, I could send it to you. Just one more question for today.

In your first essay on anxiety neurosis, you say that the affect in the phobias of anxiety neurosis cannot be fought by way of psychotherapy.[3] Do you still hold the same opinion? This interests me in connection with one of my two cases.

The practice is going quite well; at any rate better than that of most beginners. I often attend Oppenheim's polyclinic. Unfortunately there is no understanding of the psychological there. In the last few days, for instance, some particularly strange cases of tic in boys passed completely unnoticed in the bustle of the institution. The diagnosis is registered, and arsenic, the waters, and gymnastics are prescribed.

I could tell you of another scientific plan that is occupying me very much these days, but I would like to wait until it has become more tangible in order not to bother you too much. It will be something truly Freudian.

Now I add my best regards for you and your esteemed family, and I wish your daughter a rapid recovery. We are extremely sorry that the expected visit, which we had taken for certain, had to be cancelled for the time being.

Your very devoted

*Karl Abraham*

1. Abraham, 1908[11].
2. Otto Juliusburger [1867–1952], German psychiatrist and psychoanalyst in Berlin. Founding member of the Berlin group [1908], from which he later resigned. He emigrated to New York in 1941. (Cf. Juliusburger, 1909a.)
3. "[T]he affect ... turns out to be *not further reducible by psychological analysis, nor amenable to psychotherapy*" (Freud, 1895b [1894]: p. 97), because anxiety, in these neuroses, "can be traced to *no psychical origin*" (ibid.: p. 107). "Anxiety neurosis ... is the product of all those factors which prevent the somatic sexual excitation from being worked over psychically" (ibid.: p. 109), like abstinence, unconsummated excitation, coitus interruptus, etc.

## 20F

Vienna IX, Berggasse 19
16 February 1908

My dear Colleague,

After the end of a rather stormy period and the recovery, more or less, of the domestic patients,[1] I take advantage of a peaceful Sunday to answer your letter of 29 January.

The news that you are satisfied with the beginnings of your practice came as no surprise to me, but was as gratifying as the confirmation of a conviction always is. I look forward with pleasure to seeing you again in Salzburg. I am naturally in full agreement with your intention to put the libido in the foreground. I have not received the Juliusburger review, resp. the paper itself, and I shall be glad if you will get him to send it to me.

As for the question of the reducibility of anxiety in anxiety neurosis, you will find full information in Stekel's new book on anxiety hysteria[2] (to be expected in April). I would still regard the old position as theoretically unassailable, but I see that pure cases of anxiety neurosis are great rarities and perhaps once again only abstractions, and that the not really typical phobias permit and call for a ψanalytic resolution. That there is always also a bit of hysteria is just the way things are. In practice what happens is that actual therapy is first attempted,[3] and then, what turns out to be resistant, is tackled with Ψtherapy. Forming one's own opinion experimentally is certainly justified in every case. True, when the actual therapy is omitted or cannot be undertaken, one finds that the emptied forms are again and again filled afresh, so that one never comes to an end.

The new scientific project you mention makes me very curious. Will it be ready to be discussed in Salzburg?

The series in which the study of Gradiva appeared (Vol. 2, Riklin,[4] *Fairy-tales*, Vol. 3, Jung, *Content of the Psychoses*)—in which we should be very glad to publish something by you sometime—is now published by F. Deuticke.[5] My little paper from the new *Zeitschrift für Sexualwissenschaft*[6] must have reached you by now.

Among the small novelties—there are no large ones at present—you might be most interested by "Character and Anal Eroticism", which I gave to Bresler for his little weekly.[7] It tries to advance into new territory and therefore will create displeasure enough.

My wife's journey is off for the time being. I hope that your small family is well and send you my most cordial greetings.

Your most devoted

*Dr Freud*

1. In addition to Mathilde's abdominal troubles, several members of the family had had influenza.
2. Stekel, 1908, to which Freud wrote a foreword (Freud, 1908f). Wilhelm Stekel [1868–1940], Viennese physician. As Freud's analysand he was one of the first of his students and had prompted the founding of the Wednesday Society. Author of numerous popular articles and books about psychoanalysis. Co-editor, with Adler, of the *Zentralblatt*, which, after his break with Freud [1912], he continued on his own until 1914. Although Freud later had not one good word for Stekel, he viewed his numerous contributions to the investigation of symbols as fundamental and also integrated them into *The Interpretation of Dreams* (Freud, 1900a).
3. "In such cases it is natural that the physician should first consider 'actual' therapy, some alteration in the patient's somatic sexual activity" (Freud, 1910k: p. 224)—i.e. giving up coitus interruptus, for instance.
4. Franz Riklin [1878–1938], Swiss psychiatrist; collaborator on Jung's association studies. First secretary [1910] of the International Psychoanalytic Association [IPA] and, with Jung, editor of the *Korrespondenzblatt*. Riklin followed Jung after the latter's break with Freud.
5. *Schriften zur angewandten Seelenkunde* [*Papers on Applied Psychology*] [= *Schriften*], a monograph series edited by Freud. The first two numbers, published by Hugo Heller, were Freud's "Gradiva" study (1907a) and Riklin's on fairy-tales (1908). Heller [1870–1923] was the first publisher of *Imago* and the *Zeitschrift* and also a member of the Wednesday Society. His salon was a centre for liberal artists and intellectuals. Another Viennese firm, Franz Deuticke [1850–1919], publisher of the *Jahrbuch*, took over the *Schriften* with Jung's work (1908), the third number.
6. Freud, 1908a. The paper was originally intended for Magnus Hirschfeld's *Jahrbuch für sexuelle Zwischenstufen*, but was transferred by Hirschfeld to a new periodical just started by him. Hirschfeld [1868–1935] was the central figure of German sexology and a prolific author, best known for his struggle for the legalization of homosexuality. He became an original member of the psychoanalytic group in Berlin [in 1908]; he withdrew in 1911 [see letter 116A, 29 October 1911]. (Cf. letter 26F, 19 April 1908; Freud's letters to Jung, 25 February 1908, 14 April 1908, Freud & Jung, 1974 [1906–13]: pp. 125–126, 138; Herzer, 1992.)
7. Freud, 1908b. The article appeared in the *Psychiatrisch–neurologische Wochenschrift*, edited by the psychiatrist Johannes Bresler [1866–1936].

## 21A

Berlin
23 February 1908

Dear Professor Freud,

Your last letter contains little specific news about how your family is getting on. You speak about patients. Since I have had the pleasure of getting to know all your family, I do also take a further interest in them. I should therefore like to beg you from the bottom of my heart to keep me up to date on what is happening there too. I hope next time the news will be really favourable.

The plan I hinted at has come nearer to its realization. It had been my intention to send you the finished manuscript and to ask you to accept the paper for the *Sammlung*,[1] but you forestalled me by asking for a

## 1908 February

contribution. The title is to be "Dream and Myth", or something along those lines. I want to deal with the symbolism of language and of the myth, and especially with the numerous analogies between dreams and myths. I do not know how far Riklin goes in this respect; according to a short paper in the *Psychiatrisch–neurologische Wochenschrift*,[2] he appears to confine himself to proving wish-fulfilment. I should especially like to develop a number of other aspects: infantilism, condensation, censorship, repression, identification, etc. I should like to prove that ~~like the individual in the dream,~~ these concepts are not merely important with regard to individual psychology, but that they are also of great importance in ethnopsychology. As a paradigm, I shall take first of all the myth of the Descent of Fire, or rather its interpretation by Adalbert Kuhn,[3] and try to show that all important aspects of this interpretation resemble dream interpretation. Other myths will be dealt with briefly as well, to confirm various statements through them. If all goes well, I hope to finish in about six weeks. I believe the topic is suitable for the series.[4] Perhaps you would indicate to me the minimum or maximum length that you find acceptable?—A great many interesting questions arise in the course of the work, today I am confining myself to outlining the essentials and shall leave the details till later. I very much hope that you will approve of my plan.[5]

Many thanks for your essay on hysterical phantasies.[6] Like every single one of your writings, it comes as a relief to me insofar as things that I would not yet have dared to tackle are made clear to me. Indeed, I am even more curious to see the next. Anal erotism will have the effect of a small bomb. The lack of understanding is so great that this work, too, will not bring anyone into our camp. At least the time of killing us through silence [*Totschweigen*] is at an end. However full of misunderstanding Friedländer's collective review in the *Journal für Psychologie und Neurologie*[7] may be, it does show that the ideas are being discussed. I find from conversations with my colleagues that indifference is increasingly giving way to enmity. This enmity, however, does not always mean a poor prognosis. I have brought two of my colleagues to the point where I can debate with them, and one of them already gets me to interpret his dreams. I hope that the establishment of a Freudian Society, like those in Vienna and Zurich, is not too far off.

I have great hopes of Salzburg. I have received a very valuable confirmation concerning the subject of my talk. At a party I made the acquaintance of a poet, highly talented but undoubtedly suffering from dementia praecox. In him I found the *auto-erotism* in a sublimated form: he starves himself for days, as the Indian fakirs do, in order to bring on visionary states; then he gets into a state of supreme ecstasy which he describes as an infinite enjoyment of himself. The external world remains far behind him; nothing but he himself interests him; he revels in the feeling of being detached from the world and from human beings. He considers this to be the most dignified and highest form of enjoyment of life, which he obtains completely from himself alone.—The turning away of the libido from the external world could not be more beautifully illustrated.

With cordial greetings to you and your esteemed family, also from my wife, I remain

your gratefully devoted

*Karl Abraham*

1. The *Schriften*.
2. Riklin, 1907.
3. Adalbert Kuhn [1812–1881], German Indo–Germanic scholar, founder of comparative mythology. In his work, Abraham relied heavily on Kuhn (1859).
4. *Schriften zur angewandten Seelenkunde*.
5. This project, often discussed in the following letters, was to lead to Abraham's study *Dreams and Myths* (1909[14]), which appeared as No. 4 of the *Schriften*.
6. Freud, 1908a.
7. Friedländer, 1907–08. Adolf Albrecht Friedländer [1870–1949], German psychiatrist, titular professor in Berlin. Although he vehemently criticized psychoanalysis in public, he visited Jung on 14 October 1909 (Freud & Jung, 1974 [1906–13]: pp. 250, 253, 296) and later also Freud (see letter 88F, 5 June 1910). (Cf. Jones, 1955: p. 117.)

## 22F

Vienna IX, Berggasse 19
1 March 1908

My dear Colleague,

Yesterday my daughter left for Merano to convalesce.[1] All the others are back to normal again.

Your plan interests me greatly. I will await the work with much interest and shall publish it as Vol. V. The fourth in the series deals with a similar subject, the myth of the birth of the hero (Cyrus, Romulus, Moses, etc.), which is given a completely psychological interpretation. The author is our young secretary, Herr Otto Rank,[2] and a little of it will be mine. But I think you ought to take a good look at the astral meaning of myths, which now, since the discoveries of *Winckler*[3] (*Jeremias*,[4] Stucken*[5]) about the ancient oriental world system, can no longer be ignored. We were confronted with the same task. Apart from that, I believe there is room for a ψ explanation, because, after all, the ancients only projected their phantasies onto the sky.

The Anal Eroticism, which I expect daily, will surely not be very effective in winning people over, in that you are right. But if we can only get the matter securely under control. The others will come over in the end, whether still in my life-time or not, I have no misgivings about that.

In Salzburg we will strengthen each other, will we not? That is the main thing.

I hope your practice is making progress and yielding the empirical material from which imperative warnings originate.

With cordial greetings,
Yours,

*Freud*

P.S.: Both your dreams, mislaid with the cooperation of the Ucs., have been found and will be sent back to you again.

1. Mathilde spent half a year recovering in Merano, where she became acquainted with her future husband, Robert Hollitscher [1876–1959], a merchant.
2. Rank, 1909—this paper was to appear after Abraham's as No. 5 of the *Schriften*. Otto Rank (originally Rosenfeld) [1884–1939], a trade-school graduate, had introduced himself—by arrangement with his personal physician Alfred Adler—to Freud and became one of his first students and perhaps his most intimate collaborator. He was paid secretary and scribe for the Wednesday Society. With Freud's support, he undertook a course of study [Ph.D., 1912] and became editor of the periodicals *Imago, Zeitschrift für Anwendung der Psychoanalyse auf die Geisteswissenschaften* [= *Imago*], and *Internationale Zeitschrift für (ärztliche) Psychoanalyse* [= *Zeitschrift*] [1912–24], as well as head of the Internationaler Psychoanalytischer Verlag [= *Verlag*] [1919–24]. Around the time of publication of his book, *The Trauma of Birth* (1924), he gradually became estranged from Freud. In 1926 Rank went to Paris and in 1934 to the United States, where his ideas on the artist and on "will therapy" exerted a strong influence on psychotherapy and social work. (Cf. Lieberman, 1985.)
3. Hugo Winckler [1863–1913], German orientalist, from 1904 on professor in Berlin. (See also Freud, 1900a, addition 1909: p. 99.)
4. Alfred Jeremias [1864–1935], Assyriologist and professor in Leipzig. Jeremias (1904) was quoted by Freud in his article on anal erotism (1908b: p. 174), which he had just finished.
5. Eduard Stucken [1865–1936], German writer and linguist, expert on Syria and Egypt, author of *Astralmythen* (1907; quoted by Freud, 1913f: p. 291).

## 23A

Berlin
8 March 1908

Dear Professor Freud,

Very many thanks for your letter and for returning the dreams. I had not actually expected you to send them back. Should the mislaying of which you write mean taking possession of them, I shall be glad to send them to you again. I am delighted that you approve of my plan. I am going to get hold of Winckler's paper,[1] and I am anxious to know whether and where it confirms or overturns my results. But I scarcely believe that it can add anything better to my special paradigm (Prometheus) than Kuhn's classic interpretation. Do you know it? I wish

Riklin's and Rank's papers were already out, as I could refer to them on some points. I have now written down quite a large portion; at any rate, I am hurrying the work as much as I can.

As usual, I now have some questions. I have noticed in two mentally ill women a symptom that is familiar to me from other cases: they both complain of a tense, puckered feeling around the mouth, as if it were constricted. In the case of one of them, this sensation gradually leaves the mouth and moves to cheeks and forehead. It is obvious that this is a displacement upwards. Well, I know that both patients have an aversion to their husbands (in one of them repressed). One of them hardly tolerates any sexual intercourse and might react at times with physical symptoms of revulsion and disgust. Could the constricting sensation around the mouth perhaps stand for displaced vaginismus? The latter is, after all, also only an expression of revulsion. Have you come across similar phenomena in other cases?

Now a question about the *Interpretation of Dreams*. On p. 217 you speak of the expression of logical relations, inter alia of the "either–or".[2] I have seen a very instructive case in this connection. We had a visit from a friend of ours, a lady who is of Jewish descent on the paternal side and who had become engaged to a Jewish young man.[3] From both families strong resistance against this match could be expected. They were secretly engaged for years until they decided to marry. The lady visited us at the time when the arguments were at their most difficult with both families. She had a dream on the first night of her visit, which I was able to interpret immediately. This interested her greatly, and on the following morning she said to me: "Last night I had five dreams." She could relate them all very clearly; she had obviously dreamt them with the wish that I should interpret them. All five dreams were naturally concerned with the marriage, but each dealt with the subject from a different point of view. Thus, the five dreams presented the following five possibilities. (1.) they could live together in concubinage. (2.) they could marry in a register office without either of them having to give up their respective faiths. (3.) *he* could be baptized. (4.) *she* could become Jewish, but with only a civil marriage both in this case and in the previous one. (5.) *she* could change her faith and they could marry according to Jewish rites. In each of the dreams the couple were represented by relatives or friends who fitted the case. The interpretation was easy for each case, and I could not but see the five dreams as an expression of all future possibilities. I find this manner of expressing an "either–or" very remarkable, and I should like to know whether my interpretation is correct.[4]

I was very glad to learn that your family are all better. I hope that your daughter will soon make a complete recovery in Merano. Please

accept, for yourself and your esteemed family, kind regards from my wife and myself,
   your very devoted
   *Karl Abraham*

1. Probably Winckler, 1902, quoted in Abraham, 1909[14]: p. 206.
2. Freud, 1900a: pp. 316–318.
3. Judaism is matrilineal, so a woman whose father is Jewish is considered to be Gentile.
4. Abraham reported this case briefly (1909[14]: p. 195).


## 24F

Vienna IX, Berggasse 19
13 March 1908

Dear Colleague,

As usual you make it easy for me to reply, as in both cases I only need to say yes. I should also take the feeling of constriction round the mouth as displaced vaginismus; the patient herself must tell you about the more special determinations.

Your dream interpretation is certainly correct, and a complement to the passage you quote. There it says: "or" in the dream is to be replaced by "and" in the [dream] thoughts[1]; you add: "Or" in thoughts is shown by simply stringing them together (["]and["]) in the dream. Drawing apart in five single dreams is quite a charming manner [?],[2] and particularly transparent; usually the different possibilities are composed one over the other (in each other).

I am now reassured about your Salzburg lecture, about the missing of which I have been worried; I am supposed to talk a little casuistics according to Jung's wish.

Reading about the Babylonian matter[3] will in any case stimulate you very much. I, too, think it will not disturb our circles.[4]

In my family nothing is quite right these days. We cannot escape from the children being ill. My daughter writes very favourable reports from Merano.

With cordial greetings,
Yours,
   *Freud*

1. Freud, 1900a: p. 317.
2. Reading uncertain.
3. Referring to Winckler, 1902.
4. "*Noli turbare circulos meos*" [do not disturb my circles], Archimedes [287–213 BC] is said to have said to an intruding soldier.

25A

Berlin
4 April 1908

Dear Professor Freud,

This time you have had to wait a long time for my reply. I deliberately delayed my letter until the manuscript of *Dreams and Myths* was finished. It was finally sent off today by registered post and should reach you in a few days. The work on myths gave me great pleasure, especially since my former philological interests were revived a little.[1] The material certainly merits much fuller treatment. I feel like doing some work on a specific cycle of myths possibly sometime later. First of all, though, I wait to hear your opinion. My expositions are, naturally, based entirely on yours, and I very much hope that you will agree with the conclusions I drew for the myth from the interpretation of dreams, etc. I am naturally very interested to know whether the paper will appear soon. Or do I have to wait until Jung and Rank are published? Rank's subject is certainly very fruitful. If you have not come across it yet, I should like especially to draw your attention to the Samson legend and to Steinthal's[2] paper on it (*"Die Sage von Simson"*, Zeitschrift für Völkerpsychologie und Sprachwissenschaft, Vol. 2, 1862). Riklin's paper reached me just as I had finished mine. It is a pity that the style is so irritating; it does not do justice to the content.

Now I must thank you for the two reprints. A few days before I received the "Sexualmoral",[3] I heard a lecture on *"Medizin und Überkultur"* by our new clinician, His[4] (successor to Leyden[5]), which is the complete opposite of your paper. Not one word on sexuality in the whole lecture! Yet it was a most learned paper, which drew on all sorts of material not directly connected with medicine. *Summa summarum*,[6] only a spate of words as a cover for sexual repression. Soon after that I read *your* paper. How differently this sign strikes me![7]

I had already found the paper on anal erotism in the journal a few days before your parcel arrived. It will arouse a great deal of headshaking.[8] The description precisely fits one of my relatives—a peculiar bachelor. Furthermore, it fits a case of hysteria analysed by Jung with which you will undoubtedly already be acquainted from his description.[9] The loving interest in their defaecation displayed by men who have exhausted their sexuality early certainly belongs in this context, as a way of returning to anal erotism. Would not the following also belong here? Before puberty, lavatory humour plays the same role as sexual humour does later. There are people who never rid themselves of the first kind, whose greatest pleasure is to make jokes referring to defaecation in the most unsuitable surroundings. Are such people not anal erotists? It seems to me that old men as well, after their potency disappears, also return to lavatory humour.

1908 April

I am analysing a nice case at the moment—compulsive ideas of having missed something, obsessional washing, swearwords in prayer, etc. I am very well satisfied with the success of the first sessions.—Now a question, as usual. Do you know a psychological cause for the so-called "Ictus Laryngis" (Charcot)?[10] I saw a case in Oppenheim's polyclinic: in an otherwise apparently healthy man, attacks of coughing over the last twenty years with dyspnoea and increased pulse rate. There must be something psychological behind it.

There was a lively discussion about Freud the other day at a party at Professor Liepmann's.[11] Only doctors and their wives were present. In the course of the battle it so happened that two groups formed in two different rooms. While I defended the wish-fulfilment theory of dementia praecox in one room, my wife had to defend the theory of repression in the other. Otherwise there is little opportunity for propaganda. I am planning before very long to arrange a course for physicians in order to discuss the theory of neuroses and the dream. What do you think about this?

You write in your last letter that you are now reassured about my paper. Did it originally not appear on the programme?

I hope that all your family are well again now and add my kind regards to all of you.

Your gratefully devoted

*Karl Abraham*

1. Abraham's great interest in comparative linguistics and etymology dates back to his adolescence (cf. H. Abraham, 1974: pp. 37–38).
2. Hajim (Heymann) Steinthal [1823–1899], German philologist and philosopher. Pioneer of a psychological view of language. Co-editor [from 1859 on] of the *Zeitschrift für Völkerpsychologie und Sprachwissenschaft*; from 1863 on professor at Berlin University.
3. Freud, 1908d.
4. Wilhelm His [1863–1934], Swiss general practitioner, professor in Basel, Göttingen, and Berlin, where he held a Chair of Medicine at the university clinic, the Charité.
5. Ernst von Leyden [1832–1910], prominent German general practitioner, physician of Tsar Alexander. Known for his works on the pathology of the heart, lung, kidneys, the nervous system, and particularly on dietetics. Editor of numerous medical journals.
6. Latin: "sum of sums", "all in all". From the Roman dramatist Plautus [ca. 254–184 BC].
7. *Wie anders wirkt dies Zeichen auf mich ein!* (Goethe, *Faust I*, "Night", verse 460).
8. A jocular quotation from the *Jobsiade* of the very popular German artist and humorist Wilhelm Busch [1832–1908].
9. These seem to refer to Sabina Spielrein, who had been Jung's patient between 1904 and 1909; this had led to a love-affair, of which Freud was also informed (cf. Carotenuto, 1980; Kerr, 1993). Spielrein [1885–1941], born in Russia, had studied medicine in Zurich [from 1905 on] and in 1911 became a member of the Vienna Society. In 1912 she moved to Berlin, then to Munich, Lausanne, Châteaux d'Oex, and Geneva, where Jean Piaget was in analysis with her for eight months in 1921. In 1923 she returned to the Soviet Union and became a member of the Society there. In 1941 she was murdered by the Nazis, along with her two daughters.

10. Ictus laryngis or tussive epilepsy (Charcot), sudden loss of consciousness after heavy coughing.
11. Hugo Karl Liepmann [1863–1925], professor of neurology at Berlin University and psychiatrist at the Charité.

## 26F

Vienna
19 April 1908

Dear Colleague,

A few words, before we meet in Salzburg, about your work, which I am happy to accept as the fourth volume of the *"Schriften"* etc. [the publisher's consent is still to be formally sought].[1] I have read it with pleasure and especially enjoyed the decisiveness with which you speak up for our cause. The basic thought, the way you conceive the myth, is obvious to me; an off-print that is going off to you at the same time will tell you that I have already stated it, without any proof.[2]

What follows now are suggestions for alterations, which you will kindly understand as an effort to make your work appear as favourable as possible:

1. I should like to ask that polemics, my name, psychiatry etc. should retreat a little in favour of the myth itself, as readers will be much more interested in that than in our disputes. In other words, what was written for you and me is to be transcribed for the public.

2. It would be a natural consequence that the sober scientific form would change to the style of a lecture or essay.

3. It would be wonderful if you could deal briefly with one additional myth or the other.

I will take the manuscript to Salzburg for you, and there we can discuss the details. I shall easily induce Herr Rank to let you precede him. His work is also mythological, it borders on yours but does not clash with it. Form and technique are quite different in him, so that the smooth and immediate sequence of the two papers remains quite possible. We should consider September as the date of publication, as two issues have just been brought out and midsummer is said to be unfavourable. Jung's "Content of the Psychosis", brief but very well done, has been in my hands for a few days.

I might also tell you that Dr Magnus Hirschfeld, who visited me here recently, has asked for your address in order to get in contact with you. I hope you will not be influenced by the opinion of the official mob in Berlin about him.

Until we meet again in Salzburg,[3]

Yours cordially devoted

*Freud*

1908 April

1. Square brackets in original.
2. Freud, 1908e [1907]: p. 152.
3. On 26–27 April the first international meeting of psychoanalysts took place in Salzburg. Jones had wanted to call it "International Psycho-Analytical Congress" (Jones, 1955: p. 39), in Jung's printed circular invitation it read "First Congress for Freudian Psychology", on the programme "Meeting in Salzburg" (Freud & Jung, 1974 [1906–13]: pp. 110, 571), while Freud simply regarded it as private gathering and not to be mentioned in public (see letter 28F, 3 May 1908). Freud spoke on "Case Material", the analysis of the "Rat-Man" (Freud, 1909d, 1955a [1907–8]) and Abraham on "Psychosexual Differences between Dementia Praecox and Hysteria" (Abraham, 1908[11]). It was also decided that a journal, the *Jahrbuch für psychoanalytische und psychopathologische Forschungen* [*Jahrbuch*], the first psychoanalytic periodical, should be published, under the direction of Freud and Bleuler and the editorship of Jung. The atmosphere was friendly and relaxed, except for a conflict between Abraham and Jung (see the following letters) and Bleuler's reserved attitude (see letter 27A, 30 April 1908, n. 2).

27A

Berlin
30 April 1908

Dear Professor Freud,

I am sorry to have to bother you with a question. Today I am sending the paper of my talk to Gaupp[1] to be printed. I noted under the title of the work: "Paper read at the First Congress for Psycho-Analytical Research in Salzburg on 27.4.08." Is that description all right with you, or would you prefer another? I would not like to give the Congress a name on my own authority. I will make the alterations you asked for in the proofs, which I am expecting in about a fortnight. Many thanks in advance!

Salzburg was good. I only have great regrets about Bleuler's behaviour.[2] I am convinced that we cannot expect anything more from him towards our efforts.

With cordial greetings,
your gratefully devoted

*Karl Abraham*

1. Robert Eugen Gaupp [1870–1953], German psychiatrist, professor in Tübingen [1906–1936]; editor of the *Zentralblatt für Nervenheilkunde und Psychiatrie*, in which Abraham's article then appeared.
2. From the beginning, Bleuler had great reservations about a psychoanalytic "movement". Calling the Salzburg meeting a "congress" "represented an attitude which presently was to give his [Jung's] chief, Bleuler, a handle for criticism" (Jones, 1955: pp. 39–40). Bleuler's difficult relationship with Jung, who was, at that time, an enthusiastic advocate and promoter of such a movement, added to the strained atmosphere.

## 28F

Vienna IX, Berggasse 19
3 May 1908

My dear and esteemed Colleague,

I am very glad that you regard Salzburg as a gratifying event. I am in no position to judge, since I stand in the midst of it all, but my inclination is also to consider this first gathering a promising try.

I can answer your question straight away: the Congress is not to be publicly mentioned at all. Thus also not under the title of your forthcoming publication.

In connection with the latter, I would make a request to you, on the fulfilment of which all sorts of things may depend. I recollect that your paper led to a slight conflict between you and Jung, or so at least I concluded from a few words you said to me afterwards. Now, I consider a rivalry between the two of you to be inevitable, and also quite harmless within certain limits; in dealing with the matter at issue I did not hesitate to say that you were in the right and to attribute Jung's sensitiveness to his vacillation. But I would not like any serious bad feeling to come between you. We are still so few that disharmony, especially because of any personal "complexes", should be out of the question among us. It must also be of importance for us that Jung should find his way back to the views he has just forsaken, which you have stood by so consistently. I believe there are prospects for this; Jung also writes to me that Bleuler shows signs of being very much influenced and almost inclined to abandon again the concept of the organic nature of dementia praecox.

So you would virtually do me a personal favour if you informed him in advance of your publication and asked him to discuss his former objections with you so that you would be able to take them into account. Such an act of courtesy will certainly nip the nascent disagreement in the bud, would greatly please me, and would show me that all of us are capable of also drawing practical benefit for our own mental activities from the practice of psychoanalysis. Do not take the little victory over yourself too hard.

Be tolerant, and do not forget that really it is easier for you to follow my thoughts than it is for Jung, since to begin with you are completely independent, and then you are closer to my intellectual constitution through racial kinship, while he as a Christian and a pastor's son finds his way to me only against great inner resistances. His association with us is therefore all the more valuable. I was almost going to say that it was only by his emergence on the scene that psychoanalysis was removed from the danger of becoming a Jewish national affair.

1908  May

I hope you will give your attention to my request and send you the most cordial greetings.

Yours,

*Freud*


29F

Vienna, Berggasse
9 May 1908

Dear Colleague,

Still without response to my last request, I am writing to you again to reinforce it. You know how gladly I put what I have at your disposal as well as that of others, but nothing would be more painful to me than that sensitivity about priority among my friends and followers should be the result. If everyone contributes his mite, it must be possible to avoid these things. I expect that you will manage to do so both for the sake of the cause and myself.

With cordial greetings,

Yours,

*Freud*


30A

Berlin
11 May 1908

Dear Professor Freud,

I was about to write to you when your letter of the 9th reached me. It was merely in the interest of the cause that I had not answered earlier. When I read your *first* letter, I was not in agreement with all of your points, and therefore let it rest for a few days. Then I was able to read it *sine ira et studio*, and I convinced myself of the correctness of your arguments. After that I delayed no longer in writing to Zurich, but I did not post the letter at once. I wanted to make sure after a few days' interval that there was not something concealed in it somewhere that would have turned the *rapprochement* into an attack. I know how hard I find it to avoid polemics altogether, and the subsequent reading of the letter proved me right. So yesterday I brought the letter into its final form. I hope it will now serve the cause. I wanted to write to you, dear Professor, only after dealing with the letter to Jung. Thus, you will surely excuse my silence. Now that I look upon this matter calmly, I have to thank you for your intervention and at the same time for the confidence you placed in me. You need not fear that the matter will leave me with any kind of bad feeling. I hope that the way I acted will have the desired success; in any case, I shall keep you informed of further developments.

Actually I became involved in the conflict quite innocently. In December I asked you whether there was any risk of my colliding with Jung on this subject, as you had communicated your ideas to him as well. You dispelled my doubts at the time. My manuscript for Salzburg contained a remark that would certainly have satisfied Bleuler and Jung; following a sudden impulse, I omitted to read it out. I deceived myself for the moment by a cover-motive—saving time—while the true reason lay in my animosity against Bl.[euler] and J[ung]. This came from their latest all too conciliatory publications, from Bleuler's address in Berlin,[1] which made no reference to you *at all*, and from various trivialities. That I did not mention Bl. and J. obviously means: "Since they turn aside from the theory of sexuality, I really will not cite them in connection with it."—It naturally did not come into conscious thought at that moment that this omission might have serious consequences.

According to your wish, the publication of my paper will contain ~~nothing~~ not a word about the Congress.

I hope I have now settled everything as you would have wished. As far as I am concerned, the harmony shall not be disturbed. I should like to ask you from the bottom of my heart to criticize me frankly also in future. I shall always try to follow your views. As with so many theoretical questions where at first I could not follow you but later became fully converted to your view, I shall surely also succeed here in future, too. I freely admit that I find it easier than Jung does to go along with you. I, too, have always felt this intellectual kinship. After all, the Talmudic way of thinking cannot disappear in us just like that. Some days ago a small paragraph in *Jokes*[2] strangely attracted me. When I looked at it more closely, I found that, in the technique of apposition and in its whole structure, it was completely Talmudic. In Zurich, incidentally, I was always pleased that Bleuler and Jung overcame the resistances based on their different constitutions so successfully. All the more painful is the change!

The alterations asked for in *Dreams and Myths* are already partly completed; the others will be done in the course of the week.—I called on Dr Hirschfeld and gained an impression that is far better than his reputation. Among other things, he asked me to collaborate with him on the revision of a questionnaire, which he said he showed to you, too.[3] Some days after my visit to him he sent me a homosexual patient for psychoanalysis.

With cordial greetings,
your devoted

*Karl Abraham*

1. See letter 15A, 8 January 1908, n. 8.
2. Freud, 1905c.
3. Hirschfeld had suggested to Freud and his circle that they should collaborate on a questionnaire for sex research. On 15 April 1908, the Wednesday Society agreed to do so; Freud himself wanted to work out the questionnaire. On this occasion the group around Freud publicly called itself "Psychoanalytic Society" for the first time.

## 31F

Vienna IX, Berggasse 19
15 May 1908

My dear Colleague,

I thank you, and shall not forget that you have allowed me this influence. I hope that you too will be satisfied.

I await your paper in its revised form and shall duly submit it to the publisher.

Our *Jahrbuch* is secured, under favourable conditions, and is to appear in two half-volumes; the decision still hovers between Deuticke and Marhold.[1] The first issue shall contain a survey of the hitherto published ψanalytic works. Jung will deal with the publications from Zurich, Maeder with the French, Jones[2] with the English-speaking literature, and the purely negative and hostile achievements will, I think, be referred to a special reviewer. For the Vienna publications, mine included, and the contributions from Germany, Jung has suggested you, so that I can now inquire directly of you whether you will accept.[3] If my publications are too much of a burden for you, I can shift the load to Rank, who is, as it is, very well attuned to me, though his *Matura*[4] is just ahead. The reviews will, of course, be paid for, 50 marks a sheet.[5] I shall probably contribute a case history in each half-yearly issue.[6]

With cordial greetings and thanks,
Yours,

*Freud*

1. Carl Marhold, publisher in Halle am Saale, Germany.
2. Ernest Jones [1879–1958], Welsh neurologist. He had met Jung in 1907 at the Neurological Congress in Amsterdam, and shortly thereafter he had spent a short time at the Burghölzli. He had met Freud and Abraham for the first time at the Salzburg meeting. Jones played an extremely significant role in the psychoanalytic movement and its historiography. He was an initiator of the "Secret Committee", founder of the American and London—later British—Psychoanalytic Societies, president of the IPA with the longest term [1920–1924 and 1934–1949], as well as the author of the well-known Freud biography (Jones, 1953, 1955, 1957). Among Jones's scientific writings are a large number of works on the dissemination of psychoanalysis, as well as on specific themes— on psychoanalysis and religion and Hamlet, among others. His writings on female sexuality gave rise to a number of controversies. Perhaps his most lasting contribution is the concept of "rationalization", first presented in Salzburg.

3. This plan was carried through, with the exception of reviews of the French and of the critical literature (cf. Abraham, 1909[15], 1909[16]; Jones, 1910a; Jung, 1910a).
4. The qualification examination for admission to Austrian universities.
5. Holograph: [*Druck-*]*Bogen* [printed sheet, signature], which has 16 pages.
6. The case histories of "Little Hans" (Freud, 1909b) and the "Rat Man" (Freud, 1909d).

32A

Berlin
19 May 1908

Dear Professor Freud,

By the time you receive this letter, your wife will already have given you our regards. My wife and I were so pleased with her visit and only regretted that there could be just this one short meeting.

My reaction to the inquiry in your last letter can only be one of glad acceptance. However, I shall be able to say whether or not I can manage on my own the work allotted to me only when I know more precisely what it involves and also how much time I shall be allowed for it. I assume that I would first have to give a collective review of all your writings. As far as I know, I have them all. But I do not have exact knowledge of all the other papers contributed from Vienna. Could I perhaps have a list? I assume that the Psycho-Analytic Society is in possession of all the papers. Perhaps Herr Rank would be kind enough to draw up such a list for me. Could I possibly also borrow from the Society's library those papers that I cannot obtain here? The *German* literature contains very few positive contributions indeed, and these I can find myself.

First of all, then, I should like to see how much work is involved and how much time I may take over it. Then I can easily judge whether I can manage by myself, or whether I would have to ask Herr Rank for his help. To the work itself I am very much looking forward.—I cannot give you any news about the Jung affair, as I am still waiting for a reply.

The elaboration of the Soma myth is, after all, taking up more time than I had expected, as Kuhn only gives an incomplete interpretation on this point. I therefore have to work off on my own bat and, consequently, must be doubly careful. The interpretative work is most interesting, though, and also yields the same layers and the same wish-fulfilments as the Prometheus myth. I am most grateful to you for your advice to include this myth.[1]

In connection with *Jokes,* I have arrived at some further understanding of the psychology of mental illnesses, especially the behaviour of the so-called [paranoid] querulant.[2] I shall tell you about this on some future occasion. I have promised Dr Hirschfeld a contribution to his

Journal ("On the Sublimation of the Sexual Instinct").[3] So, for the near future, there is enough work to do.

My practice is doing fairly well. The analysis of the homosexual is making quite good progress and shows noticeable results. I still doubt, however, that I shall succeed in making him potent in his marriage. He is almost 40 years old and has been married for eight years.

With cordial greetings from house to house,
your very devoted

*Karl Abraham*

1. Abraham, 1909[14], chapter XI: pp. 200–204.
2. In German the word *Querulant* describes a patient diagnosed as having predominantly paranoid ideas and litigious tendencies, covered in English by the term *paranoid querulant*. Abraham's interest in paranoia querulans persisted (cf. letter 356A, 5 June 1919).
3. Abraham did not publish such a work.

## 33A

Berlin
27 May 1908

Dear Professor Freud,

The manuscript has just gone back to you again. I have dealt with the Soma legend in a special chapter, and in the rest of it I have made the alterations about which I have already written to you. On the whole the work still has the character of a scientific treatise, whereas you would rather have the style of an essay. The difficulty is that actually there is a great deal in it that must first rest on a scientific basis before it is ready to be dealt with in an essay. I hope the work does not suffer too much from this. It now contains quite a number of examples, and this, I believe, will make it digestible for lay people also.

With kind regards,
your very devoted

*Karl Abraham*

## 34F

Vienna
29 May 1908

Dear Colleague,

Many thanks for the notice about your work, the arrival of which I need not confirm to you.

I am especially glad that you have accepted the task of doing an authentic survey of the Viennese literature [perhaps also the German][1] for the *Jahrbuch*, as, in this case, it is mainly I who am under consideration. I think brevity will be very desirable. Perhaps you will also allow me to read the reviews dealing with my works in manuscript so as to shorten or emphasize. Herr Rank will be told next Wednesday to contact you and to send you a complete list of the other Viennese contributions along with the contributions themselves, from our private library or from the authors.

The first half-volume should appear on 1 January 1909. So you have time with the manuscript until October. Everything else is in order. Deuticke has gone through a great deal of trouble to get the publication. Bleuler will, I hope, as co-editor, now feel committed and disprove your bad prognosis. His paper on dementia praecox at the Berlin Congress was, it is true, not *"fameux"*.

My wife has told me a great deal about the cordial welcome she received at your house. I seem to have made a good diagnosis with regard to your family life.

With a friendly greeting,
Yours,

*Freud*

1. Square brackets in original.

### 35F

Vienna IX, Berggasse 19
7 June 1908

Dear Colleague,

On this rainy Whitsunday I have read your revised paper for the *Schriften zur vergl angewandten Seelenkunde,* and as the first reader I shall not withhold from you my thanks and full appreciation, particularly as I do not know whether you will get these from other quarters. It is all so clear, well based and constructed, full of conviction and free from misunderstanding and misunderstandability. I liked the piece very much. You are right, it is not an essay but a treatise, but that, after all, is what you chose to make it, and perhaps the persuasiveness of the whole has only gained thereby.

I was very much struck by the fact that you found such far-reaching agreement with our views and statements among the great ethnopsychologists.

May I make one or two small suggestions to you? To make use of the very conclusive detail in connection with Moses's staff when he appears before Pharaoh that the transformation from the stiff wood to the flexible snake is nothing but an unconcealed (reversed) representation of

1908 June

*erection*, which is in a way the most striking phenomenon encountered by man.[1] Also perhaps to mention what I say about myth in the lecture "Creative Writers and Day-Dreaming", which fits in very well with what you say.[2] The vitalizing effect of semen is to my knowledge directly expressed in Indian erotic literature. I know of one allusion to it in *Fuchs, Das erotische Element in der Karikatur*, pp. 29–30.[3] Furthermore the Soma potion seems to contain the important presentiment that all our intoxicating liquors and stimulating alkaloids are merely a substitute for the unique, still looked for toxin of the libido that rouses the ecstasy of love.—

Herr Rank is getting the literature together for you. I shall send your work off to be printed before the beginning of the holidays; I must allow the publisher a few weeks' peace.

Personally (the catchword just fell), I am counting the weeks till I have got as far myself. We have booked in Berchtesgaden, where part of the family will be going at the end of June, and I shall join them on 15 July. The literary work there is nothing but pleasure in comparison with the hard professional grind.[4]

Hoping that "whitewashing"[5] the nervous will soon be as disagreeable to you as it has become to me, I send you my most cordial greetings.

Your most faithfully devoted

*Freud*

1. Cf. Abraham, 1909[14]: p. 203.
2. Freud, 1908e [1907]: p. 152, then quoted by Abraham (1909[14]: pp. 154–155). Freud's paper was first presented as a public lecture in the salon of Hugo Heller.
3. Eduard Fuchs, noted historian of erotic art.
4. In Berchtesgaden, Freud prepared the second edition of the *Interpretation of Dreams*, worked on the final draft of the case history of "Little Hans" (Freud, 1909b), and wrote two articles (1908c, 1909a [1908]). On 15 August, he was joined by Ferenczi for what would be the first of many joint holidays.
5. An expression going back to Jeremias, 13:23 already used by Freud earlier (Breuer & Freud, 1895, German edition: p. 262; [omitted from *Standard Edition*]).

36A

Berlin
11 June 1908

Dear Professor Freud,

Your appreciative words gave me great pleasure. I do hope the success with regard to its persuasiveness will bear out your prognosis. I shall put your suggested additions into the proofs. If I should write another contribution for the collection, I may perhaps succeed in adopting a style more to your taste. I am, incidentally, becoming more and more convinced that a work can be useful to our cause only if the author unreservedly stands behind it. I believe that the reviews in the *Jahrbuch* should also allow the reviewer's opinion to emerge. I have started on this work. The *Three Contributions*[1] are finished; I am now engaged on *The Psychopathology of Everyday Life*.[2]

Yesterday I received an invitation from Moll to collaborate in a new journal. He tells me that you have agreed to contribute.[3] I have done likewise and furthermore shall have a discussion with M. on this matter.—It will interest you to know that Oppenheim has sent me a patient for psychoanalysis; true, the patient herself wanted this treatment. But it is remarkable that he did not dissuade her. In general, the practice is going satisfactorily. It is not yet keeping me so busy that I could wish for a holiday, nor that I could afford one. But the beginning is encouraging. I wish you and your esteemed family a very pleasant holiday, even if for the time being you yourself have to be content with the anticipation of it.

I intend to hold a course for doctors in the autumn, and the reviews serve as a kind of preparation for this. Or do you think such a course is too daring a venture here, *in partibus infidelium*?[4]

Now, you will certainly be waiting to hear something about the outcome of my affair with Jung. To my sincere regret, I cannot tell you anything, since, after more than a month, I have still not had a reply.

Finally, two more questions. (1.) Who is Alfred Polgar,[5] who in his stories in *Simplicissimus*[6] always uses your nomenclature? Dr Graf,[7] by any chance? (2.) In the *Psychopathology of Everyday Life*, second edition, p. 40, example i,[8] is the *Klapperschlange* [rattlesnake] not determined by *Klapperstorch* [stork], which also bites?

The subject of the Soma potion is one that I should like to take up again at some later date in order to go into the psychology of intoxication in greater detail. But some other subjects attract me first.

With cordial greetings,
I remain your gratefully devoted

*Karl Abraham*

1. Freud, 1905d.
2. Freud, 1901b.
3. Albert Moll [1862–1939], German neurologist, pioneer of sexology. The periodical mentioned is the *Zeitschrift für Psychotherapie und medizinische Psychologie*, in which Freud's paper (1909a [1908]) was to appear.
4. Latin: "in the lands of the unbelievers"; appended to the titles of bishops who were ordained but were not allowed to act as such in the countries they were ordained for.
5. Alfred Polgar [1873–1955], Austrian writer and critic. Master of small prose pieces such as sketches, feuilletons, etc.
6. Famous German political satirical weekly [1896–1944, 1954–1967].
7. Max Graf [1875–1958], noted musicologist, critic and writer; member of the Wednesday Society and a friend of Freud's. He was the father of "Little Hans", Herbert Graf.
8. Freud, 1901b: pp. 65–67.

## 37F

Vienna[1]
14 June 1908

[D]ear Colleague,
[A qu]ick reply to your questions:
[1. Pol]gar is—he himself; is considered the [most?] talented of the *Jung-Wiener*;[2] I do not know him.
2. The rattlesnake, as far as I know, goes [back] only to Cleopatra and the youth phantasy of becoming a Wolter[3]; behind that is the "snake".
I have very little news of Jung, he seems to be busy "day and night" with Otto Gross.[4] The reviews very short, right?
Your cordially devoted

*Freud*

P.S.: I have given M.[oll] your name as well as those of other fellow-workers, it is a question of a *Zentralblatt*, in which we too are to be represented. Otherwise—*caveas!*[5] M. bites too.

1. Postcard with the corner cut out—presumably in order to keep the stamp.
2. *Jung-Wien* or *Junges Wien* [Young Vienna]: a circle of avant-garde writers around Hermann Bahr, ca. 1890–1900. Among the members were Hugo von Hofmannsthal, Arthur Schnitzler, Felix Salten, Richard Beer-Hofmann, Peter Altenberg, and Karl Kraus.
3. Charlotte Wolter [1834–1897], famous German actress at the *Burgtheater* in Vienna (cf. Freud, 1901b: p. 66).
4. Otto Gross [1877–1920], son of Hans Gross, renowned professor of criminology at the University of Graz. In 1902 Gross, addicted to cocaine and morphine, was at the Burghölzli for the first of many drug cures. In 1908, at Freud's request, he was ana-lysed—unsuccessfully—by Jung. On 25 May 1908, Jung had written to Freud that he "spent all . . . available time, day and night, on Gross" (Freud & Jung, 1974 [1906–13]: p. 153). In 1914 Gross went back into therapy with Stekel. Gross was considered to be one of the most brilliant and creative analysts, while being suspect because of his drug addiction, life style, and anarchistic ideas. (Cf. Green, 1999; Hurwitz, 1979.)
5. Allusion to the Latin *"cave canem"* ["beware of the dog"].

## 38A

Berlin
9 July 1908

Dear Professor Freud,
Your card pleased me very much. I take it that I may definitely expect Myths to be published in the autumn. Gaupp will publish the Salzburg paper on 15 July. A little while ago I gave Hirschfeld a short essay on the "Psychological Relationship between Alcoholism and Sexuality". A further paper is in preparation and will deal with the psychology of marriage between relatives.[1] This has been regarded for many years as a cause of nervous illness. I want to prove the reverse: namely, that neu-

rotically disposed persons have a preference for marrying blood relations because they cannot detach their libido from its earliest object — father or mother.* I have found some very interesting material[2] but will not trouble you with it just now before the holidays.

The practice, though numerically small, is at least therapeutically satisfying. I have achieved a very nice success in a case of severe anxiety hysteria. The [male] patient, a very intelligent Ph.D., showed excellent comprehension and is now also scientifically interested in the cause. The wife also had anxiety symptoms and has lost them. This couple is at the same time an excellent example of my theory about intermarriage between relatives.

I do not want to write anything about Zurich today. You will draw the right conclusions about it for yourself in any case. Oppenheim, on the other hand, seems to show signs of coming round. Recently he asked me in the polyclinic *coram publico*[3] to investigate a boy psychoanalytically! His earlier resistance seems to be changing into tolerance. Perhaps we shall yet live to see "signs and wonders".[4] But I do not rush anything and can see that reserve gets me further than propaganda.

I wish you a very pleasant holiday; I myself am staying in Berlin and shall write the reviews for the *Jahrbuch*.

With cordial greetings,
your very devoted

*Karl Abraham*

\* and can most easily find an object with similar qualities within their own families.

1. Abraham, 1908[12], 1908[13].
2. Much of which came from Abraham's own family.
3. Latin: "before the public".
4. Exodus 7, 3.

## 39F

Vienna IX, Berggasse 19
11 July 1908

Dear Colleague,

Please do not make too heavy going of the review for the *Jahrbuch*. After all, it should be as brief as possible. Have I already drawn your attention to Warda's papers? One is in the *Archiv für Psychiatrie*.[1] It would be best for you to ask him for them.

I have little news from Zurich, that is to say, from Jung, and know nothing that would concern you. I greatly deplore your quarrel. If I have the opportunity to talk to Jung in the autumn, I shall take thorough soundings. I am afraid that there is a lack of desire for a satisfactory harmony on both sides, although, to be sure, with the exception of what you did recently to please me. I must reconcile you for the sake of the cause; you are both too valuable to me.

Your idea about marriage between close relatives is certainly correct and worth describing. It has already been mentioned in our group, but of course you need take no notice of that. A girl cousin very often takes the place of the sister. I believe the prognosis for such marriages to be generally rather favourable.

Your reserve in relation to Oppenheim is very appropriate. Let us do as we do in relation to associations in analysis: not to run after one that is unwilling.

On the 15th I am leaving for *Berchtesgaden Dietfeldhof.*

I feel in great need of the holiday. At your age things were different with me too.

With cordial greetings,
Yours,

*Freud*

P.S.: Recently I have come to understand the flood myths and traced them back.

1. Dr Wolfgang Warda, psychiatrist in Blankenburg, Thuringia, Germany, participant at the Salzburg meeting, charter member of the Berlin Society [1910]; withdrew in 1911. The article (Warda, 1909), along with some others by Warda, was mentioned by Abraham in his review for the *Jahrbuch* (Abraham, 1909[16]: p. 594).

## 40A

Berlin
16 July 1908

Dear Professor Freud,

I really ought to leave you in peace just now at the beginning of your holiday, but I do have to reply to some points in your letter. My brief reference to Zurich in my last letter was *not* meant to refer to my personal disagreement with Jung, but to the whole present attitude adopted in Zurich. To deal with the former first: I have not the slightest wish for an estrangement from Zurich. My letter to Jung was as accommodating as possible (I could send you a copy). Not to reply is really rather rude. But should harmony be re-established, now or later, either through your mediation or in some other way, I for my part will certainly not be the sulky one! On the contrary, I should like to keep in touch with the Burghölzli. Even though a number of unpleasant things happened before I left, I brought so many agreeable memories away with me that I certainly do not wish to disturb the peace.

Actually, the matter goes deeper. Jung's behaviour to me is, after all, only a symptom. I believe all the gentlemen in Vienna had the impression in Salzburg that not much more could be expected from Zurich. I have news from a reliable source about the latest developments, and it was under the impact of this that I wrote to you last time. I do not wish to pester you with details. But the sudden death of the Freudian evenings, so well attended until April, is striking. Jung seems to be reverting to his former spiritualistic inclinations. But please let us keep this between ourselves! However, if Jung gives up for this reason and for the sake of his career, then it is simply over at the Burghölzli. Bleuler, however efficient he may otherwise be, will do nothing on his own. He is a very complex personality, a mass entirely of reaction formations. His external simplicity and often exaggerated modesty cover strong grandiose tendencies. Salzburg was no help to the latter. The others are of little account. Riklin is Jung's creature. Only Maeder could be counted on; he is both intelligent and independent. Eitingon[1] is rather unsuitable for active collaboration, although he shows the best understanding. So, my remark referred to all these matters and not to my personal affair.

I will make the reviews as short as possible, but surely they must not be too short either? After all, there is no sense in selecting only a few findings from your papers. The most important lines of thought that lead to the conclusions and to our present point of view do have to be made clear. Actually, a short review is no less work than a long one. The review of *Jokes*, which I am just writing, will be approximately one and a half printed sheets long.—Rank has sent me everything I wanted. I shall take Warda's papers into consideration.

I have already received the first proofs from Deuticke.—May I ask you to reply to my recent question? I should like to know whether you agree with my plan of organizing a course for doctors.

I hope you will have very pleasant days in Berchtesgaden, and add, also in my wife's name, kind regards to you and your esteemed family.

Your devoted

*Karl Abraham*

1. Max Eitingon [1881–1943], German physician of Russian extraction. During his internship at the Burghölzli in 1907, he had visited the Wednesday Society and Freud as his first foreign adherent (Nunberg & Federn, 1962). Eitingon later became a founding member of the Berlin Society [1910], a member of the Secret Committee [1919] and founder of the Berlin Psychoanalytic Polyclinic [1920]—where he introduced the tripartite structure of psychoanalytic training (training analysis, supervision and theory)—and president of the IPA [1925–1932], as well as of the International Educational Commission [1925–1938]. In 1933 he went to Palestine, where he brought the Psychoanalytic Society of Palestine into being. His significance lies above all in the organization and financing of the psychoanalytic movement. (Cf. Pomer, 1966.)

1908 July

## 41 F

Berchtesgaden
17 July 1908

Dear Colleague,

I am taking advantage of the fact that I was sent the proof sheets of your fine work to make a few suggestions that would probably have occurred to you.

p. 1. It should probably read: objects and points of view of the *psycho*analytic etc.[1] Below, add to the quotation from the *Interpretation of Dreams*: 2nd ed., 1909.

p. 1. below, "*these* apparently heterogeneous["] instead of the[2]

p. 3. Here insert my statement on myths from "Creative Writers and Day-Dreaming" if it does not suit you better later on?[3]

p. 10. The realization of two [intimately connected or something similar][4] childhood—etc.[5]

p. 11. In some versions the punishment for Kronos is also emasculation.[6]

p. 12. Branches?

I really am expecting to read a work of yours dealing with love of inanimate objects as a valuable complement to the sexual theory.[7]

p. 19. Analogous to sexual repression, the (house)-serpent, honoured as a *god* in ancient times, has also become a devil-beast since Christianity. Just like the worship of the phallus.[8]

p. 20. The apple of Babylonian myth meant *only* the pomegranate.[9] Our apple of today then *unknown*. (Cf. Kohn, *Culturpflanzen und Thiere.*)

p. 29. Through the movements of coitus is missing here (capable of moderation).[10]

p. 30. In German the consonance of *geboren* [born] with *Bohren* [drilling holes] gives the child a cause for interesting phantasies?[11] Are these also possible in other linguistic material?

Cordial greetings,
Yours,
  *Freud*

1. Abraham, 1909[14]: p. 153. The reference is to the title of the first chapter: *Objekte und Gesichtspunkte der psychoanalytischen Forschung nach Freud* [in the translation: "The subject-matter and theory of Freudian psycho-analysis"].
2. ". . . these apparently unrelated products" (Abraham, 1909[14]: p. 153).
3. Abraham, 1909[14]: pp. 154–155.
4. Square brackets in original.
5. Abraham, 1909[14]: p. 160.
6. Abraham, 1909[14]: p. 160.
7. Abraham speaks of his intention "to deal in detail in another publication with the

ramifications of sexuality and in particular with deviations in this realm [of inanimate objects]" (Abraham, 1909[14]: p. 166).
8. Cf. Abraham, 1909[14]: p. 167.
9. Cf. Abraham, 1909[14]: p. 167.
10. Reference unclear.
11. Cf. Abraham, 1909[14]: p. 175.

## 42F

Berchtesgaden
20 July 1908

Dear Colleague,

I like your work better with each printed sheet. Please permit me to point out that the secondary elaboration (p. 46) is not quite correctly described, but this could easily be corrected in accordance with the *Interpretation of Dreams*. It is restricted too much to its last part, the distortion that takes place in the telling, while the essential point is the false distribution of emphasis in the whole dream content.[1]—I shall write to you about Burghölzli more fully next time; I am thinking of going to Zurich at the end of September; I think a great deal more favourably about Jung, but not about Bleuler. On the whole it is easier for us Jews, as we lack the mystical element.

Forgive me for not answering your question about the course for physicians. I should be very glad of it, but make sure of Oppenheim's feelings in the matter; I would not like to see you coming to any harm.

Cordial greetings,
Yours,

*Freud*

1. Cf. Abraham, 1909[14]: p. 188; esp. n. 1.

## 43A

Dr med. K. Abraham
Specialarzt für nervöse und psychische Krankheiten
Berlin W. 35. Schöneberger Ufer 22
Tel. Amt VI, 13245
Sprechst. 9–10, 4–6. Sonntags 9–10[1]

23 July 1908

Dear Professor,

I have seen to the additions and corrections you wished. I am glad that you are still getting pleasure from my work; for my part, reading the proofs has thoroughly put me off it. I want to deal especially with

1908 July 53

the love of inanimate objects at some other time. First there are a few little things about which I wrote to you recently, then a new subject, accident neurosis, is dear to my heart.[2] I believe that the connection with sexuality can easily be demonstrated.—It will interest you that Moll has invited me to give a lecture on a Freudian theme in the Psychological Society. As he told me, he had expected the announcement of such a talk from another quarter, but instead of the unfavourable criticism to be expected he would rather have a positive lecture.—May I ask you, *when you have the chance*, to let me know the present address of Dr Sadger,[3] and that of the old staff doctor in the Wednesday Society?[4] In Salzburg I promised both of them a copy of the paper of my talk.

With cordial greetings,
your devoted

*Abraham*

1. Pre-printed letterhead in different font from that used previously.
2. No publications of Abraham's about these two topics have been found.
3. Isidor Sadger [1867–194?], Viennese physician and member of the Wednesday Society since 1906. Fritz Wittels's uncle. He published, among other things, psychobiographies and matters related to homosexuality. He disappeared during the Nazi regime.
4. Edwin Hollerung [1847–1921], staff doctor of the Austrian army; participant at the Salzburg meeting (see Mühlleitner, 1992: pp. 159–160).

## 44F
## PROF. D^R FREUD
### BERCHTESGADEN; DIETFELDHOF[1]

23 July 1908

Dear Colleague,

Thank you very much for your paper on dementia praecox and hysteria,[2] which arrived today. I value the resolute tone and clarity of your writings so highly that I must ask you not to think that I overlook their beauty. May I say that it is consanguineous Jewish traits that attract me to them? We understand each other, don't we?

You also know what it is that mars my pleasure in your paper. It makes manifest your latent quarrel with Jung. You certainly had every justification for writing in that way, but it would have shown greater delicacy of feeling not to have made use of it. At the time I gave the same suggestion to each of you and had no intention other than that each should take it up and work on it independently. In picking it up, you are to an extent forcing him to the other side.

When I go to Zurich as arranged at the end of September, I shall try to make good what can be made good. Please do not misunderstand me; I have nothing to reproach you with; I nurse a suspicion that the suppressed anti-Semitism of the Swiss that spares me is deflected in reinforced form upon you. But I think that we as Jews, if we wish to join in anywhere, must develop a bit of masochism, be ready to suffer some wrong. Otherwise there is no hitting it off. Rest assured that if my name were Oberhuber,[3] in spite of everything my innovations would have met with far less resistance.

I prefer not to share your unfavourable prognosis with regard to the co-operation of the Burghölzli. Certainly, the failing of the evening discussions struck me too; but I do not know whether it is final. Bleuler I surrender to you; in Salzburg I got an uncanny feeling from him, the situation cannot have been to his liking, and your description seems to prove me right. But with Jung it is a different matter, there is a personal sympathy that binds me to him, and he writes to me about his superior—the same that you said, in fact in the same words. Moreover, he can hardly back out, he could not undo his past even if he wanted to, and the *Jahrbuch*, of which he is the editor, is a bond that cannot be broken. I hope that he really has no intention of severing the tie with me, and that you, for reasons of a competitiveness that has not been overcome, do not see the situation correctly.

I am busily writing the case history of the boy of five,[4] which I hope will interest you greatly. In-between I am correcting the second edition of the *Interpretation of Dreams* and reading the galleys of *Dreams and Myths*. I am more and more convinced that you are right and that we share the honour of resolving mythology. Cheers!

Why cannot I harness you two, Jung and you, together, your sharpness and his *élan*?

With cordial greetings,
Yours,

*Freud*

1. Pre-printed letterhead.
2. Abraham, 1908[11]; paper presented in Salzburg.
3. A distinctly non-Jewish name.
4. Freud, 1909b.

## 45A

Berlin
31 July 1908

Dear Professor,

I am very sorry that not only my work but also my personal affairs are taking up your time and efforts. But since the subject of Zurich has been broached, I must add something further to it. You think that I should have used more tact in the ~~lecture~~ formulation of my paper. I

1908 July 55

myself believe that some things now look more pointed in print than they sounded when spoken. I did not have the intention to offend; true, however, that while writing it, my feelings towards Zurich were not very rosy. Shortly before going to Salzburg, I received Jung's Amsterdam paper[1] and Bleuler's and Jung's reply to E. Meier[2] and heard Bleuler's paper at the Congress here. These three performances did certainly astonish me. Now, I understood Jung's defeat in Amsterdam.[3] In his talk, Bleuler avoided anything relating to psychoanalysis (and how much he could have said!), and, as for their joint publication, I found it really outrageous. The sub-division into primary and secondary symptoms as the only result of years of analysis of the mentally ill! And a hair-splitting about toxins, etc. Should they not instead have held out the prospect that the problem was soon to be approached on the basis of the theory of sexuality? Not a word about Freud or the theory of sexuality. But Meier! (He has a chair at Königsberg, and is known to both authors as a total dead loss.) On the journey to Salzburg, Eitingon told me of this change and also that Jung's paper on dementia praecox[4] would contain *nothing* Freudian. I had long before informed Jung how I conceived my subject and that I had added some new points of view to those formerly discussed. One would have thought from his talk that he had never heard of auto-eroticism, etc. We talked at cross purposes. You yourself have put the reason for Jung's subsequent ill humour in the best possible way. There was universal surprise at the behaviour of the Zurichers. Everyone saw it as a turning away. Can one then say that I stole a march on Jung by using a suggestion that we had both received from you? In my opinion, the matter is as follows: I used the idea, and Jung deliberately *suppressed* it. I cannot help seeing it that way. Later events confirm it. I received the following comment some weeks ago from someone who knows nothing of my conflict with Jung: "At the Burghölzli, Freud seems to be a point of view that has been superseded." Why do people who are not involved arrive at this opinion? And how could all the tact in the world on my part have helped? I have had no reply to my letter in which I expressly referred to your wish. In my opinion, out of respect for *you*, Jung should not have ignored this letter.

I have been hesitating all this week whether or not to write all this to you. I have tried to make your opinion my own. I cannot be so optimistic in this matter. Nobody could have been more pleased than I was about Jung's first appearance. That is why the change pains me so much. Your last letter, dear Professor, contained so many kind and appreciative words, that I find it difficult to write this one. But it is precisely those personal sympathies you mention that force me to do it.—If you are successful in Z[urich] in September, I shall be very pleased. If Jung wants to, he can be of extraordinary service to the cause, and I fully understand your wish to keep him. It would also be very unfortunate if the enemies were able to say that the only clinic supporting us[5] had now left us again. But if this conclusion is to be avoided, it is necessary for something fruitful to come *soon* from those quarters. The prognosis for Berlin is not that bad, favourable signs are increasing.—I should be glad to talk to you sometime about traumatic neurosis; for the present, however, we seem to be restricted to correspondence. As soon as I find the time, I shall compile the main points. A great number of other subjects are crowding in on me. The proofs of the Myth are finished, so nothing will prevent publication in September. My short essay[6] will appear in Hirschfeld's journal in a fortnight.

With cordial greetings,
Yours,

*Karl Abraham*

1. Jung, 1907a.
2. Bleuler & Jung, 1908.
3. The "Premier Congrès International de Psychiatrie, de Neurologie, de Psychologie et de l'Assistance des Aliénés" [First International Congress of Psychiatry, Neurology, Psychology and Care of the Insane] had taken place on 2–9 January 1907, in Amsterdam, and Jung had read a paper about "Die Freudsche Hysterietheorie" [The Freudian theory of hysteria]. He had run over his allotted time, had had to break off the lecture, and had been sharply attacked in the discussion. (Cf. Ellenberger, 1970: pp. 796–98; Jones, 1955: pp. 112f.)
4. Jung's Salzburg paper was not published (cf. his abstract in the *Zentralblatt*, 1910, *1*: 128).
5. The Burghölzli in Zurich.
6. Abraham, 1908[12].

46A

Berlin
21 August 1908

Dear Professor,

Things are moving! On the 27th the Berlin Psycho-Analytic Society will meet for the first time. For the time being, the following gentlemen (all of them physicians) will take part: Hirschfeld, Iwan Bloch,[1] Juliusburger, and Koerber (Chairman of the *Monistenbund*).[2] I believe others will soon join in. Dr Juliusburger in particular is very keen; he is *Oberarzt* [senior staff physician] in a private institution and is introducing psychoanalysis in spite of his superior's opposition.

Now I have various business questions. I have finished the review of your writings for the *Jahrbuch*. Shall I send the manuscript now, or would it be better in October?—I shall now start on the other reviews. How should I behave towards *Friedländer*? The one publication is a

1908 August

polemical collective review[3] and so is unsuitable. But the other[4] is based on his own observations, it is completely negative all the same. Still, I believe I should review them (without becoming polemical myself). Is that what you think too? Furthermore: I published *my* first works on sexual traumata[5] in Switzerland. As papers from the Zurich clinic, do they now fall into Jung's competence, or should I review them together with my later work? May I also ask what the *Jahrbuch* will contain in addition to reviews and your casuistic contribution?[6] Is there possibly still room for original articles, or have we all the material we need?

Finally, another question about the *Myth*, which, as you know, is to come out in September. You wrote to me quite a long time ago that Deuticke was going to contact me. Apart from the proofs, I have had nothing from him. So I do not know at all whether there still have to be some arrangements made between the publisher and me, or whether you have settled everything already.

My paper on sexuality and alcoholism[7] has just appeared, but I have not received the offprints yet. Meanwhile, I have learned many interesting things about the sexual basis in the use of sleeping pills from the psychoanalysis of a colleague. In this patient, the narcotic serves as the substitute for masturbation, which had been given up with difficulty; the analogy holds good down to the smallest detail. The weaning from sleeping pills meets with great resistances. Today he brought a neat confirmation of my views: after two nights without sleeping drugs he suddenly felt a return of the infantile urge to suck![8]—The practice is very quiet now during the summer but gives me much satisfaction, both scientifically and therapeutically. I have had an extremely nice success with a married couple and may tell you something about this sometime.

With cordial greetings to you and your esteemed family,
your devoted

*Karl Abraham*

1. Dr Iwan Bloch [1872–1922], dermatologist in Berlin and a pioneer of sexology.
2. Heinrich Koerber [1861–1927], general practitioner and *Sanitätsrat* [member of the Board of Health] in Berlin. Koerber's house was a meeting place for avant-garde artists, writers and psychoanalysts. His writings deal mostly with sexuality; he also gave a lecture series on psychoanalysis. He was president of the Berlin section of the *Monistenbund*, founded by Haeckel, which propagated a monistic *Weltanschauung*, based on the natural laws, as the religion of the future. The *Monistenbund* later adopted socialist and pacifist views, fighting against anti-Semitism and racism.
3. Friedländer, 1907–08.
4. Not identified.
5. Abraham, 1907[9], 1907[10].
6. Freud, 1909b.
7. Abraham, 1908[12].
8. Abraham described this case and this incident in his paper on the oral phase (1916[52]: pp. 266–268).

47F

## PROF. DR. FREUD
~~WIEN, IX., BERGGASSE 19~~

Dietfeldhof[1]
24 August 1908

Dear Colleague,

I congratulate you on this beginning. Berlin is difficult but important soil, and your efforts to make it cultivable for our purposes deserve every praise. Of the members probably only Juliusburger will be a pure gain, because the others have other guiding complexes, but even if they are only touched by [psychoanalytic] components, it will still be valuable.

I can answer your business queries only partly, as I have nothing to do with the editing of the *Jahrbuch*, which is entirely in Jung's hands. So please address yourself directly to him; it is possible that you will not get a reply before the middle of September, for he wrote—at the same time as you[2]—that he had gone on holiday until 8 September to some lonely peak in Säntis; however letters will be forwarded to him. I am thinking of visiting him around 20 September, and you know what I want to reproach him for. Please send the manuscript directly to him as well. He will then probably answer you himself and tell you where he is thinking of inserting your work; I rather think with the Swiss. Hostile publications, thus also Friedländer's, should according to earlier statements be dealt with in a special review; but I do not know of anything more recent.

I know no more than you do about the composition of the first half-volume; but wait—Binswanger's analysis of a case of hysteria, with his uncle's preface,[3] will be going in. In any case, I shall let you know from Zurich anything I can find out, so that your communication with Jung can be limited to business matters.

I have already seen *Dreams and Myths* advertised on the jacket of the new edition of the *Studies*.[4] Nothing more needs to be done, it is Deuticke who decides when it will appear, probably at the beginning of October; he will send the royalties of 60 crowns per sheet directly to you. I hope to bring out the next issue, by Rank, at Christmas.

Your paper on alcoholism will certainly have given you confirmation of the Soma interpretation. Your observation on the substitution series: auto-erotic satisfaction in phantasy before going to sleep–sleeplessness–sleeping drugs, is of course completely accurate.

Apart from working on the 2nd edition of the *Interpretation of Dreams*[5] and the article for the *Jahrbuch*,[6] I have written here a paper "On the Sexual Theories of Children", which is to appear in *Sexual-Probleme*,[7] and a short article, "Some General Remarks on Hysterical Attacks", for

1908  August

*Moll's* new *Zentralblatt*.[8] I shall let you know whether I shall be going to England on 1 September,[9] because if I do so my movements will be uncertain until then, and I shall not be reachable until I go to Zurich.

With cordial greetings and best wishes for the thriving of your undertaking,

yours in friendship,

*Freud*

1. Hand-written above pre-printed letter-head.
2. Letter of 21 August 1908 (Freud & Jung, 1974 [1906–13]: pp. 169–170).
3. Binswanger, 1909. The paper had no introduction by his uncle Prof. Otto Binswanger but was subheaded *"Aus der psychiatrischen Klinik in Jena (Geh. Rat Prof. O. Binswanger)"* and closed with a quotation from him and an expression of thanks to him.
   Ludwig Binswanger [1881–1966] had participated as an assistant physician in Jung's association experiments and in 1910 was first president of the Zurich branch society of the IPA and from 1911 to 1956 headed the Bellevue Clinic in Kreuzlingen on Lake Constance. He was interested simultaneously in psychiatry, psychoanalysis and philosophy, which, in his opinion, complemented each other. Despite their partly diverging views, Freud and Biswanger maintained a life-long friendship. (Cf. Binswanger, 1956; Freud & Binswanger, 1992.)
4. Breuer & Freud, 1895d (second edition 1909).
5. Freud, 1900a (second edition 1909).
6. Freud, 1909b.
7. Freud, 1908c.
8. Freud, 1909a [1908].
9. On 1 September Freud left for England to visit his half-brother Emanuel [1833?–1914] and his family.

48A

Dr med. K. Abraham
Specialarzt für nervöse und psychische Krankheiten
Berlin W. 35. Schöneberger Ufer 22
Tel. Amt VI, 13245
Sprechst. 9–10, 4–6. Sonntags 9–10[1]

29 August 1908

Dear Professor,

Many thanks for the various pieces of information. On one point there is probably a misunderstanding. You asked me earlier to send you the reviews of your writings before they go to Jung, to look through them. It was only for *this* purpose that I asked now whether you would like to have them immediately or only after the holidays.—With regard to the provisional members of our Society, you are quite right. But at least we have made a start.

And now one more modest question. Does the journey to England go through Berlin?

With cordial greetings,
Yours,

Karl Abraham

1. Pre-printed letterhead in different font from that used previously.

49F

Vienna IX, Berggasse 19
29 September 1908

Dear Colleague,

Having arrived here this morning from Lake Garda,[1] I am writing to you at once in spite of the fatigue of the journey, as I found an inquiry from you waiting for me and owe you some amends.

First about business matters. I could not write to you from Zurich; I was never alone until late at night; we spent up to eight hours a day walking and talking. So let me recapitulate: the first half-volume [of the *Jahrbuch*] is to include, apart from my paper, Binswanger's analysis, and your review, only a number of short reviews. Opponents' works are to be dealt with separately and dismissed briefly. You will hear directly about whatever you wish. I think it unnecessary for you to send your review to *me*, unless you especially wish to do so because of some point or other. That can also be done at proof stage.

Now to the main thing! I am glad to say that you were only partly right, that is to say, only about Bl[euler]. As for Jung, he has overcome his vacillation, adheres unreservedly to the cause, and also will continue to work energetically on the dementia praecox question along our lines. That is highly welcome to me, and I hope it will please you also. It will come to nothing with Bl., his breaking away is imminent, the relations between Bl. and J. are strained to breaking-point. Jung is giving up his position as assistant but remains head of the laboratory and will work completely independently of Bl.

It was a great satisfaction to me that Jung did not make it difficult for me to prepare the ground for the reconciliation with you that I wish to bring about. His high regard for your scientific work was of great assistance here. He spoke only in hints, but I was able to conclude that he is sorry if you have ideas about him that do not correspond to reality, and the reasons for which came from another quarter. I do not want to stand between you, but I hope that in direct communication with each other you will soon find it possible to resume the friendly and collegial tone which alone befits cooperation and mutual respect. So I left the Burghölzli the richer for this valuable expectation.

Now for my transgression against you. I was actually in Berlin for 24 hours and did not call on you. I could not, because I crossed from England with my aged brother and visited my sister who lives in Berlin,[2] and between the two camps of fond relatives I saw as little of Berlin as I did of you.

For certain reasons I gladly confess to you that Jung found this incomprehensible—in retrospect, I do not know either how the day passed. I only remember that I could not leave the hotel before 11 a.m., and that at 11 o'clock in the evening my train left, so that the 24 hours become—12. But now I do know that because of my brother and sister I shall soon be going to Berlin again, and I hope that until then you will have forgiven me the appearance of unfriendliness.

Today I can only send you my cordial greetings,
your most devoted

*Freud*

1. After his trip to England, Freud travelled by way of Berlin to Zurich and was Jung's house-guest at the Burghölzli [18–21 September]. Subsequently he spent a few days with his sister-in-law, Minna Bernays, at Lake Garda.
2. Marie (Mitzi) [1861–ca.1942], married to Maurice (Moritz) Freud [1857–1920]. She died in the Treblinka concentration camp.

## 50A

Dr med. K. Abraham
Specialarzt für nervöse und psychische Krankheiten
Berlin W. 35. Schöneberger Ufer 22
Tel. Amt VI, 13245
Sprechst. 9–10, 4–6. Sonntags 9–10[1]

4 October 1908

Dear Professor,

I am very glad to hear that your holidays finished so well in Zurich; and I am grateful for the trouble you have taken on my behalf. I received two cards from Jung, which clearly show your influence! I am very pleased indeed that, with that, the unpleasant situation has been brought to an end. You may rest assured that in my correspondence with Jung I shall not refer in any way to what is past. It is true, I see some things at the Burghölzli differently from you; in three years of constantly being together[2] one gains insight into a great deal. But I shall welcome it as a valuable result of your Z.[urich] visit if Jung is actively working with us again. I am now sending the reviews directly to him.—Heartfelt thanks to your Fräulein daughter for her provisional reply to my inquiry.[3]

Now, I must beg you, dear Professor, not to imagine that I took offence at your passing through Berlin. If you reproach yourself for this reason, there is a simple way to make amends. When next you come to Berlin, please give my wife and myself a good deal of your time!

I am sending you *Dreams and Myths* together with this letter. You mentioned some time ago that you had analysed the Flood myths. I have also been working on this and am quite certain that it is a symbolic representation of pregnancy. That is your opinion too, I take it? There are amazingly fine symbolisms contained in it, and I regret that I was unable to include this legend in my book.—The first paper on psychoanalysis in the Italian literature (as far as I know) has now been published. I have only read a review; the author is Baroncini, whose judgement is very favourable.[4] For my talk before the Psychological Society I have given as subject: "Childhood Phantasies in the Mental Life of the Adult".

With cordial greetings from house to house,
Yours,

    *Karl Abraham*

1. Pre-printed letterhead, as on letter of 7 July 1908.
2. At the Burghölzli, the doctors and their families had their apartments in the institution and lived together with the patients and their colleagues. They had to ask for special permission to leave the hospital grounds.
3. Missing.
4. Baroncini, 1908. Baroncini was a psychiatrist in Imola.

## 51F

Vienna IX, Berggasse 19
11 October 1908

Dear Colleague,

I thank you for so amiably accepting everything mentioned in my last letter, but I do not want to burden you with too much self-oppression and prefer to state that I owe you a debt that should be paid off one day.

You know it was not easy for me between you both. I do not want to spare either of you, yet I can actually let neither of you share my feeling of how much liking I have for the other. You would make it very much easier for me if you made friends with each other, or at least got along well together. It is just the fact that I find it easiest with you [and also with our colleague Ferenczi[1] of Budapest][2] to come to an understanding that warns me not to concede too much to racial preference and therefore neglect the Aryan, which is basically more alien to me. I do not ask either of you to make sacrifices for me personally, but for the significant cause.

1908 October

*Dreams and Myths* is now about to serve that cause. We shall hear what people will say about it. You are certainly right with your interpretation of the Flood myths, but you were not able to grasp the whole because you did not reach it by the right path. This path leads by way of the myths "of the birth of the hero" (exposition at birth: Romulus, Cyrus, Moses, etc.), with which Herr Rank is to deal in the next issue.[3] The same motifs appear in this as in the other. I am quite content that you have reserved the interpretation of the Flood myths for this context.

On Friday evening—your superior[4] and his wife were our guests here. They were very kind, in so far as his unapproachability and her affectation permitted. He had not yet read *Dreams and Myths*. They both tried to take me by storm; I should not talk of "sexuality", but should find another name for what does not, in any case, coincide with sexuality in the popular sense. All resistance and misunderstandings would then cease. I replied that I did not expect anything to come of such little household remedies; and besides, they were unable to give me this other word.

There is still little scientific news. The second edition of the *Interpretation of Dreams* is ready and is to appear in November. The "Fragment of an Analysis of a Case of Hysteria" is also to undergo a resurrection in some form or other.[5]

Does your little Society still meet regularly, and what form is its activity taking?—I trust I shall hear about your lecture as soon as possible.

With cordial greetings to you and your wife,
Yours,

*Freud*

1. Sándor Ferenczi [1873–1933], neurologist in Budapest, employee of the medical insurance company and expert witness at the Budapest court. Freud and Ferenczi established a close relationship after the latter's first visit on 2 February 1908, and Ferenczi became, together with Otto Rank, Freud's closest disciple. Their correspondence consists of more than 1,200 letters (cf. Freud & Ferenczi, 1992, 1996, 2000). Ferenczi was founder of the IPA [1910], founding member of the Secret Committee [1913], co-editor of the *Zeitschrift* [1913], president of the IPA [1918], and the world's first professor of psychoanalysis [1919]. Many of his early writings are considered as classics; his later work, in the 1920s and 1930s, was and is controversial. While some consider it unimportant—a scientific regression—and attribute it to an alleged mental illness of Ferenczi's, others value it as a pioneering work in therapeutic practice and object relations theory.
2. Square brackets in original.
3. That is, the next volume of the series, *Schriften zur angewandten Seelenkunde* (see Rank, 1909).
4. Eugen Bleuler, who had participated at the Third International Congress for the Treatment of the Insane, Vienna, 7–11 October 1908.
5. Freud, 1905e [1901], second printing 1909, in the *Sammlung kleiner Schriften zur Neurosenlehre*.

## 52A

Berlin
10 November 1908

Dear Professor,

I have postponed my reply longer than usual because I wanted to tell you without delay what happened yesterday evening. I spoke to the *Berliner Gesellschaft für Psychiatrie und Nervenkrankheiten* on "Intermarriage between Relatives and Neurosis".[1] To sum up first of all: the evening was quite successful on the whole. The subject proved suitable for this first attack because I did not have to touch on certain points that would be most likely to raise people's temperatures. I chose a few remarks of Oppenheim's as a starting point and stressed the correspondence between his and your views concerning certain observations on neurotic children. I avoided mentioning several important points (for instance, the connection with homosexuality) because these would have aroused unnecessary opposition, but stood very firm on all my references to sexual theory. I think you will also agree that I did not mention your name too often. It acts like a red rag to a bull, and people knew what I was aiming at in any case. The audience remained attentive to the end, and, in spite of the late hour, a discussion followed. First Oppenheim: very appreciative in several respects. He would be quite convinced on some new points. It was only against the Freudian view of infantile sexuality that he could not but take a "most brusque and resolute stand". Then *Ziehen*.[2] While O. had on the whole remained factual, Ziehen rode his academic high horse. "Wild assumptions", "What Freud has written is all nonsense", and so forth.—Then two speakers (Schuster, Rothmann), who made factual contributions. And now the star turn: a very pushy colleague, Braatz,[3] whose conversion to Christianity has proved only partially successful, assumed a moralizing tone that would have been more suited to a public platform. I had, *inter alia*, mentioned Konrad Ferdinand Meyer (as had Sadger) as an example of love for the mother.[4] That would be outrageous; the German ideals would be at stake. Even the German fairy-tale should now be something sexual, etc. It was very gratifying that authorities such as Z. and O. had taken such a determined stand against Freud; the whole Association should express their disapproval of this new trend. Liepmann, declaring himself a scientific opponent, replied to him in a very reasonable and dignified manner and rejected the presumptuous tone. I avoided all acrimony in my final summing up in order not to damage our cause. I only hit out at Ziehen, because he had been so very rude. I stood in lonely opposition to the well-attended gathering. Juliusburger, who would certainly have seconded me, was prevented from coming at the last moment. After the meeting, quite a number of colleagues told me

## 1908 November

that they had enjoyed hearing something new as a change from the eternal demonstration of anatomical preparations. I have the impression that quite a few of them went home at least *half* convinced. At any rate, the ground has been prepared, and perhaps I might advance in the second half of the winter with heavier artillery. The advice you gave me a year ago has proved useful. I waited almost a year before coming forward and even then was more moderate than in fact I felt comfortable with. I think it was just the crudity of some opponents that swung the mood of the meeting in *my* favour. Oppenheim, whose goodwill is very important to me, expressed his appreciation in *private*. True, he said he did not want to hear anything about infantile sexuality, but in many respects he agreed with me and even suggested publication in the *Deutsche Zeitschrift für Nervenheilkunde* (of which he is co-editor!). So one can get by without making concessions as long as one does not put forward too many things that are alien to people all at once.

Our psychoanalytic meetings are shaping up quite nicely; I hope that soon some more interested colleagues will join. We meet every two or three weeks.—You probably know already that I sent yesterday's paper, in a somewhat extended form, to Jung for the *Jahrbuch*. I believe the *Jahrbuch* comes out under favourable auspices. Stekel's book[5] has been widely read in Berlin; it was very suitable for propaganda, and I know of a number of doctors whose further interest has been aroused. The new editions you mention are surely also another good sign.

The *Gesellschaft Deutscher Nervenärzte*, which met recently in Heidelberg for the second time, will have its next congress in Vienna. Should one not [be] there? What do you think? Would you not like to intervene personally once again?—Moll's recently published book (*The Sexual Life of the Child*)[6] shows a greater lack of understanding than I have ever come across.

Your report on Bleuler's visit was very interesting for me. Let me thank you cordially for all the personal things you wrote in your letter.

With best regards for you and your esteemed family—also on behalf of my wife,

Yours,

*Karl Abraham*

1. Abraham, 1908[13].
2. Theodor Ziehen [1862–1950], German psychiatrist and experimental psychologist with a special interest in child psychology, former assistant of Kahlbaum in Görlitz and Binswanger in Jena. Member of faculty of psychiatry and neurology in Jena [1886–1900], Utrecht [1900–1903], Halle [1904–1912], and Berlin [1917–1930]. Co-editor of the *Monatsschrift für Psychiatrie und Neurologie*.
3. Emil Braatz (1865?–1934). Berlin psychiatrist.

4. Conrad Ferdinand Meyer [1825–1898], important Swiss writer, novelist, and poet (cf. Abraham, 1908[13]: p. 27; Sadger, 1908).
5. Stekel, 1908.
6. Moll, 1908; see the minutes of the meeting of 11 November (Nunberg & Federn, 1967: pp. 43ff).

## 53F

Vienna IX, Berggasse 19
12 November 1908

Dear Colleague,

Your account of the evening of the talk was very interesting. Things are really not easy for you, but I think you are applying the right technique—treating those people like patients in psychoanalysis, ignoring their "no" with superior calmness, continuing to develop one's view yet not telling them anything from which they are too far because of too much resistance. . . . After the clear, resolute stand in *Dreams and Myths* no one can accuse you, of all persons, of making concessions.

The resistance to infantile sexuality strengthens me in the opinion that the *Three Essays*[1] is a work of similar value to that of the *Interpretation of Dreams* (the second edition of which you will, I hope, be receiving next week; the book is out, but I have no copies yet). Moll's piece is as pitiful as it is dishonest. You see that I am in form today. I did not know, incidentally, that you had sent Jung your paper.

Unless the most improbable changes take place in the meantime, I will stay away from the Congress in Vienna and will also prevent my hotheads here from making an appearance. If you wish to present something, that is a different matter; you possess the necessary self-control and superiority. But you will not derive much pleasure from it either, and I do not want to grant my dear Viennese the pleasure of a battle in which we will be shouted down. But our absence will annoy them, and that suits me just right. As an opportunity to have you with us here again, this time with your wife, the Congress would suit me very well, however.

I am now working on a "General Methodology of $\Psi\alpha$".[2,3] Where it is to be published is not yet settled, but in any case it will appear—perhaps exclusively—in the second volume of my *Schriften zur Neurosenlehre*.[4] Unfortunately I have so little time that work is making only very slow progress. A happy event in my family, my daughter's engagement to a young man of her choice,[5] also does not exactly increase leisure time. But one is not only a literary and medical workhorse.

My sister-in-law has already been negotiating for quite a long time with a [female] friend in Berlin about a treatment that would be of some importance for you. But you will only hear something more about it if the attempt at persuasion has been a success.

With cordial greetings and thanks,

Yours,

*Freud*

1. Freud, 1905d.
2. See letter 16F, 9 January 1908, n. 1.
3. Ψα = psychoanalysis; ψα = psychoanalytic, in accordance with German usage (except in titles, where it is capitalized).
4. *Sammlung kleiner Schriften zur Neurosenlehre* [*Collection of Shorter Writings on the Theory of the Neuroses*].The first volume of this series appeared in 1906, followed by four more volumes, 1909, 1913, 1918, and 1922.
5. Robert Hollitscher. The wedding took place on 7 February 1909.

## 54A

Berlin
23 November 1908

Dear Professor,

I read with great pleasure the news about your eldest daughter's engagement. To the person most involved I expressed my congratulations some days ago; now I should like to repeat them to you. At the same time, I should like to thank you most sincerely for the *Interpretation of Dreams*. It is really rare for a book with a poor initial sale to go into a new edition after so many years. Interest must be growing after all. I am waiting eagerly to see all that you are going to write in the next few months.—I, too, have always taken the resistance against the *Three Essays* as a sign of their importance. I might add that this work has always been my favourite over all the others because it contains so very many ideas that still require detailed elaboration, while the *Interpretation of Dreams* is so well rounded and finished that there remains nothing for any of us to do. Also, what I especially like in the *Three Essays* is its denseness; much is hidden in every sentence.

As for the Vienna Congress, something can probably be done later. And how about *our* congress? It would be nice if it were to come off well again.

The psychoanalysis you mention would be very welcome, since I do not have a suitable case at the moment. In the case of a lady I was quite successful with a partial analysis which, for external reasons, I had to combine with another type of treatment. Unfortunately, I am always short of young and fresh cases. At the moment a mentally ill lady takes up hours of my time every day. A series of reports of court cases also keeps me busy. Relatively speaking, I am very satisfied with the result of my first year's practice, i.e. the income surpasses my expectation but lags naturally still far behind the expenses.

The mentally ill lady just mentioned, in whom I can observe the development of delusions at their beginning, clearly shows the mechanism of the so-called melancholic delusions. I am always hoping that I may someday soon have a chance to work on the psychogenesis of the various forms of delusions.

With cordial greetings,
Yours,

*Karl Abraham*

Have you read the nice *lapsus linguae* in the *Reichstag*? *Rückgratlos* instead of *rückhaltlos*.[1]—The following slip of the pen is also very neat: a lady has to undergo painful treatment by a woman dentist with whom she is clearly in love. Reporting this to her family, she writes: "I have just returned from this wonderful creature"—instead of procedure!

1. "Spinelessly" instead of "unreservedly"; used by Freud in the *Psychopathology of Everyday Life* (1901b: pp. 95–96, addition of 1910) and in his *Introductory Lectures* (1916–17: p. 62).

## 55F
### Prof. Dr Freud
Vienna IX, Berggasse 19[1]

14 December 1908

Dear Colleague,

Only a greeting today, so as not to interrupt our correspondence. Just now I am very taken up with hard work.

You will have received my last communication. The review in the *Neurologisches Centralblatt* reminded me of you today. Some day Z.[iehen] will pay dearly for the "nonsense".[2] No hurry, it tastes better cold. Our *Jahrbuch* is already being printed.

Your turning towards psychiatry is very much appreciated as we here cannot enter into it with you; there, however, one can only apply what one has experienced with the neuroses.

With cordial greetings,
Yours,

*Freud*

1. Pre-printed letterhead.
2. Referring to the official minutes of Abraham's talk on 9 November and Ziehen's statement in the discussion that what Freud had written was all "nonsense" (both in *Neurologisches Centralblatt*, 1908, 27: 1150–1152).

## 56A

Berlin
18 December 1908

Dear Professor,

You must not assume that I expect you to reply letter for letter. The reprint you sent was in itself a sign of life that gave me much pleasure. The review in the *Neurologisches Centralblatt* does not, of course, give an accurate picture of the discussion after my lecture. My reply to Ziehen was sharper; I did not put the exact words into my own report, because the printed word gives a quite different impression from the spoken word. In Berlin the signs of a germinating understanding are increasing. After a session this week, for example, several professional colleagues offered me observations from their practice, and the points of view I was expounding to them were not rejected at all. In Oppenheim's polyclinic, which I often visit, I have the same experience. I have high hopes of the psychoanalysis of a case that I began a week ago. It is that of a seventeen-year-old boy belonging to the Jewish aristocracy. For five years he has suffered, among other symptoms, from an obstinate localized backache, and also from sexual neurasthenic troubles. He was in the hands of orthopaedic surgeons etc. for nearly five years; then under Oppenheim, who treated him with radium etc., and who finally referred him to me. He is related to two of Oppenheim's assistants. It would make a great deal of difference if I were successful in this case, which has been given a very unfavourable prognosis by everyone. The beginning looks promising. I am taking particularly exact notes because the case is of the greatest interest, especially concerning the appearance of certain symptoms within one family. No other analysis has yet given me so much pleasure. The patient, whom O. described as very inaccessible, is very interested and very happy to have been freed from his nightly anxiety attacks and pollutions since his second session with me.

A strange endemic cluster of Freudians has been in existence for about a month in Charlottenburg. One of my first patients was a very intelligent philologist, a teacher at a newly opened school in Charlottenburg. He is very grateful and shows an excellent understanding of analysis. As the result of a certain incident with some pupils, he gave your writings and mine to the headmaster. The headmaster has been poring over them for the last four weeks, and demands of the school doctor that he familiarize himself immediately with the whole of the theory of sexuality and—examines him on it! And the teachers have to do the same. My informant says: those who do not know these works are considered old-fashioned by the headmaster: and what teacher wants to be that?—Incidentally, I was told by a bookseller that the *Interpretation of Dreams* is selling very well.

Naturally, there are also some less pleasant incidents. Some months ago I sent a revised version in English of my earlier publications on Sexual Trauma to Morton Prince (*Journal of Abnormal Psychology*).[1] I had written to him in advance informing him of its subject. He asked me to send him the manuscript, saying he would look at it, while adding that he would not be in favour of publishing things that had already been published elsewhere previously. This already looked very much like an excuse, since simultaneously he himself let a word-for-word translation of a paper be printed in a German journal. After a long delay, I received an evasive reply and finally a rejection slip from the assistant editor, which I enclose. The reasons given are precious. The manuscript was returned at the same time, enriched by many grease spots.

I found a communication from Jung perhaps even more disagreeable. Only now, after the *Jahrbuch* has gone to press, does he tell me that he has postponed publishing my reviews—which he has had in his hands for over two months. He says that, for reasons of propaganda (!), he wanted to make the first issue as varied as possible. I can scarcely be wrong in assuming that at the last moment he substituted a paper of his own for my reviews. I find it inconsiderate in the highest degree to have this put to me as a *fait accompli*. He could have seen to the variety of the contents somewhat earlier. I have answered Jung in a calm and factual manner and suggested that, in the circumstances, I withdraw the reviews on the German and Austrian literature, but have urged him to print the reviews of *your* papers *now*. I know that many colleagues are very interested in an objective, collective review, and the natural place for this is surely the first issue. I assure you that I would have preferred to prohibit the publication of the three manuscripts altogether so as to show Jung that his arbitrary behaviour must have its limits. I believed, however, to act in accordance with your wishes if I were as moderate as possible in my requests.

I am enclosing a picture,*[2] which will undoubtedly interest you. It corresponds exactly to Jensen's[3] description of how Gradiva steps from stone to stone. One might perhaps be able to get some interesting information from the deaf-mute sculptor.

With cordial greetings,
your devoted

*Karl Abraham*

* you need not return it.

1. Morton Prince [1854–1929], psychiatrist and psychotherapist, known for his work with hypnosis and on multiple personality disorder. 1926 associate professor at the new Department of Abnormal and Dynamic Psychology at Harvard. With Henry A. Murray, Prince established the Harvard Psychological Clinic [1927–1957]. He was the founder and editor of the *Journal of Abnormal Psychology*.

2. Not identified.
3. Wilhelm Jensen [1837–1911], North German playwright and novelist, author of *Gradiva* (1903; cf. Freud, 1907a).

## 57F

Vienna IX, Berggasse 19
26 December 1908

Dear Colleague,

I reply without delay to your interesting letter, which contains pleasing and unpleasing news side by side, as happens indeed in life itself.

In the first place, many thanks for the woman of Pompeii. It would be really interesting to know whether the sculptor knew Gradiva or worked independently. Unfortunately I have not even a trace of foot worship, and that is why I am so completely at a loss about the whole problem. Now for the painful part. I am very sorry that you are again at loggerheads with Jung. In Zurich I pressed him hard, found him accessible, and he wrote to me only recently, saying he was glad to have come to an easy relationship with you. Now, this time I cannot agree that you are in the right. Jung made a decision that plainly falls within his powers as editor, and in my opinion someone who assumes responsibility and labour should be allowed a certain amount of elbow-room for this. His act has certainly nothing hostile to you in it; you are, as far as I know, represented in the first half-volume with your paper on the intermarriage of relatives, and the postponement of your review to the second can really not be regarded as a snub to you. I fear you have rather too much mistrust of him, a trace of a persecution complex. I should be very sorry were you to give grounds now for justifying his earlier behaviour towards you. I have deliberately refrained from exercising any influence on the contents of the *Jahrbuch*, and think you could well do the same without compromising your dignity. I also remind you that your prognosis about Jung's future behaviour with regard to our cause did not turn out to be correct. You see from this how important it is to me that in these affairs, in which each of you judges the other, *both* of you should turn out to be wrong and I to be right; I really cannot tolerate that "two such fellows"[1] both of whom are so close to me, should not get on with each other.

The hostilities by which we are surrounded also remind us to hold together. Morton Prince, who has always been a kaleidoscopic character, is this time really lamentable. Where do the Americans expect to get with this fear of public prudery? Unless you specifically forbid me, I shall warn Brill[2] and Jones, who are being continually bombarded with requests from M.P., to expound our theories in a series of articles for the

*Journal of Abnormal Psychology.* He always begins by over-compensating for his cowardice and then withdraws into it. Actually, he also wanted to come to Salzburg.[3]

My warmest congratulations on that patient of yours whose analysis gives you so much pleasure! Radium has raised my spirits for hours today; really a miraculous element! There is only one worry in my mind that I should like to mention. It has often been my experience that precisely those cases in which I took an excessive personal interest failed, perhaps precisely because of this intensity. When such a "test" case succeeded, however, I found that the previously constituted jury withheld its approbation by its silence. The opportunity of demonstrating our skill will come eventually, even if it should fail in this particular case. Do not lose heart! Our ancient Jewish toughness will prove itself in the end here, too.

At Christmas I am expecting our colleagues Stein[4] and Ferenczi, of whom the latter had conquered a place in the hearts of all of us in Berchtesgaden. If Dr Abraham of Berlin joined us, it would be a splendid little assembly, and a great refreshment in this period of hard work. Because of the amount of energy consumed by my practice, I am not managing to get on with the "General Methodology of Psycho-Analysis", which has been stuck for weeks on page 36. The slightest extra load, for instance physical troubles, turns the scale. That is what things are like when "all is well".

The Charlottenburg endemic is priceless. There seems to be a similar centre of infection in Munich, and it seems to have affected the craziest artists and the like.[5] No doubt one day there will be a great deal of noise, if the appropriate impulse is given. But that is nothing to look forward to. Every theory sacrifices so much that is of value when it becomes popular.

I have the manuscript for the next issue of the *Schriften zur angewandten Seelenkunde* already. *The Myth of the Birth of the Hero*[6] will certainly interest you greatly as an advance that continues your own. I expect a huge defensive din to arise from the case history of the boy of five[7] that is to open our *Jahrbuch* and the proofs of which I have here for correction at the moment. Again some German ideals in danger! Our Aryan comrades are really quite indispensable to us, otherwise psychoanalysis would fall victim to anti-Semitism.

With many cordial greetings,
yours in friendship,

*Freud*

1. An allusion to Johann Peter Eckermann [1792–1854], *Gespräche mit Goethe in den letzten Jahren seines Lebens 1823–1832*, 12 May 1825.
2. Abraham Arden Brill [1874–1948], psychiatrist of Hungarian-Jewish origin, emigrated alone at the age of 14 to New York, where in 1903 he began a course of study in

medicine. After an internship at the Burghölzli and a brief analysis with Freud he returned to the United States in 1908, where in 1911 he founded the New York Psychoanalytic Society and became its first president. Brill was Professor of Psychiatry at the College of New York University and Lecturer in Psychoanalysis at Columbia University. He translated many of Freud's and some of Jung's works into English. (Cf. Romm, 1966.)

3. That is, in the end he did not come.
4. Philipp (Fülöp) Stein [1867–1918], Hungarian psychiatrist and neurologist; proponent of the temperance movement. He had visited Freud together with Ferenczi on 2 February 1908. The visit had been arranged by C. G. Jung, in whose association experiments at the Burghölzli Stein and Ferenczi had collaborated. Stein later distanced himself from psychoanalysis.
5. The central figure of this "infection" was Otto Gross, who publicly "analysed" in coffee houses and pubs.
6. See letter 51F, 11 October 1908, n. 2.
7. Freud, 1909b.

# 1909

## 58F

Vienna IX, Berggasse 19
10 January 1909

Dear Colleague,

I told you not long ago that I owed you some amends. I remember this as I write to you today, though your long silence points to your feeling seriously offended by the criticism in my last letter. You know that that criticism is consistent with the friendliest feelings towards you or, rather, derives from those feelings, because it was from my liking for you that I assumed the right to draw your attention to a wrong emotional turning along which I saw you making your way. Permit me to hope that you are not capable of taking frankness amiss for long, and show this soon

to your cordially devoted

*Freud*


## 59A

Berlin
12 January 1909

Dear Professor,

You are indeed wrong. The reason for my silence was illness. During the last few days since I have been up again, I have had no time to write to you, because a great deal of work has accumulated, particularly reports on court cases. My sincere thanks for your kindness, and I hasten to assure you that there is no question of my taking offence. If possible, I shall write more fully later today.

With kind regards,
your gratefully devoted

*Abraham*

## 60A

Berlin
13 January 1909

Dear Professor,

You will by now have received my brief note of yesterday, which will surely have convinced you that I am in no way offended. Your last letter reached me just before Christmas. I then went to visit my parents for a few days, and on my return to Berlin I had to go straight to bed. The influenza epidemic did not spare me. Your card,[1] with Stein's and Ferenczi's greetings, reached me in bed. Once I was up, there followed, for the first time in my practice, a somewhat overwhelming influx of patients, and I also had to write some psychiatric court reports in a hurry. In short, I did not find the desired leisure to reply to your letter which had given me particular pleasure in every way. It was perhaps wrong of me not to send you at least a few lines as an interim reply, but I hoped from day to day that I should at last be able to get down to answering it properly. And now, dear Professor, once and for all my assurance: I shall never take offence at your criticism of me. Nor do I think there is anything for which you have to make amends. I am, after all, aware of your personal interest in every one of your letters. The most recent one demonstrates it yet again. I would therefore have no reason to sulk and, in any case, it is not my way to react like that. The whole matter does, however, offer one comfort: I am not the only one who occasionally goes wrong in interpreting motives.

I should have been so glad to accept your invitation to come to Vienna at the same time as our colleagues from Budapest. The card from the Café Riedl[2] awakened many memories. I think it will be possible to meet soon. I assume from your remarks that you will shortly be visiting Berlin, and after that it will be time for our spring meeting in Salzburg or elsewhere. It will presumably take place?

You are, of course, free to tell Brill and Jones about the letter from Morton Prince. Where is Jones, incidentally? I heard that he had emigrated to Canada.[3]

The psychoanalytic case I wrote you about last time is progressing well; unfortunately, family circumstances may intervene to make its further course unfavourable. *Radium*, too, still keeps interfering. Oppenheim sees the patient at infrequent intervals, but the patient does not prove accessible in these emanations.

I have reason to be pleased with the results of my first year's practice. The new year has also started well, so that the hope of being able to earn my living in this way no longer seems so distant. During the past months I have had a number of court and other reports to write, mostly through the good offices of Dr Hirschfeld, who altogether takes the kindest interest in me.

I look forward to the *Jahrbuch* and Rank's paper.
With the most cordial greetings,
your gratefully devoted

*Abraham*

1. Missing.
2. A meeting-place for psychoanalysts after Freud's lectures.
3. After two—probably unfounded—charges of indecent professional behaviour, Jones felt that his reputation in England was damaged for several years to come and seized the opportunity, at the invitation of Dr C. K. Clarke, Professor of Psychiatry and Dean of the Medical Faculty in the University of Toronto, to establish a psychiatric clinic there. After a stay in Paris and a brief return to England in September, he arrived in Canada in October 1908.

61F

Vienna IX, Berggasse 19
17 January 1909

Dear Colleague,

I am delighted to have been wrong, and I am always willing to be wrong if it can be so to such advantage. But you will find that I tend to acquire prejudices that turn out to be very resistant to opportunities for shaking them.

I gladly answer your questions. There is to be no congress this year, but it will take place again next year, to make it easier for our gallant Americans to attend. Also, the accumulation of material worth communicating can be only desirable. Jones is in *Toronto*, Canada, *35 Chicora Avenue*, from where he writes very interesting, sarcastic letters in which his countrymen come off badly. He thinks we shall come to grief there on Anglican prudery.

You will certainly have read Strohmayer's good and certainly effective paper,[1] which is very pleasing. I was also pleased to see from the proofs of the *Jahrbuch* that Jung has given your contribution first place after the analysis of little Hans.

No. 5,[2] with Rank's work, is already at the printer's. During the period when you were missing, I received an invitation to deliver four to six lectures at the twentieth (!) anniversary celebrations at Clark University, Worcester, Massachusetts, in the first week of July, and they offered to pay my fare. I had to decline, as I am not rich enough to be able to sacrifice three weeks' earnings in Vienna. But I was sorry, and at least one can talk about the invitation here in Europe.[3]

The news of your practice is excellent. Hirschfeld is certainly an agreeable colleague because of his well-sublimated homosexuality. Perhaps you will gradually be able to convince him of the incorrectness of

1909 January

his theoretical assumptions about the origin of homosexuality, if he is sufficiently uninvolved.

I have no news of Moll's new journal, and I had to write to him recently because my intended contribution to it is now to appear in the second series of the *Sammlung [kleiner Schriften] zur Neurosenlehre*.[4]

Things are moving everywhere. Hold out valiantly, and write to me soon again, pending an opportunity for a more extensive exchange of ideas.

Your cordially devoted

*Freud*

1. Strohmayer, 1908. Wilhelm Strohmayer [1874–1936], physician and *Privatdozent* [a German academic title, roughly the equivalent of Associate Professor], and, from 1910 on, Professor in Jena.
2. Of the *Schriften*.
3. In a letter of 15 December 1908, Granville Stanley Hall [1844–1924], Professor of Psychology and Education and President of Clark University, Worcester, Massachusetts, had invited Freud to give a series of lectures on the occasion of the twentieth anniversary of the opening of the University. Freud declined, for the time being, for financial reasons, but he later accepted when Hall nearly doubled the honorarium and when the date of the celebration was changed from June to September (Hall's letter of 16 February 1909). (Cf. Rosenzweig, 1992.)
4. Freud, 1909a [1908], appeared in Moll's journal, after all.

## 62A

Berlin
31 January 1909

Dear Professor,

You are probably busier than usual owing to the forthcoming family celebrations.[1] All the same, I should like to ask your help concerning a few psychoanalytic difficulties. Please do not trouble to reply for the time being to anything else contained in this letter.

The young patient[2] about whom I have already written to you has suffered from anxiety since his childhood. He is particularly frightened of speaking or eating in the presence of a stranger. He will eat in front of the family; he just manages in the presence of friends if he is alone with them. However, as soon as strangers join the family circle (or a stranger sits at the family table), he cannot eat or talk. Nor can he ever speak to several members of his family at once, but only to one person at a time. If someone else joins in, he becomes silent. (He has, incidentally, become much more accessible since he started analysis.) His fear of strangers is certainly partly based on a repressed scoptophilia, which is, incidentally, only directed towards the male members of his family and towards male strangers. I cannot find a suitable explanation for his inability to eat. There is no nausea whatsoever. (He only feels aversion towards certain dishes—for instance, fish and certain fluids, such as white wine, champagne, and coffee.) I have tried in various ways to explain his fear of talking but cannot make any headway. Perhaps you could advise me a little on this point. The patient shows strong unconscious homosexual masochistic trends. His main symptom (the one for which he came to me) is pain in a certain spot beneath his right shoulder blade. It is linked with his anxiety. Pain and anxiety are both tied up with a "sensation of dread" that is both frightening and sensuous. He also experiences this feeling in certain anxiety dreams (especially in dreams of falling). But it is particularly connected with the relationship he had up to his thirteenth year with his elder brother, who showed strong sadistic tendencies. (Lying on top of each other in bed, kissing, biting, licking, and then hitting each other—in all this the patient was usually the passive partner.) I have uncovered much important material concerning the origin of the pain, but so far its localization remains puzzling. (I only know that the "sensation of dread" has moved from the perineum to that region, but why does it stop just there?) The last fortnight the patient spent with his brother, before the latter was sent away and soon afterwards committed suicide, is subject to an almost complete amnesia. I suspect that this is where the most important clues are to be found, for the pain first appeared after the brother's departure. I cannot give you all the other related details. The case is extremely complex because other pains later supervened, which the patient took over from his sister, while she in turn took over certain pains from him. His backache once disappeared for ten days—after his first successful coitus—but it returned. Apart from anxiety and pain, he has from early infancy suffered from feelings of exhaustion and somnolence, which do not seem to me to be sufficiently accounted for by masturbation. I hope that this will give you a rough outline and that you will be able to let me have some hints along which lines I should search further.

As for the aversion to fish, I have just had an interesting illumination from another patient and I should like to know whether it has general validity. The patient, bisexual and referred to me by Hirschfeld for analysis, has gone through the typical transference onto his mother and the subsequent turning away from her. He lost his father at the age of six and thereafter shared his mother's bedroom and felt repelled by the menstrual smell. The smell of fish, especially smoked and salted herring and such-like, reminds him of this. Have you come across similar instances?

There will be plenty of life in the journals now. I shall read Strohmayer. Stegmann's work[3] is also nice. I have not seen Frank's[4] yet. Hirschfeld is very amenable to psychoanalysis and is, for example, very interested in my results with the patients I have mentioned.

1909 February

I shall save the rest for another time. So, for today, my thanks in advance and cordial greetings,
your gratefully devoted

*Abraham*

1. The wedding of Mathilde to Robert Hollitscher on 7 February 1909.
2. Abraham described this case (1910[17]: pp. 109–110; 1916[52]: pp. 268–270).
3. Arnold Georg Stegmann, court physician and psychiatrist in Dresden; participant in the Salzburg meeting [1908] and founding member of the Berlin Society. He died in the First World War. Abraham is referring to Stegmann, 1908, which he reviewed for the *Jahrbuch*.
4. Ludwig Frank [1860–1935], an adherent of Forel's, was a neurologist in Zurich and practised a variation of the original Breuer–Freud cathartic method. Abraham refers to Frank (1908), about which Freud commented to Jung: "Frank . . . carries his tail several inches lower and even gives it a friendly wag now and then" (11 December 1908, Freud & Jung, 1974 [1906–13]: p. 187).

63F

Vienna IX, Berggasse 19
2 February 1909

Dear Colleague,

I thank you for showing me so much consideration and hasten (relatively) to reply. Your patient obviously treats eating and talking as sexual activities. The course to follow is to search for the conditions in which his inhibitions become meaningful; and I hope you will find the problem readily soluble if you bear in mind the "displacement upwards" that you otherwise apply so skilfully and refer back to anal activity the oral activity (including speech) on which there is so much emphasis in this case. With the key of anal erotism, which is constitutionally reinforced in all homosexuals, you will be able to unlock the closed doors easily.

Little work has been done on food fads, but very often they have the same root as in your second patient. In the course of time you will increasingly fall in with the inevitable trend to trace back more and more to sex, to genital and functional details.

I know nothing about Stegmann's paper. Is Frank's paper the earlier one? Our *Jahrbuch* must be ready in a few days.[1] Rank's *Heldengeburt* is already being printed.

I eagerly await further news from you.
With cordial greetings,
Yours,

*Freud*

P.S.: In a few days the joyous turmoil here in the house will be at an end.

1. The first *Jahrbuch* was published on 25 February (Jung to Jones, 15 February 1909, LOC).

64A

Dr med. K. Abraham
Berlin W. 35, Schöneberger Ufer 22
14 February 1909

Dear Professor,

First of all, many thanks for your advice. It proved perfectly correct. I was able with the help of anal erotism to explain my patient's fear of eating and several of his other symptoms. For two sessions there was still an embittered resistance, then the associations followed in plenty. I think I am dealing with a particularly difficult case with whom the proven method—to let the patient bring associations freely and uncritically—fails. He is quite intelligent but obstinately declares himself to be stupid, and when I ask him to bring me his associations in this way, he asserts that each time the fear of saying something stupid as well as his aversion to speaking in general arise. I hope that this will change when I have found, in anal erotism, the explanation of the latter symptom. The idea of his stupidity is mainly derived from the fact that his sadistic elder brother constantly showed him up—he is masochist—as the stupid one. The desire for physical and mental ill-treatment by the brother, who has since committed suicide, pervades his whole illness.

Unfortunately it is so difficult to discuss these things by letter. Are you not coming to Berlin soon? I take it that family reasons have kept you in Vienna until now. As there is to be no congress this year, it would be very pleasant indeed to see you sometime in Berlin. Our scientific meetings have been quite stimulating on the whole, but were generally of more sexological character. All the same, there has been a lively interest in psychoanalysis. Hirschfeld has now begun a longish recreational journey that will probably bring him to Vienna, too. Both he and Bloch are very receptive to our efforts, but can naturally not make them their main interest. In this respect Juliusburger is greatly to be praised. He is not only a very likeable, dependable, and loyal person, but has a very subtle understanding of psychology and stands completely by our cause. You will probably have received his last publication.[1] In the private institution in which he works he is seeking to raise the interest of his other colleagues. One of them, Wulff[2] by name, is already very well versed. We have meetings now and then at which we exchange our experiences and especially seek to put psychoanalysis to good use in psychiatry.

I am planning to give another talk next term in the *Berliner Gesellschaft für Psychiatrie und Nervenkrankheiten* [Berlin Society for Psychiatry and

Nervous Illnesses], as I did this term. I think half a year is the right interval but would like to have your opinion. I do not want to tire people—that would do much harm to the cause.

There is activity everywhere. Not even mentioning the *Jahrbuch*. Frank's paper "On Psycho-Analysis"[3] is new; it is in the Festschrift for Forel[4] (special issue of the *Journal für Psychol. und Neurol.*). Stegmann ("Asthma in Children") came out in *Medic. Klinik*, 1908, No. 29.[5] In Gaupp's *Zentralblatt*[6] there is a rather stupid criticism of your theory of obsessional neurosis. The author is a Russian called Skliar; he came out with something similar in another journal.[7]—The invitation to America is, all the same, a delightful thing to happen—what a pity that you cannot follow it up. Incidentally, here is something else remarkable: Bleuler has published a short article in the *Centralblatt*[8] in which he once again takes up a position in your favour. This, admittedly, is only a secondary topic in the article; the subject offered no opportunity to go into it in detail.

The practice is going on rather satisfactorily; it seems to progress quietly, without too much vacillation. Last week the builder from Breslau whom you referred to me over a year ago came to see me. It seems he will come to Berlin for a time at the end of February for treatment. The prognosis is doubtful; he told me that he did not want to give up his sexual activity (sadistic phantasies). There could also be dementia praecox in the background. I suggested a trial period of eight days.

A Russian journal has invited me to contribute a short article on psychoanalysis, and I shall probably take this up.

Some time ago I wrote to you of my wish to write on traumatic neurosis. This is something I would very much like to discuss with you. I consider it a very important subject, because so far it has always been used as counter-evidence against the sexual basis of neurosis. I now believe that it is definitely a sexual neurosis. I shall, as soon as I find it opportune, look for further material in Oppenheim's polyclinic. Do you not also feel that this work is desirable? I have, for some time past, been very much intrigued by another subject, a psychoanalytic study of Giovanni Segantini,[9] whose personality and works can be understood only with the help of the theory of sexuality. I should also like to discuss this with you personally. It is astounding how great a role is played here by the sublimation of component instincts, the repression of incestuous phantasies, the transference onto non-human objects, etc.

To conclude, one more question concerning foot fetishism. Though I am familiar with the symbolic significance of foot and shoe, it does not seem to go far enough. I have just come across a case (six-year-old girl) where the foot is of great significance. The sister and brother practised mutual masturbation by touching each other's genitals with the *foot*. Do you happen to know whether this is a frequent practice?—And could it be of significance for the explanation of foot fetishism?—Now I have again troubled you a great deal, dear Professor. I conclude with cordial greetings to you and your esteemed family.

Your devoted

*Abraham*

1. Not identified.
2. Mosche Wulff [1878–1971], Russian psychiatrist. After having studied in Berlin with Abraham and Juliusburger, he returned to Odessa in 1909. Member of the Vienna Society [1911]. In 1927 he re-emigrated to Berlin and in 1933 to Palestine, where he was co-founder and, after Eitingon's death, president of the Psychoanalytic Society there.
3. Frank, 1908.
4. Auguste Henri Forel [1848–1931], noted Swiss psychiatrist and psychologist, who also made a name for himself with his research on ants. Bleuler's predecessor as director of the Burghölzli and, like Bleuler, champion of the temperance movement.
5. Stegmann, 1908, reviewed by Abraham in the *Jahrbuch*.
6. Robert Gaupp [1870–1953], German psychiatrist; 1906–1936 professor in Tübingen. Co-editor of the *Zentralblatt für Nervenheilkunde und Psychiatrie*.
7. N. Skliar. His thesis, *Über Gefängnispsychosen*, was published in 1904. Grinstein only notes a work of 1911.
8. Bleuler, 1909.
9. Giovanni Segantini [1858–1899], Italian painter, from 1886 on in Switzerland. Abraham's interest was to lead to a psychobiographical study (Abraham, 1911[30]), often discussed in the following letters.

## 65F

Prof. D$^r$ Freud
Vienna IX, Berggasse 19
18 February 1909

Dear Colleague,

The fact is, it is very uncertain that we shall see each other so soon in Berlin, but this should not relieve me of the pleasant obligation of writing to you. As you know, I am the slave of money for nine-and-a-half months of the year, which is to be earned only in small portions and therefore does not permit any real lavishness or freedom of movement.

First, your questions: I agree that half a year's interval is enough; one can gradually get bolder, however. Consideration for Opp. will bring little success, for he will all the same go deeper and deeper into opposition [I am referring to Oppenheim[1]].[2]

I believe traumatic neurosis to be difficult to tackle, and, apart from a remark in the *Theory of Sexuality*,[3] I have no suggestions about linking it with our theories. If you have a definite or anticipatory idea that you can link with it, you are naturally fully justified in trying it. Scientific work, like ψα technique, must follow the path of least resistance.—In stereotypes like those of your patient who will not talk for fear of saying something stupid, the difficulty can be overcome by exercising rather more patience than usual without having to change the technique, which always leaves a feeling of uncertainty behind. The aversion to talking is ultimately based on the other intended (sexual) uses of the mouth, and that can be stated, and also repeated a few times.

As it happens, I am in a position to give you some orientation about foot fetishism, thanks to some investigations during the past few days. The use of the foot (heel, knee) for masturbation is not quite uncommon, either as a solitary or as a mutual practice. But that explains only the element: foot in the symptomatology, not the fetishism. [In one of my cases a paralysis was the understandable consequence.][4] The fetish comes about as follows: it is the result of a special kind of repression that could be described as partial; part of the complex is repressed, and in compensation for that another part pertaining to it becomes *idealized*. [A historical parallel: the mediaeval with its contempt for women and the exaltation of the Virgin Mary.][5] In our case we have an original olfactory pleasure in the foul-smelling foot [which the pervert therefore always prefers to a clean one].[6] This olfactory pleasure is driven out, and the foot, the former provider of the pleasure, is elevated into a fetish instead. We then hear no more of its smell. I also know clothes fetishists, in whom the connection is even closer. They are former voyeurs, watchers of undressing scenes, for whom clothes were once very much in the way. The normal clothes fetishism of women is also connected with the passive drive to be seen, with exhibitionism. I am still waiting for more examples before going public with this conclusion, and I shall be delighted if you are able to unlock some cases with this key in the meantime.[7]

If you are serious about your study of Segantini, I will try to take hold of it immediately to decorate the *Schriften zur Angewandten Seelenkunde*. *Dreams and Myths* has made an excellent impression on everyone to whom I spoke, and these testimonials to the many-sidedness of your abilities make me very proud for you.

I have not received all the papers you mention. For Juliusburger's brave intervention I have already thanked the author. So I know that at least you are no longer completely isolated in Berlin. A Dr Weiss from Vienna may perhaps look you up sometime soon.[8] He has heard my lectures and finally shown a really good understanding of them. However, in his case, too, $\Psi\alpha$ is not the chief interest; he wants to learn Frenkel's[9] treatment of ataxia.

Today came a paper by Maeder, in French, from *Coenobium*, a review published in Lugano, very intelligent and with excellent original examples.[10]

The *Jahrbuch* will at last come out next week. There were complications in the printing of Binswanger's paper.

An offprint of Moll's first issue[11] is going off to you by the same post. Apart from that, I do not think our relations will develop very amicably. The paper on hysteria[12] makes me suspect that Moll means to oppose us in this journal and, in accordance with his somewhat malicious nature, needs to wear a veil of impartiality. Several passages in the *Sexual Life of the Child* would actually have merited a charge of libel, but they are best answered with prudence and silence. In any case, *hic niger est, hunc tu Romane caveto*.[13]

With cordial greetings,
your most faithfully devoted,

*Freud*

1. In German, the "he" in the subordinate clause about the growing opposition grammatically refers to "success".
2. Square brackets in original.
3. Freud, 1905d: p. 202.
4. Square brackets in original.
5. Square brackets in original.
6. Square brackets in original.
7. Shortly afterwards, on 24 February, Freud gave a talk about this case to the Vienna Society (Freud, 1988k [1909]). Abraham used this communication of Freud's in a later publication (Abraham, 1910[18]: p. 129; cf. Lobner, 1909.)
8. Karl Weiss [1879–19?], Bohemian physician in Vienna, from October 1911 on member of the Vienna Society. Emigrated to London in 1938 (see Mühlleitner, 1992: pp. 362f).
9. Probably Henri Frenkel [1864–1934], Parisian ophthalmologist.
10. Maeder, 1909a.
11. Freud, 1909a [1908].
12. Not identified.
13. "This is a black [soul]; O Roman, be aware of him" (Horace, *Satires*, 1, 4, 85).

66A

Dr med. K. Abraham
Berlin W. 35, Schöneberger Ufer 22
9 March 1909

Dear Professor,

This time I have to thank you for your detailed letter, which contained so much that is pleasing to me personally, and also for the offprint and the *Kleine Schriften*.[1] Your statements about the hysterical attack, which I find particularly illuminating precisely because of their being short and sharp, caused an attack from Oppenheim while he was examining a hysterical woman in the polyclinic yesterday: it would simply be outrageous, etc. That very day one of his assistants suggested to him that one might ask the patients of the polyclinic a little about their sexual life—but he rejected this with strong affect. So you hit the mark with your opinion of O. Berlin psychotherapy is altogether some-

1909 March 85

thing very "nice"; the enclosed cutting[2] shows you how an obviously psychogenic case of migraine is treated here.

I will not start to work yet on the traumatic neuroses. I simply cannot involve patients in O.'s polyclinic in discussions of their sexual life just now. So I will probably have a go at Segantini first. If the work turns out well and is long enough to appear as an independent small volume, then, of course, I should like to publish it nowhere else than in the [Schriften zur] angewandten [Seelenkunde], and I thank you already in advance for your invitation to do so. I have not yet read anything about Dreams and Myths, apart from one short note in a newspaper. I am all the more pleased that you have heard favourable comments.—You will probably have received a short paper of Wulff's[3]—quite a good but not thorough analysis.

My analysis of a bisexual with a great preponderance of homosexuality will soon be finished and has been very successful. The case of hysteria about which I recently asked for your advice will also soon be concluded; that is to say, the strongest resistances have been resolved, and the therapeutic results are already quite far-reaching.—As far as I have heard, a collective review of your publications has appeared in the journal edited by Stern in Breslau.[4] There is nothing else to report today.

With kind regards, your devoted

*Abraham*

1. The second volume of Freud's *Sammlung kleiner Schriften zur Neurosenlehre*, Leipzig and Vienna: Deuticke, 1909.
2. Missing.
3. Probably Wulff, 1909, reviewed by Abraham in the *Jahrbuch* (1909, 1: 594).
4. William Stern [1871–1938], German psychologist and philosopher, Professor in Breslau and Hamburg [1916], editor of the *Zeitschrift für Angewandte Psychologie*. In 1933 he emigrated to the United States, where he taught at Harvard and at Duke University. Stern is one of the pioneers of modern psychology. The review has not been identified.

67F

PROF. D^R. FREUD
WIEN, IX. BERGGASSE 19

Vienna IX, Berggasse 19
9 March 1909

Dear Colleague,

Oppenheim is too limited; I hope you will manage without him in time. The *Jahrbuch* is in everyone's hands now; are there any cries of indignation reaching your ears, too?

Your review in the second half-volume should make up for all the collective reviews that are now suddenly sprouting.

I have the best expectations of your Segantini, following the example of *Dreams and Myths*. I know that the latter is widely read and highly praised in our circles. Other circles have not yet taken much notice of the [*Schriften zur*] *angewandten* [*Seelenkunde*] at all!

Jung wants to come for a visit on the 19th of this month. He writes to me that a Dr Häberlin in Basle has announced a course of lectures on "Reading F.'s *Interpretation of Dreams*". H. is a lecturer on psychology and runs an educational establishment.[1]

And now for the big news. I have accepted the repeated invitation of Clark University, Worcester, Mass., near Boston, to give a series of lectures there in the week beginning 6 September on the occasion of the university's twentieth anniversary celebrations; and I shall be leaving at the end of August. My brother,[2] and probably also Dr Ferenczi of Budapest, want to come as well. I am very curious what sort of experience it will be and about the outcome of these lectures. The journey may certainly be mentioned, it is as sure as anything human can be. Perhaps it will annoy some people in Berlin as well as in Vienna. That will not do any harm.

I know you will be pleased about it, and send you my cordial greetings.

Yours,

*Freud*

1. Paul Häberlin [1878–1960], Swiss philosopher and professor of philosophy in Berne and Basle.
2. Alexander Freud [1866–1943]. Without an academic degree, he became a sworn specialist at the Court of Commerce, an Expert of the Ministry for Freight, Transport, and Tariff Affairs, and Imperial Counsel. He was a lecturer at the Consular Academy and editor of the periodical *Allgemeiner Tarif-Anzeiger*. Dispossessed by the National Socialists, he died in exile in Canada. The intention of the brothers—who normally took many trips together—to travel together to the United States in 1909 was not realized.

## 68A

Dr med. K. Abraham
Berlin W. 35, Schöneberger Ufer 22
7 April 1909

Dear Professor,

The eagerly awaited *Jahrbuch* has now been in my hands for a few days. It only became available in German book-shops a week ago. I read your analysis[1] at one sitting, and I am still completely under the impression it made. I have not heard any other opinions yet; and as I know in advance what they will be like, I am not at all curious. It is certainly very gratifying to find again so clearly in the child what we have reconstructed from the analyses of adults; this feeling speaks from every line.

1909 April

This is at least some compensation for the lack of understanding on the part of professional colleagues.—It is remarkable that the remaining contents of the volume all come from the Zurich school. Maeder's paper[2] seems very valuable to me. I had heard a great deal beforehand about Jung's contribution[3] and therefore expected something very original. I am afraid he disappointed me somewhat because he does not seem to shed any new light on the question under discussion. Incidentally, are you also of the opinion that the *father* is so predominant? In some of my analyses it is definitely the mother; in others one cannot decide whether it is the f.[ather] or the m.[other] who is of greater importance. It seems to me to depend very much on the individual circumstances. Binswanger[4] is unfortunately rather too long-winded. How much more is there still to come in the next volume? Incidentally, I think it technically wrong to report the second part of an analysis after an interval of a half a year. Those who read the first part now will not be able to understand the second then.

I am delighted that the American trip is taking place after all; the people whom I told about it along the lines you suggested were unfortunately not sufficiently annoyed. Incidentally, does the journey there or back lead through Berlin? That is what interests me particularly in this matter.

Here there is still nothing moving. Only Juliusburger is very interested and is analysing diligently. Recently, however, he has put himself under analysis with me; it has brought out some quite peculiar results. At the moment he is on a journey; it is not impossible that he may pass through Vienna. (The reason for the analysis was a state of nervous anxiety; naturally to be treated with discretion!) Recently Eitingon visited me; as always he was full of the finest observations; unfortunately he does not make use of them by writing anything. He drew my attention to a passage in the 2nd edition of the *Interpretation of Dreams*. The footnote on p. 181 contains two mistakes ("*vergleichende Seelenkunde*" and "*1809*"). I can hazard a guess about the wrong year. But why is poor Rank the victim in both instances?[5]

What you write about Oppenheim is absolutely right. But, then, he has to be judged more leniently. He went through an illness last summer which the doctors treating him could not understand at all and which was wrapped in a thick cloak of mystery. At that time, hearing the description, I had the impression of a severe anxiety neurosis or anxiety hysteria. Since then O. has been repressing with great energy but often suffers from all kinds of physical symptoms. In short—his refusal is understandable. I ask you, dear Professor, to treat this information as confidential too.—The analysis of the young man, about which I have repeatedly written to you, had already led to very fine therapeutic results when it was abruptly broken off because of an event in the family. But the patient will take it up again in a few weeks. In the meantime I have begun two new analyses, and I notice that from each treatment I gain a better understanding of the following ones. I have tracked down a symptomatic action in myself. While I am analysing and am waiting for the patient's reply, I often cast a quick glance at the picture of my parents. I know now that I always do this when I am following up the infantile transference in the patient. The glance is always accompanied by a particular guilt feeling: what will they think of me? This has of course to do with my separation from them, which was not too easy. Since explaining this symptomatic action to myself, I have not caught myself at it any more.—Another observation of our little girl,[6] aged two years and four months. On two occasions I had to give her a glycerine enema. Since then, she has told me every day that she does *not* want another injection, but she says this without real affect and, on most occasions, even with a rather arch smile. So obviously she wants to get the injection. Apart from this, she does not show any anal-erotic tendencies.

So much for today.
With cordial greetings,
your devoted

*Abraham*

1. Freud, 1909b.
2. Maeder, 1909a.
3. Jung, 1909a.
4. Binswanger, 1909.
5. Referring to the note (Freud, 1900a, addition 1909: p. 256), in which Freud quoted Rank (1909), published in the Schriften zur angewandten Seelenkunde. The mistake, to be sure, is not to be found in later editions. Ferenczi, too, had noticed the wrong year and had ventured an interpretation (15 December 1908, Freud & Ferenczi, 1992: p. 30). Interestingly, in the same footnote Freud tried to correct an error in the main text, on which he commented (1901b: p. 218).
6. Hilda C. Abraham [1906–1971], later psychoanalyst in London, co-editor of *Dialogue* (cf. Abraham's posthumously published "Little Hilda: Day dreams and a Symptom of a Seven-Year-Old Girl", Abraham, 1976).

69F

Vienna IX, Berggasse 19
27 April 1909

Dear Colleague,

I was very glad to read a letter from you after a longish interval. Then the reply was delayed by all sorts of disturbances, such as conjunctivitis and my daughter's falling ill again, which led to an operation, but hopefully also to a final recovery. She is already doing very well.[1]

## 1909 April

First of all, let me say that everything you tell me in confidence will be treated confidentially, *personalia* in particular. I willingly grant you the preponderance of the Zurich school, to which, after all, you belong yourself. I would like to make the same comments as you did on the problems that Jung dealt with. Up to now, I have believed the parent of the same sex to be more important for the person concerned, but can also adapt to greater individual variations. Jung has taken a part out of the whole, but he has done so very effectively.

My trip to America starts on 21 August from Trieste, only the return journey will be by way of Hamburg and Berlin and will bring about a brief reunion with you. There is really nothing to be done with the Berliners if they are not annoyed even by this.

As for visitors, we had Jung and his wife here at the end of March[2] and Dr Pfister[3] during these last few days. Half an hour before him Moll was here, with whom things ended badly. It came to harsh words, and he left suddenly, with a great deal of rapidly secreted venom. I almost had the impression that he thought he was patronizing us, and at that I let myself go a little. Probably you will now feel the repercussions. Never mind.

I should now prepare the third edition of the *Everyday Life*,[4] but because of the pressure of medical work cannot get round to anything. Also, my health has left something to be desired during these past few months. Perhaps it is a good thing if you young people take good care of the cause.—Rank's paper will have been of special interest to you because of its mythological content, and I would like to hear your comments. The mistakes referring to it in the *Interpretation of Dreams* have already been explained, but I have forgotten the explanation! Just that it was no special vindictiveness against Rank!

Cordial greetings from your

*Freud*

1. The operation on Mathilde, necessary because of the residues of an appendectomy in 1905, had taken place on 22 April.
2. 25–30 March.
3. Oskar Pfister [1873–1956], Protestant minister in Zurich, in correspondence with Freud since January 1909 (Freud & Pfister, 1963). He was active as a psychoanalyst all his life and a pioneer in the application of psychoanalysis to the ministry and to education. Pfister became and remained a close friend of the Freud family. (Cf. Zulliger, 1966.)
4. Freud, 1901b (third edition 1910).

## 70A

Berlin
16 May 1909

Dear Professor,

I hope by the time this letter reaches you the various illnesses you mentioned some weeks ago will long have been things of the past. I answer your letter only today because I wanted to report to you on my talk to the Psychological Society, under Moll's chairmanship. It is not a professional association but a rather mixed audience. I spoke about "Infantile Phantasies in the Mental Life of the Adult". M. was very kind (as always) and declared that he did not want to take part in the discussion because his reply would probably turn out to be too temperamental! I was glad that frictions were avoided in this way. M. also talked about his visit to you, naturally completely differently from what you told me about it. In the future I shall keep away from him as much as possible. This type of person does not appeal to me, and from other quarters too I keep hearing unfavourable things about his character. His part in the patient-catching affair also prejudices people against him. In the discussion one of the speakers, the psychologist Vierkandt,[1] showed quite good understanding.

What gave me most pleasure in your letter was the hope of seeing you here in the autumn. Perhaps I may ask you already now to be generous in apportioning your time! I am so looking forward to it, and in the course of time such a great deal has accumulated that I want to discuss with you!

My practice, which from the outset has developed more favourably than I had dared hope, has recently surprised even me by its progress. I am busy for the greater part of the day with ongoing treatments; in the morning there are nine patients on my agenda, six of them psychoanalytic cases! A year and a half ago I would not have dreamt of this. Admittedly I am not yet sought out by the public. I owe most of the cases to other doctors or to personal contacts. For several months I have had no support from Oppenheim, as he has either been ill or away, but in spite of this the practice has not declined during that time. I now see, incidentally, that psychotherapy can be a very exhausting business, and if it remains like this the ample free time for my private work will be a thing of the past. If finances permit, I should like to go away for some weeks in mid-summer with my wife and our little one. Have you decided yet where you are going? Perhaps there will be a chance to meet during the holidays after all.

I like Rank's book very much. I am only sorry that the Flood has not been dealt with more fully. It has so many connections with the birth legends. In addition—at least in the biblical form—it is such a particularly good demonstration of the effects of repression. This might well be a subject on its own.

Do you not agree that it might be worth while sometime to work on a special study of agoraphobia? I am currently dealing with several such cases that very nicely demonstrate the fixation on mother or father.[2] I would like to know your opinion on several points. I find in these patients that during their anxiety states they feel very small, would like to crawl on all fours, and have the impression at the time that other people are terribly large. Here the phantasy—of being a child who is unable to move—is transparent. Some such patients, however, describe a feeling as if they were shrinking and sinking into the earth. At home they shut themselves into as small a space as possible. I assume that this stands for the wish to be an embryo, to return to the mother's womb. Do you approve of this interpretation? It fits my cases very well. Of course there is no hurry about answering this question. There are several other matters from my practice that I would like to put before you, dear Professor, but every letter must come to an end. So, just accept the most cordial greetings

from your devoted

*Karl Abraham*

1. Probably Alfred Vierkandt [1867–1953], German sociologist. Co-founder of the German Society for Sociology in 1909; from 1913 on Professor in Berlin. After the Nazi era, during which he was not allowed to lecture, again lecturer in sociology [1946] at the University of Berlin.
2. Abraham described one such case (1910[17]: pp. 94ff).


71F

Vienna IX, Berggasse 19
23 May 1909

Dear Colleague,

I am highly delighted at your good news, not least at your independence of O., who is a hopeless proposition in any case.

Now to the most important matter, our next meeting. On the outward journey I shall probably be travelling direct from Munich to Bremen (21 Aug. "George Washington" N[ord]D[eutscher] L[loyd]). On the way back, I want to stop briefly in Hamburg; then break the journey in Berlin. There I have a very jealous and incredibly youthful and energetic 75-year-old brother,[1] from whom I shall conceal my presence for half a day in order to have the chance of talking to you and catching a glimpse of your hospitable home. The rest we shall see. Probable date, towards the very end of September.

In the summer we shall very probably take rooms in the Hotel Ammerwald (on the borders of Tyrol and Bavaria), two hours by carriage from Oberammergau, if we can still get rooms there. I am longing for the lovely leafy solitude I was promised there, also I should finish a paper off there.[2] So I cannot offer you hospitality, but if you want to disturb me you will be cordially welcomed.

*Ad vocem*[3] Moll: the man is not a physician but a shyster. I am forcing myself to tell you something more as a warning. Naturally he soon started talking about you, and immediately came up with the insinuation that your enthusiasm for psychoanalysis seemed to be on the wane, as your lectures were no longer so frequent. I interrupted him with the dry comment that we had agreed that you would not come forward more often than once every six months. Looking back, it seems to me that he wanted to induce *me* to initiate a similar purifying action in the matter of the patient-catching affair in Vienna; I quickly turned the talk to other subjects, which shattered his illusion. A spiteful, shifty fellow, capable of every dirty trick, who compensates with official ethics!

Vierkandt has exchanged letters with me several times. You might perhaps attempt to draw him into your circle. I also hear so much that is favourable about Marcinowski[4] (I cannot guarantee that that is the name—he heads an institute) that I would heartily recommend acquiring him as well.

The tracing back of agoraphobia to infantile spatial impressions is known to me and is certainly important. You will never miss the father–mother fixation in any future case. Ambitious phantasies gone to ruin seem to be the specific factor in agoraphobia. More when we talk!

I am of course too tired to work, but am otherwise well again. My wife and my second daughter are in Karlsbad.

With cordial greetings to you and your dear family.

Yours,

*Freud*

---

1. Freud's half-brother Emanuel from Manchester, who had accompanied Freud to Berlin in September 1908.
2. Probably Freud meant to write his *General Methodology of Psychoanalysis* there. It seems, however, that he did not write anything at all during his holidays before the trip to America.
3. Latin: "as regards", "as to".
4. Jaroslaw Marcinowski [1868–1925], medical director of a sanatorium in Holstein, Germany. Marcinowski later belonged not to the German, but to the Vienna Society [1919–1925].

## 72A

Berlin
15 June 1909

Dear Professor,

I do not want to delay answering your last letter any longer, and I am sending you a few lines, as there is not very much to report. It is not very likely that I shall come to the region where you are having your summer holidays; *if* we go away we shall probably go to a Danish sea resort (Gillelege). On the other hand, it is very probable that at the time of your journey to America I will be in Bremen, where my parents live. If you have no other claims on your time, we might perhaps be able to see each other. Otherwise, a bit later in Berlin! The practice is so busy again at this very moment that I am most anxious for a little relaxation.

I know you will be pleased when I tell you that in the first half of this year the practice has already brought in a good 4,000 M. I can add that on the difficult ground of Berlin most people are progressing very much more slowly. Incidentally, Oppenheim has recently been kind enough to take care of me again; only the times during which he is repressing particularly strongly are unfavourable to me.

The literature is now growing greatly, and the papers are buzzing with reviews of the well-known kind. Have you read the "Hysterische Bellen" [*Hysterical barking*] of Frl. Chalewska in Zurich?[1] A new adherent appears to be Stockmayer in Tübingen; I saw a good review by him of the 2nd edition of the *Interpretation of Dreams*,[2] and a number of others. I am corresponding with Marcinowski. He has not lived in Berlin for two years. Our association here has been dormant for quite a long time. Hirschfeld has been away since February, Juliusburger is ill and away; of the others, who had taken part more as audience, nobody asked about a meeting, and so nothing could be done recently. I have hopes for the autumn.—As far as Moll is concerned, the assertion that my lectures were becoming less frequent is a spiteful invention. As it is, I have given a single one in November, and one in May in "his" "Psychological Society".

For the last few days I have been treating a young colleague who is a foot and clothes fetishist;[3] we corresponded on this question some time ago. I shall let you know my results later. I should be glad only to know whether you have seen any therapeutic influence on such patients.

Recently I spoke to our colleague Wittels here. His sudden marriage came as a great surprise for me.[4]

With cordial greetings, also from my wife, who is looking forward to seeing you, dear Professor, in our home.

Your devoted

K. Abraham

1. Chalewsky, 1909. Dr Fanny Chalewsky was engaged to Alphonse Maeder for a short time (14 October 1909, Freud & Jung, 1974 [1906–13]: p. 252).
2. Stockmayer, 1909. Wolf Stockmayer [1881–1933] had, together with Ernest Jones, been in training under Kraepelin. Between 1908 and 1909 he was at the Burghölzli, where he collaborated on word associations and became a personal friend of Jung's. Then he returned to Tübingen, where he was Gaupp's assistant at the University Clinic. Gaupp was co-editor of the *Zentralblatt für Nervenheilkunde und Psychiatrie*, in which the review appeared. From the end of 1913 on, Stockmayer was in Berlin; later active as an analytical (Jungian) psychologist in Stuttgart.
3. Cf. Abraham, 1910[18].
4. Fritz Wittels [1880–1950], Viennese physician and writer, from 1907 on a member of the Wednesday Society. From 1908 until 1922 he was resident-physician at the Cottage-Sanatorium of Rudolf von Urbantschitsch. His pointed, polemical contributions and publications (e. g. Wittels, 1907) and his crossing swords with Karl Kraus (Wittels, 1910) unleashed heated controversy. Wittels left the Vienna Society in 1910, joined Stekel, and wrote a critical biography of Freud (Wittels, 1924). Around 1927 he was readmitted into the Vienna Society with Freud's support; in 1928 he emigrated to New York, where he became a professor at the New School for Social Research. He married Yerta Pick, the daughter of a famous psychiatrist from Prague; she died one year later (Mühlleitner, 1992: p. 370; Timms, 1995).

## 73F

Vienna
11 July 1909

Dear Colleague,

The term is in its death-throes, so that I am happily occupied with the prospect of the delightful interval. So I shall really be in Ammerwald *Post Reutte* Tyrol until 18 August, on the 20th I have to be in Bremen, and on the 21st the G. Washington casts off. If you are in your home-town around this time, perhaps you will let me know your address in advance or leave me a message in the ND Lloyd office. Ferenczi will be with me; it is not yet decided whether we will meet Jung, who as you know is also invited, on the ship or beforehand. If not Bremen, then certainly Berlin at the end of September. I am very pleased about your favourable news, that is to say, your favourable view of the situation. As you are the only one in Berlin, it should work out for you even better; it will come to pass.

Cordial greetings, nothing scientific today, I am already too tired.

Your faithfully devoted

*Freud*

## 74A

Berlin
13 July 1909

Dear Professor,

Today I would like to thank you only briefly for your letter, so as not to go away owing letters. We are leaving in a few days. My address during the next few weeks is: Pension Frl. Dahlerup, Hornbach, Denmark. A meeting in Bremen is unlikely, as I am back in Berlin on the 13th or the 14th. But do you perhaps go through Berlin on the way to Bremen? Otherwise I count on September. I, too, would very much like to make the trip to America. I had no idea that Jung had also been invited.

In contrast to this happy event, unfortunately there has recently been a whole series of the most stupid attacks. The number of publications this year has given the critics plenty to do. Oppenheim's attack in the *Berliner Klinische Wochenschrift* is very regrettable, and it has already borne fruit. An article with psychoanalytical content was sent back by return of post to a colleague (Wulff, Juliusburger's assistant) by this very journal.—I myself recently spoke on "Psychoanalysis and the Interpretation of Dreams" in a circle of Russian doctors. In October I am to speak in a circle of Oppenheim's assistants. I am planning an attack on a larger scale in the *Neurolog[ische] Gesellsch[aft]* [Neurological Society] for November.

But now the peace of holidays! I wish you and your esteemed family a very pleasant rest. With kind regards,
your devoted
*Abraham*

## 75F

21 August 1909[1]

See you again on the way back!
Yours,
*Freud*[2]

1. Postcard.
2. Freud, Ferenczi, and Jung met in Bremen on 20 August and departed the following day. After their arrival on the 29th, they first spent a week in New York and then drove to Worcester, Massachusetts, to Clark University. During the following week Freud gave five lectures (Freud, 1910a [1909]), which he sketched out each morning on walks with Ferenczi. At the closing celebration Freud and Jung received honorary Doctor of Laws degrees. After a visit to Niagara Falls and a stay in James Putnam's camp in the Adirondacks, the three men embarked on 21 September and reached Bremen on 29

September. While Jung immediately went home, Freud and Ferenczi stayed briefly in Hamburg and Berlin, where Freud also visited the Abrahams. The trip has been described numerous times (e. g. by Clark, 1980: pp. 264ff; Hale, 1971a; Jones, 1955: pp. 53ff.; the most complete description is by Rosenzweig, 1992; a comprehensive depiction can be found in Freud & Jung, 1974 [1906–13]: pp. 245f).

## 76A

Berlin
10 November 1909

Dear Professor,

Now it is time to abreact! The day before yesterday there was the battle in the Neurological Society. The "Dream States"[1] met with a far worse reception than I had expected. To be sure, Ziehen as Chairman had, in quite a perfidious way, done all he could to make my talk fall flat. While I was speaking, I was confronted only with faces wearing that well-known supercilious smile. Then Ziehen prevented any discussion, only allowing himself time to deliver a short but furious attack on my "hotchpotch". I have never in any neurotic patient seen such crude and poorly disguised resistance. I merely replied that, in view of Z.'s prejudice, I would abstain from a rejoinder. Very characteristic: the only colleague who took an objective view was—as I heard privately—a surgeon who had strayed into the meeting by mistake. This man is able to satisfy his aggressive desires with the help of the knife and does not, like the neurologists, need to air it in petty animosities.

But otherwise I am well, and I sincerely hope that this is so with you, too, by now. My wife and I were very sorry that in the circumstances we could offer you so little hospitality. But, once again, I want to thank you most cordially for the hours you gave us.

As regards my practice, I can report that the public is gradually finding its way to me under its own steam. In the course of the next few months I shall also have to appear as an expert in several major lawsuits; among others, I shall probably have to give an expert opinion concerning a spiritualist medium about whose unmasking there was a great deal in the papers.—It is very amusing that two nerve specialists have recently moved right into my neighbourhood and a third will soon follow their example. Whatever success one achieves—it must not be due to psychoanalysis. So this time it is the district!

A Russian colleague by the name of Wulff, who has been Juliusburger's assistant in a private institution for some time, is now going to settle in Odessa. He is very interested in psychoanalysis and, because of this, lost his last job in Berlin after a few weeks. I know him to be a diligent and trustworthy man who is, however, in a very critical financial situation. Perhaps you (or one of the colleagues there) could occasionally refer patients to him? I assume he will write to you personally

1909 November

as he has asked me for your address. In addition, he would like to do translations into Russian, as I hear from Juliusburger.

With cordial greetings, also to your esteemed family, your devoted

K. Abraham

1. Abraham, 1910[17].

77F

Vienna IX, Berggasse 19
23 November 1909

Dear Colleague,

Only the fact that I am forced to use every free minute to put to paper the Worcester lectures[1] has made such a bad correspondent of me and caused me so long to delay thanking you for making another appearance with the "Dream States". Surely we will get them for the *Jahrbuch*? You are just the man to take as little notice of the general opposition as I did in Vienna at the time, and to find sufficient compensation in our interest alone.

I thank you for your kind reception and your dear wife for her[2] hospitality. You will remember how rushed I was, and that only the train journey gave us the hour of undisturbed discussion for which we had been waiting for so long.[3] Our colleague Eitingon will long since have told you the news from our house[4] and given you the bad photograph,[5] which at least shows how heavy the demands were that America made on me physically.

I am well again now, except for the usual symptoms due to overwork.

The practice was never so busy as in these last two months, but also never so dreary and scientifically sterile; also, the flow of would-be patients that usually enabled me to pass on cases to younger colleagues has so far not materialized.

The appearance of the second half-volume[6] is imminent; it is to contain all sorts of things.[7] You will also be shortly receiving from me the third edition of the *Everyday Life*. The second one of the *Sexual Theory*[8] will come next. It will be *some* time, I think, before a short paper on Leonardo da Vinci[9] that so far only Eitingon knows about will enrich the *Schriften zur angewandten Seelenkunde*. I would like to see your Segantini there. There would then be two advances into biographical writing in our sense.

I am trying to win over to the ψα points of view a young mythologist, also called Oppenheim.[10] I have not seen your O., who is staying here at the moment, but actually do not miss him much. I am now giving my lectures in the form of a seminar, and I shall soon have one of your works presented and discussed, probably the one on the differences between hysteria and dementia praecox.[11]

In the hope that this delay will not have frightened you off, and with best regards to your little family.

Yours in friendship,

*Freud*

1. Freud, 1910a [1909].
2. In original: "Ihre" [your] instead of "ihre" [her].
3. Abraham had accompanied Freud on the train for part of the journey.
4. Eitingon had been in Vienna from at least 12 October until about the middle of November. He had attended the meetings of the Wednesday Society (cf. Nunberg & Federn, 1967) and had also been "analysed" by Freud on walks "twice a week after dinner" (22 October 1909, Freud & Ferenczi, 1992: p. 85).
5. Taken by Freud's future son-in-law, Max Halberstadt, in Hamburg (reprinted in Ernst Freud, Lucie Freud, & Ilse Grubrich-Simitis, 1974, no. 202).
6. Of the *Jahrbuch*.
7. Among others, Abraham's two collective reviews (1909[15], 1909[16]) and Freud's case history of the Rat Man (1909d).
8. Freud, 1905d (second edition 1910).
9. Freud, 1910c, which appeared at the end of May 1910 as no. 7 of the *Schriften*.
10. David Ernst Oppenheim [1881–1943] was a teacher of Greek and Latin at the Academic Gymnasium in Vienna. Co-author with Freud (1957a [1911]). Between 1910 and 1911 member of the Vienna Society, then an adherent of Adler's. He died in the Theresienstadt concentration camp.
11. Abraham, 1908[11].

## 78A

Berlin
24 November 1909

Dear Professor,

When our colleague Dr Eitingon brought me your picture some days ago, I would have thanked you at once, had he not told me that there was the beginning of a letter to me lying on your table, which I would shortly be receiving. Now I can thank you for both at the same time. I was particularly delighted with the picture; it most faithfully mirrors your appearance seven weeks ago. It now stands on my working desk in a frame that accentuates it very well and surveys the coming into being of the "Dream States" with a critical eye. These are to be published in the next half-yearly volume.

Your new plans, of which Eitingon has already told me, make me curious. The neighbourhood of your Leonardo will, however, be slightly discomfiting for my Segantini. But written it certainly will be, and that as soon as possible. The letters and writings of Segantini, for which I have been waiting, have just appeared, and I think I will be able to start work in a week or two.

1909 November

To characterize our enemies, I have something more to report. As I heard from a very reliable source, Ziehen told a colleague that he let my talk fall flat in the way he did in order show the present foreign guests what one thought of Freud in Berlin! (My informant would not like this to be spread around.)

What you write about your seminar interests me not only because of the discussion of my paper but mainly because of the course of lectures I am planning for January. I am still very uncertain which form I should choose for it. The one now chosen by you seems to be suitable only for an advanced audience.

A short paper by Juliusburger has just come out.[1] He is very zealous; but it is not easy for him to detach himself from some other authorities whom he admires, and then this always ends up in a compromise. I have traced this characteristic of his, psychoanalytically, to infantile transferences. It is clearly recognizable in the publication.

Recently there was a short article in the *Schaubühne* by an authoress called Riemann, who through reading the *Interpretation of Dreams* gained some insight into her own dream life and now discusses, in the form of a dialogue, whether such knowledge makes one happier or not. The authoress thinks the latter and seems to have a personal grudge against you, for instead of your name she always writes just Professor F.

I hope you feel quite well again by now, and also your daughter, about whose illness I was very sorry to hear. With my own and my wife's most cordial greetings to you and your family,
   your devoted
   *Karl Abraham*

1. Probably Juliusburger, 1909b.


### 79A

Berlin
30 November 1909

Dear Professor,

Please accept my heartfelt thanks for the 3rd edition. I have already read it with much pleasure.

There is nothing new yet. Only that for a few days I have been analysing a most interesting case of incest between siblings. More details when the occasion arises.

Kind cordial greetings,
   your devoted
   *Abraham*

## 80A

Berlin
22 December 1909

Dear Professor,

Thank you very much for your letter and, at the same time, for the offprints of my reviews. I am at the moment very busy with several reports on court cases; as soon as I can, I will write you something about the obsessional neurosis and other scientific matters. At the beginning of January I start my course, which we discussed in September. Seven participants have already registered, and I am expecting more still.

With cordial greetings from house to house,
your devoted

*Abraham*

# 1910

### 81 F

Vienna IX, Berggasse 19
20 January 1910

Dear Dr Abraham,

A patient, the sister of one of your latest patients, had to show me an advertisement in a Berlin paper announcing the beginning of your courses. That reminded me of how long it is since I last wrote to you.

Recently I have been in a position three times to mention your name here, twice to patients whom I wanted to refer to you and once to a Finn who was referred to me by a circle of young doctors and philosophers in Berlin (!). I let these gentlemen know that they should, rather, get in touch with you and extend your circle of pupils. As regards the patients, I have unfortunately learnt that the number of shots that score hits is still very small; but he who sits it out will have good times ahead.

You are probably following how eagerly the Americans are participating in the cause. Jones is working very eagerly, and Putnam is just publishing a series of articles on our visit to Worcester in the *Journal of Abnormal Psychology*.[1] Stanley Hall will devote the whole April issue of the *American Journal of Psychology* to us.[2] Both of them recently gave the confused and dishonest Boris Sidis a thorough rebuff at a meeting of American psychologists.[3]

Our Congress in Nuremberg is fixed for 30 and 31 March, that is, just after Easter. The invitations will be going out very soon. We Europeans will, I hope, be present in full force. This time the subject will be primarily questions of principle and organization.[4]

We have been extending hospitality to L. Binswanger and his wife[5] since Sunday, as far as Viennese hospitality can possibly go in these days of hard work. My wife obviously prefers the memory of another ψα couple who have not fully been our guests so far. But please do not pass this on.

I cannot do any work at all now. Handicraft work such as the preparation of the 2nd edition of the *Sexual Theory* and of the German edition of the Worcester lectures, letters, the seminar, the Wednesday meetings—that is all. Not a line on Leonardo for weeks. I gladly yield precedence to Segantini.

I send you my cordial greetings and hope that you and your little family are very well.

Yours in friendship,

*Freud*

1. James Jackson Putnam [1846–1918], Professor of Neurology at Harvard University; co-editor of the *Journal of Abnormal Psychology*. He was a participant in the celebration for Clark University and host to Freud, Ferenczi, and Jung in his lodge in the Adirondacks. In 1911 he founded and was first president of the American Psychoanalytic Association. He was interested in combining psychoanalysis and philosophy. (See Putnam, 1909–10.)
2. *American Journal of Psychology* (1910), *21*, containing the Worcester lectures of Freud (1910a [1909]) and Jung (1910b), as well as papers by Ferenczi (1909[66]) and Jones (1910b).
3. Eighteenth annual meeting of the American Psychological Association, Cambridge, Massachusetts, 29–31 December 1909. The afternoon of 29 December was given over to abnormal psychology and psychoanalysis. Sidis "deprecated the present prospect of a Freud cult in this country and said it seemed likely to be a passing craze but that people would get over it" (Hall's letter to Freud of 30 December 1909; in Rosenzweig, 1992: p. 367).

    Boris Sidis [1867–1923], a political refugee from Russia, studied psychology with William James at Harvard. From 1896 to 1901 associate psychologist at the Pathological Institute of the New York State Hospitals; he practised in Brookline, Massachusetts, between 1904 and 1909, when he established the Sidis Institute for Nervous and Mental Disorders in Portsmouth, New Hampshire. Associate editor, under Morton Prince, of the *Journal of Abnormal Psychology*. He was a vehement opponent of psychoanalysis.
4. Having played with the idea that psychoanalysts could join the "International Order for Ethics and Culture", founded by the Swiss pharmacist Alfred Knapp, or even to join a "certain [political?] party in practical life" (letter to Adler, undated, LOC), Freud had finally proposed, in letters to Jung and Ferenczi, "a tighter organization with formal rules and a small fee" (1 January 1910, Freud & Ferenczi, 1992: p. 119). Ferenczi was to work out the statutes and present them at the congress.
5. Hertha, née Buchberger, a psychiatric nurse with whom Binswanger became acquainted during his stay in Jena [1907/08]. The couple had married on 2 April 1908 (cf. Fichtner, 1992: p. xviii). Their visit to Freud is described by Binswanger (1956).

## 82A

Berlin
23 January 1910

Dear Professor,

When your letter arrived yesterday, I had been about to write myself. As I know how many claims there are on your time, it goes without saying that I do not settle accounts with you "an eye for an eye".[1] I thank you from my heart for all the kindness contained in your letter.

At the moment I am not quite so isolated in Berlin, as I often meet up with the peripatetics (Karpas,[2] Eitingon etc.). The course is turning out very well. I have nine participants, all of whom seem to be quite interested. Oddly enough, the four doctors from here who had registered definitely did not appear at all!

1910 January

Frau Dr Meyer, my new patient, whom I have actually seen only once, is attached to you with a textbook transference. As soon as I know more, I will report to you about the case.

I am very much looking forward to Nuremberg. At present, however, I do not know what questions of principle are to be discussed.—Who is taking on the organization in N.[uremberg]? I have a fairly good knowledge of the hotels and the general situation there and can perhaps advise in one way or another.

I have sent the "Dream States" to Jung.[3] Now Segantini should be coming—*should*, but at present I am forensic psychiatrist "in full-time office", that is to say I am overburdened with reports on court cases. I like this activity very much next to psychotherapeutic work, and for the sake of my income I cannot do without it either. The general outcome of 1909 was very encouraging, I have brought it up to over 8,000 M.—Segantini is going to make me go also into the question of flying,[4] and it is actually not to my liking to anticipate Leonardo. Recently—unfortunately only for too short a time—I analysed a highly intelligent writer who, because of infantilisms, was intensely concerned with the problem of flying; he also has his sublimations very much in common with Segantini.

The opposition in Berlin will probably show itself in a very unpleasant way in the near future. Ziehen is letting one of his doctors give a "critical" review in the *Gesellschaft für Psychiatrie und Nervenkrankheiten* [Society for Psychiatry and Nervous Diseases], and—Moll, I hear from a reliable source, is preparing some dirty trick or other. No matter. In South Germany the situation seems to be much better. I hear about America quite often from Karpas. My general review of your writings—assuming you agree—will perhaps be translated into Russian by Dr Wulff in Odessa.

I have only partly read the last *Jahrbuch*, to be exact, *wholly* only your work, which reminded me vividly of the lecture in Salzburg.[5] I hope this year's Congress will be really satisfactory. I have recently collected many interesting single observations, about which I should like to talk to you, but especially about a few theoretical points that seem important to me. Could you not perhaps come to N. a day earlier? The town is very attractive and very suitable for conversations while walking. Rotenburg ob der Tauber might possibly be a very suitable place for an excursion. I hope you and your family are well. Is your dear wife not perhaps coming to Nuremberg? My wife would very much like to go with me. There were a few ladies at the first Congress, too. The "psychoanalytical couple" here will probably not come to Vienna for the time being. With cordial greetings,
  your devoted

  *Karl Abraham*

1. 2 Moses 21, 24; 3 Moses 24, 20; Matthew 5, 38.
2. Morris J. Karpas [1879–1918], a charter member of the New York Psychoanalytic Society. He had been in Vienna from April to July 1909 and had attended a number of the Wednesday meetings. The "peripatetics" perhaps refer to Eitingon's—and Karpas's?—"analysis" with Freud during walks.
3. Abraham, 1910[17], to be published in the *Jahrbuch*, edited by Jung.
4. Cf. Abraham, 1911[30]: pp. 239ff., dealing with the question of why Segantini painted the *Voluptuaries* as well as *Dea Pangana* as floating in the air.
5. Freud's analysis of the Rat Man (1909d), about which he had spoken in Salzburg. The second half-volume of the *Jahrbuch* had come out in November 1909.

## 83A

Berlin
22 February 1910

Dear Professor,

I have announced a talk on fetishism[1] for Nuremberg. You told me in September that you might put your notes on an analytic case at my disposal. If it is no trouble to you, I would now like to ask you for them. But should I take up too much of your time with this request, I would rather restrict myself to my own case; perhaps you would then tell us something about your experiences in an eventual discussion? This one case has naturally not given me complete understanding, but I can put forward a number of new viewpoints.

I enclose the clipping of an advertisement that you may consider a favourable symptom. Several colleagues have asked me to arrange another course.

---

In March, I intend to arrange another four weeks'

### Course on Freud's Theory of Neuroses

(including the theory of sexuality and dream analysis), twice weekly, on evenings still to be specified, from 8: 30 to 10. Begin: Monday, 28 February, 8: 30 p.m., in my apartment. Fee: 30 marks. Written or verbal (in the afternoon) applications are requested.

Dr med. K. Abraham
Berlin W. 35, Schöneberger Ufer 22
Tel. Amt VI. 132345

---

Did you happen to see the article on dream interpretation in the *Frankfurter Zeitung*? The author is one of my patients. The article is very intelligently written, only at the end does resistance appear, against

1910 February

wish-fulfilment, of course. You will probably receive a copy direct from the author.

With cordial greetings from house to house,
your devoted

*Abraham*

1. Abraham, 1910[18].

84F

Vienna IX, Berggasse 19
24 February 1910

Dear Colleague,

I am uncommonly pleased at being able to help you in something. Unfortunately it is only very little, but make any use of it you wish.

I have investigated only one case in detail; of others in which the subject of fetishism was instructively touched on I have only the results, not the notes.

The case was that of a highly educated, elegant, and sophisticated man of 25, who carefully adjusted the creases in his trousers before lying down for the first time on the $\psi\alpha$ couch.[1] He turned out to be a clothes fetishist in the better sense of the word, attached great importance to elegance and taste in his own clothes, and found a female person "impossible" if her dressing did not meet his ideal demands. He suddenly lost all interest in a girl who had greatly attracted him when she turned up for a rendezvous unsuitably dressed.

He was $\psi$ impotent[2] and, according to analysis, fixated on his mother, who had for years made him watch her dressing and undressing, at least up to the penultimate point, who is completely in love with him and would still be inclined to such intimacies to the present day, in spite of his withdrawing from them now. (During the treatment he achieved excellent potency but remained $\psi$ anaesthetic.) He was also a boot fetishist, also not of the crudest kind. His childhood was full of unusually intense *coprophilic* activity. At the age of eight to ten, for instance, he managed to keep a hard sausage hanging from his rectum, from which he kept breaking off little bits in the course of the day. He still was an over-sensitive "smeller". In the years of puberty he was a voyeur, his masturbation began with his spying on undressing American women[3] in a Swiss hotel.

I have learnt from other cases that boot fetishism goes back to an original pleasure (olfactory pleasure) in the dirty and stinking foot. As it is, this object also recurs in the positive perversion. I regard *coprophilic olfactory pleasure* as being the carrier of most cases of foot and boot fetishism.⁴ In addition, it must be emphasized that the female foot is probably a substitute for the painfully missed, prehistorically postulated, penis of the woman. A substitute for the same thing seems to be the plait. Cutting off plaits thus stands for the castration of women, "making" women, as it is through castration that one becomes a woman.

I have not analysed glaring cases of fetishism.

———

Your advertisement delighted me. You are standing on the most arid soil in Germany, and it will bear fruit for you.⁵ About the Congress I know only the following: apart from your lecture, *Adler*⁶ on hermaphroditism,⁷ full of all kinds of delusive lights, *Marcinowski* on sejunctive processes as the basis of psychoneuroses,⁸ probably also somewhat out of line, *Ferenczi* on organization and propaganda⁹ (having discussed it with me, he wants to suggest that we form an association and issue a little bulletin through which single members and the societies in Zurich and Vienna can get into touch with each other), *Jung*¹⁰ on the reception of Ψα in America; *myself* on the future chances of ψα therapy.¹¹

Jung writes today that he has 22 registrations up to the present, including only two Viennese, of whom, however, 10–15 will come. I do not expect, incidentally, any substantially larger numbers than in Salzburg, but a more intimate alliance between the faithful.

My Viennese are not giving me much pleasure. Actually, the heavy cross I have to bear is with the older generation—Stekel, Adler, Sadger; they will soon think of me and treat me as an obstacle, and I cannot believe that they will have anything better to replace me with.

I am now writing on the *Leonardo at odd times*¹²; from next week onwards there will be a decrease in my practice, and then at last I want to get on with it. Otherwise I have nothing in store for the *Sammlung*. I will have to send back as flat and boring an essay by Riklin on Goethe's "beautiful soul".¹³

As an epilogue to the American journey I shall probably be going to Karlsbad on 15 July to take the cure. Otherwise I am keeping pretty well. Hardship has been great so far, the opposition fierce, and the friends far away. Ferenczi was the one who did most for me; on one occasion I went to see him in Budapest, and he came to see me on a Sunday in return.¹⁴

I received the clever article in the *Frankfurter Zeitung* and did not actually believe the assurance that it had been written before reading the book.

Have I already mentioned to you that Stanley Hall is producing an issue of the *American Journal of Psychology* on 1 April that is to be filled exclusively with our lectures?

1910 March 107

I send my cordial greetings to you and to your dear wife,
Yours,

*Freud*

1. Freud later used this incident to illustrate that the "patient's first symptoms . . . may . . . betray a complex which governs his neurosis" (1913c: p. 138).
2. That is, impotent for psychic reasons.
3. *Amerikanerinnen*, which can mean both American girls and women.
4. Freud had already alluded to this case and given his interpretation of fetishism in letter 65F, 18 February 1909.
5. Cf. Matthew 13, 3–9; Mark 4, 3–20; Luke 8, 5–15.
6. Alfred Adler [1870–1937], Viennese physician and psychologist, in contact with Freud at least since 1899 (letter of Freud to Adler of 27 February 1899, LOC), had been a member of the Wednesday Society from its beginning [1902]. In 1910 he became president of the Vienna Psychoanalytic Society and—with Wilhelm Stekel—editor of the *Zentralblatt*. From 1911 on he went his own way and founded what he called "individual psychology", which views itself as a unique movement, different from psychoanalysis, emphasizing, among other things, the role of aggression, of rivalry among siblings, and social factors. (Cf. Handlbauer, 1992; Hoffman, 1994.)
7. Adler, 1910 (based on a talk in the Vienna Society on 23 February 1910—Nunberg & Federn, 1967).
8. Marcinowski, "Sejunktive Prozesse als Grundlage der Psychoneurosen und andere Behandlungsarten in der nervenärztlichen Praxis" [Sejunctive processes as the foundation of psychoneuroses and other methods of treatment in the practice of the nerve doctor].
9. Ferenczi, 1910[69], 1911[79].
10. Jung, 1910c.
11. Freud, 1910d; the final programme is reprinted in Freud & Jung, 1974 [1906–13]: p. 573.)
12. Italicized words in English in original.
13. Freud had received, on 12 February 1910, a manuscript of Riklin's, "Bekenntnisse der schönen Seele" [Confessions of a beautiful soul], a monograph about Book VI of Goethe's *Wilhelm Meisters Lehrjahre* (1796), for the *Schriften zur angewandten Seelenkunde*. The paper was based on a talk given to the Swiss Society [1907] and was not published. (Cf. also Freud to Ferenczi, 13 February 1910, Freud & Ferenczi, 1992: p. 137.)
14. At the end of November 1909, Freud had been for a "consultation in Budapest, which gave [him] an opportunity to see Ferenczi and share in his work" (2 December 1909, Freud & Jung, 1974 [1906–13]: p. 270). Ferenczi, in his turn, had visited Freud on 30 January 1910.

85A

Berlin
14 March 1910

Dear Professor,

In return for your last letter, which contained various manifest and latent complaints, I want to give you a sign of life once again. Above all, please accept my sincere thanks for your scientific information. I hope

Nuremberg will be a real pleasure and compensate you for some of the unpleasantness. I am so very sorry that you are still not satisfied with your state of health. If Vienna were not so far away, I should have been glad to do the same as Ferenczi; would you not like to come to N. a day earlier? I should be glad to fit in with that, and we could continue the conversation that was interrupted six months ago in the train. I do not know if my suggestion is convenient for you; I, for my part, should be extraordinarily pleased if you accept it.

The Nuremberg programme is very varied, but the scientific part is not entirely as I would have wished. Incidentally, Juliusburger has also announced a paper. You have probably already heard of the subject in the meantime (on Feuerbach and Freud).[1] The foundation of an Association and of a bulletin is very much to my liking.

My course, which this time has only four participants, ends before Easter. I derive much pleasure from it. In neither the first course nor this one has a participant missed one session. My present audience consists of a 60-year-old member of the Board of Health, a senior doctor at the Epileptic Institute in Potsdam, a doctor from a spa in the Schwarzwald, and a colleague from here named Dreyfus, a psychiatrist who is at present assistant to Oppenheim.[2] He is on the way to becoming an adherent, does analyses on his own initiative, and is independent enough not to bother about the general resistance in Berlin. I expect the best from him. He cannot come to Nuremberg, because he is going to Paris for study purposes.

The course takes up part of my evenings; in addition, there is the activity as expert witness for the court, which has become remarkably predominant since the beginning of the year. Oppenheim sends me few patients—perhaps he is piqued by the courses—and even then such as are certainly unsuitable for analysis; and if one is suitable, he asks me in writing *not* to use analysis. The court reports leave me hardly any time at all for scientific work. Segantini is barely progressing, and I shall not be able to get down to the paper on fetishism until Easter.

The author of the article in the *Frankfurter Zeitung* is now on his way to accepting wish-fulfilment. At the same time he is making progress in therapy.

Hirschfeld, who has returned from his lengthy journeys, told me yesterday that people often asked him about you in France and England. He intends to come to the Congress too.

This summer I will probably not be able to get out of Berlin because of our move and because of a happy event to be expected in late summer.[3]

With cordial greetings from house to house,
your devoted

*Abraham*

1. The talk was not held.
2. Probably Daniel K. Dreyfuss, later psychoanalyst in Israel.
3. The birth of Abraham's son in August (see letter 94F, 30 August 1910, and n 1).

## 86A

B.
21 March 1910[1]

Dear Professor,

I am very glad to hear from you,[2] and I too shall be in Nuremberg on Tuesday morning. My train gets in at 7.45, yours, if I am not mistaken, an hour earlier.[3]

With cordial greetings,
Yours,

*Abraham*

1. Postcard.
2. Missing.
3. The Second International Psychoanalytic Congress took place on 30–31 March in Nuremberg. Freud opened it with a lecture on "The Future Prospects of Psycho-Analytic Therapy" (1910d), and Abraham spoke second, on "The Psychoanalysis of Fetishism" (1910[18]). The main event was the decision to found the IPA. Freud's and Ferenczi's plan to move its seat permanently to Zurich and to vest in Jung exceptional powers as president for life—every lecture or article was supposed to be presented to him for approval—encountered resistance, especially from Adler and Stekel. The power of the president was thereupon lessened and his term of office limited to two years. In addition, the *Korrespondenzblatt* [Bulletin], edited by Jung as President and by Riklin as Secretary of the IPA, was founded as the official organ of the Association. Back in Vienna, Freud offered Adler the chairmanship of the Vienna Society and accepted the editorship, with Adler and Stekel, of a new *Zentralblatt für Psychoanalyse: Medizinische Monatsschrift für Seelenkunde* [*Zentralblatt*], on the condition that he "could exercise the right of Veto against any article to be published" (Freud to Jones, 23 October 1924, Freud & Jones, 1993: p. 557).

## 87A

28 April 1910

Dear Professor,

I assume that you returned from Nuremberg feeling completely satisfied. The greatest pleasure for me was the mood in which all participants left the Congress. I travelled back with Eitingon, Hirschfeld, and Koerber, and during the whole of the nine hours' journey we did not stop discussing our impressions for one moment. Tomorrow I shall open the proceedings of our local Society with a introductory talk.

Meanwhile, you have once again given me new cause for gratitude. So far I have only read the first of the five lectures and glanced through the others.[1] They come in very handy as an introduction for the many people who have recently become interested. The Americans, however, were the fortunate ones, being able to hear all this in the spoken word.— Moreover, you have my best thanks for recommending me to a patient. I do not yet know whether Herr Strasser is coming here from Budapest; according to his letter, however, that may well be possible.

Psychoanalysis has recently been flourishing in my consulting-room. I have started four new treatments in rapid succession, three of them in a very strange way. One of your former patients—I think his name is Rudolf Foerster[2]—has introduced analysis here to a small circle of neurotics. From this circle, first a very intelligent young woman arrived, who is getting better very nicely in treatment, and soon she sent her best [female] friend; then some days ago she sent still another friend who once discussed treatment with you in Vienna. His name is Mueller, and he is noticeable for his extreme Germanic blondness. These three are most interesting objects indeed; also, there is one case of actual parent-incest among them.[3] From these cases, and from one other that Hirschfeld sent me for analysis, I have had nice results concerning the question of "flight from race", mixed marriage, etc., which I intend to publish soon.[4]—Official resistance in Berlin is stronger than ever.

I hope that everything is going as you would wish with you and yours, especially your eldest daughter. Here preparations for things to come are taking up a great deal of our time, otherwise I would have given you some sign of life earlier. At least the question of an apartment is now settled.

With cordial greetings from house to house,
your devoted

*Karl Abraham*

1. Freud, 1910a [1909].
2. Dr Rudolf Foerster [?–1924] from Hamburg (cf. Abraham's obituary, 1924[105d]; not included in the bibliography of his writings).
3. Very probably, Abraham refers to Karen Horney (see letter 118A, 5 December 1911), her friend "Idchen" (Ida Behrmann), and Carl Müller-Braunschweig (Quinn, 1987: p. 143).
    Müller-Braunschweig [1881–1958] had been in Vienna in 1908 to ask for an analysis with Freud, which, however, turned out to be too expensive (Maetze, 1976–77: p. 419). By 1921, lecturer at the Berlin Psychoanalytic Institute, and in 1925 member of the Executive Committee of the Berlin Society. He, and even more Felix Böhm, were to play a highly controversial role during the Nazi regime, more or less collaborating with the Nazis and being the principal exponents of the "Aryan" psychoanalysts who had not emigrated. (Cf. Brecht, n.d.; Goggin & Goggin, 2001.)
4. Abraham, 1914[45], in which the "patient of fair, north German type" is mentioned briefly (p. 49).

1910 June

## 88F

Vienna IX, Berggasse 19
5 June 1910

Dear Dr Abraham,

Apart from being ill and having to work,[1] my long silence has been due to the delay in the appearance of *Leonardo*, which I had expected from one week to the next. L. is out at last, my digestion is improving under medical care, but I still have to work for another 40 days. At least my eldest is very much better. Wife and second daughter returned from Karlsbad today.

Your good news pleased me very much. Otherwise you are just the man to stick things out. Attacks still do not disturb my mood. Our latest reaction,[2] the foundation of the *Zentralblatt*, will soon turn out to be biologically advantageous. Privy Councillor Friedländer (!) recently spent four hours with me one evening; I kept him for such a long time in order to study him. As a result of the examination I ask you to take it [it really need not be kept secret][3] that he is a liar, a scoundrel, and an ignoramus.

Yesterday I had a much more pleasing visit from Ossipow of Moscow,[4] who has a good mind and is a convinced follower. He came to get permission to publish the Worcester lectures in Russian in his journal.[5]

If your small group should be showing signs of despondency, then comfort them with the news that the *third* edition of the *Interpretation of Dreams* is to appear this winter, that is to say, only a year after the second.[6] The interval between the first and second ones was nine years. *Nonum prematur in annum.*[7]

I have of course been able to do only a small amount of work. Just now I am preparing a trifle on love life for the *Jahrbuch*.[8] We will probably put the Nuremberg talk into the first issue of the *Zentralblatt*.[9]

Jung is having great difficulties in Z.[urich] at present.[10] The *Jahrbuch* is delayed through Deuticke's fault, the organization is moving slowly. There are such times, but the standstill is only apparent.—Do the domestic news refer only to your changing apartments?

I send my cordial greetings to you and your dear family,
Yours,

*Freud*

My collegial greetings to the gentlemen of the local Society.

1. Freud had "thirteen patients, nine hours a day" (22 April 1910, Freud & Jung, 1974 [1906–13]: p. 310); in addition, he had caught influenza (17 May 1910; ibid.: p. 317).
2. Reading uncertain.
3. Square brackets in original.
4. Nikolai Jewgrafowitsch Ossipow [1877–1934], chief physician at the Psychiatric University Clinic in Moscow. Co-founder of the Russian Psychoanalytic Society, and

Freud's translator. In 1920 he emigrated to Istanbul, and in 1921 to Prague where he became docent for psychoanalysis. Ossipow had come forward with reports about psychoanalysis as early as 1908. (Cf. Wulff, 1910–11.)
5. Freud, 1910a [1909], trans. Ossipow (Moscow: Nauka, 1912 [*Psikhoterapevtikcheskaia biblioteka*, vyp. 1]).
6. The third edition of Freud, 1900a, was published in early 1911.
7. Referring to Horace's "*Nonumque prematur in annum*" (*Art of Poetry*, 388) ["And it must remain hidden until into the ninth year"]—namely the masterpiece on which the poet is supposed to be working that long.
8. Freud, 1910h. The gist of the paper had already been given before the Vienna Society on 19 May 1909 and was discussed a week later.
9. Freud, 1910d, in the first number of the *Zentralblatt* (1910, *1*: 1–9).
10. With Bleuler, who did not want to join the newly founded IPA—of which his collaborator Jung was president. In particular, Bleuler objected to the exclusive attitude of the organization.

## 89A

Berlin
6 June 1910

Dear Professor,

A new work of yours always generates a somewhat anxious suspense—whether it will yet again be an advance on earlier ones. The suspense has now been resolved. The analysis is so delicate and so perfect in form that I do not know anything quite like it.

I can best express my thanks for the book by getting on quickly with my Segantini. But the material overwhelms me by its diversity, and I am only making slow progress.

The practice is improving greatly. A Herr Dr Sachs has come to me on your recommendation. His mother-in-law, Frau Henschel, has corresponded with you. Please accept my sincere thanks for this, too!

Our local group is doing well. Stegmann is coming from Dresden for the session on the 8th; last time Warda was here. That does show a gratifying interest. You have surely read about the heresy trial in Hamburg[1]; almost like the new Encyclical. But you can see from it that psychoanalysis is in the air; Deuticke must notice it most, at least that is what book-sellers here are saying.

With sincere thanks and regards,
Yours,

*Abraham*

1. At the meeting of the Medical Society of Hamburg on 29 March 1910, several neurologists—above all Weygandt—had spoken out in favour of a boycott of clinics where psychoanalysis was practised (see Jones, 1957: p. 116; the reports in the *Hamburger Ärzte-Correspondenzblatt*, 4 April 1910, and the *Neurologisches Centralblatt*, 1910, *29*: 659–662).

## 90A

Berlin
20 June 1910

Dear Professor,

Our letters crossed the last time. I was sorry to see from yours that your health was giving you cause for complaint. I hope that is now over. Where are you going in the holidays? I am staying here this summer. My wife is expecting in August, and we are moving in September. I have now been away for a week, not, indeed, for pleasure, but as expert witness in a lengthy judicial hearing in a little town in Westphalia.

I have good things to report of our little circle. Stegmann came over from Dresden for the second session. Körber talked about a case he was analysing—incomplete, it is true. Even if he has not yet grasped the subtleties, he is a straightforward, reliable person who will support the cause if need be. Next time Eitingon is to talk about the critical objections of our opponents; Hirschfeld speaks on symbolism in fetishism. After the summer holidays we want to organize an autumn session in Dresden—at Stegmann's suggestion—in order to mobilize the interested people scattered about Central Germany a little more.—The colleagues return your greetings sincerely.

As I conclude from the Circular, the difficulties in Zurich are still going on. It must surely be about Bleuler? I have not heard any details yet, though.—The fact that the *Interpretation of Dreams* is coming out in yet another edition is a particularly clear sign of progress. The *Jahrbuch* is far too unpunctual this time!

I am working on Segantini, but the practice has recently become so lively that I have only little spare time. I have plans for so many new subjects to work on that I should be glad to have a few weeks to spend only in writing.

To amuse you, I am sending you with this a new effort by Hellpach[1] out of the *Tag*. The underlined passage shows clearly the correctness of the tactics followed up to now.

With cordial greetings from house to house,
your devoted

*Abraham*

1. Willy Hellpach [1877–1955], German physician, psychologist, and politician. Contributions to medical, ethnic, social, cultural, and religious psychology. His attitude towards psychoanalysis was characterized by a mixture of approval, rejection, and misunderstanding.

## 91F

Vienna IX, Berggasse 19
3 July 1910

Dear Dr Abraham,

Many thanks for the good news from your circle, which is small but perhaps particularly distinguished by reason of its homogeneity and unity. In Zurich there really are difficulties, with Bleuler at their centre. They do not want to join the Society, and attend the meetings only as guests. I cannot envisage how this should work out at the next congress. Of course I am also not fully in the know. I hear from Jung that Binswanger, who is now the president, is standing by the dissidents.[1]

Hellpach's prattle was soon put in the shade by Hoche's profound performance.[2] These are really valuable signs of the uneasiness in which our opponents are floundering. The reviews in the new *Zentralblatt* will in all such cases be strictly unemotional, plain, and laconic, at least as far as my influence[3] can reach.

The *Jahrbuch* is really behaving carelessly. The next issue of the *Sammlung [Schriften]* will be Pfister's study on Count Zinzendorf.[4]

About us personally I can say that all of us are already very tired of the city. As we have nothing as delightful as you have to look forward to in August, we are already longing for 15 July. But so far we have no idea where we shall turn to until 1 August, the day on which our lodgings in Noordwijk (near Leiden) will be ready. My bowels have improved, but there is no time for real well-being now.

If you write to me, go on using my address in Vienna until I can give you another.

I have received the first review of the *Leonardo*, Havelock Ellis in the *Journal of Mental Science*,[5] friendly as always. It [*Leonardo*] pleases all our friends and will, I hope, disgust all outsiders.

In the year that is now ending,[6] America stood out above all. Let us now seek some rest and refreshment against the hardship of the next.[7]

With many congratulations to your dear wife,
and cordial greetings,
Yours,

*Freud*

---

1. It had proved difficult to find a president for the newly constituted Zurich branch society. Finally, Binswanger declared that he would accept the vote, but only if all meetings were open to non-members. Despite Jung's opposition, the vote went through (Jung to Freud, 17 June 1910, Freud & Jung, 1974 [1906–13]: p. 329).
2. Alfred Hoche [1865–1943], professor of psychiatry at Freiburg im Breisgau, one of the bitterest opponents of psychoanalysis among the German psychiatrists. At the Congress of South-West German Psychiatrists, 28 May, he had spoken on "An Epidemic of Insanity among Doctors" (Hoche, 1910) and railed against the "strange medical frenzy movement" of psychoanalysis, from which one should "dissociate oneself most emphatically".

3. On Adler and Stekel, the editors.
4. Pfister, 1910. Graf Ludwig von Zinzendorf [1700–1760], German religious reformer, leader of the "Moravian Brethren" sect. In his monograph, Pfister related Zinzendorf's religious fanaticism to perverse eroticism.
5. Havelock Ellis [1859–1939], pioneering British sexologist; author of *Studies in the Psychology of Sex* (6 vols., 1897–1910; suppl. 1928). He concluded his otherwise rather critical review (Ellis, 1910) by saying: "if . . . Freud sometimes selects a very thin thread, he seldom fails to string pearls on it, and these have their value whether the thread snaps or not".
6. That is, the end of the working year.
7. On 17 July Freud and his sons Oliver [1891–1969] and Ernst [1892–1970] went to The Hague; on 1 August they went on to Noordwijk, a Dutch seaside resort, where they were joined by the other family members, who had come from Hamburg. Only Minna Bernays had stayed in Hamburg with her mother, Emmeline Bernays, who was fatally ill; she died on 27 October.

## 92F

Noordwijk
22 August 1910

Dear Friend,

I must take your latest piece of work[1] as an opportunity to congratulate you heartily on all the contributions you render to the cause of psychoanalysis. I do not know of anything to place beside them for clarity, inner solidity, and power of evidence. I am convinced that that is the impact on all readers on our side. The others, with Ziehen at their head, may see for themselves how they cope with them.

My stay in N., where I have not been able to work at all, is nearing its end. Dr Jones, who was my guest for two and a half days,[2] shook me into action a little. I heard from him, and by letter from Putnam, that the American group will come into existence.[3] Ferenczi, with whom I shall be travelling during the whole of September, arrives here on the 27th. We want to see a few towns in Belgium and then travel by way of Basle and Rome to Sicily. We will do much work on $\Psi\alpha$ then. I am greatly looking forward to it, because I am already taking the idleness badly.

Be so kind as to send me the expected domestic news from your house by way of my wife, who is staying in Holland until about 15 September. On 1 October I go back to work, to which one becomes reconciled again after a long break.

On the whole, I think, our cause is going very well, and is no longer for my four eyes only.[4] Progress will now be more difficult, however, the surface has been creamed, the final, decisive results are perhaps not yet clearly visible, and defence is required not only against enemies but also against rash fellow-workers. But perhaps it is only I who have an impression of an unavoidable slowing-down, while there will come energetic advances from the younger ones.

I send my cordial greetings to you and your dear family,
Yours,

*Freud*

1. Abraham, 1910[17]; contained in the eagerly awaited *Jahrbuch*, which Freud had finally received on 17 August (Freud & Ferenczi, 1992: p. 205).
2. Around 11/12 August. A sister of Jones's common-law wife Loë Kann had a house in Noordwijk.
3. Putnam's letter (end of July, 1910) in Hale, 1971b: pp. 102–104. The American Psychoanalytic Association was founded on 9 May 1911.
4. Perhaps a play on the German saying *"unter vier Augen"*—something should be said, kept, etc., "among four eyes only"—that is, between two people only.

## 93A

25 August 1910

Dear Professor,

Many thanks for card[1] and letter! Your appreciative words gladdened me very much. I hope to be able to justify your good opinion through two more works in the course of this year. Fetishism (from Nuremberg) is to appear in the next half-yearly volume; if only I could finish Segantini off too in the next few months. It could then be printed before Christmas.

I will spare you the promised scientific communication for now; I did not know that you would be leaving Holland so soon. I now wish you a very enjoyable journey. The expected event has not yet happened but is very near. I will eventually inform your wife, to whom I ask you to give my best wishes, and also to the rest of your family, including our colleague Ferenczi.

The quietest time for the practice is already over. Since the beginning of this week there has been quite a great deal to do. I am not going to be able to go away this year, but instead at the beginning of October I have the pleasure of the Neurological Congress here.[2] Oppenheim and Hoche are preaching on anxiety states. The latter in particular will give it straight from the shoulder. Why journey to Sicily if one can see them in Berlin—*la Maffia neurologica*!

With kind regards,
your cordially devoted

*Abraham*

1. Missing.
2. Fourth Annual Meeting of the Society of German Neurologists, Berlin, 6–8 October 1910 (see letter 95A, 18 October 1910).

1910 October

## 94F

Noordwijk
30 August 1910

Dear Friend,

I am still just in time to send you myself my hearty congratulations on the birth of your son[1] and on the completion of your fatherhood, and to express my sincere hopes for the young mother's rapid recovery. Tomorrow morning, then, off to Paris to have a look at the Leonardo,[2] then on to Italy.

Your most faithfully devoted

*Freud*

1. Abraham's son, Gerd, later emigrated to London; forced to change his profession, he joined the British Army and fought during the war in India, then returned to London.
2. Leonardo's *St Anne with Two Others* in the Louvre, reproduced and interpreted in Freud's essay (1910c: pp. 111ff). Freud probably wanted to see the original to check Pfister's idea that the outline of a vulture can be seen in the white cloth around the body of Mary. (Cf. Freud, 1910c: pp. 115f., addition 1919; Pfister, 1913.)

## 95A

Berlin W., Rankestrasse 24
18 October 1910

Dear Professor,

I have left your kind congratulations on the birth of our son and the various postcards from your journey[1] unanswered until now. It has been a somewhat unsettled time for us. We are established in the new apartment, and I can think again about things other than worries about how to furnish it. There has unfortunately been a break of several weeks in my writing; Segantini will therefore be late—I hope not too much so.

The two congresses are over for good. One as sterile as the other. Just that the neurological one was more vicious. Oppenheim's talk on anxiety did not contain anything that could not be found in any popular article. It was in fact merely the frame for a long-suppressed outburst of affects. O. went so far as to call for a boycott of those sanatoria that use Ψα. Hoche, as discussant, was boring, nothing else. The discussion consisted mainly of a number of directors of sanatoria getting up and solemnly declaring that they did not practise Ψα. At their head Herr Friedländer, your special friend! Otherwise, only Raimann[2] from Vienna distinguished himself, who proposed, as Freud was evading a discussion, to seek out the enemy in his own camp (*sic!*) and—to make public every failed case of a psychoanalytic treatment. Boycott and denunciation. I find that the unpleasant signs are mounting up in a most gratifying way. We, the heretics in attendance (Koerber, Warda, and myself), remained silent. I need hardly mention that the jocular speeches at the banquet essentially had just one target. One evening there was a big reception at Oppenheim's. On this occasion Aschaffenburg[3] pounced on me and used me for quite a long time to let his affects loose on me. He is more intelligent than most of the other opponents, and after the resistances had faded away he became considerably more approachable. I can certainly say that the debate, which lasted about three hours, was not without its effect. Finally, he told a few tales out of school. He thought it possible that *"the three psychopaths"*, Gaupp, Wilmanns,[4] and Isserlin,[5] would change sides one day. I do not know whether he is right. Wilmanns would be very valuable. I know him from Bremen, our hometown, and know him to be a person who thinks independently.

As regards Oppenheim's resistance, I want to add in confidence that his wife suffers from severe hysteria and has given him a great deal of trouble the whole of this year, and that he himself had a severe neurosis with an anxiety state two years ago. This makes the recent intensification of his emotions indeed understandable.

Now I must tell you about Bleuler, who spent hours with me in order to abreact. You are familiar enough with his complexes. Naturally, he justifies his staying away from the Society with various scruples, for which he does not find the real motives, even with a great deal of help. All the same, I have a number of things to say in his favour and should like to ask you, dear Professor, whether it would not be appropriate now to meet him half-way, in order to make good certain mistakes and to serve our cause. I have talked much psychoanalysis with Bl., and I must say that he is taking a keen interest in the cause. During the congresses he had many discussions with Kraepelin,[6] Aschaffenburg, and others, and they all considered him, as I personally heard, a really convinced partisan. I believe his service to our cause in this respect more than outweighs the occasional harm he may have done to it by being too reserved. And, finally, the main point: both before and at the time of the founding of the Zurich group, Bl. was very obviously grossly insulted. You know that I am quite critical of Bl.; but if one makes it a principle in $\Psi\alpha$ not to insult the complexes, why should one behave differently towards Bl., of all people? Bl. *wants* a *rapprochement*. He is at odds with himself and suffers from it. Should not there be a way to come to an understanding?

And now, an encouraging symptom. I think it was Aschaffenburg who told me that on a journey through America the first question asked by all the physicians was: *What do you think about Freud?*[7]

I find our *Jahrbuch* II.1 really excellent.—Incidentally, more and more topics are accumulating that I would like to discuss with you. Starting from the antithetical meaning of primal words,[8] one could surely proceed further. In particular, the question of bisexuality in language would have to be investigated.

But I do not want to go any more into scientific matters today. With cordial greetings from house to house, your devoted

*Karl Abraham*

1. Missing.
2. Emil Raimann [1872–1949], professor of forensic psychiatry at the University of Vienna, an outspoken opponent of Freud's. He was anonymously mentioned by Freud in his "History of the Psycho-Analytic Movement" (1914d: p. 23; cf. Raimann, 1916).
3. Gustav Aschaffenburg [1866–1944], German psychiatrist. Professor at Heidelberg, Halle, and Cologne. In 1939 he emigrated to Baltimore. Author of numerous polemical articles against psychoanalysis.
4. Karl Wilmanns, German psychiatrist.
5. Max Isserlin [1879–1941], German neurologist; at that time, Kraepelin's assistant in Munich.
6. Emil Kraepelin [1856–1926], Professor of Psychiatry and Neurology at Heidelberg and Munich [1903–22], *doyen* of German psychiatry, author of an extremely influential textbook (1883).
7. Italicized words in English in original.
8. Freud, 1910e, in the *Jahrbuch* referred to.


96F

Vienna IX, Berggasse 19
24 October 1910

Dear Friend,

You have made up for the long interval by an unusually substantial letter. Cheers to the new home! How is your son thriving?

I am sorry for Opp.[enheim], a good inept man. Why does he have to fixate himself on anxiety, of all things, just to make a fool of himself in the eyes of a later generation. Ψα really has many other points on which it is assailable. I am keeping secret your explanations about his personal motives. I do not really believe in these conversions; Aschaffenburg, however, would certainly do me a great personal favour if he were to give some meaning in retrospect to his "promise/slip of the tongue" at the Amsterdam Congress.[1] Friedländer is a mendacious dog, who is not worth talking about. Perhaps Raimann will really get a rap over the knuckles before long; but perhaps I shall feel that it is not worth the trouble.

Now to Bleuler. I had decided to get in touch with him ("to make nerve-contact[2] with him") even before your letter, and since then I have been in continuous correspondence with him, the individual items running to 8–10 pages.[3]

Things are as you say. His arguments are shadowy and intangible, everything is full of alleged imponderables, and yet he seems unshakeable. I have promised him to go to Zurich over Christmas if he will give me a chance to settle matters. I have of course no intention of sacrificing the Society as such. Its foundation was too well justified. Incidentally, it was he, Bl., who first expressed the wish for a personal discussion.

The *Zentralblatt* arrived here yesterday. I hope it will make its way, though the editorship[4] may not yet have discovered all the technical mysteries of the trade. There is already a plethora of material for the next few issues, so we are forced to make contributors wait.

I am in the thick of work and have penetrated somewhat more deeply into paranoia along the path on which you have stepped.

I shall keep you informed how things proceed with Bl. as we go along. He has offered that I read his *apologia*[5] in proof in order to suggest changes that suit me better, but naturally I am declining.

With cordial greetings to your wholly new and full house,

Yours,

*Freud*

1. A play on the German word "*Versprechen*", which can mean both "promise" and "slip of the tongue". At the First International Congress for Psychiatry, Psychology, and the Assistance to the Insane (Amsterdam, 2–7 September 1907), Aschaffenburg had "made two slips of the tongue in his lecture ('facts' [of psychoanalysis] instead of 'no facts'), which shows that unconsciously he is already strongly infected" (Jung to Freud, 4 September 1907, Freud & Jung, 1974 [1906–13]: p. 83).
2. *Nervenanhang*, an expression from Schreber's neologistic "basic language" [*Grundsprache*] in his *Memoirs* (Schreber, 1903, Ch. 1), with which he described God's way of getting in contact with human beings.
3. Excerpts from this correspondence were published by Alexander and Selesnick (1965). The Bleuler letters are now accessible in the LOC, those by Freud are in the possession of the Bleuler heirs.
4. Adler and Stekel.
5. Bleuler, 1910.

## 97A

Berlin
14 December 1910

Dear Professor,

Today Eitingon brought me your greetings.[1] He did not need to remind me that I owed you a letter. I postponed writing because I wanted to send you my letter in the company of the Segantini. This latter, however, is very resistant to analysis—hence the delay. As I cannot,

1910 December

after all, send you the manuscript before Christmas, you should at any rate receive some sign of life.

The subject is really unusually difficult but I do believe I have by now solved all that is accessible to solution, and now there remain only the last two chapters to write.

I hear that you will be meeting Bleuler soon, and I am calmly awaiting the result. A pity your journey does not take in Berlin. A great number of questions have accumulated about which I should like to talk with you.

Our group is doing well. Juliusburger and Koerber have familiarized themselves very much with the work. The latter recently contributed some dream analyses that astonished me. Unfortunately we have no *young* blood. In any case, medical Berlin is taking more and more notice of $\Psi\alpha$, if only in a hostile way. A few stupid criticisms have appeared again in the journals, the most stupid of which is by Näcke.[2] The *pro* literature is growing to uncanny dimensions. Jones has given birth to quintuplets yet again, which he sent me.

As regards scientific matters, I only want to tell you today that I have analysed two cases of so-called cyclothymia[3] to quite a large extent, which, together with one other investigated previously, provide very good insight into the character of this illness. Unfortunately, I have only seen all three patients in their depressive states and know of the exalted ones merely from retrospective description. All the same, I believe I have come near to the understanding of the manic flight of ideas.

I have been very satisfied with the practice this last year. In comparison with the previous year, there has been distinct progress. Only the fluctuations are still too great. But the successes were very gratifying.

May I send you the manuscript when I have it ready, or shall I—as you are going away for Christmas—wait until the New Year? I do not want to lay a burden on you for your few days' holiday.

With cordial greetings from house to house.

Your devoted

*Abraham*

1. Eitingon had visited Freud around 6–8 December (Eitingon to Freud, 20 November 1910, SFC).
2. Paul Näcke [1851–1913], Russian-born German psychiatrist, director of an asylum at Colditz, Saxony. He published prolifically, with a special interest in sexual problems. Freud credited him with introducing the term "narcissism" (Freud, 1914c: p. 73). The criticism could not be identified; Näcke, however, had already written two rather favourable reviews of *The Interpretation of Dreams* and the *Three Essays on the Theory of Sexuality* (Näcke, 1901, 1906).
3. Manic-depressive illness.

## 98F

Vienna IX, Berggasse 19
18 December 1910

Dear Friend,

I am delighted to have heard from you again, and then something good and promising. The latter refers to your Segantini, which I would particularly like to read during the holidays. But do not rush yourself. I am hardly having a vacation; except for the two days of Christmas, every day is the same for me, and only Sunday a real holiday. Also, I would not be able to have it printed right away, because that is what is now happening to the German translation of *Jones's* study of Hamlet,[1] and after that I have accepted a legal paper (the first) by a talented young Zuricher named *Storfer*.[2] But your Segantini will of course follow as soon as possible after that.

A meeting with Bleuler has been arranged in Munich,[3] at any rate so far as I am concerned; I still have no reply from him. He is a strange customer. I am expecting to read his *apologia* this week in the *Jahrbuch*.

Our *Zentralblatt* would like to publish a nice contribution from you.

My own work, just finished, has dealt with *Schreber's* book and has tried, using it as a point of departure, to solve the riddle of paranoia. As you can imagine, I followed the path indicated by your paper on the psycho-sexual differences between hysteria and dementia praecox. When I worked these ideas out in Palermo, I particularly liked the formula that megalomania was the sexual overestimation of the ego. In Vienna I found that you had already said the same thing very trenchantly. I have of course had to plagiarize you very extensively in this paper.[4]

I think that I am able to clear up the difference between dementia praecox and paranoia also in the stricter sense of the word.

I should be delighted to discuss all these things with you again, but there is no respite from the necessity of earning money.

In America things are going very well. Brill has now translated the *Theory of Sexuality* too, and Putnam provided a superb introduction.[5] That old gentleman is altogether a magnificent acquisition.

Your wife and progeny are very well, I hope?

Cordial greetings,
Yours,

   *Freud*

1. Jones, 1910c, for the *Schriften*.
2. Storfer, 1911. Adolf (after 1938, Albert) Josef Storfer [1888–1944], journalist and writer of Romanian origin, studied philosophy, psychology, and linguistics at Klausenberg and Zurich, where he also began the study of law. He went to Vienna in spring of 1913 and later became the business manager of the Verlag [1925–1932]. He was co-editor of

## 1910 December

Freud's *Gesammelte Schriften* [1924–1934] until the penultimate volume and, until 1932, editor of the journals *Die psychoanalytische Bewegung* [1929–1933] and *Almanach der Psychoanalyse* [1926–1938]. After the *Anschluss* he fled to Shanghai and from there to Melbourne, Australia, where he died in poverty.

3. Freud had originally wanted to visit Bleuler in Zurich in order to convince him to join the Zurich Society of the IPA, and he would also have used this occasion to see Jung. In order for Freud not to have to meet Bleuler and Jung—between whom there was disagreement—simultaneously, Jung had proposed that Bleuler and Freud meet in Munich, where he himself arrived after Bleuler's departure.

4. It was Jung who had drawn Freud's attention to the *Memoirs* (1903) of the judge Daniel Paul Schreber [1842–1911]. Freud used the book to develop his theory of paranoia (Freud, 1911c [1910]). Two days earlier, Freud had written to Ferenczi that "this step in psychiatry is probably the boldest that we have taken so far" (Freud & Ferenczi, 1992: p. 243). The Schreber case is probably the one most often cited in the history of psychiatry—specifically, there is a growing literature critical of Freud's interpretations. (For the explanation of megalomania, see Abraham, 1908[11]: p. 75; Freud, 1911c [1910]: p. 65.)

5. Freud, 1905d, translated by Brill, under the title *Three Contributions to the Sexual Theory* (New York, 1910) (Putnam, 1910a).

# 1911

## 99A

Berlin W.
11 January 1911

Dear Professor,

Segantini is finished and is coming to you as soon as it has been copied.

Many thanks for your letter. I am glad that the *Schriften zur angewandten Seelenkunde* are succeeding each other so rapidly. Today I have to ask you something related to them.

In the last session of our local group, a Russian doctor, Frl. Dr Rosenthal, who had already been our guest on several occasions, gave a talk: "Psychoanalytical Remarks on Karin Michaëlis's 'The Dangerous Age'".[1] The lecture was—particularly for a beginner who was in Zurich for a short time and had a little more experience with me—quite outstanding and really deserves to be published. The question is, *where*. According to the calculations of the authoress, two to three printed sheets could come out. As the subject is topical, it would be desirable for it to appear soon. I thought I might do it like this: I will go through the work in detail with Frl. Dr R., then send it to you and ask your opinion as to whether the paper is suitable for the *Sammlung* [*Schriften*] (and whether we would have to wait not too long for publication). Otherwise I would ask you to hand the manuscript on to the *Zentralblatt*. Do you agree with this?

I am quite pleased with our group. In February Stegmann—who comes from Dresden every time—is speaking on asthma.

The main question that interests us here is the next congress. Presumably it will again be at Easter? Do you know something definite about it already?

Recently I had a visit from a doctor from Stockholm, who was on his way to you.[2] He was very well-informed. My ambition as President of the local group is to extend it as soon as possible to Scandinavia.

With cordial greetings from house to house,
Yours,

*Abraham*

1. Rosenthal, 1911, which later appeared in the *Zentralblatt*; Michaëlis, 1910. Tatiana Rosenthal [1885–1921], born in St Petersburg, studied medicine in Zurich. Member of

1911 January　　　　　　　　　　　　　　　　　　　　　125

    the Vienna Society [1911–21]. Around 1914 she returned to St. Petersburg, where she practised as a psychoanalyst, lectured on psychoanalysis, and headed a polyclinic as well as a children's clinic. In 1921 she committed suicide at the age of 36. (Cf. Mühlleitner, 1992: pp. 275f.)
        Karin Michaëlis [1872–1950], Danish writer, lived in the United States during the Second World War [until 1946]. She wrote novels about adolescent girls, centring on their psyche.
2. Poul Carl Bjerre [1876–1964], Swedish psychiatrist and psychotherapist. It was he who introduced Lou Andreas-Salomé to psychoanalysis and brought her to the Weimar Congress [1911]. He later withdrew from psychoanalysis and in the mid 1930s became a collaborator of Jung's. Bjerre had been guest at the meeting of the Vienna Society on 4 January 1911.

## 100F

Berggasse 19
20 January 1911

Dear Friend,

A ridiculously hectic period, complicated by an accident of my eldest, who broke a thigh skiing (not a complicated fracture, fortunately taking a normal course),[1] has meant that the reply to your letter has had to be put off for such a long time. I scarcely know now with what I should catch up.

I believe I know Frl. Rosenthal from a brief correspondence with her. If you send me the work, I will read it at once and then make a decision about it. Your Segantini is most welcome. Its position is as follows: The translation of Jones's Hamlet is to appear very soon, followed two months later by a paper on parricide by a Zurich doctor of laws, and then comes your Segantini's turn. I cannot expect Deuticke to accept more than five or six volumes a year.

Dr Bjerre was in Vienna for a week and at first made things difficult for me by his taciturnity and stiffness, but finally I worked my way through to discovering his serious personality and good mind. I advised him to join the Berlin group as a member, and I hope he will do so. Scandinavia is, after all, your natural hinterland.

Have I already told you that I spent Christmas in Munich with Bleuler and then with Jung? No, I certainly have not, my brain is clearly weakening. With Bl. things went well, I was so tired that I acted quite naturally, and that worked. We parted as friends, and he has since joined the Z.[urich] Society. So the schism there has been healed. With Jung I discussed the Congress. As a result I think the date will be changed to the end of September, because of the Americans; and perhaps it really will take place in Lugano. The most important event of the moment, Bl.'s *apologia*,[2] is already in your hands. The *Zentralblatt* would very much like to publish something by you. Juliusburger has done a very good thing with the quotations from Schopenhauer,[3] but my originality is obviously on the wane.

My sister-in-law Minna Bernays[4] is thinking of going to Berlin next week and has promised to see for herself if you and yours are happy in your new home.

Cordial greetings
from your

*Freud*

1. Martin Freud described this incident (1958: pp. 175ff). Through Freud's intervention Martin, serving in the army at that time, did not come into a military but, rather, into a private hospital, which probably saved his leg from having to be amputated.
2. Bleuler, 1910.
3. Juliusburger, 1911.
4. Minna Bernays [1865–1941], Martha Freud's sister. After the death in 1886 of her fiancé Ignaz Schönberg, a boyhood friend of Freud's, Minna had worked as a companion. At the beginning of 1896, after the birth of Anna Freud, she had moved into the Freud family household, where she remained until her death. She was interested in the subject of psychoanalysis and accompanied Freud on numerous trips.

## 101A

Berlin
11 February 1911

Dear Professor,

The Segantini manuscript goes off to you together with these lines. I send it to you with a request for your criticism that seems particularly necessary to me this time, as it is a piece of work with some personal complexes behind it. Besides, I would like to have your opinion about a question of layout: Would it be useful to include some of the main pictures, since they are not as generally known as some of the works of Böcklin[1] and other modern painters? I would suggest one of the pictures pertaining to the mother-complex and one of the mystical ones (the wicked mothers). If you are in favour of illustrations, would you kindly discuss this with the publisher?

We had the pleasure of seeing Frl. Bernays twice in our home. I heard from her in more detail about the doings of you and your family. I hope that your patient is as well as one can be after so unpleasant an injury.

You will soon be receiving Frl. Dr Rosenthal's paper; I have spoken to her, and she is in perfect agreement with its publication in the *Zentralblatt*, as the *Schriften* are probably too full up for the time being. So you could perhaps save yourself the trouble of reading it and pass the manuscript on direct to Stekel or Adler. Or I could send it direct. Our group is doing splendidly. The day before yesterday Stegmann spoke on asthma, and I spoke about a case of obsessional neurosis. Interest is constant. Next time Koerber is speaking on narcissism.

Bleuler's paper is gratifying on the whole; but the second half is much inferior. I am glad that unity has been re-established in Zurich, at least outwardly. In the last few days I have heard of various things that must have made it very difficult indeed for Bl. to meet us halfway. But now for peace.

At the moment I find myself in a dilemma. The other day I mentioned to a colleague that I had found, in a very striking way, masculine and feminine periods[2] in a mild case of circular psychosis. She spoke of this to Fliess, with whom she is friendly, and a few days later told me of Fliess's request that I should visit him. On the one hand, I would not like to be discourteous; on the other, I find it unpleasant to have to force myself to adopt as much reserve as is necessary in this case.

To conclude, a little satyric play from Ziehen's clinic: a demonstration of a case of obsessional neurosis. The patient suffers from the obsessional idea that he must put his hands under women's skirts in the street. Ziehen, to audience: "Gentlemen, we must carefully investigate whether we are dealing with an obsessional idea with sexual content. I shall ask the patient whether he also feels this impulse with *older* women." The patient, in answer to the question: "Alas, Professor, even with my own mother and sister!" Thereupon Ziehen: "You see, gentlemen, that there can be nothing sexual at all at work here." To his assistant: "Note in the case history: Patient suffers from a *non-sexual but senseless obsessional idea!"*—

With cordial greetings from house to house,
Yours,

*Abraham*

1. Arnold Böcklin [1827–1901], Swiss painter.
2. Fliess had developed a comprehensive theory about the role of periods of 28 (female) and 23 (male) days, to whose influence he believed the entire organic world to be subjected.

## 102F

Vienna IX, Berggasse 19
13 February 1911
In haste

Dear Friend,

I am replying by return of post because of what you say about Fliess, and I am taking the liberty of giving you my advice unasked, that is, telling you my attitude in the matter. I cannot see why you should not call on him. In the first place, you will meet a highly remarkable, indeed fascinating man, and on the other hand you will perhaps have an opportunity of coming scientifically closer to the grain of truth that is surely contained in the theory of periodicity, a possibility that is denied to me for personal reasons. Now, he will certainly try to sidetrack you from Ψα (and, as he thinks, from me) and to guide you into his own channel. But I am sure you will not betray both of us to him. You know his complex and are aware that I am the centre of it, and so you will be able to evade it. You know from the outset that he is basically a hard, bad man, which took me many years to discover. His talent is exclusively one of exactitude, for a very long time he had no idea of psychology, at first he accepted everything literally from me, and he will by now, of course, have discovered the opposite of it all. I warn you particularly against his wife.[1] Wittily stupid, malicious, a positive hysteric, therefore perversion, not neurosis.

I am eagerly awaiting your post.

Could you not make up your mind to let me use the priceless story about Ziehen in the *Centralblatt*?[2] Z[iehen] has no claim to mercy. Please reply by postcard, but without feeling forced.

With cordial greetings to you all,
Yours,

*Freud*

1. Ida, née Bondy [1869–?]. In his conversations with Marie Bonaparte about his relationship to Fliess, Freud called her a "*böses Weib*" ["malicious skirt"]—this quote only in the German edition of Freud (1985c [1887–1904]: p. xv)—and maintained that she, "out of jealousy, did everything possible to sow discord between the two friends" (Masson, in ibid.: p. 3).
2. No question mark in original.

## 103A

Berlin
17 February 1911

Dear Professor,

Many thanks for the letter and the cards.[1] Your information about Fliess was very welcome. I will get in contact with him and exercise the necessary caution.

I got the story about Ziehen recently from our colleague Maier[2] from Zurich, who was here, visited the clinic, and told the story at our session in the evening. As I was not an ear-witness, I cannot vouch for the wording. I will ask Maier about it once again in writing, and then there will be no more obstacles to its publication.

I see, incidentally, that we have recently taken a somewhat different stand vis-à-vis our opponents. Your "Wild Ψα",[3] then Bleuler's defence, Jung's remarks to Mendel[4]—this means a step forward out of reserve. If only it carries on with such caution, it will help rather than harm.

1911 February

I had a great deal of trouble translating Dr Rosenthal's manuscript into readable German (she is Russian). It will probably be ready in a few days. I myself now believe that it is best suited for the *Centralblatt*.

Did you read that Segantini's son Mario was arrested in Berlin for fraud? Another deserted from the Army a few years ago and deserted then shot himself. The third is an idler. Only the daughter seems to be worth anything. It is remarkable that the sons completely lack the father's capacity for sublimation.

With cordial greetings from house to house,

Yours,

*Abraham*

1. The cards are missing.
2. Hans Wolfgang Maier, M.D. [1882–1945], pupil of Forel and Aschaffenburg; first assistant at the Burghölzli, the staff of which he had joined in 1905. Later Professor of Psychiatry in Zurich, and, from 1927 on, Bleuler's successor as director of the Burghölzli.
3. Freud, 1910k.
4. Mendel had written an "unforgivably impudent" (Jung to Freud, 7 June 1909, Freud & Jung, 1974 [1906–13]: pp. 231–232) review of Chalewsky (1909), to which Jung replied (1910a).

    Kurt Mendel [1874–19?], Berlin psychiatrist, editor of the *Neurologisches Centralblatt*, founded by his father Emanuel. Freud knew Kurt Mendel, and from 1886 on had abstracted the Viennese neurological literature for the *Centralblatt*.

## 104F

Vienna IX, Berggasse 19
23 February 1911

Dear Friend,

Your Segantini is fine and beautiful, it goes deep without causing offence, and is probably also discreet. I was very much struck by the similarities of character with Leonardo (anarchism due to an absence of paternal authority, fixation on the mother, influence of the chance events of childhood, but different results because of the death of the mother, jealousy of the brother). On a second reading I shall of course get even greater pleasure from it. The manuscript is now with Deuticke, with whom you should get in touch in order to arrange the matter of the two illustrations, which have naturally been accepted without any difficulty. Your work is being printed at the same time as a legal article by a young Swiss named Storfer, which will be ready before yours because it is shorter.

Things are on the move in the Society here; there have been agitated discussions about Adlerian theories. Adler and Stekel have resigned, and I shall probably have to take over the presidency.[1] Putnam[2] will certainly have given you pleasure too. In due course I shall be sending you some reprints for distribution. Brill reports that he has founded a branch society in New York with 16 members, of which he is the president.[3] The enemies are rather quiet at the moment.

With cordial greetings to you and your family,
your faithfully devoted

*Freud*

1. On 16 November 1910, Hitschmann had proposed a detailed discussion about Adler's views and their relation to those of Freud. Freud agreed, with the stipulation that Adler himself talk about the relation of masculine protest to the theory of repression (Nunberg & Federn, 1974: p. 59). Adler accepted. The discussions were continued on 8 and 22 February 1911, and ended with Adler's and Stekel's resignation as president and vice-president, respectively, of the Vienna Society. On 1 March, Freud was elected the new president by acclamation. It was further unanimously resolved to thank Adler and Stekel and to inform them that the greatest value was being placed on their continued collaboration, and it was resolved by a majority that the Society would refrain from recognizing the incompatibility between their scientific positions and their functions, which had been cited by Adler and Stekel as grounds for their resignation (ibid.: pp. 178ff).
2. That is, Putnam's article (1910b), which had appeared, in Freud's translation and with a supplementary footnote by Freud (1911j), in the *Zentralblatt*.
3. Independently of the impending foundation of the American Psychoanalytic Association [on 9 May 1911], Brill had founded the New York Psychoanalytic Society on 12 February 1911.


105A

Berlin
26 February 1911

Dear Professor,

I thank you for the trouble you have taken with my *opus*, and I am pleased that it could go straight into print. You remark that the work is "discreet" on some points. This is quite true, particularly concerning the question of the homosexual component. There was too little material in this respect. The similarities to Leonardo had struck me right from the beginning; perhaps I could insert a note about this in the proofs.

Now I must tell you about Fliess. I had a very friendly reception. He refrained from any attacks aimed at Vienna. He has closed his mind to the more recent results of $\Psi\alpha$ since the conflict but showed great interest in all I told him. I did *not* get the fascinating impression that you predicted (Fl. may have changed in the last few years), but, nevertheless, I did get the impression of a penetrating and original thinker. In my opinion he lacks *greatness* in the strict sense of the word. This is also borne out in his scientific work. He proceeds from some valuable ideas; all further work just revolves around the proof of their correctness or on their more exact formulation.—He met me without prejudice, has meanwhile visited me in turn, and I must grant him that he made no attempt to draw me (in the way feared) to his side. I have heard many interesting things from him and am very glad to have made his acquaintance—perhaps the most valuable I could make among Berlin doctors.

I am so sorry for you about the inner conflicts of the Society, the more so since, up to now, everything has been progressing most pleasantly here.—Putnam also pleased me, as did Brill's organization. The whole business is progressing, at any rate. I have been amazed several times recently at how much has already penetrated into wider circles.

This week I am beginning another four-week course, provided that there are people to take part. The practice has been rather lively for quite a long time, so that I am usually busy for eight hours.

I am writing an article on blushing for the *Centralblatt*.[1] I will let you have it soon, together with some short communications.

With cordial greetings, also to your esteemed family,
your devoted

*Abraham*

1. Probably never published.


## 106F

Vienna IX, Berggasse 19
3 March 1911

Dear Friend,

I inform you that I have taken over the leadership of the Vienna group again after Adler's and Stekel's resignation. Adler's behaviour was no longer reconcilable with our ψα interests, he denies the role of the libido, and traces everything back to aggression. The damaging effects of his works will not take long to make themselves felt.

I ask you once again to make the little scene in Ziehen's clinic available for the *Centralblatt*. It is too priceless.

You must not think Fliess so crude as to betray any intention in the first hour. Unfortunately he is the opposite, sly or, rather, vicious. You will certainly come across his complex. Do not forget that it was through him that both of us came to understand the secret of paranoia (cf. psychosexual differences).[1] What you say about the nature of his work strikes me as remarkably true; I once loved him very much and therefore overlooked a great deal. Above all, beware of his wife.

Stekel's dream book[2] appeared a few days ago. There will be a great deal in it to be learned from, a great deal to be missed, and a good deal to be criticized.

Let me draw your attention especially to the last issue of the *Journal of Abnormal Psychology*. Jones[3] is correct and understanding, Morton Prince[4] impudent and stupid, Friedländer[5]—the old pig.

I also thank you and your dear wife for the friendly reception that you gave to my sister-in-law who returned today.

Yours cordially,

*Freud*

1. Referring to Abraham, 1908[11], Abraham's paper for the meeting in Salzburg, in which he acknowledges his debt to Freud for "many of the ideas" (p. 65). Freud probably alludes to the connection between auto-erotism, delusions of persecution, and megalomania drawn therein (pp. 74–75).
2. Stekel, 1911.
3. Jones, 1911.
4. Prince, 1911.
5. Friedländer, 1911 [1910].

107A

Berlin
9 March 1911

Dear Professor,

Heartfelt thanks for the further information about Fliess, to whom I have not yet spoken again, and also for the Putnam reprints. I hope to get the new publications you write about before long. I have already had part of the Segantini proofs. Deuticke is in touch with the Photographic Union in Munich about the illustrations.

As regards the Ziehen affair, I wrote to Dr Maier at the Burghölzli and received the enclosed letter from him. I cannot say that he is in the wrong. It was fortunate that I wrote to him first, for publication would surely have generated an irritation in Zurich (i.e. the Burghölzli)—after all, the rift has only just been mended. Now we have to pass the story on by word of mouth.

I can hardly regret Adler's resignation. In spite of one's respect for his good qualities, he was certainly not the right man to lead the Vienna Society. His more recent papers are not at all to my liking. It is true that I dare not give a definitive judgement because I cannot detach myself from an antipathy to Adler's style and exposition. There is the danger of rejecting this or that out of indolence, so as not to have to immerse oneself into his work. I do not think, however, that I do him an injustice if I find the "aggressive drive" very one-sided. The giving up of the libido, the neglect of all we have learned about erotogenic zones, auto-erotism, etc., appear to me as a retrograde step. The pleasure principle is lost entirely. On top of that, he relapses into surface psychology, such as "over-sensitivity", etc. The one-sidedness of his interpretation is very evident to me when he gives an example. The fundamental fact of overdetermination is completely neglected, as, for instance, in the note (to the Nuremberg talk) in which he does away with erythrophobia.[1] The "masculine protest" seems to me to be a valid point of view in certain cases; I do not, however, find anything basically new in it. I would say that it is an idea that is already contained in your *Three Essays* (about the masculinity of the libido),[2] stated exaggeratedly and pushed onesidedly to its extremes. The "masculine protest" must have its roots in his unconscious. In spite of all these objections, one always finds something valuable, so that one tends to regret that it is all in such a sketchy, fragmentary, and insufficiently explained form.

The practice has been turbulent for some time, almost every day eight analytic hours and a few other things as well, so that I have little time for science. I am thinking of taking a little rest at Easter.—I shall perhaps write to you soon about some—as far as I know, new—results.

We were very pleased with Frl. Bernays's visit, and we had her give us a detailed account of everything concerning your family. With cordial greetings to you and yours, also from my wife,

Yours,

*Abraham*

1. "In *compulsively blushing* (*ertyhrophobia*), for example, the patient reacts to felt or feared disparagement with (male) rage and displeasure. But the reaction is done with female means, with blushing or fear of blushing. And the meaning of the fit is: 'I am a woman and want to be a man'" (Adler, 1910: p. 89; editor's translation).
2. Freud, 1905d: p. 219.

## 108F

Vienna IX, Berggasse 19
14 March 1911

Dear Friend,

I am returning Dr Maier's letter herewith. I think you could not have acted otherwise, and if he cannot make up his mind, we have still nothing to reproach him with. He is not very close to us. The delicacy could be mingled with caution. In any case, I am sorry to let the bite go.

Your judgement of Adler coincides completely with mine, and particularly with my judgement before the discussions. Since then, it has become more trenchant; a great deal of confusion is concealed behind his abstraction, he dissimulates a much more far-reaching opposition and shows some fine paranoid traits. Nothing is going to come out of all my Viennese, with the exception of little Rank, who is becoming someone decent and remarkable.[1]

I am glad to hear that your practice is doing so well. Your success at your difficult post deserves all respect and reward. I have had a less busy week and am therefore feeling quite refreshed.

With the most cordial greetings,
Yours,

    Freud

1. Holograph: ". . . der etwas Ordentliches wird".

## 109A

Berlin W.
9 April 1911

Dear Professor,

You have presumably already heard from Jung about his visit to Berlin.[1] The result for me was that a few days ago I was called in as consultant to a case in the Kraus clinic. I hope that is the beginning of the outward progress of our cause here in the tough North! After Easter I shall try to teach the clinic doctors, *privatissime*, a little about $\Psi\alpha$. Some of them are certainly interested.

For the Congress in the autumn, after discussion with the members here, I have suggested Weimar, and I hope that you agree and Jung as well. It is favourably situated, that is, it can be reached from both Zurich and Vienna by direct express train without changing (Vienna–Aachen express without overnight journey). We in Berlin would have a slight advantage, it is true, but we would take over the arrangements. The town as such will be congenial for all. I can probably soon make inquiries about a venue for the meetings myself; as far as I know, everything we need is there. If we should make progress in Berlin in the near future, a place so convenient for North Germany could be especially recommended.

Meanwhile I visited Fliess, who referred a woman patient to me for analysis once again. He recommended both analysis and me to the patient in a very nice way. As yet, we have not discussed scientific matters again.

On Wednesday the 12th I am going on holiday for a short time; I am very much in need of rest, as the practice has made extreme demands on me in the last few months. I am going to Bad Schandau near Dresden; on 18 April the Berlin group is meeting in Dresden for a session at our colleague Stegmann's house. The members in Thuringia thus have the opportunity to participate.

I have not yet read Stekel's dream book, but even in advance I find it too voluminous in comparison with the work it is based on. But now I

1911 April

understand why St. in the last *Zentralblatt* quotes Swoboda's platitude about "brilliant imitative creativity".

I hope that the differences in the group there have been smoothed out again to some extent.

If you have anything to tell me (about Weimar, for instance, which I shall probably be passing through), my address is Hotel Forsthaus, Bad Schandau a/Elbe (from 12 to 18 April).

With cordial greetings to you and yours,
your devoted

*Abraham*

1. Between 29 March and ca. 1 April, to the Charité, headed by Friedrich Kraus [1858–1936] (cf. Freud & Jung, 1974 [1906–13], letter of 28 February 1911, and the following ones: pp. 397–413), where Jung found the "whole clinic infected with $\Psi\alpha$" (31 March 1911, ibid.: p. 412).

## 110F

Vienna
11 April 1911

Dear Friend,

I do not begrudge you your well-earned leave. The prospects opening up in Berlin are very fine. It was an extraordinary achievement on your part to base your existence on representing $\Psi\alpha$ in Berlin.

Weimar suits me very well, and there is also much sympathy for it in the Vienna group. Stekel's dream book is in some respects shameful for us, although it contains much that is new. I shall give an actually unfavourable criticism of it to the *Jahrbuch*. He is unfortunately ineducable. In Vienna we have a rather unpleasant situation, and a few quite crazy members.

You will have been informed about what has recently been going on in the Association (America, Munich[1]) through Jung's visit. My work on paranoia, which takes up again your "$\psi$sexual Differences", is already printed. If you wish, I can send you proofs long before the *Jahrbuch* comes out.

I am meeting Ferenczi in Bozen for Easter.[2]

With cordial greetings to you and your dear wife,
Yours,

*Freud*

1. The founding of the New York branch society [on 12 February 1911], and the impending founding of the Munich [on 1 May] and the American [on 9 May] societies.
2. Freud and Ferenczi spent 16 and 17 April together in Bolzano in South Tyrol.

## 111A

Berlin
14 May 1911

Dear Professor,

You congratulated me four weeks ago on Segantini's birth, but I did not receive the copies until a few days ago; you will meanwhile have received one. Many thanks for the proofs. Unfortunately, I have not yet found the time to read the two papers at leisure, but even a cursory reading has given me particular pleasure. The postulation of the two principles[1] is unusually illuminating and helpful; it seems indispensable to me for the understanding of the development of the libido. I should like to go into it in greater detail once I have read the paper again.

You have succeeded wonderfully well in the Schreber analysis and in further developing the theory of paranoia. There is a great deal in this paper that I would like to discuss with you in greater detail. Could you possibly reserve some time for me in the autumn just before or after the Congress? So much has accumulated that is difficult to discuss in letters.—I must thank you for the incidental profit of pleasure I have gained from several of your comments!

For a short time I have been treating the lady—Frl. Eibenschütz—whom you so very kindly referred to me. Her strange fear of speaking has a very interesting aetiology. After my return from the short Easter holidays the practice has increased again very rapidly; analyses keep me busy from morning to evening.

If your time permits, I should like to ask you to comment briefly on a passage in the *Three Essays*, namely on the last paragraph of the 2nd essay ("The same pathways" etc.).[2] I was questioned about it a short while ago but was unable to give a satisfactory reply.

With cordial greetings from house to house,
your devoted

*Karl Abraham*

1. Freud, 1911b.
2. Freud, 1905d: p. 206.

## 112F

Vienna IX, Berggasse 19
18 May 1911

Dear Friend,

It is true that I received the first copy of your Segantini weeks ago. Opinions of your work in my immediate circle are *extremely* appreciative, and I hope that our opponents will also have to speak of it with respect.

I shall be very glad indeed to meet you for an undisturbed private meeting before or after the Congress, and look forward very much to the rare opportunity. You would make things much easier for me if you would prefer the *later* of the two possible dates for [the Congress in] Weimar; I could then spend the day *before* with you and afterwards go to Zurich for the inspection I have had in mind for a long time. For highly private family reasons 16 September is a very inconvenient, *nearly* impossible date for me,[1] though I am loath to arrange the date of the Congress according to my personal requirements.

The passage in the *Sexual Theory* cannot but sound oracular, because no clear idea hides behind it, only a hypothesis. There are ways, unknown in their nature, in which sexual processes exercise an influence on digestion, blood formation, etc. The disturbing influences of sexuality travel by them, and thus probably the conducive and other usable influences normally travel by them too. You see, I can really give you only a paraphrase of the dawning suspicion.

With cordial greetings and many good wishes to your wife and children,

your most faithfully devoted

*Freud*

1. Referring to the Freuds' twenty-fifth wedding anniversary on 14 September.

## 113A

Berlin
28 August 1911

Dear Professor,

Many thanks for your lines from Klobenstein![1] We have been back here for eight days after a lovely holiday in Denmark; business is already in full swing, almost more than one would wish for in this heat.

I am sending you today a prospectus of our Weimar headquarters; it looks as though we shall be well received there. If you have special requirements with regard to the room, please let me know. I am delighted that you are keeping the day after the Congress for me.

I have announced a talk on the psychosexual basis of agitated and depressive states,[2] and I believe I shall be able to present some ideas that are new, or at any rate not yet published.—My Segantini has caused some stir. Servaes[3] has already written to me unfavourably about it and notified me at the same time of an article that has appeared in the *Frankfurter Zeitung*, of which he promised me a reprint. The article appeared, but not the reprint. In another paper a local colleague expressed violent indignation and called on all the neurological saints. And a poem, *Wissenschaft und Stumpfsinn* [Science and Stupidity], appeared in the *Jugend*.[4]

Otherwise, the summer's peace has only been interrupted by seven new papers by Jones. I will not disturb yours any further. Your kind regards and those of Dr Ferenczi are most cordially reciprocated by my wife and myself,

Yours,

### Karl Abraham

1. Missing. On 9 July, Freud had gone to Karlsbad and from there, around 1 August, to Klobenstein near Bolzano, where he had joined his wife. Ferenczi had joined the party on 20 August for a fortnight.
2. Abraham, 1911[26].
3. Franz Theodor Hubert Servaes [1862–1947], German writer, biographer of Segantini (Servaes, 1907).
4. Munich weekly [1896–1940], which gave the *Jugendstil* [art nouveau] its name.

## 114F

Klobenstein
30 August 1911

Dear Friend,

Many thanks for your letter and enclosure. If I am to express a wish, it would be for a room *with* bathroom.

I have followed the fortunes of your Segantini with interest. You know, it is very much appreciated in our circles and bought in quantity at Deuticke's. I have read the article by Servaes. If you do not know it, you have missed nothing. Exactly what anyone could have made up for himself. People feel the uneasiness that arises from the dissolution of sublimations and make us pay for it.

Each of your greetings evokes for my family a pleasant memory of your home and your wife. They send their thanks.

I am thinking—if possible—of leaving others to do the talking at the Congress. I have nothing actually ready to be said.

With cordial greetings and looking forward to seeing you again,
 your faithfully devoted

*Freud*

## 115A

Berlin
12 September 1911

Dear Professor,

Heartfelt thanks for your letter! I have informed the hotel of your wish.

Up to now about 35 rooms have been booked; but the number of participants will probably be substantially larger. Jung wrote to me recently that there was a shortage of papers. This is probably connected with the fact that participation from Vienna is so weak. For at the previous congresses the Viennese have always provided an important contribution to the programme.

If only because of this shortage, you, dear Professor, will surely not keep to your intention of remaining silent. But you would not be so cruel as to disappoint the participants in their greatest expectation.

I am therefore keeping the 23rd free and am much looking forward to this day. As far as I can see, I shall arrive in Weimar at noon on the 20th.[1]

With cordial greetings—also from my wife—to you and yours.

Yours,

*Karl Abraham*

1. Because Ferenczi had to go back to Budapest to work, Freud went alone to Zurich in the middle of September and spent three days at Jung's house in Küsnacht, from where he continued on—probably in the company of Putnam, Jung and his wife—to the Third International Psychoanalytic Congress in Weimar [21–22 September]. There Freud presented a brief postscript to the Schreber case (1912a), and Abraham gave the announced talk on manic-depressive psychosis (1911[26]); these and the other lectures were abstracted by Otto Rank for the *Zentralblatt* (1911, 2: 100–105). Jung and Riklin were re-elected by acclamation to their posts as President and Secretary, respectively, of the IPA, and the *Korrespondenzblatt,* which had been published independently up to then, was incorporated into the *Zentralblatt.* Furthermore, the American Psychoanalytic Association was recognized as a branch society of the IPA, along with the New York Society. After the Congress, Freud remained briefly in Weimar to be able to talk with Abraham.

## 116A

Berlin
29 October 1911

Dear Professor,

I have not written to you since Weimar. You will see from the enclosure[1] that since then there has been a conflict within our group. Hirschfeld declared his resignation and has stuck to his decision in spite of all attempts at persuasion. At his request, I am sending you his letter. It is a question of resistances that link up with an external cause (Jung's behaviour towards him[2]), but this is definitely not their source. At a lengthy members' meeting, during which Weimar was discussed, he displayed an ignorance about Ψα that was outright shocking. It is true that something completely different had originally made him join us. It was most probably only the emphasis on sexuality that made analysis attractive to him, especially at a time when his own sex research met with hostility. Basically, Hirschfeld's defection is no loss to us, for the work of our group it is, rather, a gain. On the other hand, I regret his decision for personal reasons. The Congress aroused much irritation also in Koerber and Juliusburger, but this has virtually died down by now. In order to prevent our meetings this winter from becoming too superficial, I have suggested, and won through, that we all work through the *Three Essays* in the form of reports and discussions.

Despite these unpleasantnesses, I recall the days in Weimar with great pleasure. I have followed up the private discussion we had on the last day and found out a number of interesting facts about totem animals.[3] I shall report when my observations are more complete. I have sent two small communications to Stekel for the *Zentralblatt*.[4] Now I am occupied with the finishing strokes on my Weimar paper, and this will soon follow. After that, a little essay on a strange ceremonial[5] is to come: women who every evening before going to bed dress up as brides—brides of death. I could analyse such a case in detail and have a second quite analogous case.—I have undertaken one issue of a new series called *Beiträge zur Forensischen Medizin* [*Contributions to Forensic Medicine*]. It is to be entitled "The Child's Instinctual Life and Its Relation to Delinquency". Later sometime about other plans that were furthered by the hours I spent with you!

I was gratified to hear that our third journal will not have the title originally intended.[6] I am eager to see it.—Bleuler's *Dementia Praecox*,[7] which I read recently, is as contradictory as the man himself. In many ways the book is excellent; yet, at the same time, it contains half-truths like those that abounded in his Weimar paper.

I hope you have not taken the toothache back with you to Vienna and that you and your family are enjoying the best of health. Please give them all most cordial greetings from myself and my wife.

Herr Schönlank, whom you referred to me in the summer, has not yet been to me, whereas his son is very keen and is making good progress. It is still rather quiet in the practice. I hope it will become more lively in November.

With the most cordial greetings,
your devoted

*Abraham*

1. A (missing) letter of Hirschfeld's.

1911 November                                                             141

2. It seems that Jung had objected to Hirschfeld's homosexuality.
3. Evidently, Freud had talked to Abraham about the ideas that were to lead to *Totem and Taboo* (Freud, 1912–13a). First hints of this project are found in letters to Ferenczi of 21 May 1911 and 20 July 1911 (Freud & Ferenczi, 1992: pp. 281, 296).
4. Abraham, 1911[28], 1911[29].
5. Abraham, 1912[32].
6. This refers to a plan for a new psychoanalytic journal, devoted to non-medical topics. Several names were under discussion—among them, still on 13 November, "Psyche" (Freud & Ferenczi, 1992: p. 310). It was finally called *Imago, Zeitschrift für Anwendung der Psychoanalyse auf die Geisteswissenschaften*, edited by Otto Rank and Hanns Sachs under the chief-editorship of Freud. The first issue appeared in 1912 with Hugo Heller.
7. Bleuler, 1911.


117F

Vienna IX, Berggasse 19
2 November 1911

Dear Friend,

I too remember fondly the beautiful days and face a relatively unsatisfactory present. The practice is not as full as it was last year, I can still pass on very little. To begin with Herr Schönlank cancelled, as you know; so he has not yet translated his motives into action. It is to our great detriment that we have no $\psi\alpha$-led institution here in which I could place all four assistants and train new ones. But Vienna is not the ground on which anything can be done.

What gave me most pleasure in your letter were the numerous germs of works, some of which you trace back directly to Weimar. I too am using a period of relative leisure to go more deeply into the work I mentioned to you.[1] I already have the major results beforehand, but reading and collecting in order to provide proof for them is very tedious, and the end is not in sight for some time to come. Anything in the nature of a pleasure gain can only arise at the stage of final shaping, and God alone knows when I shall be able to get to that.

To maintain the parallel still further, let me tell you that I have completed the purge of the Society and sent Adler's seven followers packing after him.[2] The decrease in numbers is of no importance, work will be much easier now, but, with the single exception of Rank, I have no one here in whom I can take complete pleasure. Perhaps Sachs,[3] the second editor of the still unborn journal, will rise to the occasion. My spirits have not been improved by the fact that my offer to publish it has been rejected in three (actually, four) quarters. Perhaps it will work out with our member Heller[4] now.

Hirschfeld's resignation is really no loss. His personality is not prepossessing and his receptivity equals zero. In your difficult position, however, I would have rather you had additions. I shall write H. a few friendly lines. I enclose his letter. I hope our correspondence will be able to deal with more pleasant things in the course of this year.—My tooth is forgotten, it was annoying that it took so much out of me in both Zurich and Weimar. In the hope that you and your little family are very well,

your cordially devoted

*Freud*

1. Freud, 1912–13.
2. Freud had written to Bergmann, the publisher of the *Zentralblatt*, that the latter would have to choose between Adler and himself. Bergmann brought this letter to Adler's attention, whereupon Adler drafted a declaration in which he announced his resignation from the Editorship (*Zentralblatt*, 1910–11, *1*: 433). "I have finally [in original: 'endlessly' (*endlos*, instead of *endlich*)] got rid of Adler", Freud had written to Jung on 15 June (Freud & Jung, 1974 [1906–13]: p. 428). David Bach, Stefan von Maday, and Baron Franz von Hye also left the Society with Adler. On 20 June 1911, Karl Furtmüller, Margarete Hilferding, Franz and Gustav Grüner, Paul Klemperer, David Oppenheim, and Josef Friedjung wrote a declaration in which they termed Adler's resignation as an "out-and-out provocation" and condoned his actions; but they further expressed the wish to remain "diligent members" of the Society (Handlbauer, 1990: p. 140). At the special general meeting of 11 October it was decided, however, to declare that memberships both in the Society for Free Psychoanalytic Investigation, which had been founded in the interim by Adler, and in the Psychoanalytic Society were incompatible, whereupon the aforementioned—with the exception of Friedjung—announced their resignations (Nunberg & Federn, 1974: pp. 281–283).
3. Hanns Sachs [1881–1947], Doctor of Laws, from October 1910 on member of the Vienna Society. In 1912 he, along with Rank, became editor of the newly founded *Imago*. He was a member of the Secret Committee and a training analyst at the Berlin Institute [1920–32]. In 1932 Sachs emigrated to Boston, Massachusetts, where he became a prominent but somewhat isolated representative of non-medical analysis. Sachs was one of the first to become interested in the application of psychoanalysis to the humanities. (Cf. Moellenhoff, 1966.)
4. See letter 20F, 16 February 1908, n. 5.

## 118A

Berlin
5 December 1911

Dear Professor,

The peace of Christmas is letting me carry out the long-desired intention of writing to you. First of all I can answer your news with similar ones in turn. Our little group has once again suffered two "losses". At my request to pay the increased yearly contribution, Warda and Strohmayer promptly left. I cannot say that our scientific life would be affected by it. Despite all personal difficulties—for example, Juliusburger has sulked in the background since the Congress—it seems to me to be better than before. Actually there are only five of us, i.e. Eitingon,

1911 December

Koerber, Stegmann, and myself and recently a very intelligent young woman doctor, Dr Horney,[1] whom I cured of fairly severe hysteria two years ago. She is very zealous, and as soon as she is familiar enough with the work, she will set herself up as an analyst. What I need is someone who does not remain purely receptive. Berlin is an all too sterile ground. Ziehen's impending retirement will also scarcely change things, for every successor will also take a refractory attitude. A little praise must be given to Kraus's intern clinic, several doctors of which are taking at least a sympathetic interest, as they come to our meetings. I hear favourable news rather from non-medical circles. I know that the Director of the National Gallery here and his co-workers have completely accepted my Segantini. At present there is a very lively interest there in your *Leonardo*. Among teachers and lawyers the interest is also clearly increasing. A few evenings ago, at the invitation of the Russian Medical Association (= Russian doctors who are staying here for further training) I spoke on "The Practice of $\Psi\alpha$" in front of a fairly large and very attentive audience.

The new journal, as Rank wrote me, will surely come into being. This undertaking is very much to my liking. I am preparing a work that is in a line with your present interests; but I should prefer not to say anything about it until I know whether I can carry it through successfully.

The actual progress of our research will for the moment have to make up for our poor success outside. I would wish the coming year to bring you very much pleasure in that sphere at least. The rest will follow; there can be no doubt that everywhere things are in a ferment. Incidentally—my good wishes for you and yours are not only for psychoanalysis.

One more question: could Reik's dissertation on Flaubert, parts of which I read in "Pan",[2] not appear in the *Schriften zur angewandten Seelenkunde*?

With many cordial greetings—also from my wife—to you and your house,

Yours,

*Abraham*

---

1. Karen Horney, née Danielsen [1885–1952]. She attended a secondary school in Hamburg, studied medicine in Freiburg and Göttingen [1906–09], then moved to Berlin to complete the final year of medical school at the Charité. She began analysis with Abraham at some time early in 1910 and continued it until the summer of 1910; she soon became a member of the Berlin Society. In 1920 she was a founding member of the Berlin Institute and the first woman to teach there. She also was a member of the Berlin education committee from its inception, and of the education committee of the IPA [1928]. Her second analysis was with Hanns Sachs. In 1932 she left Germany for Chicago, becoming associate director of the newly formed Institute for Psychoanalysis (Franz Alexander) [1932–34]. In 1934 she moved to New York [1934–52] and became

a member of the Society there and a popular teacher at the New School for Social Research, building a following of her own. She had regular contact with Harry Stack Sullivan, Clara Thompson, and William V. Silverberg. Her books *The Neurotic Personality of Our Time* (1937) and *New Ways in Psychoanalysis* (1939) unleashed a storm of controversy, and in 1941, on the instigation of Lawrence Kubie and Gregory Zilboorg, the education committee voted that her status should be changed from that of instructor to lecturer. Together with Harmon Ephron, Sarah Kelman, Bernard Robbins, and Clara Thompson, she resigned from the New York Society, causing the first split in American psychoanalysis. She founded the *Association for the Advancement of Psychoanalysis*, including Thompson, Erich Fromm, Sullivan, and Silverberg; within two years, the AAP itself split, and Fromm, Thompson, Sullivan, and Janet Rioch left to found the William White Institute in New York City. Horney is a prominent exponent of so-called neo-analysis; she is best known for her groundbreaking papers on female psychology, making her perhaps the first critic of Freud's views on femininity. (Cf. Quinn, 1987.)

2. Reik, 1911; the dissertation appeared as Reik, 1912. Shortly before, he had been elected to membership of the Vienna Society (15 November, Nunberg & Federn, 1974: pp. 310–319). Theodor Reik [1888–1969] was born in Vienna and studied psychology, German, and French literature there. In 1914/15 he underwent a—cost-free—training analysis with Karl Abraham. In 1915 he became Rank's successor as Secretary of the Vienna Society and retained this function until he moved to Berlin in 1928. In 1934 he emigrated to Holland, and in 1938 to New York, where, as a non-medical analyst, he was "strongly admonished" by the Psychoanalytic Society there "against practising, or rather forbidden to practise, psychoanalysis" (Reik, 1974: p. 656). Reik worked as an analyst just the same, and in 1948 he founded his own group, the National Psychological Association for Psychoanalysis.

# 1912

## 119F

Vienna IX, Berggasse 19
2 January 1912

Dear Friend,

Having filled the holidays with the writing of two and a half treatises[1] (which I do not like) and all sorts of private discontents, I at last come round to sending my best wishes for the prosperity of your wife and children and yourself that you so well deserve and the fulfilment of which would give me so much pleasure. Shared interests and personal liking have tied us so intimately together that we have no need to doubt the genuineness of our good wishes for each other.

I know how difficult a position you have in Berlin and always admire you for your unruffled spirits and tenacious confidence. The chronicle of our undertaking is perhaps not always pleasant, but that may be true of most chronicles; it will yet make a fine chapter of history. The latest favourable signs, strangely enough, have come from France. We have gained a vigorous helpmate in Morichau-Beauchant in Poitiers (see his article in the *Gazette des Hôpitaux*, 1911, p. 1,845),[2] and today I received a letter from a student of Régis in Bordeaux, written on his behalf, apologizing in the name of French psychiatry for its present neglect of $\Psi\alpha$. He announced his willingness to come out with a long paper about it in *Encéphale*.[3]

For myself I have no great expectations; gloomy times lie ahead, and recognition will probably come only for the next generation. But we have the incomparable pleasure of the first discoveries. My work on the $\psi$ of religion is going ahead very slowly, so I should prefer to remove it from the agenda altogether. I have to write something in the nature of a preliminary communication for the new journal *"Imago"*, something from the $\psi$ of savage peoples.[4] Reik's work[5] is too long for the *Sammlung*, and I heard only just today from the author (who is a member of ours) that it is to appear as a book.

Farewell, and do not write too seldom
to your faithful

*Freud*

1. Freud, 1912c, 1912d; also very probably the beginning of work on the "psychology of religion" (*Totem and Taboo,* Freud, 1912–13), mentioned later in this letter.
2. Morichau-Beauchant, 1911. Pierre Ernest René Morichau-Beauchant [1873–1951], professor of clinical medicine at the École de Médecine in Poitiers, was instrumental in introducing psychoanalysis to France. He had already written Freud a letter at the end of 1910 in which he had referred to himself as Freud's pupil (Freud & Jung, 1974 [1906–13]: pp. 377–378; cf. also Freud, 1914d: p. 32). In January 1912 he joined the Zurich group.
3. Emmanuel Régis [1855–1918], Professor at the Clinique des Maladies Mentales in Bordeaux, and his assistant, Angelo Louis Marie Hesnard [1886–1969]. They would indeed publish a long article about "The Theory of Freud and His School" in *Encéphale* (1913).
4. *Imago, Zeitschrift für Anwendung der Psychoanalyse auf die Geisteswissenschaften* [*Imago, Journal for the Application of Psychoanalysis to the Humanities*] (named after a novel by the Swiss writer Carl Spitteler), edited by Otto Rank and Hanns Sachs under the general editorship of Freud. The first issue came out in 1912 with Hugo Heller, containing Freud's "The Horror of Incest", which was to become the first chapter of *Totem and Taboo.*
5. See letter 118A, 5 December 1911, n. 2.

## 120A

Berlin
11 January 1912

Dear Professor,

Only a few lines today to thank you very much indeed for your kind wishes and encouraging words! The latter have helped; I have just completed the preparatory work on my paper for the new journal. I know that its theme will interest you: it is about Amenhotep IV and the Aton cult.[1] The subject has a particular attraction for me—to analyse all the manifestations of repression and substitutive formation in a person who lived 3,300 years ago. The Oedipus complex, sublimation, reaction formations—all exactly as in a neurotic today. I did the preparatory work partly in the Egyptian department of the Berlin Museum and was reminded more than once of the first instruction of Egyptology that I enjoyed in Vienna in December 1907.

That is all for today. In accordance with your wish, I did not want to keep you waiting too long for news. With cordial greetings also to your family from my wife and myself,

your devoted

*Abraham*

1. Abraham, 1912[34].

## 121F

Vienna IX, Berggasse 19
14 January 1912

Dear Friend,

Well, well! Amenhotep IV in the light of Ψα. That surely is already a great advance in "orientation". Do you know that you are now regarded with Stekel and Sadger as being among the *bêtes noires* of Ψα, against whom I have always been warned? Evidently since your Segantini, and what will it ever be like after Amenhotep? But you will not let it worry you. The reason why I am in such a good mood is that I have just managed to finish a paper for the *"Imago"* on the horror of incest among savages. What is so splendid is not that I think it good, but that it is finished.

The work to which I referred above is "On the Ψ Theories of Freud and Related Views", by Arthur *Kronfeld*, of Berlin, published in book form as No. 3 of Vol. II of the *Papers on Psychological Paedagogics*.[1] In its tone it is quite decent, but it proves philosophically and mathematically that all the things over which we take such a great deal of trouble simply do not exist, because it is impossible that they should exist.[2] There we are.

Shortly, I am going to have to write an English essay on the *unconscious*[3] in Ψα which has been asked for by the Society for Psychical Research,[4] or read Bleuler's manuscript on autistic thinking,[5] which I received today. But reading is even worse than writing.

Cordial greetings to you and your dear wife,
from your

*Freud*

1. Kronfeld, 1911, previously published in a journal. Arthur Kronfeld [1886–1941], psychiatrist in Heidelberg, later in Berlin. A critical review of Kronfeld's work, at Freud's instigation, appeared in the *Jahrbuch* (Rosenstein, 1912).
2. *Weil, so schließt er messerscharf, nicht sein kann, was nicht sein darf.* Often quoted line by the German poet Christian Morgenstern [1871–1914].
3. This word in English in original.
4. Freud, 1912g, written by Freud in English and published in the *Proceedings of the Society for Psychical Research* (26: 312–318).
5. Bleuler, 1912.

## 122A

Berlin
25 February 1912

Dear Professor,

I wish to begin my long-postponed letter with the pleasant news that I am up to my neck in psychoanalyses. Since January the practice has been overwhelming, never less than ten hours a day. This has also brought about the desired effect that I am independent of Oppenheim's support, for what I receive from him now is no longer worth mentioning. I do owe him a debt of gratitude, but the present state of affairs, with its full independence of action, is far preferable. Recently I had to refuse a few cases because I really could not take on any more; I passed one on to Eitingon who does every now and again treat a patient. The lack of a colleague is gradually making itself felt, and I do not know where to find one. Certainly, work will not go on at this rate right through the whole year, but it would nevertheless be desirable to have someone else with me. You will be interested to know that the $\Psi\alpha$ of the young Schönlank (whose father you referred to me in the autumn) has ended and was a great success. The compulsion to doubt, impotence, and everything else neurotic are eliminated. I am also very pleased with the material of patients: almost all of them intelligent people with very individual forms of neurosis, so that the work is never monotonous.

I have very little time for private work. The Egyptian research for *Imago* progresses only at a snail's pace. I always wonder how you manage to write so much in addition to your practice. Heartfelt thanks for the reprints!

For today, only one theoretical comment: one of my patients who has been in analysis for quite a long time already has recently gone through a hysterical twilight state of several days' duration, during which the patient developed a persecution mania. I succeeded in understanding it, in part during the twilight state and in part afterwards, when the patient had become clear and reasonable. It is rare to have such an opportunity of observing delusion formations *in statu nascendi*, and of analysing after full insight has been reached. Here I was able to prove, with really striking transparency, everything that you deduced from the Schreber case.[1] I want to publish the whole thing when I find time.

Our small Berlin group is leading a quiet life. The last meeting was pleasant, due to a talk held by Dr Horney about sexual instruction in early childhood.[2] The paper showed, for once, a real comprehension of the subject; unfortunately something rather infrequent in the talks in our circle.—Recently our colleague Brecher[3] paid us a visit; he struck me as rather neurotic, and was more wavering than ever in his stance to $\Psi\alpha$ purely because of complexes.—One more request! Would you, dear Professor, write me in a few words sometime what the prognosis is, from your experience, in cases of impotence in neurotics, when there is a strong tendency towards fetishism? These cases seem particularly unfavourable to me.

With cordial greetings from house to house,
your devoted

*Abraham*

1. Freud, 1911c [1910].
2. Horney, 1912.
3. Guido Brecher [1877–19?], member of the Vienna Society [1907–1919]. Physician at the spas of Bad Gastein and Merano.


123F

Vienna IX, Berggasse 19
22 April 1912

Dear Friend,

Only business today, too tired for anything else.

Prof. Kalischer of the Technical College will consult you about a $\Psi\alpha$ for his 28-year-old daughter—typical Berlin intelligence, Jewess, nervous asthma for nine years, only one year of improvement in between, physical side rather dealt with by nasal therapy, psychical trigger excitement before an examination, later resistance on the father's part against a plan to go on the stage. Mother died a year ago.—Mostly continuous restriction of breathing, which is occasionally aggravated to the point of severe attacks.

Father is serious about treatment, made a slip of the tongue, "wife" instead of "daughter". Have opted in favour of one year.

Wish you great success—if they come.

Cordial greetings,
Yours,

*Freud*


124A

Berlin
28 April 1912

Dear Professor,

There has not been anything special to report lately, that is why I have not taken up your time with correspondence. Your letter, received some days ago, gives me a reason for writing, above all to thank you for the patient—though she has not arrived yet—and for the offprint from *Imago*.[1] And at the same time to send you my congratulations on this third child! I am delighted with the tasteful presentation; everybody likes it. Your contribution is particularly important to me because of my own gradually maturing interests. *My* own long-overdue contribution to *Imago* (Amenhotep) is almost ready. The practice, which remains almost constantly on the same high level, is absorbing me. In addition there are quite a few family matters—first a serious illness of my father, from which he has now reasonably recovered. My wife and I were in Bremen to congratulate him on his 70th birthday, for which he had just got out of bed. After we got home whooping cough set in; both children are suffering from it, and, to make matters worse, they infected my wife and the children's nurse.

I am quite glad that the Congress is not to take place until next year, only spring would suit me far better than autumn. There is not much news from our group; as far as Berlin is concerned, however, public interest in $\Psi\alpha$ is on the increase. In any case, you will be interested to hear what I was told happened after the meeting of the Kant Society in Halle. There was an unofficial debate on $\Psi\alpha$ during which many people showed themselves to be well informed and where the general atmosphere was favourable rather than not.—Have you read the *"Die Intellectuellen"* by Grete Meisel-Hess?[2] Stekel recently proved in the *Zentralblatt* that it was untenable that a woman would commit suicide as a consequence of a $\Psi\alpha$. Recently I have seen both the authoress and the heroine who committed suicide—quite cheerfully together, a fact that reassured me enormously!

One of the visitors to the Weimar Congress, Frau Lou Andreas-Salomé,[3] has just spent some time in Berlin. I have come to know her very closely and must say that I have never before met with such an understanding of $\Psi\alpha$, right down to the last details and subtleties. She will visit Vienna in the winter and would like to attend the meetings there.

My *Dreams and Myths* has recently appeared in Russian and will shortly appear in English in the *Journal of Nervous and Mental Diseases* in America.[4]

I hope you and your family are well, and enclose the most cordial greetings, also from my wife,

your devoted

*Abraham*

1. See letter 119F, 2 January 1912, n. 4.
2. Meisel-Hess, 1911. Grete Meisel-Hess [1879–?], known for her popular writings on sexuality and partnership (cf. her report on sexual reform in the *Zentralblatt*, 1911/12).
3. Lou Andreas-Salomé [1861–1937], born in St Petersburg, married to the Orientalist Friedrich Carl Andreas [1846–1930]. She was then a popular writer, champion of women's rights, and, later, psychoanalyst in Göttingen, although today she is best known for her friendships with Friedrich Nietzsche, Rainer Maria Rilke, and Freud. After she had participated in the Weimar Congress in September 1911, she decided to study psychoanalysis in Vienna (cf. Andreas-Salomé, 1958). Her correspondence with Freud was published in an abridged version (Freud & Andreas-Salomé, 1966).
4. In a translation by William A. White, as No. 15 of the *Nervous and Mental Diseases Monograph Series*, New York: Nervous and Mental Diseases Publishing Company, 1913.

## 125F

Vienna IX, Berggasse 19
2 May 1912

Dear Friend,

Many thanks for your good news. I was very pleased to hear about the English and Russian translations. Your domestic news was less pleasing, but fortunately does not go beyond what one is prepared for.

*Imago* is eagerly awaiting your Amenhotep. Will you not want to include a portrait of the interesting king?—On the strength of your recommendation Frau L. A.-Salomé will be very welcome; she is said to have sent Jung a paper for the *Jahrbuch* which has been promised me for a reading too.[1]

Kalischer, I thought, for once, was a serious case, and so I hurried with the letter. Is not one always taken in.

*Imago* is indeed getting a pleasant reception in general; only in Vienna the interest is slight. There are now some innovations in the *Zentralblatt*: Open Forum and "Children's Corner" are going to be activated,[2] the former for exchanges of ideas and for internal criticism. Your "Bride of Death Ceremonial"[3] is priceless and in many respects overwhelming. It is correct to identify the father with death, for the father is a dead man, and death himself—according to Kleinpaul[4]—is only a dead man. The dead are universally thought of as coming for their own.

At the Society yesterday we had talks on the last two issues of the *Zentralblatt*, and we are to make our $\psi\alpha$ literature the subject of regular discussions. Your paper on melancholia was very sensibly criticized by Federn,[5] and then all sorts of things dawned on me which may lead further. We are still only at the beginnings in that respect.

At home things are going well, but I am rather over-worked, i.e. dim-witted, and the work on taboo is going very badly. The "totem"[6] will have to wait for a long time.

With cordial greetings and wishes for the recovery of your wife and children,

your faithfully devoted,

*Freud*

1. Andreas-Salomé, 1913, which she at first submitted to the *Jahrbuch* but then took back; it was finally published in *Imago*.
2. Two rubrics in the *Zentralblatt* for brief communications: *Offener Sprechsaal*—at the instigation of James J. Putnam—and *Psychologisches aus der Kinderstube*.
3. A ceremonial that Abraham described and analysed (1912[32]; see letter 116A, 29 October 1911).
4. Kleinpaul, 1898. Rudolf Alexander Kleinpaul [1845–1918], noted German philologist and linguist (cf. Freud, 1912–13: pp. 58–59).
5. Abraham, 1911[26], critically discussed by Federn, half-defended by Freud (Nunberg & Federn, 1975: pp. 99–100).

Paul Federn [1871–1950], general practitioner and a prominent member of the Wednesday Society. He joined the Social Democratic Party in 1918. He was Freud's representative after the latter's operation for cancer [1923] and was vice-president of the Vienna Society from 1924 until its dissolution by the Nazis [1938]. In 1938 Federn emigrated to New York, but it was not until 1946 that he became recognized as a physician and consequently as a member of the Psychoanalytic Society there. After his wife's death and when he became ill with cancer, he took his own life. His contribution is significant because of his version of "ego-psychology" and he played a pioneering role in the investigation of psychoses and in popularizing psychoanalysis and its application to adjacent disciplines.

6. That is, the fourth and last chapter of *Totem and Taboo*: "The Return of Totemism in Childhood".

## 126A

Berlin
28 May 1912

Dear Professor,

Following your suggestion, I shall add two pictures to the Amenhotep—who is now with Rank in the form of a manuscript—the king himself with his consort, and his mother. I hope Heller will have no difficulty in obtaining permission to reproduce the two pictures from Breasted's *History of Egypt*.[1]

I am pleased to hear about some innovations in the *Zentralblatt*. I have a few charming contributions for the "Children's Corner", which I am sending to Stekel as soon as I can.[2] I rested for once a bit around Whitsuntide. In the next seven weeks, until we go on holiday, there is still a great deal of work to be done, as the practice constantly remains at the same high level I described in my last letter. On 19 July we are going to Kurhaus Stoos above Brunnen (Lake Lucerne). I shall then have the opportunity to visit Zurich again after five years.

On the question of melancholia, which you touched on in your letter, I can report that I have for some time past had a particularly instructive case of "cyclothymia" under observation. In this patient everything lies unusually close to consciousness, and she is particularly aware of her own inability to love. Physically as well as psychologically she is thoroughly "intermediate stage",[3] very masculine in physical appearance, manner, voice, movements, etc., as well as in her thinking and feeling. The mixture of male and female in her is such that she is too masculine to love men; but she also fails to achieve full transference onto women. Thus she never reaches a satisfactory attitude either to a man or to a woman. Reaction to this: vivid substitute gratification in phantasy (prostitution phantasies) and masturbation, which are, however, not sufficient. Hence, repeated lapses into depression, alternating with rapid manic exaltation. I am really quite stuck in this case. The patient lacks the type of transference usually met with in neurotics.

1912 May                                                                     153

The case I described in greater detail in my paper[4] is now giving me trouble again. He did quite well for approximately four months, but then he went through a depression lasting some time, which, though not as severe as some of his earlier ones, continued for 6–7 weeks. I myself have the impression that I have not got to the bottom of this case. You hint that a thing or two dawned on you. I should be very grateful for any suggestions, as I would very much like to give the pitiable patient another try.

I have recently analysed in two patients a disorder that is a complete counterpart of Schreber's ability to look into the sun without being blinded.[5] The *fear of light* proved to be directly connected with the father. One of the cases, a dementia praecox, forces one to assume that fear of light has an underlying unconscious delusion of grandeur. If the patient firmly makes both eyes converge, he first has a visual hallucination (under closed lids) of two eyes, which then suddenly merge into one *sun*. So, he *himself* is a sun, just as good as the father. I suspect that Schreber's idea also has the connotation that he himself (his eye) is a sun more radiant than the paternal sun. Thus the latter cannot blind him. Naturally, I see this merely as a possible complement to your explanation.

I like to hear about the work of the group in Vienna, but always with the regret that I can obtain so little stimulus through the exchange of experiences. Our sessions have indeed grown, but the right people are missing.

Recently I went through the neurological literature of the past months, as I do about every half-year. It is frightening how unproductive it is. It is interesting that among the journals, the *Zeitschrift für die gesamte Neurologie und Psychiatrie* does not review us at all any more, and the *Neurologisches Centralblatt* does almost the same (the only critically active journal is Ziehen's *Monatsschrift [für Psychiatrie und Neurologie]*). So they are giving up their "refutations".

I spoke briefly the other day in a discussion in the *Berliner Gesellschaft für Psychiatrie und Nervenkrankheiten* [Berlin Society for Psychiatry and Nervous Diseases], not *propagandae fidei causa*[6] but in order to carry some of the speaker's (Kohnstamm's[7]) psychological amateur work *ad absurdum*.

With cordial greetings, from house to house,
your devoted

*Abraham*

1. Breasted, 1905.
2. Abraham did not carry out this intention. After the break between Stekel and Freud, which happened shortly afterwards, Freud and his followers withdrew from the *Zentralblatt*, which was edited by Stekel.

3. *Sexuelle Zwischenstufe* [sexual intermediate stage], a term coined by Magnus Hirschfeld for describing people with strong features of the opposite sex, supposedly linked to homosexuality (cf. the *Zeitschrift für sexuelle Zwischenstufen*, edited by him).
4. Abraham, 1911[26].
5. As analysed by Freud and traced back to the father relation, in the postscript to the Schreber analysis (Freud, 1912a).
6. Latin: "for the sake of propagating belief".
7. Oskar Felix Kohnstamm [1871–1917], German psychiatrist, known for his work on the psychopathology of memory and the so-called Kohnstamm phenomenon. Author of works on psychopathology, psychotherapy, hypnosis, the unconscious, art, and the soul.

127F

Vienna IX, Berggasse 19
3 June 1912

Dear Friend,

I have read your Egyptian study with the pleasure that I always derive both from your way of writing and your way of thinking, and should like to make only two objections, or, rather, suggestions for alteration.[1] Firstly, you claim that when the mother is particularly important, the conflict with the father takes milder forms. I for my part have no evidence of this and must assume that you have had special experiences in this respect. As the matter is not clear to me, I ask you to revise this passage. Secondly, I have doubts about presenting the king as so distinctly a neurotic, which is in sharp contrast with his exceptional energy and achievements, as we associate neuroticism, a term that has become scientifically inexact, precisely with the idea of being inhibited. After all, we all have these complexes, and we must beware of not being called neurotic. If we have successfully stood up against them, we should be spared the name. Perhaps nothing of value will have been sacrificed if you call your work a character study and leave the neurotic as an object of comparison in the background. I cannot judge from my knowledge of the literature how positive the evidence for real neurotic symptoms in Amenhotep IV is. If you have such evidence, do quote the accounts in full.

In cyclothymic cases you should just go on digging; one can see more the next time. The difficulty lies not in finding the material but in linking up what has been found and grouping it according to its layers. Yet, I have also got the impression from your paper, which I value so highly, that the formula is not assured and the elements not yet convincingly linked. If I knew any more than you, I should not withhold it from you, but you will learn more from the cases themselves.—

I am glad to hear that you continue to be satisfied with the practice. I notice that the beginnings of our holidays coincide. I am going first to

1912 June

Karlsbad with my wife. In the middle of August we want to meet the others, but it is not at all certain where. There is not enough time left for Switzerland.

Over Whitsuntide I was in Constance for two days as Binswanger's guest. Zurich could not be fitted in.[2] I am now resting from more serious work. The *Taboo*[3] is to appear in the next issue of *Imago*. You will just have received the last technical paper in the *Zentralblatt*.[4] The Society has adjourned its sessions. Jones is expected for the middle of June.[5]

Most cordial greetings, to you and to your dear wife and children, your

*Freud*

1. Abraham modified his paper (1912[34]) in accordance with Freud's suggestions (see letter 128A, 9 June 1912).
2. From 25 to 28 May 1912, Freud had visited Ludwig Binswanger, after the latter's cancer operation (cf. Binswanger, 1956: pp. 38–43; Freud & Ferenczi, 1992: pp. 376–377; Freud & Jung, 1974 [1906–13]: pp. 508ff). Jung had been of the opinion that Freud had not informed him in a timely fashion about this visit in Kreuzlingen, which is not far from Zurich. He had not been at home, however, when Freud's letter of 23 May arrived (in those days mail between the major cities of Central Europe usually took no more than one day). This "Kreuzlingen gesture", as Jung termed it, was to play an important part in the alienation between Freud and Jung.
3. "Taboo and Emotional Ambivalence", later the second chapter of *Totem and Taboo*.
4. Freud, 1912b.
5. Jones accompanied his morphine-addicted mistress, Loë Kann, from Toronto to Vienna, where she started an analysis with Freud (see Freud & Ferenczi, 1992: pp. 486–387; Freud & Jones, 1993: pp. 134ff).

## 128A

Berlin
9 June 1912

Dear Professor,

I had already heard from Herr Rank about your two objections to my paper and immediately asked him to return my manuscript. I shall revise it as soon as I get it back. I shall merely compare Ikhnaton with the neurotic, as I did with Segantini. I shall look into the other question further with the help of my clinical material. There is some truth in my statement, but it is untenable in the general form in which I put it forward.

I hope that, after all, something useful will emerge in the end.

Many thanks for the reprint! I enjoyed every word of the essay. This same issue of the *Zentralblatt* celebrates the inauguration of the "Open Forum" with something by Marcinowski,[1] to which I must reply out of politeness. If one knows him, one knows what resistances lie behind it.

This particular sort of grandiosity complex is difficult to put up with. He would like to act as the final censor of Ψα.

*Imago* certainly comes at the right moment! Interest in Germany is rapidly increasing, except among doctors.

I am longing for the holidays. Ten hours of analysis are ample in this heat. What a pity that our holiday destinations are so far apart!—I hope to do some preparatory work on a linguistic subject during the holidays.

For today, cordial greetings to you and your family, also from my wife,

your devoted

*Abraham*

1. Marcinowski, 1912, in which he criticized Abraham's article on depression (1911[26]).


## 129F

Vienna IX, Berggasse 19
14 June 1912

Dear Friend,

Many thanks for your willingness to consider my suggestions concerning the Pharaoh. The work will, I hope, be an adornment for *Imago*, which is, incidentally, going surprisingly well. 230 subscribers on account from the first issue on, mostly from Germany. Vienna has *very little* part in it.

I too think you have a right to holidays. This year I have been more productive than in earlier years and am visiting Karlsbad again also for this reason. September, as I have perhaps already said, is still quite uncertain; so it is not at all improbable that we shall meet again in that month.

The Open Forum in the *Zentralblatt* is certainly a good institution. I felt very little sympathy for Marcinowski, but the last time he was here he conquered much ground. That he does not join is a symptom of his neurosis, with which his censorious cravings, which astonish you, are probably also connected. But I learn a bit more tolerance every day, and I am satisfied if someone has only a few good sides, which is certainly the case with M.

Your approval of the last technical article was very valuable to me. You will probably have noticed the critical intentions. At present my intellectual activity would have been limited to correcting the proofs of the 4th edition of *Everyday Life*,[1] if it had not suddenly occurred to me that the opening scene of Lear, the judgement of Paris, and the choice of caskets in the Merchant of Venice are based on the same motif, which I

have to track now.² I have also the most lively interest in your projected escapades. Departure from Vienna: 14 July.
With cordial greetings to you and your whole house,
your devoted
*Freud*

1. Freud, 1901b, fourth edition 1912.
2. Freud, 1913f.

## 130F

Vienna IX, Berggasse 19
3 July 1912

Dear Friend,

It is excellent that you should so soon have reached the utmost in your practice, but now turn the tables and start to defend yourself against the blessing. The first rule, if the flow continues, must be to increase your fees, and you must find time to work and rest. The answer to your question how I manage to write in addition to my practice is, simply, that I have to recuperate from $\Psi\alpha$ by working, otherwise I do not endure it.

Your superb contributions to the *Zentralblatt*[1] please me very much for the reader's sake, and I look forward with special personal excitement to the recently announced contribution on paranoia.[2] It would, after all, be nice if we were right about this topic, and theoretically important. But the *Imago*, which is a youngest and most favourite child for me, not least because of the editors,[3] should not be neglected in any case. I am working with my last, or penultimate, ounce of strength on my article on taboo, which is to continue the horror of incest. In addition, I hope to have thrown analytic light on guilt-feelings and conscience, but this shall make its appearance only later.

I have no special experience of impotent fetishists. Your prognosis is quite probable; yet, each case is different. Masochists have given me poor results.

Kronfeld's work is now really stirring up opinions against us. I can find nothing in it but a laudable decent tone, the "logic" in it is not worth mentioning.

Could not Eitingon take patients off your hands to a greater extent? He has sent me a case on which he had begun incredibly correctly.

With cordial greetings to you and your dear house,
your faithfully devoted
*Freud*[4]

1. Abraham, 1911[28], 1911[29], 1912[32].
2. See letter 126A, 28 May 1912.
3. Rank and Sachs.
4. Shortly afterwards, on 15 July 1912, Freud left for Karlsbad.

## 131A

Kurort Stoos ob Brunnen
24 July 1912

Dear Professor,

Your last letter is already six weeks old and still unanswered. You have now been in Karlsbad for a while—I hope with good results—and I may disturb your holiday peace with a few lines. Above all I am interested to know how you imagine a possible meeting in September. Are you perhaps coming to Berlin? I shall be there again about 21 August. Naturally a rendezvous somewhere else would suit me too, if it is not too far from Berlin. At any rate I am already looking forward to it very much. In view of this possibility of a discussion, I will not go into scientific matters today.

To my great joy, the new editions are succeeding each other at a rapid rate. [ . . . ][1] at last the "Jokes" is among them too.[2] I had been waiting for that for a long time. And first of all the quick success of Imago is a favourable sign. Shortly before I left, Ferenczi and Rank visited me.[3] I got the latter to tell me things in more detail. He also brought me the *Incest Motive*.[4] I have taken it with me on holiday. I cannot yet say much about it; only that it gives the impression of a mature work, and that it definitely will be of great service to the whole cause.

Shortly before I left, Ikhnaton went off, in a revised form, to the editorial office of *Imago*. I am expecting the proofs here.

I am enjoying the peace to the full here. Since the short Christmas holidays I have done my ten hours of analysis a day. The practice has also become more lucrative. Up to now the months of 1912 have already brought me 11,000 M. But I will soon go for my first rise in fees. You see, even in Berlin it is no longer a martyrdom to be your follower.

With cordial greetings to you and your wife from my wife and me.
Your devoted

*Abraham*

1. One word illegible.
2. Freud, 1905c, second edition 1912.
3. Ferenczi had been in Berlin, approximately between 26 June and 3 July, to conduct experiments with a clairvoyante, Frau Seidler. We have no details about Rank's visit.
4. Rank, 1912.

1912 August

## 132F

Karlsbad
29 July 1912

Dear Friend,

It is wonderful that you have such good news. But now it is time for you to put your honorarium up, or you are harming the "cause" doubly if you do not get down to work. My travel plans are very complicated this year as a result of various circumstances. Until 10–12 August here, then from the middle to the end of August in Karersee,[1] Latemar Hotel. There we shall be visited by a young man from Hamburg, who has been *publicly* engaged to my daughter Sophie since yesterday, Max Halberstadt, photographer, Neuer Wall, a very nice, refined man, and now very much in love.[2] From 1–8–10 September, S. Cristoforo on Lake Caldonazzo, where Ferenczi is coming as well. Then a journey to England, perhaps with Brill. Jones has promised to show us London in any case; he will be back from the congresses by then. I should be glad to see you at any of these stops, naturally I can promise you least for Karersee. If none of this fits, I can think of coming back through Berlin, so as to see you and make up for the cancellation of this year's congress, although I know that you yourself will then be at work. I am waiting for your further comments.

That you want to leave me in peace as far as scientific matters are concerned is nice, but not sufficient. I am preoccupied with what is going on in Zurich, which seems to prove the truth of an old prediction of yours, which I willingly ignored. I shall certainly contribute nothing to the break, and I hope that the scientific companionship can be sustained.

With cordial greetings to you and your wife, and best wishes for your holidays.

Your faithfully devoted,

*Freud*

1. Karersee/Lago di Carezza, in the South Tyrol.
2. Sophie [1893–1920], Freud's second daughter, and Max Halberstadt [1882–1940] married in 1913. The couple had two sons, Ernst Wolfgang [b. 1914], now a psychoanalyst in Germany, and Heinz Rudolph ("Heinerle") [1918–1923]. Sophie died in the influenza epidemic after the First World War when she was pregnant with a third child.

## 133A

Kurhaus Stoos ob Brunnen
9 August 1912

Dear Professor,

In the time between my last card and today's letter, there fell a rather long bronchial catarrh, which has embellished my holiday. In practice, however, it made little difference, as it has been raining so hard for the past week that it was impossible to go out of doors in any case. I hope you are having a pleasanter time and that you also get the expected results from the cure.

Now for the question of our meeting! We are leaving here tomorrow for Brunnen, from there on the 17th to Zurich for a day, then to Bremen to my parents, and on the 23rd we shall be back in Berlin. There is quite a great deal of work waiting for me at home, and I cannot really interrupt it again straight away in order to meet you in the Tyrol. Other considerations, too, make it impossible for me.

I should like most of all to go to London with you, but for that too I should need a long enough holiday. So I will count on your return journey through Germany. I should be particularly happy to see you in Berlin. But you should not orientate your plans to mine, if it is inconvenient for you. I could, for example, travel in your direction, meet you in some town, etc. In any case, I shall see to it that I have the necessary time free.

I have heard quite a few things about Zurich in the last few weeks. Details had better be left for discussion when we meet. My prognosis is not too unfavourable. Jung's resistances are reminiscent of Adler's in their motivation but, since we are dealing with a person without a paraphrenic tendency, it might well all change again, just as it did four years ago. Unfortunately, he wavers between the rejecting behaviour of recent times and an uncompromising go-aheadedness. I believe the latter has cost us *more* than the former. I do not only have Bleuler in mind. I am glad that we are not having a congress just now; I think everything will have smoothed itself out by next year.

The scientific points I hinted at recently are very varied in character and are therefore hardly suitable for a holiday letter. I only wish to mention briefly one question that has occupied me for some time. It concerns a case of hay fever[1] cured by $\Psi\alpha$, and the theoretical conclusions to be drawn from it. I was treating the patient last spring for a neurosis. During the first months of analysis he suffered from severe hay fever and particularly from hay-asthma. I did not discharge him without searching for the psycho-sexual roots of the hay fever too. I have recently heard from him that—in addition to the general improvement—he has also remained free from hay fever this year.

I am now awaiting more news, dear Professor. My address from tomorrow until the 16th: *Brunnen* (Switzerland) poste restante, then *Bremen*, Uhlandstr. 20.

With cordial greetings to you and your wife,
your devoted

*Abraham*

1. Cf. letter 220A, 16 June 1914.

## 134F

Karlsbad
11 August 1912

Dear Friend,

I am replying immediately in order not to miss you in this migratory period. As you say, our meeting will have to take place in Berlin on the way back, or somewhere on the way. What would be most delightful would be your joining us in London between 10 September and the 18th or thereabouts.

I am glad you accord a good prognosis to the relationship with Jung, I know you are not exactly an optimist in this respect. But still, it is not the same as four years ago. Then the vacillation took place behind my back; when I found out about it, it was surmounted. This time I have felt obliged to react to the changed behaviour towards me and in so doing to lay down the armour of friendship in order to show him that he cannot at his pleasure assume privileges like no one else. How he will take this, I cannot foresee. So far he has expressed a firm determination not to stage an external break.

The last week of our stay is being spoiled by the appalling weather. We hope to be at the Hotel Latemar, Karersee, on the 16th inst., from where you will hear from me.

With cordial greetings to you and your dear wife, and with thanks for your congratulations.

Your faithfully devoted

*Freud*

## 135A

Bremen[1]
19 August 1912

Dear Professor,

Many thanks for your letter; I hope you are now having a pleasant after-cure in the Tyrol.

On the 21st I am back again in Berlin and hope to hear there about your plans for your journey. I have heard more in Zurich about transformations of the libido[2] there. I would rather tell you about that when we meet!

I wish you and yours very happy vacation days. The greetings, which I also add in my wife's name, are also especially for the bridal couple.

yours, as ever,

*K. Abraham*

1. Postcard.

2. Allusion to the title of Jung, 1911–12, a work that was to bring about the scientific break with Freud.

## 136F

Karersee
24 August 1912

Dear Friend,

If the loss of the letter in which you asked for a honorarium has had any consequences, *I* am not convinced that it went down with the Titanic. Jelliffe,[1] in fact, is one of the worst American businessmen, translate: crooks, Columbus has discovered.

In *any case* you should demand an honorarium for the independent edition. Whether it is correct to do so without asking the Viennese publisher, I do not know.

It would be best to ask Deuticke himself, who is in such things very decent and—resigned.

I am very well here.

In unchangeable[2] libido,
Yours,

*Freud*

1. Smith Ely Jelliffe [1866–1945], M.D., from New York City, important medical editor, pioneer psychoanalyst, one of the earliest advocates of psychosomatic medicine. He had not yet met Freud but had become acquainted with Abraham in 1908 in Berlin, where he had studied with Ziehen and Oppenheim. In 1907 he had founded, with William A. White, the *Nervous and Mental Disease Monograph Series*, in which Abraham's *Dreams and Myths* (1909[14]), originally published by Deuticke in Vienna, appeared in 1913. (Cf. Burnham, 1983.)
2. Play on the German word *unwandelbar* [unchangeable, unable to be transformed], picking up Abraham's allusion to Jung in the previous letter.

## 137A

Berlin
13 September 1912

Dear Professor,

I gather from the enclosed card that you were so kind as to give my address to a lady. The card was marked by the Post office as undeliverable, and by mistake was not sent back to you, but delivered to me. I have tried to forward it to the lady; but no such name exists in the directory. There must be some mistake.

1912 October

I heard from Ferenczi that you are not going to England. I hope soon to hear something about the changed programme![1] With cordial greetings to you and yours!
Yours,

*Karl Abraham*

1. Freud had originally planned to travel to London with Ferenczi and Rank for a week in the autumn and to Scotland with Ferenczi for an additional week. On 30 August the Freud family travelled to Bolzano, where Ferenczi met them. Afterwards, they all wanted to go to S. Cristoforo, in the vicinity of Trento. But Freud's daughter Mathilde fell ill in Vienna during this time, and so both men went to her. Once Mathilde was better again, they caught up with Freud's family in S. Cristoforo. Instead of going to Great Britain later, Freud and Ferenczi opted to stay in Rome.

## 138A

Berlin
13 October 1912

Dear Professor,

The last weeks have been a sorrowful time for us. A fortnight ago my father-in-law died from the after-effects of a stroke after being unconscious for nine days. Now that we have got back into somewhat calmer waters again, I can at last reply to your news and greetings from Italy. I hope that you and your family have all come back refreshed from your holiday!

First I must bore you with those translation matters once more. I wrote to Deuticke as you advised; he asked for M. 15.– per printed sheet, M. 80.– in all, and a few copies of the translation. I asked the same for myself, and I do not think I have claimed anything out of the ordinary (20 dollars for Deuticke and myself together). You have rated Jelliffe quite rightly; the enclosed letter[1] shows that. Now how should one answer this naughty boy? I should like to ask you at the same time to be so kind as to bring the letter to Deuticke's notice. Would it not be a good thing in any case to have our literature protected in all such cases by reserving the copyright?

Owing to the upsets of the last weeks, I have scarcely found the time to read the new papers in the *Jahrbuch*, etc., with the exception of your short paper,[2] which I have studied with pleasure and admiration.

I, too, should like to publish something on the subject of impotence before long. During this year I have treated two men with *potentia coeundi* but who, over the course of many years, have never had an emission. Both have been cured by $\Psi\alpha$. One, whose marriage had been childless, is now looking forward to becoming a father. I cannot find anything about the mentioned symptom in the literature, but merely mention of delayed emission in contrast to premature ejaculation.[3] I assume that you have also come across such cases and would ask you, if it is not too much trouble, to let me have a few words about them sometime.

I very much regret that our meeting never took place. There is so much from the various scientific fields that I should have liked to talk over. I have been wondering whether I could make a short trip to Vienna during the winter. Could you, dear Professor, tell me now when I would disturb you least, perhaps just before Christmas, or between Christmas and the New Year, or after the New Year?

With cordial greetings from my wife and myself to you and your family,

Yours,

*Abraham*

1. Missing.
2. Freud, 1912d. The *Jahrbuch* had come out in September.
3. Abraham did not devote a paper to the topic but briefly mentioned these two cases of *impotentia ejaculandi* in his 1917 paper on *ejaculatio præcox* (1917[54]: pp. 297–298).

## 139F

Vienna IX, Berggasse 19
21 October 1912

Dear Friend,

Your letter has been with Deuticke for a long time; I myself have been prevented from replying for a few days; I also know why. It is hard to know what to do with the American, and what is more, the fellow is impudent. You could refer to your supposed part in the misfortune of the Atlantic (but she has a different name!), in the end you will have to give in.

My condolences on the tragic event in your family; it is to be hoped that your dear wife has recognized as some consolation the advantages of a quick death.

I like your Amenhotep in its revised form very much better, it is an adornment of our *Imago*, which continues to count on you.

I have heard in quite a number of my cases of an absence of ejaculation as a $\psi$ disturbance, but at the time of the analysis the disturbance was already over and had given way to a common anaesthesia with excellent motor potency. I have not treated cases like yours.

Now to what preys on my mind. I find it embarrassing to think that we should get on so well because we meet so rarely. (With Ferenczi it goes just as well, incidentally, despite our frequently being together.) So

1912 November

I should most willingly accept your offer to come to Vienna, were it not for my daughter's engagement, which is already known to you, to the young man from Hamburg, which would affect just the time you have in mind. We are expecting his visit around Christmas, before the wedding, which has been arranged for February. There is, however, again a consolation, as I shall certainly be going at least once a year to Hamburg to see the child, and that will provide the most excellent opportunity to pay you a visit in Berlin.

I am now in deepest labour with the continuation of the "points of agreement"[1] and with technical papers for the *Zentralblatt*.[2] The taboo will soon greet you in the form of an offprint. The political worries are also troubling us much, but I take them coolly. Jones, whose wife I am now treating—he himself is in Italy—has become personally very attached.

I send my cordial greetings to you and your whole house,
your faithfully devoted

*Freud*

1. I.e. *Totem and Taboo*, which had originally appeared in four parts in *Imago*, under the general title *Über einige Übereinstimmungen im Seelenleben der Wilden und der Neurotiker* [Some points of agreement between the mental lives of savages and neurotics].
2. Freud, 1912e; the following technical papers by Freud appeared in the *Zeitschrift* (see letter 126A, 28 May 1912, n. 2, and the following letter).

## 140F

Vienna IX, Berggasse 19
3 November 1912

Dear Friend,

Just a brief official note that I am no longer editor of the *Zentralblatt* and that Stekel is going his own way. (I am so glad about it; you cannot know what I have suffered under the obligation to defend him against the whole world. He is an unbearable person.) The occasion for the split was not a scientific one, but a presumption on his part against another member of the Society whom he wished to exclude from the reviews in "his paper", which I could not permit.[1]

I of course have in mind starting a new journal to take the place of the *Zentralblatt*, and ask you to withdraw your name from the latter and no longer to direct the papers from your group to it. In the next few days a circular letter will ask you to take these steps and to cooperate with the new organ. I was about to offer you the editorship of the latter and let myself be deflected only by the consideration that luckily your practice already keeps you busy to the point of excess. I have therefore turned to Ferenczi, but should much like to hear your views on this proposal.

Be it you or Ferenczi—at a time when Ψα is in danger of splintering and discussions with adherents come on top of the battle against those outside, such a journal means a great deal to me, and the expulsion of such a doubtful character as Stekel remains a blessing.

I shall keep you informed of how things develop with the publishers, etc.

In greeting you cordially,
your faithfully devoted,

*Freud*

1. Victor Tausk [1879–1919] became a lawyer and judge in Croatia after studying law in Vienna; from 1906 to 1908 he was active as a writer and journalist in Berlin. In 1908 he went to Vienna, and, in order to be able to become a psychoanalyst, he studied medicine and became a psychiatrist [1914]. Tausk is considered to be a pioneer in the psychoanalytic investigation of the psychoses. (Cf. Tausk, 1919, in Roazen, 1991. For the relations between him, Freud, and Lou Andreas-Salomé and for the motives for his suicide, see Roazen, 1969, 1990 and Eissler, 1971, 1983.)

    Tausk was supposed to take over the discussion section of the *Zentralblatt*, but Stekel declared that "he would never concede to having Dr Tausk write in *his* journal" (Freud & Ferenczi, 1992: p. 418; see also Jones, 1955: p. 136). According to a version of the story presented by Freud and Federn in 1929 (Nunberg & Federn, 1975, only in German edition: pp. 108–109), Stekel provoked this incident in order to force Freud out of the *Zentralblatt* and to be able to take it over himself.

    The break between Stekel and Freud is described from the latter's point of view by, among others, Jones (1955: pp. 136–137), Clark (1980: p. 357), and Gay (1988: p. 232). Stekel's version can be found in his autobiography (1950: pp. 142–145). His resignation from the Society was announced on 6 November. Freud founded the *Internationale Zeitschrift für ärztliche Psychoanalyse* (Vienna: Hugo Heller) as the new official organ of the IPA; he was the director, and Ferenczi, Rank, and Jones were the editors. It was published six times a year, beginning in January 1913. The *Zentralblatt* continued to exist under Stekel's sole leadership until September 1914, when it folded.

## 141A

Berlin
5 November 1912

Dear Professor,

It is very painful for me that once again you have to suffer from ruthlessness from one of those who owe you everything.

I had the following idea after receiving your letter today. If Ferenczi takes on the editing, I might be able to help in some other way. If he declines, then I am at your disposal. Should the proposal be put to me definitely, then what would be most congenial to me would be to collaborate with Ferenczi—if that is technically feasible.

My other work should not be a reason for declining the offer in this case. I have, incidentally, already talked to Eitingon, who says that he is ready to help in any way possible.—At the moment I am not clear what is to happen to the *Zentralblatt*, and whether the new journal will be the official organ. I shall probably learn that from the circular letter.

It is so difficult to discuss all this by letter. If you, dear Professor, should wish for verbal negotiations, I could manage it on a Sunday (for instance, on 24 November). The journey to Vienna does, of course, take a great deal of time, and I cannot easily leave my practice for a period of several days. Perhaps, though, we could meet halfway (Prague or Breslau). We could travel on Saturday afternoon, have the whole of Sunday, and travel home during Sunday night.

That is all for today. I am in a hurry and shall therefore not go into your letter of 21 October, for which many thanks.

With cordial greetings,
Yours,
*Abraham*

## 142F

Vienna IX, Berggasse 19
21 November 1912

Dear Friend,

So I can expect to see you sooner than intended, on the 24th inst. in Munich.[1] Meanwhile a bitter cup has passed you by. Ferenczi and Rank have undertaken the editorship of the new journal. For your kind willingness I owe you an explanation of the choice. I had begun negotiations with a Berlin publisher,[2] which seemed promising. If they had come to anything I should have asked you to undertake it, with Eitingon's help. But the Berlin publisher let me down and, as I had to decide on Heller, the publisher of *Imago*, I could only choose the editor in the neighbourhood of the publisher. I know that you will not take this amiss.

I have had a great deal of worry and anger over the affair. All our internal and external colleagues have come with us, only Jung (!) and Juliusburger, who does not seem to be informed at all and therefore does not wish to sever the connection with the *Zentralblatt*, have declined.[3] In addition, one Viennese has also expressed certain reservations.[4] But the bliss of being rid of Stekel is worth some sacrifice.

I hope there will be an hour for an intimate exchange of thoughts in Munich, and send my cordial greetings to you and your whole house,
cordially yours,
*Freud*

1. At the meeting of heads of the local psychoanalytic societies, at which it was agreed to leave the *Zentralblatt* to Stekel and to found the *Zeitschrift* as the official organ of the IPA. Present were, apart from Freud and Abraham, Jones, Jung, Ophuijsen (representing

Maeder), Riklin, and Seif. (Cf. Freud & Ferenczi, 1992: pp. 433–435; Freud & Jung, 1974 [1906–13]: pp. 521–522.)

Alphonse Maeder [1882–1971], Swiss psychotherapist, chairman of the Zurich Society. He followed Jung after the latter's separation from Freud.

Johan H. W. Ophuijsen [1882–1950], Dutch psychiatrist, at the Burghölzli 1903–1913. Co-founder [1917] of the Dutch Society. In 1934 he emigrated to New York.

Franz Riklin [1878–1938], Swiss psychiatrist, collaborator on Jung's association studies. After the Nuremberg Congress [1910] he became secretary of the IPA and, with Jung, editor of the *Korrespondenzblatt*, which was founded there. Like Maeder, he supported Jung after the break.

Leonhard Seif [1866–1949], neurologist in Munich, founder [1911] and head of the Psychoanalytic Society there. In 1913 he separated from Freud and joined Adler.

2. Erich Reiss [1887–1951], publisher of the journals *Zukunft* and *Schaubühne*. He was interned in 1937; after his release, he emigrated to Sweden, then to England, and eventually to New York.
3. At the Munich meeting, however, Jung went along with Freud unreservedly.
4. Herbert Silberer [1882–1923], sports journalist, balloonist, and private scholar, member of the Wednesday Society from October 1910 on. He was interested in the investigation of dreams and symbols, alchemy, and occultism. (Cf. Freud to Ferenczi, 14 November 1912, Freud & Ferenczi, 1992: p. 431.)

## 143A

Berlin
1 December 1912

Dear Professor,

Now that a week has passed since the conference in Munich, I hope that you too will have come to the conclusion that the end result was a favourable one. Being liberated from Stekel has brought with it the advantage of narrowing the rift between Vienna and Zurich. If, as I hope, I come to see you in a few weeks, perhaps we can talk more of this than the short time in M.[unich] allowed.

Today, reluctant as I am to take up your time, I have to make two requests. On Thursday we have a session in which I have to give a report on the *Zentralblatt* business. As Stekel has in the meantime made further attempts to turn matters in his direction, I should like some really accurate information in order to be able to deal smoothly with all questions. There are two points that came up in M.[unich], which I do not now remember exactly: (1.) in what way did Bergmann[1] break the contract? (2.) how far did Stekel take advantage of the wishes for a falling-off of the Zurichers? I should be glad of some more information on this. If the two questions cannot be answered quite briefly, perhaps you will ask Dr Rank to write to me what is necessary.

Now the second request. As long as Ziehen held the Chair here, I could not carry out my long-standing plan of writing my *Habilitation*.[2] The present Professor, Bonhoeffer,[3] is a much pleasanter person. To him

I have a very good recommendation from Professor Liepmann. I know from your report that Kraus is becoming increasingly sympathetic to our cause. If both Bonhoeffer and Kraus were to support me, the chances would not be entirely bad. (The anti-Semitism of the Faculty does, naturally, remain an obstacle.) My request is this: would you send a few words of recommendation to Kraus about me, so that if Bonhoeffer approaches him he will know what it is all about?

Although I had already buried these plans regarding the *Habilitation*, two considerations induced me to take them up once again: apart from the usefulness to my practice to be expected from it, above all there is the hope that I might be able to awaken interest in our cause among the students—something I could not do so far among the doctors.

I thank you, dear Professor, in anticipation of your kindness. I am saving up everything else to tell you personally.

With the most cordial greetings to you and yours, also from my wife, your devoted

*Abraham*

1. The publisher of the *Zentralblatt* in Wiesbaden (see also letter of 3 December). Finally, for 652 marks in damages, the title of official organ of the IPA was removed from the *Zentralblatt* (Freud to Ferenczi, 9 December 1912, Freud & Ferenczi, 1992: p. 440; see also the note to this effect in the first issue of the *Zeitschrift*, 1913, *1*: 111). A year earlier, Bergmann had already been approached by Freud with the injunction that he would have to choose between Adler, then still co-editor of the *Zentralblatt*, and Freud himself, whereupon Adler had announced his resignation.
2. A prerequisite to being eligible for tenure.
3. Karl Bonhoeffer [1868–1948], noted German psychiatrist, professor in Breslau and Berlin, where the psychiatric clinic is named after him. Father of the theologian Dietrich Bonhoeffer, who was murdered by the SS in 1945.

## 144F

Vienna IX, Berggasse 19
3 December 1912

Dear Friend,

Gladly, gladly will I give you the warmest recommendation to Kraus, *as soon as* you wish. I only fear that nothing will come of it, because that would be too good. I do not know Kraus personally, and, until the acceptance of the two chapters for his book,[1] I have had no relations with him whatsoever. But we will try it, particularly if you promise that in the event of success you will greatly increase your fees.

To complete your information: (1.) B[ergmann]'s breach of contract, if you want to call it that, consists in the fact that he replied to my question, as to whether I could dismiss St.[ekel] or rather sent word, that everything should remain as it was this year; next year he would in any case not keep the paper any longer. (2.) Stekel showed Riklin's Congress Report[2] around in Vienna and commended it as a proof of the impending falling-off of the Z.[urichers]. I believe that is why he chose just that point in time for his trial of strength.

I shall be very delighted to see you here already before Christmas. You must, of course, include a Sunday.

With cordial greetings,
Yours,

*Freud*

P.S.: I received a very kind letter from Jung[3] shortly after returning from Munich, but have not yet had any news about the outcome of his trip to Wiesbaden.

1. Friedrich Kraus had invited Freud to contribute to a new encyclopaedia of internal medicine. For various reasons (cf. Jones, 1955: pp. 248–249), this project did not come to fruition, and the work (Kraus & Brugsch, 1919–1927) was published after the war without psychoanalytic contributions.
2. Presumably the report of the Third Psychoanalytic Congress in Weimar [21–22 September 1911] in the *Zentralblatt* (1912, 2: 231–237).
3. Letter of 26 November 1912 (Freud & Jung, 1974 [1906–13]: pp. 522–523).

## 145F

Vienna IX, Berggasse 19
12 December 1912

Dear Friend,

The letter to Kraus has long since reached its destination; but whether also its purpose?

Come to us when you can. I shall in any case benefit from you only on Sunday, but then in plenty. Let me know for when I can book a room for you at the Hotel Regina.[1]

Tell your dear wife that we do not want you to get indigestion anywhere but with us.

Otherwise all at last is quiet.

I look forward to seeing you again.

Yours cordially,

*Freud*

1. Most of Freud's visitors usually stayed in the Hotel Regina—which still exists today, at the present Sigmund Freud park—five minutes' walk from Freud's apartment.

## 146A

Berlin[1]
18 December 1912

Dear Professor,

I intend to arrive in Vienna on Saturday morning. It is very kind of you to offer to book accommodation for me; I accept your offer with gratitude.

Looking forward to seeing you again soon, I send my warmest regards to you and yours, also on behalf of my wife.

Your devoted

*Abraham*

1. Postcard.

## 147A

Berlin
27 December 1912

Dear Professor,

It is only today that I find time to send you a sign of life. The indisposition that began in Vienna worsened somewhat over the next few days. Now I am better and do not want to delay any longer in sending you, first of all, my thanks. What for is, however, difficult to enumerate. And it is almost impossible to thank with words for the warm reception in your home, and for all the personal interest you showed in me. If a recent criticism made of you is justified—that you treat your followers like patients[1]—then I have to reproach you with several grave technical errors. First, you *spoil* your patients, and it is well known that one should not do so. Second, you have given presents to the patient, which might give him a completely wrong idea of the treatment. And finally, before my departure from treatment, you had secretly been in my hotel to pay the bill. "If you had been a psychoanalyst", you would not have done such a thing, since, at the end of the cure, the patient should know as much about his case as the physician. You, however, kept a secret from me. And you do know, after all, how easily a feeling of guilt can lead to a hostile attitude! But since I was in general satisfied with the "treatment", I shall not make a complaint, and can only give you once again my heartfelt thanks for everything. Please give the enclosed lines[2] to your wife!

There is not yet much else to say today. I shall, if possible, despatch the grandparents paper[3] within the next few days. After that, a short article about a screen-memory[4] is to follow very soon.

Yet another request, on my wife's behalf. She would be happy to translate English and French articles that come in for one of the two journals. Up to now, I believe, the editors have mostly done it themselves; perhaps they would be glad of such a lightening of their work load.

With cordial greetings, also from my wife,
your devoted

*Abraham*

1. As claimed by Jung.
2. Missing.
3. Abraham, 1913[40].
4. Abraham, 1913[38].

# 1913

148F
Vienna IX, Berggasse 19
1 January 1913

Dear Friend,

Thank you for your friendly lines. The hospitality we are able to provide in Vienna, and what I in particular am able to do in that respect, is so little.

Now accept my cordial good wishes for the New Year, which will certainly not be an easy one for us. The past year achieved something nice on the very last day with a letter from Fr. Kraus, from which I gather that he asked you to call on him and is by no means disinclined to your cause. He still counts on "Bonhoeffer's approval" and confirms that you have a good reputation—even among the opponents. The letter was very decent, exceptional for someone who will soon be a privy councillor. Will you keep me informed about how things develop?

Stekel is to give a talk in Berlin on the 6th of January. Stöcker,[1] as I told you, excused herself to me on the basis of ignorance of the state of affairs, which was forgivable at that time and expressed her opinion that nothing can be done now. That may be so, but he should still feel that he has an anachronism to thank for his invitation, and he should feel inhibited to some extent in his productions. Firstly, he will lie shamelessly about the reasons for his resignation. I have already prepared Stöcker for this. Secondly, he will obviously preach Adlerism, as he is now in their employ, and politeness need not go *so* far as to acclaim everything he says. He should be reminded of the change of conditions. So have another word with Stöcker, and think how anxious he might be made in his godlikeness.

Forgive the nasty affair; politics corrupt the character.

Yours cordially,

*Freud*

1. Dr Helene Stöcker [1869–1943], German feminist, sexual reformer, and pacifist, had become a member of the Berlin Psychoanalytic Society in June 1912. She had been acquainted with Lou Andreas-Salomé since 1900. Shortly afterwards, on 5 March 1913, she was a guest at the Vienna Society (Andreas-Salomé, 1958: p. 112; Nunberg & Federn, 1975: p. 172). Stöcker was co-founder of the *Bund für Mutterschutz* [League for Mothers' Protection] and editor of its journal, *Mutterschutz*. In 1933 she emigrated to New York.

## 149A

Berlin
5 January 1913

Dear Professor,

Many thanks for your letter and your good wishes, which I heartily reciprocate.

Kraus asked me just before the New Year to go to see him. In the course of my visit he told me that he has made enquiries about me and that the replies were favourable, and he advised me in any case to submit a *Habilitation*. He promised to do what he could and asked for a list of my earlier, non-psychoanalytic papers. By this, he has at least shown a friendly interest. His influence within the Faculty is very great, although Bonhoeffer will have the final say in my case. I shall now work on a most innocuous theme. Then I will have to mobilize my old contacts. Bleuler might be able to influence Bonhoeffer favourably; it is also important for me to win over one or two other members of the Faculty. Keibel, my former teacher in Freiburg,[1] could give me an effective recommendation to one of the two anatomists; one of them—Waldeyer[2]—has a great deal of influence. In prehistoric times I did several years of microscopic work under Keibel. In spite of all this, I am not too optimistic about this matter.

Now for the Stekel affair. I would have followed your suggestion if circumstances had not intervened in the meantime, as you will see by the enclosure.[3] Yesterday I spoke to Frau Dr Stöcker by telephone about it. In any case, we can be indifferent about Stekel's lecture to the *Bund für Mutterschutz* on January 6th. Before the conflict in Vienna, Stöcker had already asked Stekel to reserve an evening for a social gathering. Recently Juliusburger dealt privately with Stekel, agreed with him that the lecture would be on the 5th, and saw to it that Stöcker should put the lecture and the social gathering together in one evening. Who is going to grace this scientific evening is still not clear to me. I myself have naturally refused Stöcker's invitation on the grounds that I felt far too repulsed by Stekel's behaviour. At the same time I expressed to her my displeasure that two members of our group should arrange such an evening, bypassing the existing organization. She then rang me, and I had with her the conversation I mentioned above. She was very embarrassed that she had taken part in the rather peculiar event and approved absolutely of my standpoint.

It is a bad thing that we are completely without useful people here. We must overlook a great many of Juliusburger's faults, i.e. put them down to his neurosis. He is utterly loaded with ethics, and besides has a great need for fathers, for whom he is fired with enthusiasm, only to go off each of them after a while. After his correspondence with you he was full of resistances, indeed he had not been short of them before either. Unfortunately a year ago he brought in Stöcker; it would have been better if she had not joined.—I hope that in a while we shall be over the whole wretched affair.

You will probably see from the account above, dear Herr Professor, that I cannot exert any influence on Stekel's reception in Berlin. The only thing is to stay away; I know that is what Eitingon is doing too.—

Time permitting, I shall send some small contributions to Ferenczi[4] in the near future.

With cordial greetings,
your devoted

*Abraham*

1. Franz Karl Keibel [1861–1929], lecturer and then professor [1892] of embryology and histology in Freiburg and later in Berlin. Having begun his studies in Würzburg [1895], Abraham had finished them in Freiburg [1901], with a thesis on *Beiträge zur Entwicklungsgeschichte des Wellensittichs* [Contributions to the Developmental History of the Budgerigar] under Keibel, who had also co-authored Abraham's first scientific publication (1900[1]).
2. Heinrich Wilhelm Gottfried von Waldeyer [1836–1921], noted German anatomist, professor at the universities of Breslau [1865] and Strassburg [1872], 1883 head of the anatomical institute at Berlin University.
3. Missing.
4. I.e. for the *Zeitschrift*, of which Ferenczi was co-editor.

## 150A

Berlin
29 January 1913

Dear Professor,

Everything should now be running normally again after last Sunday's event,[1] and so I may write to you today about some political and scientific matters.

Following Stekel's non-public talk—and presumably at his suggestion—a committee of people with a talent for resistance was set up in order to establish an Association for Sexual Science.[2] I was invited to the preparatory meeting. This will certainly not do us any harm, perhaps one might even use it to overthrow one or the other prejudice. I only mention it because I saw an interesting letter from Stekel, which seems to suggest that the *Zentralblatt* is about to collapse. St. offers his journal to the new Association as its organ and wants to extend it to a *"Zentralblatt für analytische Seelenkunde, mit besonderer Berücksichtigung der Sexualpsychologie und Sexualbiologie"* [*Journal for Analytical Psychology with Special Reference to Sexual Psychology and Sexual Biology*], with which the publisher is said to be in agreement. He recommends this new title as "excellent" with the profound reason that "every unravelling of an illness is an analysis". The offer has, however, been declined with thanks. This attempt to join an association that is as yet unborn proves how little the *Zentralblatt* is viable. There is a particularly nice postscript with which Stekel tries to entice the sexual researchers: "*The gentlemen['s names] will all be on the cover*". One would like to say with Adler: a unique opportunity for being on the top.[3]

It was with great pleasure that I received the first issue of our *Zeitschrift* today. Contents, editing, and general appearance are excellent. It makes a much better impression than the *Zentralblatt*. I assure you of my further active collaboration.—

I took down verbatim the following sentences in an analysis of a paranoid patient: "I at first try to come close to everyone, but am prepared for the break of the relationship from the very beginning." "I am prepared from the very beginning to find in everyone every possible bad intention against me." I find that these statements fit in extremely well with the views described in your Schreber paper. I have certain reasons not to publish anything from this analysis for the time being.

On the other hand, I would ask you to make use of the following, if you wish. In Vienna you discussed with me the deification of the murdered father. A patient brought the following neat confirmation of this. Over an extended period he had a number of Oedipus dreams concerning the possession of his stepmother and his father's death. A series of these was followed by one in which the patient ascends to heaven, where he finds God on his throne, looking like his father. The ascent to heaven obviously has two meanings: (1.) coitus with the stepmother, (2.) the patient convinces himself that the father is in heaven, that is, dead, and then elevates the dead man to being a god.

Nothing new in the matter of my *Habilitation*. I shall shortly start on a thesis and will probably undertake association experiments in cases of senile dementia. An innocuous topic in any case.

With cordial greetings from house to house,
your devoted
    *Abraham*

1. The marriage between Freud's daughter Sophie and Max Halberstadt on 25 January (Jones, 1955: p. 98, gives a wrong date).
2. Shortly afterwards, on 21 February 1913, the *Ärztliche Gesellschaft für Sexualwissenschaft und Eugenik* [Medical Society for Sexology and Eugenics], the first scientific sexological association ever, was founded in Berlin by Iwan Bloch [1872–1922] and Magnus Hirschfeld; Albert Eulenburg (see letter 172A, 10 October 1913, n. 2) was president. Its organ was the *Zeitschrift für Sexualwissenschaft* [Journal of Sexology] (not to be confounded with the short-lived journal of the same name of 1908), founded in 1914 by Bloch and Eulenburg.

3. In original: *Obensein* [be on top, be above], homonym of *oben sein* [here: be on the cover]. According to Adler, in every neurotic symptom one recovers "the feeling of effeminacy, of inferiority, of being 'down,' and the masculine protest, the fictitious manly goal, the feeling of being 'above'" (Adler, 1912: p. 353).

## 151A

Berlin
6 February 1913

Dear Professor,

Please forgive me for being importunate and writing again. I am sending the enclosed paper direct to you (instead of to Ferenczi) because it is a contribution to the specific question put by you.[1] As noted in the introduction, the case does not fully conform to your demands. I do not know therefore whether you will be able to use it.

This time nothing else, only cordial greetings from your

*Karl Abraham*

1. Abraham, 1913[42]. Still in the *Zentralblatt*, in the rubric *Offener Sprechsaal* [Open Forum], Freud had called for papers on "patients' dreams whose interpretation justifies the conclusion that *the dreamers had been witnesses of sexual intercourse in their early years*" (Freud, 1912h: p. 4). Freud's interest had evidently been stimulated by the famous dream of the "Wolf Man" (Freud, 1918b [1914], chapter 4).

## 152F

Vienna IX, Berggasse 19
14 February 1913

Dear Friend,

I have to thank you for two valuable communications, and I do so belatedly because I have to use all my time for drudgery again.

The infantile dream, clinically particularly interesting, is already with the *Internationale Zeitschrift*. The dream about God will be stored.

Spielrein has told me of a striking partisanship for $\Psi\alpha$ by Kraus.[1] So there is ground for hope for you.

Yours cordially,

*Freud*

1. Spielrein (see letter 25A, 4 April 1908, & n. 9) had moved to Berlin in 1912. Her letter to Freud is missing in Carotenuto, 1980, where Freud's answer of 9 February 1913 is printed.

## 153A

Berlin
3 March 1913

Dear Professor,

First of all, many thanks for your lines and for the reprint![1] I am amazed at all the new ideas and points of view contained in this series of papers. I have also received the two reprints from the *I.[nternationale] Zeitschr.[ift]*[2]; I should like sometime to make a few small additions to the technical paper.

I have to let my psychoanalytic pen rest for the time being, as I am now occupied with preparatory work for my *Habilitation*. I have therefore provided the *Zeitschrift* with several small contributions. *Imago* must wait for the time being.—I am working on associations in normal old age and in mild cases of senile dementia. It will be a good old Prussian piece of work, forcing open doors. If only it would also force the door to the University. In fact, things do not look quite so bad for me as I first thought. Kraus has become very interested. For two days running he discussed Ψα in detail in his clinic. But the best is the following. I had asked Professor Liepmann (the aphasia–apraxia researcher) to explore my chances with Bonhoeffer. L.[iepmann] let me know by letter at the time that B.[onhoeffer]'s reaction had been thoroughly negative. In a personal meeting I asked Liepmann to tell me about the matter in more detail, and then it came out that B. had actually said: if I wrote a good paper he would not be opposed to it on principle! This strange contradiction, which is interesting in the matter of "testimonies", is due to the fact that, in spite of his recognized ability, L. himself did not get the chair he longed for. He has already been suggested four or five times for different universities. He has become very pessimistic and despite his otherwise good intentions towards me has let his complex get mixed up with my affairs.

I am attaching a programme of the psychiatrists' congress.[3] You probably know about this event already. There is perhaps not much point in going there; if you, dear Professor, were in favour, then I would perhaps go to the Congress nevertheless. Please let me know your opinion when you have the opportunity!

Meanwhile, the *Sexualwissensch.[aftliche] Gesellsch.[aft]* [Association for Sexual Science] has been founded. It will not disturb our circles. Otherwise, there is nothing much happening here.

I heard by chance that Jung is soon going to America again, and for some months at that.[4] I am afraid that this will once again make for difficulties in preparing the Congress. It would be a good thing if someone were to do whatever is necessary in his place.

## 1913 March

Just one small scientific comment today. In the *footnote* on page 5 of the new paper in *Imago*, you mention the biblical ban on making images, which refers chiefly to the worship of images.[5] I have found a couple of times in the $\Psi\alpha$ of patients an analogous "ban" referring to the *parents*. The patient is capable of recalling the features of all his relatives and friends with great visual clarity; it is only his parents' features that he cannot recall, even when he had just left them. The most pronounced case was that of an obsessional neurotic with very severe compulsive brooding. The repression of *scoptophilia* had led to the most bizarre obsessional symptoms: for instance, brooding about the appearance of invisible things (what the conscious and the unconscious looked like in the brain, what his neurosis looked like, etc. etc.; he wanted to *see* everything.*[6] Might not the biblical prohibition of worshipping God as an image be connected with the repression of scoptophilia? Looking on God is in fact punished with death or blindness.

As soon as I find a little time, I shall send the *Zeitschrift* a very interesting observation about mouth eroticism in a case of hebephrenia.[7] A patient who at the age of 14 had to wean himself from sucking milk and who often masturbated—at least this was the conscious reason—only because he could not get any milk to drink at night! This is the same patient about whose "mouth pollutions" (dribbling saliva while dreaming) I already spoke to you in Vienna.

Incidentally, it is a pleasure to see how keenly the editors of the new *Zeitschrift* are setting about their work! No. 1 is excellent and can easily compete with the "inferior organ".[8]

Putnam sent me a lady (Miss Stevens) (a former patient), who is studying children's speech defects in Berlin. She would perhaps like to go to Vienna for the winter and said that she would ask you whether you would admit her to your lectures.—She is a nice, intelligent person, and I do not think she would be a burden to you.

I assume that *Dreams and Myths*[9] will have reached you!

Naturally, I do not expect a reply to this letter, dear Professor! I know how heavily burdened you are with correspondence and would only ask for a few words about Breslau sometime!

Cordial greetings to you and yours, also from my wife!

Your devoted

*Abraham*

---

*For example, also his own birth. He envied Pythagoras for having experienced his own birth three times. Severe incestuous fixation of the scoptophilia could, of course, be demonstrated.

1. "Animism, Magic, Omnipotence of Thoughts", the third part of *Totem and Taboo*, first published separately in *Imago*.

2. Freud, 1913c (first part), 1913a.
3. *Jahresversammlung des Deutschen Vereines für Psychiatrie* [Annual Meeting of the German Psychiatric Association] at Breslau in May, which was to be characterized by a heated polemic against psychoanalysis by Hoche and a critical evaluation of it by Bleuler as discussant. (Cf. Eitingon's report in the *Zeitschrift,* 1913, *1:* 409–414; letter 157F, 13 May 1913.)
4. On 4 March, Jung went to America for five weeks (Freud & Jung, 1974 [1906–13]: p. 545). On 27 March, he lectured at the Liberal Club in New York (*Zeitschrift,* 1913, *1:* 310).
5. Freud, 1912–13: p. 80.
6. Cf. 15A, 8 January 1908, & n. 3.
7. The paper containing this case, which is today considered a classic and was to win the Freud prize in 1918, appeared only a couple of years later (1916[52]); cf. letter 288A, 13 February 1916.
8. Allusion to the *Zentralblatt* and to Adler's (its former co-editor's) concept of "organ inferiority" [*Organminderwertigkeit*].
9. See letter 136F, 24 August 1912, & n. 1.

## 154A

Weimar[1]
25 March 1913

Dear Professor,

After a lovely spring tour through Thuringia I have landed with my wife in Weimar, where I am now reviving memories of autumn 1911.[2] On the reverse is the castle courtyard, in which you then told me for the first time about the totem.

With kind regards to you and yours from
Your devoted

K. Abraham

Best regards!

Hedwig Abraham

1. Picture postcard.
2. Of the Third Psychoanalytic Congress.

## 155F

Vienna IX, Berggasse 19
27 March 1913

Dear Friend,

Your beautiful Easter greetings from Weimar reminded me that I have made use too long of the permission you gave me not to reply. Having returned yesterday from Venice, whither I had guided my sin-

1913 March

gle[1] little daughter,[2] and being slightly more rested, I hasten to chat with you.

First of all, the satisfaction that things do not stand so badly with regard to your *Habilitation*. I should *really* wish for it; Kraus's letter to me has actually made me hopeful.

Next I should like to suggest that you finish your comments on the ban on making images for the *Zeitschrift*. It would cost you only an hour after all, and would be very valuable to us.

Miss Stevens will be welcome, on the grounds of your and Putnam's recommendation.

Whether or not you should attend the Congress in question, I can really advise you only on secondary grounds. Perhaps yes, so that we could have a report on it in the *Zeitschrift* with some strong words in it, and that you get two days of rest. You have not mentioned whether you have carried out the plan to increase your fees. I am afraid that that is the only point in which you—wrongly—refuse to follow me!

Jung is in America, but only for five weeks, that is, he will soon be back. In any case, he is doing more for himself than for $\Psi\alpha$. I have greatly retreated from him and have no longer any friendly thoughts for him.[3] As it is, his bad theories do not compensate me for his disagreeable character. He is following Adler, without being as consistent as this latter pest.

I am pretty overworked, but in the months from now until the holidays still have to finish the totem job of which you remind me. In the end, nothing of oneself will be left.

Ferenczi was ailing, and is now in Corfu.[4] Rank is extraordinarily good.

I send my cordial greetings to you and your dear wife and want to hear good news about you.

Your faithfully devoted

*Freud*

1. That is, unmarried.
2. Anna [1895–1982]. Originally an elementary-school teacher, Anna—analysed by her father—was the only one of Freud's children to become a psychoanalyst. She was a pioneer in child analysis. From 1922 on she was a member of the Vienna Society, and from 1924 on a member of the Committee. When her father fell ill with cancer, she became his nurse, secretary, and adviser and remained so until his death. She was co-editor of the *Zeitschrift für psychoanalytische Pädagogik*. In 1935 she took over from Helene Deutsch as director of the Training Institute of the Vienna Society. She was head of the Hampstead Nurseries [1940–1945] and the Hampstead Clinic [from 1952 on]. In 1945 she founded the journal *Psychoanalytic Study of the Child*. In her works she represented—in contrast to Melanie Klein—the pedagogical trend within child-analysis advocating a clear differentiation between the analysis of children and of adults.

Anna had been staying in Merano during the five previous months (thus missing her sister Sophie's wedding). Freud had met her in Bolzano on 21 March, and they both went

by way of Verona to Venice, from where they returned to Vienna five days later (Jones, 1955: p. 99; Freud to Anna Freud, 10 March 1913, LOC).
3. In fact, Freud and Jung had already ended their personal relationship in January, on a bitter note (cf. Freud & Jung, 1974 [1906–13]: pp. 538ff).
4. Instead of going to Vienna for an analysis with Freud, as Ferenczi had originally planned, he accompanied his friend Miksa Schächter to Corfu for three weeks.

## 156A

Berlin
5 May 1913

Dear Professor,

If one only considers external events, then the outlook for psychoanalysis is very grim again. Just when I was about to write to you, the enclosed reached me. The last bit of desire to attend the Congress left me when I read Bleuler's contradictory stuff.[1] It is best to stick to our old ways, and to keep ourselves to ourselves. As far as I know, only Wanke,[2] who has also announced a paper, is going there. He is honest and will certainly stand up for the cause, but he will not make any impression. I shall ask him to write a report of the Congress.

I am now busy with preparation work for my *Habilitation* thesis; that is to say, I take down associations of patients suffering from senile dementia in the hospital for incurables. Otherwise, every day brings ten hours' work. I can reassure you, dear Professor, on the question of fees. Last autumn I had started putting up my fees from 10 to 15 M and recently made the jump to 20 for the first time. The income is about to rise correspondingly; i.e. to 18,000 M last year; this year I may count on about 25,000 M. As soon as I have carried through the increase in fees totally, the best time for which is after the holidays, I shall shorten my working day by one hour in order to have more time for scientific work. So much is ready to be written down; and in addition the thesis for the *Habilitation* is another hindrance at the moment.

You ask me to work on the ban on images; this shall be done too, but, I would prefer not to communicate this as such, but, rather, in a broader context. I should like to speak at the Congress[3] on the transformation of scoptophilia.[4] Surely, you will agree if I leave the triviality unpublished until then. I should very much like to know whether your work on totem will be published before Munich; I would have to refer to it in my paper. I would perhaps like to ask you to let me read the proofs, as you did in an earlier case too.

Unfortunately, I cannot but agree with what you write about Jung; all the same, I do not believe that Adlerism[5] has come to stay in Zurich.

What are your plans for the summer? We are going somewhere on the North Sea, for the children's sake. After that I should like to go

1913 May 183

to South Tyrol for a short while with my wife, and from there to Munich.

With cordial greetings to you and yours,
your devoted

*Abraham*

1. Probably the (pre-circulated?) key statements of Bleuler's paper (Bleuler, 1913a) for the congress in Breslau (see *Zeitschrift*, 1913, *1*: 411–414).
2. Dr Georg Wanke [1866–1928], a psychiatrist who practised psychoanalysis as medical superintendent at a sanatorium in the Harz mountains; one of the earliest supporters of psychoanalysis in Germany.
3. The Fourth International Psychoanalytic Congress in Munich (7–8 September).
4. Abraham, 1914[43].
5. *Adlerei*—a pejorative form of *Adlerismus* [*Adlerism*].

157F
Vienna IX, Berggasse 19
13 May 1913

Dear Friend,

The totem job is finished,[1] apart from corrections and supplements from the literature. It is to go to the printer's on 13 June,[2] and I shall then send you the galleys as soon as I have them. It is to appear before the Congress, in the August issue of *Imago*, and will serve to neatly eliminate anything Aryan–religious. Because that will be the consequence.

I am very much in agreement with your proposed lecture and with your economic reforms. Your *Habilitation* seems to me particularly important at this moment; now that we must reckon with the breaking away of Zurich and Munich, a school in Berlin would be the only proper compensation.

For all its ambivalence,[3] Bleuler's concoction clearly shows the regressive trend. Indeed he accepts far less than he did two years ago. He also used to add the modest flourish that, when he contradicted me, subsequently he so often found that I was right, that etc. . . .

Our summer plans: 14 July to 10 (or 12) August—Marienbad, then, until the Congress, S. Martino di Castrozza in South Tyrol. Was the latter region not on your programme as well?

I have learned with great satisfaction that you are corresponding with Rank about our affairs. Politically I am paralysed and see all salvation for Ψα as we understand it in the unity of the four or five men who are closest to me, among whom you seem to count yourself.[4]

Cordial greetings to you and your dear wife,
from your faithfully devoted

*Freud*

1. The fourth and last part of *Totem and Taboo*: "The Return of Totemism in Childhood".
2. Reading uncertain; Freud had probably written 15 and then corrected it to 13.
3. A term coined by Bleuler.
4. The so-called Secret Committee—founded in 1912 against the background of the conflicts with Adler and Stekel but, above all, Jung—then consisting of Abraham, Ferenczi, Jones, Rank, and Sachs. This small select group of "paladins", as Freud referred to them, were to guard and protect the core of psychoanalysis. (Cf. Falzeder, 1993; Grosskurth, 1991; Wittenberger, 1995.)

## 158A

Berlin
23 May 1913

Dear Professor,

Of all that is going on in Zurich I only receive murky tidings here, but then I can more or less imagine it. I do not know whether, as you indicate, the break is unavoidable. As far as it lies in my power, Berlin shall offer compensations. Naturally no further developments have taken place concerning my *Habilitation*, except that I am working on my thesis. I have to collect the material gradually, hope to finish the whole thing in the summer and to submit the paper in the autumn. All the rest lies then in the lap of the Faculty gods. I am as sceptical about this as before. If I fail, something else will have to be attempted. I will not be on my own any more in the winter. First of all Stockmayer is settling here, with whom, I believe, something could get going. Up to now we have always been short of young blood. I do have various ideas of what can be done. If the *Habilitation* succeeds, the place will be livened up.

I am delighted to be getting the proofs of the totem work. I have a number of very interesting observations for the Congress lecture, which, however, I can only present if I have read your work beforehand.

Breslau was bad. According to Eitingon, who was there, Bleuler behaved most unpleasantly. E.[itingon] will surely tell you about this personally. Only Stegmann was present from our side. It seems he behaved very correctly and nicely. Hoche did get the laugh on his side; however, I have talked to several people who, though not supporters of $\Psi\alpha$, felt greatly repelled. It is a good thing that after the neurologists (in 1910)[1] the psychiatrists have now also given vent to their wrath. Things will be getting all the better for our cause after this. I often have occasion to notice with amazement how much interest in $\Psi\alpha$ has grown in Germany. One thing is certain: no topic in the realm of medicine and psychology is at present so widely discussed in professional circles as $\Psi\alpha$, and no doctor's name is mentioned as often as yours—and be it with three crosses.[2] It is similar in lay circles!

I received an inquiry from Jung, addressed to our group, whether the subject for discussion chosen in Munich (the function of the dream) still stands.³ I see no reason against it. Should any reservations regarding this subject come from the Vienna group, I should like to hear particulars. In that case I would ask you to let me know all that's necessary through Rank.

I am at present reading Hitschmann's Schopenhauer⁴ and am glad that the journals are going so well, while the *Zentralblatt* sinks to a lower level with each issue.

Our plans for the summer have changed. We have to give the children a longer holiday by the sea, and we shall probably choose Noordwijk, which you know.⁵ My wife is going away with the children at the beginning of July, and I am not going until the end of July; I shall have a few weeks' rest and then I shall visit the Dutch and Belgian towns with my wife for a fortnight. In the meantime the children will remain in Noordwijk, and we shall be near them. We would not be able to give them so long a holiday by the sea if we were to go south. So it seems that nothing is going to come of that. I intend to go direct to Munich from Holland. Perhaps we could arrange a rendezvous before the Congress; I am very ready to receive suggestions! Perhaps something could be arranged by *word of mouth*, if you visit Hamburg in the summer and then pass through Berlin.—If it is not too much trouble for you, I should be very grateful for a very short account of how satisfied you were with your hotel in Noordwijk.

Unfortunately, I have to bother you yet again, dear Professor. Frau Dr Stegmann⁶ has asked me to analyse her. She will not, of course, be able to come to Berlin for an indefinite length of time, only for about two months. Do you advise me to take this on? And what do I do in this case about the question of fees? Have you any idea in what sort of circumstances the woman is living since her divorce?

Please do not be annoyed about all these questions. I shall be very satisfied with quite a short answer in telegram style.

With cordial greetings from house to house,
your devoted

*Abraham*

1. In 1910, prominent German neurologists had on two occasions called for a boycott of clinics where psychoanalysis was practised: at the Meeting of the Medical Society of Hamburg on 29 March 1910, and at the Fourth Annual Meeting of the Society of German Neurologists in Berlin on 6–8 October 1910.
2. Making the sign of the cross three times for protection against demons. Freud often used the symbol of three crosses before the names of persons towards whom he was ambivalent.
3. At the meeting of organization heads in Munich it was suggested that the theme for discussion at the forthcoming congress be "On the Teleological Function of Dreams", a concept particularly stressed by the Zurich group. In Jung's invitation circular of June

1913 (Freud & Jung, 1974 [1906–13]: p. 547) it was subsequently formulated more openly as "The Function of Dreams".
4. Hitschmann, 1913. Eduard Hitschmann [1871–1958], general practitioner, member of the Wednesday Society from 1905 on. He was head of the psychoanalytic outpatient clinic in Vienna from 1922 until the Society was disbanded by the Nazis. In 1938 he emigrated to London and in 1940 he moved to Boston, where he was active as a training analyst.
5. Freud had spent part of his summer holiday there in 1910 with his family, before going to Sicily with Ferenczi.
6. Margarete Stegmann [1871–between 1935 and 1937], neurologist in Dresden, from 1912 on a member of the Berlin Society; former wife of Arnold Georg Stegmann.

## 159F

Vienna IX, Berggasse 19
1 June 1913

Dear Friend,

Excuse my lateness due to the greatest demands in dreadful heat.

The hotel in Noordwijk was actually good, all the small meals ample: butter, cheese, drinks, etc., the longer ones, meat, vegetables, in the coarse Dutch style, basically unpalatable. Food in the big Huisterduin Hotel is said to be not good either. Our house was called Pension Noordzee, proprietor van Beelen.

I do not know much about Frau Dr Stegmann, can imagine that she has nothing. Very unpleasant to get mixed up with the divorce, as it has already been forced upon me!

You will already know by now that we are to meet in Munich on the day before the Congress (Saturday, 6 Sept., in the morning).—Jung is crazy, but I am not working for a separation, should like to let him reach rock bottom first. Perhaps my totem paper will hasten the breach against my will. You will of course receive the galleys as soon as I have them (from the middle of the month onwards). I shall be presenting it to the Society on Wednesday[1]; now I have grave doubts about it, the reaction after the enthusiasm.

Jones is off today for two months' analysis with Ferenczi. I enjoy the thought that your marriage shows that $\Psi\alpha$ does not necessarily lead to divorce.[2]

Bleuler has nicely developed backwards. I suspect that the last motives were the $\psi\alpha$ papers on the synaesthesias,[3] which raised tremendous resistance in him (see the *Zeitschrift für Psychologie*, last issue).[4] A proof perhaps that Pfister and Hug are really right in this matter.

With cordial greetings to yourself and your dear wife,
Yours,

*Freud*

1913 June

1. On 4 June, at the last meeting of the working year 1912/13. Minutes and attendance list missing in Nunberg & Federn (1975: p. 204).
2. Jones underwent an analysis with Ferenczi during June and July for two hours a day, which overlapped with the analysis of his common-law wife, Loë Kann, with Freud. As Freud had written to Ferenczi, Kann, "as a consequence of the analysis, no longer wants to remain his wife" (4 May 1913, Freud & Ferenczi, 1992: p. 482). She had fallen in love with a man by the name of Herbert Jones, whom she later married.
3. Hug-Hellmuth, 1912; Pfister, 1912. Hermine Hug-Hellmuth (orig. Hug von Hugenstein) [1871–1924], a teacher, was the first child analyst. She was the editor of the *Tagebuch eines halbwüchsigen Mädchens* (1919), the authenticity of which was later disputed; and she was director of the advisory board of the Vienna Psychoanalytic Outpatient Clinic [1923]. She was murdered by her nephew, the observation of whom had provided material for many of her works. (See Huber, 1980; MacLean & Rappen, 1991.)
4. Probably Bleuler, 1913b.

## 160A

Berlin
29 June 1913

Dear Professor,

I have now read the totem paper twice, always with increasing enjoyment and continually growing conviction of the correctness of your view. I do not want to go into detail today; I want to express my gratitude through the paper that I announced for the Congress, which will bring some additions—not inconsiderable ones, it seems to me—to the subject. Today I only want to say that I find rich confirmatory material in my psychoanalyses. Only yesterday I discovered something I did not know until now: a perfectly clear tree-totemism in a neurosis, whereas so far I had only encountered animals. It becomes evident in this case, just as in the totems of primitive peoples, that we are not dealing with something as primary and elemental as animal totemism.

Recently I have scarcely been able to write a line. My ten hour-a-day stints are likely to last until the holidays; yet various long-planned papers, which I should like to send to the *Zeitschrift*, are pressing upon me. The preparatory work on the *Habilitation* paper is naturally taking up what little free time I have.

Thank you very much for your information on Holland! We found accommodation in Noordwijk. My wife is travelling with the children on 8 July; I myself am not going until the end of July and shall remain there until the end of August. I shall have 1 to 1½ weeks free before the Congress. If it could be fitted in with your programme, I should be very happy to meet you sometime and somewhere, but it goes without saying that you should not upset your plans in any way. The day before the Congress in Munich will be given over to tiresome inside politics; after the Congress you will, like myself, certainly want to get home as soon as possible. So the only opportunity for scientific conversations would be *before* Munich.

Last week there was, for once, an opportunity to speak in public in Berlin about Ψα. In the "*Ärztliche Gesellschaft für Sexualwissenschaft*" a bad paper by Rohleder[1] was followed by a discussion on masturbation, in which first Koerber and then I firmly upheld Ψα. The preceding week brought me a few unpleasant days as an expert witness at court in the case against the *Anthropophyteia*.[2] Whatever could be said in its favour, I said. But unfortunately I had to realize that some of the authors are scientifically very poorly qualified, and serious objections against Krauss as a person can also be raised.—Bjerre from Stockholm came to see me today on his way to the Tyrol. He is very well informed and a really serious and reliable man; he made a perfectly correct assessment of Jung and Adler all on his own.

With cordial greetings from house to house,
your devoted

*Abraham*

1. Dr Hermann Rohleder, sexologist from Leipzig, co-editor of the *Zeitschrift für Sexualwissenschaft* [1908]; author of a book on masturbation (1912).
2. *Anthropophyteia, Jahrbuch für folkloristische Erhebungen und Forschungen zur Entwicklungsgeschichte der geschlechtlichen Moral*, a periodical founded and edited by the Viennese ethnologist Friedrich Salomon Krauss. It assembled principally anthropological material of a sexual character. (Cf. Freud's letter to Krauss on *Anthropophyteia*, Freud, 1910f.)

## 161F

Vienna IX, Berggasse 19
1 July 1913

Dear Friend,

Your opinion of the totem paper was particularly important to me, as after finishing it I had a period of doubt about its[1] value. But Ferenczi, Jones, Sachs, Rank have expressed opinions similar to yours, with the result that I have gradually recovered my confidence. The way in which you want to show me the value of the work, through contributions, additions, and conclusions, is, of course, the most marvellous. I am prepared for vicious attacks, which will naturally not sway me in any way. The rift with the Swiss is likely to be substantially widened.

I am counting the days until the beginning of the holidays, and lo! there are 12.[2] But I am not working any more—apart from the 11 hours of practice. On the evening of the 13th we are going to Marienbad, four weeks later from there to S. Martino di Castrozza (behind Trient).

1913 July

Should you like to come there, you will also meet Ferenczi, who is travelling with me to Munich on the 5/6 September.³ It is really the only opportunity for discussion.

Frau von Salomé has, in her own words, "laid a small egg for *Imago*".⁴ In any case, it is welcome. Of the papers for the Congress I know of *Tausk*, on narcissism, *van Emden* (who is here now): analysis of a pseudo-epilepsy, *Jones* on the technical behaviour of the analyst on questions of sublimation, *Ferenczi* on a subject still to be decided. I shall not speak.⁵

It would be a good thing to arrange our meeting in Munich a long time in advance. Shall we stay at the same hotel or somewhere else? I have still not received any information about the venue.

I send you my cordial greetings and wish you and yours the best course of a well-earned holiday.

My address in Marienbad is Villa Turba, but the Vienna address can also be depended on throughout the whole summer.

Yours,

*Freud*

1. One word heavily crossed out. Freud probably first started to write *Ihrem Werte* instead of *ihrem Werte*, i.e. "doubt about your value" instead of "its value".
2. Allusion to Friedrich von Schiller's "Lied von der Glocke" (which every schoolchild had to learn by heart).
3. Freud, his wife Martha, Minna Bernays, and Anna arrived in San Martino di Castrozza on 11 August, where Ferenczi joined them four days later. Abraham did come to visit for a few days. Freud and Ferenczi then went together to Munich for the Congress.
4. Andreas-Salomé, 1914.
5. Eventually, Tausk spoke about "The Psychological and Pathological Significance of Narcissism"; van Emden on "On the Analysis of a Case of Ostensible Epilepsy in a Child"; Jones about "The Attitude of the Physician Towards Current Conflicts" (Jones, 1914); and Ferenczi on "On the Psychology of Conviction" (Ferenczi, 1913[109]). Freud did give a paper, "The Problem of Choice of Neurosis" (Freud, 1913i).
   Jan E. G. van Emden [1868–1950] from the Hague, later president of the Dutch Society. Analysed by Freud, he had become a friend of the Freud family, and he and his wife spent several holidays with them.

## 162A

Berlin
6 July 1913

Dear Professor,

Today, only very briefly, many thanks for your information, particularly for the invitation to come and see you in San Martino. If nothing intervenes, I shall be there at the end of August, and I am looking forward to meeting you and yours, as well as our colleague Ferenczi, then.

For our *pre*-meeting in Munich I have already suggested to Rank that we should stay in the hotel in which the meetings are taking place, so as not to give an impression of deliberate separation. For our discussion we should meet somewhere else. I suggest that we should all meet on 6 September in the morning and perhaps go together for an excursion into the Isar[1] valley.

With best wishes for a good rest, and greetings to you and your whole house.

Yours,

*Abraham*

1. The river running through Munich.

## 163A

Berlin
20 July 1913

Dear Professor,

I do not want to disturb your holiday peace with a long letter. I would like to refer to just one point in your last letter, now that you have enjoyed a week of holiday and therefore will surely have become more receptive to my arguments.

You wrote that you would not be speaking in Munich. I hope you only wrote this while overly tired out with work in the last weeks in Vienna. For, if this were your last word, it would not be a proper congress any longer. I believe I act on behalf of the circle, which will assemble already on 6 September, if I ask you most sincerely to ensure the importance and effectiveness of the Congress by giving a paper. Who knows how much unpleasantness will occur? There is nothing that would be more suitable as a counterweight. You remember the effect your personal appearance had in Munich in November, and there it was only a report on the irksome politics. How much more favourable will the effect of a scientific paper be in the present situation! I do not want to pursue it further. Eitingon, who is visiting you today, will surely succeed in persuading you to change your mind. My best blessings go with him.

That is all for today. I am here until 26 July, then my address will be: Pension "Ozon", Noordwijk aan Zee. Perhaps you might send me there your address in San Martino.

With cordial greetings to you and yours,
your devoted

*Abraham*

1913 July

## 164A
Noordwijk aan Zee, Pension "Ozon"
29 July 1913[1]

Dear Professor,

After Eitingon had told me your views about a possible paper, I turned to Jung to find out his intentions regarding the discussion. I reminded him that already in Munich we had said that perhaps only the main paper, not each individual one, should be followed by a discussion. I have just received the reply, which I enclose. Unfortunately it does not meet with your wishes.[2] But I think this need not be decisive. After all, we are having our preliminary meeting on 6 September. It would be so simple if one or two of us were to undertake any necessary replies to unpleasant remarks in discussion, so that you would not have to bother with them! You might, in fact, just have to make a short closing statement.

I do hope you are willing to make the Congress into a real congress by reading a paper.

I do not wish to use many more words to plead with you, dear Professor, to do so. I would just like to remind you that presumably this time quite a number of young people will come to the Congress. The Congress would lose its most attracting force if you were there as a silent listener.

I hope you and yours feel really comfortable there; now the weather is probably more favourable than it was at first. We are splendidly looked after here; we shall spend the next weeks partly resting by the sea and partly visiting the old towns.

With cordial greetings to you and yours, also from my wife,
yours devotedly,

*Abraham*

1. Typewritten postcard.
2. "[T]he freedom of discussion that Jung has set up doesn't suit me", Freud wrote to Ferenczi (3 August 1913, Freud & Ferenczi, 1992: p. 502). At previous Congresses no allowance had been made for discussion of the lectures.

## Addendum
[Jung to Abraham]

Küsnacht[1]
28 July 1913

Dear Colleague,

I have taken note of the announcement of your paper on "Neurotic Limitations etc."[2] I want to limit the time for the talk to a *maximum* of 25 min. If at all possible, the individual papers should also be discussed, not only the main papers. Mere listening to papers is too barren. It will be up to the president and the good will of the assembly not to stretch the discussions too much, so that the whole matter can be dealt with.

With collegial greetings,
your devoted
Dr Jung

1. Typewritten postcard.
2. Abraham, 1913[41].

## 165F

Marienbad
31 July 1913

Dear Friend,

This morning a reminder arrived from Jung[1] to announce a paper, together with various complaints about misunderstandings and some supercilious lecturing that is incomprehensible to me. In view of these never-ending misunderstandings, I can only regret that the Zurichers have lost the ability to make themselves intelligible.

This afternoon your letter, from which I see how much you want me not to make a demonstration by abstinence. This repetition of the request transmitted by Eitingon was decisive for me, in spite of the unfavourable arrangements for speaking at the Congress. So I shall present a short communication on the problem of the choice of neurosis. You will see that though I wish to avoid the discussion, I am not afraid of it.

For us it is a pleasant thought that you are now enjoying our beautiful Noordwijk too. Above all the sunsets were magnificent. Wind and dunes I did not like. The small towns are delightful. Delft is a little gem. You have to go a long way to find an Egyptian collection like the one in the museum in Leiden. The Attic burial steles are also outstandingly beautiful.

I hope your wife and children will have a good rest there.

Do not forget that you have promised to be in S. Martino di Castrozza on 1 August. Let me know when I can book a room for you in the Hotel des Alpes.

Cordial greetings,
Yours,
    *Freud*

1. Letter of 29 July 1913 (Freud & Jung, 1974 [1906–13]: p. 548).

## 166A

Noordwijk aan Zee
6 August 1913

Dear Professor,

No better news could have reached me here than that contained in your letter. Since you tell me that my repeated requests were the decisive factor, I want to thank you sincerely for your decision. Incidentally, you will surely not be subject to the time-limit. We also had a time-limit of half an hour at previous congresses; yet I still remember with great pleasure the two hours you filled with your paper in Salzburg. Surely no one will notice when the first 25 minutes are up! I would like to ask you not to restrict yourself to a short communication, especially since Eitingon has made me very eager to hear about your new ideas on the question of choice of neurosis; but I shall gladly be content with what I have achieved by my previous letter.

We like Noordwijk very much indeed. Just today we visited the Museum of Antiquities in Leiden; I have seldom taken such pleasure in walking through a collection; there is too much in it for one visit.

I shall not forget to come to San Martino. As I am not yet absolutely certain of the day I arrive, may I ask you not to book a room for me in advance. After all, around 1 September accommodation is available without advance booking.

I wish you and your family a good move to the Tyrol, and add my kind regards to you all, also on behalf of my wife.

Your devoted

*Abraham*[1]

1. The Munich Congress took place on 7 and 8 September, with 87 participants present. The atmosphere was especially tense because of the burgeoning conflict with Jung; on his re-election as president, two fifths of the members abstained from voting. After the Congress Freud, along with Minna Bernays, who met him in Bologna, went to Rome for 17 days.

## 167F

Rome[1]
13 September 1913

The Jew survives it!
Cordial greetings and Coraggio Kasimiro![2]
Yours,

*Freud*

1. Picture postcard of the Arch of Titus, Rome. Titus Flavius Vespasianus [39–81] was supreme commander in the first Jewish–Roman War [66–70], which led to the destruction of Jerusalem. Roman emperor from 79 until 81.
2. This refers to the following event: Two guides with whom Abraham had climbed a mountain had taken some raw meat with them to eat. By the time they reached the hut and set about cooking it, it had gone off, and one of them encouraged the other to eat it with the words: *"Coraggio, Casimiro."* Freud and Abraham subsequently often quoted this remark.

## 168A

Berlin
17 September 1913

Dear Professor,

From your encouraging postcard, for which I thank you very much, I take it that you are very happy in Rome and that you have thrown off the unpleasant memories of Munich. I may say for myself that in some ways I now feel better than before the Congress—the heart-to-heart talk came as a relief.

The old work has started again, the day is already almost fully occupied. Beside that I am toiling at my *Habilitation* thesis, and for respite I turn to the work of which I read a part at the Congress. I have obtained such rich new material that I shall extend the subject. In order to be able to publish it in the *Zeitschrift* (the *Jahrbuch* does not appeal to me any more),[1] I shall have to split it into several small sections, which can then appear as a series, like your technical recommendations, for instance.

Deuticke informed me that *Dreams and Myths* is now being translated into Dutch by Stärcke.[2]

I often think back to the pleasant days I spent in your family circle in San M.[artino].

The enclosed card of the Pyramids near Euseigne in the Valais is sure to be of interest to you.

While wishing you further pleasant days, I beg you to give Fräulein Bernays best wishes from my wife and myself, and with the same for yourself, I am,
 your cordially devoted
  *Abraham*

1. Shortly afterwards, Jung resigned from his editorship of the *Jahrbuch*, which then continued publication for one more year under a slightly altered title, edited by Abraham and Hitschmann; it contained Abraham's Congress paper.
2. August Stärcke [1880–1954], Dutch psychoanalyst. In fact, the translation of Abraham's *Dreams and Myths* (1909[14]) was done by S. C. von Doesburgh (Abraham, 1909[14]; Leiden, 1914).

## 169F

Rome, Eden Hotel
21 September 1913

Dear Friend,

Many thanks for your friendly words and good news, in particular for the promise to serve our *Zeitschrift*, which we must now keep going entirely on our own resources.

In the incomparably beautiful Rome I quickly recovered my spirits and energy for work, and in the free time between museums, churches, and trips to the Campagna finished a foreword to the book on totem and taboo,[1] an expansion of the Congress paper,[2] and the sketch of an article on narcissism,[3] as well as a proof of my propaganda article for *Scientia*.[4] My sister-in-law, who warmly returns your and your wife's greetings, sees to it that the real Rome work is kept within moderate bounds. She has put up unexpectedly well with all the inevitable exertions, and it is a pleasure to see her succumbing increasingly every day to enthusiasm for Rome and to feeling at ease.

Yesterday there arrived, *post festum*, a letter—assuring me of admiration from Maeder, with the addendum: Here I stand, I can do no other[5] (which is well suited to someone taking a risk, but hardly to someone withdrawing from one). He will get a cool, not very detailed reply.[6]

The whole Roman décor will, alas! be laid aside in a week and be replaced by a more sober and familiar one.

I send you my cordial greetings and hope to hear continuing good news from you and yours.

Your faithfully devoted

*Freud*

1. Freud, 1912–13a: pp. xiii–xiv.
2. Freud, 1913i.
3. Freud, 1914c.
4. Freud, 1913j.
5. *Hier stehe ich. Ich kann nicht anders. Gott helfe mir! Amen!* [Here I stand. I can do no other. So help me God! Amen!], Martin Luther is said to have said at the end of his great speech in his defence at the *Reichstag* at Worms [18 April 1521]. The words are engraved on the Luther monument at Worms (1868).
6. Maeder, 1988 [1912–13]; Freud, 1956j [1913].

## 170A

Berlin
27 September 1913

Dear Professor,

I must particularly thank you for writing to me at such length from Rome. At the same time, I want to tell you how glad I am that Rome has done so much for you, and—according to your report—also for psychoanalysis. When you get this letter, you will surely have just returned to your *lares* and *penates*.[1]

My work is already back to its usual ten-hour schedule. I hope soon to be able to refer some patients to the new colleagues. Yesterday we had our first meeting. I gave a report on Munich, and the schism was then discussed. It is a good thing for our small group that Juliusburger is turning back to us. I do not think he will give Stekel any more contributions. It looks as if life within our group will pick up this winter. The *"Ärztliche Gesellschaft für Sexualwissenschaft"* provides us with an increasing number of contacts from a wider medical circle. Koerber and Juliusburger are in its committee; we take a lively part in its discussions and lectures. I should like to take this opportunity to point out to you that Moll is trying to found a rival Society[2] and wants Löwenfeld[3] to lend his name to it. You will probably also be approached now. I mention this because earlier on you once warned me against Moll.

If you want to pass a happy hour, dear Professor, you absolutely must read the last issue of the *Zentralblatt* (especially Birstein[4])!

In conclusion, I only wish you a winter made easier by shorter working hours! I add cordial greetings to you and all of yours, also on behalf of my wife!

Your devoted

*Abraham*

1. Roman household and tutelary gods.
2. Only a few months after the founding of the *Ärztliche Gesellschaft für Sexualwissenschaft und Eugenik*, Albert Moll did in fact establish a rival society, the *Internationale Gesellschaft für Sexualforschung* [International Society for Sexual Research].
3. Leopold Löwenfeld [1874–1924], psychiatrist in Munich. In 1895 Freud had been involved in a scientific controversy with him, which ended "in our becoming friends and we have remained so to this day" (Freud, 1916–17a: p. 245). Löwenfeld was editor, with Hans Kurella, of the series *Grenzfragen des Nerven- und Seelenlebens; Einzeldarstellungen für Gebildete aller Stände* [Questions at the Frontier of Nervous and Mental Life: Individual Presentations for Educated Persons of All Classes] (Wiesbaden: Bergmann), in which Freud had published a paper (1901a). (Cf. Freud, 1904f, 1906a, written at the instigation of Löwenfeld, to be included in his book *Sexualleben und Nervenleiden*.)
4. Not identified. J. Birstein contributed eight short articles and one book review to the 1913 *Zentralblatt*.

1913 October

## 171F

Vienna IX, Berggasse 19
8 October 1913

Dear Friend,

Thanks for your lines on my arrival in Vienna, which, because of immediate inundation, I am answering only today and for a current reason.

I received the enclosed letter from the *Gesellschaft für Sexualwissenschaft*, and I am asking you whether I should join it. Löwenfeld has spoken to me about Moll's foundation, and, *discreetly*, informed me of his disinclination to have any part in it. I dealt with the letter that came from Moll's faction by not reacting.

From Rome I brought with me the deepest well-being and the draft of the narcissism. Here I acquired a head-cold, like all Viennese, and have not yet been able to take the n[arcissism] out again. All well and satisfactory at home, my son Ernst is getting ready to move to Munich.[1]

The group in London is said to have been founded,[2] we have had no more news from Switzerland. Today we had our own first meeting, at which I gave a very honest account of Munich.[3]

It is a quarter to one in the morning. Reason to wish you and your dear wife the finest days ahead.

Your faithfully devoted

*Freud*

1. Freud's youngest son, Ernst [1892–1970], went to Munich to study architecture. See letter 372A, 4 April 1920, n. 5.
2. On 4 and 14 October, Jones informed Freud of plans to establish a branch society; on 3 November he reported its foundation, on 30 October, with himself as president, Douglas Bryan as vice-president, and David Eder as secretary.
3. Meeting of 8 October; the minutes are missing in Nunberg & Federn, 1975: p. 205.

## 172A

Berlin
10 October 1913

Dear Professor,

I think I should *advise* you to join the *Ärztliche Gesellschaft für Sexualwissenschaft*. It is the first medical corporation to accord our discipline equal rights with all the others, and at the same time, as I have already written in my last letter, it is a good opportunity to propagate our views. Two members of our group are on the committee. Our colleague Liebermann,[1] who recently opened a practice here, is speaking in November at Eulenburg's[2] instigation on "Freud's Doctrine of the Erogenous Zones".

I may add that with my psychoanalytic contributions to the last discussions I found more interest than any other speaker. I could think of no serious objection why you should *not* join. Your membership would, I believe, create further sympathy for us; your not being a member, on the other hand, would certainly be interpreted wrongly in one way or another.

With regard to Adler's[3] proposal that you should give a talk in Berlin, I should like to ask you, dear Professor, to tell me at your convenience whether you are at all willing to do something of the sort. I have purposely never made such a suggestion to you, but I have already often considered whether a talk arranged by our local group might not be received with very great interest by the Berlin doctors. Perhaps on the occasion of your going to Hamburg? You could count on a very large audience.

I am eagerly looking forward to the narcissism. I found the last two issues of the *Zeitschrift*, which I have read now, *very* satisfying, though naturally not all the contributions equally so. Today I sent Ferenczi a short paper on the auditory passage as an erotogenic zone.[4] Apart from my *Habilitation* thesis and the paper on scoptophilia,[5] I am working on a few more small things like the latter. A brief essay will deal with neurotic exogamy,[6] along the lines of your *Imago* paper.[7]

Our group here has already had its first meeting. We are at the moment very worried about our member Koerber. He became ill a short while after the session and was taken to hospital the same night, where, after he had been under observation for eight days, his left kidney was removed. Multiple papillomas were found in the renal pelvis. If he survives the next few days, there is hope; but it looks very serious.

I am glad to have good news of you and yours. You write about your son Ernst; did he get a job in Munich? What is it? My congratulations are no less heartfelt, despite my complete ignorance.

Many thanks for the *Scientia* article, and many good wishes, also from my wife!

Your devoted

*Abraham*

---

1. Dr Hans Liebermann [1883–1931], former analysand of Abraham's. He became addicted to cocaine after using it as a pain-killer during the First World War. (See Eitingon's obituary in the *Zeitschrift*, 1931.)
2. Dr Albert Eulenburg [1840–1917], nerve specialist in Berlin, prolific author, "Nestor" of German sexology.
3. Otto Adler, secretary of the *Ärztliche Gesellschaft für Sexualwissenschaft*.
4. Abraham, 1914[46].
5. Abraham, 1914[43].
6. Abraham, 1914[45].
7. See letter 157F, 13 May 1913, n. 1.

1913 October

## 173F

Vienna IX, Berggasse 19
12 October 1913

Dear Friend,

I have to thank you for your well-motivated advice and will declare my membership to Adler as soon as I have changed the necessary 5 Mk note.

Naturally, I would not like to give a talk before the doctors in Berlin; much rather in your group, should the opportunity arise. I want to go to Hamburg around Christmas, but as time is so limited, I really cannot break my journey more than for being with you for a few hours, on the way there or back.

You will receive a third volume of the *Kleine Schriften zur Neurosenlehre* in the next few days; it contains the three big analyses and a few smaller essays.[1]

My son Ernst is going to Munich because the technical faculty in Vienna offers too little for his study of architecture. He is still very far from getting a job, he has only two years of study behind him. I feel very sorry for Koerber, his comments at the Congress have brought him closer to me again. Should you manage to see him, please express to him my firm intention that he should recover.

The matter of your lectureship certainly touches me very closely, but may perhaps plunge me into a conflict. In the last post from Kraus and Brugsch, the editors of the new *Pathology and Therapy*, I find, surprisingly, behind my space, the following:

Hysteria and Obsessional States—Freud
item Dr Kutzinski[2] (Berlin).

"Before dinner it read differently".[3] On the 5th of this month, therefore, I asked Brugsch, very politely and without giving away any of my purpose, what this dual treatment meant, whether the space allotted to me may suffer from it, whether we should show consideration for each other, etc. Up to now no reply! That doesn't look kosher! I have not yet written again. My own inclination is naturally to withdraw from such utterly uncommon treatment; the reservation to that is that your relationship with Kraus would probably be endangered by such a step. I should like to know your opinion here too; will certainly put your interests first.

I greet you with wife and children cordially.

Yours,

*Freud*

1. *Sammlung kleiner Schriften zur Neurosenlehre* [Collected Smaller Papers on the Theory of the Neuroses], third volume, Leipzig and Vienna, 1913; containing, among others, the three major analyses of Little Hans (Freud, 1909b), the Rat Man (1909d), and Schreber (1911c [1910]).

2. Arnold Kutzinski [1872–19?], assistant to Bonhoeffer, psychiatrist at the Charité, known to be antagonistic to psychoanalysis. His contributions, unlike Freud's, did find their way into the Kraus encyclopaedia. (Cf. Kutzinski, 1910.)
3. *Vor Tische las man's anders* (Friedrich von Schiller, *Die Piccolomini* [1800], IV, 7).

174A

Berlin
14 October 1913

Dear Professor,

It does not seem to me to be such a difficult business. Kutzinski, who has been attached to you, is Bonhoeffer's assistant. So I imagine that Kraus gave in to the influence of his colleague B., who is not really favourably disposed towards Ψα.

Kraus promised me his support, giving as reason that scientifically and personally he had heard only good of me. In this light, his intercession for me would be an act of personal friendliness rather than a support of Ψα. If Bonhoeffer has now influenced him also against me *personally*, then there will not be much that can be done about it. If such influence has not taken place, I believe that Kr. would not change his behaviour towards me, even if you clearly told him the truth about your business. For, as I have said, the event does *not* seem to originate with Kraus; that seems to me to be the main thing.

I hope you, dear Professor, will not come into a position where you would give precedence to my interests. Perhaps the situation will become clearer after the reply from Brugsch. I should naturally like to see this. Perhaps you could simply put it into an envelope and send it to me, so that you will not have the trouble of writing another letter! I thank you very much for the information and for your intention of showing consideration for me. I really should prefer to ask you to leave my interests completely out of account, if my *Habilitation* were simply my personal affair. But I do hope for something from it for Ψα.

Thanks in advance for the 3rd volume of the [*Kleine Schriften zur*] *Neurosenlehre*!

I have taken over the review of Jung's American lectures.[1] It is only after very detailed study that one can see exactly what it is all about.

Koerber seems to be a bit better.

I am looking forward to your visit at Christmas, however short.

With cordial greetings from house to house.

Yours,

*Karl Abraham*

1. Abraham's trenchant review (Abraham, 1914[47]) of Jung's Fordham lectures (Jung, 1913; cf. Freud & Jung, 1974 [1906–13]: p. 513), in which Jung set forth in detail his chief departures from Freudian principles.

## 175F

Vienna[1]
19 October 1913

Dear Friend,

Your arguments are very clear to me. Incidentally—so far no reply from B.[rug]sch. After your letter I wrote (on the 17th) a second time, by registered post. I shall send you the reply, which I expect to be fishy.

Cordial greetings,
Yours,

*Freud*

1. Postcard.

## 176F

Vienna[1]
23 October 1913

Dear Friend,

No reply from Brugsch for a week (to the second registered letter). He may easily be away. Today I have sent the question directly to Kraus, and if I get a reply I shall let you have it.

Yours cordially,
Your

*Freud*

1. Postcard.

## 177F

Vienna IX, Berggasse 19
26 October 1913

Dear Friend,

The letter to Kraus has resulted in my receiving a reply from Brugsch, which I enclose. A fishy reply, which nevertheless makes possible the continuation of negotiations. I was already thinking I had hit on a special university technique for "disgusting people out of business"[1] and would be granted no answer at all. The best thing in the whole business seems to be Kraus himself.

I shall not make up my mind about the next step until I have heard from you and have your approval. You are so very much affected that you are allowed to have the first say.

These are gloomy times in other ways too, or perhaps only a time when gloomy moods predominate. I shall have to say to myself: Coraggio Casimiro!

Rank and Sachs are very good and great supports for the cause. Yesterday Ferenczi sent in an exceptionally trenchant and pertinent criticism of Bleuler's negative article in the *Zeitschrift für Psychiatrie*.[2] Your criticism of Jung's theory in the *Jahrbuch* should follow it, we declined to have it reviewed by Eder.[3] The question now is the extent to which Jones will be able to steer the new London group into our channel; all further "political" steps depend on that.

At the first lecture yesterday[4] I realized the complete analogy between the first running away from the discovery of sexuality behind the neuroses by Breuer[5] and the latest one by Jung. That makes it the more certain that this is the core of $\Psi\alpha$.

I send my cordial greetings to you and your dear family and await your communication.

Yours,

*Freud*

1. *Hinausekeln.*
2. Ferenczi's review (1914[150]), of Bleuler 1913a.
3. David Montague Eder [1866–1936], founding member and secretary of the London Society. In early 1913, he had come to Vienna. Disappointed in his hopes of an analysis with Freud, he had gone for a brief period to Viktor Tausk. He became increasingly sympathetic to Jung's views, although eventually he remained in Freud's camp and was analysed by Ferenczi. (Cf. Freud, 1945a [1939]; Hobman, 1945; Roazen, 2000.)
4. Freud's Saturday lecture at the university.
5. Josef Breuer [1842–1925], fatherly friend and mentor to young Freud, co-author of Breuer & Freud (1895d). According to Freud, it was Breuer who "brought psychoanalysis into being" (Freud, 1910a [1909]: p. 9; for a critical evaluation of the legendary accounts on his "running away from the discovery of sexuality", see Hirschmüller, 1978).

## 178F

Vienna[1]
28 October 1913

Dear Friend,

Urania, of Vienna, is a distinguished lecturing institute, whose invitations are accepted by the best people.

I am curious to know your communication with regard to B.[rugsch]–Kr[aus].

Yours cordially,

*Freud*

1. Postcard. A communication of Abraham's is evidently missing.

## 179A

Berlin
29 October 1913

Dear Professor,

Once again I have little to say. Brugsch's letter confirms that Bonhoeffer is behind the whole thing. My chances depend mainly on Bonh.; it seems to me that whatever stand you take with Kraus and Brugsch will have little effect on my prospects. I am therefore glad that I can ask you not to make any special allowances for me.

Br.'s diplomatic letter does at least have the advantage of leaving the matter open for further negotiations. If only one knew whether he means everything he says. Could you not take him at his word and offer to deal with the other theories of hysteria as well? That would dispense with Kutzinski. I thought one of the Viennese colleagues could perhaps undertake this piece of work as a critical and historical prelude to your exposition. (I do not know whether this suggestion is useful; it just occurred to me as I was reading Br.'s reply.)

On a recent journey to Bremen on a Sunday, I carefully studied Jung's work once again. I shall soon start to work out the critique.

Our group is becoming more lively. We are probably going to have our meetings every fortnight. The younger elements are very keen. Stockmayer, who is very friendly with Jung and greatly influenced by his views, will not, I believe, make any great difficulties.—Koerber is out of danger, but he is still very weak and confined to bed for weeks.

I am returning Brugsch's letter, with many thanks for sending it to me.

With kind regards from house to house,
your devoted

*Abraham*

## 180F

Vienna IX, Berggasse 19
2 November 1913

Dear Friend,

Two questions:

[1.] Jung, while putting on a display of injured innocence, has resigned the editorship of the *Jahrbuch*,[1] evidently with a view to securing sole control after getting rid of the editorial directors.[2] Our friends here are unanimously of the opinion that we should not abandon this position, and I am prepared to keep the *Jahrbuch* if you are willing to undertake the editorship. You can have Hitschmann as a helper specifically for all negotiations and work in Vienna. The *Jahrbuch* would be reduced in size to between fifteen and eighteen signatures, it would appear only once yearly, its title would be simplified, all boring laboratory papers would be declined, and it would become a real yearbook of $\Psi\alpha$, that is, it would contain, apart from some selected original papers, critical accounts of the literature, a survey of progress in the various fields, and reports of events in the $\psi\alpha$ movement. Thus it would become an essential tool to everyone interested in $\Psi\alpha$. Please let me know whether you will accept.

2. We think the time has come to think of a severance of all ties with Zurich and thus to the dissolution of the International $\Psi\alpha$ Association. As the best way of bringing this about we have in mind forwarding to the central office a resolution proposing dissolution, signed by the three groups in Vienna, Berlin, and Budapest.[3] If Jung does not accept this, these groups can then resign and promptly form a new organization. Primarily, we do not want to strive for resignation, because that would again mean abandoning a position to them, and Jung would remain president. Similarly, in the event of our resignation, the new organization would be constrained to elect me as president to put an end to the hoax of the Zurichers.

We therefore ask you for your comments on how you stand in this matter, on the question of the resolution to be submitted to the central office, and on the foundation of a new organization, and hope you are in full command of your group.

The matter is urgent. We are already in communication with Jones to explore the prospects in America. Please keep the matter secret for the time being.

With cordial greetings and in haste,
Your faithfully devoted

*Freud*

---

1. On 27 October Jung had written to Freud that he had learned from Maeder that Freud doubted his *"bona fides"*, and that he was therefore "lay[ing] down the editorship of the *Jahrbuch*" (Freud & Jung, 1974 [1906–13]: p. 550). Subsequently, Bleuler resigned as co-director. Under the general direction of Freud alone, Abraham and Hitschmann took over as editors, and the *Jahrbuch* continued publication for one more year in this form. (Cf. the note to this effect in the *Jahrbuch*, 1913, 5: 2.)
2. Bleuler and Freud.
3. "Jung had not yet recognized the British Society, so it could not act" (Jones, 1955: p. 150).

## 181A

Berlin
4 November 1913

Dear Professor,

I am answering you by return and therefore in haste, without giving your *second* question sufficient and calm consideration.

Your first question is quickly answered. If you are willing to entrust me with the editing, I would (with Hitschmann's collaboration) undertake it naturally and gladly. Jung's resignation from the editorship is a good thing for us, and one must definitely not leave the *Jahrbuch* in his hands by your giving up the directorship. I fully approve of the programme as you are planning it. I believe that if all three journals are edited in the same spirit, this can only benefit psychoanalysis. Unfortunately, we know nothing of Jung's real motives. He will certainly not give up his position unless he has some other plan.

The question of the dissolution of the Association is a most delicate one. Our rules do not contain a paragraph dealing with this contingency. On going through them, I even notice that the president is elected for a term of *two* years. We could not, therefore, elect a different president in the autumn of 1914! This is an uncomfortable state of affairs, but I do not see how it should have changed since Munich. Unfortunately I hear very little here about it all. If nothing has happened since, I wonder whether it is wise to choose precisely this moment to adopt a new policy. The proposal made by three groups can too easily come to nothing. We would then be forced to resign, and I would consider this a great mistake. The existing association, known as such, must remain a truly psychoanalytic one, and *you* in particular must not leave it. What is of more practical importance is that I cannot be certain of Berlin. Of 18 members, only 9 are in Berlin. How are we to come to a decision? It could not be done in one meeting, as we would then be making our decision over the heads of those who live elsewhere. It would be a precarious move to inform these members by letter. They are either shifty fellows or would offer well-meant peace proposals. The group would suffer a schism. This is due to the special circumstances in the group. I must add the following points in the interest of our group. Two colleagues have recently settled here, one of whom—Stockmayer[1]—is very much under Jung's influence, or at least is still close to him. I had great hopes for our group from these two members, both of whom are keen and whom I will surely win over in the course of time. Berlin may become very important in the future, and it would be a pity if political differences were to occur in our circle just now when it is beginning to develop!

At any rate, the result of a vote in our group would be doubtful. That is why I cannot unreservedly urge you to this action. It is true, however, that I do not at present have any better suggestion. What a pity that we cannot meet to talk things over. I shall give this matter further thought and shall let you know should something occur to me.

If I have come to a wrong judgement due to insufficient information, you could ask Rank to let me have further details! The above are only some doubts from a particularistic viewpoint!

As soon as I am certain of the rightness and inevitability of your suggestion, I shall of course do everything to ensure its success.

With cordial greetings,
Yours,

*Karl Abraham*

P.S.: Thank you very much again for the information re. "Urania"!

1. The other colleague referred to is evidently Liebermann.

## 182F

Vienna IX, Berggasse 19
6 November 1913

Dear Friend,

My heartfelt thanks for your willingness. Jung obviously gave up the *Jahrbuch* only in order to gain sole control of it after my withdrawal. Deuticke[1] is inclined towards him, and it is probable that he will succeed; at the present moment D. finds himself between two offers, the Jungian and ours, and he will shortly have to decide between them. If D. declines, we shall remember that Heller is very anxious indeed to have the modified *Jahrbuch,* and we shall probably do it with him.

An imprudence on my part which D. rapidly exploited encouraged his coming to an understanding with Jung. Relations between D. and J. have developed with uncanny speed.

On the second question, I know that all your misgivings are justified. On the other hand, however, there is something oppressive about the situation, and both affectively and practically it calls for a solution. Under the terms of the contract we can, for instance, do nothing if Zurich requires us to publish all its rubbish in the *Korrespondenzblatt*,[2] or to publish special papers. Formally the difficulties are slight. The passage in the rules which says that the purpose of the Society is the cultivation of Freudian $\Psi\alpha$ gives us a smooth handle to call for its dissolution, as a statement by me that the Zurichers do not do this cannot reasonably be set aside. Of course J. would make difficulties nevertheless. In the event of the secession of our three groups we should be obliged to found a counter-organization, and our groups would lose about a third of their membership. Perhaps even that risk would have to be accepted. We cannot have regard for our external members here either.

If the dissolution came about from Jung, all difficulties would be removed. But it would have other disadvantages.

I shall let circulate your letter among the friends. Then you and all the others should consider the most advisable course. I feel very uncertain in the matter and must no longer give in to my inclinations, which, however, would certainly be an unambiguous guide.

After the return of Brugsch's letter on your part, I wrote to him politely, but not without reproaches. I made him two proposals, either to let me withdraw or to allow me to make another contribution, which would be called, quite generally, "The $\Psi\alpha$ Theory of the Neuroses", and at the side of which the individual descriptions of the neuroses in the old style, as wished by the befriended neurologists, may remain standing. We shall soon see whether the whole thing was a manoeuvre to "disgust me out of it". Up to now, no reply.

Unfortunately all these affairs disturb one's energy for work, in addition to wasting the time for it.

With heartfelt thanks and in expectation of hearing from you further. Yours,

*Freud*

1. The publisher of the *Jahrbuch*, who would nevertheless bring out the sixth and final volume.
2. The bulletin containing news of the activities of the branches of the IPA incorporated in the *Zeitschrift*.

## 183A

Berlin
7 November 1913

Dear Professor,

Your letter, which reached me a few hours ago, has quickly converted me to a radical point of view. I consider it unethical for the president of the Association to negotiate with a publisher behind our backs, as Stekel once did, in order to lay his hands on the *Jahrbuch*. I can spare myself giving reasons for this view. In my opinion the Association cannot tolerate such underhand activity. Since, however, we cannot shake Jung off in any other way, I am in favour of taking extreme measures, but I could not decide on this until I knew of the most recent developments.

The main thing now is to bring about the action of secession without friction and with the least possible loss of membership among the seceding groups. The following method seems to me the most practicable. There should be a *uniform* action of the three groups. A memorandum would serve this purpose best, to be signed by the presidents of the three groups and sent to all their members. It should give objective grounds for the procedure. Subsequently, each president would have to call a business meeting to arrive at a decision—these meetings should, if possible, occur simultaneously at the three places, and the result should be immediately forwarded to Zurich.

The memorandum would have to state our point of view incisively and take a stand against the false rumours. Sachs seems to me the right man to draft it.

I think I could bring about an almost unanimous vote at our meeting. The objections raised in my last letter referred to members outside Berlin, particularly those from abroad. We are likely to lose some of them. On the other hand, Berlin as well as Vienna might expect some additional members through resignations from the Zurich group (Binswanger, Oberholzer, Gincburg,[1] Pfister(?)).

Are you, dear Professor, already sure whether you will go to Hamburg at Christmas? In this case, any editorial matters concerning the *Jahrbuch* could be discussed then. I am completely at your disposal. If, for instance, you do not have enough time for Berlin, I could accompany you part of the way on the train. Should you not be going, I could come to Vienna if necessary.

For the rest, we will do as Casimiro! With cordial greetings from house to house, and also to your loyal collaborators there,

Yours,

*Karl Abraham*

1. Dr Emil Oberholzer [1883–1958]. After the break between Freud and Jung he became the co-founder, in 1919, of the Swiss Society for Psychoanalysis, serving as its first president until 1927. In that year he founded his own purely medical psychoanalytic group, which dissolved after his emigration, in 1938, with his wife, the child analyst Mira Gincburg [1887–1949], to New York.

### 184F

Vienna IX, Berggasse 19
9 November 1913

Dear Friend,

Events have followed each other so rapidly that a great deal of what you suggest no longer applies. Under the impact of your letter and a very similar one from Jones, Rank and Sachs have agreed to a postponement of the operation against the Association, and Ferenczi, who has

1913 November

been the hothead in the whole business, will no doubt agree to it too. You know that in these matters I gladly let myself be advised by friends, because since being taken in by Jung my confidence in my political judgement has greatly declined. I enclose Jones's letter.[1]

So the *Jahrbuch* has remained ours. Deuticke was simply over-hasty, he seems to have made no secret agreements, and had at first misunderstood me. I shall soon be sending you the detailed plan for the volume I should like to bring out on about 1 July, and shall myself take a substantial part in the work. I shall tell Hitschmann on Wednesday and ask him to get in touch with you. We shall all put our best efforts into making the new *Jahrbuch* a testimonial to what we are capable of, and you will automatically find yourself in an extremely influential position. True, the material benefit will be very slight.

I see already that the whole situation boils down to squeezing out of us everything that we have. There is the cause, and we shall sacrifice ourselves for it without complaint. C.C.!

At the same time the business with Brugsch has been cleared up in a not unpleasing way. He has released me from hy[steria] and agrees that I should contribute to the compilation a section on "The $\Psi\alpha$ Theory of the Neuroses", of the same length or a little more. That, however, throws good light on Kraus's reliability.

On the way back from Hamburg I propose to spend the afternoon (Sunday, 28 December, from midday to the night train) in Berlin, where we shall then discuss everything.

I send my heartfelt greetings to your whole family, and am delighted to be able to regard you officially as what you have always been, one of my best helpers.

Your faithfully devoted

*Freud*

1. Letter of 4 November (Freud & Jones, 1993: pp. 234–236).

## 185A

Berlin
13 November 1913

Dear Professor,

I am glad that we are not going to make politics for the time being. I find Jones's exposition most congenial. I hope we shall make good use of all our energies for creative purposes in the near future. Despite heavy pressure, I am looking forward to my work for the *Jahrbuch* and sincerely thank you for your kind remarks on this occasion. I always have the feeling that I cannot really do *enough* for our cause, since my debt to you is too great in various respects. I feel this with every new stimulus I receive either from you or from Ψα, and the increasing success of my work evoke this thought no less again and again.

The agreement with Brugsch is very gratifying. Kraus really is worth our trust. For example, he has now succeeded in getting a Jewish woman doctor, an assistant in the clinic, the title of professor, the first in Germany. That means an important influence in our Faculty! Perhaps he will use it for me too.

It is not quite certain whether I shall be in Berlin on 28 December, as there are several other things happening around that date. Should I not be here, we would have to find another way. As soon as I know more definitely, I shall come back to it.

As with each of your communications, I welcomed *Totem and Taboo*[1] with great pleasure. It looks very good in this edition and will certainly arouse wide interest. Many thanks!

I am returning Jones's letter and send cordial greetings from my wife and myself to you and your house,

Yours,

*Abraham*

1. The book edition (Vienna: Heller, 1913).

## 186A

Berlin
8 December 1913

Dear Professor,

What a great and unexpected pleasure you gave me today with your picture! The reproduction is excellent. It is only the lateness of the hour that limits me to a few short words of thanks!

I am glad to be able to reciprocate with the enclosed return gift,[1] which has just been finished. This copy is meant for you, Rank, and Sachs. Ferenczi and Jones will receive one each. In this way we can agree quickly on alterations. If you only have small changes to make, would you please correct the text directly and send it to the printer. Ferenczi's copy is carefully corrected for spelling mistakes; the enclosed copy (not intended to be printed) is only made roughly readable. I have put a great deal of work into this unpleasant review but I do not regret it, because only by doing it have I come to recognize the complete sterility of the Jungian "school".—What I have always guardedly called an "incorrect exposition" would actually have deserved a different name.

Now I must apologize to you, dear Professor, that in a paper that I recently sent to Ferenczi (agoraphobia), I committed an unconscious plagiarism. I refer to the remarks on railway phobia, which I found, to my amazement, already in your works (when reading the *Three Essays* for the purpose of the Jung review). I shall make the necessary amendment in the proofs.[2]

It is *possible* that I shall not be in Berlin on the 28th. Would it perhaps suit you, dear Professor, to stop in Berlin *on the way there*? (Naturally I should like that only if it does not interfere with your plans in any way!) If necessary I could make yet another suggestion.

Many thanks for the reprints which I have not yet read, and with cordial greetings from house to house!

Your devoted

*Abraham*

1. The draft of Abraham, 1914[47].
2. Cf. Freud, 1905d: p. 202; Abraham, 1914[44]: pp. 242–243.

## 187F

Vienna IX, Berggasse 19
10 December 1913

Dear Friend,

As today is Wednesday, I shall not be free to study your paper in the evening, but I have skimmed through it and seen that it would deserve a civic crown if such distinctions existed in science! It is, in short, excellent, cold steel, clean, clear, and sharp. Moreover, God knows that it is all true. I shall pass it on to Rank and Sachs and, if a comment could be fitted in somewhere, I shall give you suggestions for it. You cannot imagine what pleasure the co-operation of five such people[1] gives me.

It makes no difference to me whether I stop in Berlin on the way there or the way back, it can also be left undecided until a few days beforehand. Provisionally this is the plan: I shall arrive at 8:08 in the morning of Thursday 25th, go into the hotel only to make myself human, will already be with you for breakfast, and stay until the afternoon train at 3 o'clock (7 o'clock in Hamburg). I shall bring the plan of the first volume of the *Jahrbuch* with me.

My cordial greetings to your wife and children, whom I shall thus soon be seeing.

Your faithfully devoted

*Freud*

1. The Secret Committee.

## 188A

Berlin
14 December 1913

Dear Professor,

Your opinion of my review gives me great satisfaction. Jones has meanwhile already returned his copy, with comments. I hope that, after using all the suggestion that I will still get from Vienna and Budapest, something will emerge that will not fail to make an impression.

Your suggestion about Thursday, 25 December, suits me extremely well. I have unlimited leisure then, so that the best use can be made of these few hours. I do not know how much else you have to do in Berlin. If time runs too short, I could accompany you part of the way to Hamburg. Just for reasons of "insurance"[1] I would add that you will, of course, be our guest for lunch.

My wife and I are delighted to be seeing you here again after a break of years. I assume from your letter that you are coming alone, but should your wife be coming with you, of course every word applies to her also.

With cordial greetings,
Yours,

*Karl Abraham*

1. *Sicherung.* An allusion to Adler's concept that neurotics defend their outward "façade" by various "insurances" against being looked through.


## 189F

Vienna IX, Berggasse 19
21 December 1913

Dear Friend,

I am leaving, then, on Christmas Eve, shall arrive in Berlin at 8:08, Anhalter Station, go to the Excelsior Hotel, which is opposite, to make myself presentable, and ask you to breakfast without me. I then have two visits to make in Berlin, to Eitingon and to my sister,[1] which I can do alone or already in your company, and I hope that until 3 o'clock we shall find time for all we have to talk about. I shall be very glad to be your guest for lunch, and I am looking forward to seeing your wife again and making the acquaintance of your children. The little girl has surely grown big since I saw her last; I assume—no *déjà vu?*—that I saw her once for a moment. On Sunday at 5 o'clock I am travelling straight back from Hamburg.

I am bringing your Jung criticism with me, together with a multilayer encrustation of marginal notes, with which you shall please do whatever you like. I am also bringing Hitschmann's outline of the material for the *Jahrbuch*.

It only remains for me to wish you the best of health for these few days,

your faithfully devoted

*Freud*

1. See letter 49F, n2.

# 1914

## 190A

Berlin
7 January 1914

Dear Professor,

First something unpleasant—politics. Jung is asking about the venue for the Congress.[1] On second thoughts, I myself find my suggestion (Schandau near Dresden), which had been accepted, not to be a good idea, in so far as the place is only good in fine weather. In bad weather we should be confined to the hotel and have nothing else to do. I believe therefore that *Dresden* is the right place. The Viennese colleagues will certainly be pleased with it because of the good [train] connections day and night. I would see to the arrangements. If this suggestion does not seem good to you, please let me know; our group will vote on 17 January. I have just written to Ferenczi and Jones to the same effect.

My negotiations with the reviewers for the *Jahrbuch* went well.—I am spending every free moment on the scoptophilia paper.[2]

Your communications about the genesis of masochism[3] have, in the last few days, led me onto a trail that seems promising. It concerns solving the question of exhibitionism (as a *perversion*, not the general exhibitionistic tendencies of neurotics). The connection with castration anxiety seems quite striking to me. It would stand for exhibiting that part of the body about which one is anxiously worried for several reasons, probably mostly composite ones:

1. Compulsion with strong anxiety; one exhibits oneself anxiously (because of the threatening castration) and, like the masochist, follows one's unconscious impulse and wish to be castrated.
2. Defiant exhibiting: in spite of the threat, I still have the penis!
3. The wish to impress the woman, or, rather, to frighten her. The attempt to incite the woman to similar activity, as the diminished sexual activity (castration anxiety!) does not allow for any other mode of behaviour. (Usually impotence is to be found simultaneously.)

According to my analysis, exhibitionism is certainly originally directed towards the mother. An attempt to compete with the father.

It is late, and I would therefore ask you to excuse this poor presentation!

1914 January

My wife thanks your daughter Anna very much for her letter. For the rest, cordial greetings from house to house and best wishes for 1914!
Yours, as ever,

Karl Abraham

1. Circular letter of January 1914 to the heads of the branch societies, with a hand-written draft of a reply by Abraham, criticizing Jung for not mentioning that Schandau had already been accepted as the venue for the next congress (LOC).
2. Abraham, 1914[43].
3. Evidently on the occasion of Freud's visit to Abraham at Christmas (see also Freud's remark about masochism on 5 November 1913, in the Vienna Society, Nunberg & Federn, 1975: p. 213).

191F

Vienna IX, Berggasse 19
12 January 1914

Dear Friend,

So we all vote for Dresden. Our meeting is on the 14th.

Your remarks about exhibitionism (for which your son provided the impetus) seem to me to be very pertinent. I think matters will turn out to be similar for all perversions, and new viewpoints for therapy and understanding are opening up here.

I am writing on the history of the $\psi\alpha$ movement[1] and am completely absorbed in it. It will be quite vigorous and plain-speaking. I am asking for your help, for the time being with the following points:
(a) When did Eitingon first come to me in Vienna?
(b) When did the Freud Society in Zurich first become active?
(c) When did interest in $\Psi\alpha$ in Bleuler's clinic first begin?
With cordial greetings and thanks,
your faithfully devoted

Freud

1. Freud, 1914d.

192A

Berlin
15 January 1914

Dear Professor,

In reply to your questions[1]:

1. Eitingon, according to his own statement, visited Vienna for the first time at the end of January 1907.[2]

2. The "Freudian Association" must have had its first meeting sometime in the *middle* of the year *1907*. I myself read a paper at one of the first meetings (on the experiencing of sexual traumas), which was published in *November* 1907. It must have been presented late that summer.

3. The third question is hard to answer. When I came to the Burghölzli in December 1904, interest in psychoanalysis already existed. The following years saw a rapid increase in this interest. The following events definitely *preceded* this:

(i) Jung's "Occult Phenomena" (*1902*),[3] in which your *Interpretation of Dreams* is quoted (p. 102).

(ii) Jung's attempt at an analysis of the patient B. St., published in the appendix to the Psychology of Dementia Praecox.[4]

(iii) Several of the studies on association had already been published.

(iv) A case of hysteria (Spielrein) had been analysed by Jung (*definitely* 1904).

I assume that stronger interest probably started in 1903, or possibly only in 1904.

In haste, with cordial greetings,
your devoted

*Abraham*

1. Freud quoted the following information in "On the History of the Psycho-Analytic Movement", as stemming from "the evidence of a colleague who witnessed developments at the Burghölzli" (1914d: p. 28).
2. Eitingon, then assistant at the Burghölzli, was the first pupil from abroad to visit Freud. He was guest at the meetings of the Wednesday Society on 23 and 30 January 1907 (Nunberg & Federn, 1962).
3. Jung, 1902—his doctoral dissertation.
4. Jung, 1907b; C.W. 3, pars. 198ff.

## 193A

Berlin
11 February 1914

Dear Professor,

Everything seems to be going smoothly with the *Jahrbuch*; I hope the reviewers will all send their work in on time. Sadger's review has already arrived. I myself am still busy on "scoptophilia", hope to finish in a week or two, and will then write my review.[1]

We had a very satisfactory meeting of our group a few weeks ago, with four talks about the Jung affair. The best of unity reigns; Stockmayer behaved very well, i.e. he gave the main talk in a purely factual way. He is causing no trouble in any case. I believe that should there be any action within the next few months, I can rely entirely on our

1914 February

group. Indeed, something must happen soon; personally, I would want to throw out the *Munich* lot even more than the Zurich one.

Today there was one real ray of light among the gloom. Renterghem[2] sent me a newspaper carrying a detailed report of the inaugural address given by the Leyden psychiatrist, Jelgersma.*[3] As you may not have heard about it yet, I shall report to you briefly that J. (*nota bene* the most distinguished psychiatrist in Holland) fully accepts the dream and neurosis theories, calls them a great achievement, also fully supports sexuality, and ends by speaking of the enormous impression that the rediscovery of the Oedipus complex made on him. All in all, a very comprehensive review and whole-hearted appreciation without any reservations. I immediately sent a short excerpt of the Dutch report to Ferenczi with the suggestion that Jelgersma's permission should be sought for a translation of his paper for the *Zeitschrift*.

I am gradually beginning to think about plans for the summer. Unfortunately the Engadine, which I love more than anything else, is out of the question for us, as there is an epidemic there of spinal poliomyelitis; last summer there was also a great deal of scarlet fever. Would you perhaps have any suggestions for South Tyrol? We are ready for anything.

In haste, with cordial greetings from house to house,
Yours,

*Abraham*

* on the Unconscious

1. Sadger, 1914; Abraham, 1914[51]. Abraham is referring to the reviews for the *Bericht über die Fortschritte der Psychoanalyse in den Jahren 1909–1913* [Report on the progress of psychoanalysis in the years 1909–1913] in the *Jahrbuch*.
2. Albert Willem van Renterghem [1845–1939], neurologist and psychiatrist, one of Freud's first adherents in the Netherlands; head of the Institute for Psychotherapy in Amsterdam.
3. Gerbrandus Jelgersma [1859–1942], professor of psychiatry [1899–1930] at Leyden University. On 9 February 1914 he had given a rectorial address, "Unconscious Mental Life", at the celebration of the 339th anniversary of the foundation of the university; it was subsequently published as the first supplement to the *Zeitschrift* (Jelgersma, 1914). In 1920 Jelgersma founded the Leyden Society for Psychoanalysis and Psychopathology, which had friendly relations with the Dutch Psychoanalytic Society.

194F

Vienna IX, Berggasse 19
15 February 1914

Dear Friend,

Jelgersma really seems to be an event. I had already received his pamphlet and the copy of the newspaper through Renterghem before your letter arrived. The following day I received a letter from him that corroborated all your information and was really very kind. So here is an official psychiatrist who swallows Ψα hook, line, and sinker! The things one experiences!

I shall send you his letter as soon as I have it back from Ferenczi and it has been read to the Wednesday meeting. Heller intends writing to him and arranging a German edition. I do not think it is anything for the *Zeitschrift*, as it does not go one word beyond the *Interpretation of Dreams*. The "Contributions to the History of the Ψα Movement" were finished, in draft, an hour ago. They are now going to Budapest, from where they will be sent to you as my first contribution to the *Jahrbuch*. It was hard work. I have nothing to say to you about it but the celebrated words: Coraggio, Casimiro! If you have any comments or amendments to suggest, I promise to be very grateful for them. Ferenczi will be doing the same.

Our summer plans are still entirely amorphous. We are no longer a family, only three old people. Even my little daughter wants to go to England by herself this year, as your dear wife still recalls. What sort of revolution the expected guest[1] in Hamburg will bring about is also still unknown. So we may show ourselves really in an anaclitic mood, but we will put off planning until the last moment. The elevation in South Tyrol makes it impossible for my sister-in-law; it is still possible that my wife and I may go there for part of the time (Madonna di Campiglio?).

If you could do something for poor Reik, who is not getting anywhere here, it would be a very fine thing. He has obvious faults, but he is a good modest boy of great devotion and strong conviction, and he can write well.[2]

With cordial greetings to you and yours,
your faithfully devoted

*Freud*

1. Freud's daughter Sophie was expecting her first child, Ernst Wolfgang, b. 11 March 1914.
2. Reik was to move to Berlin shortly afterwards, where Abraham helped him and analysed him free of charge.

## 195F

Vienna IX, Berggasse 19
27 February 1914

Dear Friend,

I think of you a great deal, because I am writing on the "Narcissism". The contributions to the ψα movement[1] have been with Ferenczi for a week, they are probably already with you. Please send your critical remarks separately and order three copies of the proofs from Deuticke so that I can also call upon Rank, Sachs, and Jones to make their comments.

Hard work is being done to make up for time lost because of the strike.[2] I hope to see two issues finished by the first week of March.

I shall be very grateful to you if you can do anything for Reik. We must not desert our people. Perhaps he can help you in some way with your work.

We have begun a joint research and discussion project in the Society on the Oedipus complex in the child. The first meeting passed off very well.[3] Might it be possible for your group to take part or to co-operate in the publication (No. 3 of the *Diskussionen*[4])?

All are well here, hope the same is true with you, and send you my cordial greetings.

Your faithfully devoted

*Freud*

1. Freud, 1914c, 1914d.
2. A strike, which had begun on 27 December 1913, as a result of a wage dispute in the printing trades, had shut down the presses. It ended on 30 January 1914.
3. Meeting of 25 February (Nunberg & Federn, 1975: pp. 231–238).
4. Freud is referring to the series of writings *Diskussionen des Wiener Psychoanalytischen Vereins* [Discussions of the Vienna Psychoanalytic Society], which was edited by the leadership of the Society and published by Bergmann (Wiesbaden), and in which two volumes—about suicides of pupils (1910) and masturbation (1912)—had already been published. No third volume was to appear.

## 196A

Berlin
9 March 1914

Dear Professor,

When these lines reach you, you will perhaps already be a grandfather; I heard by chance that your wife had gone to Hamburg. So—at the risk of being a little bit too early—I send my heartiest congratulations to you and yours!

A small parcel will be posted to you tomorrow containing a long-overdue gift in return for your picture. Some time ago I received a request from Stanley Hall to present my photograph to the psychological seminar in Worcester.[1] I am sending you a copy of the photograph I had made for that reason.

Your manuscript has been with me for more than a week. I have read it several times. I have no factual comments to make except that every word you write conforms to my innermost thoughts. It is a relief that for once everything has been brought out into the open, and the way you have done this is the particularly gratifying thing about it.—I shall only mention a few very minor points:

1. On p. 21 you relate how Rank joined you, but his name is omitted. I do not know whether this is intended, but wished to draw your attention to it in any case.

2. On p. 27 there seems to be an omission: "Havelock Ellis, who has followed its development with sympathy *from*". The words "the beginning" are probably missing here.

3. Might the adjective you assign to Hoche not lead to unpleasant consequences? You are certainly right about him, but would it not be better to omit it?[2]

That is all I have to say, except that I enjoyed my editorial privilege of reading the manuscript before anyone else. It compensated me for the hard work of the last few months.

My scoptophilia paper has just been finished. Now I have to complete my review in record time. I hope to receive all the contributions in the course of this month.

I am enclosing Jelgersma's letter, which Jones sent me. I am very pleased with it.—You will have heard that I am in frequent correspondence with all the members of the Committee.—I am doing everything possible for Reik, but it is not easy to find anything for him.

I shall ask our group whether they are prepared to take part in the research on children, and shall let you know then.

With cordial greetings,
your devoted

*Abraham*

1. Letter of 2 January 1914 (LOC).
2. Freud did eventually mention Rank by name, wrote about "Havelock Ellis, who has followed its [psychoanalysis] development with sympathy though without ever calling himself an adherent", and changed "that filthy genius, Hoche" into "evil genius" (1914d: pp. 25, 30, and 45).

## 197F

Vienna IX, Berggasse 19[1]
9 March 1914

Dear Friend,

Today Deuticke enquired about the progress of the preparations for our *Jahrbuch*. Perhaps you might give him a brief report too.

1914 March

My "Contributions" must already be in your hands. Narcissism will follow in less than a fortnight.
My wife is in Hamburg.
Cordial greetings,
    Freud

1. Postcard.

## 198A[1]

Dear Doctor,
When you have read this, will you pass it on to Prof. Freud and Dr Rank.
With best regards,
A.

---

Confidential!
After various proposals for action against Jung have proved not feasible, I should like now to submit a new proposal to the members of the Committee.

At present our *Zeitschrift* contains a variety of firmly disapproving criticisms of Jung's innovations from, as far as I know, Jones, Ferenczi, Eitingon, and myself. Several others are still to follow. In addition, Freud's thorough reckoning with Jung will appear in the *Jahrbuch*,[2] and also an enlightening article by Sachs and Rank ("What Is Psychoanalysis?").[3]

As soon as the greater part of the articles will have appeared, which will probably be towards the end of April, it seems to me that the time has come for action, as outwardly our moves will then already have sufficient foundation. There are no substantial disagreements between the local groups in Berlin, Vienna, Budapest, and London. A detailed discussion has taken place in the group here and will be continued in small supplementary talks in the following sessions in order to keep the members' interest alive. I believe that everywhere the ground has been smoothed for our action.

I now make this proposal: In May at the latest the four groups give their official position towards a resolution to be brought in by the presidents, which will I imagine be something like this:

"The local group in . . . has after thorough discussion arrived at the opinion that the direction taken by Jung and his followers has lost all inner connection with psychoanalysis. In these circumstances we declare it inadmissible that the sitting President should continue to represent the I. Ps.A. A. to the outside world. We therefore call upon him to give up his office immediately."

All four groups send this or a similar decision to Jung at the same time. The relating decisions of the groups will be published in the next issue of the *Zeitschrift* to appear.

In my opinion Jung will have to yield to this sharp vote of no confidence. But he will then resign from the Association and take his followers with him. For us that would be the desired outcome, far better than if we ourselves resigned.

The loss of members is easy to put up with now; for our *Zeitschrift* in particular it is of little importance. We are not losing any collaborators. As far as pure numbers are concerned, the fast-growing London group and some increase in the Berlin group are already providing a certain substitute. A small number of the Swiss will also remain loyal to us.

This document is going—one copy each—to Vienna, Budapest, and London. If the proposal seems debatable, please say what you think.

With kind regards,

*Abraham*

1. Undated typed circular letter, probably sent to Ferenczi. Note on top and signature in Abraham's handwriting. It evidently belongs here in view of its content and Freud's response. (See also Ferenczi's letter to Freud of 16 March 1914, Freud & Ferenczi, 1992: p. 546.)
2. Ferenczi's programmatic critique of Jung's *Wandlungen und Symbole der Libido* (*Zeitschrift*, 1913, *1*: 391–403) and the adversarial discussions of his works by Abraham, Eitingon, Ferenczi, and Jones in the next volume of the *Zeitschrift* (1914, *2*: 72–87, 99–104)—referred to by Freud as "the salvo in the *Zeitschrift*" (Freud to Ferenczi, 24 April 1914, Freud & Ferenczi, 1992: p. 55), as well as "the bomb in the *Jahrbuch*" (ibid.), Freud's "On the History of the Psycho-Analytic Movement".
3. No such article could be found. This probably refers to the paper Rank and Sachs finally withdrew from the *Jahrbuch* (see letter 208F, 24 April 1914).

## 199F

Vienna IX, Berggasse 19
16 March 1914

Dear Friend,

Tomorrow I am sending you the narcissism, which was a difficult birth and bears all the marks of it. Naturally, I do not like it particularly, but I cannot give anything else at the moment. It is still very much in need of retouching. (You see what my thoughts are lingering on.)[1] Please choose the passage where I have to mention your first (Salzburg) paper yourself;[2] I shall be grateful to you for this, as grateful as I am for any kind of objections. Your comments on the contributions will be taken into account in the proofs.

1914 March

Your proposal of an aggressive action against Jung will be discussed tomorrow evening with Rank and Sachs. What I am most curious about is the reply from London, where difficulties could easily arise.

In Hamburg I gather things are going very well, my daughter seems to continue to behave bravely and sensibly. She already has milk, but the little mite is not yet sucking properly. Strange that these vital instincts should also awaken with such difficulty! I once thought that Mephistopheles's speech to the student *So nimmt ein Kind der Mutter Brust im Anfang widerwillig an*—[So does a child take unwillingly to the mother's breast] was not true. But it is unmistakably true, and so, I hope, is the continuation: *Doch bald ernährt es sich mit Lust* [But soon it feeds with pleasure].[3]

Your picture will return tomorrow from the framer's and will then take the place of Jung's. It does not quite do you justice, but I thank you very much for it. Deuticke has developed a very healthy respect for your work as editor. We have really all been putting every ounce of strength into the work. I must also mention how excellent your locomotor paper[4] is. Even in the Sexual Theory I found no better argument for "muscular eroticism" than the analysis of the abasias,[5] which culminate in the phantasy memory of making the first attempts to walk on the maternal body (the earth).

I send my cordial greetings to you and your dear wife,
Yours,

*Freud*

1. The birth of his first grandchild.
2. Freud, 1914c: p. 74, quoting Abraham, 1908[11].
3. Goethe, *Faust I*.
4. Abraham, 1914[44].
5. Freud, 1905d: p. 203, footnote added in 1910.

## 200A

Berlin
18 March 1914

Dear Professor,

Today the Narcissism arrived, but I have not yet read it. Many thanks for your letter!

In reply to my proposal against Jung, I promptly received from Jones the enclosed declaration, the contents of which are very painful to me.[1] Jones's argumentation is as clear and sharp as ever, and I fear we must give up the action we planned. But perhaps something might yet occur to one of us. The thought of the Congress is extremely unpleasant to me. I should like to cut the tablecloth beforehand. But how?

I shall be glad once the *Jahrbuch* is complete at the end of March. I hope that I shall then be able to find a compensation for the past few months, overburdened with work as they have been, by giving myself about ten days' leave. If nothing happens to prevent it, I want to visit Lake Garda, Venice, and Padua with my wife. As I know that you were in Venice last year, I should be grateful if you could suggest a place to stay that you could recommend!

Before leaving I am sending the manuscripts to Hitschmann. I assume that you also think that a short preface is necessary, to call attention to the change in form and the new editorial principles.[2] I shall write it, and ask you to alter anything that you find necessary.

At the moment I am taken up with the work on the review. That too will have an end.

I am glad to hear that you have such good news from Hamburg. I should like to take this opportunity to express my modest wish that your wife will have a little time left for us on the return journey!

The situation with Reik, from whom you have perhaps heard directly, is all right now. The many efforts to get him a post all failed. But I was able to help him to get some work with two publishers of newspapers—or journals—and he himself found something in addition. He is now very busy writing articles and is sure to make a livelihood for himself gradually. I will continue to stand by him as much as I can.

With cordial greetings, also from my wife,

Yours,

*Abraham*

1. Letter of 13 March 1914 (LOC), in which Jones advised against the action planned by Abraham, stating that "[t]he only member of our [London] group that could be counted on to support the resolution is myself" and: "There are nine groups, counting the new additional one in New York. You could not count on more than three out of these nine sending in a petition to Jung."
2. *Vorbemerkung der Redaktion* [Editorial preface] (*Jahrbuch*, 1914, 6: 263–266).

## 201F

Vienna IX, Berggasse 19
25 March 1914

Dear Friend,

Enclosed Jones's letter. It is quite remarkable how each one of us in turn is seized with the impulse to kill, so that the others have to restrain him. I suspect that Jones himself will produce the next plan. The role of co-operation in the Committee is however, very well illustrated by this! We shall discuss all this. The critical issue of the *Zeitschrift* has now appeared and will perhaps spare us many a decision.

You do not mention when you are going on your well-earned little journey. The last few times I was in Venice, I stayed in the Britannia, very good, always very full. Book a long time in advance! Danieli is said to be very good too. At Easter everything is full up now.

Many thanks for the trouble you took over Reik, which seems to have been successful. Now we have to wait and see whether he will not ruin what he has all over again. He is suffering the recoil of the violent death-wish against a tyrannical father-in-law to be!

Since finishing the Narcissism, I have not been having a good time. A great deal of headache, intestinal troubles, and already an idea for a new work, which is an added difficulty in the summer because it precludes staying at a hotel and requires a quiet place where one can work. So far our summer is utterly sphinx-like.

According to the news from Hamburg the mother is very well, the little boy still very "shabby", as we say. He has not yet quite grasped the idea of drinking and putting on weight. Today he is two weeks old.

I send my cordial greetings to you and to your dear wife,
your faithfully devoted

*Freud*

## 202A

Berlin
2 April 1914

Dear Professor,

Yesterday I sent off to Hitschmann the contributions to the *Jahrbuch* that had come in to me and asked the latecomers to send their manuscripts direct to Hitschmann to save time. I did not really need to look through these manuscripts, because they came from our most reliable collaborators (Jones,[1] Sachs,[2] Ferenczi[3]). My manuscript has a rather variegated look, part hand-written, part typed. But I had no time to do it better. I shall have to polish it further when the proofs are corrected. I think we ought to ask Sadger to shorten his review of Stekel's work; there is no point there in writing so many words. I have not written to him about it myself, because I wanted to hear your opinion first.

Now, to your two manuscripts. I have already written to you about the "History". I have read it over and over again and have increasingly come to see how important a weapon it is. After giving it much thought, I have also come to the conclusion that everything personal should stay as it is. There is only one expression that I would like to have changed. You say about Adler how much he complained about your *persecution*. I am afraid this word might cause harm. A. will protest against being called paranoid. An expression with a less pathological implication—such as "hostility"—would be preferable.[4]

I cannot understand why you should be dissatisfied with the "Narcissism". I find the work brilliant and completely convincing throughout. I do not wish to go into details of your train of thought, but will only emphasize one point: namely, the particularly successful analysis of the delusion of being watched, its relation to conscience, etc.[5] Your expositions about the ego-ideal are especially valuable for practical purposes. These expositions had been in my mind for a long time already, and with every sentence I read I was able to guess what was coming next. In particular, the distinction between ego-ideal and true sublimation[6] is something that I have always explained to my patients, but without putting it in so precise a form. Might I add a suggestion here? I think this is where the contrast between Jung's therapy and $\Psi\alpha$ can be most pointedly stressed. The "life task" and all similar concepts (including the prospective tendency of the unconscious)[7] are in fact nothing but an appeal to the ego-ideal and thereby a path that by-passes all real possibilities of sublimation (with the unconscious intention of avoiding them). Perhaps a passage referring to this might be useful?

I am now eagerly awaiting the "Moses",[8] but do not quite understand *∗*.[9] Do you not think that the lion's paw will be recognized all the same?

I received a message from Jung that Dresden had been chosen as the venue for the Congress, with 44 votes, against 36 cast for Munich. It is not clear to me how the vote works out, as Berlin cast 18 votes and London 15 for Dresden, and I can scarcely believe that Vienna and Budapest cast only 11 between them. Jung proposes 4/5 September as the Congress date, taking into account the International Neurological Congress in Berne (7 September and the following days).[10] As I have still not given Jung a definite answer on the latter question I would welcome your opinion.

In May our group will have a meeting on the subject of the Oedipal attitude in infancy.[11] I hope at least some of the contributions will be worth publishing.

Pollak's etching[12] arrived a few days ago. I find the posture a particularly good likeness, whereas it takes some time to get used to the facial expression. But then it is good. The whole composition, especially the distribution of black and white, is very well done.

By chance, I recently acquired your work on cocaine (1885)[13] from an antiquarian, and read it yesterday.

I hope, dear Professor, that your health has improved in the meantime. Your grandson, too, I hope, is making good progress and no longer fails to recognize the pleasure value of sucking. Incidentally, we had this difficulty with both our children!

1914  April

Our planned trip to Italy can unfortunately not take place. Three weeks ago our little one got tonsillitis, and after that an infection of the lymph glands, was feverish for a fortnight, and has only just recovered. At the moment the elder one is in bed. My wife cannot leave the children now, so we have put off our journey until the end of the summer holidays, and if the children can travel we shall go with them on Sunday for a week in the Frankenwald, where we have found, in an old castle, romantic quarters that I hope will also be good. We are not clear yet about what will happen in the summer. Perhaps the little one will have to go to the seaside, then my wife might travel with the children; after that, the two of us could visit the Tyrol and North Italy; we could entirely adapt to possible suggestions from you.

With cordial greetings, also from my wife, to you and yours,

Yours,

*Karl Abraham*

1. Jones, 1914b.
2. Sachs, 1914.
3. Ferenczi, 1914[148].
4. Freud finally wrote about "the 'persecution' to which he [Adler] asserts he has been subjected by me" (1914d: p. 50).
5. Freud, 1914c: p. 95.
6. Freud, 1914c: pp. 95–95.
7. According to Jung, the neurotic suffers from having shrunk back from the demands of reality, the "life task". Therapy should be guided by the question of which task the patient does not want to fulfil, and which difficulty he or she seeks to avoid. The unconscious, particularly as expressed in dreams and "collective" symbols, would have a teleological, "prospective" tendency—a reference to neglected duties and to reality rather than a fulfilment of repressed wishes. Similar views had been expressed by Janet, Adler, and Maeder.
8. Freud, 1914b.
9. Freud published the work anonymously. In the pre-publication announcement in the *Zeitschrift* (1914, 2: 205), to which Abraham seems to refer, and in the publication itself in *Imago*, the author's name was replaced by three asterisks: *⁎*.
10. The International Congress for Neurology, Psychiatry, and Psychology was scheduled for 7–12 September in Berne, Switzerland. Like the planned Psychoanalytic Congress, it was not held because of the outbreak of the First World War.
11. Meetings of 17 and 27 May (*Zeitschrift*, 1914, 2: 410).
12. Max Pollak [1886–?], noted Viennese painter and graphic artist. His etching of Freud is reproduced in Ernst Freud et al., 1974: p. 202.
13. Probably Freud (1884e), which had originally appeared in 1884 in a journal but was subsequently published separately in a revised and enlarged edition in 1885.

## 203F

Vienna IX, Berggasse 19
6 April 1914

Dear Friend,

Hitschmann telephoned this morning to say that the patient from Berlin[1] had arrived, thus putting an end to a minor worry. Your parcel with the manuscripts was considered overdue, and we did not dare to imagine the situation that it had perished.

Do not let yourself be bothered at all with regard to Sadger and insist on the elimination of everything digressing or spiteful. S. is seldom tolerable without censorship, and it is really superfluous to make publicity for Stekel.

"Persecution" is the term used by Adler himself. I shall replace it in accordance with your wish. Instead of the "filthy" genius of A. Hoche I will insert "evil" genius.[2]

That you also buy the Narcissism from me affects me deeply and binds us still more intimately together. In this case I have a very strong feeling of awful inadequacy. I shall incorporate the comment you would like on the bypassing of sublimation in the Zurich therapy.[3] The Moses is anonymous partly as a pleasantry, partly out of shame at the obvious amateurishness which it is hard to avoid in the *Imago* papers, and finally because my doubts about the findings are stronger than usual and I published it only as a result of editorial pressure.

I cannot explain Jung's election arithmetic. Vienna had 16 votes for Dresden, Budapest 3 or 5.

That would be:
```
Berlin      18
London      15
Perhaps London was not unanimous?
Vienna      16
Budapest     3
            ──
            52
```

I did not answer Jung, as his letter had the character of a provisional note and did not appear to demand a reply.

Your opinion about the etching coincides with that of many here. I have heard more severe and more enthusiastic opinions.

I am still going through a dull and stupid period. Our trip to Brioni,[4] which I hoped would give me a push forward, has had to suffer an alteration. My little girl has caught whooping cough and cannot come with us. Rank is going instead of her. I am very sorry that you had to postpone your plans, and also for the reason for it. Instead, I will tell you about a summer project that has surfaced here and which you also might perhaps consider. In 1907 we spent half of August and a bit of

1914 April

September in Annenheim on Lake Ossiach, one stop before Villach.[5] Lake resort, house, forest, air, general atmosphere were so excellent that we decided to return as soon as the then proprietor, who was running a scandalous place, had wrecked himself. That has now happened. The doctor I know who goes there guarantees that the new owner's intentions are good. We would not mind spending the whole summer there. Some time ago my sister was on Lake Ossiach for the whole summer and really never found it too hot. The warm bathing might do your children no less good than the sea. I should work a great deal and take many walks in the fairy-tale forests above the house. In any case, keep the project in mind.

The little "Dream" appeared yesterday in an English translation by Eder.[6] Otherwise nothing new. Perhaps the calm before the storm.

I send my cordial greetings to you and your dear wife, and wish for a quick going through the inevitable diseases of childhood, which are, as we see, best got rid of sooner rather than later.

Yours,

*Freud*

Postscript

The first issue of the *Zeitschrift für Sexualwissenschaft*[7] has reached me. I decided to make my contribution to it dependent on the attitude to $\Psi\alpha$ that it displayed. This turns out to be not very alluring. There is an extremely shabby note in Eulenburg's article (p. 9) and a review by Saaler[8] that regards Stekel's work on fetishism as representing the present status of $\Psi\alpha$. This strengthens my intention to go on maintaining reserve.

The Society is designed to achieve recognition for Fliess.[9] Rightly so, because he is the only ingenious mind among them and the possessor of a bit of unappreciated truth. But the subjection of our $\Psi\alpha$ to a Fliessian sexual biology would be no less a disaster than its subjection to any ethics, metaphysics, or anything of the sort. You know him, his psychological incapacity and his physicalistic consistency. Left hand = woman = *Ucs.* = anxiety. We must at all costs remain independent and take our stand with equal rights. Ultimately should be able to meet all the parallel sciences.

*F.*

1. The contributions to the *Jahrbuch* that Abraham had sent to Hitschmann on 1 April.
2. See letters 196A, 9 March 1914, & n. 2; 202A, 2 April 1914, & n. 2.
3. Freud did not carry out this intention, however.
4. Freud, his daughter Anna, and Ferenczi had planned to go to Brioni (an island in the Adriatic) at Easter, 9–13 April. Rank eventually went along instead of Anna.
5. In Carinthia, in the south of present-day Austria.
6. Freud, 1901a (London: W. Heinemann).

7. See letter 150A, 29 January 1913, n. 2.
8. Dr Bruno Saaler; he had previously published several of articles in the *Zentralblatt*, later lecturer at Hirschfeld's *Institut für Sexualwissenschaft* in Berlin (Herzer, 1992: p. 122).
9. Fliess was a founding member of the *Ärztliche Gesellschaft für Sexualwissenschaft und Eugenik* and contributed an article for the first issue of the *Zeitschrift für Sexualwissenschaft* (Fliess, 1914).

## 204A

Berlin
8 April 1914

Dear Professor,

Many thanks for your detailed letter! I do not want to answer it now, but only to tell you what I would have written to you in any case today.

Our little daughter's illness turned out on Sunday to be measles; in the meantime it has already passed, having taken a very mild course. But a journey together with wife and children is now out of the question. As I can now go away alone for a few days without worries about the children, I had the idea of spending Easter in Vienna. I was just going to ask you whether I would not be coming at an inconvenient time for you, when I heard from you that your youngest daughter is ill, and then you mention something about a journey you have planned, about which I have no details.

I am asking now for some brief information (by telegram, if you like) as to whether you are going away over Easter, when you are going, and in this case whether I can meet you somewhere on the way. As I have reasons for being back here on Tuesday, a journey too far south would, of course, not be worth while. Personally, I am most anxious to know whether I would not disturb you.

It goes without saying, as the state of health is still a little uncertain here, that I could not guarantee that I would appear, and so I beg you not to orientate your plans towards mine in any way!

With best wishes for your health and for your daughter's quick recovery, and with cordial greetings,
Yours,
*Karl Abraham*

## 205A

Berlin[1]
14 April 1914

Dear Professor,

Many thanks for your telegram and the card from Brioni![2] I should have been glad to come, and I would not have shrunk from even a rather long journey. But after receiving the telegram I could not have left before 11 at night, would have been in Pola the following night at 12 o'clock, and as far as I can see I could not have reached Brioni before Saturday morning. I should then have been much too short of time. I have been in the Harz Mountains for three days and came back just in time to see the beginning of measles in our little boy.

I shall answer your letter at the end of the week. I hope this card will reach you despite the lack of a more detailed address.[3]

Cordial greetings to you, Rank and Ferenczi, whom you will be so kind as to remind, gently, about his review!

Yours,

*Karl Abraham*

1. Postcard.
2. Both missing.
3. The card is addressed to "Prof. Dr S. Freud from Vienna, Brioni near Pola".

## 206A

Berlin
19 April 1914

Dear Professor,

I am replying today to your detailed letter of the 6th, assuming that you are now back in Vienna. I hope the short trip has brought you the desired rest. If you have received my card—but surely even if you have not—you will know how much I would have liked to come. But three days' travel so as to be there for a day and a half seemed too much. Many thanks once again for your telegram and card! I hope your "little one's" whooping cough has been as mild as our two "little ones'" measles.

To go on with the subject of travel—you suggested Lake Ossiach. I have only two reservations. Firstly, I do not know whether its low height above sea level will improve the children's health as much as the high mountain region; all other requirements seem to be splendidly fulfilled there. Secondly, my wife and I had set our hearts firmly on the Dolomites. These, admittedly, can be reached by rail in a few hours from there. So if we are there for some time, I might be able to have a tour of the Dolomites with my wife and leave the children there in the care of the governess.—Wolkenstein (Gröden) is especially recommended to us from various sides. Would you not be in favour of such an elevated place, or is there a health reason for the choice of lower height? Of course we shall comply with your suggestions as far as possible, only the above reservations because of the children are disturbing.

Jung's *Jahrbuch*[1] is rather mediocre. I think the new one will be far superior, and I am glad it will appear as early as June. I hear from Hitschmann that you have somewhat qualified what I said in the preface concerning the exclusion of case material. (I perfectly agree with that.)[2] Some time ago Sadger submitted a larger casuistic essay on inversion for the *Jahrbuch*, also containing some basic general notions. I declined for the time being. Should we accept it after all?[3]

I should also like to remind you to let me know which days you, or rather the Vienna members, suggest for the Congress. Jung suggested 4 and 5 September on account of the subsequent International Neurological Congress in Berne.

The new *Zeitschrift für Sexualwissenschaft* does not greatly impress me. Eulenburg, incidentally, is quite senile; I have therefore spared him in recent discussions.

In May our group will have the session in which the Oedipus phenomena in infancy are to be discussed. I myself must resume work on my *Habilitation*, which has had to rest throughout the winter. I would much rather turn to a few subjects that interest me more. Perhaps I can combine both.

One of the last issues of *Simplicissimus*[4] contained a joke which brilliantly illustrates your essay on narcissism, especially with regard to the significance of hypochondria—I therefore enclose it. And in addition cordial greetings, also from my wife, to you and yours,
Yours,

*Karl Abraham*

1. The last issue edited by Jung (1913, 5, part 2).
2. It finally read in the preface: "[The *Jahrbuch*] will only bring original works that communicate new results of research or take position in controversial problems, but will, as a rule, exclude articles dealing with casuistic material" (1914, 6: p. v; translated for this edition).
3. Sadger's paper was not included.
4. See letter 36A, 11 June 1908, n. 5. The clipping is missing.

## 207A

Berlin[1]
22 April 1914

HEARTFELT CONGRATULATIONS ON THE ZURICH NEWS[2]
ABRAHAM EITINGON +

1. Telegram.
2. Two days earlier, Jung had written to Freud: "Dear Mr. President, The latest developments have convinced me that my views are in such sharp contrast to the views of the majority of the members of our Association that I can no longer consider myself a

suitable personality to be president. I therefore tender my resignation to the council of the presidents of the branch societies, with many thanks for the confidence I have enjoyed hitherto. Very truly yours, Dr C. G. Jung" (Freud & Jung, 1974 [1906–13]: p. 551).

## 208F

Vienna IX, Berggasse 19
24 April 1914

Dear Friend,

You were certainly just as surprised as I was at how meticulously Jung carries out our own intentions. Our reserve has now indeed borne fruit; somehow we will get rid of him, and perhaps of the Swiss altogether.

I immediately assumed the role of summoner of the conference of presidents and arranged for Rank to send out a circular letter which should make possible a decision by correspondence, thus saving travel. The action is being carried out in two steps, first among the friends, and only once these have reached agreement, steps will be taken officially by all the presidents (i.e. two more[1]). Please support the proposal to entrust you with the leadership until the Congress.[2]

About plans for the summer: we have almost definitely settled for Annenheim. We have reservations because of the high cost, 15 K per person per day, which does however guarantee select company and good food. A family would naturally find other conditions. We have six rooms for three persons. In my experience and judgement warm water and mild air are far better for children than extreme heights (apart from the sea, of course); I know Wolkenstein, having been there myself. It is splendid; in the Längsthal edelweiss grows in the streets, but accommodation is not easy to get, and it is hardly possible to extend one's stay for more than two to three weeks. The weather is far from constancy (not the one on the lake[3]), and if it is not fine, one is miserably cold, as we remember very well. I am giving you this to think about, without wanting to influence you decisively; I know how difficult the problem of summer is.

I am glad to hear that your little ones have got over the statutory measles so easily; with ours, the superfluous whooping-cough was nothing like as easy, but it is departing now.

I enjoyed Brioni very much, but had to struggle with an indisposition I could not account for, which broke out on my return as a severe tracheitis–laryngitis. I am by no means well, and in particular I am quite inactive intellectually. Perhaps it is also the intoxicating spring which one feels in one's bones.

Hitschmann says that he already has too much material for the *Jahrbuch*, so Rank and Sachs have withdrawn their contributions. Sadger can be accepted and put in store.

Last week I talked to two members of the American group from Ward's Island (the most serious one),[4] and they assured me that Jung's influence is quite unimportant with them. It seems that only Jelliffe, that crook, is a firm support for him.

With cordial greetings to you and your dear wife and good wishes for the new Jungless era,
Yours,

*Freud*

1. Maeder of Zurich and Seif of Munich.
2. On 30 April Freud sent letters with the same text to each of the presidents of the European branch societies with the request "to nominate that person among the six eligible presidents of the branch societies whom you wish to entrust with the leadership of the Association until the election of a president, whereby you do not need to exclude yourself . . . I, myself, am inclined to choose Dr *Abraham* as the provisional head of the Association, because from his place of residence he can most easily make preparations for the Congress, which will take place in Dresden" (LOC). Freud's suggestion was accepted.
3. . . . *weit entfernt von Konstanz (nicht a.[m] B[odensee]*); the German *Konstanz* can stand for Constance on the lake to which it gave its name or for constancy.
4. The American Psychoanalytic Association; president, August Hoch [1868–1919] (Ward's Island), secretary, John MacCurdy [1886–1947], council, Abraham Brill, Louville E. Emerson [1873–1939], and William A. White [1870–1937].

## 209F

Vienna IX, Berggasse 19
7 May 1914

Dear Friend,

You are now our President. We have the Association in our own hands and shall not soon let go of it.

Maeder agreed in a very obliging fashion; and Seif did so laconically.[1] The official announcement of the result of the vote will probably be sent out by Rank tomorrow.

I now suggest to you the preparation of a *Korrespondenzblatt*, which can come into the 4th issue of the *Zeitschrift*. (The 3rd is as good as finished.) In the preamble to your proclamation please do not omit to mention that the previous headquarters ceased all activity since Munich and did not even produce a Congress report.[2]

Perhaps you will find yourself justified in altering the ill-chosen date of the Congress. In fact it cuts right across our holidays. If we have to be in Dresden for 4/5 September, what shall we do afterwards? I have to

1914 May                                                                  235

give a lecture in Leyden at the end of September,[3] fetch my youngest from England,[4] and pay my visit to Hamburg. Can it not be arranged that the Congress is postponed until the third week in September or the beginning of the fourth? For many this would be much more convenient. You see, no sooner have you taken office than the petitioners come. We can probably have our own private meeting the day before the Congress.

I am still unwell and without pleasure for work, and am waiting for the proofs of the *Jahrbuch*, which fail to arrive in spite of all reminders. There is a good deal that I shall sharpen, and several things I shall soften.[5]

I still know nothing about the summer.

Heller is complaining vigorously about the bad state of the subscription list of both our journals. Certainly the printers' strike did us a great deal of harm. But we must see it through.

I hope your children have now fully recovered, and that you and your wife are as well, as is appropriate to your youth and harmony.

I turned 58 yesterday.

With cordial greetings,

Yours,

   *Freud*

1. To Freud's suggestion of making Abraham interim president.
2. See *Zeitschrift*, 1914, 2: 405–406.
3. Jelgersma had invited Freud to lecture at the University there (Jones, 1955: p. 105).
4. Anna was to leave for Hamburg on 7 July, from where she went on to England on 15 July. Caught there at the outbreak of the war, she could return to Vienna only on 26 August 1914, with the Austrian ambassador, after 10 days' journey and a 40-hour train ride by way of Gibraltar–Genoa–Pontebba.
5. In the "History of the Psycho-Analytic Movement", which first appeared in the new *Jahrbuch*.


# 210A

Berlin
10 May 1914

Dear Professor,

Only today can I thank you for the telegram[1] and your written communications, as the bandage at least leaves my fingers free. I have been suffering all week from a boil on my right wrist, with very unpleasant lymphangitis. It is healing now. And as it was not a "dog-bite",[2] the consequences for our correspondence are already almost removed!

It gives me great pleasure and satisfaction that you, dear Professor, and the closest friends, wish me to be President, and I sincerely thank you all for your confidence. I had already stated my readiness to take over temporarily, but you seem to want me as permanent President. I have given this much thought. I am not reverting to my earlier proposal (Jones), because I realize that London is too far away from the centre and it would be particularly difficult to direct the *Korrespondenzblatt* from there. The most important objection to *my* being President really comes from you. If a splinter group misuses the name of Ψα, then you personally should be at the head of the legitimate movement, so that everyone is aware which is the Freudian Ψα. That was your own view when we discussed it in the winter. On the other hand—and I have talked about this with Sachs during the last few days—you ought not to be burdened with new duties. I have therefore thought of a solution, and I hope you will find it feasible. The actual presidential duties will be taken over by myself, or whoever else is finally elected; however, my suggestion would enable you to stand officially at the head and to lead the scientific part of the congresses. I think we ought to make you a permanent Honorary President—as is also the practice in other scientific associations. As far as I am concerned, I shall not say too much about feelings of insufficiency, for I feel confident that I can do better than my predecessor. Thinking back to the first congresses, though, I realize that the excellent atmosphere, and much else besides, was due to your leadership. With the best will in the world, none of us others can restore the character that the Congress lost in Munich. The business report and the chairing of the business meetings would be the actual President's job, as well as all business during the year. You would assume office only on the two Congress days and could even be relieved then if it proves too much for you—which is hardly likely. Sachs immediately approved of this suggestion. I should be very happy if you agreed as well.

I was glad to see that you are now interested in the date of the Congress. Jung had proposed 4/5 September. I replied to him at the time that I would first of all ask round our group. Jung wanted these days because the Berne International Neurological Congress is immediately afterwards (7–12 September). To that we can reply that the German Neurological Congress begins precisely on the 5th, also in Berne. So we cannot begin before 13 September. Our group was all for 13/14 September. However, a somewhat later date, something like 19/20 or 20/21, would certainly also suit all of us. Or would you prefer 26/27? I intend to leave the decision as to which date seems the most favourable to the European groups. Can you give me your opinion on a card?

I am also preparing the *Korrespondenzblatt* as fast as I can. I shall ask the groups for their reports. I am a bit at a loss with regard to a secretary. Eitingon has offered himself; I am only afraid that he may not work quickly enough. Reik has offered himself too. I shall probably take on Dr

1914 May

Horney, who has proved a very good secretary to our group; that is to say, she can have all duplicating and other work done in her husband's office. I think it is very important that everything should function promptly at this stage.

I thought the printing of the *Jahrbuch* was proceeding well as I received the proofs of Federn's paper a long time ago. I hope there will be no delay.

Reik gave a very nice paper in our last meeting about the male puerperium. He wants to submit the expanded work to the *Jahrbuch* under the title of "Father Rites".[3] Stär[c]ke has sent me the big manuscript with 18 plates which had already previously been in Jung's hands. I am looking through it very carefully, but it is unlikely that we shall be able to accept it, not even parts of it, as St. now suggests.[4]

Our holiday plans are gradually taking the following shape. At the beginning of the school holidays (4 July) my wife will probably go with the children to a Baltic resort in Mecklenburg and stay there for four weeks. I shall start my holidays on about 25 July, and first of all stay a week at the seaside with my wife and children. Then we shall bring the children home and go, the two of us, to the Tyrol. We should like to do a walking tour in the Dolomites and then find our way to you, wherever you and yours are.

I believe that by the time we meet in the summer, everything will have been decided in Switzerland. Your "History" in the *Jahrbuch* will induce Jung (and with him his followers) to resign. We shall then be able to enjoy the Congress.

I am preparing a paper for *Imago* on forms of greeting.[5] At the Congress—if it turns out as we wish it—I should like to give a talk about the ψα therapy of mental diseases. Cordial greetings to you and yours, also from my wife!

Yours,

*Karl Abraham*

1. Missing.
2. Just when a serious conflict had arisen between Freud and Jung (concerning a patient; cf. Falzeder, 1994), Jung had stopped writing to Freud. Freud then learned that Jung had been bitten by a dog and had been in great pain (Freud & Jung, 1974 [1906–13]: p. 479).
3. *Über Couvade ("männliches Wochenbett")* [On Couvade ("male puerperium")], at the meeting of the Berlin Society in April (report in *Zeitschrift*, 1914, 2: 410); subsequently published not in the *Jahrbuch*, but in *Imago* (Reik, 1914).
4. No paper by August Stärcke that might fit this description appeared in any of the psychoanalytical journals.
5. Apparently never published.

## 211A

Berlin
12 May 1914

Dear Professor,

A card from Rank, which arrived today, has answered my question about the time of the Congress, so that I delayed no longer to draft and despatch the enclosed circular.

At the same time I am approaching Riklin[1] for a short report on the Congress, which will contain only the names of the papers and the tenor of the decisions.

So everything will appear in one issue of the *Korrespondenzblatt*.[2] I anticipate having all the material together at the beginning of June at the latest, so that printing can follow quickly.

In haste, with cordial greetings,
Yours,

*Abraham*

Today a section of your "History of the $\Psi\alpha$ Movement" came from Deuticke. I assumed that I was only to take note of it and had nothing further to do.

1. Re-elected secretary of the IPA at the Munich Congress.
2. *Zeitschrift*, 1914, 2: 405–407.

## 212F

Vienna IX, Berggasse 19
13 May 1914

Dear Friend,

Many thanks for your rich letter! I had no suspicion of a "dog-bite". Meanwhile I have been ill again myself and have been having a bad time in general, as if worry and work were at last wearing me down!

My last bout of intestinal trouble caused my personal physician[1] to take the precaution of carrying out a rectoscopy, after which he congratulated me so warmly that I concluded that he had regarded a carcinoma as highly probable.

So this time it is nothing. I must struggle on. Our summer is still not settled at all. If, as Rank suggests, you manage to have 20–21 September (Sunday!) accepted as the date of the Congress, we can have our private meeting beforehand on the 19th, I shall be able to postpone my lecture in Leyden to, say, the 23rd, and then move on to see my daughter and grandchild in Hamburg. My little one can cross over from England and

1914   May

join me in Holland, and then there will be more time for us in Berlin than the interval between two trains.

Meanwhile I firmly accept your promise of a visit after your tour of the Dolomites. Perhaps we shall travel to Dresden together.

It is true that it is my personal wish to see you as our definite President. I know what to expect of your energy, correctness, and devotion to duty, in most agreeable contrast to your predecessor. From other quarters it is pointed out that relations with America and regard for capturing the young London group speak in favour of Jones. In these circumstances I wish to leave to all of you the decision that will have to be made at our pre-congress. To decide now would be premature. We do not know yet whether the Swiss will really resign after the appearance of the *Jahrbuch*, and this must necessarily influence the election of the president. I myself would like to be excluded, or rather held in reserve for some undetermined extreme emergency. Your *honourable* suggestion does not appeal to me; in the first place, there is a flavour of "retd." [retired] about it, and in the second the present bad and crisis-ridden times do not seem to me to be appropriate for conferring an honour. But I must not refrain from heartily thanking you for the friendly idea. In quiet, successful times I should gladly have accepted. For the time being the institution of a president and vice-president seems to me to be indispensable, and the sharing of the two functions between you and Jones at brief (two-yearly) intervals advisable. However, as I mentioned, I am positive that the Committee will itself be able to settle this question without being disturbed by personal ambition.

What rather offends me is my lack of desire or incapacity for work, which has persisted since Easter. This week I at last finished the proofs of the first third of the "Contributions to the History of the Ψα Movement", the part in which there was practically nothing to alter. I have only added a motto, *fluctuat nec mergitur*,[2] and inserted Rank's name into an anonymous praise. I think of changing a great deal in the third section.

I welcome all your work projects with full sympathy. I expect to hear about you and Berlin from Sachs tomorrow.

Do not take amiss the low level of morale in this letter and accept cordial greetings for you and yours from
Your

*Freud*

1. *Leibarzt*, a play on the possible double meaning of the word *Leib* in composite words: doctor for the body, or favourite doctor.
    Walter Zweig [1872-after 1954], *Privatdozent* in Vienna, specialist for diseases of the stomach and intestines.
2. "It is tossed by the waves, but it does not sink" (motto of the city of Paris).

## 213A

Berlin
15 May 1914

Dear Professor,

In my last letter I did not really take much notice of your state of suffering, since I thought it was not serious. This is what happens if one is narcissistically restricted by one's own complaints. I now hasten to join your doctor wholeheartedly in his congratulations. I hope to hear from you at the next opportunity that you are once again fully satisfied with your health and your achievements—this would be the most reassuring news in view of the demands you make upon yourself. Meanwhile, you might perhaps apply to your own health the motto you mentioned! Since there really seems to be no reason for pessimism.

As regards the matter of the presidency, I fully agree with you. I cannot, however, see why my suggestion concerning your Honorary Presidency should have the flavour of "retd"., since it would, on the contrary, make you once again the active leader of our congresses. It goes without saying that I should like most of all to see you as *full* President. The best solution to the problem will probably be found within the intimate circle of friends.

Riklin, whom I asked for some material on the past Congress, responded with the enclosed writing,[1] which I should be glad to have back sometime. I replied at once, most politely, of course. I am doing everything to keep the correspondence calm, so that nothing on my part can exacerbate the situation. If the Swiss take part in the Congress, they shall have nothing in hands to hold against us.

This letter, dear Professor, needs no reply! Do not trouble yourself unnecessarily just now. I should like to add to my recent communications that I am working on a short paper "On the Relationship between the Oral and Sexual Drives".[2] The *Zeitschrift* should not be completely without contributions from me.

More about plans for the summer as soon as I know something myself! I should like to know sometime when your holidays begin—the middle of July, or later?

With cordial greetings and good wishes,
Yours,

*Karl Abraham*

1. Missing.
2. Abraham, 1916[52]; see letter 153A, 3 March 1913, & n. 7.

## 214F

Vienna IX, Berggasse 19
17 May 1914

Dear Friend,

I am answering you by return, so that I can send you back Riklin's letter. It goes without saying that as long as we are in power we shall never imitate Jung's brutality.

I can consider myself cured of my last attack. If one pauses with production for a few months, it is perhaps not such a misfortune. I am planning to begin the holidays this year on 19 July; the decision as to whether we are going first to Karlsbad will be made on Monday.

There was another very intelligent article by Putnam in defence of sexuality in the interpretation of dreams in the *Journal of Abnormal Psychology*, April–May '14.[1] It is just that he has to show such hellish reverence for Adler, which is quite out of place in this context.

It will interest you that we recently discovered that my little one[2] translates English poets very beautifully into German verse. As a test I set before her some of Byron's *Hebrew Melodies*,[3] and cannot deny that her version pleased me almost more than that of Gildemeister. It is a very fine little creature.

As far as Reik is concerned, I assume that you have long understood that he must not be allowed to get into real poverty, and if you notice that he does, act quickly on my behalf and debit the cost to me. I had started in Vienna with a regular subsidy when he left, and perhaps that too was a motive for him. For he is noble and decent.

With cordial greetings and please do not worry.

Your faithfully devoted

*Freud*

1. Putnam, 1914; cf. Freud's letter to Putnam of the same date (Hale, 1971b: pp. 173–174).
2. Anna.
3. Italicized words in English in original.

## 215A

Berlin
19 May 1914

Dear Professor,

These hasty words will not serve as an answer to your letter of Sunday; they are only to draw your attention to a point in your history of the ψα movement.

On the paragraph beginning "Just as Adler's investigation..." on proof 63, or rather on proof 61 (first indication of the defection of Zurich),[1] it can be commented from a historical point of view: The articles you mention by Riklin in the popular press appeared after the attack on Ψα in the Zurich daily press. At that time (end of 1911 or 1912) the "Keplerbund", induced by the ethics specialist Foerster, organized a public assembly against Ψα, in which a doctor made a fiery speech. The reviews in the daily press were followed by a bitter feud, in which Jung took part, and in which, Forel, among others, intervened. That lasted for weeks. Then, when things were somewhat calmer, Jung began his retreat, i.e. those articles by Riklin appeared.[2]

Of course I do not want to say anything about whether this event should be mentioned. But perhaps it may seem not unimportant to you.—I have read the whole work once more with the greatest of satisfaction; I hope the printing errors which distort the sense will all disappear.

I received from Riklin material for the *Korrespondenzblatt*. I am writing to Rank about it, to make the burden of correspondence lighter for you. Hearty congratulations on your recovery!

Yours,

*Karl Abraham*

1. Freud, 1914d: p. 61, referring to p. 58: "Adler's secession took place before the Weimar Congress in 1911; after that date the Swiss began theirs. The first signs of it, curiously enough, were a few remarks of Riklin's in some popular articles appearing in Swiss publications." Freud might be referring to Riklin, 1912a, 1912b.
2. Friedrich Wilhelm Foerster [1869–1966], German philosopher, pedagogue, and pacifist. Having had to leave Germany for having committed *lèse-majesté*, he had become a professor in Zurich in 1901. Foerster was considered a pedagogical and moral authority. He had already once polemicized against psychoanalysis in 1909 (cf. Freud & Ferenczi, 1992: p. 99).

    The *Keplerbund*, founded in 1907 in answer to the *Monistenbund* (see letter 46A, 21 August 1908, & n. 2), sought to overcome pseudoscientific speculations in the name of science.

    On 15 December 1911, Dr Max Kesselring, Zurich neurologist, had given a public lecture under its auspices, attacking psychoanalysis. In its wake, a series of polemical articles had appeared in the *Neue Zürcher Zeitung* during January 1912 (see Ellenberger, 1970: pp. 810–814; Freud & Jung, 1974 [1906–13]: p. 482).

## 216F

Vienna IX, Berggasse 19
20 May 1914

Dear Friend,

I know the context of what went on in Zurich, and have always had the same opinion of it as you, and I have made no secret of this understanding to Maeder in my letters. There is an allusion to this in the article at one single point, where I talk about adaptation to reality which goes too far. I could not say more without direct denunciation.

In the narcissism I must rewrite the passage on hypochondria[1]; it has turned out too confusing.

At last I can tell you about the summer. Karlsbad from 12 July to 2 August, then probably Seis am Schlern,[2] until we leave for Dresden.

I am still working hard.

With cordial greetings,

Yours,

*Freud*

1. Cf. Freud, 1914c: pp. 82ff.
2. Village in the southern Dolomites.

## 217A

Berlin
2 June 1914

Dear Professor,

Yet another boil on my wrist has forced me to make you wait for a reply. Last week I could only attend to the most urgent business affairs with Hitschmann and Rank. Now it is all right again. I hope that in the meantime you have quite recovered; Karlsbad will have to do the rest. At the next opportunity please give me an exact report on how you are!

The *Jahrbuch* proofs are going quite quickly, but not quickly enough to ensure publication in four weeks, although Deuticke did hold the prospect out to me in a letter. I am eagerly awaiting the alterations to your two articles; I read them again in the proofs with the greatest gratification.

The date of the Congress, 20/21 September, is now as good as decided.—After asking and waiting in vain, I have at last received a report from Zurich for the *Korrespondenzblatt*. Munich, on the other hand, is on strike. I wish it could be an indication of their resignation! The disorder in the old Central Office verges on the grandiose. No cash report can be got out of Riklin. Putnam's announcement of the founding of a group in Boston[1] has been left without a reply. Jung knew absolutely nothing about it. Jones wrote to me that a new group, Ward's Island,[2] was accepted by Jung in the autumn. Jung denies knowing about it. It is like that with everything. The contributions @ 3 M. from Munich are showing no signs of coming in. I shall now press a bit harder, so that some order may reign in all respects by the time of the Congress. Next Sunday I am going to Dresden to make the first preparations for the Congress.

Our holiday plans are now as follows: My wife is going with the children to Arendsee in Mecklenburg on 5 July. I shall follow on the 26th, and we shall stay there until about 2 August, go to Bremen for about four days to see my parents, then bring the children to Berlin and travel to the Tyrol around 8 August. I shall give myself leave until the end of August.

I am very pleased to hear what you write about your "little" daughter. Is she in England already? Or are the translations still growing in the soil of home? In any case, my wife and I are looking forward very much to welcoming her here on the way back with you.

With regard to Reik, I have repeatedly and tactfully offered him my help. But he has always said that he could manage for the next few months. He intends to marry soon. I doubt whether neurotic reasons are not playing a part in this, rather than the practical considerations he gives. He has a great tendency to make difficulties for himself. In any case, you can be sure, dear Professor, that I shall be at his side as soon as it is necessary.

There must be something fishy going on with Stekel's *Zentralblatt*. Bergmann asked recently in a circular for several issues of the 3rd and 4th annual volumes to be given back, to be exchanged for replacement issues. (All of you in Vienna have probably not received this letter, because by the time these issues appeared, you had already cancelled your subscription). I have sent Bergmann a reply postcard and asked him for information about the meaning of this, but after three weeks I have still not had a reply. It must be something very shady, since Bergmann wants to take back even bound volumes and replace them with new ones.

With kind regards to you and yours and best wishes for your well-being.

Yours,

*Karl Abraham*

1. The Boston Psychoanalytic Society was founded in 1914 with Putnam as president and Isador Coriat [1875–1943] as secretary. See *Journal of Abnormal Psychology*, 1914, 9 (April–May): 71.
2. See letter 208F, 24 April 1914, & n. 4.

## 218F

Vienna IX, Berggasse 19
5 June 1914

Dear Friend,

I read your paper for the *Jahrbuch*[1] yesterday and cannot refrain from congratulating you on it. I think it the best clinical contribution that has appeared in any of the five volumes, unequalled in assurance, correctness, many-sidedness, and interest. Vivant sequentes![2]

Rank will have written to you about the immediate political affairs that are engaging our attention. I do not share your confidence that the Zurichers and their Munich appendage will resign before the Congress. In any case, the uncertainty remains and disturbs our preparations for it. For should they attend, the preparations will have to be different from what they would be should we be left peacefully among ourselves.

I shall now make another attempt to spare ourselves the difficulties in question. I have made an appointment with Deuticke for Monday, and I shall ask him to make up and print my polemical historical contribution before anything else, so that the offprints can be dispatched before July. (Like you, I think it improbable that the *Jahrbuch* can come out so early.) I hope the editorial board agrees with this preferential treatment. I shall naturally send them out very generously. The advantage of this would be that we could be informed of the reaction of the Swiss before you send out the questionnaires on the Congress.

Another way would be for you to ask Maeder and Seif (at the right time) outright whether their groups propose to attend or not, and also emphasize particularly that your motivation is the necessity of determining the subject for discussion.

I am thinking of making it "The Objects and Aims of a $\Psi\alpha$ Society", in order to justify the association's existence, rebut the objections relating to restrictions on scientific research, and give a *consilium abeundi*[3] to the Swiss, should they be present. In the event of our being undisturbed by them, the subject could still stand. I am not concerned about the effect on the American groups, who in any case will never be able to really join in our unity. London will, I hope, remain with us.

I thought it very noble of you not to have attacked the Zurich slovenliness more specifically in your *Korrespondenzblatt*,[4] and defended you for this against Rank. But at the Congress you need not mince your words.

The case with the *Zentralblatt* is not what you suppose. A certain Kaplan, a lamentable schlemiel, has published at Deuticke's a book on $\Psi\alpha$[5] that cannot appear because some people exploited in it have obtained legal seizure. For the same reason, certain issues of the *Zentralblatt* with contributions from this Kaplan are being withdrawn. Ill weeds grow apace.

I have surely already told you about our plans for the summer: 12 July Karlsbad, 4/5 August Seis am Schlern, 24 September, lecture in Leyden.

My health is fortunately less interesting than it might have appeared. I have nearly recovered from a clearly multiple intestinal affection (or infection) without any suspicion of carcinoma. If I am not very fond of writing, this will need no particular explanation.

My little one has completed her poetical accomplishments here, and at the beginning of July she is going to England. Her whooping-cough is better. She has hay-fever instead. It can be foreseen that she will have all sorts of troubles in life. On the whole, however, she is very sweet.

I hope now that you will not let yourself be bitten by boils[6] any more, and that your family will be very well again until the approaching holidays.

With cordial greetings,
your faithfully devoted

*Freud*

P.S.: Only one correction in your article. Your informant from Leyden is probably Dr Debruine, whom we know. You have deprived him of his first syllable.[7]

1. Abraham, 1914[43].
2. "Long live those that follow!" [Latin blessing].
3. The advice given to a student to leave an institution of learning in order to avoid being expelled. Freud had already used this expression in connection with Adler (Freud & Ferenczi, 1992: p. 285).
4. See letter 209F, 7 May 1914, & n. 2.
5. Dr Leo Kaplan [1876–1956], born in Russia, lived in Zurich from 1897 until his death. He studied mathematics, physics, and philosophy. Then from approximately 1910 on he began to occupy himself intensively with psychoanalysis but did not belong to any psychoanalytic organization. His book (Kaplan, 1914) is one of the earliest systematic summations of Freudian doctrine.
6. Allusion to the "dog-bite" (see letter 210A, 10 May 1914, & n. 2).
7. Abraham, 1914[43]: p. 188. Jan Rudolf de Bruine Groeneveldt [1872–1942], Dutch physician. "He is said to have arranged the place in Leyden where Freud had an analytic consultation with the composer Gustav Mahler" in August 1910 (McGuire in Freud & Jung, 1974 [1906–13]: p. 209).

## 219F

Vienna IX, Berggasse 19
14 June 1914

Dear Friend,

Having read practically all the proofs of the new *Jahrbuch* today, I must express my thanks for the tremendous pains you have taken in the interests of our cause. It will be an impressive demonstration by our little community, about whom there will be no lack of obituary notices in the near future.

Most of the reviews[1] are very good, and some outstanding. I do not have to stress which. The homogeneity of direction in all of them is very pleasing. Perhaps some of the very good ones are too short, there is a lack of uniformity in the allocation of space. Sadger is too quick to find fault, Hug cannot but be long-winded. I have written to Tausk to urge him to withdraw the suggestion about the connection of both ψ systems with time and place. It is a remark that I dropped in the Society[2]; it is only important for a later work and does not belong in a review at all. This man's hastiness and passion for priority are unfortunately very great. I should like to ask you to phrase rather more cautiously the passage about my question in the Schreber analysis whether the concept of the libido should be changed, so that it does not seem to justify Jung's misinterpretation. I asked it purely dialectically, in order to be able to answer it in the negative, as Ferenczi has correctly interpreted.[3] But I have no other misgivings to add.

We are now of course awaiting the effect of the "bombshell" that has not yet been laid. Deuticke has promised to do his utmost to hurry things. As for myself, I have to report that I feel quite well again. Bowing to this time of need, I am working from 8 in the morning until 9 at night.

I answered Spielrein, who wrote me an ambivalent letter, with a request to make up her mind one way or the other.[4]

With cordial greetings and thanks,

Yours,

*Freud*

P.S.: There was a reference in a review to a treatment of "ambivalence". But this important subject does not appear anywhere (Ferenczi? Hitschmann?).[5]

1. Freud is referring to the contributions for the *Bericht über die Fortschritte der Psychoanalyse in den Jahren 1909–1913* contained in the *Jahrbuch*, by Sadger (1914), Hug-Hellmuth (1914), Tausk (1914), and Abraham (1914[51]), among others.
2. On 25 November 1914 Freud wrote to Ferenczi: "I have finally found the solution to the riddle of time and space" (Freud & Ferenczi, 1996). Referring to this, Jones (1955: p. 175), obviously mixing up the two concepts, is of the opinion "that the former concept [time] is related to the topographical nature of the mind, particularly of the unconscious, while the latter [space] is absent in the unconscious and is confined to the more conscious layers".
3. Jung (1911–12, reprint p. 134) had claimed that Freud "had found himself compelled, simultaneously with myself, to extend the concept of libido". This refers to Freud's raising the question, in the Schreber analysis, whether "a general detachment of the libido from the external world would be an effective enough agent to account for the 'end of the world'" as experienced by the psychotic (1911c [1910]: p. 73). If not, Freud went on, one would have "to assume that what we call libidinal cathexis . . . coincides with interest in general" (ibid.: p. 74). Eventually, however, Freud stated it would be "far more probable that the paranoiac's altered relation to the world is to be explained entirely or in the main by the loss of his libidinal interest" (ibid., p 75)—which alternative Ferenczi duly emphasized in his review of Jung (Ferenczi, 1913[124]: pp. 254–255).
4. That is, between Freud and Jung. Freud had invited Spielrein to have her name put on the cover of the *Zeitschrift*, but had made it clear that this would be "a very clear sign of partisanship. . . . You will be heartily welcome, if you stay with us, but in this case you

must also recognize the enemy on the other side" (letter of 12 June 1914; Carotenuto, 1980: pp. 126–127). Spielrein's name did not appear on the cover of the *Zeitschrift*.
5. Cf. Ferenczi to Freud, 19 June 1914: "With regard to the—*very*—justified—wish to take up the important relation of the *ambivalence* of savages and of neurotics in my paper [Ferenczi, 1914(148)], I have already done what is necessary" (Freud & Ferenczi, 1992: p. 558).

## 220A

Berlin
16 June 1914

Dear Professor,

A chance free hour enables me to answer you at once. It is wonderful that you yourself now write so contentedly and confidently about your well-being. I hope you will already be completely recovered when I meet you in Seis in August. Naturally it will still be somewhat uncertain up to the last moment whether my wife can leave the children for long enough to make a journey to the Tyrol worth while. We are hoping to find a good substitute for her, but it is still uncertain. I myself could of course make the journey, and am coming in any case.

I am certainly glad to hear that you are satisfied with the *Jahrbuch*, only you do not have to thank me for it, dear Professor. I really believe that all the reasons for gratitude are on my side. True, it was a great deal of work, especially in the last few weeks again, as the proofs were so bad (in my general review two pages of manuscript were simply left out). But we have got over that now, and I believe we shall all be happy with the finished volume. I did notice the shortcomings of some single reviews, but we could not expect any more in so short a time. I am glad none of our collaborators failed us.

I am sending with this the passage relating to the withdrawal of the libido, in an altered form. If you approve of it like this, simply send it back to me in an envelope. If necessary, make any changes. I shall use them for the 2nd proofs.

I am still going to write to Ferenczi; I observed the same deficiency as you (ambivalence).

I am not as satisfied as you with my contribution to the *Jahrbuch* (scoptophilia). I could really have shaped some things better, but I did not have the time.

I have given the answers to the political questions in your last letter directly to Rank. I have had an afterthought about my planned letter to Maeder and Seif. I deliberately wrote as calmly as possible; that now contrasts much with the "bombshell". It could thus look like duplicity, if I ask both groups, quite charmingly, for their opinion. But perhaps only the wording of the letter needs to be altered; besides, I really think this is the only right way.

1914 June

The group here is doing quite well. At any rate, everyone is of the same opinion with regard to Jung. Only Stockmayer has kept away from the meetings since our discussion in January (about Jung) and has given absolutely no sign of life. I believe he is not staying in Berlin. He is a pleasant, decent man, but it is no loss to us if he is not there.

For the next *Jahrbuch*[1] there is up to now a useful contribution by Sadger (on inversion). Reik promised me a more extensive work on the theory of affects. The review part will of course be much smaller than this time, yet will, I hope, meet all demands. Towards the end of the year I shall have all the writings that appeared in 1914 card-indexed and will give every reviewer his allotted task. It seems to me that the volume should come out in April 1915, so the deadline for contributions should be set at the end of January. There cannot be all that much work for the reviewers, so that 1 to 1½ months will be enough.

What do you say about Pfister? He has obviously gone completely over to Jung. Reik told me about a new work in which Pf. says so directly. Recently I had from him an article, "Echnaton",[2] which corrects a few mistakes I had made but then also attacks what is indisputable and loses every $\psi\alpha$ point of view, instead flowing out into theological bombast. When we get rid of the Swiss, the elimination of the theologians will not be the least of the advantages.

When we meet in the summer I will bring with me some lovely material concerning "slips of the pen". A few months ago I left the abstinent doctors' association. From the correspondence that ensued, a letter from Maier in Zurich[3] is quite priceless.

I hope your daughter's hay-fever did not take a turn for the worse. I will also take the opportunity to mention that my case of hay-fever analysed in 1911 (it is our colleague Liebermann here) is still very well. In 1912 he was completely free, in 1913 there were some quite negligible symptoms; this year in response to severe psychological influences there were slight symptoms, for example, mild asthma once during a visit from his mother. But the situation is such that his capacity for work is not suffering.

I am overburdened with treatments up to the holidays, and so in my so-called hours of leisure I do not get around to anything but proofs and writing letters, etc. The works announced some time ago have been lying untouched for several weeks.

Most cordial greetings from house to house.

Yours,

*Karl Abraham*

1. There would be no other *Jahrbuch*.
2. Pfister, 1914a.
3. Hans Wolfgang Maier [1882–1945]; at the Burghölzli from 1905; from 1927 on, Bleuler's successor as director.

## 221F

Vienna
18 June 1914

Dear Friend,

In haste, without intending to answer your letter, a few words on our business affairs.

a) Herewith my suggestion for your review.[1]

b) Deuticke is still causing us trouble with the naming of the new *Jahrbuch*. If we were to do as he wants and begin a new series with this volume, there would be unspeakable difficulties in its wake. I have advocated to him that it should be called simply: *Jahrbuch der Psychoanalyse* VI, allowing him to put it in parentheses under the main title (*des Jahrbuchs für psychoanalytische und psychopathologische Forschungen Neue Folge* [New Series of the Yearbook for Psychoanalytical and Psychopathological Research]). Today I am correcting the narcissism in accordance with this.

Hitschmann, on my advice, is putting something about Jung in his review on the theory of drives.[2]

We want to clip Sadger's wings here.

c) I am expecting on Saturday the reprints of the bombshell and will send them on at once. Your arguments for postponing the circular are completely accepted. We shall also need to keep some distance.

Cordial greetings from work,
Yours,

*Freud*

1. Missing.
2. Hitschmann, 1914.

## 222A

Berlin
21 June 1914

Dear Professor,

Today I have only a few communications. I take it that I need say nothing more about the title of the *Jahrbuch*.—I am eagerly awaiting the bombshell; perhaps already tomorrow.

Ferenczi agrees to do the paper for the Congress, but thinks it will have a point only if the "schismatics" come.[1] I have written to him about it. He delivered the addition to the review (ambivalence) quickly; it is already with Deuticke.

In my review I shall make the changes you wish in the second proofs. The fact that the second proofs are coming so slowly has probably

1914 July

something to do with your work being printed beforehand. But I do hope that the whole lot will be ready at the beginning of July.
Most cordial greetings!
Yours,

   *Abraham*

1. "I will naturally assume the task of presenting a paper on the topic of 'The International Psychoanalytic Association,' but I hope it won't come to that; I wrote to Abraham to that effect" (Ferenczi to Freud, 19 June 1914, Freud & Ferenczi, 1992: p. 558).

## 223F

Vienna IX, Berggasse 19
25 June 1914

Dear Friend,

So the bombshell has now burst, we shall soon discover with what effect. I think we shall have to allow the victims two to three weeks to collect themselves and react; incidentally, I am not sure they will respond to the blandishments bestowed upon them by resigning.

Rank has shown me that the familiar demon has played a small trick on me. So I am sending you a correction for the last page of the *Jahrbuch*; perhaps you yourself will have something to add from other papers. [ . . . ][1]

[p.] 45 in the offprint is then to be replaced by the page number in the volume.
Most cordial greetings,
Yours,

   *Freud*

1. A paragraph cut out.

## 224A

Berlin
5 July 1914

Dear Professor,

The proof-correcting is almost finished. Your correction (with regard to Adler), the alteration of my review in the direction required, and the insertion of Ferenczi's supplement to the review have been taken care of.

I have heard nothing yet from Zurich or Munich. Unless you wish otherwise, I shall send off the letter to Maeder and Seif next Sunday!

Last Friday, at the end of the summer term, I gave a talk to the *"Gesellschaft für Sexualwissenschaft"* on incest, marriage among relatives, and exogamy.[1] I met with more understanding and appreciation than I had anticipated.

Now I must ask for your advice. I had already written some time ago that I would like to talk in Dresden on the treatment of psychoses. I have meanwhile come to feel that it would be preferable to have a bit more experience before going public with it; perhaps this subject could be treated in the main talk at one of the next congresses. Now another topic suggests itself to me. With the help of several analyses conducted during this last year I have, I believe, succeeded in explaining *ejaculatio praecox* almost completely, that is, back to the earliest roots in the first two years of life.[2] I should like to present the results to the Congress. Now I should be glad to know whether you think the subject suitable. Furthermore, I would mention that I should have to go into castration anxiety in some detail, and what you told me at Christmas on the journey to Berlin[3] has not yet been published! The most pleasant solution would be, naturally, if you yourself would speak about these matters in Dresden, and if I could then demonstrate their application, so to speak, to a specific problem. This derivation from castration anxiety is, incidentally, only *one* of the results obtained.

After business, now comes pleasure. My wife and I will presumably leave on 9 August and arrive in Seis on the 10th. So I should like to ask you for details of the hotel!

Your holiday is now approaching. In case I have no opportunity to write to you beforehand, I will wish you and your family already now a pleasant journey and a good rest. Incidentally, I should also like to have your address in Karlsbad.—Tomorrow my wife leaves with the children for the Baltic.[4]—

With the most cordial greetings from both of us to you all,
Yours,

*Abraham*

A reply to the above question is not urgent!

1. Paper read to the *Ärztliche Gesellschaft für Sexualwissenschaft* on 3 July, entitled "Eigentümliche Formen der Gattenwahl, besonders Inzucht und Exogamie" [Peculiar forms of choosing a partner, in particular incest and exogamy] (*Zeitschrift*, 1914, 2: 410). In the discussion, Iwan Bloch supported Abraham's views (Rank to Freud, 9 July 1914, Archives Judith Dupont).
2. Cf. Abraham, 1917[54].
3. See letter 190A, 7 January 1914.
4. One week before Abraham wrote this letter, Archduke Franz Ferdinand, successor to the Austrian throne, and his wife had been murdered by Gavrilo Princip and other assassins belonging to the Young Bosnia movement in Sarajevo (a fact not mentioned by either correspondent). This set in motion a rapid and furious chain of events, leading finally to

1914 July

the outbreak of the First World War. Naturally, all plans for holidays, congresses, etc. became obsolete.

## 225F

Vienna
5 July 1914

Dear Friend,

A bad time for letter-writing. The most intensive work of the entire year (8 [a.m.] to 10 in the evening), and with it a paralysing heat, which one can bear only because one has no time to worry about it. I have stood up to it very well, am now waiting for the end of the week that starts today.[1] Unfortunately our departure has itself now become uncertain. I am finishing work in any case by the said deadline. My sister-in-law took to her bed eight days ago with very severe influenza, is still feverish today, and is developing focuses of bronchopneumonia, the course of which, as is well known, is particularly lengthy and insidious. If eight days from now she is free from fever and convalescent, we shall bring her to a sanatorium and go to Karlsbad; if not, everything is of course uncertain.

I assume that you too have had no reaction yet to the bombshell. We can still wait a fortnight, about up to the date of the day of the Congress,[2] then you will probably have to come out with the direct inquiry, which you so nobly formulated. Every further step depends on the success of this one.

Among the written replies to the sending of the "bombshell", those of Lou Salomé[3] and Liebermann seemed to me to be the most sincere. Attitudes in Vienna are "ambivalent".

Our meeting in the summer is still on. It cannot yet be decided whether it can be in Seis, as absolutely everything has now become uncertain. But you probably will not mind changing your last travel plans according to where we are.

*The Interpretation of Dreams* is finished but has not yet appeared.[4] Your Dutch *Dreams and Myths* pleased me very much.[5]

I hope all is well with you and send cordial greetings,
Yours,

*Freud*

My little one has got over her hay- and whoop-, as she says, and intends to go via Dresden/Hamburg to England on 7/7.

1. 5 July 1914 was a Sunday.
2. That is, until the 20/21 July, two months before the planned Congress.
3. Only Freud's reply of 29 June 1914 has been published, in Freud & Andreas-Salomé, 1966: pp. 17–18.

4. Fourth, enlarged edition (Vienna: Deuticke); like the three following editions, with contributions by Otto Rank.
5. See letter 168A, 17 September 1913, & n. 2.

## 226F

Vienna IX, Berggasse 19
10 July 1914

Dear Friend,

The danger about which I wrote in my last letter is fortunately over. My sister-in-law is going into a sanatorium for further convalescence, and we can travel on Sunday evening. You will get my address—which I do not know myself yet—from Karlsbad.

I have the two most difficult weeks of the year behind me and have withstood them well. I note that the bit of sympathy that the friends have been showing me on the occasion of the "bombshell" has, after all, done me a great deal of good. No reaction from Zurich yet! Did I suggest to you that you should wait with your circular letter until the 20th?

Lou Salomé has sent me an exchange of letters with Adler[1] that shows her insight and clarity in an excellent light, but also Adler's venom and meanness, and with such riffraff, etc.![2] In such circumstances, sometimes even Casimiro loses heart.

Your travel plans have thrown me into confusion. I had somehow concluded from your earlier letters that I could expect your visit in Seis at the beginning of September. I would have preferred that time to 9/10 August, of which you now write, for we shall not get there until after 4 August, and I should like to stay a few weeks in isolation to do the difficult work for Kraus. It was with this misunderstanding that I made a remark in an earlier letter, in which I said that I might ask you, instead of coming to Seis, to go a little further. That is to say, were I to be ready ahead of time, it is possible that we may go to one of the North Italian lakes in the week prior to the Congress; it is a very pleasant place to stay with women. Now you will be able to put my remark in its place—you must certainly have misunderstood it.

*The Interpretation of Dreams* arrived today and will soon be with you.

It will be possible to do something about the papers for Dresden only once we are sure of the non-Swiss. In *those* people's presence we shall not say one word. In that case premature ejaculation would seem to me to be a very suitable subject. Deal with the castration question just in so far as it has been useful to you. For me the time for publication has not yet come. The question has grown more complicated and magnified, and thus the solution has receded, so that I must also ask you for restraint in the interest of prudence.

Hotel in Seis: Pension Edelweiss.

1914 July

I have had some insights into the primordial structure of human early sexuality with which I shall bother you then. But after a fortnight of 12 to 13 hours' work daily I am incapable of any synthesis, and am panting for the holidays.

It is possible that my grand-patient Frau Hirschfeld[3] may approach you in the near future. She will be staying in Berlin for some time. I ask you not to refuse her, but to let her feel that no one who is not in the know can intervene in so very complicated a matter. Besides, she does not tell anyone anything useful; the whole thing is partly a demonstration of faithlessness and partly a need for someone who is not in opposition to me. Today she mentioned that she might possibly stay permanently in Berlin. Then you would of course be the qualified person whom I would inform as best as I can. But there would probably be little pleasure in it.

Hoping that yours are now enjoying themselves on the Baltic, your cordially devoted

*Freud*

1. Letters of 12 and 16 August 1913; in Andreas-Salomé, 1958: pp. 175–180.
2. "Such riffraff I have to deal with!", Friedrich the Great is said to have exclaimed at the battle of Zorndorf [1758], when ragged Cossacks were brought before him as prisoners of war.
3. Elfriede Hirschfeld [1873-?], whose case was mentioned by Freud in at least six papers (1913a [of which she is the unnamed co-author], 1913g, 1913i, 1941d [1921], 1925i, 1933a) and in many letters. In addition, Freud had written an "essay about her illness" (Freud to Pfister, 9 February 1912, LOC), which seems to have been lost. Freud referred to her as his "grand-patient" (also to Ferenczi, 23 June 1912, Freud & Ferenczi, 1992: p. 406), "main customer" (25 February 1910, ibid.: p. 157), or "chief tormentor" (27 April 1911, Freud & Jung, 1974 [1906–13]: p. 417). Frau Hirschfeld had also played a major role in the conflict between Freud and Jung. Her name is given anonymously as "C–" in Freud & Jung (1974), "A." in Freud & Abraham (1965), "H." in Freud & Pfister (1963), and "Gi." in Freud & Binswanger (1992). (Cf. Falzeder, 1994.)

## 227A

Berlin
10 July 1914

Dear Professor,

Our last letters crossed. While I was asking you for information about Seis, you wrote to me about the illness in your house. I should like first of all to ask after your sister-in-law's health; as I know these bronchopneumonias are long-drawn-out things, I have delayed this question for a few days, but I am now hoping for good news. Of course, quite a brief note will suffice!

You are surely glad now to be able to stop working. And now this very day I have to bother you with a matter that is urgent for me. It is about Reik. He will marry on the 31st. He had prospects of being taken on at the "*Morgen*" in Vienna; nothing came of it. He wanted to rent a small flat here; now he will not get the furniture offered to him by a relative of his wife. I had hoped to help him with his furniture and was going to ask for your assistance—now he is moving with his wife into a furnished room temporarily, so that there is no point in contributing anything towards his furnishings.—He is living on very slender means, i.e. he has at times been actually starving, and despite many offers he would never take money (a good part of which was pleasure in suffering); today at last he accepted a small contribution. I think one should do something for him, to give him as much security as possible, and also to make the situation bearable for his wife. He is really very industrious and has worked very well here (couvade[1] and other things). He is now, I know, comparing himself with Rank, whom the Association helped for such a long time. (I know this and a great deal more, highly subjectively coloured of course, because I have been analysing him since the beginning of the week; he was in an extremely bad state of depression.) I think now that we could do as follows: the Central Office of the Association will have a credit balance of at least 400 M. We could decide at the Congress to give one of the younger workers a similar sum in recognition of his work. With that he would be helped for a while. But there are still two months to go until then. Have you any advice, dear Professor? He is so very sensitive, but certainly more towards me than you. If you have no time to write, get our colleague Hitschmann, to whom Reik is very devoted, to tell me your views!

In case you are travelling on Sunday, my best wishes go with you and your family. My wife and children have been away since Monday.—I am writing tomorrow to Zurich and Munich. In haste, cordial greetings from your

*Abraham*

1. Reik, 1914.

## 228F

Karlsbad, Villa Fasolt
15 July 1914

Dear Friend,

Today I sent Rank a letter to be circulated which I had from Pfister.[1] He expresses his willingness to separate from Jung and enter the Viennese group if the Zurich people walk out, *as they plan to do*. So we had wrong reports of him, and the chances of reaching our goal are good.

Of course I have not the slightest intention of dropping Reik. The first thing I did was to send him 200 Mk and give him a bit of a dressing-

1914 July

down in a letter.[2] I hope he will then take something regularly and give up working against himself so persistently. He is a good chap, intelligent and modest. But he cannot really compare himself with Rank. It is true that the Association has done a very great deal for Rank. But R. would not have gone under if none of us had bothered about him. He would have found others; I know of few people who can make themselves so generally loved and deserving. Also, Rank was there earlier. Perhaps Reik has a sibling rivalry complex in this respect. He was astonished to hear that he has completely withheld several brothers from my knowledge.

Your suggestion of putting in a claim for a prize for him at the Congress is very much to my liking. Of course, only if we are among ourselves at the Congress. Up to then we will not let him suffer any deprivation, even if I cannot make him rich. Has his wife not brought anything with her?

We have settled in very comfortably here and are consuming the expected royalties for *The Interpretation of Dreams*. It is just appallingly hot, but probably not only in Karlsbad.

Do not be sparing with your news, which I always rate so highly, and keep me up to date with your holiday plans.

With cordial greetings to you, with wife and children,
your faithfully devoted

*Freud*

1. No letters between Freud and Pfister dated between 11 March 1913 and 9 October 1918 have survived.
2. Letter of 15 July 1914; in Reik, 1956.


## 229A

Berlin
16 July 1914

Dear Professor,

How nice that our letters did not cross again. I appreciate with great satisfaction the prospect of the early resignation of the Swiss. With Eitingon's assistance I have now dealt promptly with the further preparations for the Congress; that is to say, I have drawn up a circular that is going to all members, together with reply cards on which there are three questions to be answered: participation in the Congress, intention to read papers, and booking of rooms. It is already being printed. Tomorrow shall come the proofs, on Saturday evening it will be delivered. We shall send it out on Sunday.—Today I am adding a small enclosure relating to the Congress.[1]

Bleuler's letter,[2] which I received from Jones today, reminds me of the best times at the Burghölzli. Jung's secession from the Association is surely a bridge for Bl., which he *may* use to return to us. Did you note the concluding sentence? I think Bl. would like to be approached to take over the leadership in Switzerland again. We shall certainly invite him to the Congress; let's see there what happens. His taking sides with us would make good before the outer world for anything the schism may have caused us.

On the other hand, dear Professor, I take a completely opposite view from yours about Pfister! We were not given wrong information about him, as you think. But recently he made a declaration in the *Theologische Literatur-Zeitung*:[3] Ψα has nothing to do with sexuality. I agree with Jung!—His attitude in other writings is quite feeble. A while back he sent me a paper on Echnaton,[4] which, according to Jung's procedure, drops all ψα points of view. For example: after I had shown in my article that the king's struggle against Amon was actually against his father, Pfister discovers that the enmity against his father is actually against the god Amon. I think Pf. is completely unreliable. His letter quoted in the "History"[5] was written in opposition to Jung; with his change of attitude he returns to Jung, and now back to you again! I think we could well afford to lose him; the theologians do find it much too difficult to adopt Ψα completely. In any case, we should not make any effort to win Pfister over!*

Did you know that Oberholzer has already left the Zurich group?

It is kind that you have helped Reik; it is particularly hard for him to accept anything from me during the analysis. In the meantime we are making good progress, and I hope to be able to help him. His attitude toward you, toward Rank, toward me, etc. is distinctly neurotic, fluctuating between tender devotion and extreme sadism. He is making life sour for himself and for his bride as well. Incidentally, *she* is bringing almost nothing to the marriage; she has scarcely 1,000M.—I have rarely seen a person who would like to rage against the whole world and himself to such an extent as Reik does.

I hope that Karlsbad will do you and your wife much good again! As far as our plans are concerned, the misunderstanding is surely entirely on your side, dear Professor! I have always given the same dates. I could not possibly have had any doubt about *August*, especially as Ferenczi recently wrote in reply to my question that he would be in Seis in August! I think that you had already been planning for quite a long time to do the work for Kraus in August, but were too considerate to put me off for August, and so the repressed tendency was expressed in the mistake that *I*, on my part, intended to leave you undisturbed in August and to come only later. The proposal to meet further south, which you mention, surely referred to Ossiach? But even then, I always understood

1914 July

that it would be August. Another suggestion for further south did not come to my notice.[6]

Now it would be very painful for us to disturb you in the slightest! Well, I feel that the relationship between us is such that you need not be afraid to speak out now quite openly. We cannot, for various important reasons, postpone our journey to any great extent, by a few days at the most. But as we are planning a walking tour in the Dolomites, we could do this first and then push on to you. That would still also be in August, but not until the second half, probably the last week of the month. I should be glad to know—without mincing matters—whether it would be inconvenient for us to come then, and I promise you that I shall not take anything amiss! So tell me briefly what you wish; and we shall act accordingly!

I am very curious about the latest on infantile sexuality!—Frau Hirschfeld telephoned me from Vienna; otherwise I do not know anything about her yet.

Another 10 or 12 days and then I shall be off. Cordial greetings to you and your wife,

Yours,

*Karl Abraham*

\* If Pfister's circular letter gives me a better point of view, I shall be very pleased.

1. Missing.
2. Bleuler had sent a letter to Freud on 4 July 1914 (LOC), giving a generally positive reaction to the "History of the Psychoanalytic Movement", which was then circulated.
3. Pfister, 1914b.
4. Pfister, 1914a.
5. In the printed version, no letter of Pfister's is quoted.
6. This sentence inserted later.

## 230A

Berlin
17 July 1914

Dear Professor,

A letter from Maeder, which has just arrived, is the occasion to disturb your cure once again. I am enclosing a copy of the letter,[1] which is very hard to read, and am at the same time sending a copy each to Rank and Jones for circulation (so there is no need to return it).

The end of the letter is very mystical, but not difficult to grasp. I think they are planning a circular of indignation to form the basis of their resignation.

The Zurich group's session on 10 July took place immediately *before* I sent my letter. I believe that it was a good thing to send it nevertheless, as the reactions of Zurich come extremely slowly.—We send out the invitations to the Congress on Sunday, but will leave those meant for Z.[urich] and Munich for a few more days; perhaps we shall have the notices of resignation in the meantime.

I am not of course giving Maeder an answer to his letter. Both the content and the handwriting ooze spitefulness.

Today Pfister's letter came from Rank. It reminds me of many an analytic session. The patient comes with resistances, but as soon as he is at the doctor's he very quickly finds positive contact again. Thus the *first* page of Pfister's letter is full of hidden resistances, and after that his attitude to you and $\Psi\alpha$ becomes more and more positive. I know that Pf. has some very estimable qualities; he was very sympathetic to me personally at the Weimar Congress. But he is inwardly insecure. So I cannot be unrestrictedly pleased about his well-meant letter.

Reik is very pleased with your attitude!
With cordial greetings,
Yours,

*Abraham*

1. Missing.


## 231F

Karlsbad, Villa Fasolt
18 July 1914

Dear Friend,

I cannot suppress a Hurrah. So we have got rid of them then! We shall print their manifesto of indignation in the next issue of the *Korrespondenzblatt*, in which you, hopefully as definite president, will make a statement on the matter.[1]

I enclose two letters, a statement by Putnam[2] and also a letter from Maeder,[3] which remains unanswered, like the one to you. The *Zeitschrift* will be glad to get rid, in addition to Maeder, also of Riklin, Seif, and the rest.[4] My bombshell has worked well, then. But it is good that your circular letter has already arrived. So once again we shall have a good Congress.

In the matter August/September you are surely right, but one of the warring sides may be wrongly identified. The fear of being disturbed is not in opposition to the fear of hurting you, but to the tendency to chat with you instead of doing the hard work. Well, come whenever you like. I have to see how to fit it in with work. I don't even know whether I shall have any desire for work. Saying no to you was also made more difficult by the fact that I originally had proposed that we should spend the whole summer together, at a time when I was not yet thinking of the work during the holidays. Meeting later refers to a plan to show my wife Lago Maggiore at the beginning of September.

I am warned not to contradict you too easily in your judgement of people. So also in the case of Pfister. But after the letter we did have to accept him for the time being. He did not—cautiously—send me the Echnaton work, as he did with all the rest. Thus cleverness combines with saintliness.

Do not be afraid of disturbing my cure many more times. Such news is good for me.

Cordial greetings and thanks,
Yours,
*Freud*

2 *circulars*

F. Alcan has just announced a book on Ψα by Régis and Hesnard.[5]

1. In the following *Korrespondenzblatt* there was a note of Abraham's stating that "the branch group of Zurich decided on 10 July, with 15 votes, to leave the Association—on the grounds that freedom of research would no longer be secured within our organization. In times like these, it does not seem to be appropriate to counter this allegation by a criticism. But we may expect that the controversies, which have so thoroughly disturbed our last Congress in Munich, have come to an end through the mentioned decision of the Zurich group" (*Zeitschrift*, 1914, 2: 483).
2. On Freud's "History of the Psychoanalytic Movement", calling it *"very fine* and impressive" and "a model . . . in the way of clear thinking and intelligent expression" (7 July 1914; Hale, 1971b: p. 177).
3. Missing.
4. Of those included on the cover of the *Zeitschrift* in 1913 as regular co-workers, Alphonse Maeder and Franz Riklin from Zurich and Leonhard Seif from Munich were, in fact, missing from the 1914 volume.
5. Régis & Hesnard, 1914, the first book on psychoanalysis published in France, critically reviewed by Ferenczi (1915[175]; cf. also letter 119F, 2 January 1912, & n. 3).

## 232A

Berlin
23 July 1914

Dear Professor,

I have now also reached the point where I am groaningly completing the last few working days. On Sunday morning, off on holiday (address: Brunshaupten in Mecklenburg, Hotel Dünenhaus).

The two letters are being circulated. Putnam could say more as to facts; nevertheless, his statement is valuable because it proves that no danger threatens our organization in America. Maeder's letter is at least courteous in tone. His lecturing reference to types, meaning in fact differences in race, does not become more intelligent by repetition. This is a comfortable position, making things easy, since one is unassailable. The manifesto announced to me by Maeder has not yet arrived. Seif has not replied to my letter (sent a fortnight ago) at all. So we would still be dependent on circumstantial evidence leading us to assume that the Zurichers will not participate in the Congress, had the invitation circular not already provoked some characteristic reactions.

From Stockmayer came a "No", underlined. (St. has behaved very strangely. After our debate about Jung in the January session, he has not appeared at any more of sessions and has also broken off all personal relationships. I hear that he is leaving Berlin.) His cancellation is certainly not on his own initiative, but is a symptom of the non-appearance of the Swiss. No reply as yet from Zurich, but I did send those two days later, after all. Only one Zurich member living in Germany[1] sent a card with *No*. From Munich—the group has eleven members—three have replied. *Ludwig*[2] is coming; but he is always attached to both opposing parties simultaneously. Böhm,[3] a new member, is also coming. Gebsattel,[4] who is a bit of an outsider,[5] is probably coming.

Papers have been offered by (apart from yourself): *Ferenczi* (main paper and also something about infantile sexuality), *Rank*, *Jones* on a subject still to be announced, Frau Dr *Stegmann* ("Studies on Art and Literature on the Basis of Formal Psychology". Could you not dissuade her from this? After all, what we are doing is not formal psychology. The subject is a pretty revelation of megalomania). Also *Liebermann* (phantasies of the womb). *Reik* (belief in the transmigration of souls),[6] *Abraham* (ejaculatio praecox).[7]

The publication of a French work on $\Psi\alpha$ is a good sign, and an even better one is the new edition of *The Interpretation of Dreams*. Many thanks for sending me a copy! I hope to be able to read in it during the holidays. At the same time, my congratulations!

I am giving Dubois a postponing reply.[8] I shall ask Jones, our congress missionary, whether he is going to Berne, and shall possibly ask him to take my place; otherwise perhaps Binswanger.

I called on Frau Hirschfeld at the hotel. She talks of staying in Berlin. I was surprised to learn from her that she is the disposition to obsessional neurosis.[9]

I shall be staying with my wife and children in Brunshaupten until 3 August; from there I will travel to Bremen, will be back here on 7 August, at which time I will send off the final Congress programme with Eitingon. On the 9th or 10th we leave for the Tyrol. More specific arrangements I will still discuss with my wife. Heartfelt thanks for your friendly attitude; I am very much in agreement with the interpretation of the September misunderstanding! We do not yet know whether we are travelling directly to Seis or whether we will start a walking tour somewhere which will take us to Seis. In any case, dear Professor, we shall keep you to your work as far as we can! Could you tell me when you have the chance whether it is still absolutely necessary to book a room in Seis for 10 August? The German holidays end exactly then, and I think one might easily get accommodation.

After this extensive interruption of your cure, I can only add my most cordial greetings to you and your wife. Please inform me at your earliest convenience how your sister-in-law is getting on.

Yours,

*Karl Abraham*

1. Possibly a Dr E. Lenz, who had changed his membership from the German to the Zurich group in 1912 (cf. *Zentralblatt*, 1911/12, 2: 545).
2. Dr A. Ludwig from Munich, participant at the Salzburg meeting in 1908.
3. Felix Böhm; see letter 87A, 28 April 1910, n. 3 .
4. Victor Emil Freiherr von Gebsattel [1883–1976], psychiatrist. Originally influenced by Adler and Jung; friend of Lou Andreas-Salomé. Gebsattel was later a training analyst at the Berlin Central Institute for Psychotherapy and Depth Psychology.
5. This word in English in original.
6. Cf. Reik, 1915a.
7. Abraham, 1917[54].
8. Paul Charles Dubois [1848–1918], professor of Neuropathology at Berne, known for his treatment of neuroses by "persuasion". Abraham is referring to the planned congress for neurology, psychiatry, and psychology in Berne.
9. Freud, 1913i, Freud's paper at the Munich Congress.

## 233A

Berlin
24 July 1914

Dear Professor,

The reply card system has now borne fruit at last: we have received cards with *no* from Riklin and Mensendieck,[1] and also one from Pfister with very meandering reasoning. Ophuijsen[2] has agreed to come. No harm is done if one or another from "over there" is at the Congress; they can see then that things don't have to go the same way as in Munich. I am even very pleased about Ophuijsen, partly because he does not belong absolutely to Jung's adherents, and partly because in Holland the schism might perhaps be avoided, so that we may soon have a new group there.

As we now *know* that the Swiss are not coming, there is surely nothing more to stop you from determining the subject for your talk more precisely!

I am glad to be certain of the non-participation of the Swiss still before leaving.

With cordial greetings,
Yours,

*Abraham*

1. Otto Mensendieck [1871–19?] from Hamburg, lay member of the Zurich Society until 1914, when he returned to Germany.
2. See letter 142F, 21 November 1912, n. 1.

## 234A

Berlin
25 July 1914

Dear Professor,

At the same time as your telegram, for which I sincerely thank you, there came this stupid manifesto from Zurich.[1] I am sending it to you because it seems to have been sent only to the people in Zurich and Munich as well as to my address.

I have replied to it by asking Riklin to transfer the [Association's] money, which is still there, to my bank. I think, with this, the relationship is definitively settled.

I am leaving tomorrow morning.
Cordial greetings!
Yours,

*Abraham*

1. Both missing.

## 235F

Karlsbad
26 July 1914

Dear Friend,

Simultaneously with the declaration of war,[1] which transforms our peaceful spa, your letter arrives, at last bringing the liberating news. So we are at last rid of them, the brutal, sanctimonious Jung and his parrots! I feel impelled now to thank you for the vast amount of trouble, for the exceptional, goal-oriented activity, with which you supported me and with which you steered our common cause. All my life I have been searching for friends who would not exploit and then betray me, and now, not far from its natural end, I hope I have found them.

1914 July

I can now satisfy your recently expressed wish and tell you what my subject is: aspects of ψα technique. Please put me in somewhere once the people have warmed up.

It will not be difficult to comment on the motivation of the Swiss' refusal with regard to the programme of the International Ψα Association.

It is of course impossible to foresee now whether conditions will permit us to hold the Congress. If the war remains localized in the Balkans, it will be all right. But one can say nothing about Russia.

My three sons are fortunately not affected. Two have been definitely rejected. The third has just been put into the reserves for the second time.[2] However, perhaps for the first time in 30 years I feel myself to be an Austrian and would like to try it once again with this not very hopeful Empire. Morale everywhere is excellent. The liberating effect of the courageous action and the secure prop of Germany contribute a great deal to this.—One observes the most genuine symptomatic actions in everyone.

I wish you undisturbed enjoyment of your well-earned holiday.

Your cordially devoted

*Freud*

1. On 23 July the Austrian government had directed an ultimatum at Serbia, giving a 48-hour deadline. Although the Serbian response of 25 July had partially acceded to the demands, Austria–Hungary had responded on the same day with a breaking-off of diplomatic relations and a partial mobilization. On 28 July Austria– Hungary declared war on Serbia.
2. In fact, however, Martin [1889–1967] volunteered in August 1914 and served in Galicia, Russia, and Italy. Oliver [1891–1969] served as engineer, and Ernst [1892–1970] fought in Italy from April 1915 on.

## 236F

Karlsbad
29 July 1914

Dear Friend,

Where are you and what are you thinking of doing? Did you expect your rest *re bene gesta*[1] to be like this? Can you perhaps tell me whether in a fortnight's time we shall be thinking half ashamedly of the excitement of these days, or whether we are close to the decision of destinies that has been threatening us for decades? Do you know whether we shall be able to meet at an intimate Congress this year?

No one knows all this, and the abundance of uncorroborated news, the ebb and flow of hope and fright, is bound to disturb the emotional balance of each of us.

We are here, lonely while waiting for letters that arrive late and writing letters that leave irregularly, hope to be able to leave Karlsbad on Monday the 3rd, as traffic with Germany remains open, and after some hold-ups to get to Seis after all by way of Munich. We are overjoyed that none of our sons or sons-in-law[2] is personally affected, and yet actually ashamed of this in view of the multitude of sacrifices all round us. The weather is as appalling, as if it were merely a projection of human moods in these times. Eitingon wanted to visit me, but the uproar of war intervened; our telegrams took 24 hours, and so I asked him to give it up. The great struggle would stifle all interest in the minor one, which we have now happily ended.

I am glad to have finished two technical articles while it was still quiet, one on transference love and the other entitled: Remembering, repeating and working through.[3] I think my way of presentation has changed, since the showdown I have become more honest, bolder, and more ruthless. I cannot yet imagine myself beginning anything new.

First a change of scenery. For your amusement I quote verbatim what Jones writes to me today:[4] "I had a long talk with Mrs Eder[5] last week, who has just had a month's analysis with Jung. . . . You may be interested to hear the latest method of dealing with Übertragung.[6] The patient overcomes it by learning that she is not really in love with the analyst but that she is for the first time struggling to comprehend a Universal Idea (with capitals) in Plato's sense: after she has done this, then what seems to be the *Übertragung* may remain."

*Risum teneatis*, Casimiri![7]

Eagerly looking forward to your news,

Your faithfully devoted

*Freud*

1. Latin: "after a successful fight".
2. Max Halberstadt, husband of Sophie, would fight in France. He was wounded on 23 February 1916.
3. Freud, 1914g, 1915a.
4. Letter of 27 July 1914 (Freud & Jones, 1993: p. 296). The quote is in English in the original.
5. Edith [?–1945], second wife of David M. Eder, sister of the British analyst Barbara Low [1877–1955].
6. Transference.
7. Allusion to *Risum teneatis, amici?* [Could you, oh friends, help laughing?] (Horace, *Ars poetica*, verse 5).

## 237A

Ostseebad Brunshaupten
29 July 1914

Dear Professor,

Your letter of the 26th reached me here on the day after my arrival. I should like to respond to the gratitude you express by doing everything I can to ensure that the Congress will fully compensate you and us all for Munich. You, too, surely have no doubt that the small circle of "Five"[1] will do everything possible and give of their best, not only at the Congress, but also in the future.—I shall schedule your talk for the best possible time. I believe we shall have a full and varied programme.

Here too everyone is solely preoccupied with the question of war. I do not think any of the powers will bring about a general war. But there is a strong universal feeling of alarm, in spite of a very friendly attitude towards Austria. We cannot yet tell at all what will happen to our plans. Rank wrote to me yesterday that he would have to advise strongly against going to the Dolomites. It would be a great pity if the meeting were to fall through. If the worst came to the worst, we could meet in Switzerland.—The Congress, too, has become somewhat problematical. I hope the next few days will bring a quick decision.

I have just got back the suggested guest list. Jones has proposed van Eeden.[2] I think you have his address; so please would you let me have it at the earliest opportunity.

Our *Jahrbuch* arrived yesterday from Deuticke. I am very pleased that we managed to get it ready within six months, despite all the difficulties. I shall start preparations for the next one as soon as I return to Berlin. It should certainly appear in the spring of 1915.

Cordial greetings to you and your wife, also from my wife!

Yours,

*Abraham*

1. The Secret Committee.
2. Frederik Willem van Eeden [1860–1932], an old acquaintance of Freud's; Dutch neurologist, poet and social reformer, founder of the socialist-communist colony Walden in Bussum [1898]. According to Jones (1955: p. 368), he and Freud had tried in vain to win him over to psychoanalysis.

## 238A

Brunshaupten
31 July 1914

Dear Professor,

I am replying straight away. We know nothing here. It is possible that we shall leave still today or tomorrow. Because there are strong indications that general mobilization will take place tomorrow or Sunday.[1] It is out of the question to remain here if war breaks out. One cannot make any further plans. So we shall probably wait and see in Berlin. I must not be away if war comes, since I am liable for military hospital service. I have no other duties.[2]

This place is already half empty; officers on the active list and men on leave have already been recalled. If you were to stop in Munich, it might not be impossible to meet, but who knows?

One tends to assume that none of the powers wants to start the war. All the same, things look very serious. The papers are only allowed to print half of what is going on.

All I can promise you today is to keep in regular communication with you. Your letter postmarked the 30th has, incidentally, reached me very quickly. My best wishes for us all go with this letter on its way.

I am looking forward to your new papers with as much anticipation as is possible at the moment!

With cordial greetings,
Yours,

*Abraham*

Did you not receive my last letter?

1. After Austria-Hungary's declaration of war on Serbia on 28 July, Serbia's protector, Russia, had partially mobilized on 29 July. Secured by the German General Staff, the general mobilization of Austria–Hungary was signed and announced by the Kaiser in Vienna on the morning of 31 July. One day later, the general mobilization in Germany and Germany's declaration of war on Russia followed.
2. Because of emphysema of the lungs in childhood, Abraham had not done his military service and was therefore only in the reserves.

## 239F

Karlsbad
2 August 1914

Dear Friend,

Your letter received today (dated 31 July) has been overtaken by events, so I am writing to you to Berlin again. I thank you for your promise to keep me amply provided with news, and I shall try to do the same with you. We shall probably stay here for another week; travelling to Vienna during the period of mobilization is hardly feasible, and to Munich it is impossible. Incidentally, our Ernst is in Salzburg with his brother Martin and will probably be unable to return for the time being.

We can safely dismiss from our minds all worry about the Congress, etc. All interest now goes elsewhere. At the time of my writing the great war can be regarded as certain; I should be with it with all my heart if I did not know England to be on the wrong side.

I should very much like to get to work on a nice topic that has begun to plague me, but I am still too tense, too distracted, I must wait for a *definitivum*, a *fait accompli*. Meanwhile I also feel ashamed at enjoying all the refinements of the cure at charming Karlsbad with my good wife while the world is quaking like this. No more white bread is being baked in Vienna. What is perhaps more worrying is that savings- and other banks are not paying out deposits over 200 crowns. It will become evident to what extent it is possible to do even without money in everyday life.

We cannot fall out of the world,[1] that is the greatest safeguard.

I hope that you and yours have arrived safely and that your war service will not take you too far from home.

With a cordial shake of the hand in the distance,
Your faithfully devoted,

*Freud*

1. *Ja, aus der Welt werden wir nicht fallen. Wir sind einmal darin* [Indeed, we shall not fall out of this world. We are in it once and for all], says the hero who is facing a self-inflicted death in Christian Dietrich Grabbe's [1801–1836] *Hannibal* (1835). Quoted by Freud in 1930a: p. 65.

## 240A

Berlin[1]
3 August 1914

Dear Professor,

We arrived back here last Saturday after a very exhausting journey. What are you and yours doing? I shall probably do some locum work for the time being. There is no question of our meeting unless you can come here.

With cordial greetings,
Yours,

*Abraham*

1. Postcard. Addressed to: "Herrn Prof. Dr S. Freud, Karlsbad/Böhmen, Villa Fasolt, Wien, IX Berggasse 19" with the remark: "Please forward, if departed!", which was evidently done, because the Bohemian address is crossed out.

## 241A

Berlin[1]
8 August 1914

Dear Professor,

I have just received your letter of 2/8, after it had travelled around for six days. I am answering only briefly today, and will write in more detail when I know for certain that you are in Vienna, but I am sending a duplicate of this card to Vienna.

We are well. Do your sons and sons-in-law have to go into the *Landsturm* [Territorial Reserves]? Eitingon is in the Austrian *Landsturm* as a doctor, I think in Eger.[2]

Only provisional greetings for today!, also from my wife, for all of you!

Yours,

*Abraham*

1. Postcard. Same double address as in letter 240A, 3 August 1914.
2. Max Eitingon had—as an Austrian citizen—volunteered for the army (Eitingon to Freud, 24 August 1914, SFC). From August on he was first stationed in the Prague garrison hospital, then at various locations in Hungary—Kassa, Igló, Hatvan, and Miskolcz, among others.

## 242A

Berlin[1]
8 August 1914

Dear Professor,

Your letter of 2 August has just arrived! As I do not know whether this card will still reach you in Karlsbad, I am sending two copies of it, to K. and Vienna. In a few days, when I know for certain that you are in Vienna, I will write more.

We are also well. What are your sons doing? *Landsturm*? Here morale has risen very high through the brilliant success of Lüttich.[2] More soon, today only cordial greetings from my wife and me!

Yours,

*Abraham*

Eitingon is with the Austrian *Landsturm* as a doctor, I believe in Eger.

1. Postcard.
2. After the declaration of war on Belgium on 3 August (because Belgium had refused to let German troops march through her territory), German troops under General von Emmich had, on 7 August, conquered Liège/Lüttich, the portcullis guarding the gateway into Belgium from Germany (see Tuchman, 1962).

## 243A

Berlin
14 August 1914

Dear Professor,

I presume that by now you are back in Vienna. Unfortunately, I have had no news from you for some time; what may have happened to you all in the meantime? Did your sons have to join the *Landsturm*? What has happened to Rank, Sachs, Ferenczi? Our lively correspondence has come to a complete standstill. I still have to wait, am *Landsturm* and volunteer physician. I shall probably be employed in this latter capacity quite soon. I know no particulars as yet.

The first great victories have done very much to raise morale here. We have had practically no news from the battle-fronts since the day before yesterday. Presumably great things are happening even now. So we are in a state of utmost tension.

The practice has, to my surprise, increased somewhat again this week. This was supposed to have been the holidays, and we should be in the Tyrol just now! But in times like these, one has to give up holidays for the sake of a little more financial security. I am working three, four hours a day. There is too little tranquillity for scientific work. We are living from one newspaper to the next; scarcely satisfied with one lot of news, one already longs for the next.

My family is well; I hope it is the same with you. For a long time now I have not heard how your sister-in-law's convalescence has progressed.

In the hope of receiving good news soon (postcard or open letter[1]) and with the most cordial greetings from house to house.

Yours,

*Abraham*

1. Open because of the censorship during the war.

## 244F

Vienna IX, Berggasse 19
25 August 1914

Dear Friend,

If I could expect this open letter ever to reach you, I should say: at last news from you (the last were from 2 August). Since then I have written to you repeatedly, obviously in vain. I have heard from Eitingon in Prague that you are probably staying in Berlin.

Our news is as follows. We returned here from Karlsbad on 5 August, my sister-in-law, who is at last recovering, was back before us, as her sanatoria had closed.[1] Oli turned up a few days later, and for 12 days we were unable to find out whether Ernst had managed to get back to Munich from Salzburg, where he had made an excursion. Eventually he reached Vienna from Munich as a passenger of the Austrian consulate there, with 1 mark, 55 pf. travelling money, but here he was deferred with thanks, and since then he has been living with us. Annerl is so-to-say a prisoner-of-war in England; after some long, anxious days we managed to get in touch with her via the Hague through Dr van Emden. We have learned that she remains unmolested at her institute on the coast and is in contact with our friends in London, who will certainly look after her in case of need. She is said to be well, and to be behaving very pluckily. Living in an enemy country can scarcely be without its thorns.[2]

Martin completed his court practice in Salzburg before the outbreak of war. When the storm broke he volunteered, proved that he had fully recovered from his broken thigh,[3] and managed to be posted to the same unit in which he had once served as a One-Year Volunteer[4] (41st Field Artillery Regiment). His reason, according to what he writes, was that he did not want to miss the opportunity of crossing the Russian frontier without changing his faith.[5] He was expecting to remain in Salzburg for several weeks' training but reported today that he has left. We do not know of course where to, whether south or north.

My son-in-law in Hamburg[6] has received his calling-up papers for 7 September.

Now for the others. Rank and Sachs are here. Rank, as cheerful as ever, has, as we are all for the time being incapable of scientific work, found himself work arranging and cataloguing my library. Ferenczi has been called up; he is awaiting employment as a physician and wants to visit us in the next few days.[7] We remaining members of the Society want to meet in the café tomorrow, Wednesday. I know of Federn that he was on the "Kronprinzessin Caecilie", which turned back off the coast of France after receiving a warning and so took him back again to New York!

At last I have the marvellous leisure in my own study that I have always longed for. But see what happens to wishes when they come true! I find it completely impossible to do anything sensible. Like everyone else, I live from one German victory to the next, and in the meantime torment myself with fear of fresh complications, breaches of neutrality, etc. The really unheard-of achievements of our allies seem actually already to have saved us. These are great and terrible times.

Of all my plans for the summer and autumn there is one only I wish to hang on to. I want to see my grandson in Hamburg and so will come to Berlin too, as soon as travelling becomes tolerable again. This is likely to be early in September. Recent experiences, of course, frighten one from making any plan or project.

1914 August

"What becomes of the hopes,
what becomes of the plans,
built by Man,
that transient creature!"
(Or something of the sort.)[8]
I am delighted to hear that you and yours are well, and only hope that correspondence between the allies will be facilitated again. But *forsan et haec olim meminisse juvabit*, as we read in Virgil.[9]
Most cordially in the name of us all,
Yours,

*Freud*

1. See Freud's letter of 6 August 1914 (LOC) to Sophie and Max Halberstadt: "In Karlsbad one couldn't comprehend the total seriousness of the situation, either. But Aunts Minna and Mathilde, who had already returned to Vienna earlier, gave us no peace until . . . we departed on the evening of Tuesday the 4th with the last evening train that was even permitted to run. . . . The impressions of these two days can't be put into a letter."
2. Anna Freud had actually already left England and arrived in Vienna on the following day after a long and difficult journey.
3. In January 1911, Martin had broken his thigh on a ski tour (cf. Martin Freud, 1957: pp. 175ff.; Freud & Ferenczi, 1992: p. 251). He had subsequently been deemed unfit for military service.
4. As he was a university student, Martin had become a so-called "one-year volunteer" [*Einjährig-Freiwilliger*] with the artillery. Those who were not students had to serve in the military for three years.
5. Jews were not allowed to enter Tsarist Russia.
6. Max Halberstadt.
7. Ferenczi cancelled his trip, however.
8. *Was sind Hoffnungen, was sind Entwürfe, die der Mensch, der vergängliche, baut?* (Friedrich von Schiller, *Die Braut von Messina*, 3, 5). Also quoted by Freud in letter 278F, 3 July 1915, and in his obituary of Anton von Freund (1920c: p. 268).
9. Latin: "Perhaps remembering this, too, will be pleasant one day" (Virgil, *Aeneid*, 1, 203).

## 245A

Berlin
29 August 1914

Dear Professor,

You have evidently not received various letters I sent you. Now I am glad to hear from you at last and at some length; letter and postcard took only three days to get here, and I hope mine will take no longer.

So you all are well. I have often wondered how your youngest would do in England, and correctly assumed that van Emden would be the intermediary. Besides, ladies are being allowed to leave England. An American living here, for example, has brought several young girls out of London. There are various ways of getting news from England, including via Denmark. I am giving you, just in case, the address of a good friend who, if you mention my name, will certainly pass on any news (she knows German well). "Fröken Ellen Lauritzen, Kjobenhavn Ø, Strandboulevard 66".—A brother of my mother's in London sent a card which duly arrived in Bremen. It was addressed to the postmaster in Vlissingen. There was only a request to him on the text side to forward the card to Bremen with an altered address.

My best wishes go with your Martin into the field! I hope that all will go well with all of you in these difficult times, particularly your sister-in-law.

All is well with us here. I have volunteered for hospital work, perhaps also abroad, or for hospital trains. I very nearly went off to Dirschau (mouth of the Vistula) a week ago. But it was decided otherwise, and I remain, for the time being at least, at the military hospital on Grünewald racecourse. I have plenty of work, mainly surgical, but later on I am possibly to take over the Psychiatric and Neurological Department. The practice is now very restricted. I still feel too unsettled for scientific work. The need to help in the common cause, and the uncertainty of the first weeks of war overshadowed everything else. Now, however, the news is excellent. The German troops are barely 100 kilometres from Paris. Belgium is finished, so is England on land. The same is happening with Russia. The Austrian successes came at the right moment during the days when we were deeply very worried about East Prussia.[1]

My kindest regards to Sachs, Rank, and Ferenczi, as well as to all the other friends in Vienna. I have heard nothing about Hitschmann. What is he doing?

None of us has news of Jones, I take it? Do you also find it such a strange feeling that he belongs to our "enemies"?

Now I am very eager to hear when you are going to Hamburg! The express train connection with Vienna is fairly reliable again. Via Berlin, of course, and we shall be pleased to see you, rather than the Cossacks, marching in (who, according to some anxious minds, are due to be here soon). A compensation for Seis, if only a very abbreviated one! My wife and I offer you our cordial welcome in advance.

With cordial greetings to you and all of yours.

Yours,

*Abraham*

[Postscript from Frau Abraham]

Dear Professor,

My husband was already on his way to hospital for night duty when your two cards[2] came. I telephoned the contents to him, and he asked

1914 September

me to congratulate you and your dear family on Fräulein Annerl's[3] safe return home! I join most cordially in these congratulations, and at the same time I send you all my best wishes! In the hope of seeing you, dear Professor, in our home very soon, I remain
Your devoted

*Hedwig Abraham*

1. On 24 August, the Austro-Hungarian army had defeated the Russians near Lublin. Shortly afterwards, a successful German counter-offensive defeated the Russian army at Tannenberg [on 30 August].
2. Missing.
3. Diminutive of "Anna".

246F

Vienna IX, Berggasse 19
3 September 1914

Dear Friend,

At last a proper letter from you, and with a charming postscript from your wife! It was on the way from 29 August until today, so Berlin is still a long way away.

Thank you very much indeed for your offer, which has fortunately been overtaken by events, and for the news of your family, which I shall do my best to reciprocate. We are all well; the only ill person (my sister-in-law) has almost completely recovered. Martin is in Innsbruck, I want to visit him on Sunday; he counts on leaving by the middle of the month.[1] My son Ernst will probably be taken at the call-up on the ninth. To the young this means nothing but wish fulfilment. The barriers between army and civil population have, incidentally, practically disappeared, only the barriers of age remain.

The German victories provided a firm basis for our morale, and we have been shaken in the worst way by the expectation of ours. Things seem to be going well, though, but there is nothing decisive yet, and we have given up hope of a rapid end to the war by means of catastrophic strokes. Endurance will become the chief virtue. In these circumstances, interest inclines a bit towards scientific matters again. Rank, with whom I spend a great deal of time because he is now arranging my library, will be writing to you about this. We count on a similar "positive" inclination with you. We wish to show, while we are cut off from our foreign colleagues, that we alone can do something good, and we want to bring out respectable issues of *"Zeitschrift"* and *"Imago"*.

Hitschmann is a happy father, Federn finally back from New York after great adventures, and now seems to be moving upwards. True,

Jones is our "enemy". Unfortunately correspondence with van Emden and hence through him is also very unsatisfactory.

I like to think that I shall be in Berlin and Hamburg this month. These days we hardly dare express a firm intention.

A paper from the Flechsig clinic in Alzheimer's journal[2] shows the beginning of a changed attitude to $\Psi\alpha$ also in Germany.

With kindest regards,
Yours,
 *Freud*

Write again soon!

1. Freud was in Innsbruck on 6 September, then returned to Vienna. On 16 September he left for Hamburg to see the Halberstadts, stopping in Berlin in both directions to visit Abraham. He returned to Vienna on 27 September 1914.
2. Paul Emil Flechsig [1847–1929], German psychiatrist and neurologist, from 1882 on professor in Leipzig, physician of Daniel Paul Schreber (cf. Freud, 1911c [1910]). Alois Alzheimer [1864–1915], German neurologist and psychiatrist, who described the disease that was named after him. He edited the *Zeitschrift für die gesamte Neurologie und Psychiatrie*, of which he was co-founder. The paper was not identified.

## 247A

Berlin
9 September 1914

Dear Professor,

These lines are only to ask you how things are with you, especially what news you have of Martin.

All is well with us. At the moment I am very busy again at the hospital. Today I had to do dressings for about eight hours.

Morale here is entirely optimistic. In the West things look brilliant in spite of the difficulties, which are still great. We are now waiting for great events in the East, preceded already by all sorts of rumours. The collaboration of Germans and Austrians will certainly achieve the aim here too. Then England remains to be taken care of; but we put our hopes in Krupp and Zeppelin.

I hope the time will soon come when we can again correspond scientifically in peace. Today is the precise anniversary of the Munich Congress! From this point of view we do feel better now.

With cordial greetings from my wife as well, for you and all your family!

Yours,
 *Karl Abraham*

What about the visit to Hamburg?

1914 September

## 248A

Berlin
13 September 1914

Dear Professor,

I must assume that several cards and at least one of my letters have not reached you. Postal services are still difficult. Your letter, dated and stamped 3 September, arrived yesterday, having taken nine days to get here.

I am glad to hear that you are all well and that your sister-in-law is on the way to recovery. My best wishes go with your two sons. Many thanks, incidentally, for the card that you and Martin sent me.[1]

All is well with our family. There are, on the whole, few signs of war here in Berlin. We have been greatly reassured by the complete defeat of the Russians in East Prussia,[2] and are hoping for favourable news in the very next days about the battles on the Marne. Once these are decided in our favour, France is virtually finished; that is to say, the capture of the south-eastern fortifications will only be a question of a relatively short time. This evening we heard of the Austrian withdrawal near Lemberg [Lvov]; I expect that the fortifications and the Carpathian mountains will halt the Russian advance.

Now to the smaller world of our own interests! I wrote a card to Rank on Tuesday, promising him a short paper. Still on the same evening, I had news that very early the next day a transport of wounded would arrive at our hospital, which is situated a long way out of town. That meant that I had to get up at 4.30 a.m., was standing in the operating theatre without a break till 2 p.m. and then spent some hours in my own practice in the afternoon. As the next few days were just as full, I could not even make the smallest beginning on my paper. Perhaps it will be better this week.—I don't feel like starting on the bigger piece of work at all, an excerpt of which I had planned to present as my Congress paper. All the more I am glad to be able to put my ideas to you when you come to Berlin. I shall arrange to be hindered as little as possible by my work at the hospital during your visit.

I add the most cordial greetings to you, yours, and all the friends,
yours, as always,

*Karl Abraham*

1. Missing.
2. See letter 245A, 29 August 1914, n. 1.

## 249A

Berlin
21 September 1914

Dear Professor,

The report is enclosed.

I hope we shall see you again at our home in a few days. If in any way possible, I shall see to a victory!

Morale is improving here! The chances in the West are more favourable. There are rumours of an imminent action against England. And then Hindenburg[1] has gone to Galicia, with, they say, about 100,000 men.

Cordial greetings, also from my wife, to you and yours! Looking forward to seeing you again soon,

Yours,

*Karl Abraham*

1. Paul von Beneckendorff und von Hindenburg [1847–1934], German field marshal [from 1914 on] and later president [1925–1934]. On 22 August 1914, along with Erich Ludendorff [1865–1937], he had assumed the leadership of the Eighth Army, which recorded great successes on the Eastern front. At the end of August 1916 both assumed the Third High Command, which, strongly influenced by heavy industry, presided over the strategic planning and leadership of the war. After the defeat of Germany he lost nothing in popularity, and, despite his monarchical stance, he became the second president of the Weimar Republic; it was in this capacity that he appointed Hitler as chancellor in 1933.

## 250F

Hamburg
22 September 1914

Dear Friend,

Thank you very much indeed for the preparations you are making for my second stay in Berlin, in particular for those aimed against England. Having regard to them, I propose to leave here early on Friday and to arrive in Berlin at 1.10, where I can stay until six in the evening. The time is perhaps too short for a meeting of the group, should rather be saved for our being together, if you can manage it.

I hope I shall still be in time to forward to Rank the manifesto you sent,[1] which pleased us very much.

This is not the first time I have been in Hamburg, but it is the first time I have been here not as in a strange town. I live with my children, talk about the success of "our" loan,[2] and discuss the chances of "our" battle of millions, with a faint memory of discussions about an earlier gigantic battle, which, after some partial successes, ended quite drearily.

It is like remembering an earlier existence according to the doctrine of the transmigration of souls.

My grandson[3] is a charming little fellow, who manages to laugh so engagingly whenever one pays attention to him; he is a decent, civilized being, which is doubly valuable in these times of unleashed bestiality. A strict upbringing by an intelligent mother enlightened by Hug-Hellmuth[4] has done him a great deal of good.

My son-in-law has every now and then to portray a departing hero or to enlarge the portrait of a dead hero, but otherwise he can devote himself to his family, so that the days pass very happily.

I think I shall be arriving from the station just in time for your lunch, counting on your family hospitality as an unvarying factor.

Hoping that this letter will reach you before I do myself, I send my cordial greetings to you, your dear wife, and your swarm of children, who, I hope, have now fully recovered.

Yours,

*Freud*

1. Probably Abraham's presidential note on the secession of the Zurich group (see letters 231F, 18 July 1914, & n. 1; 252F, 18 October 1914).
2. Subscriptions to the German war loan were as high as 4.5 billion marks.
3. Ernst; see letter 194F, 15 February 1914, n. 1.
4. See letter 159F, 1 June 1913, n. 3.

## 251A

Berlin[1]
11 October 1914

Dear Professor,

Many thanks for your postcard! I postponed writing until today. Now that Antwerp has been taken[2] and our tension has lessened, I must at least send you a sign of life. I should be glad to hear soon how you all are and, in particular, to know what news you have from your Martin!

It is doubtful whether my trip there will come off. My work at the hospital takes up more time now than when you visited us. I must not conclude without thanking you, also on behalf of my wife, for the time you spent with us!

With cordial greetings from house to house,

Yours,

*Karl Abraham*

1. Postcard.
2. After a siege of 12 days, German troops had conquered Antwerp on 9 October.

## 252F

Vienna IX, Berggasse 19
18 October 1914

Dear Friend,

At last a sign of life from you! The Antwerp news is fine, at any rate a good sign. It is to be hoped that things are going the same way elsewhere, where we do not suspect it. We too breathe more freely here.

Martin is expected here on sick leave with catarrhal jaundice. Eight days ago Ernst left for Klagenfurt[1] as a one-year volunteer for the artillery. He has been deferred four times this year, but was taken at the general examination and then asserted his rights as a volunteer. My third son Oliver is not having his turn; he is surveying ground for building barracks.

The volume of the *Zeitschrift* has appeared with your *Korrespondenzblatt*, unfortunately showing signs of serious negligence by the printer's proof-reader. An issue of *Imago* is expected daily. I am working on the big and difficult case history for the *Jahrbuch*[2] and on the third edition of the "Sexual Theory".[3] I do not enjoy the hack work required for this. It is never like something that comes in one stroke.

I am now doing 5½ hours' analysis daily, of which practically none is of long duration, only a couple of weeks are secured. One's heart is also elsewhere.

Today I also had a card from Jones, through Dr van Emden.[4] He is well, and has seven hours' work; he tells me that Eder has dropped out. So we put him in with the others. The circle is moving closer together. Binswanger has announced his joining our group.[5]

Ferenczi is still here, and is spending his holidays here,[6] as he is missing nothing in Budapest.

In these unfriendly times we enjoy making plans for the summer. This year the plan for the house in Berchtesgaden shall be carried out at last. Sophie wants to run it, contribute the child and the servants. It would be an opportunity for once to spend some time peacefully with one's friends. Karlsbad will, alas, be one of the extravagances of the "good old days".

I send my cordial greetings to you, your dear wife, and both your children, and I always think with unclouded satisfaction of the days I spent with you.

Your faithfully devoted

*Freud*

1. Provincial capital of Carinthia, in the south of present-day Austria.
2. The "Wolf Man" analysis (1918b [1914]), written in October/November 1914.
3. 1905d, 3rd edition 1915.
4. Jones had sent three evidently identical cards on 10 October 1914, via Holland, Sweden, and Italy (Freud & Jones, 1993: p. 300).

1914 October

5. That is, to the Viennese group (letter to Freud of 28 July 1914, Freud & Binswanger, 1992: p. 142). Freud announced this in the first session of the working year 1914/15 (Nunberg & Federn, 1975, only in German edition: p. 257).
6. In fact, on 1 October Ferenczi had begun the first of three periods of analysis with Freud; it had to be discontinued after three and a half weeks because he was called to military service.

## 253A

Berlin
28 October 1914

Dear Professor,

This letter is to accompany the manuscript[1] I have owed you for so long. I am still deeply immersed in hospital work, and the few remaining hours are taken up by the practice. Perhaps Rank will be good enough to undertake the small job of proof-reading, to avoid posting to and fro in these uncertain times.

Your Martin will certainly get better quickly under his mother's tender care. I send all my best wishes to your two sons in the army! And naturally to the peaceful members of your family as well. I am curious to know what will happen with Reik. Do yet others of our friends have to go into the Territorials? I have heard nothing of Eitingon for a long time. Do you know anything about him? I myself am here for the present. But it is not impossible that I may have to go to a foreign hospital. What is Ferenczi's situation in this respect?

The practice is taking its quiet course, three to four hours per day. I recently started treating one of your former patients, Dr Veneziani[2]. I have not heard anything more of Frau Hi....[3] I am still occupied with your niece's[4] affairs. Her fiancé has again suffered serious attacks outside Berlin, and lay for quite a long time with stitched-up wounds. She has come to see reason and is ready for renunciation, only the mode to a solution is difficult.

The thought of peaceful journeys in the future is wonderful. But one hardly wants to think about it. We would also be very much in favour of Berchtesgaden. Let us wait and see with $\psi\alpha$ patience!

I intend to call an informal meeting of our greatly reduced group. There will hardly be any scientific activity.

These are hard days at the front. But people are, on the whole, full of confidence. Even the sense of humour is dawning again. A shop selling uniforms and fashion goods displays a placard saying: "Field grey, the fashionable colour for 1914." Among the funny Germanizations of English words and names there is one very good one: How do you translate Shakespere [sic] into German? Answer: "Schütte-Lanz".[5]

Another of the amusing moments of these serious times is a letter from Stockmayer *from the front* in which, after hesitating for ten months, he announces his resignation: he says that as a result of mobilization he has not been able to get down to it until now.

As I was writing this, Deuticke's honorarium arrived. To my pleasant surprise he has now calculated the printed sheet at M. 60, and has also added to the editor's honorarium M. 25 as a lump-sum payment for expenses.

With cordial greetings, also from my wife, to you, your family, and our friends,

Yours,

*Karl Abraham*

1. Not identified.
2. Bruno Veneziani, a brother-in-law of Italo Svevo, the great writer. Later he also went for an analysis with Edoardo Weiss. (Cf. Veneziani Svevo, 2001; friendly communication by Paul Roazen.)
2. See letter 226F, 10 July 1914, n. 3.
3. Margarete; see letter 257A, 6 December 1914.
4. *Schüttle* [*die*] *Lanz'* [shake (the) spear]; Schütte-Lanz was the name of a German factory that manufactured airships and aeroplanes.

## 254F

Vienna IX, Berggasse 19
31 October 1914

Dear Friend,

Your letter was like a refreshing breeze. We are very pleased just now about the Triple Alliance, given us anew as a result of the Turkish decision.[1] Otherwise we learn the same things in the newspapers, I assume.

Your little work was welcome; a proof of my next paper for the *Zeitschrift*[2] is on the way for you. I am again hard at work on the large case history, in which I let myself go at length into discussing things. I now realize that the only reason why I wrote in such concise a style in recent years was that I had so little time. (!) How shall I get the paper to you when it is finished? You will have to come to Vienna to fetch it, or I shall have to go to Berlin again if, as I hope, you stay there.

Otherwise I have very little to do, I have not been able to get more than two patients, and in the long run there are likely to be fewer rather than more.

As for Frau Hirschfeld, I am able to inform you that she is with her husband in Nassau—interned as an Englishwoman. This will not be very oppressive to her; on the contrary, she will enjoy being guarded by the state now. She, too, is, after all, a victim of British perfidy. I have noticed in general that obsessional people feel better now in wartime, we have descended to their level.

Venez.[iani] is a bad case; you are his fifth doctor: Sadger, myself, Reitler,[3] Tausk. He is an enigma, probably a *mauvais sujet*, up to now nothing could be done with him. My son Martin is going back on 8 November; of Ernst there is good news. My little one[4] is busying herself very much in the day-nursery and public soup-kitchen, and is continuing with her Latin at the same time.

From Pfister there was a precious article on Adler,[5] which you will surely also have received. He simply glosses over my remarks about him, but manages to make an unholy praise out of the same material that would have served someone else for an annihilation. I did not know until now that one could be of such service to science through one-sidedness and obstinacy.

Binswanger has sent in a good paper on Jasper [sic] and $\Psi\alpha$, but makes too much of Jasper too.[6]

An Italian, Levi Bianchini, *Dozent* [Associate Professor] in Naples, who has a part in the *Manicomio*, intends to begin an international psychiatric library in Italian with the translation of the five lectures.[7] Perhaps I have already mentioned that to you.

Ferenczi—as I have perhaps mentioned to you also—has gone to Pápa in Hungary for local service with a regiment of Hussars. Eitingon's last letter is from Igló (Hungary). Fer.'s address is the Hotel Griff. Which brings me to the end of my news.

I send you my cordial greetings and hope that your wife and children are well—which you have not mentioned this time.

Your faithfully devoted

*Freud*

Have seen Reik only once, on Wednesday.

1. On 21 October, Turkey had entered the war alongside the Central Powers. The so-called Triple Alliance had been a secret treaty [1882] between Germany, Austria–Hungary, and Italy, essentially directed against Russia. It contributed to the formation of the Triple Entente between Russia, Great Britain, and France [1907].
2. Freud, 1914g.
3. Rudolf Reitler [1865–1917], Viennese physician, founding member of the Wednesday Society, and probably the first to practise psychoanalysis after Freud.
4. Anna.
5. Probably Pfister, 1914c.
6. Freud also mentioned this paper in his letter to Ferenczi of the previous day (Freud & Ferenczi, 1992: p. 22); it could not be identified.
    Karl Jaspers [1883–1969], famous German existential philosopher and psychologist, professor at the University of Heidelberg. Between 1937 and 1945 he was forbidden to lecture; from 1948 on he was professor in Basel.
7. Marco Levi-Bianchini [1875–1961], Italian psychiatrist, professor at the University of Naples and editor of the journal *Il Manicomio*. Cofounder, with Edoardo Weiss, of the first unofficial Italian psychoanalytic group; then founding member [1925] and, up to his death, honorary president of the Società Psicoanalitica Italiana, but remaining a member of the Vienna Society [1922–1936] as the Italian Society was not affiliated with the IPA.

He was an adherent of the Fascist party, but, as a Jew, he was relieved of his duties in 1938, although he did not emigrate. His translation of Freud (1910a [1909]) was published in 1915 as the first volume of the Biblioteca psichiatrica internazionale, which he founded.

## 255A

Berlin
28 October 1914

Dear Professor,

The proofs you sent showed me that the wheels of science are not completely at a standstill. The paper is very convincing, both as a whole and in all details. However, in the interests of the beginner, I should like to suggest that *one* paragraph be expanded a little. Page-proof 3, lines 7–12[1] describe an experience that the initiated immediately understands, while the inexperienced will miss a somewhat fuller explanation.

These technical papers always come in the nick of time. This most recent one gave me some good advice during the last few days in the treatment of a difficult case!

As a rule I work at my practice three or four hours a day. My experience is that at the moment there is only *one* type of patient who goes into treatment (or, more precisely, who is, for financial reasons, *able* to): unmarried men with inherited money. This applies to all my patients.

Dr Venez.[iani], about whom you wrote to me, will very soon leave treatment; there is no getting at his narcissism.

*Zeitschrift* and *Imago* have arrived, as well as the *Psychoanalytical Review*,[2] but I have read only a very little of them.

I hope everything will continue well for your two sons at the front. At the moment the general mood here is very positively expectant. I would like to go on about quite a few things, but that is, as we know, not possible by letter.—I should like to come to Vienna to go through your large manuscript, but I do not know yet whether I shall be able to travel in the foreseeable future. Perhaps between Christmas and the New Year.

Many thanks for news of our friends! Liebermann, who is in the Vosges, asked recently whether he could send you a card, that is, whether you would not find it importunate. I encouraged him; he would certainly be very glad of a few lines from you. I have heard nothing from Eitingon himself for a long time. Yesterday I learned that Stegmann was wounded and a prisoner of war in France, as has already happened to a number of doctors.

I am very busy at the hospital with my 50 patients. The work in itself and its results are very satisfying.—All is well with us. Cordial greetings to you and yours, also from my wife!

Yours,

*Karl Abraham*

1. Freud, 1914g (the paragraph on pp. 149–150).
2. *Psychoanalytic Review*, American psychoanalytic quarterly founded by William A. White and Smith E. Jelliffe in 1913 (cf. Burnham, 1983: pp. 61–63), a venture not particularly welcomed by Freud (cf. ibid.: pp. 195–196).

## 256F

Vienna IX, Berggasse 19
25 November 1914

Dear Friend,

Your last letter arrived unopened. Can the censorship have been reduced for you? The proofs you sent unfortunately arrived too late for me to use your suggestion. In any case I am glad that you have found something useful in this article too.

Little is happening in the intimate circle. Both young ones are writing industriously for money and good remittances. The practice has not risen above 2½ patients. My wife went to Hamburg for a fortnight out of longing, for no particular reason, spending just one hour in Berlin. I am very rested, despite all burdens on my feelings physically very well, and am working very easily with a rested head, interrupted by attacks of laziness. The large case history is finished, it is waiting for you, if you really can come for Christmas. In addition I have begun a larger comprehensive work[1] which has in passing produced the $\psi\alpha$ solution of the problem of time and space and the clarification of the mechanism of anxiety.[2]

Today van Emden sent me a long letter from Jones, from which it appears that he has difficulty in warding off the Jung disciples in the Association, which incidentally is fairly unimportant, as we have to start from the beginning in any case. He writes about the war like a real Anglo.[3] There will have to be a few more *Überdreadnoughts*[4] sent to the bottom or a few more landings made, otherwise their eyes will not be opened. An incredible arrogance has taken possession of the island. It is highly probable that Rank will become free at recruitment. With Sachs it is not yet certain.[5] Ferenczi is striving for a transfer to Budapest. I should be very pleased to have a card from Liebermann. Landauer[6] is, as we know, in Lille, behind the front line. The sentencing of the German army doctors by the French courts is one of the most disgusting farces of this war.

I send you my cordial greetings and hope that you and your family will continue to be well.

Your most faithfully devoted

*Freud*

1. A first allusion to Freud's attempt at a great synthesis, an extensive book on psychoanalytic metapsychology, later abandoned (cf. editor's introduction in *S.E. 14*: pp. 105–107). Eventually, he wrote 12 metapsychological papers, of which only 5 (1915c, 1915d, 1915e, 1916–17f, 1916–17g) were published; the others (on consciousness, anxiety, conversion hysteria, obsessional neurosis, sublimation, projection and paranoia, and the transference neuroses) were presumably destroyed. A draft of the last one finished, "Overview of the Transference Neuroses" (in English, *A Phylogenetic Fantasy*), which he had sent to Ferenczi on 28 July 1915, was published in 1985 (Freud, 1985a).
2. Regarding the time–space problem, see letter 219F, 14 June 1914, & n. 2. With respect to the mechanism of—the release of—anxiety, cf. *Inhibitions, Symptoms, and Anxiety*, 1926d [1925], *passim*, esp. p. 93; cf. also Freud's letter to Ferenczi of the same day, Freud & Ferenczi, 1996: pp. 30–31.
3. Letter of 15 November (Freud & Jones, 1993: pp. 302–305). Constance Long, and Edith and David M. Eder, in particular, defended the view "that Jung's method constitutes a variety, and legitimate evolution, of Ps-A" (ibid.: p. 303). Freud took exception to Jones's view that "obviously Germany cannot win nor can she be really crushed" (ibid.), a judgement made "with the narrow-mindedness of the English about the outcome of the war" (Freud & Ferenczi, 1996: p. 30).
4. As opposed to (German) submarines (*über* [over, above]) [translator's note].
5. Rank was "defending himself *against* the fatherland like a lion" (2 December 1914, Freud & Ferenczi, 1996: p. 33). Hanns Sachs had been mustered out because of nearsightedness, but, like Rank, he was called up in the summer of the following year (Jones, 1955: pp. 176 and 181).
6. Karl Landauer [1887–1945], M.D. He had had analysis with Freud in 1912 and had become a member of the Vienna Society in 1913. After the war he moved to Frankfurt, where he founded, with Heinrich Meng, Frieda Fromm-Reichmann, and Erich Fromm, the *Frankfurter Psychoanalytische Institut*, which closely collaborated with the *Institut für Sozialforschung* (Horkheimer, Adorno, Marcuse). After the coming to power of the Nazis he fled, first to Sweden, and then to Amsterdam, where he and his family were arrested. Landauer starved to death in the Bergen-Belsen concentration camp (Mühlleitner, 1992: pp. 205–207; Rothe, 1991).

## 257A

Berlin
6 December 1914

Dear Professor,

Your last letter contained much that greatly pleased and interested me. One generally hears of nothing but trenches, numbers of prisoners, etc., and then, for a change, there comes a sign that our science is still alive. I am extremely curious to know what new ideas have matured in the short time since we met and hope fervently that I can come to Vienna between Christmas and the New Year; this is, however, rather doubtful. I do not even know whether I shall remain in my present hospital post.

In the meantime, we may possibly have the pleasure of seeing your wife on her return journey from Hamburg here with us. We should be very pleased if she could spare a few hours for us.

It is good to hear that you feel so much like working. I am also doing quite well in this respect. In spite of having had no summer break, I am standing up to the large quantity of work quite well. The practice still occupies me for 3–4 hours a day. It is possible though that the recruiting of the Home Guard may make inroads in my small group of patients.

You may well continue to keep me up to date with news about Rank and the other friends. Scientifically speaking, I can now do nothing here with our association, as they are almost all away, and the few who have stayed behind are, especially now, not sufficiently interested.

What is to happen about the next *Jahrbuch*?[1] So far I have only one paper by Sadger. I assume that I can expect the long paper you mentioned several times. Reik informed me that nothing will come of his contribution. The reviews could be dealt with, but I think we would be short of original papers. I personally cannot promise to get anything ready in the next few months. The hospital takes up too much time. Besides, this year's volume will not have had much of a sale, and Deuticke might make difficulties, too. What is to be done?

Liebermann wrote to me that he has little to do and would be glad to read some psychoanalysis. As I would not like to entrust the *Jahrbuch* to the post just now, I am asking you to send him an offprint of Narcissism[2] if you have one to spare. His address is: *Oberarzt* Dr H. Liebermann, poste restante, Schirmeck in the Alsace.[3]

Your niece Margarete has, to my great regret, drawn back again from the decision she had already made to separate, and is insisting in a very ignorant way on marriage.

There has been very little news of the war in the last few days. In spite of that, morale remains steady here. Let's hope for good reports soon! I am especially nurturing the wish that you will have further good news of your sons!

Cordial greetings from my wife and myself for you and all your family!

Yours,

    *Karl Abraham*

1. There was to be no more *Jahrbuch*. On 27 October 1913 Jung had resigned from his editorship of it (Freud & Jung, 1974 [1906–13]: p. 550). Only one further volume appeared in 1914, with a slightly altered title, under the sole general editorship of Freud, with Abraham and Hitschmann as working editors. Freud's "long paper", the analysis of the "Wolf Man" (1918b [1914]), did not appear until 1918 in the fourth series of his *Sammlung kleiner Schriften zur Neurosenlehre*.
2. Freud, 1914c, which had opened the last volume of the *Jahrbuch*.
3. Here a page of the original ends. In the previous editions of this correspondence, there follow passages (about the *Jahrbuch*, Reik's work, Freud's pessimism, the six brothers of Lou Andreas-Salomé) that clearly do not fit in here but are a reaction to Freud's next letter of 11 December. Obviously the endings of the present letter and of that of 15 December (with the news about Freud's niece, also beginning on a new page) were transposed.

## 258F

Vienna IX, Berggasse 19
11 December 1914

Dear Friend,

Correspondence is now so slow and sluggish that it is best to answer straight away. I understand that you are unwilling to hold out the hope of coming to see me at Christmas. Everything is too uncertain. My case history will remain lying for a long time to come.

With regard to the *Jahrbuch*, things are difficult. As it is, we shall have to abandon the idea of an annual report. The question is whether we have enough papers to form a volume and whether Deuticke will be prepared to bring one out at all in 1915. I have not talked to him yet, but incidentally I also fully expect Heller to propose ceasing publication of *Imago* and the *Zeitschrift* after the completion of the current year. We really have no material and are hardly in a position to demand anything else.

The situation is one of continual crumbling, in the face of which it is not easy to do what your Kaiser rightly called for, that is, keep "good nerves". After some nice results, my own works have plunged into deep darkness; I go on because one cannot remain without "something to do besides" (*que haceres*, as the Spaniards say), but often without enthusiasm and with only a slight expectation of solving the very difficult problems. My way of working used to be different, I used to wait for an idea to come to me. Now I go out to meet it, and I do not know whether I will find it any more quickly for all that.

Rank and Sachs have both been deferred. Rank is making very fine progress with the problem of the epic, which he intends to use for his *Habilitation*.[1] Reik is also very productive—in advance of his imminent call-up. I shall send the reprint to Liebermann.

My sons write cheerfully and indifferently, they are completely taken up in their training.

As you notice, I am not always in a radiant mood; apart from general circumstances, I am tormented by my own particular intestine, which has shaken off the effects of Karlsbad after four months.

Lou Salomé has written a touching reply to a letter of mine. Her optimism is too deeply rooted to be shaken. As you know, she had six big brothers, all of whom were kind to her.[2]

My wife came back without touching Berlin. We now have an influenza epidemic in Vienna and in the family.

I hope you and yours remain well.

With cordial greetings,

Yours,

*Freud*

1. Rank, 1917a, 1917b; he intended this to be his *Habilitation* thesis.
2. Letters of 25 November and 4 December 1914 (Freud & Andreas-Salomé, 1966: pp. 20–22). The "six brothers" are a "frequently repeated reference of Freud's to the fact that for Lou A.-S. . . . the feeling of 'solidarity' with her brothers . . . 'extended to all men . . . it always seemed that a brother was hidden in each one of them'" (ibid.: p. 217). In fact, Lou had *five* older brothers.

## 259A

Berlin W. 15, Rankestrasse 24
15 December 1914

Dear Professor,

Yesterday I got up for the first time after being ill in bed for a week, and was gladdened on this occasion by your letter. My trouble was the same as is reigning in your house, too. I have already had a great deal of experience of influenza, but I have never yet gone through such a bad infection as this. Today I am trying to work a little again, but it does not quite work yet. I hope yours are all well again, and you yourself have again overcome the intestinal attack!

I also think that we cannot demand that Heller publish the journals, should he refuse. He is taking over a considerable risk. Apart from the fact that a number of buyers (the Swiss) are falling off, and there is now no replacement for them, he cannot send to England and get money from there. Quite a number of members from the Berlin group are away, and it will be difficult to get the money also from them. We can of course hope that peace will come in the course of time, but when?—We are short of contributions, so it is all the more correct to let the journals lapse for now.

I should like to suggest the following: we could prepare the 1914 yearly report now for the 1915 *Jahrbuch*. It is true that some co-workers who helped last year are missing, but the report will make much less work and can be done with rather fewer workers. We could also collect the original writings produced in the course of the next few months. In these times, when everything is absorbed by the war, there is no doubt that only the narrowest circle of our collaborators—naturally, also the most reliable—will contribute something. A survey of the products of this circle could easily be acquired. A good *Jahrbuch* 1915 could be put together out of this, and it would then be our only organ for this year. It could be edited jointly by Ferenczi, Rank, Sachs, Hitschmann, Jones, and myself (with you as chief editor, of course). The printing could be done by the sheet during the war. If peace comes, and interest turns towards our cause again, we can immediately present a finished, and certainly splendid volume. Putting together the journals in that way seems to me more effective than delivering them for another few months and then breaking off, as they would now meet with only moderate interest!

I know that you, dear Professor, already have a long manuscript ready. In your last letter you mentioned that Reik had written something; moreover, his couvade[1] has not yet been printed. We could ask Jones via van Emden whether he has anything. Ferenczi, Rank, and Sachs are sure to contribute. I already have a manuscript from Sadger. I intend to start the formulation of the *ejaculatio praecox*.[2] Some miscellaneous items could be added to all this. Anything further that may be forthcoming during the next year could form the basis of our three periodicals for the year 1916, when they can all be published separately again. Should this suggestion appear reasonable to you, will you discuss it with our friends in Vienna?

Your present pessimism would sadden me, had it not followed upon a time of special productivity. Findings such as those you hinted at recently do not drop from the skies every day, and it is equally certain that there will be more. If, as I hope, I see you before very long, you will surely have new ideas and discoveries to tell me about. Admittedly, not everyone is as lucky as Frau Salomé, with her six big brothers. But you do have, at any rate, some six small but loyal collaborators[3] who make a point of lifting your spirits at such times.

I believe that the war is going more in our favour than we know. The Russian army in particular appears to be generally demoralized. We often hear that our enemies want peace, but one does not know how much importance to attach to this. The present reversal in Serbia[4] is unfortunate, it must be assumed that the Serbs have had reinforcements from outside.

I hope next time to hear only good news about you and your family and also about your sons, and am, with cordial greetings from my wife and myself to you all,

Yours,

*Karl Abraham*

1. Reik, 1914.
2. Abraham, 1917[54].
3. Allusion to the "Secret Committee" around Freud, then consisting of Karl Abraham, Sándor Ferenczi, Ernest Jones, Otto Rank, and Hanns Sachs.
4. On 3 December the Serbs had started a counter-offensive, and on 15 December Belgrade had to be given up without a battle.

## 260F

Vienna IX, Berggasse 19
21 December 1914

Dear Friend,

I should like to hazard the paradox that your letters are always pleasing, even if you [they][1] have uncheering things to report, as your last one. I hope you have now fully recovered, as have the patients in my house.

You are right, I need someone to give me courage. I have little left. In your letter I cherish all the qualities our allies impress us with, and in addition your own personal qualities, your Coraggio Casimiro! Sometimes I dread the meal. If you can really manage to come and see me, you will be doing a great service to my morale, and we shall be able to discuss everything easily. Your proposals about the journals will be the subject of consultation by everyone involved as soon as one of the publishers has communicated with us. We do not want to take the words out of anybody's mouth.

The only thing that is going satisfyingly is my work, which does indeed lead from interval to interval to respectable novelties and conclusions. I recently succeeded in finding a characteristic of both systems, *Cs.* and *Ucs.*, which makes both almost tangible and, I think, provides a simple solution to the problem of the relationship of *dementia praecox* to reality.[2] All the cathexes of *things* form the system *Ucs.*, while the system *Cs.* corresponds to the linking of these unconscious representations with the *word* representations, by means of which the possibility of coming into consciousness is brought about. Repression in the transference neuroses consists in the withdrawal of libido from the system *Cs.*, that is, in the dissociation of the thing and word representations, while repression in the narcissistic neuroses consists in the withdrawal of libido from the unconscious thing representations, which is naturally a far deeper disturbance. That is why dementia praecox changes the language first and on the whole treats word representations in the way in which hysteria treats thing representations, that is, it subjects them to the primary process with condensation, displacement and discharge, etc.

I might finish a theory of neuroses with chapters on the vicissitudes of the instincts, repression, and the unconscious[3] if my enthusiasm for work does not finally succumb to my disgruntlement.

My eldest[4] is to move out already in the first days or weeks of January. Ernst is still in training. My son-in-law in Hamburg has also been accepted for the Infantry, but not yet called up. Ferenczi came in uniform yesterday evening from Pápa.[5] Left again this evening. He took with him the manuscript of the paper for the *Jahrbuch* to read. Reik has again presented a good paper on puberty rites.[6]

It now takes seven days for a letter to arrive from Hamburg! How is it that you are already able to send letters in sealed envelopes? We know nothing of such progress towards liberty.

Trigant Burrow[7] yesterday assured me tenderly of his sympathy because of the plight of my country,[8] and seriously offered me his house in Baltimore as a place of refuge! That is how they think about us in America.

I do not know whether I have already told you that Rank has brilliantly solved the problem of Homer.[9] I want him to make it his *Habilitation*. I want to see him, you, and Ferenczi as university lecturers in order to enable $\psi\alpha$ theory to survive the bad times ahead.

With kind regards to you, your wife and children,
Yours,

*Freud*

1. "You" [*Sie*] is obviously a slip of the pen of Freud's for "they" [*sie*].
2. See Freud, 1915e, esp. pp. 201–204.
3. See letter 256F, 25 November 1914, & n. 1.
4. Martin.
5. Locality in Hungary, about halfway between Vienna and Budapest, where Ferenczi was stationed as a physician with the Hungarian Hussars.
6. At the meeting on 16 December 1914 (Nunberg & Federn, 1975: p. 271; cf. Reik, 1915b).
7. Trigant Burrow [1875–1950], Baltimore psychiatrist, an analysand of Jung's [1909], charter member of the American Psychoanalytic Association [1911]. He later veered from both the Freudian and the Jungian schools, becoming a pioneer of group therapy. (Cf. Burrow, 1958.)
8. These three words in English in original.
9. See letter 258F, 11 December 1914, & n. 1.

## 261A

Berlin
26 December 1914

Dear Professor,

Your letter dated 21 and postmarked 22 December reached me on the 24th. Postal services seem to be improving. Of course, letters from here to Austria must also be sent unsealed. The fact that my last letters arrived in closed envelopes must have been due to the censorship department. Your letters also sometimes arrive sealed, with the censor's stamp on the reverse.

I am glad to hear that your family is well again; I myself am still not quite well; the catarrh refuses to budge. My wife has been ill in bed since Tuesday: influenza, tonsillitis, and a rash like scarlet fever, but certainly benign. I only hope it will not be the children's turn next. My travel plans have become doubtful because of this; at least, they will have to be postponed. There is another obstacle to my visit to Vienna. When I have one or two days free, I must urgently go to Bremen to visit my parents. A 76-year-old sister of my father's,[1] who lives with my parents, had a stroke last summer and is now quite helpless and psychologically disturbed, and I must go there to discuss with my parents what is to be done with her. But I am keeping the projected journey to Vienna in mind and shall gladly come as soon as it can be arranged, especially as I know that I may be of some small personal use to you.

I found the scientific part of your letter very illuminating, as far as I could already think myself into it. I am, however, not yet quite clear on some points. I assume the remainder will be equally convincing, once I have mastered it. I should like to keep this for our meeting, which I hope will take place soon.

Your news about Rank is very pleasant; although I do not yet know what he has solved of the Homer problem, I am delighted for him, and for all of us, for his consistency and success. I have no idea yet what will happen about the *Habilitation*. I hope perhaps during the war to be able to do some work on psychoses, but the case material has not been suitable so far. The [*Habilitation*] paper I had previously begun has also reached a stagnation through lack of suitable material. I therefore do not yet know what will happen after the war.—I gather from your letter that Ferenczi is well. I have heard nothing from Eitingon for a long time. I had a card yesterday from Jones via van Emden; its tone is as friendly as one could only expect, coming from enemy territory. He does not write anything new. I find Trigant Burrow touching.

I scarcely need to assure you that my best wishes go with your sons and your son-in-law when they go to the front. I send cordial greetings to you and yours!

Yours,

*Karl Abraham*

Should the *Zeitschrift* continue to appear in the New Year, Rank will kindly give me early information. Here, two members have dropped out, who are no longer entitled to have it sent to them, and it is impossible to send it to several members whom I could name.

1. Johanne Abraham [20 August 1936–3 March 1916]; in fact, 78 years old (kind communication from Bettina Decke).

## 262F

## INTERNATIONALE ZEITSCHRIFT
## FÜR ÄRZTLICHE PSYCHOANALYSE

[International Journal for Medical Psychoanalysis]

Vienna
30 December 1914

Dear Friend,

I am very sorry to hear that you are not yet well and that your wife is now ill too. These are times in which one should at least be in good health. Our domestic epidemic has come to an end, but Ernst is in bed in Klagenfurt with severe tonsillitis, from which, no doubt, he will recover only slowly. One can naturally do nothing for him. According to his letter today, he is back in barracks, though feverish.

I have always hated helplessness and penury most of all, and I am afraid we are now approaching both.

Deuticke has told me that he does not want to publish the *Jahrbuch* in 1915, as he has not yet been able to distribute the 1914 edition. He says that everything is bolted, and quotes the example of renowned German publishers who in many cases have ceased their business entirely for the duration of the war. I suspected something of the sort when I read of your intentions in your last letter but one.

We have not yet heard from Heller, but have nothing different to expect.

When you come here—I am delighted you have not abandoned the intention—you can talk this through with D.[euticke] in detail. I shall postpone till that happy occasion telling you about Rank's findings on Homer. My own work is resting. I have not got beyond certain difficulties, and as a consequence of my state of mind I no longer like my previous findings so much. Because of this estrangement I am often quite at a loss what to do with myself. The obvious remedies are of course those that are now generally recommended: wait-and-see and hold out.

Today I had a kind letter from Spielrein, from Zurich;[1] Eitingon is back in Igló in Hungary; Jones writes tirelessly in his old tone; I do not know whether he receives my replies.

You will perhaps receive the *Sexual Theory*[2] sooner than this letter.

Wishing you all a speedy recovery,

your cordially devoted

*Freud*

1. Not in Carotenuto, 1980.
2. Third edition of Freud, 1905d.

# 1915

## 263A

Berlin W., Rankestr. 24,
Tel. Steinpl. 3566[1]
10 January 1915

Dear Professor,

All is well again with us. I hope it is the same with you, your Ernst included! This card will only serve for keeping up our correspondence, for there is nothing important to tell you about. Rank asked me to lengthen the small manuscript for *Imago*[2]; I shall try to see whether I can do it. Many thanks for the 3rd edition. I am studying it at the moment.

Whether I can get to Vienna is very doubtful. Whether I stay in Berlin is equally so. For the time being I shall not need to leave, but in a few weeks it may be different.—In Berlin everything is unchanged: the same confidence as since the beginning. Cordial greetings to you and yours, from my wife as well!

Yours,

*Abraham*

1. Pre-printed letterhead.
2. Not identified. Abraham's next contribution to *Imago* appeared only in 1918.

## 264F

Vienna IX, Berggasse 19
25 January 1915

Dear Friend,

Such a long time has passed since your last meagre and unpleasing postcard that I must write to you again.

First about myself. Physically I am well again and in steady spirits, but am not working and have dropped everything on which I had started, including some things that were very promising. I still think it is a long polar night, and that one must wait for the sun to rise again. Whether this is part of a progressive development or just of an organic periodicity that comes to light now, in so much deprivation, can be decided only later on.

About other things I have good news for you. I was afraid that Heller would decline to continue publication of the two journals. That has not happened. The final decision will not be made till next Thursday, but we have agreed insofar that the new annual series of both shall begin in a slightly reduced form, the *Internationale Zeitschrift* with 6 issues as before, each of 4 signatures, and *Imago* with 4 issues of 6 signatures. Thus our expectations with regard to the journals have been reversed. Naturally we of the inner circle shall have to write everything ourselves and we count to a large extent on you.

I saw my son Martin in the guise of a smart corporal last Wednesday morning between two trains before he left for the Galician theatre of war. I thought in total clarity about the doubt there is whether and how we shall ever see him again.

Medical activity permanently reduced to a quarter; otherwise no news. In the last issue of his Dutch weekly van Eeden[1] printed a comment about the war for which he had asked me, in which I naturally let $\Psi\alpha$ have its say.[2]

I send my cordial greetings to you and yours and await your news, I hope from Berlin.

Yours,

*Freud*

1. See letter 237A, 29 July 1914, n. 2.
2. Freud, 1915g [1914].


## 265A

Berlin
30 January 1915

Dear Professor,

You have obviously not received my last letter. I have *also* been waiting for a reply from you daily! Let us hope *this* letter will reach its destination.

I am glad to hear that our journals will continue to appear. Heller is taking a certain risk, of course, as many subscribers are away from home for an indeterminate time. I will see how much I can collaborate. Recently I have been completely taken up with the hospital and the practice. I could have considerably more patients for analysis if I did not have the hospital. In the last four weeks I had a great many consultations. Perhaps Liebermann, who has been in the Vosges for five months, will soon be posted back to Berlin and will be able to back me up again. Incidentally, he has been awarded the Iron Cross.

Unfortunately there is no way of getting news about Stegmann; no one knows what has become of him.

To return to our journals: I have started a small paper about the relation between hunger and libido,[1] which is chiefly to contain analytically established facts and conclusions drawn from them instead of theories à la Jung. As you know, it depends little on me when I shall be able to finish it.

It seems that now everybody in your house is fit again, as we all are here. I should like to ask you especially to tell me in your next letter what news you have of your sons.

The lost letter contained, among other things, my thanks for the *Three Essays*, as well as some remarks about them. I am therefore repeating my thanks.

It is striking how few people in the hospital are affected by genuine neuroses. I have seen a number of traumatic neuroses, well known to us from peacetime, in a typical form. They were all people who had had an *accident* at the front, such as being run over; they had not been wounded through being shot. I have seen several severe cases of hysteria in people knocked unconscious by an explosion. They generally have aphasia–abasia and hysterical attacks.

A few weeks ago I heard from Eitingon from Igló. Otherwise I have heard nothing from anybody.

I am not giving up my plan to go to Vienna, but it will have to wait some time.

With cordial greetings—also from my wife—to you and yours, both in Vienna and at the front,

Yours,

*Karl Abraham*

1. This refers to his work on "The First Pregenital Stage of the Libido" (Abraham, 1916[52]), a project already mentioned in letters 153A, 3 March 1913, and 213A, 15 May 1914.

## 266F

Vienna IX, Berggasse 19
18 February 1915

Dear Friend,

I received your letter of 30 January on 12 February and your postcard of 16 February[1] today, so things seem to be better again. However, a previous letter from you seems to have gone astray. We were quite disconsolate at being cut off, we were without news from Hamburg for 28[2] days.

It is pleasing that all goes well with you again. It is the same with us, apart from small troubles. Martin is writing assiduously from his anonymous abode in Galicia, and greatly praises his condition; he is now in a ruined castle somewhere, quartered with German infantry. Ernst is kept under strict discipline in the training school in Klagenfurt; Oli, the last remaining one, will be called up on 3 March, but will probably volunteer beforehand for a rifle battalion. He would prefer to go into a railway regiment as a qualified technician, but cannot find a way in.

I cannot report any further development of the practice. At the end of this week my daily sessions will be reduced from 4 to 3. I have finished something new on melancholia, it is now with Ferenczi, who will forward it to you.[3] The first issue of the *Zeitschrift* is at the printer's; the introductory article is a technical contribution by me[4] which I am sending you so that you may kindly let me know what you think of it. I propose to send as much as possible to the *Zeitschrift*. We know that we can count on you as far and as soon as you can.

Pfister is drawing very close to us, and has contributed a critical paper on the "arson" of the splendid Z. Schmid[5]; and he has also sent us a short essay by a new worker, who draws an analogy between our libido and Plato's theory of Eros. (A Dr Nachmannsohn of Zurich.)[6]

Rank showed me a letter from Jones yesterday. He is very well, is doing ten *analyses* a day, etc. His group has suspended its meetings and appears to be seriously split.[7]

All interest is concentrated on events that are to begin on the 18th, that is to say, today.[8] May they bring us victory and therewith liberation and peace. This time I am inclined towards optimism.[9]

I send my cordial greetings to you and to your dear wife, and hope to be hearing from you more often from now on.

Yours,

*Freud*

1. Missing.
2. Reading uncertain, but likely.
3. A draft of "Mourning and Melancholia" (Freud, 1917e [1915]), sent to Ferenczi on 7 February, who then forwarded it to Abraham. I found this hitherto unknown draft at the Freud Archives (LOC, container B7) and reprinted it in the second volume of the Freud/Ferenczi correspondence (1996: pp. 47–49) [E.F.].
4. Freud, 1915a.
5. Pfister, 1915—a polemical review of a paper on arson by Dr Hans Schmid, which had appeared in the *Psychologische Abhandlungen*, edited by Jung. Pfister particularly criticized Schmid's methodological errors and his "unmistakable tendency to belittle Freud and to elevate Jung" (pp. 152–153).
6. Nachmannsohn, 1915. In 1921, Nachmannsohn moved to Göttingen in Germany and joined the Berlin Society (circular letter, 1 July 1921, BL).
7. In the London Society, controversies persisted during the war years; some members, among them David Eder, the Secretary, approached Jung's ideas. "Our society has not met since last autumn, owing to Eder's attitude. . . . I hope to get him to resign his position so that we can meet without him in October", wrote Jones to Freud on 17 June

1915 (Freud & Jones, 1993: p. 310). Jones's efforts to establish a unified direction foundered, whereupon he finally dissolved the Society and re-established it on 20 February 1919 as the British Psycho-Analytical Society, this time without Eder.
8. Probably an allusion to Germany's declaration of the U-boat warfare and a blockade against England the previous day.
9. This word in Latin characters and in English in original.

## 267A

Berlin
28 February 1915

Dear Professor,

This time I received your letter within three to four days. I hope mine will also reach you without difficulty.

I must first of all thank you for the proofs. I found nothing to criticize, from the first word to the last. To my great satisfaction, everything in this paper corresponds with my own experiences. When I say that this is the first of your papers that did not give me anything new, this should naturally only mean that this time I have not been compelled to learn anything anew. On the other hand my own observations were not yet so clearly organized; I therefore could still learn quite a great deal from the way the paper is structured.

I can only occasionally find time for writing. I am working on the short paper on pleasure from sucking. If I can carry the plan out, I should like to publish it as No. 1 in a small series, which is to deal with the pregenital organizations. I recently began treatment of a relatively simple case of obsessional neurosis that overwhelmingly confirms the theory you put forward in Munich.[1] I should like to present this as No. 2 of the series, and No. 3 would then contain some contributions on the symptomatology of anal erotism.[2]—I have only just been able to study at leisure the new edition of the *Three Essays*. I have always had a preference for this work. I like it just as much in its new form. The findings of the last ten years fit in very well with the earlier ones.[3]

I often think how the war saved us from unpleasant discussions with the Swiss. When it is over we shall go our separate ways.

We too are wondering what our blockade against England will achieve. There are no authentic reports so far, but in the light of previous experiences, we may expect amazing facts to be disclosed one day. Our new war loan will probably be another complete success.[4]

It is still uncertain what is going to happen to *me*. For the time being I am still working at the hospital. However, the younger doctors in our hospital have gradually been called up, and it might be my turn at any time.

I hope you will have further good news of your sons; please do keep me up to date about their situation.

With cordial greetings, also from my wife, to you and all your family,

Yours,

*Karl Abraham*

1. Cf. Freud, 1913i.
2. Abraham's interest in pregenital stages of libido development would result in several articles, assembled in his classical books (1924[105], 1925[106]).
3. For a list of the additions to the third edition of Freud, 1905d, see the note in Freud & Ferenczi, 1996: pp. 30–31.
4. The second German war loan brought subscriptions of 9 billion marks.

268F

Vienna IX, Berggasse 19
4 March 1915

Dear Friend,

The means change, but the result is the same. When you say that my last contribution taught you nothing new, it is as gratifying to me as your usual emphasizing of the opposite. I believe this contribution to be the best and most useful of the whole series, so I am prepared for it to evoke the strongest opposition.

Your announcement of a series of articles, which I take as a definite promise, is highly welcome. After all, we do wish to keep the journals alive at all costs during the war and to manage them in such a way that later we shall be able to come up with them with satisfaction. But the authors are very few. We shall have to do everything ourselves. I have decided to publish three chapters of my germinating summary (drives, repression, Ucs.)[1] gradually in the *Zeitschrift*. For *Imago* I am even writing a piece of topical claptrap about war and death[2] to keep the self-sacrificing publisher happy. All this naturally against inner resistance.

"My heart's in the Highlands, my heart is not here."[3] Namely in the Dardanelles, where the fate of Europe is perhaps being decided; in the classical country,[4] the inhabitants of which are supposed to be about to declare war on us in the next few days,[5] with the result that the places that I have most enjoyed being in will be closed to me for my remaining years; and on the North Sea, on which it will be a long time before one can travel again. Enough!

Only the best of news comes from Martin, who is shooting somewhere in Galicia. Ernst is probably staying in Klagenfurt for another few weeks. Oli was rejected at the medical examination for military service yesterday and so has a few months to take his final exams. My son-in-law in Hamburg has also been deferred for the present. The tension under which we are living is often unbearably high. I should like to go to Berlin and Hamburg again, but the mark now stands at over 135. So we cannot travel.

I send my cordial greetings to you and to your dear wife, and hope you will be allowed to remain in Berlin, where, after all, doctors are also needed.

Yours,

*Freud*

1. Freud, 1915c, 1915d, 1915e; see letter 256F, 25 November 1914, & n. 1.
2. Freud, 1915b.
3. First lines of a poem by Robert Burns [1810–1876] (Burns, 1986: p. 390).
4. Referring to the offensive of the allied troops at Gallipoli near the Dardanelles (and also near Troy), which had started on 19 February 1915 and lasted until 19 January 1916.
5. Turkey would remain with the Central Powers, however.

## 269A

Berlin[1]
5 March 1915

Dear Professor,

This is only to tell you that I have received the small manuscript on melancholia from Ferenczi. Once I have studied it in detail I shall send it back to you.

With cordial greetings,
Yours,

*Karl Abraham*

1. Postcard.

## 270A

Allenstein[1,2]
13 March 1915

Dear Professor,

I arrived here yesterday and shall be doing surgical work, though I hope to have more time for my own work than I had at home. I have brought with me the paper I recently promised you. My address is: Allenstein (East Prussia), garrison hospital I, Hohensteinerstrasse.— What is your news, what do you hear from your sons? I hope that here too I shall hear from you frequently.

With cordial greetings to you, your house, and the friends there,
Yours,

*Abraham*

1. Postcard.
2. Allenstein/Olsztyn, about 175 km north of Warsaw, in today's Poland.

## 271F

Vienna IX, Berggasse 19
15 March 1915

Dear Friend,

Our warmest good wishes accompany you in your new work, which I hope will give you the opportunity to see your family and sometimes also leisure to do your intended writings.

I ask you to retain the presidency, which is now a sinecure in any case. If you agree, we propose to announce, in the first issue of the *Zeitschrift* on which we are now working, that because of your call-up, publication of the 1915 *Jahrbuch* is now doubtful, but that publication of the two other journals will continue.[1] When I have finished this letter I shall begin to write out "Instincts and Their Vicissitudes".[2]

You will have heard that we consider peace in the south to be certain. If we ever see San Martino again, we shall be able to visit it only as guests. Mind you, I preferred Karersee,[3] which remains with us.

In eager expectation of your news,
Your faithfully devoted

*Freud*

1. *Zeitschrift*, 1915, 3: 64.
2. Freud, 1915c.
3. Two locations in the South Tyrol, which as a whole became part of Italy after the war.

## 272F

Vienna IX, Berggasse 19
27 March 1915

Dear Friend,

I eagerly await your news from your new abode, but I myself have little to tell you.

I am working slowly and steadily on the papers for *Imago* and the *Zeitschrift*, and have found confirmation of the solution of melancholia in a case I studied for two months, though without visible therapeutic success, which, however, may follow.

My son[1] writes from the North that he is living in unpleasant and difficult conditions and has not felt well since his typhus vaccination, but hopes to improve. The other one is still awaiting his destiny in Klagenfurt.

1915 March

The summer problem is naturally more difficult this year than ever, in fact as a result of all the uncertainties it is actually insoluble. We have to wait.

How are you and your work? What do the children say about papa's absence? How is your dear wife managing alone?

With cordial greetings from us to all of you,

Yours,

*Freud*

1. Martin.

## 273A

Deutsch Eylau
31 March 1915

Dear Professor,

I have long postponed commenting on your outline of a theory of melancholia—and not only because I have no real peace for work. Some years ago I myself made an attempt in this direction[1] but was always aware of its imperfections, and was therefore afraid that my attitude to your new theory might well be too subjective. I think that I have now got over this difficulty and am able to accept all the essentials in your work. I do think, however, that one element from my earlier work should be more heavily stressed than it is in yours and should like to put forward a suggestion that may solve the question left open by you. Important questions do naturally remain unresolved, and I have no explanation for them at the present time.[2]

I should like to remind you—not in order to stress any priority but merely to underline the points of agreement—that I also started from a comparison between melancholic depression and mourning. I found support in your paper on obsessional neurosis (the Rat Man),[3] which had just been published, and stressed that sadism was important because its intensity does not allow the capacity for love to arise; and I deduced depression from a perception of one's inability to love. I had to leave completely unanswered the question of why melancholia develops in one case and obsession in another. At the time, two important papers of yours were still to be written: "Narcissism"[4] and "Pregenital Organizations".[5] I recently wrote to you to say how completely convinced I was, particularly by this new concept of obsessional neurosis. If therefore, as you will surely acknowledge, there is a relationship between obsessional neurosis and melancholia, the new insight into obsessional neurosis will also shed light on melancholia.

Of the two important factors in the genesis of obsessional neurosis—sadism and anal erotism—I strongly stressed the importance in melancholia of the former in my paper of 1911. I must still hold to this view. Too much violence and criminality was uncovered in the analyses of my melancholic patients. The self-reproaches do indicate repressed hostile feelings. The complete motor inhibition leads one also to assume that strong motor impulses have had to be made harmless. The same tendency is manifest in the way the melancholic torments those around him. Added to this is the reappearance of the most open sadism in the manic phase. These are only *a few* of the reasons why I still rate this factor as highly as ever.

On the other hand, I think, reconsidering my cases, that one should *not* assume that anal erotism is of extraordinary significance in melancholia. If I am right in this assumption (which still needs to be confirmed, because at the time of the analyses of the cases in 1911 I had no knowledge yet of the importance of anal erotism in obsessional neurosis and may possibly have overlooked it in melancholia), *then this may well be the point where these conditions, which in other ways are so closely related, diverge.*

To proceed further from here, I must revert to what you say in your paper under (3).[6] Even though I do not yet see that the melancholic displaces onto himself all the reproaches that are aimed at his love-object and that serve to denigrate it, all that you say about identification with the love-object is perfectly clear to me. Perhaps I could not fully grasp this because of the compression of your arguments. With my patients it appeared to me as if the melancholic, incapable of loving as he is, desperately tries to get possession of a love-object. In my experience, he does in fact identify with his love-object, cannot tolerate its loss, and is hyper-sensitive to the slightest unfriendliness, etc. from that side. He often allows himself to be tormented by the loved person in masochistic self-punishment. He reproaches himself for this instead of reproaching the loved person because unconsciously he has done far greater harm to that person (omnipotence of thought). That is how I deduced it in my analyses. But as you well know, dear Professor, I am ready to re-learn. I only regret that our discussion has to be carried on by letter.

What harm has the melancholic in fact done to the object with whom he identifies?

The answer to this is suggested to me in one of your recent papers—I think it is the one on narcissism (?). There you discuss identification and you point to the infantile basis of this process: the child wants to *incorporate* its love-object: to put it briefly, it wants to *devour* it.[7] I have strong reason to suspect that such cannibalistic tendencies exist in the melancholic's identification. It may be safely assumed that this identification has an ambivalent meaning—a manifestation of love as well as destruction.

1915 March

The first argument I would advance is the melancholic's fear of *starvation*. Food has taken the place of love here. I would assume that the role played by the anal zone in obsessional neurosis is assigned to the mouth in melancholia. In menopausal depressions in particular, the fear of starvation plays a dominant role. A further dominant symptom is the *refusal of food*. In other calmer and more chronic cases, food in the positive sense is of excessive importance.

Also of interest is the classic form of depressive delusions found in earlier centuries, called lycanthropy. This is the delusion of being a werewolf and of having eaten men! Such delusions are not so rare even nowadays. I should mention here a characteristic and rather curious expression, which, up till quite recently, somewhat crude psychiatrists would use towards patients believed to be suffering from delusional self-reproaches they did not wish to reveal. They would say the following: "What have you done, have you perhaps devoured small children?" Such so-called jokes have to be rooted somehow in real experience.

I think that the impoverishment of the ego becomes more comprehensible in this way. The ego does not, as it were, get the food it wants. It has lost its content (that is to say, that which it wanted to incorporate).

It seems to me that we ought to agree easily, provided the above ideas are not too wrong. The basic points of your exposition: the melancholic has lost something but does not know *what*; the impoverishment of the ego and all that is connected with it; the identification with the love-object; the localization of the process of mourning in the ego-cathexes; the dissolving of object-cathexes in narcissistic identification—all this should definitely stand. I think sadism and oral eroticism should be added.

I should like to ask you, dear Professor, for unsparing criticism, but also for a more detailed explanation wherever I may have misunderstood your very condensed arguments.

I shall probably stay here in Deutsch Eylau only until 5 April; I will then be back in Allenstein. I shall give you my address there, and ask you not to write to me earlier, so that your letter is sure to reach me.

Otherwise I am well. Both Allenstein and Deutsch Eylau are in midst of beautiful country, which I am enjoying very much. The work is not unbearably heavy.

Hoping to receive good news from you and yours—such as I have from my own at home—I am,
Yours,
*Karl Abraham*

1. Abraham, 1911[26].
2. Most of the following points were raised and discussed at greater length in Abraham, 1916[52].

3. Freud, 1909d.
4. Freud, 1914c.
5. Freud, 1913i.
6. "One often gets the impression that the self-reproaches of melancholia are none other than reproaches against someone else, which are directed away from him onto one's own ego. There is thus an *identification* of the ego with the libidinal object. The ego mourns because it has lost its object through devaluation, but it projects this object onto itself and then finds itself devalued. The shadow of the object falls on the ego and obscures it. *The process of mourning is not carried out on the object cathexes, but rather on the ego cathexes*" (in Freud & Ferenczi, 1996: p. 48).
7. In the third edition of the *Three Essays on the Theory of Sexuality* (which had just appeared; cf. letter 267A, 28 February 1915), Freud had introduced, for the first time, the concept of an oral-cannibalistic organization of the libido, the aim of which "consists in the incorporation of the object—the prototype of a process which, in the form of identification, is later to play such an important psychological part" (1905d: p. 198). He also raised this point in "Instincts and Their Vicissitudes" (1915c: p. 138), which he was just in the process of writing.

## 274A

Allenstein[1]
17 April 1915

Sender: Dr Karl Abraham
Allenstein (East Prussia)
Zeppelinstr. 1, Pension Graw.[2]

Dear Professor,

This is only to give you the news that I am back in Allenstein and am looking forward to your news.

Cordial greetings to you and yours from your

*Karl Abraham*

1. Picture postcard with Schloß Allenstein.
2. Reading uncertain.

## 275A

Allenstein, Garrison Hospital
26 April 1915

Dear Professor,

Your card of the 19th[1] reached me fairly quickly, as did the parcel with the proofs.[2] I have so far cursorily read through the latter once and should therefore prefer to say nothing about them today. At any rate, it is good to know that the concepts we constantly use are being properly clarified for once. I enjoyed reading the short paper on war[3]; my wife is at present reading it in Berlin. You were wrong when you wrote deprecatingly about this work some time ago. There can scarcely be any disagreement between us concerning our viewpoint on these matters. I shall therefore only add that I liked this paper very much and that I am eagerly anticipating the chapter on death. While reading your work, I was struck by an interesting parallel. What is forbidden to the individual in normal circumstances, he *must* do in such times as these, and in fact in company with all other men. Exactly the same applies to the totem meal, where the whole community consumes the animal that the individual is usually not permitted to touch.

I am glad to know that all is well with you and your family. Please do keep letting me know how your sons get on! I am getting on quite well here. Beside my work I have enough free time to myself; I am using it partly for the promised paper on the oral phase,[4] which is now largely finished. I am expecting my wife to visit in eight days, though she can stay here only for a short time. If I should have to spend the summer in A., my wife and children will choose this town for their summer holidays. Allenstein is very prettily situated in a region with forests and lakes only about 40 kilometres west of the Masurian lakes. We will perhaps take furnished rooms and keep house here.

One of your letters, dear Herr Professor, which you wrote to me soon after I was posted here, arrived very late because it was inadequately addressed. In this letter you asked me about my children's reaction to my leaving. I have some nice stories to tell about our little boy. In fact my daughter was also delighted with my uniform, which I had been wearing for some time in Berlin. She was particularly impressed by the soldiers' salutes. The little boy took the matter in a very different way, in accordance with his gender and age. He was most impressed by my rapier. I promised that I would let him wear it sometime. He was speechless with delight when I put the weapon on him. The impression stayed with him. The next day he said in front of the whole family at dinner: another father would not have done that—given me his rapier to wear. This harmless incident must have served to change the child's hostile feelings into their opposite. What he said probably means: if *I* were in possession of this precious weapon, I would not have given it to anyone else. He was obviously struck by my magnanimity. During the following days he was extremely affectionate, but there was something in his behaviour that illuminated for me the psychology of vassals. For example, on one occasion I was pacing up and down in the room. Because of my heavy army boots, my gait was different from what it usually is. The little fellow immediately fell into step with me, walked behind me, and imitated the length, rhythm, and heaviness of every step I took. He has obviously identified with me ever since I lent him the sword. This is also apparent from games he is now playing at home.

In the hospital I am working with a *Privatdozent* at Binswanger's clinic in Jena,[5] Dr H. Schultz, who wrote a criticism of $\Psi\alpha$ in the *Zeit-*

*schrift für angewandte Psychologie* [*Journal of Applied Psychology*][6] some time ago. I have naturally not touched on the subject of Ψα but have let him approach, and at the moment am busy with demonstrating to him his easily recognizable resistances.

In the last few days reports from the West are very satisfying. It is odd how the diametrically opposed parts of the theatre of war—Flanders and East Galicia/Bukowina—are the only ones in which field warfare is going on.

I add my cordial greetings to you and your family and to the friends in Vienna.

As always,
Yours, as ever,

Karl Abraham

Please address letters to:
Allenstein (East Prussia)
Garrison Hospital

1. Missing.
2. Probably of Freud, 1915c.
3. Freud, 1915b, Part I, "The Disillusionment of the War". Part II, "Our Attitude Towards Death", is a slightly altered version of a lecture Freud had given at the B'nai B'rith Lodge on 16 February 1915 (cf. Meghnagi, 1993: pp. 11–39; letter 268F, 4 March 1915, & n. 2).
4. Cf. letter 267A, 28 February 1915, & n. 2.
5. See letter 15A, 8 January 1908, n. 10.
6. Schultz, 1909. Johannes Heinrich Schultz [1884–1970], German psychiatrist and psychotherapist, from 1919 on professor in Jena, from 1936 on director of the Berlin Institute for Psychotherapy; introduced autogenic training.


## 276F

Vienna IX, Berggasse 19
4 May 1915

Dear Friend,

A fortnight of being cut off from Germany has at last ended. Today I received, together with your nice letter, 12 postcards from my wife in Hamburg! I now hasten to send you the long-delayed reply.

Your comments on melancholia were very valuable to me. I unhesitatingly incorporated in my paper those parts of them that I could use. What was most valuable to me was the reference to the oral phase of the libido, and I also mention the link with mourning.[1] Your request for severe criticism caused me no difficulty; I liked practically everything you wrote. I should like to make only two points: that you do not bring out sufficiently the essential feature of the assumption, that is to say the topical element, the regression of the libido, and the abandonment of the

## 1915 May

unconscious object cathexis, but instead put into the foreground sadism and anal erotism as explanatory motifs. Though you are correct in this, you overlook the real explanation. Anal erotism, the castration complex, etc., are ubiquitous sources of excitation that have their part in *every* symptom. Sometimes one thing comes of them and sometimes another; it is naturally always a task to find out what has become out of what, but the explanation of the illness can be derived only from the mechanism, seen from the *dynamic, topical,* and *economic* point of view. I know that soon you will agree with me.

The work is now taking shape. I have five essays ready: that on *Instincts and their vicissitudes*, which may well be rather arid, but indispensable as an introduction, also finding its justification in those that follow, then *Repression*, the *Unconscious, Metapyschological supplement to the theory of dreams,* and *Mourning and melancholia*. The first four are to be published in the just started volume of the *Zeitschrift*, all the rest I am keeping for myself. If the war lasts long enough, I hope to get together about a dozen such papers and in quieter times to offer them to the ignorant world under the title: *Essays in Preparation of a Metapsychology*. I think that on the whole it will represent progress. Manner and level like the VIIth chapter of the *Interpretation of Dreams*.[2]

I finished the paper on melancholia a quarter of an hour ago. I shall have it typewritten[3] to send you a copy. In exchange, you promise further comments.

My eldest is doing well in Galicia, has reached the highest NCO rank and calls himself a fireworks-maker. I do not yet know whether he was involved in the last affair. His card of 26 April sounded still quite idyllic. Ernst, still in Klagenfurt, has taken his officer's examination with particularly good results and is waiting. He will probably soon become a platoon leader (*\**\*). You can guess what he is waiting for. There is bound to be a decision soon with regard to Italy, and the indications are that it will not be a peaceful one.[4] What a pity that the victory celebrations of these days,[5] for which we have been waiting for so long, are marred by this prospect. Our admiration of our great ally increases daily!

It was very nice of you to like even the "Thoughts for the Times". You will soon receive the continuation about "Death". Your remark about the analogy with the totem meal is absolutely accurate. It is interesting how the slightest trace of affective mood in the author restricts the view. What you write about your children is very pithy. There is always something to see and to understand.

We have all managed with an unexpected adaptability to get used to the war, with the result that we too can say we are well. The biggest surprise to me is my ability not to miss my practice and earnings. I fail to see how I shall ever again get used to a working day of six or eight hours—I had been used to 10. Is one's elasticity equally great in both directions? We like to quote an advertisement that is very common here:

"It is easy to get used to the pleasant taste." By the time you read this, I shall be 59 years old, which should perhaps give me a right for comfort, but I have no way of staking my claim to it. So C.C.! and let us leave something for those who will follow, too.

I hope that you too will make frequent use of the reopened postal connection, and please give your dear wife my cordial greetings.

Your old

*Freud*

1. Cf. Freud, 1916–17e: pp. 243 and 250.
2. See letter 256F, 25 November 1914, & n. 1.
3. English in original.
4. On 4 May Italy had denounced the *Dreibundvertrag* of 1882; on 23 May she would declare war on Austria–Hungary.
5. Referring to the breaching of the Russian front at Gorlice-Tarnow [2 to 7 May], followed by an offensive in Galicia and the recapturing of Przemysl [on 3 June].

## 277A

Allenstein, Garrison Hospital
3 June 1915

Dear Professor,

You are right—it is indeed a long time since I last wrote to you. Your reminder will now at least have a result. I shall first tell you about all that has happened in the meantime. My wife spent the first week of May with me. We had some beautiful days together, although my duties kept me fairly busy. Shortly after my wife's departure your letter arrived, but, almost at the same time, came the news that our little boy had fallen ill with diphtheria immediately after his mother's return. That gave me a worrying time, mitigated only by the fact that I could telephone Berlin every day. At times, indeed, even this was not possible because of a communications block. Two serum injections helped our patient very well. He is already quite lively again, but must still be kept quiet and suffers still from a quite mild albuminuria and paresis of the soft palate.—For the last fortnight I have been overwhelmed with work, sometimes even at night. I waited in vain for a day of peaceful writing. Today, because of the Feast of Corpus Christi, it is Sunday working in the hospital, which lets me carry out my intention at last.

I will first continue my report of last time and tell you some more about our small son, who really is a pillar of $\Psi\alpha$. I think I did not tell you what his parting words were when I left for Allenstein in March. You may remember that I had gained his confidence and admiration through the incident with the rapier. When saying good-bye, he only said: "Papa, perhaps you will win the battle!" The best he has produced so far came after my wife's return from Allenstein. On the day after her

1915 June

arrival, my wife's siblings came to dinner. During the meal, the little chap asked to speak: "Mummy, while you were in Allenstein I kept having a dream" ("dream" is what both children call their daydreams). My wife unsuspectingly asked him what he had dreamt. The answer: "I kept on thinking when mama comes back from papa whether there would soon be a baby growing inside her." I should mention that our children have been told about pregnancy and birth in a matter-of-fact way but not about conception. They have never asked about it. I have no idea where else the child could have heard about it, and I think that he must have put two and two together for himself. I have already told you of his jealousy and his wish to have his mother all to himself. This omnipotent position also includes having children with the mother. Our bedroom has always aroused his curiosity; in the morning he has often tried to look through the keyhole. There can definitely be no question of his having observed anything at night. The following shows that nevertheless he had the right ideas. When he had diphtheria, he was kept in isolation in his room. During the subsequent disinfecting my wife was forced to take him into our bedroom for two nights before he could return to his sister. He was beside himself with delight. Already beforehand he had asked questions such as: Does papa allow this? And then: Does he allow me to put my hanky under his pillow, too? (This surely seems to be an obvious displacement of his real wishes onto something "very small"?)[1] When the night he had waited for arrived at last, the bedside table with the chamber-pot in it had a magical attraction for him. He woke frequently during the two nights only in order to use it. Here one of the frequent infantile theories plays a role.[2] I suspect the "dream" is explicable from that point of view. There is other evidence for this, but it would take too long to report it all.

As regards the question of melancholia, I am now fully in agreement with you on *one* point—that I had not sufficiently appreciated the mechanism, that is to say the topographical aspect. One other point remains: the postulation in your short manuscript that reproaches that are actually directed against another person are transposed to one's own ego. I am not yet convinced of this. I do not remember your bringing detailed proof in your paper. If it does not involve too much trouble, I should like to have a letter from you explaining more exactly what you mean and how you account for it.

I read with great pleasure of your plans for further work, especially in connection with your remark about your 59th birthday. You have, naturally, dear Herr Professor, my good wishes on this occasion. Omnipotence of thought is, however, not yet sufficiently established for us to expect much benefit from good wishes alone.—Many thanks for the paper on "Death". It has only one fault, that it is not a little longer. I mean this in two ways: (1) because I would have liked to read more of it, and (2) because the extremely short résumé of the taboo-totem paper may not be convincing to outsiders. I had the impression that writing this paper did not give you the satisfaction you usually get and that this accounts for its brevity. It is different with the "Vicissitudes". I must agree with your own judgement—that it is somewhat "arid" but that it makes an excellent basis for what is to follow!

I hope to hear only good news about you and yours, especially about your warring sons. Are your sons-in-law now on the field too? My wife's brother has for a short time been near Königsberg. Perhaps I will see him sometime.

Since 1 June I have been living in the hospital as medical officer on night duty. There is a slight possibility that a Psychiatric Department may be set up sometime, and I shall probably be in charge of it. However, everything is still uncertain. Also, whether I will stay in Allenstein.

I watch the great events as optimistically as ever. Morale here has not even been shaken by Italy. One would never have imagined what a nation is capable of in wartime when attacked from all sides. It reminds one of analogies in the life of the individual.—We may expect further rapid progress after the fall of Przemysl.

With the most cordial greetings to you and yours,
Your

*Karl Abraham*

1. Cf. Freud, 1909d: p. 241, 1912–13: p. 87.
2. That is, infantile notions of conception and of "being married" (cf. Freud, 1908c: pp. 222, 224, 1918b [1914]: pp. 92–93).

## 278F

Vienna IX, Berggasse 19
3 July 1915

Dear Friend,

My having failed to answer you for so long is due not to one single motivation, but to a very multiple one, which I shall now try to break down into its component parts. First of all there was probably an intention to imitate you in your long silence, which had already caused me concern. This was, indeed, not groundless, as your child's severe illness fell into that interval. Then there was the impact of our splendid victories, which expressed itself in increased working ability, with the result that today I am already working on the 11th of the intended 12 papers. As a result of the interval I got into a muddle and do not know what I have already sent to you. Some of what has already passed the manuscript stage is indeed transportable. I am in a similar situation with Ferenczi, who is so much nearer and turns up in Vienna occasionally. Our correspondence undergoes the strangest interruptions, and I cannot remember what I have told him and what I have not. I think I regard the situation as a repetition of the initial one, when I was productive and—isolated. All my friends and helpers have now really become soldiers, and it is as if they were removed from me. Even Rank, who has remained in Vienna, has not appeared since his call-up. He is serving with the heavy artillery. Sachs will be going into the army service corps in Linz.[1]

Now, to continue by association: my son Martin tells me that he is finally on Russian soil, but gives hints that can only mean that he will soon have a finer summer abode—in Know'st-thou-the-land,[2] or first of all in the foreland. Ernst is still unoccupied in Wiener Neustadt and often visits us. Oli, who is still free, has in the meantime taken his last engineering examination and is at present helping his uncle[3] in his empty tariff office. On the same day as he, my last daughter qualified as a certificated primary-school teacher. So we have been an industrious family.

On top of all this there was added a third motivation, an absence of several days from Vienna while I was in the country of Berchtesgaden. I liked it so tremendously, it so far exceeded the memory of the five summers I spent there, that the only explanation I can offer is that my libido, having been set free by the loss of Italy, would want to settle there. Our plans for the summer have now taken shape. The two of us will be going to Karlsbad a fortnight today, from there probably to the Königsee or Berchtesgaden, with an interruption in August for a visit to Ischl on the occasion of my mother's 80th birthday. (My father reached the age of 81/2, my eldest brother the same age—gloomy prospects!) Naturally in these times all plans are rather uncertain. "What becomes of the hopes, what becomes of the plans, built by Man, that transient creature!"[4]

I should gladly tell you more about melancholia, but could do it *properly* only if we met and talked. Have I not sent you the typed[5] manuscript of "Mourning and Melancholia"?

A book by Putnam called *Human Motives*[6] appeared yesterday; it is a popular work forming part of a series, Jung-free but in the service of his own hobby-horse. I enclose half of the cover, should it pass the censoring. Otherwise I hear only of neutral (and Hungarian) attempts at translation.

I shall be very glad to hear that your hopeful young son has fully recovered and that you are really working in a psychiatric department. My cordial greetings and good wishes to you and your dear wife.

Yours,

*Freud*

1. Town on the Danube, approximately 150 km west of Vienna.
2. That is, Italy. *Kennst du das Land, wo die Zitronen blühn?* [Know'st thou the land where the lemon trees blossom?]; song of Mignon in Goethe's *Wilhelm Meisters Lehrjahre* (3, 1);

also set to music by Franz Schubert; in Ambroise Thomas's [1811–1896] opera *Mignon* [1866].
3. Freud's brother Alexander.
4. See letter 244F, 25 August 1914, & n. 8.
5. In English in original.
6. Putnam, 1915.

279A

Allenstein
6 July 1915

Dear Professor,

I was just going to write to you to ask about the reason for your silence, when your letter arrived. I am glad to hear that it was only delayed for psychological reasons. One so easily fears other reasons in these times. I fully understand your feeling of scientific isolation, and am myself one of those who is failing to liberate you from it. But it has been weeks since I was able to add a line to my still unfinished paper. The hospital work takes up almost all my time. My duties as a psychiatrist are, incidentally, only a side-line. In the main, I have become a surgeon, not only an assistant or dresser, but an operating surgeon, too. The psychoanalyst in me stands amazed while I operate on a hydrocele or carry out a rib resection because of empyema. But war is war.

I have recently regained my good spirits. There was a very worrying period again between my last letter and this one. About a fortnight ago I had most alarming news from Bremen about my father, had to rush off there and found him very ill. He had severe neuralgia of the left arm, partly connected with his heart, and was greatly weakened by the resultant sleeplessness, morphine, and accompanying feverish bronchitis. When I arrived, the illness had already passed its climax, and he recovered so much before my eyes that I was able to leave after a few days. He is now slowly improving. On my return journey, I stayed one day in Berlin. Our boy is still rather weak after his severe illness, he still had paresis of the soft palate, which made eating difficult. The albuminuria is over. My wife has been in Fürstenberg (Mecklenburg) with the children for a short time, where the forest and the water will do them good. Unfortunately we are completely restricted to telegraphic communication; my wife has not had one line from me for eight days. Anyhow, you know these occasional disturbances there too. Great events cast their shadows before.[1]

I hope to be able to have 8–14 days' leave in August to be with my family. Your travel plans awoke great longing in me. I should be only too glad to go to the Alps, and I would not mind visiting you in Berchtesgaden. But we cannot plan anything yet.

Regarding your new papers—I am amazed at your productivity during recent months—I have only read what has appeared in print in the meantime. We have only corresponded about mourning and melancholia. I look forward to all that is to come! Incidentally, I shall in my virtually completed paper on the mouth zone make some allusions to the connections I mentioned to you some time ago. When the manuscript is ready, I shall send it to *you* and not to Rank. This seems safer at present.

Some more about psychology. My son is recently disowning me in a characteristic way. When my wife once said to him, "Hilde is papa's daughter and you are papa's son", he strongly denied this. On being asked who he thought he was, he replied: "I am papa's half-brother". On my journey to Bremen during the night after receiving the bad news, I had a very nice dream, with my dead *dog*, which has recurred since childhood, with all the signs of infantile hostility. You will be interested to hear of a slip of the pen in your letter which arrived today. You mention the forthcoming 80th birthday of your mother and add that your father reached the age of 8½ years.

I spend the little free time I have enjoying the beautiful woods of these surroundings. East Prussia offers great natural beauties, especially because of the large lakes lying between wooded hills.

We are pleased here about the successful defence of the Austrian Alps, and no less about the great victories in Galicia.[2] In spite of the fact that one cannot see the end anywhere in sight, morale remains firm and confident.

With many cordial greetings and best wishes to you all at home and at the front,
Yours,

*Karl Abraham*

1. "'Tis the sunset of life gives me mystical lore, / And coming events cast their shadows before", from Thomas Campbell's [1777–1844] *Lochiel's Warning*. Lord Byron chose this as motto for his *Prophecy of Dante* (1821).
2. Particularly the recapturing of Lemberg, the capital of Galicia, on 22 June.

## 280F

Karlsbad, Rudolfshof
1 August 1915

Dear Friend,

I was delighted to hear from you at all, though not all your news is pleasing, but as variegated as life itself is now. Fortunately none of it was definitely bad, however. The psychoanalyst may be surprised, but must adapt.

We arrived here a fortnight ago and found that this bubble-town still keeps its old magic: the food is good, and the place is much quieter than it used to be. Officers with Iron Crosses instead of the ladies[1] in crazy dresses. Apart from a disturbance caused by my wife's having some tooth trouble, we can say that we are very well. We are actually thinking of staying on for an extra week. In the middle of August we want to be in Ischl for grandmother's 80th birthday (incidentally, 81/2 was not a slip of the pen, but my usual way of writing 81–82, taken over from the dream notes, e.g. "dream of 8/9 August"). Our daughter is already in Ischl.

Ernst should have left for Galicia yesterday. Martin has been through some severe fighting, a bullet grazed his right arm and another went through his cap, both without disturbing his capacity for action. He has been praised for bravery. In his last postcard he mentions the possibility of a fortnight's leave. He has been out there since 20 January.

I have completed my 12 papers here. ("War-time atrocities", like a great many other things.) Several, like for example that on consciousness, still require thorough revision. Censorship seems now to have made the sending of manuscripts much more difficult. What else will still have to befall before the book can go to print, one cannot say.

Correspondence is silent. Lou Andreas has promised a paper on "Anal and Sexual".[2] The editorial board of *Imago* bristles with arms. My house in Vienna is open, and is thus the best address for correspondence.

I hope this letter will be forwarded to you in Mecklenburg.
With cordial greetings
Your faithfully devoted

*Freud*

1. In English in original.
2. Andreas-Salomé, 1916.


## 281A
Fürstenberg in Mecklenburg, Villa Undine
27 August 1915

Dear Professor,

A week ago I began a fortnight's leave and am here with my family, all of them are well and I am recovering from the over-strenuous efforts of the preceding time quite well. I am staying here until the morning of Monday the 30th and then going to Bremen—my father, unfortunately, is still not well after a bad attack of pleuritis exsudativa[1]—and will probably be back in Berlin on Wednesday, or Thursday 2 September at the latest. I am hoping to get another week of extra leave and would like

1915 September

to ask you whether it would be possible to meet. I should like to spend the extra leave (always providing I get it!) with my wife outside Berlin. However, I cannot travel far. I have to be prepared for a possible summons by telegraph, even though it is not probable. Now, I do not know how long you are staying in Ischl—incidentally my hearty congratulations to you and yours for the family festival you are celebrating there!—and whether you are then going to Berchtesgaden. The latter would be difficult for me with the current poor connections, over 24 hours from Allenstein. Would you and your wife, dear Herr Professor, like a rendezvous between Berlin and Munich? For example, Lauenstein Castle near the express train station of Probstzelle, exactly halfway between B[erlin] and M[unich], would be lovely. I once told you about this splendid little place; you stay there in the wonderful castle chambers furnished in the old-fashioned style. It is very beautifully situated, surrounded by much forest. The food is plain and good. Perhaps you will also be attracted by the abundance of mushrooms and berries in the region. The post and telegraph offices are close at hand. Only transport is not as good as in peacetime. As far as I can see, an express train leaves Munich at 8:20 in the morning; ~~arrives in Bamberg at 11:52 where one now has to change trains~~ you would have to take this to Saalfeld, that is, a little beyond Probstzelle; you would arrive in S. at 2:20, and we at 2:44, and then we would go together for the short distance that is left. To walk from Probstzelle to the Castle takes 1½ hours, but we can also go by car. Saturday 4 September would suit us best; I would then have four days. (It is safer in these times to make more precise enquiries concerning the train.)

I hope you have more good news about your sons and are in the mood to follow up my suggestion. In the meantime my wife and I greet you both most cordially!

Yours,

*Karl Abraham*

Will you, dear Herr Professor, please reply to *Berlin*! If I do not get extra leave, I shall naturally tell you straight away.

1. An inflammation of the pleura with effusion, usually combined with tuberculosis.

## 282F

Königsee *Upper* Bavaria[1]
8 September 1915

Dear Friend,

It is a pity that we had completely lost touch! We have been here for three weeks. Your letter arrived *today*. Any chance for a meeting is probably over! We[2] are going through Munich and Berlin on the way to

Hamburg, perhaps on the 13th or 14th. Send me a telegram here if anything can still be done. Good news of sons. Cordially,
Yours,

   *Freud*

1. Postcard.
2. Freud was accompanied to Berlin by his sister-in-law, Minna Bernays.

## 283A

Allenstein
24 October 1915

Dear Professor,

Not only did we not meet at the beginning of September, as we had hoped, but we have even also lost letter contact for quite some time. Up till a few days ago, I have done practically nothing but hospital work day and night. At last the work has begun to ease off a little. Yesterday afternoon, for the first time, I had a few free hours when I did not have to catch up on sleep, and I finally unearthed my manuscript and wrote a few pages. I tell you this today as a good omen and hope to be able to resume our correspondence as well as my writing.

My wife was especially delighted with your and van Emden's visit, and I, too want to repeat my thanks—although I had already thanked you briefly some time ago. It is over a year since we have seen each other, unfortunately I do not at present see any possibility of arranging a meeting. I hope that you and yours, both at home and at the front, are as well as one could wish! Our news is also good—even my father, at the age of 73, has recovered from his severe attack of pleurisy, though he is still very weak and suffers from the residues.

I hear little from our acquaintances; our correspondence has gradually faded to nothing. I have not received a line from Eitingon and Ferenczi for a long time. Did you know that Stegmann had been killed in action? He was long considered missing in action.

I am very pleased that both journals are continuing. As I mentioned, I hope to be able to send in a contribution soon—about two printed sheets long. I hardly dare say this since I have so often made this promise to you. As soon as I have more leisure, I should also like to contribute something to *Imago*.

The fact that Sachs remains in Vienna[1] and that Rank is also still there, as well as some older members, means that our work has not completely stopped there, as it has here. Rank wrote that you will be having the first meeting of the winter about now[2]; meanwhile, I must sit here *in partibus infidelium*,[3] and am developing more and more into a surgeon!

I hope to hear from you again soon, dear Herr Professor! You will surely have—as always—lots of news, while I am ashamed to have nothing positive to report as far as scientific work is concerned. However, it may be different from now on.

With cordial greetings to you and all your family,
Yours,
*Karl Abraham*

29 October

This letter was returned to me because I had sealed it.

1. "Sachs has returned unfit for military duty after ten days' duty" (Freud to Ferenczi, 7 September 1915, Freud & Ferenczi, 1996: p. 78).
2. Minutes missing in Nunberg & Federn, 1975. The German edition, however, in contrast to the American one, contains the attendance lists and the topics for discussions of the meetings from 5 January 1916 to 19 November 1918.
3. See letter 36A, 11 June 1908, n. 4.

## 284A

Allenstein
13 November 1915

Dear Professor,

Your letter of the 7th[1] took only three days to get here; the proofs followed yesterday. Many thanks for both. I am particularly glad that so far your sons have safely and honourably survived all dangers.

I have been able to breathe more freely for the last few days. For the past eight months I had the most exhausting job at this hospital, but I have now left the Surgical Department for good. I am at present organizing an observation ward for psychopathic soldiers and shall probably very shortly be doing only psychiatric and psychotherapeutic work, as has long been my wish. It is likely that I shall have to write a great many reports for the court, but I am sure I shall have time for analytical studies. In these few days, during which I have been busy with about a dozen patients, I have already made some interesting findings about the origin of paralyses in the war-wounded. If things go as I wish, many cases of psychosis should pass through my hands, and I hope the scientific result will prove useful to us.

You are quite right, dear Herr Professor, when you write in your letter of my "awakening". But while I was working ten hours and more every day, often with disturbed nights as well, and with many other things on my mind, I could do no more than vegetate for months on end. If circumstances permit, then certainly nothing on my part will stand in the way of things being different from now on.

Your short communication[2] gave me much pleasure, even though I was familiar with the case. You told me about it in Lehrter station in Berlin in the winter before the war on your way to Hamburg. In future, I shall make a particular point of investigating this and similar questions in the material from my patients.

I am glad to see that our journals keep going, in spite of the difficult times. I hope I shall soon be able to re-enter the ranks of contributors. I have read practically nothing for months, with the exception of *your* papers.

Is there any chance of your travelling to Berlin or Hamburg again? I very much hope to have a week's leave at Christmas, which is barely enough for Berlin and Bremen. Should I have a little more time, though, a meeting in Breslau, for example, might be arranged, but everything could naturally turn out quite differently.

I have good news from home. My wife is putting up bravely with the long separation; the restrictions imposed by the war are also not easy to bear. But that does not matter. In principle, the war has already been won. The other side just does not want to admit it yet. This is similar to what we see in some difficult cases. But we are used to the fact that these resistances, too, yield in the end.

With cordial greetings, also to your family and the friends in Vienna,
Yours,

*Abraham*

1. Missing.
2. Freud, 1915f.

## 285A

Berlin
28 December 1915

Dear Professor,

Contrary to all my expectations, I did get leave, which I am spending partly here and partly in Bremen. I had planned to use the present free time to write to you when I was surprised by the announcement of your son's wedding,[1] and now I can begin my letter with my wife's and my heartfelt congratulations to all of you. It is pleasing to be able to congratulate somebody in these times. When you have time, I should be glad to hear how this happened so quickly.—I hope I can assume that your sons at the front are well; how are your sons-in-law?

I can report that I am at last working as a specialist once again. I hope shortly to have a psychiatric department of my own, for the observation of patients about whose mental state there is some doubt, for the treatment of nervous patients, particularly those with hysterical paralyses, and for the observation of epileptics.

My long-promised paper for the *Zeitschrift*[2] is now finished. I only have to add a conclusion and shall send it off to you from Berlin. It will probably amount to two and a half printed sheets. I should like now to make a request. I should very much like the proofs to be corrected *there*. When I am back at the hospital, there are all sorts of difficulties with the post. As the manuscript is clearly written, it should not be too much trouble. Perhaps Dr Sachs would be so kind as to take it on. (I suppose Rank is no longer there?)[3] I should only like to see a proof before the final printing; then the manuscript, of which I have no copy, would not need to travel. In the course of time there have been so many difficulties with shipment that I should be very grateful to have the correcting carried out there!

Our acquaintances are still scattered to the four winds; I hear very little of them.

We are all very well, and I am especially enjoying the children during my short holiday. The little boy in particular has developed very well in my absence, and constantly tries to prove your theories with nice examples. I shall be back in Allenstein—garrison hospital—on 3 January and hope to hear from you there. With best wishes for the New Year to you and all your family and also to the friends there,

Yours,

*Karl Abraham*

1. Oliver Freud and the medical student Ella Haim were married in Vienna on 19 December 1915. The marriage lasted for only a short time, however; Oliver came to Vienna at the end of May 1916 on account of divorce formalities mandated by the state. The marriage was ritually dissolved on 10 September 1916. (See Hoffer, 1996: pp. xxxi–xxxii.)
2. Abraham, 1916[52].
3. On 6 January 1916, Rank left for Cracow, where for three years he served as editor of the *Krakauer Zeitung*, the only German daily in Galicia.

# 1916

## 286A

Allenstein[1]
12 January 1916

Dear Professor,

Your letter of the 8th[2] has just arrived. I shall answer it in detail soon, but for the moment will only tell you that the promised work is *ready*. A copy is in Berlin, my wife is typing the copy and will then send you the finished opus. I had already told Rank about this; as I now hear from you, he is no longer in Vienna, so I am repeating the news directly. I am very glad that you have such good news of your sons.[3]

In haste, with kind regards,
Yours,

*Karl Abraham*

1. Military postcard [*Feldpostkarte*].
2. Missing.
3. On 1 January 1916, Ernst had become *Fähnrich* [cadet] and Martin lieutenant (Freud's calendar entry, LOC).

## 287A

Allenstein
23 January 1916

Dear Professor,

Due to my wife's rather lengthy indisposition—she had a painful inflammation of the mucous membrane of the mouth—the manuscript is not yet finished, but I hope it will be ready this week. In a few days, too, I am going to take up my new psychiatric post. I have recently had many interesting experiences, especially on traumatic neuroses. In February I shall be speaking here on hysteria in an "Evening on Medicine in Wartime".

It does not surprise me that activity in the Association in Vienna is falling off. On the contrary, I am astonished that it has remained quite high for so long.—I think it is very right of you to have rejected a few scientific contributions from Switzerland. I have long regretted the fact that Pfister, for example—who is probably the person in question—was still one of our collaborators. He wavers here and there, and his changes in position are entirely dependent on his personal attitude to you and Jung. His letter, which you quoted in the "History of the Psychoanalytic Movement"[1] was indeed factually correct, but it was written in a period of personal resistance against J., and with his changed attitude all his fine discernment has vanished again.

I am glad to hear such good news about your sons. My brother-in-law, who has been in Russia since December, has also advanced pleasingly. How is your Hamburg son-in-law in the West? It is a pity that he cannot do X-ray photography, or he would now be of capital use everywhere. Is your Viennese son-in-law still there?

As soon as I am settled in my new post, I hope to find time for a small work for *Imago*.

Cordial greetings to all of you, at home and at the front!
Yours,

*Karl Abraham*

Would you kindly forward the enclosed?[2] I have not got Reik's address here! Many thanks in advance!

1. No letter of Pfister's is quoted therein (but cf. letters 228F, 15 July 1914; 230A, 17 July 1914).
2. Missing.

## 288A

Allenstein
13 February 1916

Dear Professor,

I hope you have fully recovered from influenza, and also that you have satisfying news from all your family!

I am naturally very pleased that my paper meets with your approval.[1] Incidentally, I personally felt, on the last reading, that the work was good. This is undoubtedly due in part to the slow way in which it matured. In the course of writing it piecemeal over the last seven or eight months, the whole train of thought could be worked through in my mind. In a few days, when I am rid of my official talk on hysteria, my wife will visit me for a week or so. After that, I may put pen to paper again, probably first of all something for *Imago*.

I recently received the issue of *Imago* with Reik's excellent paper on "Puberty Rites",[2] and then the *Zeitschrift* with your *Unconscious*,[3] the first half of which I have already read. I would rather wait until I have read the whole work before making any comment. Incidentally, Heller sent one copy to Berlin and one to Allenstein; I conclude from this symptomatic action that he would like to publish twice the editions he does.

You are quite right, dear Herr Professor, in remarking that I could have given more consideration in my paper to hysterical anorexia. I can explain why I only mentioned this condition in passing and did not investigate it in detail by the fact that I have not yet thoroughly analysed such a case. But there must be a deeper personal reason, just as you consider your passion for smoking to be a hindrance in your investigation of certain problems. I know from experience that my reaction to unpleasant events regularly makes itself felt by a loss of appetite. Therefore, inadvertently, I have avoided analysis of this symptom. However, I believe I have analysed it quite fully in myself and therefore could have taken myself as an example! Instead of this, I paid tribute to repression while working on the paper. Perhaps it will be possible to make a small addition to the text before the final printing.[4]

With cordial greetings to you and all your family, near and far,
Yours,

*Karl Abraham*

Reserve Hospital II Bahnhofstrasse

1. Another letter of Freud's is missing.
2. The first part of Reik, 1915b.
3. Freud, 1915e.
4. Cf. the concluding sections VII and VIII of Abraham's paper (probably added later) and letter 273A, 31 March 1915.

## 289A

Allenstein
1 April 1916

Dear Professor,

During the last few weeks I have spent my somewhat limited leisure time studying your new paper on the Unconscious. I am not quite sure how many times I have read it. I had the same experience as with the *Three Essays* ten years ago. Once again I am amazed how you have succeeded in saying everything of importance so concisely and systematically and linked it all up to form a complete structure. As with the earlier work, every subsequent reading uncovered for me something new that I had not yet assimilated in previous readings. It is probably the most fundamental and important of your papers for a long time; it provides a final and firm foundation for our whole science, leaving none of the familiar concepts unexamined and developing new concepts so naturally from the old ones that one has occasionally to remind oneself how different they had been before. My only regret is that this exceptionally important paper should appear in wartime, when it cannot attract the attention it deserves. But I take it that the whole series will appear in book form as soon as the war is over?

I hope in the next few weeks to be quite productive myself. Incidentally, on my ward here I am able to make many interesting observations, which I should like to use later on; they concern in particular the neuroses following explosions, etc.

I hope all of you, including those at the front, are as well as is possible in these times. I have already spent more than a year here. In May I intend to bring my wife and children here. There is a chance that I shall take a furnished flat. Since there are lovely woods in the neighbourhood, Allenstein is to be the place for this year's summer holiday. My wife was really down for a while with ulcerous stomatitis and ulcerations on her fingers. It looked as though she had caught foot-and-mouth disease, but it turned out to be a pneumococcal infection. She is now quite well again.[1]

I am enclosing a newspaper cutting[2] that has some interesting bits.

With cordial greetings,
Yours,

*Karl Abraham*

1. Interestingly, Abraham had asked Wilhelm Fliess to treat his wife (Abraham to Fliess, 2 March 1916; Abraham, 1991: pp. 249–251).
2. Missing.

## 290A

Allenstein
15 April 1916

Dear Professor,

Yesterday I received your letter of the 10th,[1] for which I thank you very much. I am answering soon. Today I am only sending you a very small contribution[2] for our journals. I leave it to you which one you put it in.

In haste, with cordial greetings,
Yours,

*Karl Abraham*

1. Missing.
2. Probably Abraham, 1917[53].

## 291A

Allenstein, Kreuzstrasse 2 pt.
1 May 1916

Dear Professor,

I have just moved into "our" flat and am expecting my wife and children in a fortnight's time. It is a five-room, furnished flat on the ground floor of a fairly old house entirely in midst of nature, a reasonable substitute for a summer holiday. My first task is to write to you so that these lines will reach you in time. In accordance with your wish, your birthday[1] shall be celebrated very quietly. Surely, however, I may participate in this celebration—in the absolute silence imposed by distance—by sending my most sincere good wishes to you and all your family. Nevertheless I wanted to give you at least a small sign of my affection and gratitude. Since the *Festschrift* that was originally planned has not materialized, I have taken the liberty of preparing a small issue all on my own. I am sending the manuscript[2] by registered post at the same time as this letter. The work was in preparation for a long time, which is all to the good, but was put to paper hastily, within a few days, and then only in the rare hours of leisure. I hope it will contribute to keeping our journals going. (I expect it to cover at least 20 printed pages.) It does in fact contain some new ideas, for instance on narcissism.

When I think, dear Herr Professor, of the abundance of original ideas contained in every one of your new publications, I see all the more clearly the difference between our achievements, that is to say the achievements of your five closest followers,[3] as compared with your own. The five of us, however, seem to be able to accept this fact well enough and to be quite immune from the Jungian type of reaction. The undeniable fact that you have passed your 60th year appears completely irrelevant to me in the light of the continuous and upward progress your papers have shown over the last few years. It is something conventional, rather like putting the clocks forward one hour, as we did last night. May you retain for many years the brightness and creative enthusiasm that are the envy of many a younger man!

My wife asks me to convey to you her sincere good wishes. I send greetings, also in her name, to you and yours, and remain, as always,
Your faithful and devoted

*Karl Abraham*

1. Freud's 60th birthday on 6 May.
2. Definitely Abraham, 1917[54], *not* the (1916[52]) paper on the oral phase and depression sent shortly before, as is sometimes stated in the literature (e.g. in Abraham, 1969: p. 84). Consequently, Freud's remarks in the following letter refer to the former, not to the latter.

3. The members of the Secret Committee (cf. Grosskurth, 1991; Wittenberger, 1995): Abraham, Ferenczi, Jones, Rank, and Sachs.

## 292F

Vienna IX, Berggasse 19
8 May 1916

Dear Friend,

I have just got round to answering your letter last of all, though it was the first to arrive. Because of announcements in the Berlin papers the day could not be kept as secret as I should have wished, and it was just those in the middle distance, who knew nothing about my wishes, who did the most and thus gave me a great deal of work. I have also received so many flowers from Vienna that I have lost all claim to further funeral wreaths, and Hitschmann slipped me an "undelivered speech" that was so moving and laudatory that when the time comes I shall be entitled to ask to be buried without a funeral oration.

The paper with which you presented me is as excellent as—everything that you have been doing in recent years, distinguished by its many-sidedness, depth, correctness, and, incidentally, it is in full agreement with the truth as it is known to me. It is so crystal clear that it seems to cry out for a graphic representation of the intersecting and merging mental forces. It shall not, however, remain mine in the sense of being kept from others. Shall we keep it in reserve for a while in case our *Jahrbuch* is resurrected? Otherwise we shall print it into the *Zeitschrift*.

I have little news to tell you. I have probably already written to you that my second son's marriage will be formally dissolved in a few weeks.[1] It is no misfortune, although he is taking it rather hard, but quite the contrary, besides it is quite a respectable simple business. The girl, who had beforehand thought that she could cope with all possible difficulties, is a runaway, and took flight from the task of combining her medical studies with his engineer's life. We only hear from the other two with a fortnight's delay. My son-in-law is still convalescing in Hamburg; he has had a bit of a traumatic neurosis. I do not know whether it will be taken into account. My daughter and grandchild are naturally staying there.

We are all tremendously pleased that you have your wife and children with you again. Give them my cordial greetings and accept my taciturn thanks for all you have said to me.

Your faithfully devoted

*Freud*

1. See letter 285A, 28 December 1915, n. 1.

## 293A

Allenstein
19 June 1916

Dear Professor,

Your last letter has lain unanswered for a month. In the meantime my family has settled here completely. In the little town, in the garden house near the forest, we feel as though we were on a summer holiday; we shall not be able to have one in the true sense this year. After a separation of 1¼ years we are happy to be together again. We have removed our little girl completely from school for the summer and are having her privately taught here for a while. The boy, who is developing splendidly, is still a source of psychological education for me. The various tasks of moving here in these hard times, and, besides, the hospital work, which is still strenuous, have stopped me from writing for a long time.

I must thank you for your kind words about my last article. I do not mind at all where it is published. First of all the work I sent first will probably appear in the *Zeitschrift*. We cannot for the moment think of a new volume of the *Jahrbuch*. Even if the times were more favourable to our work, we should probably be scarcely able to get the necessary contributions together. So it would probably be best to print the second article in the *Zeitschrift*, as soon as it is short of other material. I am very glad to have won your approval for the new work, too. I am sorry there is now no opportunity to discuss these subjects. Are the sessions of the Vienna Association actually still taking place?

I am eager to hear more about how all your family is getting on, at home and in the field. I hope your next letter will bring good news. Are you making plans for the summer? And what are they? Karlsbad first of all? Are you coming to Germany at any time? And then will there be a chance to meet? I shall probably be coming in September to the Neurologists' Congress in Munich, that is to say in an official capacity. Then it might be possible to meet in Salzburg or in some other place.

From a scientific point of view I have hardly anything new to report. So I add, on behalf of my wife also, only the most cordial greetings to all of you!

As always,
Yours devotedly,

*Abraham*

## 294A

Allenstein
16 July 1916

Dear Professor,

The first issue of your *Lectures*,[1] together with your greetings, arrived the day before yesterday. I have already read the three of them to my wife, and we both sincerely thank you for some stimulating hours. This paper is of particular interest to me in view of the future. Since I have held an official psychiatric post here, I hope it will be easier for me to achieve the *Habilitation* later in peacetime, and through the reading I am learning a bit how it is done. Unfortunately I am without any other news but hope that you are all well! Did you get my last letter which must have been written some four weeks ago?

After delivering two manuscripts in the last few months, there is now a little pause in my productivity. But I am using it in a way that it will probably become the germinal phase for a new paper; in my free hours I am once again studying *Totem and Taboo* and *The Interpretation of Dreams*, always with renewed enjoyment. My medical work offers much of interest, but little that is relevant to our particular purpose. However, I am at present occupied with a court case that is psychologically most remarkable and may be worth writing up one day.[2]

My wife was in Berlin for a week. We have given up our flat and put the furniture into store with the forwarding agency. As I shall probably stay on in Allenstein, my family will stay here for the winter; we can scarcely hope for an early end to the war.

How are all your plans for the holidays, dear Herr Professor? I shall probably take a few weeks' leave at the end of August. Would it be possible to meet?

When you write to me again, please mention what has happened to our friends. I hear nothing at all any more from Reik, Rank, Eitingon, etc. Have you heard anything from Jones?

With cordial greetings to you and your family at home and at the front, also from my wife,

Yours,

*Karl Abraham*

1. On 23 October 1915, Freud had begun his famous *Introductory Lectures on Psycho-Analysis* at the University, delivered in two successive winter semesters [1915–16, 1916–17], and published by Hugo Heller in three instalments (Freud, 1916–17a). Part I, "Parapraxes", had just appeared.
2. Perhaps Abraham, 1923[95].

## 295F

Salzburg, Hotel Bristol
22 July 1916

Dear Friend,

The address will tell you everything. After a short stay in Gastein, where we wanted to stay, we were repelled, and the four of us, my wife and I and my sister-in-law and daughter, came for a longer stay here,[1] where we are at any rate uninhibited and free from food worries. It is very difficult to find accommodation in the country this year. There are a great many things that are missing, naturally, forest for instance, but who can now get all he wants? You will remember the hotel and the rooms; it is a kind of regression; this was where our first, so hopeful, Congress took place in the year 1908.

I received your letter of four weeks ago. Delayed replies call for no apology nowadays. If you are able to cross the border in August, we shall certainly not miss the chance of seeing each other again.

I am at present without news of either of my two sons; I have not heard from Martin, who is fighting the Russians somewhere, since the 11th; but from Ernst, who is still in the conquered Italian territory, I have not heard since 2 July. Perhaps our move has something to do with it, too. My son-in-law, with his wife and child, is now in the immediate neighbourhood of Marcinowski,[2] who has been very kind to them.

Perhaps I shall manage to finish one or two things here. The Dutch translation of *Everyday Life* by Stärcke[3] was forwarded to me yesterday.

Reik has just sent me a card from Trieste; he is with the medical service. We saw Rank in Vienna recently; he was happier than formerly because of certain private improvements, otherwise, naturally, unchanged. Sachs is on leave somewhere until the end of July with his beloved; about Eitingon I know only that he is in Miskolcz (Hungary). Lou still writes the most delightful, sympathetic letters. Jones has managed to get in touch again through Emden.[4] Things are different with him, he has eleven analytic sessions daily, and has now bought himself a small car and a cottage just over 50 miles from London.[5] He too is phantasizing about a meeting. I have at last heard again from Brill, who is engaged in several translations, is squabbling with the Jungians, and hopes that we shall win. Putnam has published an excellent repudiation of Adler in the latest issue of the $\Psi\alpha$ *Review*.[6] Thus interest in our science is not dying out in America.

I am delighted that you are at least constantly united with your family, and also tell myself that you are sure to build everything up again.

With cordial greetings to you and your whole house,
Your faithfully devoted

*Freud*

1. Freud had gone to the city of Salzburg on 16 July, from where he went for one day to Gastein (in the district of Salzburg) on 18 July; on 20 August he went to Gastein again, then once more to Salzburg on 12 September, and on 15 September returned to Vienna (Freud's calendar entries, LOC).
2. See letter 71F, 23 May 1909, n. 4.
3. Translation of Freud, 1901b, by August Stärcke (Amsterdam, 1916).
4. Letter of 30 May 1916 (Freud & Jones, 1993: pp. 318–319).
5. The Plat, Elsted, Surrey, south of London.
6. Putnam, 1916; cf. Ferenczi's review in the *Zeitschrift*, 1917[204].

## 296A

Allenstein
31 July 1916

Dear Professor,

I was glad to hear again from you at last. As you mention only one of my letters, a second has perhaps not arrived.

So it is in Salzburg that four of you are spending the holidays. It goes without saying that I should like to visit you there, though it is not so easy to do. But I have worked it out like this. On 22/23 September the Neurologists' Congress takes place in Munich, the main paper being neuroses after war wounds. I think it is probable that I shall be officially sent to the Congress. We could then meet before or after it. But it is very questionable whether I can cross the border to come to Salzburg. As far as I can see I will not be able to do that while I am on army leave. But there is nothing to stop me from coming to Berchtesgaden, which is so near S[alzburg]. There we could arrange a meeting! How would you feel about that? I should be very happy to see your family too. My wife is hardly likely to accompany me, partly because of the cost, partly because she would not like to go so far from the children (it is more than 24 hours by train). We no longer have a domicile in Berlin; my wife was there recently, cleared the flat, and put our things into store.

I very much hope that in the meantime you have had news—and good news—of your two sons in the field.

I was very interested in what you told me about all the acquaintances. Incidentally, I had a card from Reik this very day.

I have read to the end with pleasure the *Lectures*, for which I thanked you in my last letter!

With cordial greetings to all of you from my wife and me.

Yours,

*Karl Abraham*

## 297F

Salzburg, Hotel Bristol
10 August 1916

Dear Friend,

This time my pleasure in your letter was spoilt by the vexatious news in it. I was counting on your being able to cross the border during your leave, because the latest regulations have made that absolutely impossible for me. This year I even have to give up seeing my daughter and grandson. Here I am in Salzburg without being able to go even once to Berchtesgaden, nor shall I be able to do so in September. So of what use to me is your trip to Munich? Rank writes today that he may attend the Congress as a reporter.

Our intentions are still not definite. Perhaps we shall after all go to Gastein from 20 August to 10 September and then probably back to Vienna. So do revise your plans once more, taking into account the fact that you, belonging as you do to the army in some way or other, are more mobile than I.

We have been having some enjoyable family days here. My brother and my daughter were here for a short while, both with their other halves, as well as *both* my sons from the field, both proud lieutenants.[1] Ernst is still with us, as lively as ever. Martin we found tired this time. He went through a great deal during the Russian offensive.

Salzburg is still wonderful. This stay has been blessed with unusually fine weather. Also I am writing in my free time; five lectures, thus roughly one third, are finished. The first issue of the *Zeitschrift* is said *at last* to be on the way from Teschen![2] Sachs will hasten the second.

Otherwise—well, otherwise one tries to put oneself in a state of peace of mind, which, however, one does not have. Dreadful things are happening in the world. There is no prospect of a nice, peaceful end, and there are all sorts of dark threats to the necessary victory. C. C.! I hope you still remember (Coraggio, Casimiro!).

With cordial greetings to you and to your dear wife and in expectation of your news,

Yours,

*Freud*

1. Freud's brother Alexander and his wife Sophie [1878–1970], Mathilde and Robert Hollitscher, and Ernst and Martin. Ernst had become lieutenant on 1 August, Martin on 1 January.
2. The location of Prochaska, the printing-office, in the Carpathians.

## 298A

Allenstein, Kreuzstrasse 2
18 August 1916

Dear Professor,

It is difficult to make plans this year! I must first of all wait and see whether I am sent to the Congress. The decision on that is not made here, but in Berlin; I shall therefore know about it in some weeks at the earliest. There is also another difficulty: my hospital ward, the only one for psychiatry and neuroses in the district of the Corps, has had to be extended. I have now had for a week my own hospital, of which I am medical director, with 75 beds. I am to have a second doctor, because I cannot deal with all the work. Probably my Berlin colleague Liebermann, whom you know by name, will shortly come here to take up the post. Only *when* is still doubtful. The later he arrives here, the later he can stand in for me, so I do not even know when I shall be able to go on leave. Perhaps you will have gone off to Gastein long before my arrival in Munich. I can see only two possibilities: either I get permission to cross the border and can then visit you—no matter where—or you would have to come to Munich for the Congress, which you would be allowed to do as much as any other doctor. I will do my best to be able to tell you something more definite soon.

We were very glad to hear that you could see your two lieutenants in good shape at home: our best wishes continue to go with them! The days of being together were surely the best of the journey. I am delighted for you and for all of us that you even find time to write down the rest of the *Lectures*.

Here we go on with our semi-rural existence, content that we can be together. I have far too much to do, but am standing up to the work of an entire post, and have the great advantage of completely independent activity and a position of authority.

I have started to read Putnam's article, and I like the beginning very much. I always get the American journal as a review copy for our *Jahrbuch*, but the latter is dormant. Exactly two years have passed since it had appeared only once. As soon as peace breaks out we will catch up with what the war has delayed. I should like to believe that we shall then have more favourable ground for our research than before. After the long time during which the war has absorbed almost all interests, there will be a hunger for science that will perhaps be very good for us. I often think how we shall take up the threads again. In any case we shall behave like Casimiro.

Cordial greetings from my wife and me to you and yours, there and in the field!

Yours,

*Karl Abraham*

## 299F

Badgastein, Villa Wassing
27 August 1916

Dear Friend,

You see what has happened. I have been here with the two women for a week. My little daughter is in Aussee, both the soldiers are again in the field. Gastein is tremendously beautiful, far more so than San Martino,[1] where we were so peacefully together last time. The baths make me so tired that a rejuvenation of at least ten years is to be expected. We intend to stay here over 10 September unless—unless the spa administration drives out its remaining guests. However, there will be no water shortage in Gastein. When I am very tired, I continue writing the lectures. Seven of those on the theory of neurosis are already finished. The printing of the dream[2] is also going ahead. Two Chinese porcelain dogs are on my desk, laughing at me, I think, as I write. I spur myself on by remembering my intention to present the royalties to my grandson for his student days. My son-in-law is still doing badly. As you can imagine, giving up his studio has done him a great deal of harm materially.

I should very much like to see you, but I do not want to go to Munich. I cannot mingle with those attending the Congress, and I cannot do things like crossing the border under some invented pretext. So *ceterum censeo*: it is *you* who must cross the border, and I shall come to meet you in Salzburg or anywhere else you like, even if I have returned to Vienna by the middle of September. I hope you will get permission; my Ernst was on holiday in Hamburg and Berlin.

I think I can congratulate you on Liebermann. The best thing about these conditions is that you are able to have your little family with you. You will be interested to hear (unless I have told you so already) that Ophuijsen has written solemnly declaring himself one of us.

Eitingon wrote yesterday from Miskolcz and asked about you. I have now re-read your orality paper in print with the *greatest* pleasure.

Answer soon. Cordial greetings to you all!

Yours,

*Freud*

1. San Martino di Castrozza in the South Tyrol, where the Freuds had spent their summer holidays in 1913.
2. That is, part II of the *Introductory Lectures*.

## 300A

Allenstein
1 September 1916

Dear Professor,

Your letter of the 27th arrived today. How glad I would be to comply with your suggestion! But, from enquiries I have made in the meantime, I understand it is not possible to visit you on Austrian soil. The fact that your son had leave to visit Germany means nothing. I have been told that travel from Austria into Germany is far less restricted. There is, however, a strict blockade in the opposite direction, with exceptions made only for very special cases such as severe illness in the family. *It is therefore impossible for me* to come to Gastein or anywhere else.

I can understand that you do not wish to come to Munich. But how about meeting in some other Bavarian town? The Congress in Munich is from the 21st to the 23rd. I could keep a few days for you *before* the 22nd. As I am mainly interested in the proceedings of the 22nd, I could be with you also on the 23rd and 24th and the morning of the 25th. I have to be back in Allenstein by the morning of the 26th. I do not think you will have any difficulty, as you are no longer liable for military service. So if we could not meet in Munich, we could meet in *Nuremberg* or *Regensburg*, or naturally in any mountain region on German soil. It is some two years since we last met, and I should be so happy to see you again.

The three weeks of my leave will be spent as follows:

5–11 Sept.—with my wife on the nearby Baltic coast.

12 Sept.—Allenstein, to Bremen in the evening.

13–18 Sept.—Bremen.

~~18 or 19~~ *18th*—~~Berlin.~~ In the evening to Munich or another place to be agreed on.

I hope I shall have a favourable reply from you, dear Herr Professor. Meanwhile I send written greetings—also from my wife—to you and your family near and far, including the Chinese dogs! Letters will reach me best here, up to 12 September, and after that in Bremen, Uhlandstrasse 20.

Hoping to see you looking as rejuvenated as you promised,
Yours,

*Karl Abraham*

## 301A

Regensburg[1]
23 September 1916

Dear Professor,

So it was not to be! I am very put out to be staying here *alone* on the return journey. The town is splendid, and the Museum of Antiquities would certainly have satisfied you. So when are we going to see each other? In Munich I spoke to Dr Weiss from Vienna.[2] The Congress was just as I had expected. With many cordial greetings from your

*Karl Abraham*

On the 26th I am back in Allenstein.

1. Picture postcard: "Prehistoric-Roman museum in the Ulrich church; Roman tomb of the legionary Aurelius Patreinus (erected by his parents)."
2. See letter 65F, 18 February 1909, n. 8.

## 302F

Vienna IX, Berggasse 19
26 September 1916

Dear Friend,

It was impossible, I returned to Vienna on 16 September, and have given up the rest of the travelling season for this year. It was impossible, for various reasons, to be discussed in person. *In addition*, Ferenczi had announced a visit for the middle of this month to work on his analysis;[1] however, he was prevented and is still not here today. Rank was here until yesterday evening on his return journey from Constantinople, where he had spent his leave, and was utterly enchanted by the Orient.[2] Otherwise many of our members have been transferred, Tausk is ill, etc. We shall be a very small circle when we open in October, and then we shall only see each other occasionally.

Naturally we are keeping the journals to the last possible moment. The printing of the second instalment of the *Lectures* is now going ahead fast. Today I have had from Berlin an idiotic essay by Placzek on friendship[3] and a piece of prattle by Eulenburg on morality and sexuality.[4] So much for science.

We have had our two boys on leave in Salzburg at the same time, as you know. Since then they have both been in the South Tyrol region, and occasionally send us good news. My son-in-law drags himself around, he is not being discharged and is being given no other duties. His traumatic neurosis appears to be flourishing. He is recognized as no longer fit for field service.

Your card from Regensburg was the midwife of this letter, which otherwise would have seen the light of the censorship a few days later. Believe me, I for my part am very sorry, too, for the restriction I have imposed on myself. Also at my age one should postpone nothing. But there were certain difficulties I could not overcome.

I have finished nine of the lectures on the theory of the neuroses which I shall deliver this term. After that I propose to give no more lectures whatever.

In Gastein we shared table every evening with his Excellency Waldeyer,[5] who at the age of 80 is sound as a bell and seems to be a very nice man.

Let me have news of you again soon. With cordial greetings to your wife and children,

*Freud*

1. Ferenczi had three *tranches* of analysis with Freud during the First World War: the first started on 1 October 1914 and lasted for three-and-a-half weeks; the second was from 14 June to 5 July 1916; and the third and final period was between 29 September and 13 October 1916.
2. "Rank will leave on holidays on 4 September for Constantinople via Budapest" (Freud to Eitingon, 26 August 1916, SFC). He returned to Vienna on 18 September (Freud's calendar entry, LOC).
3. Placzek, 1915. Siegfried Placzek [1866–193?], Berlin physician, had studied under Binswanger and Ziehen, worked with Oppenheim, and wrote widely on sexual and legal problems. In 1907 he had published a complimentary review of Freud's *Sammlung kleiner Schriften zur Neurosenlehre*.
4. Eulenburg, 1916.
5. See letter 149A, 5 January 1913, & n. 2.

## 303A

Allenstein
12 November 1916

Dear Professor,

Your last letter has been waiting for weeks to be answered. The strain of work is certainly one of the reasons; but added to this is the feeling of discontent that for a long while I have been able to write about nothing but petty domestic and personal matters. It was quite different when I had the pleasure of writing to you on scientific progress, and always eagerly awaited your reactions to what I had to say.

My leave in September was rather rich in impressions. First I had eight days with my wife on the Baltic coast, which is marvellously beautiful in East Prussia. Then I spent a week with my mother in Bremen. From there I went to Munich. There is not much to report about the Congress. Dr Weiss from Vienna was the only acquaintance I met. It struck us during the discussion on neuroses how official neurology is gradually taking this and that over from us, without acknowledging the source either to themselves or to the world. After the Congress I spent one day in Regensburg and enjoyed all that I could of the Roman and mediaeval traces to be found there. Then a day in Berlin and back to Allenstein.

The collaboration of our colleague Liebermann, who had been very ardent in acquainting himself with his work, was unfortunately soon interrupted, as he fell ill with severe otitis also involving the labyrinth. He is now getting better. In the meantime I had to look after the hospital, which had been increased to 77 beds, by myself.

My family has now been with me for exactly half a year. Both the children are now going to school here; the boy is giving us grounds for great hope.

If both your sons are still in the Alps, they will have had a rather easier time recently; I am glad they are both bearing up so well in the matter of health, too. Is your son-in-law no better? And how are your family at home?

When is the 2nd instalment of your *Lectures* due? I assume that the first of my two papers will also appear in the *Zeitschrift* soon? And another question: are you going to Hamburg again at Christmas, as you did two years ago? And is there a chance of us meeting?

Adding the most cordial greetings from my wife and myself to you and all your family,
Yours,
*Karl Abraham*

304A

Allenstein, Kreuzstrasse 2
10 December 1916

Dear Professor,

I have once again just emerged from a period of excessive work. My collaborator Liebermann, who has been suffering from severe otitis, is now improving, but I had in the meantime to deal with up to 90 cases of neurosis and psychosis entirely on my own, and feel quite exhausted. Today I can breathe a little more freely as I have been given a temporary assistant. Otherwise, we are well here. I was glad to hear the same of yourself and your family. Your guests from Hamburg will certainly help you over this difficult time.[1] It is most praiseworthy of the little boy to try to thank his grandfather for his hospitality by producing "material". Incidentally, I can report that our six-year-old boy eagerly enquired today whether one can marry one's sister. Next time I hope to hear more

1916 December 339

about your sons and sons-in-law and how they are getting on in the war, and hope it will be only good news!

The *Zeitschrift* containing my contribution has not yet arrived. I am particularly pleased to hear that you have finished your *Lectures*: for your sake, because you are now once again free for something new; and for my sake, because I look forward to reading them; and for all our sakes, because a better introduction to Ψα cannot be produced. I can sympathize with your wish not to give any more lectures in future, but I regret this, since our science will then be completely removed from the academic domain, and we do not know whether anyone will get a chance to speak in the foreseeable future in Vienna or anywhere else. After the war I shall try my luck, but am doubtful of success.

I am particularly pleased that the proposal for the Nobel prize was made by Bárány,[2] one of the most original thinkers among doctors. Furthermore, this is the realization of a long-standing wish I have had for you. It is four years since I tried to get Bjerre to contact the leading authorities in Sweden in this matter. There are sufficient reasons why I would wish now more than ever that this should be realized for you!— Ophuijsen is a good acquisition if he now stands firm and does not begin to waver on account of various resistances.

Nothing more to add for today except cordial greetings and good wishes, also in the name of my wife, to you and yours, large and small, near and far. Perhaps more another time!

Yours,

*Karl Abraham*

What is Reik's present address?

1. A letter from Freud seems to be missing. On 17 November, Freud's daughter Sophie and her son Ernst had come to Vienna (Freud's calendar entry, LOC).
2. Robert Bárány [1876–1936], Austrian physician of Hungarian descent; professor at the University of Vienna, and from 1917 on in Uppsala. In 1914 he had received the Nobel Prize in physiology or medicine for his work on the physiology and pathology of the vestibular apparatus. His recommendation of Freud for the Nobel Prize was not successful. (Cf. Freud to Ferenczi, 31 October 1915, Freud & Ferenczi, 1996: pp. 86–87.)

305F

Vienna IX, Berggasse 19
18 December 1916

Dear Friend,

No. 2 of the *Zeitschrift* with your splendid paper[1] has at last appeared. The dream lectures went off to your address today. Your letter turned up at the right moment. I am delighted to hear that things are going well, or what is called that nowadays, with you and yours! I gladly give you the same news about ourselves.

My eldest is at present with the cadre in Vienna and often stays with us, he is still holding out. Ernst is in the same place on the Italian front. Oliver is now with the Engineers in Cracow, is doing his first training there, and will then come to the training school in Krems. He has settled in quite well. My son-in-law, who is in an occupation suited to him, seems to be recovering well; he is still in Hanover. The little boy is charming and amusing; if there were as much good will and understanding on the part of the Entente as there is with him, we should long since have had peace. Meanwhile he has long since passed beyond the early stages that are so instructive to us.

It pains me to hear that you are so overburdened. I have little to do, so that at Christmas, for instance, I will again have reached rock-bottom.[2] Leisure is not good for me, because my mental constitution urgently requires me to earn and spend money on my family in fulfilment of my father complex. In these circumstances, entirely against my intention, my hopes turn to the Nobel Prize, though we are all aware that there too we must count on the resistances that are ~~that are~~ so familiar to us. This makes the conflict very irritating, almost humiliating. (Perseveration![3]) C.C. is often very necessary.

Reik's most recent address known to me is *Lieutenant* Dr Th. R., k. u. k. mob. Res. Hospital Nr. 4/3, Forces' postal service 279.

I cannot vouch for its still being valid. Last month he came here on leave and asked a great deal about you. Why does he not write to you?

With cordial greetings for Christmas-time. I hope I shall hear from you again soon.

Yours,

*Freud*

1. Abraham, 1916[52].
2. On 28 December, Freud wrote in his calendar: "without income!" (LOC).
3. Referring to the crossed-out words.

# 1917

### 306A

Allenstein
2 January 1917

Dear Professor,

I received your letter and the 2nd volume of the *Lectures* over a week ago and today want to thank you sincerely for both since I have just finished reading the book. I think it will be very useful for our interests, partly because it is so elementary and yet contains everything essential, and partly because, as all historical and theoretical material has been left out, it makes far fewer demands on the reader than the earlier book on the dream. Furthermore, the perfect depiction and the certainty and serenity of the work are sure to make an impression—as soon as general interest turns back to science again. I spent a number of pleasant hours with this book, and my wife is reading it now. Otherwise, there is little stimulation in this small town. That is why I have used the holidays for avid reading, and the only dissatisfaction is that the 3rd volume is not yet out. Meanwhile, the new issue of the *Zeitschrift* has arrived, and I see myself in print again after more than two years. Incidentally, what is to happen to the other paper?[1] If only one knew that there would be peace soon and that we could publish our *Jahrbuch* again, I should like to reserve it for that. But since the future is so uncertain, it would be best if I asked you to publish it sometime when the *Zeitschrift* is short of contributions.

I should be glad to hear that you have good news of all your combatants, and that all of you at home are well too. I can say the same of us.

Not much new to report scientifically. Among my patients I have had two obsessional neuroses; without thorough analysis, both strikingly confirmed your views and those of Jones. They may be useful material later on.

Yesterday I chanced to come across a dream in *Till Eulenspiegel*[2] that is told by the *three-year-old* Till and has, as far as I know, not yet been mentioned in our literature. You might publish it under the brief communications in the *Zeitschrift* with reference to undisguised wish-fulfilment of childhood dreams. It goes as follows: "One morning Till told his father what he had dreamt the previous night. 'Father', he said, 'last night I saw a cake in my dream'. 'That is a good omen, my son', Father

Klaus replied. 'Give me a penny, and I will explain the dream to you.' 'Father', answered Till, 'if I had a penny, I would not have only *dreamt* of cake."'

More sometime soon! For today, the most cordial greetings to you all, also from my wife!

Yours,

    *Karl Abraham*

1. Abraham, 1917[54], which eventually appeared in the *Zeitschrift*.
2. German mediaeval stories about a legendary rogue, widely circulated in popular editions. A publication by Abraham or Freud could not be found.

307F

Vienna IX, Berggasse 19
13 January 1917

Dear Friend,

My warm thanks for your letter! The most important thing is that you are well and are able to enjoy your family. In such circumstances the value of a good wife, in itself inestimable, is immeasurably increased. I can well imagine that the small town offers you nothing but work, work, and not the kind of work that one desires. From another letter that arrived at the same time as yours I gather that Liebermann is again with you.

Your second, hardly less splendid paper is to appear in Number 4 of the *Zeitschrift*. Number 3 is already at the printer's, with a paper by me,[1] which I shall send you in proof as soon as the block that goes with it is ready. The situation with regard to the *Jahrbuch* is uncertain, as you know. Deuticke seems to be offended at the *Lectures* being published by Heller,[2] though I warned him a long time ago that his repeated rejections of our periodicals would ultimately have that consequence.

I have asked Karger to send the fifth edition of *Everyday Life* straight to you. According to my calculations the book must long since have been ready, but I have not yet received it.[3]

Your praise of the *Lectures* has done me a great deal of good at this moment. Living in isolation as one does nowadays, one has vigorously to remind oneself that there are still a few people for whom it is worth writing. Otherwise one would forget, and, though one does go on working for oneself, one would not commit it to paper.

Your Eulenspiegel dream will be used in the *Zeitschrift*.

My boys are for the moment out of danger. Martin is with the cadre in Vienna. Ernst, who had tonsillitis and was able to convalesce in S. Cristoforo on Lake Caldonazzo,[4] is supposed to come on leave next week, and Oli is still "enjoying" his training in Cracow. It is better not to think in advance about the painful experiences that this spring will bring the world. Little Ernst treats me as he does his father in war, he allows himself to be helped and attended to but otherwise ignores me and demonstratively sticks to his mama, aunt, and other youngish females. He is very amusing.

Cordial greetings from
Your

*Freud*

1. Freud, 1916–17e.
2. The *Lectures* were selling extremely well.
3. Fifth edition of Freud, 1901b (with S. Karger, Berlin).
4. Location in the South Tyrol.

## 308A

Allenstein
11 February 1917

Dear Professor,

Soon after your letter arrived, I received the new edition of *Psychopathology* from Karger, which I have meanwhile read. I find it enriched in many ways. I have one small reservation to make: the examples you have taken from other authors do not all appear to be as fully analysed as your own. To give one instance: the slip of the pen on p. 102, Levitico instead of Levico, does not seem to me to be sufficiently elaborated.[1] This objection only holds good for certain examples, not for those from Ferenczi, Jones, etc. A question concerning one of your own contributions (p. 96, a slip of the pen in writing about a sum of money[2])! Could this not be due to the old custom of paying tithes? I should like to take this opportunity of telling you about a nice case of mixing up letters (p. 186[3]). I was told about it by a patient who had been in treatment with colleague Ri[klin] in Zurich. After the patient had returned to his home from Zurich, he received a letter from Ri., which the latter had addressed to the canton bank in Zurich: had they already received the sum of so-and-so many francs? And in its place a letter with medical advice had been sent off in the envelope addressed to the bank. A novel form of reminder to a patient!

If I succeed in obtaining a copy of Grimm's dictionary[4] here or other relevant literature, I should like to make a small philological contribution on the same subject soon. This would represent my heartfelt thanks for your communication, which I can only express in a few words today.

You too will have been very pleased with the news from Ophuijsen.[5] Van Emden used to have doubts about founding a medical association while some of the members inclined towards Jung. Since Ophuijsen has changed sides, these difficulties seem to have been resolved. In some respects I have great hopes of this re-foundation.

I have not yet received the last issue of *Imago* but saw it at Liebermann's and am now looking forward to your article[6] in it, of which I knew nothing.

I was very glad to hear such good news from you all. Is your daughter Sophie staying in Vienna with the little boy permanently, that is to say until the end of the war? I have heard nothing more from Eitingon for a very long time. Is Rank still in Cracow?

Nothing has changed with us here, despite the long difficult cold period in the harsh region of East Prussia. May the new powerful sea action[7] bring us peace! A victory over England is certainly the most radical means for that; the prospects seem very favourable to me.

With the most cordial greetings from house to house,
Yours,

*Karl Abraham*

1. Freud, 1901b: p. 127—a communication by Hug-Hellmuth.
2. Freud, 1901b: pp. 119–120.
3. Freud, 1901b: p. 223.
4. *Deutsches Wörterbuch* (1852–1961, 32 vols.), the authoritative etymological dictionary of German started by Jacob [1785–1863] and Wilhelm [1786–1859] Grimm, better known for their collection of German fairy-tales.
5. The founding of the *Nederlandsche Vereeniging voor Psychoanalyse* [Dutch Society for Psychoanalysis] in February 1917 (see the corresponding communication in the *Zeitschrift*, 1916–17, 4: 217, which was "published with satisfaction at the international spread of psychoanalysis, which was not completely inhibited by the war").
6. Freud, 1916d.
7. The governments of Germany and Austria had announced "unrestricted submarine warfare" starting from 1 February, meaning that neutral ships would also be attacked. Thereupon, two days later, the United States had broken off diplomatic relations with Germany.

## 309A

Allenstein
18 March 1917

Dear Professor,

Since last writing to you, I have come to know two new products of your activity, written in times so unfavourable to our science. I was very interested in the "Types" in *Imago*, especially in the Shakespere [sic] and Ibsen analyses,[1] which I found completely convincing. The other paper,[2] which you sent me in proof, gave me special pleasure, not only because of its train of thought but particularly as a personal document. It is indeed a shame that there is no possibility within the foreseeable future of our meeting and discussing a great many matters. Judging from the most recent paper, you might after all be tempted to come to this furthest north-eastern corner of Germany, if I tell you that your colleague Copernicus lived in Allenstein for many years. The interesting castle, built by an order of knights, still contains some mementoes of him.

I feel quite ashamed at being able to produce so little. At least I am at present writing a *very* small contribution for the *Zeitschrift*. It will be concerned with "The Spending of Money in Anxiety States",[3] a phenomenon that you too have probably analysed in your patients. I shall, if I find the time, try to make use of some of my old notes.

Recently a journey of several days to Königsberg with my wife brought a little diversion into our existence. My wife had to go there to do some shopping, and I used the University Library.

I hope you and your family are all still well. How did your sons get through the winter on the Alpine front? Here the winter was and is unusually stubborn, which also has not been beneficial to my health. The children are well. They are making good progress at school. Our boy, 6½ years old, recently reassured my wife that he would marry her if I should die.

I have heard from Reik from Montenegro, but not from anyone else. All these contacts will one day be re-established. The moment normal conditions return, you may be sure that I shall sound the drum, summoning everyone together again. Who knows what the next weeks may bring? At any rate, we shall do as Casimiro!

With the most cordial greetings from house to house,
Yours,

*Karl Abraham*

While I was looking something up in the library in Königsberg, someone happened to ask for one of your books. It was strange that I should witness the librarian giving information about it.

1. Freud, 1916d: pp. 313–315, 318–331.
2. Freud, 1917a—in which Freud compared himself with Copernicus and Darwin.
3. Abraham, 1917[55].

## 310A

Allenstein[1]
19 March 1917

Dear Professor,

I am sending this card to follow yesterday's letter. Today I have received from a gentleman whom I treated earlier (Dr Protze in Bad Ems) a small manuscript[2] for my opinion as to whether it is ready for printing in one of our journals. I find the little work very charming and convincing, and am inducing the author to send it to you. If you approve of it too, you would do me a particular favour by writing a few words personally to the colleague. I believe we can expect more from him later.

With cordial greetings,
Yours,

*Karl Abraham*

1. Postcard.
2. Protze, 1917.

## 311F

Vienna IX, Berggasse 19
25 March 1917

Dear Friend,

You are right to point out that the enumeration in my last paper is bound to create the impression that I claim my place alongside Copernicus and Darwin. However, I did not wish to relinquish an interesting idea just because of that semblance, and therefore at any rate put Schopenhauer in the foreground.

The printing of the *Lectures* is going ahead well. The book may be in your hands in May or the middle of June, whereupon I shall ask you for your detailed private criticism.

A contribution from you, whether long or short, will be "greedily" received. Regrettably, things move very slowly with the journals, though Sachs[1] does everything possible.

What a pity I did not know when you were in Königsberg! My son-in-law was there for more than four weeks and only left it a few days ago; it would have been a relaxation for him. I myself can probably not visit you in Allenstein, as long as travelling is not permitted for outright patriotic reasons. No question that we shall all make up for it afterwards.

Our colleague in Bad Ems should just send his contribution in to us. As you have already assessed it, its acceptance is assured, and I shall be glad to thank him for it personally.

My sons are at present well. We are expecting Martin the day after tomorrow on leave from the cadre, Oli is very near, in Krems on the Danube,[2] but there is no question of visits; he will have at most the two days of Easter free for us.[3]

Ferenczi is still on the Semmering, his Basedow's disease is improving, though it may leave some permanent effects.[4] Jones has sent us news again. He is holding firm, and also personally things are going very well with him.[5]

1917 May 347

Pfister announces a little book on Ψα and education,[6] which is to appear in a few weeks' time in Leipzig. Jung is said to have published something about the unconscious,[7] but I have not got it into my hands yet. Stekel has accomplished a big book on "Masturbation and Homosexuality"[8] with an introduction that is very endearing to the initiated, etc. We are awaiting from you the official announcement about the Dutch group.

Many cordial greetings to your dear family from
Your
*Freud*

1. Who had replaced Rank.
2. About 70 km west of Vienna.
3. This is in fact what happened [8 and 9 April].
4. From February until early May 1917, Ferenczi was in a sanatorium on the Semmering near Vienna, being treated for Basedow's disease.
5. Referring to Jones's marriage with Morfydd Owen [1891–1918] (Freud & Jones, 1993: pp. 322–323).
6. Pfister, 1917.
7. Jung, 1917.
8. Stekel, 1917, 387 pp.

## 312A

Allenstein
22 April 1917

Dear Professor,

Enclosed is the promised short manuscript for the medical journal![1] I wonder whether you will agree with the conclusions?

I am writing in greater detail soon. For today, only cordial greetings!
Yours,
*Karl Abraham*

1. Abraham, 1917[55].

## 313A

Allenstein
4 May 1917

Dear Professor,

The first priority of these lines is to bring you my very best wishes for your birthday! Unfortunately, I am not in a position this time to offer you a gift in the form of a more substantial contribution to the journals. The trifle I recently sent you is in your hands, and another may follow soon.

My duties are so exacting that they prevent me from undertaking longer papers. I have had one analytic case for some time and I may shortly send you a dream of his, of the type you were previously seeking examples of.[1] I am able to report with respect to scientific matters that my psychiatric work has given me excellent proof of the correctness of your theory on paranoia. A few of the cases are so transparent that I should like to write something on them, but considerations because of my being in service would make it too difficult to publish them for the time being. As you can see, I am not completely stagnating, in spite of the war.

I impatiently await Part III of the *Lectures*. You are, as always, at work, putting all of us younger ones to shame. The three years of war have scarcely impeded your research, they were not very fruitful for me. Yesterday I passed the 40 mark. We both start on a new year of life at nearly the same time, and I have many wishes for you, dear Herr Professor, as well as for myself—I need hardly enumerate them.

Your news about Ferenczi's illness was a complete surprise to me. I knew nothing about it, and I beg you to tell me something more about him. And also about all your family. Those at the front will surely be well, in view of the quiet in the east and south, and the well-being of those at home depends on that in no small measure.

Did the little paper by Dr Protze go in? Is Rank not writing at all now? I heard from Reik from Montenegro. But from nobody else. I have heard nothing from Eitingon for a long time. Where is he?

Are you thinking of going to Germany in the foreseeable future? Or is the attraction from Hamburg still with you? I am sorry that I knew nothing about your son-in-law's stay in Königsberg. It would have been so easy to spend some time with him.

With cordial greetings to you and your house, in which my wife joins me,

Yours,

*Karl Abraham*

1. See letter 151A, 6 February 1913, & n. 1.

## 314F

Vienna IX, Berggasse 19
20 May 1917

Dear Friend,

After your last communication, with which I was supposed not to be in agreement (but why?), I had to wait a long time for your promised letter. Yesterday it arrived at last, dated the 4th inst.! My heartfelt thanks for your congratulations, though I hold that at this time of life no notice should be taken of such anniversaries, and I think with regret how different your entry into a new decade would have been, had not this disaster overtaken us all.

I see with dismay that you deprecate yourself in relation to me, building me up in the process into a kind of imago instead of describing me objectively. In reality I have grown quite old and rather frail and tired, and have to some extent turned away from work. The *Lectures* were still written in the summer holidays, and since then I have done nothing, though some short papers are still being published. Life bears too heavily on me. I talk very little about this, because I know that the other would take such statements as complaints and signs of depression and not as objective descriptions, which would be unfair to me. I believe I have had my time, and I am no more depressed than usual, thus very little, and console myself with the assurance that my work lies in the good hands of continuers such as you and Ferenczi, and perhaps some others. You in particular have written in these unfavourable conditions the two best clinical studies that we possess and have certainly compiled ample new material.

I have here an *almost* complete new edition of the *Lectures*, but it will certainly take another 3–4 weeks before I am able to send you the book. Thanks to Sachs's really astonishing efforts, the two journals are continuing; the printing of the next issue of *Imago* was held up by a sudden paper shortage. But it will be pushed through.

I do not expect to travel to Germany in the immediate future. The senseless restrictions make it quite impossible. My daughter left on the 14th inst. and joined her husband yesterday. He is in Schwerin, and she will probably soon move into a lodging-house there. It is very lonely here, as for quite a while we have had a lively family life through the child and frequent visits from the soldiers. Martin is still with the cadre[1] in Linz, Ernst in the 10th battle of Isonzo (last news on the 14th inst.), Oli still training in Krems. Ferenczi has found us lodgings in the Tatra mountains on lake Csorba, but we must get there by 1 July.[2]

Ferenczi, who has always had mild symptoms of Basedow's disease, had become weak through over-exertion and excitement, but made a good recovery after staying on the Semmering for three months. He has been back in Budapest since the 10th inst., Hotel Royal, and he will surely also sort out his private circumstances once and for all.[3] As you see, he is working very hard on the *Zeitschrift*. Rank has a very sterile and depressive time behind him but is now pulling himself together and is going to bring out a second edition of his *Artist*.[4] We have heard from Jones that he has married a young compatriot, a singer, he is very happy and regards himself as a reformed character.[5] He has also published the translation of Ferenczi's works,[6] but cannot send us the book.

Reik is still in Montenegro, Eitingon (Miskolcz, Res. Hospital, Rud. Barracks) recently asked after you and wanted your address. This very day I had the news by telegram from van Ophuijsen that Joh. Stärcke had died suddenly.[7] He was secretary of the new group; I did not know him, it is certainly a regrettable loss.

Protze's paper has gone in and allotted to the next *Imago*, which means that there is going to be a postponement of 4–5 months.

Our inner conflict here is perhaps nowhere so plainly revealed as it is by the extremely notable trial of Fr. Adler. He happens to have been born precisely in the rooms in which we live. I once saw him here when he was a boy of 2.[8]

When we meet again, we shall have many things to talk over that are now either not clear or are not communicable at a distance.

With cordial greetings to you and your dear wife and children,
Your faithfully devoted

*Freud*

1. English in original.
2. That is, earlier than Freud usually started his summer holidays.
3. Referring to Ferenczi's indecision of many years' duration whether or not to marry his mistress Gizella Pálos. The marriage would finally take place on 1 March 1919.
4. Rank, 1907 (second edition 1918).
5. These two words in English in original. Referring to Jones's sexual affairs.
6. Jones's translation of Ferenczi's papers had been published under the title *Contributions to Psychoanalysis* (Ferenczi 1916[186]) by Badger (Boston) in 1916.
7. Johan Stärcke [1882–1917], younger brother of August Stärcke, practising physician in Amsterdam, translator of Freud's *On Dreams* (1901a) and *The Psychopathology of Everyday Life* (1901b), first secretary of the Dutch Society (see Ophuijsen's obituary in the *Zeitschrift*, 1916/17, 4: 274–276).
8. The day before, the trial against Friedrich Adler [1879–1960] had ended with his being sentenced to death. Adler became an almost legendary figure by virtue of his assassination of the Austrian prime minister Karl Graf Stürgkh on 21 October 1916 and the speech he made in his own defence. He was pardoned in 1918 and subsequently assumed positions of leadership in Austrian and international Social Democratic politics; but he also made a name for himself as a theoretician in physics. His father, Dr Victor Adler [1852–1918], was a leading personality in the Austrian Social Democratic Party. Freud knew him as a student and by way of mutual friends (e.g. Heinrich Braun). The Freud family had the same apartment in Berggasse 19, where Adler's family had lived earlier and where Freud had seen the young Friedrich Adler. (See also Freud's letter of 30 October 1927 to Julie Braun-Vogelstein, Freud, 1960a: p. 380.)

## 315A

Allenstein
28 May 1917

Dear Professor,

So, your long silence was due to postal delays. Your letter of the 20th arrived here yesterday. I was pleased to learn from it that you and all your family are well and especially wish you at this moment continued good news from your warrior on the Isonzo. Many thanks for all your news. I very much regret that there is no prospect of a meeting yet.

1917 June

The *Zeitschrift* arrived at the same time as your letter; a particularly good and substantial number—amazingly good for wartime! I can make no comment on *your* paper,[1] except to agree with it. I was especially pleased with Ferenczi's essay.[2] I held a talk here on the same theme more than a year ago which coincides in every detail with what he writes. I may soon write a short supplementary paper, since it might be possible to add some important points that I have recently come to understand. The variety of his contributions to the last issue[3] proves to me that Ferenczi is well on the way to recovery. I shall write to him one of these days. It is a good thing in these difficult times that Sachs, with his characteristic devotion, can dedicate himself to the journals. Who knows what would otherwise have become of them.

There is not much new to say about us. We shall spend the summer holidays, which begin on 21 July, in Nidden on the Kurian spit of land, a little holiday resort that we already know and that offers a combination of the Baltic and a very beautiful forest. Before that I am going to Bremen for a few days, as my mother, who will soon be 70, is not well.

In spite of your appreciation of my two recent contributions, which I do not wish to belittle myself, I nevertheless feel dissatisfied with myself. It represents too small a harvest over three years, particularly since all the material on which it was based was ready *before* the war. Let us therefore continue to hope that the great change will soon come.

With the most cordial greetings from house to house,
Yours,

*Karl Abraham*

1. Freud, 1916–17e.
2. Ferenczi, 1916[189], on war neuroses.
3. In addition to the essay, Ferenczi had contributed two brief communications (1916[190], 1916[191]) as well as a book review (1917[204]).

## 316A

Allenstein[1]
17 June 1917

Dear Professor,

Very many thanks for sending the book[2] and for the short offprint[3]! I have only read a few pages of the former, but with the greatest satisfaction. You asked me some time ago for my criticism of the whole work. Would you agree if I did not put this in a letter but wrote it for the *Zeitschrift*? I could then write it during my summer holiday, which I shall probably start on 20 July. Or has somebody else already been given the review?—A second, younger psychiatrist[4] has recently been appointed to my hospital; he is interested in psychoanalysis and may settle in Berlin after the war.

With best regards from house to house,
Yours,

*Karl Abraham*

1. Postcard.
2. The complete *Lectures* in one volume (Freud, 1916–17a).
3. Not identified; perhaps Freud, 1916–17c.
4. One Dr Rudberg; see letter 322A, 23 September 1917.

## 317F

Vienna IX, Berggasse 19
22 June 1917

Dear Friend,

Have I already had an opportunity of telling you that we shall be leaving on the evening of 30 June for Csorbató in the Tatra Mountains (Villa Maria Theresia), Liptau County? Nature is said to be magnificent, everything called food is nowadays a question mark.

So far my books have never been reviewed in our journals. If you would like to inaugurate a different policy with the lectures, you would be troubled neither by objections nor competition. Your observations will be just as valuable to me, whether you make them publicly or by letter.

I can promise you an issue of the *Zeitschrift* and also one of *Imago* within the next few days. Everything now takes a long time. In any case, if one finds any energy and spirit again nowadays, one uses them up raging and grousing.

Enjoy your holiday with your family thoroughly, but write to me first.
Yours,

*Freud*

## 318A

Allenstein[1]
29 June 1917[2]

Dear Professor,

Just a few lines to greet you at the beginning of your summer holiday and to thank you for your letter of the 22nd!

Do you know that in Part III of the *Lectures* the upper part of page 284 is so misprinted that it does not make sense? (apparently because lines have been left out). The publisher could easily make a small overlay with the correct text and have it pasted into all copies.

1917 July

More soon! This time only cordial greetings to you and all your family. How are your sons at the front?
Yours,
*Karl Abraham*

1. Postcard.
2. "29. 8. 17."; without doubt, however, this letter belongs here (see Freud's following answer regarding p. 284 of the *Lectures* and Abraham's thanks for Freud's previous letter of the 22nd).

319F

Csorbató[1]
13 July 1917

Dear Friend,

This place is situated on Lake Csorba 4,000 feet up in magnificent surroundings and with beautiful forests, but it rains and storms mercilessly and we are as cold as if it were winter. I do not know whether we shall put up with it for long. Ferenczi is expected to arrive here on leave on the 24th.

The sentence on p. 284 of the *Lectures* should read that it is precisely "*a delusion of jealousy and not one of another kind. You realize the* . . ."; instead of that the printer had repeated the similarly placed sentence on p. 282 (despite the proof corrections).[2] But nothing can now be done about it, especially from here. The printing was such trouble that I will be happy if no more harm was done.

A woman patient of Jung's has sent me his new work on the psychology of the *Ucs*.[3] so that I should change my judgement on the noble character. It bears the date 1917. But he seems not to have gone beyond the crude conversion into theory of the fact that he came across myself and Adler. We meet in the "archaic".

Shortly before we left, my sister's twenty-year-old only son[4] was killed in action. Grief was beyond description. There is no news about my warriors.

Hoping that your well-earned leave will do you nothing but good and asking you for news about yourself and your dear family,
Cordially yours,
*Freud*

1. Lake Csorba.
2. Freud, 1916–17: p. 253, lines 13ff. from top.
3. See letter 311F, 25 March 1917, & n. 7.
4. Hermann [b. 1894], son of Freud's sister Rosa [1860–1942] and Heinrich Graf [ca. 1852–1908], had died at the Italian front. The couple's other child, Cäcilie ("Mausi") [b. 1899], committed suicide in 1922, while in analysis with Paul Federn.

## 320A

Nidden on the Kurian spit of land
(Address from August 17th Allenstein again!)
10 August 1917

Dear Professor,

I hope that in the Hungarian mountains, where you suffered so badly from the weather at first, you have later been enjoying yourself so much that you and your family can have a perfect rest there. I am sending this letter to Csorbató. We too have landed in a remote corner, the most north-easterly of the fatherland. Nidden is about in the centre of the spit of land about 100 km long, on the Kurian lagoon, on the shore of which I am sitting writing. In absolutely wonderful weather we are enjoying nature in this secluded spit of land with its huge forests and sand-hills. In the mornings we usually go across to the other coast, to bathe. The children are so absolutely in their element; they mostly float on the water or go with us to pick berries. Afternoons and evenings are spent in excursions, sailing, etc. As we are also well looked after, we feel very happy here and disregard some shortcomings. For me it was high time to have longer holidays after last year's very great burden of work. Last winter, which was so particularly hard, I suffered a great deal, in the harsh climate of East Prussia, from bronchial catarrh with asthmatic symptoms. Even now I am unfortunately not free from it. However, I am in general satisfied with my recovery here.

As relative quiet reigns on the Italian front, I hope that all is still well with your *familia militans* at the front. The tragic event you reported, I mean the death of your nephew, must, especially now, have had a particularly distressing effect on his mother and all of you. After three years of fearing and hoping, to lose one's only son must be particularly difficult. In my family—not, indeed, among those closest to me—a similar case occurred.

I hope you yourself and your family, among whom I may also count Ferenczi, are in good health.

Yesterday I read the third part of the *Lectures* to the end. I shall try to express my personal thanks in the form of the review I have already promised; I shall write it in the course of the next weeks, and will today only say that this, the only scientific book that I brought here with me, has only contributed to the enhancement of the joys of holiday.

With the most cordial greetings to you and yours, also from my wife.
Yours,

*Karl Abraham*

## 321F

Csorbató
21 August 1917

Dear Friend,

What you supposed has happened. Once the bad weather had been overcome, a splendid, enjoyable summer happened to set in, undeservedly delightful holidays, which my wife and daughter have also been enjoying as they have seldom enjoyed holidays before. The Hungarians are unmannerly and noisy but obliging and hospitable; friendship and loyalty are taking the form of generosity, with the result that we are able to wallow in the abundance of bread, butter, sausages, eggs, and cigars, rather like the chief of a primitive tribe. The catering of the hotel alone would not have been able to do so much, though in present circumstances it does not deserve to be criticized. I am even able to indulge in my passion for hunting for mushrooms in the forests here. I have done no work, but have been able for hours and for whole half days to forget the wretched state of the world; in addition, during this period my three warriors have been away from the front. Shortly before our departure my sister's only son, a boy of 20, was killed in the Italian theatre of war.

Sachs stayed with us here for three weeks, Ferenczi for about a fortnight. Both wives, respectively wives-to-be,[1] were also very close by. Rank came here once for a visit, over the mountains from Cracow. Eitingon was also here for a day and thanked us for his welcome with a colossal food parcel. He looks very well, has become stouter, is bored with respect to scientific matters but delighted about his wife's occupation[2]; he is probably with her now in Karlsbad. A few days later they were expecting my daughter,[3] who had travelled to an estate in the Hungarian plains to visit Ferenczi's family in Miskolcz,[4] and I have no doubt that they fed her very well.

No news scientifically. Heller has received a good fee for the Dutch translation (of the *Lectures*).[5] You know that I now need money, and nothing so urgently as money, for my family. Binswanger has sent me part of the manuscript of his book, which is to deal with the position of $\Psi\alpha$ in relation to psychology.[6]

So now your leave is behind you. I hope that it has invigorated you and your family for a long time to come! We are thinking of leaving for Vienna on the 30th or 31st. Sachs is hard at work trying to convert the standstill in the production of our journals into movement.

With the most cordial greetings to you and your dear wife,
Yours,

*Freud*

1. Grete Ilm and Gizella Pálos.
2. Mirra Jacovleina, née Raigorodsky, an actress; married to Eitingon since 1913, helped him in his work in the military hospital.
3. Anna.
4. Where Eitingon was stationed at the time.
5. Antwerp, Amsterdam: Maatsch. Voor goede en goedkoope lectuur, 1918, 1919, 2 vols. Tr., intro. and foreword by A. W. van Renterghem.
6. Binswanger did not realize his intention to write a book about psychoanalysis and psychology in this form; a first part was published in 1922 (Binswanger, 1922), the manuscript of the second part is lost (see Binswanger, 1956: pp. 63–64; Freud & Binswanger, 1992: pp. xx–xxii; cf. Freud & Ferenczi, 1996: p. 235).

## 322A

Allenstein
23 September 1917

Dear Professor,

I assume that you have been back in Vienna for some weeks just as we have been back here in Allenstein. My wife and children benefited from the holiday, and I at least had a good rest, though my old bronchial trouble somewhat spoilt my holiday. After we got back, my colleague Liebermann also went on four weeks' leave, so that I immediately had to take a great burden of work on my shoulders again. What with my bad state of health in the holidays and the overload of work, the result is that I have not completed the review of your *Lectures* as I meant to. Our financial position makes it necessary for me to carry on the practice to some extent in addition to my hospital work. Naturally my scientific interests are not getting their fair share of time. In a few days I am going (sent officially) to the Neurologists' Congress in Bonn. I shall scarcely see any of our friends. I am looking forward most to churches and museums in Cologne and Bonn. After the Congress I am going to Bremen for a few days to see my mother, who is almost past her 70th year, and on the way back to Allenstein I am having one day in Berlin. My wife is meeting me in Bremen. After that we have the endless East Prussian winter before us; so we have quickly to collect a few pleasant impressions.

On the scientific side I have hardly anything of my own to report, except perhaps that several cases of obsessional neurosis, only superficially investigated, have given me striking confirmation concerning sadism and anal erotism. The other faithful members of our small circle had the opportunity of meeting you this summer. Unfortunately *I* have had to forego this pleasure for exactly three years, as three years have passed since you and your brother were in Berlin in 1914! I constantly plan to make up for lost time, as far as possible, immediately once the war is over. But as long as "impotence of thoughts"[1] is reigning, I shall be confined to wishing.

1917 October

For a short time a young doctor called Rudberg has been working in my hospital; he is very interested in Ψα and wants to take to it altogether. I hear to my delight that interest in our cause is increasing among young doctors, and that people interested in psychiatry are cherishing the wish to be posted to my hospital.

Since I shall be unable for the time being to review your *Lectures* for the *Zeitschrift*, I should like to say a few words here. The third part is so excellent that I find it difficult to pick out any examples. So much has been placed in a new context and so many new ideas and vistas opened up that I shall have to read it again to be able to judge it as a whole. As I have very little time, I can only read it chapter by chapter, but I shall savour it more fully that way. In my opinion, the 19th chapter[2] is the climax of the whole, and I would say it has made such a strong impression on me as scarcely any of your other works. The same could be said of the *last* lectures. Only *after* the war is over shall we be able to feel properly grateful that it was in fact the war that gave you the leisure to write up the *Lectures*. We may then expect a rapid advancement in our prestige, and new followers will at last have the kind of introduction that was lacking before (though I believe that the initiated will gain far more from the *Lectures* than beginners).

During the heavy fighting on the Italian front my wife and I often thought of your sons. I sincerely hope that they have remained unhurt and that all of you at home are well too. Many thanks for your report on all our friends who visited you in Csorbató. Unfortunately one loses touch through such a long separation. I should like to know where Reik is (still in Montenegro?) and how Ferenczi is. Do you still hear from Jones? I secretly hope that one of the Dutch members will come to the Congress in Bonn.

With cordial greetings and good wishes to you all, also from my wife, Yours,

*Karl Abraham*

1. As opposed to the "omnipotence of thoughts", a formulation of Dr Ernst Lanzer (the "Rat Man"), taken over and elaborated by Freud in Part III of *Totem and Taboo* (1912–13a).
2. "Resistance and Repression".

323F

Vienna IX, Berggasse 19
5 October 1917

Dear Friend,

Your letter gave me great but painful pleasure. How much has changed since we last saw each other, and not everything for the better.

When I think of the time when you told me that it was no longer an act of martyrdom to be called my pupil.[1] The enclosure with this letter,[2] unless it remains in the hands of the censor, illustrates one of these changes. If you find me cross and annoyed, you will know why.

Csorbató was absolutely beautiful, but tomorrow we shall have been in Vienna for five weeks. We hurried because our Ernst has come to Vienna from Isonzo as a patient. So he missed the 11th battle. His suffering is a return of his earlier stomach trouble, supposedly caused by an ulcer; but it will probably turn out to be the gall-bladder. At present he is at home on leave, which he is striving to get extended, cheerful and glad of the rest. He just could not stand it any longer. Instead, Martin is now in the same area, Oli in Cracow, and perhaps after a few weeks he too will be down there.

After a few days I got a great deal of work, and am now working for 8–9 hours a day with nine patients. It amuses me and, strangely enough, has done much good to my health, to which the certainty of avoiding the otherwise inevitable bankruptcy substantially contributes. My income is now the same as before the war, but the value of money has changed greatly. My writing—I had some little things in progress—will be held up for only a short time.

Your praise of the *Lectures* pleased me greatly, though my opinion of them does not accord with yours. I hope you will still discover their great deficiencies and not leave them unmentioned in your review.

Ferenczi is working assiduously in Budapest and is close to bringing his fifteen-year-old heart saga to a happy ending. Reik really is in Montenegro. Eitingon was our guest in Vienna for a few hours on his way back from Karlsbad. Not long ago I had a good, warm-hearted letter from Frau Dr Horney. She seems to be valuable. My inner certainty against Jung and Adler has increased a great deal. Occasional letters arrive from the Dutch. Ophuijsen is entirely on our side. You will soon read an article of his in the *Zeitschrift* on the masculinity complex of women.[3] Renterghem is translating the *Lectures*, Emden is as faithful and as sluggish as ever.

Tausk and Ferenczi want to comment on your paper on ejaculatio praecox.[4] I received Tausk's contribution today; it does not agree with you entirely, but is very interesting. We now have plenty of material for both periodicals, but we cannot keep up with the printing.

Jones wrote in true English spirit a few weeks ago[5] that German resistance was still too strong, so the war was bound to last for a few years yet.

As I write to you so seldom, I do not know whether I have yet mentioned the Lamarckian work,[6] the point of which is to be that even the "omnipotence of thoughts" was a reality once.

I do not know where this letter will meet you. Hopefully it will reach you, and will soon bring me an answer, as pleasant a one as is to be had in these days.

With cordial greetings to you and your dear wife,
Your old
 *Freud*

P.S.: A slip of the pen from a letter (Martin) while the battle of Isonzo was going on: I have not understood the *Schußsatz*[7] of your letter.

1. Letter 131A, 24 July 1912.
2. Missing; see the following letter.
3. Ophuijsen, 1917.
4. Tausk, 1917. Ferenczi did not write a review of Abraham's paper but discussed it and ejaculatio praecox in his paper at the Psychoanalytic Congress in Berlin [1922] and in the first pages of *Thalassa* (1924[268]).
5. Not in Freud & Jones, 1993.
6. A plan by Freud and Ferenczi, later abandoned, to write a joint book on "Lamarck and Ψα" (22 December 1916, Freud & Ferenczi, 1996: p. 166), proceeding from Jean-Baptiste de Lamarck's [1744—1829] hypothesis that individually acquired features could be inserted into the genetic code and be inherited, and showing that "[w]hat are now neuroses were once phases of the human condition" (12 July 1915; ibid.: p. 66). Freud had already drafted some ideas in his *Phylogenetic Phantasy* (1985a [1915]), not published in his lifetime; subsequently he distanced himself more and more from the project and finally "prefer[red] to relinquish the whole thing" in a letter to Ferenczi (29 May 1917; ibid.: p. 210). Eventually, Ferenczi's *Thalassa* would contain many of these ideas.
7. Instead of *Schlußsatz* [closing sentence]; *Schuß* means "shot" [trans.].

## 324A

Allenstein
2 November 1917

Dear Professor,

The great events of the last few days[1] have often drawn my thoughts towards Vienna. Today I want first of all to express the hope that your sons have remained unhurt! They must have been through a gruelling time. May we at last be able to gather the fruits of this outstanding success in the form of favourable peace terms!

Now I have to thank you for your last letter, with the enclosed picture. Just to show that I do not always see only the good side of things, I want to stress my impression that three years of war have not passed you by either without leaving their mark. Hardly any of us will have remained completely unscathed in body and soul. You would find me too gone grey and, in spite of sufficient food, much reduced in weight. I find your photograph—apart from the changes for which the photographer cannot be held responsible—otherwise good. Perhaps I shall have an opportunity of sending you a photograph of myself. Many a thing has indeed changed. What, for instance, might have happened to Casimiro's courage during the last few days?

How is your son Ernst, who was at home recovering when you wrote, and how are you and all the others? Your letter contained some pleasant news: that you are back at work with your old vigour, that Ferenczi is approaching a wish-fulfilment, and that our Dutch colleagues are eagerly at work. I did not quite follow your hint about a paper on Lamarck. What did you mean? You have not mentioned it before, but must have thought you had done so. I am curious about Tausk's remarks on my last paper. So far I do not like his paper on deserters,[2] it is too verbose, not concise enough. Incidentally, I shall make use of my experiences in legal psychiatry over the last two years for this topic—not for a psychoanalytic paper, but for my *Habilitation* paper in order to try my luck after the war.

I forgot to tell you last time of an interesting *lapsus* of Bleuler's. In his work "The Physical and Psychic"[3] he incorrectly reproduced several things from the *Interpretation of Dreams*. I referred him to the newly published *Lectures* on the Dream. After reading the latter, Bleuler wrote,[4] inter alia: "As I have shown, Freud has for many years directed his attention only to the psychological aspects of dreams and has deliberately and consciously ignored everything else. I finished reading his latest publication only yesterday. Admittedly in this he pays more attention to other aspects which partly serve to supplement his former theories and which partly weaken them; but I must say that his previous ingenious and vigorous one-sidedness has hindered impressed me more than his present reserve . . ." (The letter was typewritten; the correction was hand-written in the original with a pencil. Do you not think the correction very instructive? Impressed instead of hindered! In fact he was *hindered* since it obstructed his ambition!)

I recently received a very interesting paper by Fliess; it contains brilliant new observations about a pituitary syndrome. Would you be interested? If so, I could send it to you.

Our life here is not subject to any great changes. My wife and the children are well. Hoping to receive good news about all of you soon, I am, with the most cordial greetings from my wife and myself,
Yours,

*Karl Abraham*

1. The 12th and last Isonzo battle, begun on 24 October, which led to the collapse of the Italian army.
2. Tausk, 1916–17. The paper was published in two parts; the second had not yet appeared.
3. Bleuler, 1916.
4. Letter of 10 July 1917 (LOC).

1917 November

325F

Vienna IX, Berggasse 19
11 November 1917

Dear Friend,

I have today been able to overcome a certain reluctance to answering your letter because we have just had the first news of Martin since the beginning of the offensive (23 October),[1] and he is well. Ernst is still with us, and Oli is building on a bridge across the Dnjester.

I have a great deal to do, with 8–9 analyses a day and some in reserve, and am very pleased at being able to avoid brooding and worrying in this way. It is still very interesting. But I am ageing rapidly all the same, and occasionally feel doubtful whether I shall live to see the end of the war, whether I shall ever see you again, etc. During the war travelling to Germany is practically out of the question. The next blow that I expect is the stoppage of our journals; Heller is not threatening this, but with the continuation of the war it will become inevitable. At any rate I behave as if we were faced with the end of all things, and in the last few days I have got ready for publication in the *Zeitschrift* two papers of the "metapsychological" series (M$\psi$ [metapsychological] Supplement to the Theory of Dreams, Mourning and Melancholia).[2] I originally intended to use these and other papers, with those already printed (Instincts and their vicissitudes, Repression, The Unconscious[3]), for a book. But this is not the time for it. It will also be a good thing for your promised review of the *Lectures* to see the light of day before the end of the world that is to be expected. With the cessation of the journals our role will for the time being have been played out.

As you see, I do not believe that the events in Russia[4] and Italy will bring us peace. I think one should take the British assurances about their intentions seriously and also admit that the U-boat war[5] has not achieved its object. In that case our future is pretty dim.

What you say about Bleuler's statement again shows how difficult it is to please people. I hope you have not received the impression that I have weakened or taken anything back. I have heard about Fliess's work, things are too uncertain to send it to me, unless you have two copies. I shall try to hunt up a copy here.

Have I really not told you about the Lamarck idea? It arose between Ferenczi and me, but neither of us has the time or spirit to tackle it at present. The idea is to put Lamarck entirely on our ground and to show that his "need", which creates and transforms organs, is nothing but the power of *Ucs*. ideas over one's own body, of which we see remnants in hysteria, in short the "omnipotence of thoughts". This would actually supply a $\psi\alpha$ explanation of expediency; it would put the coping stone on $\Psi\alpha$. Two big principles of change (of progress) would emerge; the change through adaptation of one's own body and the subsequent change through transformation of the external world (autoplastic and heteroplastic),⁶ etc.

I am not sure either whether I have drawn your attention to a book by Groddeck in Baden-Baden ($\Psi$ *Determination and* $\Psi\alpha$ *Treatment of Organic Illnesses*, S. Hirzel, 1917).⁷ Lou Andreas's paper in the *Zeitschrift für Sexualwissenschaft*⁸ will not have escaped your attention. Full of subtleties, but hardly intelligible to the general public.

Enough for today; I send my cordial greetings to you and yours.

Yours,

*Freud*

Poveretto Casimiro!

1. See letter 324A, 2 November 1917, n. 1.
2. Freud, 1916–17f, 1916–17g (cf. letter 256F, 25 November 1914, n. 1).
3. Freud, 1915c, 1915d, 1915e.
4. On 7 and 8 November the Bolsheviks had seized power in Russia (the October Revolution) and subsequently entered into truce negotiations.
5. See letter 308A, 11 February 1917, n. 7.
6. Cf. Ferenczi, 1924[268].
7. Groddeck, 1917. Walter Georg Groddeck [1866–1934], German physician and writer, founder [in 1900] and director of a sanatorium in Baden-Baden. On 27 May 1917 he had written to Freud (Freud & Groddeck, 1974: pp. 31–36), who had, in the beginning, supported Groddeck even though their relationship cooled later on. Groddeck remained outside the psychoanalytic organizations and termed himself a "wild analyst". He is considered a pioneer in psychosomatic and holistic medicine (cf. Groddeck, 1923). He saw all physical and psychic phenomena as forms of expression of the "it" (a term borrowed from Nietzsche). In therapy he emphasized the role of—above all, negative—transference and countertransference in connection with somatotherapeutic, suggestive, and dietetic techniques. He influenced psychoanalysts like Frieda Fromm-Reichmann, Erich Fromm, Karen Horney, Karl Landauer, Heinrich Meng, and Ernst Simmel. (Cf. Grossman & Grossman, 1965; Martynkewicz, 1997; Will, 1984.)
8. Andreas-Salomé, 1917.

326A

Allenstein
2 December 1917

Dear Professor,

I found it quite distressing to receive such a gloomy letter from you. It would not be psychoanalytic were I to attempt to dispel your mood with counter-arguments and I shall therefore only take up one of your worries. You think that our journals will soon cease publication. I have written to Sachs today asking him to inform you of a suggestion that seems to me to be in keeping with the times. If you both agree, a solution could be found.

I hope you have further good news from the front and that all of you at home are in good health. I have been very preoccupied with the theoretical content of your letter (Lamarck). You will remember that for several years I worked on the history of evolution and theories of heredity, etc., and therefore have a particular interest in these problems. I can hardly comment on your theory on the basis of the brief hints you have given me, but I feel extremely envious of those who have the opportunity of frequently exchanging views with you, while I can only write my *Epistulae ex Ponto*.[1]

The most recent political events in Russia seem to me well worth noting, however sceptical I may be regarding an *early* peace. When it comes, our science will be sure to rise to unprecedented heights. After these years when interests have inevitably been focused on the war, on politics, and on getting enough to eat, there will be a voracious appetite for science, and I think quite a few prejudices will have disappeared.

I cannot help saying it—we are, after all, better off than Casimiro.

For today, only hasty greetings from house to house,

Yours,

    Karl Abraham

1. Latin: "letters from the Black Sea"—i.e. from the exile.


## 327F

Vienna IX, Berggasse 19
10 December[1] 1917

Dear Friend,

I am using the leisure of a Sunday to reply to your letter of the 2nd inst. (and I am freezing so as I do so that I made the mistake of writing the 7th month). In the streets they have just called out the news of the armistice with Russia,[2] and if one had not grown so blunted, one would be glad at having survived the end of half the war.

Sachs has told me of your proposal. It is impracticable, since it involves Deuticke, who has stopped everything since the beginning of the war, and is also very ill and angry besides, because the *Lectures* are being published by Heller. Meanwhile what I feared has rapidly come true. The last issue of *Imago* (No. 2), which has been printed for a long time, cannot be distributed because no wrapping paper is obtainable, and Prochaska has already announced that he has no paper for Rank's *Artist*,[3] of which Heller wanted to produce a second edition. Officially we have not ceased publication, and perhaps we shall be able to drag on for some time yet. Sachs still hopes to avoid the ignominy of having to stop before the last issue of the *Zeitschrift* (No. 6) without being able to complete the annual series. I wanted to print in that issue the two papers from the metapsychological series about which I have already written to you.[4]

I should gladly tell you more about the Lamarck, but it would have to be on a walk. I am at daggers drawn with writing, as with many other things. Included among them is your dear German fatherland. I can hardly imagine myself ever going there again, even when it becomes physically possible again. In the struggle between the Entente and the Quadruple Alliance I have definitely adopted the viewpoint of Heine's Donna Bianca in the disputation in Toledo:

All I can say is . . .[5]

The only thing that gives me any pleasure is the capture of Jerusalem and the British experiment with the chosen people.[6]

I am very busy, and for nine hours a day on six days of the week I can exercise patience and superiority. On the seventh both generally yield.

With my cordial greetings to you and your wife,
Yours,

*Freud*

1. The "XII" in the handwriting is corrected from VII (see below).
2. On 5 December, the Central Powers and Russia had agreed in Brest-Litovsk to an armistice from 7 to 17 December, prolonged on 15 December until 14 January 1918.
3. See letter 314F, 20 May 1917, & n. 4.
4. This is what happened.
5. *Welcher recht hat, weiss ich nicht—/ Doch es will mich schier bedünken, / Dass der Rabbi und der Mönch, / Dass sie alle beide stinken* [I don't know which one is right—/ But all I can say is, / That the Rabbi and the Monk, / That both of them stink]; final lines from Heinrich Heine's [1797–1856] "Disputation" (*Romanzero*, Third Book: Hebraic Melodies).
6. The reference is to the taking of Jerusalem by British troops the day before, ending 673 years of Ottoman rule, and to the declaration by the British Foreign Minister Arthur James Balfour [1848–1930] of 2 November that "His Majesty's Government view with favour the establishment in Palestine of a national home for the Jewish people, and will use their best endeavours to facilitate the achievement of this object."

## 328A

Allenstein
16 December 1917

Dear Professor,

These days mark the 10th anniversary of my first visit to you in Vienna just after I had started my practice! It has in recent times looked rather more likely that I shall be back in Berlin in the foreseeable future and that I shall then also be able to visit Vienna again. Plans for the future are thus beginning to assume a somewhat more definite shape.

1917 December

A week ago I had to escort a sick officer from my hospital to Bremen, and therefore had the opportunity of spending two days with my mother. I made use of a short stay in Berlin to visit privy councillor Bonhoeffer and to discuss with him the question of my *Habilitation*. I knew that B. is quite generous and that he has kept apart from all attacks made against us. He was personally quite accommodating, drew my attention to all the obstacles, and, although he was honest enough to make no promises, was not in principle opposed to the idea. He said that he would enquire of Bleuler, among others, about my scientific qualifications, and he also asked me for a list of my publications. The matter thus does not seem completely hopeless to me. *One* point was not discussed but is of some importance. B. may well be afraid that a follower of an "extremist" school of thought would use his lectures to wage war against the established school of thought. It would have been appropriate to reassure B. beforehand in this respect, but I said nothing of this, either in our discussions or in a letter I wrote to him today, because I was afraid of giving a wrong impression. The thought has occurred to me that a letter from you, dear Herr Professor, mentioning not only my scientific qualifications but also my *personal* qualities along those lines, might be helpful and reassuring in this respect. I am, however, not quite sure whether this would be the best way, and I shall leave it to you to decide whether to write or not. I think a reassurance that there would be no reason to fear unpleasant incidents on my part would be appropriate. Perhaps you can think of a better way to allay such a fear?—The work on my paper for *Habilitation* is in the meantime progressing slowly. It has just occurred to me that it might be better to write such a letter to *Kraus*, with whom you have had correspondence about me before. You might ask him to talk to B. on this point! At any rate I give you both addresses: Privy councillor Professor Dr Bonhoeffer, Director of the Psychiatric Clinic of the *Königliche Charité*, Berlin NW., and Privy councillor Professor Dr Kraus, Director of the 2nd Medical Department of the Königliche Charité.

Nothing new from us! I hope all is well with you too, both at home and at the front. With many thanks in anticipation and best regards,
Yours,
*Karl Abraham*

## 329F

Vienna IX, Berggasse 19
21 December 1917

Dear Friend,

I am glad to hear that you are able to make any plans at all for the future. If I can do anything to help, I shall gladly do so. But a strong feeling warns me against writing to Bonhoeffer. If I express the thoughts that go with it, they are the following: I find nothing particularly hopeful in your account of your conversation with him. I doubt whether personal intervention by me will do more good than harm, and I am reluctant to get in touch with a stranger from whom I am not sure even of receiving at least the usual courtesies. Even Kraus, who is perfectly amicable towards me, could not bring himself to answer one of the two letters I sent him. The course that the collaboration on his handbook has taken, can have had only a cautionary effect on me, even though I let myself be guided by consideration for his relations with you.

For these reasons I think it far preferable to write again to K., with whom the ice is already broken, and, picking up the thread of my pre-war letter to him, to try to persuade him to back you with B. I shall do so this week, though I do not think it will help much. I shall write to the effect that I know you not to be one of those who turn scientific opposition into personal animosity and thus damage the dignity of science (at any rate in our sense of the word!).

Otherwise I have no news. Is it really ten years? They were significant and rich in substance enough, though not always pleasant.

My greetings to you and yours
cordially, your
　*Freud*

## 330F

Vienna IX, Berggasse 19
26 December 1917

Dear Friend,

I am afraid you may have concluded from my last letter that I was unwilling to write to Kraus and hence may be worrying that the promised letter would run aground on enigmatic obstacles. So let me reassure you by telling you that the letter has already gone off in perfect order.

It did certainly cost me some gnashing of teeth. There was one part of the complex against which one has to struggle, and another that overcame the struggling. The two parts were naturally anger at being in the position of having to ask a favour of the hostile world, and consideration that it might perhaps be useful to you. I hope that the latter may turn out to be correct.

Rank came to see me yesterday. He is now a prisoner of the editorial department of the *Krakauer Zeitung* and is in very low spirits.

If this letter reaches you in time for the New Year, may it bring you the end of exile and a new beginning of independent existence.

Cordially yours,

*Freud*

# 1918

## 331A

Allenstein
6 January 1918

Dear Professor,

Many thanks for your two letters and for complying with my wish concerning Krauss [sic]! I did gather from your *first* letter that you found it difficult to come to a decision, but I did not doubt for a moment that you would in fact write to K., and it was therefore unnecessary to set my mind at rest with the second letter! I am very sorry that my request made you feel so uncomfortable. *Perhaps* we shall both be rewarded by a favourable result!

There is nothing new to report from here. Today I received the reprints of the trifle about "Spending of Money in Anxiety States".[1] My work on the *Habilitation* progresses slowly. On the scientific front, I might mention that I am getting interesting results from the analysis of a case of obsessional brooding, which will be suitable for publication later (addenda to the anal-sadistic aetiology).[2]

I am enclosing with this letter the promised review of Pötzl.[3] I am very disappointed with the paper. The author's attitude to $\Psi\alpha$ is ambivalent, in that he agrees with everything theoretically but, at the same time, robs the concepts of their real content; thus his acceptance becomes meaningless, and in practice he is very far from using the method. I have therefore written a review that is moderate in tone but unequivocally unfavourable. Has P. become a member in the meantime? After *this* paper I should find that difficult to understand.

I am very sorry to hear that Rank is not well. Sachs on the other hand seems to be in top form. As soon as there are real hopes of peace, I feel personally ready for anything, and I already have a number of plans for a scientific get-together! That does not mean to say that the war years have passed me by without trace. Just like everyone else, I have lost some of my vigour, hair pigmentation, and weight. But I hope for a quick regeneration and not for myself alone!

Since you do not mention any details about your family, I assume that you are all well, including the soldiers at the front.

With many good wishes for 1918 (Casimiro!) and cordial greetings from house to house,

Yours,

*Karl Abraham*

1918 January

1. Abraham, 1917[55].
2. Possibly the case mentioned by Abraham (1921[70]: pp. 381–382).
3. Abraham's review appeared in the *Zeitschrift* (1919, 5: 222–224), but is not listed in the bibliography of his writings and has never been reprinted.
    Otto Pötzl [1877–1962], one of the most important representatives of the Viennese school of psychiatry, between 1905 and 1921 assistant and senior physician at the psychiatric–neurological clinic with Julius Wagner-Jauregg. On 14 November 1917 Pötzl had been accepted as a member of the Vienna Psychoanalytic Society. In 1922 he became a full professor in Prague; in 1928 he returned to Vienna as Wagner-Jauregg's successor. He "ended . . . the denial of psychoanalysis at the University of Vienna which had prevailed until then and supported, to the extent possible, Freud's pupils. But his attitude towards psychoanalysis remained ambivalent all his life" (Nunberg & Federn, 1975: p. xxii). (Cf. Mühlleitner, 1992: pp. 245–247; Roazen, 1992: pp. 119–120, 129.)

332F

Vienna IX, Berggasse 19
19[1] January 1918
*Shivering with cold!*

Dear Friend,

I am very glad you did not take my recent difficulties more seriously. Your equable temperament and indestructible willingness for life stand up well to my alternations between courage and resignation. The resistances against which it was written were probably evident in my letter to Kraus. The handwriting changed at least four times in the two pages. But at least the content was harmless. I have not received an answer this time either, but gladly put up with this if only it helps you.

Your criticism of Pötzl did him great honour, because it was completely honest. He has now become a member, and his reply to respective reproaches is that he has since gone much more deeply into analysis. Also he is soon to go to Prague as successor to Pick[2]; this too will not be a disadvantage to us.

The Dutch are now getting serious about things. We recently received from them a pile of reviews of Dutch papers and polemical writings,[3] and a quite admirably clear and definite rebuttal of Jung's latest product on the psychology of the unconscious processes (1917).[4] A new local group is about to be formed in Warsaw.[5]

Otherwise there is little news. I am reading about Darwinism without any real aim, like someone with plenty of time before him, which may be appropriate in view of the paper shortage. The practice is still very busy, and also even interesting. Successes have been good. One of my sons (Ernst) is at present nearer to you than to me, he may be visiting his sister in Schwerin today. We receive occasional news of the other two, none of it bad. If the war lasts long enough, it will kill everybody off anyway.

Reik came to see me yesterday from darkest Montenegro. He is going back there, but like so many others he is expecting to be posted to the Western Front. He looks well, asked after you, and agreed to take several things with him to review. Yesterday I also read the preface to the second edition of Rank's *Artist*.[6] Farewell, go on being a brave Casimiro for me, and accept the most cordial greetings from
Your
   *Freud*

1. Reading uncertain; it might be a 19, corrected from 18, or vice versa.
2. Arnold Pick [1851–1924], neurologist in Prague, described the illness named after him (atrophy of parts of the brain) and pontine visual hallucinations. He had written a review of Freud's *On Dreams* (Pick, 1901).
3. Cf. the review of the Dutch literature by August Stärcke in the *Bericht über die Fortschritte der Psychoanalyse in den Jahren 1914–1919,* 1921: pp. 332–347.
4. Meyer, 1917.
5. Cf. the corresponding short note in the *Zeitschrift* (1919, 5: 228). The initiative had come from Eugenia Sokolnicka (née Kutner) [1884–1934], but eventually failed. After studying natural sciences and biology at the Sorbonne in Paris, Sokolnicka stayed at the Burghölzli [1911/12]; in 1913/14 she underwent analysis with Freud and was a member of the Vienna Society from 1916 to 1926; after the First World War she underwent a second analysis with Ferenczi. In 1921, as an "emissary" of Freud's, she went to Paris; however, she was rejected by the medical circles there. In 1926 she was co-founder and vice president of the Société Psychanalytique de Paris. Isolated and impoverished, she took her own life in 1934.
6. See letter 314F, 20 May 1917, n. 4.

## 333A

Allenstein
4 February 1918

Dear Professor,
Although there is not much new to report, I do not want to delay my reply any longer. I have in the meantime studied the issue of the *Zeitschrift* that has come out.[1] What is really good in the issue is by Ferenczi.*[2] I could contribute a great deal in confirmation, drawn from the experience of the war, of his main paper and might perhaps do so later on. This may well be the best paper that F. has written so far. Besides his smaller papers in this issue, his review of Schultz[3] is excellent. I know the author personally; we worked together for quite a long time here in the hospital, and I have even mentioned him earlier in my letters.[4] He is very talented, well educated in everything to do with psychoanalysis, but without any moral foundation. This characteristic also explains the article reviewed.

Pötzl's paper on dreams, which Sachs has promised me for reviewing,[5] arrived today, sent from Lemberg. The sender does not give his

1918 February

name. The copy contains a dedication to the Vienna Association. I shall write the review as soon as I can. I use most of my spare time with preparatory work for my paper for *Habilitation*. I had a letter from Bonhoeffer that does not hold out very much hope but does not completely bar the way. At any rate I want to make the attempt. I want to thank you again for overcoming such great resistances.

Our Dutch colleagues do indeed deserve appreciation for what they are achieving in these times. This increase of interest in the East, in spite of the war, promises well for peace time. But when will peace come? You, dear Herr Professor, are mistaken if you think that I remain completely untouched by the years. At times I too feel depressed, but so far have always succeeded in accepting the inevitable.

I hope you still have good news of your two sons at the front, and that you and your family there are as well as these times allow.

What is to become of our journals, when one more issue of each of them has appeared? When is Rank's second edition coming out?

I do not know whether I wrote to you that I have moved with my hospital. Address now: Artilleries-Mess Reserve Hospital. Unfortunately we also have to change our private quarters by 1 April; it is very difficult here to get a bearable replacement. The best place would be Berlin, but at present that is unattainable.

With the most cordial greetings from house to house,
Yours,

*Karl Abraham*

\* Tausk's article[6] disappoints me. Far too many words and little substance behind them.

1. The penultimate issue of the 1916/17 volume.
2. Ferenczi, 1917[195].
3. Ferenczi, 1917[205].
4. See letter 275A, 26 April 1915, & n. 6.
5. This review of Abraham's (1919[63b]), written later but published earlier than the one mentioned in letter 331A, 6 January 1918, is also not listed in the bibliography of his writings.
6. The second part of Tausk, 1916–17, in Roazen, 1991; cf. letter 324A, 2 November 1917, & n. 2.

334F

Vienna IX, Berggasse 19
17 February 1918

Dear Friend,

Yesterday my son Martin came home on leave from Tagliamento in "excellent shape". Ernst is also here, but not at all well. Thanks to a general eczema, Oli has a rather long stay in a Galician hospital.[1]

I received a booklet from Germany a few days ago that is bound to be of special interest to you. I cannot send it to you, because I want it to be generally known here, but you will be able to get it easily. It is called "War Neuroses and Psychic Trauma. Their Mutual Relations, Presented on the Basis of Studies in Psychoanalysis and Hypnosis"[2] by

Ernst Simmel, MD
at present senior physician of the H[ome Guard?] and doctor in charge
in a special hospital for war neurotics
With a preface by
Dr Adolf Schnee
Publisher Otto Nemnich, Leipzig—Munich
1918.

This is the first time that a German physician, basing himself firmly and without patronizing condescension on $\psi\alpha$ ground, speaks of its outstanding usefulness in the treatment of war neuroses and backs this with examples, and is also completely upright on the question of sexual aetiology. It is true that he has not gone the whole way with $\Psi\alpha$, takes essentially the cathartic standpoint, works with hypnosis, which is bound to conceal resistance and sexual drives from him, but he correctly apologizes for this because of the necessity of quick results and the large number of cases with which he has to deal. I think a year's training would make a good analyst of that man. His behaviour is correct.

The booklet was written in the hospital in *Posen* and is probably intended to be only the preliminary communication of a more detailed publication. I think you should read and review it for us; it will be easy for you, and I suggest it to you as a relief from your dissertation [*sic*] which does not seem to me to be promising much success in any case.

I hope we shall be able to continue with our journals. Heller seems to be in good form. We have ample material.—The world is surely in a muddle.

With cordial greetings to you and to your dear family,
Your faithfully devoted

*Freud*

1. Ernst had arrived on 18 January, Martin on 16 February; on 16 March Martin left again, and on 12 April Ernst was declared unfit for service. From 26 February until 13 March Oli was at home on his first leave (calendar entries, LOC).
2. Simmel, 1918. Ernst Simmel [1882–1947], Berlin physician, cofounder of the Society of Socialist Physicians and, during the First World War, chief physician and medical director of a special hospital for war neurotics in Posen (now Poznan in Poland). Analysed by Abraham, from 1920 on he was a director, along with Abraham and Eitingon, of the psychoanalytic polyclinic in Berlin. In 1927 he was director of the psychoanalytic sanatorium Schloss Tegel, near Berlin—the first psychoanalytic hospital.

In 1934 Simmel emigrated to Topeka, Kansas, and then moved to Los Angeles, where, with Otto Fenichel, he brought the psychoanalytic society there into being.

## 335A

Allenstein
12 March 1918

Dear Professor,

A few days ago I heard from Sachs that at the moment you have the joy of seeing all three sons home on leave. Certainly this time, however short it might be, has had a favourable effect on your mood. May a quick end to the war enable them to come home altogether, so that they can rest on their well-deserved laurels! I often think how hard it must have been for you and your wife to bear such worries for all these years. How are your two sons-in-law?

I sent for the book by Simmel and Schnee and have just read it. I too am amazed at the achievement and even more by the courage of the conviction, of the author as well as of his protector. I shall get in touch with the author and may thus be able to contribute something to winning him completely over to our interests. I find many of my own hospital experiences confirmed in the book. Perhaps a meeting with him may be possible, as Posen lies on the way from Allenstein to Berlin.

Our journals are continuing after all! Since we have managed to keep them going for so long, they will probably stay alive until peace comes. Whenever there is a small spark of hope making one think of peace, plans for projects automatically seem to start up in my mind. I must confess to you that I am already preparing a paper for the next Congress on giving a prognosis in $\psi\alpha$ treatment. I do not have sufficient material for other *theoretical* papers, but think I can speak definitively on a practical problem of this kind on the basis of my seven years' experience before the war. There are other reasons too for choosing such a subject.

The hard East Prussian winter seems to be about to end earlier this year than it usually does. At the beginning of April we have to move into another residence, very small-town, in an old house, but at least with a big garden, which is wonderful for the children. While my wife and I think nostalgically of Berlin, the children are completely happy in the small town.

Hoping to have good news from you and your family soon, I am, with cordial greetings from house to house,
Yours,

*Karl Abraham*

March 1918

## 336F

Vienna IX, Berggasse 19
22 March 1918

Dear Friend,

There is no need to explain the slip of the pen on the envelope![1] As the great offensive has now begun,[2] I assume your spirits will have been raised, if not by the hope of peace, at any rate by that of victory, and for that reason you will think my confession to being tired and weary of the struggle all the more irresponsible. As you see, I can hardly write legibly any more. Perhaps, as I have always been a carnivore, the unaccustomed diet contributes to my listlessness.

Two of my warriors have gone back, first of all to their former postings. The third, Ernst, because of his ailments, the worst of which is pulmonary catarrh, is in a position to be graded C or B and hopes for several months' leave so as to be able to go on with his studies in Munich. If travelling were not now forbidden and subject to all sorts of penalties, I should very much like to go to see my daughter and grandson at Easter, and Schwerin is not too far from Allenstein. But it cannot be done.

If you were free now, a vast field of work would be open to you as the natural intermediary with German neurology. Today—following in the wake of Simmel—I received a monograph from Lewandowsky's collection[3] (Vol. 15), called *Delusion and Realization* by Paul *Schilder* (Leipzig),[4] which is quite analytic in its conclusions, though it dutifully ignores the Oedipus complex. Sch. naturally writes as if these gentlemen had discovered everything, or most of it, by themselves. That, in short, is the way our findings will be "adopted" by German medicine. Not that it matters.

I recently sent you the proofs of the last issue[5] of the *Zeitschrift*, both because of my metapsychological efforts[6] and because of the—not exactly distinguished—reaction of Tausk to your paper on *ejaculatio praecox*.[7] We are continuing to print the journals, but Heller is ill and inaccessible, so that we are uncertain about the future. I wanted to persuade him to publish a fourth volume of my *Sammlung [kleiner Schriften] zur Neurosenlehre* and would have given him for that purpose a long case history that has been in store since 1914.[8]

I send my cordial greetings to you and to your dear wife,
Yours,

*Freud*

1. Instead of *Kasino* [officers' mess], Freud had written *Kaserne* [barracks].
2. The big "spring offensive" of German troops on the Western Front started on 21 March.
3. *Monographien aus dem Gesamtgebiete der Neurologie und Psychiatrie* [Monographs on the Whole of Neurology and Psychiatry].

4. Schilder, 1918. Paul Schilder [1886–1940], neurologist and psychiatrist from Vienna. Before the war he had been assistant at the psychiatric clinic in Leipzig, and after the war, he returned to Vienna and became a member of the Vienna Psychoanalytic Society [1919]. He worked in Wagner-Jauregg's psychiatric clinic, advocating and teaching a combination of psychiatry, brain pathology, and psychoanalysis. In 1925 professor, in 1929 head of the department for psychoses at the psychoanalytic polyclinic. Around 1930 he emigrated to New York City, where he was instrumental in introducing psychoanalysis into psychiatry and in developing psychoanalytic group therapy. (Cf. Mühlleitner, 1992: pp. 286–288; Roazen, 1985: pp. 151, 210, 254, 284.)
5. That is, the last issue of the 1916/17 volume.
6. Freud, 1916–17f, 1916–17g.
7. Tausk, 1917, cf. letter 323F, 5 October 1917.
8. The fourth volume of Freud's *Collection of Little Essays on the Theory of the Neuroses* did appear in 1918 with Heller, containing the case history of the Wolf Man (Freud, 1918b [1914]).

## 337A

Allenstein, Bahnhofstr. 82
(Please address letters to: "Reserve Hospital Artillerie-Kasino")
16 April 1918

Dear Professor,

We have an unpleasant time behind us. First the search for a new residence, then moving from an old house into one even older. We have increasingly learned to renounce our claims to comfort, and so we are succeeding, by repressing all the desires natural to city-dwellers, in feeling tolerably comfortable in our new home. There is, however, a big orchard, so that the children are completely happy. In spite of everything we are naturally always happy anew to be able to live here together. Only the unforeseeable nature of the exile is depressing.—I am very glad that recently you have not needed to worry about your two sons at the front. I hope there is nothing seriously wrong with the one at home.

Now I have to thank you for your letter and the proofs. I have only just been able to read the latter. I wanted to read the first of your two papers[1] through twice before letting you know my reactions. It is very difficult, and I had first to adjust myself to this new way of thinking. I believe I have now achieved this and can say that I have no serious objection to make. I shall now reread the whole series of articles and after that let you know again what I think. I already knew the draft of your melancholia paper[2] so that it was less of a surprise to me. I am pleased to note that my "incorporation phantasy" could be fitted into the wider framework of your theory.[3] I have no important criticisms of this paper either[4] and can only admire your ability to complete the edifice always a little more at such a time. One very minor criticism is the following. The so-called delusion of *inferiority* found in the melancholic[5] only appears to be such. Sometimes it is actually a delusion of grandeur, as for instance when the patient imagines that he has committed all the evil since the creation of world. Even though the self-reproaches may be aimed at the love-object, they signify at the same time a narcissistic over-estimation of the *own* criminal capacities (similar to obsessional neurotics who think themselves capable of monstrous crimes).

Next week I am going (in an official capacity) to the Psychiatric Congress in Würzburg. Afterwards I shall visit my mother and also stay a short while in Berlin. If time permits I may visit Simmel in Posen on my return journey.

My colleague Liebermann has become the father of a son. Otherwise I can report from here only that I have recently begun a new psychoanalysis which promises well, a fairly mild but instructive obsessional neurosis. I have heard from Reik and Sachs and shall be answering them both soon. Pötzl's experimental work on dreams is very difficult to read. I have not yet finished it, but I shall review it in a few weeks' time.

Most cordial greetings from house to house!

Yours,

 Karl Abraham

P.S.: Tausk's review is, like everything he writes, too long-winded, but contains some good points. Perhaps I shall still have something to say about it.—Are you really in agreement with Reik's small contribution to child psychology?[6]

1. Freud, 1916–17f.
2. Freud, 1916–17g.
3. See letter 273A, 31 March 1915, Freud, 1916–17g: pp. 249–250.
4. "When Freud published his 'Mourning and Melancholia'", Abraham later wrote in his *Study of the Development of the Libido* (1924[105]: pp. 437–438), "I noticed that I felt a quite unaccustomed difficulty in following his train of thought. I was aware of an inclination to reject the idea of an introjection of the loved object. . . . Towards the end of the previous year my father had died. During the period of mourning which I went through certain things occurred which I was not at the time able to recognize as the consequence of a process of introjection. . . . It thus appears that my principal motive in being averse to Freud's theory . . . was my own tendency to employ the same mechanism during mourning." Interestingly, Abraham had not mentioned his father's death in his letters to Freud.
5. Cf. Abraham, 1924[105]: p. 246.
6. Reik, 1917.

## 338A

Allenstein
19 May 1918

Dear Professor,

Your birthday has passed without your receiving a sign of life from me. My good wishes are no less sincere for being belated! At the beginning of May I went from the Psychiatric Congress in Würzburg to Bremen, where I found my mother gravely ill, so gravely that I dared not risk leaving for days on end. It was a complete failure of heart and kidneys, severe oedemas, and also a malignant tumour was suspected. It was only because I could not stay any longer that I went back to Allenstein. In the meantime she is for the moment out of danger, but her weakness is still very serious. I still receive news of her progress every day by telegram or express letter. You will not be angry with me that in these circumstances I postponed writing.

Otherwise we are getting on well here. We have settled down in our very primitive new accommodation. The big garden is a paradise for the children. My private work has recently increased. I do two hours of analysis daily and shall shortly be doing three. One of them, a case of obsessional neurosis, is improving very nicely.

For the children's holidays, which begin as early as the end of June, I shall probably take leave. Where we are going is still uncertain, but the present travelling circumstances oblige us to remain within the province.

I spent a few wonderful days in Würzburg enjoying art and natural scenery to the full. Apart from its architecture, Würzburg offers exceptional beauties of mediaeval and later sculpture. One evening, incidentally, I made the acquaintance of our critic Isserlin[1] in a small circle of colleagues. He sat opposite me and at once paid tribute to $\Psi\alpha$ by upsetting his glass. In other ways too I found him rather neurotic; I was also astonished to find he is of our race.

I have not yet managed to get around to writing the reviews on Pötzl and Simmel for the *Zeitschrift*; perhaps soon!

For a long time I have heard nothing from you and all the Viennese. I wrote a card to Sachs from Würzburg, but it came back recently as "inadmissible" because it was a picture post-card. Please give him a special greeting! I am so little in the mood for writing just now.

What news do you have from your sons at the front, and how are you all at home? Accept the most cordial greetings for you and your family from my wife and myself,
    Yours,
*Karl Abraham*

1. Max Isserlin [1879–1941], Munich neurologist, pupil of Kraepelin. He had criticized psychoanalysis in numerous articles. He went to England as a refugee and died there.

### 339F

Vienna IX, Berggasse 19
29 May 1918

Dear Friend,

You are passing through troubled times, I can tell. How could I take amiss your not writing more often? I know that you like writing when you have anything cheerful to say, but obviously that cannot be all the time.

My mother will be 83 this year and is now rather shaky.[1] Sometimes I think I shall feel a little freer when she dies, because the idea of her having to be told of my death is something from which one shrinks back.

So I have really reached 62, still unable to achieve that quiet, firm resignation that so distinguishes you as a German, though you use an Italian motto.[2] My prevailing mood is powerless embitterment, or embitterment at my powerlessness. Perhaps you yourself will remember a recent instance of this.

A fortnight ago Reik read us an excellent paper on Kol Nidre[3]; he has hit on Bible exegesis and will remain with it for a long time. But on Thursday morning he left for Mount Asolone, where violent fighting is taking place now. He is one of our hopes. My three sons are at present out of the firing line.

Ferenczi is taking a great deal of trouble to fix us up again in the Tatras, where he can spend the holidays with us.[4] He is likely to succeed for half the holiday period, we have no plans yet for the rest. I am very busy, but am already working grudgingly.

A remarkable feature of these times which I have not yet mentioned to you is the way in which we have been victualled for one year or so by patients and friendly followers. Actually we live on gifts, like a doctor's family in the old days. Our Hungarians, with Ferenczi and Eitingon at their head, as well as some Budapest families who stick to $\Psi\alpha$,[5] keep us supplied with cigars, flour, lard, bacon, etc., either free of charge or at incredibly low prices, and I have also found other such quartermasters here in Vienna. Thus the world shows me I have not lived in vain. I am now having my portrait done by a patient who has been restored to art[6]; it is the last that I am willing to have done for posterity.

I send my cordial greetings to you and your wife, and ask for nothing better than that you in turn should write to me about yourself.

Yours,

*Freud*

1918 June

1. Freud's mother Amalie, b. 1835; she died in 1930.
2. The famous "Corragio, Casimiro!"
3. Meeting of 15 May (Nunberg & Federn, 1975, only in German edition: p. 312). *Kol Nidre*, Hebrew [all vows]: Jewish prayer at the beginning of Yom Kippur (in Reik, 1919).
4. Ferenczi had arranged a stay for the Freuds there in 1917, in Csorbató [Lake Csorba]. In 1918, Freud first went to Budapest on 8 July, and on 1 August again to Csorbató, where he met up with his wife; on 11 August Anna, who had remained in Budapest, went to meet them. On 4 September Freud went to Lomnicz, and on 25 September to Budapest for the Fifth International Psychoanalytic Congress [28/29 September 1918].
5. Mainly Anton von Freund, Kata and Lajos Lévy, and Ferenczi's relatives.
   Anton von Freund (Antal Freund von Tószeghi) [1880–1920], Ph.D., the wealthy director of a brewery in Budapest, an analysand and friend of Freud's, who intended him to become a member of the Secret Committee. In 1918 von Freund donated a sum of almost two million crowns for the advancement of psychoanalysis; as a result of inflation as well as political and administrative problems, only a part of it could be used, and that primarily for the founding of the Verlag. Von Freund died of prostate cancer in the Vienna Cottage-Sanatorium, where Freud visited him daily during his last days.
   Kata F. Lévy [1883–1969], sister of Anton von Freund. Social-worker; analysed by Freud during the following summer. Later psychoanalyst and member of the Hungarian Society. In 1954 she and her husband emigrated to London, where they were both supported by Anna Freud. (Cf. Roazen, 1995: pp. 143–165.)
   Lajos Lévy [1875–1961], renowned Hungarian general practitioner, editor of the journal *Gyógyászat* [Medical Science]; founding member of the Hungarian Psychoanalytic Society [1913]. After the First World War he was director of the Jewish Hospital. Lévy was Ferenczi's friend and at times his analysand and physician; he was also consulted by Freud in the 1920s.
6. A pencil drawing by Rudolf Kriser, which seems to have been lost.

## 340A

Allenstein
21 June 1918

Dear Professor,

I received news practically at the same time from yourself and from Sachs, and am now once more well informed about everything that is going on in Vienna. I shall therefore write about *myself* again today.

Concern about my mother is less acute at present. She is no longer in immediate danger but still suffers from the persistent oedemas. I shall visit her at the beginning of July, when my leave begins. I am staying some 5–6 days in Bremen and shall then go east again and travel with my family for a few weeks to the seaside resort Rauschen [Address: Villa Benedicta, Seaside Resort Rauschen, East Prussia].[1] Apparently we have been lucky there with our room and board. Rauschen is a spa consisting only of villas, completely surrounded by a forest, which stretches down to the sea, dropping 20–50 metres to the beach in the form of a cliff. The landscape is very beautiful. I feel very much in need of a rest. My military duties are constantly quite exhausting, and in addition, my $\psi\alpha$ practice has developed during the last few months. I have to be pleased about this from a financial point of view, but it is an extra burden of 3–4 hours daily. These cases are partly also theoretically quite productive.

After my return from leave, the hours I have available are already filled. Thanks to your recommendation, Fräulein Haas from Mainz has turned to me, and we have arranged that she will arrive here at the beginning of August. She is also bringing her nephew, aged 11, for treatment.[2] From your letter written in January, which she enclosed, I have already acquainted myself with the difficulties of this case. Strangely enough, I had intended to write to you in this very letter that I should like to do some special work on this kind of resistance (on patients who do not associate during the session but do so at home instead). I've had a small number of cases of this kind—they appear rather difficult and therapeutically less favourable. It is reassuring to hear that you too have had difficulties with this kind of resistance. I was always afraid that this is due to some lack of technique. I should be very grateful for your advice in the matter of the honorarium. As far as possible I now usually ask 20 marks per hour; what do you think in the case of H.? Can I go beyond this rate?

What you write about the return to the system of payment in kind in your practice is quite familiar to me. These are strange times.

I hope your sons are still standing up well to all the vicissitudes of war. I wish you and yours a good rest in the Tatras. I was extremely pleased with your report on Reik's scientific achievements. I think highly of him.

I have not yet quite abandoned the hope of seeing you this year, dear Herr Professor! It would be a great joy, after almost four years.

With cordial greetings from house to house,
Yours,

*Karl Abraham*

1. Square brackets in original.
2. Probably the case of a phobia mentioned in Abraham, 1918[57]: pp. 66–67.

## 341A

Allenstein
11 August 1918

Dear Professor,

I have heard nothing from you for a very long time. But you received my last letter, as I know from Fräulein Haas. I assume that you have not had much inclination for correspondence. I very much hope that the planned meeting[1] will be ample compensation for the decline in our correspondence. I also hope that you and your family are as well as circumstances allow, and that you are having a good rest in the Tatras.

Fräulein H. has been here since 1 August. We are making good progress in illuminating her resistances; I am nevertheless very sceptical about success. Her twelve-year-old nephew, whom I am also treating—my first child analysis—promises very well.

Our holiday gave us quite a good rest. My colleague Liebermann is going on leave soon. He hopes to meet you in his hometown, Hamburg.

It is now nearly four years, dear Herr Professor, since I saw you. I am looking forward to Breslau to a quite extraordinary extent, and I expect these days—apart from the pleasure of anticipation, which is already doing me good now—will leave a really intensive effect.

With cordial greetings from house to house,
Yours,

*Karl Abraham*

1. The Fifth International Psychoanalytic Congress, originally planned to be held at Breslau.

## 342F

Csorbató
27 August 1918

Dear Friend,

You are right, I have not seen you since the beginning of the war. Correspondence has been no compensation for that. I am therefore quite specially looking forward to our meeting at the Congress in Breslau and hope that I shall have no travelling difficulties.

I did not answer your last letter, I think because I was then too angry and too starving. Here I have recovered and regained my composure. The reception in Budapest by my new friends was charming, the mountain air of the Tatras did the rest, and so for a time I can venture to join again in

Bearing the world's pleasure and the world's pain.[1]

I ascribe a good share of my better spirits to the prospects that have opened up in Budapest for the development of our cause. Materially we shall be strong, we shall be able to maintain and expand our journals and exert an influence, and there will be an end to the begging we have had to do heretofore. The man whom we shall have to thank for this is not merely a wealthy man, but a man of sterling worth and high intellectual gifts, who is greatly interested in analysis; he is in fact the sort of person whom one would have to invent if he did not already exist. Faithlessness on his part is out of the question. He is a Ph.D. but a beer brewer, and I think his youthful model was Jacobsen[2] in Copenhagen.

I think Sachs has already told you something about Dr von Freund, whom I am here describing. I shall have more to tell you when we meet. It is to be expected that Budapest will now become the headquarters of our movement.

Two of my sons are near us here in the Tatras, and there is no bad news of the third.

Cordial greetings to you and yours from

Your...

*Freud*

1. "... der Erde Lust, der Erde Leid zu tragen" (Goethe, *Faust I*).
2. Jens Peter Jacobsen [1847–1885], Danish novelist.

## 343A

Allenstein
2 September 1918

Dear Professor,

Your letter gave me twofold pleasure—because it brought me a sign of life from you after a long break and because it contained good news. I am eagerly looking forward to everything I shall hear in Breslau about Dr von Freund and his plans. Even more, though, to our meeting after such a long time. The programme already seems very full. I think the participants will exceed the number originally anticipated.

Fräulein Haas and her nephew left on 31 August. With her, I had not inconsiderable success in view of the short time, and with the boy I achieved what appears to be a breakthrough. Frl. H. will probably come back in October.

No news from us. Please send my cordial regards to all your family and also to those who signed the card I recently received,[1] and accept cordial greetings for you from my wife and myself!

Everything seems to be working out with accommodation in Breslau.

Yours,

*Karl Abraham*

1. Missing.

1918 October

## 344A

Allenstein
27 October 1918

Dear Professor,

Exactly a month has passed since our pleasant days in Budapest.[1] The opportunity for discussion we had there made correspondence dispensable for a while, but I should now like to resume it.

In the meantime, the conference on the neuroses has taken place in Berlin, and, as I already foresaw in Budapest, I was delegated to it. The political situation made it impossible for Simmel and me to intervene successfully for our cause. Since an early peace was then anticipated, one could hardly expect a receptive mood towards new ideas. Moreover, I was able to convince myself that hostility from psychiatric circles has remained unchanged. I cannot even say that I am unhappy about this, for I did not like the idea that psychoanalysis should suddenly become fashionable because of purely practical considerations. We would rapidly have acquired a number of colleagues who would merely have paid lip service and would afterwards have called themselves psychoanalysts. Thus our position as outsiders[2] will continue for the time being.

On the return journey from Budapest, and also more recently in Berlin, I have become more closely acquainted with Simmel. He has not yet in any way moved beyond the Breuer–Freud point of view, has strong resistances against sexuality, which he himself does not see clearly, and has unfortunately even stressed, at the Berlin meeting, that, according to his own experience, sexuality does not play an essential part in the war neuroses and the analyses. Perhaps he will develop further. But we must by no means overrate him. The letter you showed me in B. therefore does not give the complete picture.

Political events absorb so much of one's interest at present that one is automatically distracted from scientific work. All the same, some new plans are beginning to mature. I am making progress with Fräulein H. It remains to be seen what the therapeutic success will be. I have, though, discovered something new about obsessional counting. I shall only say for now that the connected compulsion to establish symmetry is among other things directly linked with the *hands* (fingers). In these, as in some cases I have previously analysed, the hands are an important erotogenic zone. So far nothing has been written in our literature about patients who at times of libidinal excitation get congestion in their *hands*. Fräulein H. for instance, during an infantile vision of an approaching large body (father), had the feeling that her fingers were swelling.—There seems to be complete success with the patient's young nephew.

I hope you are not suffering too much from the economic poverty in Vienna about which we now constantly read.[3] Here in East Prussia we are tolerably well off in this respect. But the political future is dark.

My wife is at present in Berlin. I am expecting her back tomorrow. How are you and all your family?

The change in my handwriting has to do with the new fountain pen I had from van Emden. It has much too fine a nib, but as you cannot buy a good system here now, I must be glad to have it.

With cordial greetings to you all,
Yours,

    *Karl Abraham*

When you write to me, dear Herr Professor, please let me know how Sachs is. I should also like to have van Emden's address.

1. The Fifth Psychoanalytic Congress [28–29 September 1918], organized by von Freund and held under the chairmanship of interim president Abraham, at which Ferenczi was elected president and von Freund secretary of the IPA. It was not truly international, as only citizens of the Central Powers could participate. Freud presented a paper on "Lines of Advance in Psycho-Analytic Therapy" (1919a [1918]), Abraham was discussant in the panel on war neuroses (1918[57]), the contributions to which were published as the first book of the Internationaler Psychoanalytischer Verlag. The congress was attended by high-ranking politicians and military officers, interested in psychoanalysis as a method for restoring war neurotics to health and thus to active service. (Cf. Clark, 1980: pp. 387–389; Freud, 1919c; Gay, 1988: pp. 375–376; Harmat, 1986: pp. 65–69; Jones, 1955: pp. 197–198; the report in the *Zeitschrift*, 1919, 5: 52–57.)
2. In English in original.
3. Vienna was facing a famine, as the "non-Austrian" provinces of the monarchy no longer delivered food to Vienna.

## 345A

Allenstein
24 November 1918

Dear Professor,

I do not know whether you have received the letter I wrote several weeks ago. I am writing again today to give my agreement to the draft[1] you sent me. I could scarcely propose changes or additions. I shall only express the hope that circumstances will soon enable us to make use of the fund.

We often talk about Vienna and all of you, but have no idea of how you are, not even whether you are staying in Vienna or whether you are suffering hardship. If it comes to a union between Germany–Austria and the Reich, I very much hope for easier contact between us in the future. Here in Allenstein the revolution took its course swiftly and bloodlessly. We have no reason to complain of the present order; on the contrary, we may feel satisfied if everything goes on developing so smoothly. Only the latter is questionable.[2]

Everything concerning our personal destiny is also questionable. I do not know yet when I can go back to Berlin, and *whether* I can—whether return with the family will be advisable because of the shortage of food.

I should be glad to know how you all are, and whether your sons have all come back in good health, also where Sachs is and how he is. Are Rank and Reik there again? Dear Herr Professor, I would not at all like to ask you for a detailed report. But perhaps you would encourage one of the younger friends to write to me. I do not know who is there, or I would approach one of them direct.

With the most cordial greetings and best wishes from house to house.

Yours,

*Karl Abraham*

1. See the next letter.
2. In a rapid succession of events, the German and Austro-Hungarian monarchies had collapsed: 3 November, armistice between Austria–Hungary and the Entente; 7 November, general demobilization, proclamation of the Bavarian People's Republic by Kurt Eisner in Munich; 9 November, abdication of Wilhelm II, revolution, and proclamation of the Council Republic by Karl Liebknecht in Berlin; 11 November, armistice with Germany and end of the war.

346F

Vienna IX, Berggasse 19
2 December 1918

Dear Friend,

I received your letter of a few weeks ago, but did not answer it immediately because there was something that I wanted to let mature first, and meanwhile I wanted to send you the statutes to have your opinion on them. When the latter failed to appear for such a long time, I also postponed the other news I had for you.

You will have seen from the statutes that I have undertaken the administration of the Bárczy fund.[1] From the interest I propose to award two annual prizes, as an honour to the winners, of course, not for the enrichment or compensation of the authors. One prize is to be for an outstanding medical paper, and the other for one of the *Imago* type. Provision is made for the division of the prize if two works are of outstanding merit, but the greater or smaller cash value of the prize should not be connected with any greater or smaller estimation of the value of the work. Each prize is of 1,000 crowns, which nowadays means very little. I chose the period of war up to the Budapest Congress as the first for which prizes are to be awarded; subsequently they will be awarded annually. In order not to have to exclude the best from the potential prize-winners, I did not appoint a panel of judges. What remains is my own unvarnished arbitrary decision, the reverse of the statutes!

On this occasion, I have decided to award the medical prize for two papers: *your* investigation into the earliest pre-genital stages of development of the libido (1916)[2] and *Simmel's* familiar booklet[3] (500 crowns each). The *Imago* prize is to go to *Reik* for his work on the puberty rites of savages.[4] You will already have noted that the prizes go, not to authors, but to their works. I must ask your forgiveness for the small scale of the whole arrangement. I did not want to put a heavier burden on the fund until its potentialities and the demands that will be made on it have grown clearer. Actually the revolution has limited it for the time being to a total of 250 m[ille], and Freund is now trying to reinforce it by associating it with the larger, already existing, fund for the city of Budapest. The interest of ¼ million amounts only to 10,000 crowns, and the foundation of the publishing house will rapidly reduce the capital. It is extraordinary how much money you have to have before you can do anything decent with it. Thus the prizes are only honours, an encouragement for the younger, recognition for the mature.

As I do not know whether Simmel is still in Posen, I shall ask you to trace his address, give him the news of the prize together with comments, and send him half of the amount when you receive it from me. I shall find out whether it is now possible to transfer money from Vienna to Germany. Otherwise please wait until this can be done.

I shall now answer your questions. Sachs is in Davos Platz, Eisenlohr Hotel, writes often and is very well. He wants me to emigrate to Switzerland!! He owes many thanks to Liebermann, to whom I send my best wishes, for his advice. Reik is in Vienna. Rank is not yet completely fixed, as he has to travel between here and Budapest. His fate, and that of the publishing house, will be decided in the next two weeks. He has, to *everyone's* surprise, brought home a little wife[5] from Cracow, who up to now has not met with the approval of any of the friends. Whether it will be a big mishap will appear only gradually. A direct letter arrived from Jones by way of Zurich, with the news that he has lost his young wife, apparently in the course of an operation.[6]

My son Martin has not come home, and all the information points to his whole unit having been taken prisoner without a battle.[7] Thus this would not be the worst. We have had no news about his personal fate since 25 October. Ernst is in Munich, and Oli reached home unrobbed.[8] The restrictions are serious here, the uncertainties great, and my practice naturally minimal. The Society has not yet met. Eitingon is back in Berlin, 3 Güntzelstrasse; did you know that?

I send my cordial greetings to you and yours.

Your faithfully devoted

*Freud*

1918   December

1. Von Freund's donation, named after Dr István Bárczy [1866–1943]. From 1906 to 1917 he was mayor of Budapest, from 1917 to 1918 Lord Mayor, from 25 November 1919 to 14 March 1920 Minister of Justice, then member of parliament until 1931. He had participated in the Budapest Congress as the official delegate of the capital. There, Freud had reported that "the mayor of Budapest, who presided over the collected sum [of von Freund's fund], had placed it at his (Professor Freud's) personal disposal" (*Zeitschrift*, 1919, 5: 56–57). (Cf. Freud, 1919c.)
2. Abraham, 1916[52].
3. Simmel, 1918.
4. Reik, 1915b.
5. In November, Rank had married Beata ("Tola") Mincer (Münzer) [1896–1967], born in Poland, and for this reason he reconverted to Judaism. Beata Rank became an analyst herself, was a co-worker in the Verlag, and translated Freud into Polish. She tried to mediate in the later conflicts between Rank and Freud and maintained amicable relations with Freud. In 1926 she emigrated with her husband, first to Paris, where the two separated, and in 1936 to Boston, where she became a noted child analyst, training and supervision analyst, as well as chair of the "Educational Committee" at the Boston Psychoanalytic Institute. (Cf. Roazen, 2001a: pp. 205–215.)
6. Jones's wife Morfydd, née Owen [b. 1891], a composer and singer from Wales, had died in September 1918 amid circumstances that are not entirely clear even today (see Freud & Jones, 1993: p. 324).
7. The Austro-Hungarian High Command had ordered the cessation of hostilities for 1: 20 p.m. on 3 November 1918, but Italy complied on 4 November, in accordance with the terms agreed upon, whereby four hundred thousand Austrian soldiers—among them Martin Freud—were taken prisoner by the Italians without a struggle.
8. Referring to the revolution.

## 347A

Allenstein
15 December 1918

Dear Professor,

Your letter of 2 December has had a lengthy journey. Before taking up all its other contents, I should like to express the hope that your son Martin has in fact suffered no worse fate than being taken prisoner with his unit. Perhaps you will have had news of him meanwhile, or at least have found out more about the whereabouts of his regiment.

Now, my thanks for your award for my 1916 paper! I had not expected, as one of the older men, to be considered at all. But as it was, compared with the older ones, the younger colleagues were in fact less able to produce any scientific work during the war. Apart from your own work, there have been very few contributions to clinical $\Psi\alpha$ during these years. The sum of money, though it has little value in these times, will be used for a long-postponed wish-fulfilment—a visit to Vienna—as soon as circumstances permit. I shall write to Simmel today. The money has already been confirmed by my Berlin bank. I shall pass half of it on to Simmel as soon as I have his present address.

I was very pleased to hear good news of Sachs. And I hope that what you tell me about Rank is nothing unpropitious. I did not know that Eitingon was in Berlin.

I was discharged from the army yesterday, but shall stay here with my family over Christmas, partly because of my practice—3 analytic cases—and partly for other practical reasons. I was in Berlin at the beginning of last week and took a furnished flat on a temporary basis. I dare not, in these uncertain circumstances, enter into a long tenancy agreement for a fixed period. Our present flat is outside the city. It will also give us some indication as to whether it is possible to practise away from the centre. The address is: 6 Schleinitzstrasse, Berlin-Grünewald. We have the lower floor of a two-family villa with veranda and garden, seven rooms and entrance hall, respectably furnished. The practice promises well: two analyses certain, two probable, one still uncertain. When I have announced my return in B. there will probably be more to come. I hope that living outside town will be good for my health, which suffered from the eastern climate. It is glorious for the children, especially as there are excellent schools in the garden city.

Liebermann is staying here a little longer, as at first only one of us can be spared.

When you write again, dear Herr Professor, please write to the Berlin address, where I hope to arrive on the 30th. With the most cordial greetings from house to house and with the wish that 1919 will be better than previous years,

Yours,

*Karl Abraham*

## 348F

Vienna IX, Berggasse 19
25 December 1918

Dear Friend,

So I can write to you in Berlin again! The nightmare of war has ended for you too. I feel convinced that your practice will quickly regain its old level, and my only wish is that your health will improve to the same extent. What you say about the prize was not without a certain sting for me. Having suddenly acquired wealth, I have simultaneously to admit how inadequate it is in relation to my intentions. I did not want to make any distinction between the beginners and the masters of analysis, because in this case I should not have found the models to hold up for aspirants to follow.

The publishing house has not yet been established; like everything else one sets about doing nowadays, it is meeting with great difficulties, but I think that we shall succeed. We have appointed you and Hitschmann to be among the editors of the *Zeitschrift* and wish you in particular to concern yourself with the preparation of the annual report, which will be published as a supplement to the *Zeitschrift*. Hitschmann's special task will be to look after the reviews, which are intended to be models of thoroughness and seriousness. I am already in direct touch with Jones by way of Sachs, but we cannot yet get material from him. Rank seems to have done himself a great deal of harm with his marriage. A little Polish–Jewish woman whom nobody likes, and who does not seem to have any higher interests. It is quite sad and scarcely comprehensible.

I have no news of Martin, and still do not know where he is. That contributes to the depression of these times.

Deuticke announced today the payment for the *Danish* translation of the five lectures[1]; thus a minor victory. One of these days I shall be entrusting to the post the fourth volume of my *Kleine Schriften*,[2] directed to your new address.

Freund turned up at my house today to continue his analysis.

I wish you from the depths of my heart all the luck you deserve in the new life you are beginning!

Your faithfully devoted

*Freud*

1. Freud, 1910a [1909], Danish edition, in *Det ubevidste,* transl. O. Gelsted (Copenhagen: Martins, 1920).
2. See letter 336F, 22 March 1918, & n. 8.

# 1919

### 349A
Berlin-Grünewald, Schleinitzstrasse 6
20 January 1919

Dear Professor,

First my congratulations on the good news you have had of your son Martin! Eitingon told me about it yesterday. We are deeply happy for all of you that this great worry has been lifted from you.

In your letter you notified me of the 4th volume of the *Kleine Schriften*. I waited to write so as to be able to confirm that the book had arrived, but it did not come until yesterday. I cannot but admire the sheer quantity that you have achieved in such times. I have begun at once to read the so far unpublished analysis,[1] in the meantime thank you for the enjoyable hours you gave me yesterday evening, and I shall come back to it in the next letter.

Meanwhile I heard from Rank that the foundation of the Verlag has taken place. I heard a few more details from Reik this very day. You must excuse the fact that I have not yet got into touch with Hitschmann, nor have I sent in my Budapest paper.[2] It is not usually my way to be careless about these things. I have not been well recently because of the stubborn bronchial and nasal catarrh that I brought back from East Prussia. I have now been treated for a week by Fliess, with very good results. Until a few days ago I had bad nights and was glad when I had finished my practice. I had to use the free time for resting. But I have now done the greater part of the paper and hope to complete it in two days. I should be grateful, dear Herr Professor, if you would inform Rank of it; I shall be writing to him in detail as soon as I am no longer so tired in the evenings.

Fräulein Haas is leaving tomorrow with her nephew. She was a pillar of my practice for a long time. Her obsessional symptom has not disappeared, but in other respects she is better. The nephew has been to a large extent a success.

In Berlin we are apparently over the worst of the riots, and we are approaching the final external peace.—In our furnished flat, in the middle of the most beautiful part of the garden city, we can bear it for the present, but are longing for a permanent home. The food situation here is naturally less favourable than in East Prussia, but has at any rate not deteriorated any more in the last few months. What does it look like where you are?

Liebermann too is now discharged from the army. Dr Böhm,[3] who was in Munich up to now, is probably also settling in Berlin.

Most cordial greetings, also from my wife, for you and all your family!

Yours,

*Karl Abraham*

1. Freud, 1918b [1914].
2. Abraham, 1918[57].
3. Felix Böhm [1881-1958], member of the IPA since 1913. He worked at the Berlin Psychoanalytic Institute from 1920 to 1936 and became secretary of the German Psychoanalytical Society in 1931. His was instrumental in the "aryanization" of psychoanalysis during the Nazi regime.

## 350F

Vienna IX, Berggasse 19
5[1] February 1919

Dear Friend,

First, let me state that it is bitterly cold here in this room, and then let me add that I have heard with pleasure from various sources about your improved state of health and the arrival of your review. But I have nothing yet from E. Simmel[2]; I have had no word from him, and you do not mention him in your letter either.

The preparations to set up the Verlag are progressing very well. Rank is really outstandingly competent and keen. The second issue of the *Zeitschrift* is almost completely in type, the first is on the way from Czechia, and paper has been bought. There is talk of Rank's going to Switzerland to meet Jones there and perhaps build up the organization a little further.[3] We are delighted to be able to work in our *jardin secret*[4] while the storm lays waste to everything outside.

Activity in the societies here, in Budapest and in Holland, is lively. We hope the same will soon be true of yours in Berlin.

The last few weeks have brought me several new editions and translations, of which the most recent is the *Leonardo*.[5] The first half of the Dutch translation of the *Lectures*[6] has appeared, and a Danish translation of the American lectures is assured.

I have been lingering not unintentionally on the bright side of things. Depicting the other side would take us too far afield. I am very busy, but ———. Of Martin, who is in Genoa, we have since had no news. In any case, he would not be missing any work here. I was recently visited by an American from Wilson's staff.[7] He came accompanied by two baskets of food and exchanged them for copies of the *Lectures* and the *Everyday Life*.[8] He gave us confidence in the President.

I send my cordial greetings to you and your dear wife.

Yours,

*Freud*

1. Reading uncertain; could also be a 4.
2. Simmel, 1919a.
3. On 10 February, in a circular letter, Pfister and Mira and Emil Oberholzer proposed the founding of a Swiss Society for Psychoanalysis. The organizational meeting took place on 21 March, the first meeting three days afterwards, with guest lectures by Jones, Rank, and Sachs on "Psychoanalysis as an Intellectual Movement"; affiliation with the IPA was also decided upon there.
    The First Chair was Emil Oberholzer [1883–1958], who remained president until 1927; in that year he founded his own purely medical psychoanalytic group, which dissolved after his emigration in 1938. With his wife, the child-analyst Mira Gincburg [1887–1949], he went to New York, where he became a member of the Society there.
4. Literally, hidden garden; French expression for one's most intimate feelings and thoughts.
5. Freud, 1910c (second edition 1919).
6. Freud, 1916–17, vol. 1, transl. A. W. van Renterghem (Antwerp: Maatsch, 1918).
7. Thomas Woodrow Wilson [1856–1924], twenty-eighth president of the United States [1913–1921]. William Christian Bullitt [1891–1967], then working in the State Department as an administrative adviser to Wilson. He met Freud through his wife, who was in analysis with Freud; Bullitt himself would also become an analysand of Freud's. Bullitt and Freud collaborated on a book on the president (Freud & Bullitt, 1966), the extent of Freud's contribution to which is controversial.
8. Freud, 1901b.

## 351A

Berlin-Grünewald, Schleinitzstrasse 6
23 February 1919

Dear Professor,

In spite of the unquiet times, there seems to be much scientific activity in Vienna. I was glad to hear about the development of the Verlag, the new editions, and the activity of the societies. There is naturally only a very modest amount of scientific life to report on from here. Our group now has three meetings a month, two of them on medical subjects and one on an *Imago* topic. Last time Liebermann gave a lecture on certain bisexual phenomena in obsessional neurosis,[1] with which I was rather pleased. Simmel must first *become*. He is not yet far beyond the cathartic stage and seems to me to be in need of analysis himself. Eitingon is unfortunately too unproductive. Frau Horney is very keen, the others are scientifically scarcely worth considering. Böhm from Munich, who is probably moving here in April, will apparently be a good acquisition.

I am writing a short paper about patients who persistently avoid free association and hope to send the manuscript to Rank in a week or two.

It is a paper I read in our first meeting.[2] This week I shall speak about animal totemism in dreams.[3] My health is fairly good now so that I am able to cope well with my work. My practice is growing. It has recently provided me with various new findings, which I hope to make use of soon; among others, some contributions to the theory of the erotogenic zones, with special reference to the *eye*.[4] A most instructive case of writer's cramp gave me some nice material about the hand as an erotogenic zone.

Rank sent me the table of contents for the 2nd issue of the *Zeitschrift*. I find in it, among others, a heading "Putnam †".[5] Do you know any details about this?

The first two months of my practice have proved that it is possible to live as well as to practise away from the centre of town. I would not like to return to the centre, but it is very difficult to find suitable accommodation out here. Our current one is only a temporary solution, and after three years of Bohemian existence we should like to live comfortably again.

Have you any news from Genoa? And how are you all? It is quite like spring here already. If the weather is the same in Vienna, at least you need not suffer so much from the shortage of coal any more. In this respect we are well off, but in others living conditions are still pretty difficult here. You are right that it is as well for the time being to bury oneself in science. It is good that our science gives us such hopeful prospects for the future!

With the most cordial greetings from house to house,
Yours,

*Karl Abraham*

1. "Obsessional Neurosis and Bisexuality", 20 February 1919 (*Zeitschrift*, 1919, 5: 230).
2. Abraham, 1919[58], read on 6 February 1919 (*Zeitschrift*, 1919, 5: 230); cf. the case of Frau Haas, letter 340A, 21 June 1918.
3. Abraham, 1919[59], read on 16 March 1919 (ibid.).
4. Cf. Abraham, 1920[67]: pp. 352–353.
5. Freud's obituary (1919b) of Putnam (signed "The editor"), who had died in November 1918.

## 352A

Berlin-Grünewald
1 April 1919

Dear Professor,

I too was very sorry that the publication of the Congress volume was so badly delayed through Simmel's fault. I have urged him many times, but all in vain. In the middle of February I wrote a letter to Rank, in which I made clear to him my opinion of S. This letter came back after four weeks! My proof of the Pötzl review[1] also came back to me, and I sent it off for the second time. I hope that I too have not gained a reputation for slovenliness. You, dear Herr Professor, and Reik as well, make unclear references to Simmel. But I am interested *to know what has happened*. I even have a special interest in it, because S. wants to be analysed by me.* He should be here for the first session at this very moment but did not turn up. His resistances are *very* great. You obviously did not see them in Budapest and let yourself be deeply influenced by the one very sympathetic letter. Later I had occasion to have my view of him, which was divergent from the beginning, confirmed many times. The resistances, however, are balanced by a strong positive interest and an intelligence that grasps things rapidly. I shall tell you more later. I should like to take this opportunity to say that in my opinion yet another adept is being overestimated, namely Pötzl. I altered the review only reluctantly at the time. I have the impression that all of you in Vienna still greet every influx from the academic side with too great an optimism. In P., the resistances seem to me to *outweigh* the few positive elements in his work. He may be more positive in the sessions there; in any case, in his writings he has not risked anything up to now.

I heard from Sachs and Rank directly from Switzerland, and I am pleased that Sachs has had a good convalescence.[2] I myself am in quite good health. The practice is satisfactory as far as finances are concerned, and recently has been particularly pleasing from a scientific point of view.

We are still living in our temporary lodgings. It is very difficult to find anything definite, but I hope we shall have some success soon.

I am sending off a very short manuscript in the course of the week. It is a supplement to Ferenczi's *Sunday Neuroses*.[3] No. 1 of the *Zeitschrift* satisfied me very much. Tausk[4] is good, Ferenczi[5] as always. It was only in retrospect that I discovered in vol. 4 of your *Schriften* the new work on virginity.[6] Perhaps sometime I shall get around telling you about a few observations I made that prove your point of view very well.

I hope that you and your family are all well, and that you also have good news of Martin. Please let me have an answer to my question above about S.!

With cordial greetings from house to house,

Yours,

    *Karl Abraham*

* Especially because of his work inhibitions.

P.S.: As Simmel himself telegraphed yesterday that the manuscript has been sent off, I did not send an additional telegram.

1919 April

1. Abraham, 1919[63b].
2. At the Budapest Congress, Sachs had been stricken with a severe pulmonary hemorrhage. He subsequently went to Davos, Switzerland, where he was able to cure his tuberculosis.
3. Abraham, 1919[61].
4. Tausk, 1919; today considered a classic.
5. Ferenczi, 1919[210].
6. Freud, 1918a.

353F

Vienna IX, Berggasse 19
13 April 1919

Dear Friend,

It still is no postal service if a letter arrives on the 11th day.

In the case of Simmel, I can easily put you in the picture. We had decided to strike out his name from the notifications and bring out the booklet without him if he kept us waiting yet again. It was also a suspicious phenomenon that he did not manage to write a word in reply to the awarding of the prize. I gave the prize to the publication, not the person, and as far as that goes I am not sorry. I feel, too, that S., like Breuer at the time, can personally not endure his own findings.

With regard to an over-estimation of Pötzl, it is not as bad as that here. We rather enjoy the piquancy of the situation that the first aid of the [psychiatric] clinic associates himself with $\Psi\alpha$, but we made him spend years courting us and are very well informed about his ambiguous character. His very notable intelligence and scientific training are in his favour; if he does nothing for us, we shall put up with the situation very well. We just did not wish to let him be rejected for so long, as he was enthusiastic. Optimism regarding academic circles has no place with us.

Rank is back; in view of the uncertainties of the recent situation in Hungary,[1] he did not commit himself in any way, but he made many contacts. He found Jones as devoted to us as ever. He wants a congress, or at any rate a meeting of the committee, in Holland in the autumn. I hope it will be possible.

Your two parcels have been received with many thanks. The technical paper[2] is particularly good and topical. What is perhaps missing is that the whole attitude derives from the father complex. Printing is going ahead.

The state of our affairs is in conformity with the troubled times. Ernst is cut off from us in Munich, and from the prisoner we have rare, not unsatisfactory news.

With cordial greetings to you and your dear family,
Yours,

*Freud*

1. The Károlyi government had collapsed under the pressure of foreign and domestic policy crises. On 20 March the government had announced its resignation, and on 21 March the "Revolutionary Governing Council" under Béla Kun [1866–1939] and Sándor Garbai had assumed power and proclaimed the short-lived [until 1 August] "Hungarian Council Republic". Under these circumstances, access to von Freund's fund was threatened.
2. Abraham, 1919[58].

354A

Berlin-Grünewald
5 May 1919

Dear Professor,

This letter was meant to reach you on 7 May,[1] but it will arrive some days later after all. My good wishes are nonetheless sincere! I had hoped to be able to send you a scientific contribution in honour of the day, as I have done several times previously. The paper in question will, however, be more extensive than I had anticipated and, because of my limited leisure, will not be ready for some weeks. It uses your recent publication on the taboo of virginity as a point of departure and deals with the castration complex in women; I think it contributes something new. Some days ago I spoke in our Society about this topic.[2] We have had regular meetings since the end of the war, and they are far more productive than they used to be. I now have our colleague S.[immel] under treatment! His resistances are not, as you thought, of the Breuer type, at least not principally so, but mainly *narcissistic*. As long as he was *alone* and could feel himself a discoverer, it was all right; but he cannot bear to be a part of the organization in which he is not the first. His resistances to treatment are enormous, and I do not know whether I shall master them.

For myself, I can report that my health is now fairly satisfactory. The practice is lively and will become more lucrative in due course. I have the impression from my analyses that I have made progress in technique in spite of the long interval. My handling of neuroses and psychoses at the military hospital was certainly less intensive in each single case but gave me much insight and extended my experience.—You may be interested to hear that I have recently begun the analysis of a case of *paranoia querulans*—most instructive and fully confirming your views.

Eitingon will write to you very soon. He was in Leipzig for quite a time, as his brother died.[3] Earlier he reviewed your work on the infantile neurosis[4] for us on one evening. At the penultimate session Frau Dr Horney made an excellent analysis of a remarkable infantile female neurotic (perhaps hebephrenic).[5] Liebermann is very enthusiastic, and so is our new member Böhm.

We are still without a permanent home, as our circumstances are very difficult altogether. My family are well, and I hope you and your family are likewise.

We shall soon have to decide whether there is to be a congress and where it should take place. Holland seems to be the most suitable country, although the exchange rate makes this journey very difficult, particularly for the Austrians. I would be in favour of writing round to the societies *immediately* in order to find out whether there would be enough participants for Holland.

Is there no hope, dear Herr Professor, of you coming to Germany (Hamburg)?

With cordial greetings from house to house,
Yours,

Karl Abraham

1. Actually, Freud's birthday was on 6 May.
2. Abraham, 1920[67], presented before the Berlin Society on 17 April (*Zeitschrift*, 1919, 5: 231).
3. Vladimir or Valdemar Eitingon, Max Eitingon's elder brother, who had run the American branch of the family fur business (Mary-Kay Wilmers, personal communication). A year earlier, one of his legs had had to be amputated because of a cryptogenetic sepsis, which finally also caused his death around Easter, 1919 (Eitingon to Freud, 19 June 1919, SFC).
4. The "Wolf Man" analysis.
5. Sessions on 20 March and 8 April (*Zeitschrift*, 1919, 5: p. 230).

## 355F

Vienna IX, Berggasse 19
18 May 1919

Dear Friend,

The period of my birthday brought me a great many congratulations, dotted about all over the place from the 1st to the 7th; my own brother settled for 3 May, though he should have known better. These uncertainties contain a perfectly accurate criticism of this practice, which, like so many other things, should now be ripe for abolition. I read with much satisfaction in your letter the news about your health and your practice. What you say about S.[immel] sounds very strange. The man must at least have read Breuer when he began his work, and could not fail for a moment to recognize that he is practising the catharsis taught by Breuer. Perhaps it would be more economical to let him go; then he will never complete anything more. I have, moreover, made the acquaintance of that P. Cassian who was concerned in the business with him and Schnee. According to this witness, absolutely nothing would be left of S.'s originality.

The first book published by the Verlag now lies ready before me, that on the war neuroses. I do not regard it as an outstanding achievement, but perhaps for that very reason it will make an impression on our honoured contemporaries. Number 2, Ferenczi,[1] is soon to follow. We are completely cut off from Budapest; we know only that Ferenczi has become an official teacher of $\Psi\alpha$.[2] The embassy here has paid us out 1/5 of the fund; the remainder does not seem to be endangered. A congress this year seems to be still out of the question, as Emden also agrees, it might perhaps be possible to organize a meeting of the members of the committee or of presidents of the societies, but that too is still doubtful. Just as the war deprived us of the activity of the Berlin headquarters, so is the revolution now depriving us of the activity of the Budapest headquarters. Actually a change in organization seems to be indicated.

Kraus and Brugsch have again reminded me of my promise to produce an article on the $\psi\alpha$ theory of the neuroses for their handbook by 20 April. The recognition of $\Psi\alpha$ in the syzygiology[3] of the former is very meagre. Friedländer,[4] a real medical "subject" in Heinrich Mann's sense of the word,[5] has sent us his character-study of Wilhelm II from the *Umschau*! I conclude from this symptom that the Hohenzollerns are finally done for. Of all the rats, this Fr. is the most loathsome.

My wife is now in bed with true influenzal pneumonia,[6] but it seems to be going well; we are told not to worry.

With cordial greetings to you and your family,

Yours,

*Freud*

1. Ferenczi, 1919[223].
2. Supported by two petitions by medical students [autumn 1918 and 28 January 1919], Ferenczi had, despite strong opposition, been appointed Professor of Psychoanalysis by the new Minister of Education Zsigmond Kunfi during the Council Republic on 25 April 1919—the first professorship for psychoanalysis ever.
3. Greek: "compilation".
4. See letter 21A, 23 February 1908, n. 7.
5. Heinrich Mann [1871–1950], *Der Untertan* [*The Subject*] (1914), first novel of the trilogy *Das Kaiserreich*, a trenchant critique of German submissiveness to the authorities.
6. Martha Freud had fallen ill with a severe influenza, from which she would not recover for several months (Jones, 1957: p. 10). In 1918/19, the so-called Spanish influenza was raging in all of Europe; more people died from it than had died during the war, among them Freud's daughter Sophie [25 January 1920].

## 356A

Berlin-Grünewald
3 June 1919

Dear Professor,

Transport between Berlin and Vienna is still very slow and irregular. A direct train runs only twice a week. We have almost gone back to the time of the mail-coach. I hope with all my heart that in the time since you sent me your last letter your wife's condition has improved completely. We too have not quite finished with the influenza. If you cannot manage to give me some information in the near future about the course of the illness, you might perhaps entrust it to Rank, who often needs to write to me in any case! Your eldest son's imprisonment is probably almost at an end. The latest news gives us hope for an agreement in the course of this month after all.

*5 June.* Two very full days have prevented me from continuing my letter. Apart from work in the practice, which now fills the whole of my day, I have tried almost daily during the last five months to find a permanent home. The last two days were—besides work—completely filled with negotiations on this subject. At last we found a very suitable flat for 1 October, so we must make do with our temporary lodgings for another four months. Incidentally, these last months have proved that patients do not mind coming out as far as the Grünewald colony, and I have now rented a place very near our present refuge.

Meanwhile, the issue on war neuroses has arrived. Jones's contribution[1] interests me particularly, but I have not been able to read it yet.

As you know, among my patients there is also Dr S. He is definitely making progress. I may soon be able to give a final favourable report on him. I do not know whether I mentioned in my last letter that I have taken on the analysis of a *paranoia querulans*. It is progressing very successfully. The patient has lost interest in those things about which he was querulously complaining, has utterly changed, and is making a surprising switch-over from man to woman. He is a complete and brilliant confirmation of the theories you develop in your *Schreber*.[2] It is the sort of case where one would least expect to achieve a therapeutic influence. This man, who two months ago had no thoughts or words other than querulous ones, said to me today: "I'm feeling damned well." The speed of the improvement can probably be accounted for by only one factor—the patient's homosexuality had been very little repressed, and its significance became evident to him very rapidly.

It is weeks since I have written anything. The paper I promised on the female castration complex got stuck right at the beginning. Now that flat-hunting is over, I hope to become more productive once again.

What do you think at your end about a meeting or a congress in the course of the year? The Hague is hardly feasible while going abroad is so difficult. We here would be *very* pleased if a German town were considered, and our Society asks that this proposal should be given some thought!

I have not heard any more from Reik. He was supposed to come to Berlin some time ago.

In conclusion, I again send my best wishes for your wife's speedy recovery. With the most cordial greetings from house to house,

Yours,

*Karl Abraham*

1. Jones, 1918.
2. Freud, 1911c [1910].

357F

Vienna IX, Berggasse 19
6 July 1919

Dear Friend,

You are right, this is still not a proper correspondence. There are also weeks in which for some inner reason one cannot bring oneself to take a pen in hand. My wife has, I can say, completely recovered. She is going on the 15th inst. to the Parsch Sanatorium near Salzburg, and at the same time my sister-in-law and I are going to Gastein. (Her doctor insists on trying a high-altitude climate and a completely quiet life.) My daughter is trying to arrange a visit to Bavaria, near Reichenhall, with a friend.[1]

Do not be surprised that we are choosing such expensive holidays in these times. Everything near Vienna is even more expensive, almost prohibitive, most summer resorts are forbidden, and anything to do with foreign travel is still unbearably bothersome. And yet we do not want to give up a possible recreation as long as it is warm. Who knows how many of us will survive next winter, which is expected to be bad. And the certainty of financial decline as a result of our national situation does not encourage thrift.

We were completely cut off from Budapest for 3–4 weeks. Now Rank can speak to his journal[2] there by telephone again, and we are hoping in this way to learn the essentials about what is happening to Ferenczi and Freund.

Tausk shot himself a few days ago.[3] You remember his behaviour at the Congress. He was weighed down by his past and by the recent experiences of the war; he should have been married this week, but could not struggle on any longer. Despite his outstanding talents, he was of no use to us.

1919 August

*Interpretation of Dreams* and *Leonardo* have come out now, *Everyday Life* is expected this month.[4] Then they will certainly come to you too. Jones wants to visit me in Gastein.[5]

Rank is staying in Vienna; he is expecting to become a father soon.[6]
With cordial greetings to you and yours,
Yours,

*Freud*

1. Anna spent the holidays in Bayrisch Gmain, between Salzburg and Reichenhall, with Margarethe Rie, the daughter of Freud's friend Oskar Rie (and later the wife of analyst Herman Nunberg). Both young women were in analysis with Freud at the time.
    On 13 August, the Freud family went to Munich to visit Ernst; subsequently they went to Badersee near Garmisch-Partenkirchen in Bavaria. During this time Martin returned to Vienna after his imprisonment.
2. A newspaper of which Rank was the representative, and which he contacted by telephone every evening.
3. On 3 July (cf. Freud's obituary, 1919f).
4. Freud, 1900a (fifth edition; like the fourth, with contributions by Otto Rank), 1910c (second edition), 1901b (sixth edition).
5. Jones could not get a passport before peace was concluded; at the end of September, he and Eric Hiller were the first foreign civilians to come to Vienna after the war.
6. His only child, Helene (named after Helen of Troy), was born on 23 August 1919; she was a psychotherapist in San Francisco and Seattle, and she died in 1999.

## 358A

Berlin-Grünewald
3 August 1919

Dear Professor,

I greet you on your summer holiday and wish for you in the coming weeks as much rest and pleasant impressions as you need, according to your last letter. The same good wishes apply also to your sister-in-law. Your wife has, I hope, arrived in Salzburg in good shape and is on the road to complete recovery. We in Berlin are having such a cool summer that we do not strive to leave the city as much as usual. And besides, we live a very idyllic life in our garden city, in the woodlands so to speak, with a large veranda, garden, etc. That makes staying here much easier. At the same time, for 3¼ years we have had only what will go into suitcases for a journey. Our things are still in store, packed away so that we cannot get to them until we move into our final home. After more than three years of life à la *chambre-garnie* we long for home comforts more than for new temporary arrangements. Recently we travelled the short distance to Bremen to show my mother the children, whom she had not seen during our three years in East Prussia.

Although I too think about the future without much optimism, I do not see it *just* as black as you must in Vienna. At least at the moment we are not going further downhill here.

In case there cannot be a congress this autumn, I should be glad if we could have at least a smaller meeting—perhaps quite private, only for the inner circle, or official, for the group leaders. What place would you suggest? I should be much in favour of Lindau or Konstanz on the lake, which can easily be reached from Austria, and because Switzerland is so near, the catering is good. Binswanger could prepare everything for us there.

Things are *good* in our group. Enthusiasm is great, and achievements much better than they were. You already know from Eitingon that your appeal in Budapest fell on fertile ground. The polyclinic will be opened in the winter, and will grow into a $\psi\alpha$ institute.[1] Eitingon, the driving force of that cause, will have told you all the details. Our colleague S., about whom we were corresponding, has, following a partial $\Psi\alpha$ with me (which will be continued soon), developed decidedly more favourably. I hope for good things from him in the future, even if more from a therapeutic than a scientific point of view. He is indispensable to us for the polyclinic.

The practice continues to be lively and takes up so much of my time that I do not get anything else done. The long-lasting bronchitis, with its accompanying symptoms, which went on until the beginning of the summer, tired me out to such an extent that I do not have, in addition to my practical work, my former fitness for scientific work. The huge cost of living and the move facing us force me to work like a slave. But I hope to be completely serviceable again in a short time. From a scientific point of view I had a host of subjects to work on. I am thinking of taking several weeks off in the winter to give my breathing organs a rest from winter here. I should then like to be somewhere with much sun, Engadine, Davos, or somewhere like that.

I had not heard about Tausk's sad end. He had made a disturbing impression in Budapest. The typical neurotic, who finally turns his painfully suppressed violence against himself!

I am delighted with the various new editions that have appeared, and thank you in advance for the copies in prospect.

After the barrier has been raised, I will now write to Jones. Are you still hearing nothing more detailed from Ferenczi and Freund? What about the Institute planned in Budapest?[2] If ever you have nothing better to do in Gastein, a letter would please me very much.

My wife and I send our cordial greetings!

Yours,

*Karl Abraham*

1. "[A]t some time or other", Freud had said at the Budapest Congress, "the conscience of society will awake and remind it that the poor man should have just as much right to assistance for his mind as he now has to the life-saving help offered by surgery. . . . It may be a long time before the State comes to see these duties as urgent. . . . Probably these institutions will first be started by private charity" (1919a [1918]: p. 167). On 19 July 1919, Eitingon had proposed to the Berlin Society the foundation of a psychoanalytic polyclinic (*Zeitschrift*, 1920, 6: 100), and this took place on 14 February 1920. The clinic was financed by Eitingon and was directed by him, Abraham, and Ernst Simmel. It soon also became the first training institute.
2. Ferenczi directed a newly founded University Psychoanalytic Clinic in Budapest (*Zeitschrift*, 1919, 5: 228), wishing to transform it into a psychoanalytic institute. The whole project, as well as Ferenczi's professorship, collapsed with the fall of the Council Republic.

## 359A

Berlin-Grünewald, Schleinitzstrasse 6
14 September 1919

Dear Professor,

After consulting Eitingon, I can give you the following programme[1]:

Your train, unfortunately, does not reach Lehrter Station until 1: 40 in the afternoon, not at 12 o'clock, as my wish wanted to improve the timetable. I shall be at the station with Eitingon. He will look after your luggage and take it to Anhalter Station and bring the luggage ticket to you in the afternoon at our house. I myself will take you and your wife to Grünewald immediately by the quickest way. For lunch and supper you are our guests. If Eitingon has obtained sleeping-coach tickets, you can stay with us until about 8 o'clock in the evening.* My wife and I are vastly looking forward to receiving you both in our house again, but we must ask you in advance to excuse the fact that our temporary lodging cannot offer you as comfortable a stay as we would wish.

In the evening I shall see to it that you catch your train at the right time. Meanwhile have some really lovely days in Hamburg with your children and grandchildren![2]

I would be grateful for a short confirmation that you agree with the programme. In any case, I will point out that my telephone number is post Pfalzburg number 1684.

With the most cordial greetings to all of you from my wife and me,
Yours,

*Karl Abraham*

* The train for Munich leaves at 9: 20 in the evening.

1. On 9 September Freud and his wife went from Badersee to Hamburg to visit the Halberstadts and then to Berlin; on 24 September they were back in Vienna.
2. Ernst [b. 1914] and Heinz ("Heinerle") [1918–1923].

## 360F

Vienna IX, Berggasse 19
3 October 1919

Dear Friend,

There is already something dream-like about the times behind us, when friendly solicitude kept the seriousness of life away from us. The dreadful conditions in this city, the impossibility of feeding and keeping oneself, the presence of Jones, Ferenczi, and Freund, the necessary conferences and decision-making, and the hesitant beginnings of analytic work (5 sessions = 500 crowns) result in a vivid present in the face of which memories quickly fade. Let me tell you briefly the outcome of the committee meetings, which unfortunately had to take place in your absence. Because of the uncertainty of the situation in Hungary, Ferenczi handed over the presidency to Jones until the Congress, at which the latter is to be installed definitely. Jones is also undertaking to produce a *Journal of $\Psi\alpha$*[1] for England–America; this will remain in the closest contact with the *Zeitschrift*, and the contents of the latter will be freely available to it. The technical production will take place in Vienna, and it will be imported to London; two issues have already been assembled. I have handed over administration of the fund to Jones, and he will take the money back with him to England. Ways and means of transferring funds from London for our work in Vienna have already been found. It was Rank's idea to arrange for the fund (*Verlag*) to produce commodities here, which would then be sold in England and America. In other words, the orientation towards the west proclaimed by our Chancellor! Another point on which your opinion will be *decisive* is the following. It is proposed on the occasion of the foundation of the Berlin polyclinic to admit Eitingon to full membership of the Committee. If you too agree with this, please mention it to him without further delay.[2] In any other eventuality please let us know.

My son Martin has become engaged to a girl from a well-to-do family (Ernestine Drucker),[3] a lawyer's daughter, and through his future father-in-law's influence he will soon have a post as secretary in a newly established bank, and also a flat. No news about the others.

I send my cordial greetings to you and your dear family, and thank you all again for all the proofs of friendship you gave us during our visit.

Yours,

*Freud*

1. Italicized words in English in original. The *International Journal of Psycho-Analysis* was first published in 1920.
2. Eitingon was proposed in place of the terminally ill Anton von Freund. Abraham informed him on 12 October (Eitingon to Freud, 13 October 1919, SFC).
3. Ernestine ("Esti") Drucker [1896–1980] and Martin married on 7 December 1919, Martin's thirtieth birthday. The couple had two children, Anton Walter [b. 1921] and M. Sophie [b. 1924]. (Cf. Roazen, 1993: pp. 136–166.)

## 361A

Berlin-Grünewald, Bismarckallee 14
19 October 1919

Dear Professor,

Many thanks for the joint card from the Kobenzl,[1] for your letter, and for your photograph, which I received from Hamburg. It is excellent, true to life, and technically perfect.

I have naturally not the slightest objection to Eitingon being co-opted as a member, and he has been glad to accept. I am only too pleased to have someone here with whom I can discuss everything, should the need arise.

All the news from the Committee interested me very much and meet with my approval. There seems to be a general wish for a congress in the spring. Since most of the participants live in Germany and Austria and will not be able to afford a journey to Holland just at present, the congress will probably have to take place either in Germany or in Austria. Eitingon and I should like to propose to the Committee that the congress be held in Berlin and should further like to suggest that our closed scientific meetings be followed by a number of lectures partly on medical and partly on general subjects. We would ask you to pass on this suggestion, with our comment that there would certainly be a considerable number of participants for such a project.

After I discussed this with Eitingon, I met Federn, who broke his journey in Berlin. He said the Vienna Society was declining and expressed the hope that a congress in Vienna would revive interest there. What do you think about this? Naturally we do not want to stand in your way.—The previous objection raised against university towns is no longer valid. Berlin is clamouring for psychoanalysis, and a week of explanatory lectures would be of great service to us.

Simmel recently gave an excellent report in the Society on the $\Psi\alpha$ of a gambler.[2] He has been coming on *very* well lately.

A word about your last paper![3] I am most enthusiastic about it. It seems to me that you have never before penetrated so deeply into the uttermost depths of a problem. Moreover, the presentation is so beautifully comprehensible and clear that reading it is an outstanding intellectual and aesthetic pleasure.

To end with, my congratulations that Martin has come to such a good arrangement, and I send the most cordial greetings from my wife and myself to you and yours!

Yours,

*Karl Abraham*

How did you like Böhm's paper? It sounded very good when he presented it.[4]

1. Restaurant on a hill overlooking Vienna; the card to Abraham is missing, but on 28 September 1919 Freud, Martha and Anna Freud, Eric Hiller, Jones, and Rank had sent a card to Eitingon from their luncheon at the Kobenzl (SFC; cf. Jones, 1957: p. 17).
2. At the meeting of 14 October (Simmel, 1920).
3. Freud, 1919h.
4. Probably referring to the manuscript of Böhm's talk "On a Case of Exhibitionism" on 8 May 1919 (*Zeitschrift*, 1919, 5: 231). It does not seem to have been published. (Cf. the following letter.)

362F

Vienna IX, Berggasse 19
2 November 1919

Dear Friend,

My congratulations on your new address, which means the re-establishment of a home of your own.

I put your and Eitingon's proposal to call a congress in Berlin and in the spring before Ferenczi, Freund, and Rank at a Committee meeting. At first they were all greatly captivated by the idea, but slowly they began to share the doubt that had prevailed with me from the first. Finally we were all in agreement. The chief objection was that, particularly in view of our new orientation towards the west, we could not decide anything without consulting Jones. But Jones attaches importance to getting some Americans to come to the Congress this time and has already said that arrangements for their journey have to be made many months in advance. We also think that it would undoubtedly be better for several issues of the English journal to have been published before the Congress discusses it. So it was decided to write to Jones and ask his opinion. Moreover, I thought it better that the Congress week should fall in the autumn instead of the spring. In my opinion we should not forget that we have received an invitation to Holland, and, as the last congresses had to be quite "middle-powerful",[1] it is becoming that the next one should be moved closer, also geographically, to our Entente members. There is absolutely nothing to be said in favour of Vienna, no good is to be done here; Federn's description is correct, but nothing can be done about it. Everyone liked very much the idea of the week of lectures you would like to associate with the Congress. We should like to know whether you would not like to carry it out independently of the Congress or afterwards as a continuation. This is an idea of which something may come.

Rank is very vigorously at work here. My daughter has begun work as an assistant in the English department of the *Verlag*. Ferenczi is staying until the 8th, and Freund for an indefinite period, his condition now permits certain perhaps misleading doubts. I am analysing nine hours a day and cannot manage anything else. Dr Forsyth,[2] who is still under analysis with me, turns out to be a very notable personality; he talks much about the great interest in analysis in England. Böhm's paper is now being read by Ferenczi. I liked it. As it is too long for the *Zeitschrift*, we are now considering whether we could make a supplement of it.

The first meeting of the Society takes place today.

With cordial greetings to you and your wife and children,

Your faithfully devoted,

*Freud*

1. *Mittelmächtig*—a neologistic adjective of *Mittelmächte* [Central Powers] [trans.].
2. David Forsyth [1877–1941], founding member of the London Society, in analysis with Freud for seven weeks (cf. Freud, 1933a: pp. 48–54—"Forsyth/foresight").

## 363A

Berlin-Grünewald, Bismarckallee 14
23 November 1919

Dear Professor,

Today my wife and I tried to see your daughter[1] once more before she left, unfortunately in vain. Otherwise you would have received greetings by word of mouth in a few days. But we were very pleased to see her at our house with your sister-in-law one afternoon recently. Gradually all your family are turning up here, and we hope to have sight of one or two more of them soon. In the meantime we often think of you when we read the gloomy news about Vienna and hope that you do not have to go without too much warmth and nourishment.

I agree that it would be desirable if some Americans were to attend the Congress. It does, however, seem impossible to me to hold the Congress in Holland until the German and Austrian exchange rates have greatly improved. This can hardly be expected by the autumn, but by then it is likely that the Americans will have no difficulty in travelling to Germany! At the moment, a journey to Holland plus a few days' stay there can hardly be managed for 1,500–2,000 marks, and there are very few who can afford this. Things are even worse in Austria. Most people from there would find the *journey* alone far beyond their means. A congress that excludes most of the Austrians, Hungarians, and Germans would be no congress. Therefore, everything seems to speak in favour of Berlin.—We are waiting here to hear what Jones has to say about the Congress before arranging the week of lectures.

Eitingon will certainly be keeping you up to date with the business of our polyclinic. It seems that the plan is soon to become a reality.

If you have any news about Ferenczi and Freund, please do let me know! We are completely cut off from Budapest.

As co-editor of the *Zeitschrift*, I should like to repeat my objection against making it top-heavy. I still think it was a mistake to discontinue the *Jahrbuch*. Especially now that we have our own *Verlag*, there should be, alongside the *Zeitschrift* to which one subscribes, a *Jahrbuch* that one buys to get information about the development of our science. It seems an unnecessary weighting to include an overall view of the literature in the *Zeitschrift*. Special issues containing longer articles do not seem practicable to me. I think we should once again consider the question of resuming publication of the *Jahrbuch*.

A short paper of mine ("The Narcissistic Evaluation of Excretory Processes in Dreams and Neurosis"[2]), which is now being typed, will be sent to Rank within a few days. The paper about the female castration complex, which has been finished for some time, needs revising. I discovered, while I was churning out the reviews, that the literature already contains aspects that I had believed to be new. During the war I did not follow the literature in detail.

Reik's book[3] is excellent. The essay on the Shofar in particular is convincing and extremely penetrating. Rank sent me his book on myths.[4] His achievements are truly amazing. I am just starting to read those articles that I do not yet know.

The necessity for working very long hours unfortunately leaves me too little time for theoretical work—the same tune as the one that you, dear Herr Professor, are also singing. Added to this is the fact that I have not yet had a break this year and am therefore less keen on writing than I might otherwise have been. I shall probably take 1–2 weeks off at Christmas.

Hoping to have good news from you, I am, with cordial greetings—also from my wife, to you all,
Yours,

*Karl Abraham*

1. Mathilde.
2. Abraham, 1919[63].
3. Reik, 1919, the fifth book published by the *Verlag*, with a preface by Freud (1919g).
4. Rank, 1919, a collection of pre-war essays, the *Verlag*'s fourth publication.

### 364F

Vienna IX, Berggasse 19
1 December 1919

Dear Friend,

I do not turn a deaf ear to the weight of your arguments against Holland and in favour of Berlin, and I am actually afraid that they may

1919 December

turn the scale, but I must confess that to me there is something unsatisfactory about such a congress. Also I do not know whether it will really be possible to get the British and Americans to come to Berlin next autumn. Hostile prejudice is indeed stronger than you suppose. In any case Rank, who is now in The Hague and is travelling to London tomorrow with Emden and Ophuijsen, will be coming to see you in the course of this month, and he will give you Jones's attitude in the matter; and what the two of you then decide will be acceptable to all of us here. I am almost of the opinion that with 3⅓ crowns to the mark either journey will be just as difficult to most of the Viennese.

Your proposal to resuscitate the *Jahrbuch* will be carefully considered and should have a place in your discussions with Rank. For the time being I feel that the difficulties outweigh the demand. Because of the tremendous costs of printing, the *Verlag* already feels the maintenance of two journals a serious burden. Moreover, a third publication would be restricted to the purely $\psi\alpha$ public, which does not have much buying power. Deuticke might be persuaded to revive the *Jahrbuch*, but I am afraid that the material produced by us in the course of a year might not be sufficient to keep it going. We do not exactly have an abundance of material even for the *Zeitschrift*. A far deeper interest by a much wider circle would be necessary to create a real demand for the *Jahrbuch*. Also what England (and America) produce is henceforward to be diverted to the *English Journal of $\Psi\alpha$*.[1]

The papers you announce will be given the usual welcome! It is astonishing how much work you are still able to do in a situation in which, as I am well aware myself, all one's energy is required to maintain one's economic level.

I now have all my three sons together for a short time. Martin is marrying on the 7th inst., and the following day Ernst will be leaving for Berlin, where you will certainly see him more often. There has been hardly any news from Ferenczi since his departure, and Freund, who is here, is in a bad way. He will probably not leave Vienna alive, the metastases have now been confirmed beyond doubt.

With cordial greetings to you and your wife,
Your faithfully devoted,

*Freud*

1. In English in original.

## 365A

Berlin-Grünewald, Bismarckallee 14
7 December 1919

Dear Professor,

Your letter of the 1st inst. reached me by the 5th! Is this a sign that conditions are improving?

I want to start my reply with best wishes for your son's wedding. A telegram of congratulations that I wanted to send was refused; such telegrams are no longer being dispatched as of some weeks ago. I must ask you to pass our congratulations on to the nearest and dearest and to all your family. We hope to see Ernst here in a short time, and also Rank.

I am terribly sorry to hear about Freund's serious illness. If metastases are already present, one must be prepared for the end to come soon. Does he himself know about his condition?

I shall discuss the question of the Congress and the *Jahrbuch* with Rank.

Your praise for my productivity is not justified. In the few free hours the practice leaves me I have a marked disinclination for work. Otherwise I would get much more done. The small contributions of the last few months can be explained by the fact that I am unwilling to start on anything more extensive.

You may already have heard from Eitingon that there is a possibility of premises for our polyclinic. We shall rent it if the price is within our means. Simmel will be an excellent force for the polyclinic. He is now taking up his analysis with me again. Scientifically he is making good progress, though he has a narcissistic pride in finding everything out for himself. But I have good hopes for him for the future. The same with Böhm, who is working with great enthusiasm. Incidentally, both of them, though they have only settled in a few months ago, are already very fully occupied. We are having an unhappy experience with Körber, who embarrasses us with his superficial knowledge as soon as he comes into the public eye.

I have some additions to make to Reik's papers, which I may write down quite soon. I shall take a holiday from 24 December to 4 January but shall not go away.

With cordial greetings from house to house,
Yours,

*Karl Abraham*

1919 December

## 366F

Vienna IX, Berggasse 19
15 December 1919

Dear Friend,

Thank you for your congratulations! The wedding was a small family affair and passed off very well. The young couple have taken up life's struggle after scarcely three days of isolation.

Your contribution on the omnipotence of excreta[1] amused me greatly. After all, they really are creations, just as ideas and wishes are. At the same time I read something on the interpretation of dreams at the subjective level,[2] and once again had a strong impression of what a superfluous addition that is to the understanding of dreams. Naturally one destroys the father only because he is the "inner" father, that is, has significance for one's own mental life.

Rank has sent a telegram from London. At last! But, as he had to waste a whole week in Holland waiting for his entry permit, he will probably come back by the shortest route on a children's train[3] (before Christmas) without touching Berlin. I have therefore to report that he is definitely against Berlin and still favours Holland in the autumn. I do not even know whether that will be possible. There is no question of any improvement in communications. (Your letter of the 7th reached me today, the 15th.)

Freund's abdominal metastasis, microscopic examination of which showed the same sarcoma as had been removed from the testicle, was liquefied; it was evacuated and drained. A radium capsule has now been inserted through the drainage tube. He knows everything; he has, for instance, directed that the ring he wears is to be restored to me after his death. He has also sensed that it is intended for Eitingon.[4]

As far as work is concerned, things are no better with me than with you. Only I think that in my case it is not a phase of short duration. I think I have finished with sowing and shall probably not get to the reaping.

Cavalry Captain Schmiedeberg [sic],[5] who was Eitingon's guest, gave me a piece of news that is so good that I cannot believe it, namely that you are about to get a professorship of $\Psi\alpha$! As you have not mentioned this in your letters, I can no longer contain my curiosity. I shall naturally keep the secret if there is anything in it.

Cordially
Yours,

*Freud*

1. Abraham, 1919[63], quoting phantasies and dreams in which "the functions of excretion ... are overestimated, and in the sense of possessing great and even unlimited power to create or destroy every object" (p. 322).

2. In *The Psychology of Unconscious Processes* (1917) Jung had differentiated between dream interpretations on the objective and on the subjective level.
3. These trains brought children from the large cities of northern Germany, where infantile paralysis and tuberculosis were rampant, for convalescence, to places where the climate was more favourable.
4. Freud had presented a ring to each of the Secret Committee's original members in 1913. Eitingon, on joining the Committee in the place of the dying von Freund, received the ring Freud had himself worn, von Freund's ring being claimed by his widow.
5. Walter Schmideberg [1890–1954], from Vienna. While he was a captain in the Austro-Hungarian Army, he had met Eitingon, who introduced him to Freud. After the war he returned to Vienna, where he became a member of the Vienna Psychoanalytic Society [1919–1922]; in 1922 he moved to Berlin, where he met Melanie Klein's daughter Melitta and married her. They moved to London in 1932, where he became a training and control analyst. After the Second World War Melitta went to New York, while Walter moved to Switzerland with Winifred (Bryher) Ellerman. (Cf. King & Steiner, 1991: p. xx; Mühlleitner, 1992: pp. 289–290.)

## 367A

Berlin-Grünewald
29 December 1919

Dear Professor,

Your letter of the 15th reached me yesterday! That really does not permit the assumption that the postal services are improving. Meanwhile, your son Ernst has turned up here as a live source of news. Unfortunately we could only see him at our home once, as my wife was ill in bed over Christmas, and still is. It is a benign but stubborn catarrh of the sinuses and larynx. We are hoping that as soon as this business is finished with we shall have Ernst to see us more often. Rank passed us by; I should have been so glad to see him. There seems to be no real prospect of Reik coming either.

I very often think of poor Freund. I would like to write to him but do not want to remind him unnecessarily of his fate. Yet it does seem wrong to me to take no notice of his life and suffering, especially as he showed me so much friendship in Budapest. Could you advise me what to do? You are sure to know whether he is sensitive to his illness being mentioned.

I was afraid that Schmiedeberg would gossip prematurely in Vienna. Eitingon had told him something in confidence, and I only heard about it after S. had already left, so I could not ask him to keep it secret. Now I shall tell you the whole story, and you will appreciate why I did not want to count my chickens before they were hatched.

Through his political activities[1] Simmel has some contacts with the Ministry of Education and the Arts. Some important people there told him, partly as a result of his article in the *Vossische Zeitung*,[2] that the Ministry would be very favourably disposed to the founding of a Chair

1919 December

of Ψα. S. first discussed the matter with Eitingon and thought that *I*, Eitingon, and he himself might be considered. E. firmly declined and said that no one but I should be considered. Simmel allowed himself to be persuaded, spoke to me about it and then with the head of the department concerned in the Ministry. The latter thereupon asked me to call on him, which I did at the beginning of December. In the meantime, the very disagreeable incident occurred in Parliament concerning the Chair for tuberculosis-Friedmann, and for this reason the Ministry had to proceed far more circumspectly with the Faculty than would otherwise have been the case.[3] After a long discussion I was asked to get our *Society* to send in a detailed and scientifically based memorandum on the introduction of ψα teaching. The memorandum will then be submitted to the faculty. The outlook is therefore by no means as favourable as one might have assumed when the matter was first mooted, but it is not hope*less*. If the Ministry brings a certain amount of pressure to bear and even if only a few of the professors are definitely in favour, then the chances are not too bad. Interest in academic circles is visibly increasing. The polyclinic, which will definitely be opened in January, is arousing the greatest interest on the part of the Ministry. Of the professors I hope to win over at least Kraus and His. Even if the whole operation should prove unsuccessful, there is still hope in the forthcoming change in the Faculties' right of appeal. The memorandum must contain all the facts that serve to demonstrate the increasing interest in and need for Ψα. I shall tell you the latest news, that a young colleague from Freiburg i/B, unknown to me, who is now doing the State examination and will then be a voluntary assistant with Hoche for six months, has applied for a post at the polyclinic. A few days ago I had a query from a lady doctor, up to the present an assistant in the psychiatric clinic in Königsberg, as to whether a course in Ψα was being held. Similar expressions of interest are increasing. But I need as many facts as possible in this respect, and so I should like to ask for the following information: (1.) Has your "Obsessional Neurosis" already appeared in Kraus's handbook? (2.) What has been the frequency in recent times of your lectures and the course for doctors set up by Tausk? (3.) Is anything known about the frequency of Ferenczi's lectures in Budapest? (4.) Does Jones or Flügel[4] hold academic lectures in London? (5.) What is the name of the Norwegian psychiatrist who treated Ψα in detail in his textbook? I am sure that *Rank* will be kind enough to answer these questions for me. I have already asked him to have this letter shown to him. I would also need Rank's consent to plagiarize—I find a large part of the introductory article in number 1 of the first year of *Imago*[5] eminently suitable as a basis for our memorandum, and I expect he will be pleased to agree to this. (I would further ask him on this occasion to let me have news of Sachs's whereabouts and state of health.)

I should like to ask both of you not to discuss this matter for the time being. It would be *very* nice. I am sure the lectures would be well attended. But for the time being[6]

1. See letter 334F, 17 February 1918, n. 2.
2. Simmel, 1919b.
3. Dr F. F. Friedmann had used his political affiliation to enlist the Ministry's help in obtaining a Chair. Between 1904 and 1912 he had published numerous papers on preventive and therapeutic vaccination of animals and of men with tortoise tubercle bacilli. Well-known scientists examined and subsequently discredited his claims, and the Faculty prevented his nomination. This gave rise to a scandal.
4. John Carl Flugel (Flügel) [1884–1955], British psychologist and psychoanalyst, secretary of the IPA [1920] and analysand of Jones. Author of the popular *The Psychoanalytic Study of the Family* (1921).
5. Rank & Sachs, 1912.
6. The rest of the letter is missing.

# 1920

368F

Vienna IX, Berggasse 19
6 January 1920

Dear Friend,

I had my first business conference with Rank today and promised to write to you immediately. All your arguments in favour of holding the Congress in Berlin are sound, and yet I have to decide in favour of Holland.[1] You neglect the most important factor in the situation, the pressing need of the Verlag to win over the Americans to the English ψα journal. Failing that, we shall not be able to keep the German journals alive for more than a year. Jones now assures us that there is no chance of getting the Anglo-Saxons to come to Berlin, and that is decisive. We obviously do not have a correct picture of these people's state of mind. What is at stake in this reorientation is not a question of scientific precedence, but one of practical profit. In comparison with that, our own travel and exchange difficulties dwindle into nothing; they will in any case be partly balanced by events organized by the Dutch. I hope you will not turn a deaf ear to these considerations and will not allow the war that is soon to be wound up to flare up again in the bosom of the committee.

Perhaps there is an underground passage connecting this subject with my next. As far as I know, Schmiedeberg was directly charged with telling me the secret of your chances, and I do not see why I should not have my share in the fore-pleasure when the end-pleasure will perhaps not materialize. I too say that it would be splendid, and that it would cause the whole of Germany to collapse, but I am afraid it is too good to be true. Just think how disoriented a man must be to consider Simmel for this post besides yourself! It is too reminiscent of Ferenczi's ephemeral professorship in Budapest. For my part I shall be happy if a lecturership comes out of it for you. In the long run the faculty would not tolerate anyone imposed on them.

The questions you put for the memorandum will be partly answered by Rank. I will answer you on the first points:

1. My contribution for Kraus will not be on obsessional neuroses, but will be called "Ψα Theory of Neuroses". It is scheduled for spring 1920, but I will let them remind me, because I want to have three printed

sheets and I should like to punish the gentlemen a little for the Prussian grandiloquence they have repeatedly shown towards me.

2. I have given no lectures since the "Introduction" in 1917 and will not do so despite having been given the title of Professor,[2] because this "distinction" does not carry any teaching assignment. Tausk's courses, interrupted by the war, were attended by an average of 20–30 people. The honoraria, at any rate, were high.

3. Ferenczi lectured for one term to an audience of about 100 from all faculties, whereas generally lectures were not highly frequented.

You asked for the Spanish journal for review, did you not?[3] Delgado announces a new work, *El psicoanalisis*,[4] that is perhaps already afloat on the ocean.

It is a pity that conditions are so unfavourable to your intention to hold the Congress in Berlin. Certainly your own prospects would be improved thereby. Jones knows nothing of such a possible advantage of the Congress.—

Now at last to private matters! Today Rank unpacked the food bought in Holland. We have received notification of boxes of gifts from England and America, but of course they do not arrive. I have far too much to do, another five people have booked; I am now asking 200 K or 50 (60) marks, more naturally from the victors. An American publishing firm is offering me $10,000 for a lecture tour in the US.[5] I have no intention of accepting. The most surprising people have congratulated me on my "nomination" on 31 December. The republic has not engendered any change in the greed and respect for titles that prevailed under the monarchy.

I hope that your wife has already recovered, and that the children are growing up as happily as when we saw them in September. Now there are only three of us, and we are fairly well.

With cordial greetings and best wishes for the New Year to you and yours,

Yours,

*Freud*

P.S.: Freund is slowly withdrawing into himself. It is perhaps more advisable not to stir him up.

1. In January 1920, the secretary of the IPA, Flügel, officially announced the Sixth International Psychoanalytical Congress, 8–10 September, The Hague (*Zeitschrift*, 1920, 6: 99).
2. Freud had been appointed Full but only Titular Professor, a merely nominal title.
3. Abraham's review of the Spanish literature appeared in the *Bericht über die Fortschritte der Psychoanalyse in den Jahren 1914–1919* (Abraham, 1921[74]).
4. Delgado, 1919, the first book in Spanish on psychoanalysis. Dr Honorio F. Delgado [1896–1969], professor of psychiatry at San Marcos University, Lima [1929]—the only chair in psychiatry in Peru—and editor of the *Revista de Psiquiatria y Disciplinas Conexas*. Having become member of the British Psychoanalytical Society [1927], he gradually turned away from psychoanalysis and eventually became hostile towards it. (Cf. Engelbrecht & Rey de Castro, 1995; Rey de Castro, 1990.)

5. "To further the sales of their book [Freud's *Introductory Lectures*] Boni and Liveright offered Freud $10,000.00 in December 1919 if he would give a course of lectures in New York. They had to be in English, and that together with his unsatisfactory state of health decided him to decline" (Jones, 1957: p. 10).

## 369A

Berlin-Grünewald
28 January 1920

Dear Professor,

I have just heard that neither you nor your wife were able to travel to Hamburg. As it is therefore impossible to express my sympathy and friendship to either of you personally, I feel compelled to send you and your family a few words of deepest sympathy. Your sad news[1] has affected us as deeply as if our own family had to mourn the loss of a young life!

My thoughts are with you and I remain, in true devotion,
Yours,

*Karl Abraham*

1. The sudden death on 25 January 1920 of Freud's daughter Sophie of influenza. Sophie had been pregnant with a third child. Only five days earlier, Anton von Freund had died.

## 370F

Vienna IX, Berggasse 19
3 February 1920

Dear Friend,

I am not yet very well able to write, but I shall not delay any longer thanking you, your wife, and all the members of your local group for your heartfelt telegram of condolence. My wife, who is very shaken, appreciated all these signs of sympathy.

Meanwhile our work goes ahead under ever-increasing difficulties. We are now threatened with a paper shortage. You will soon be receiving a circular letter concerning reviewing the literature in which apologies will be made to you because of the setting up of a central editorial office in Vienna. The post between Vienna and Berlin is so bad at present that we were forced to decide on this simplification. I hope that you will be left with enough to do.

How are the prospects for the professorship?

With cordial greetings,
Yours,

*Freud*

## 371A

Berlin-Grünewald, Bismarckallee 14
13 March 1920

Dear Professor,

Our correspondence has come to a complete standstill. I kept silent for some weeks since I did not wish to put you under the obligation of replying to me so soon after your sad loss. As I have been in constant touch with Rank, you will in any case have heard what has been happening in our circle. Besides, two of your children have been able to bring you news from here. Both my wife and I were very pleased to welcome them. We are expecting Ernst back here soon and hope he will be a frequent guest. He has won lasting recognition for himself in his designing of the polyclinic,[1] which is admired by everyone. It is a good thing that we got everything settled. One cannot tell, after the radical change that took place so quietly this morning,[2] what will happen next and whether it will be at all possible to realize our plans in the near future. I have just finished the detailed memorandum on the teaching of Ψα at the university. Now we must wait and see whether such a move is feasible.

The polyclinic is well attended. I have already written to Rank about this recently: my lecture course,[3] which was not sufficiently advertised, only has ten participants, but the quality pleases me partly very much. I hope that all the teaching will soon be well organized. We have other plans as well. Eitingon wants to arrange one room of the polyclinic as a reading-room where all our literature will be available. For the more distant future there is a project to start a special department for the treatment of nervous *children*. I should like to train a woman doctor particularly for this. All our plans depend on having enough new followers, and so far unfortunately do not have them. We have no young people fresh from university, and I want to try in every possible way to gain such workers.

I found "The Uncanny"[4] very gripping. I have had a few similar cases in the last few months and came to the very same conclusions, although I did not formulate them so concisely.

At our last meeting Böhm read a paper on "Homosexuality and Polygamy",[5] which enlarged on some known points but also introduced one new aspect. Our small circle here is so unproductive that I am pleased if anything new emerges once in a while. Our activities, incidentally, have recently been very much restricted. Liebermann lost both his parents within a week and was in Hamburg mostly for weeks at a time. Frau Dr Horney has been ill since December with parametritis after a gynaecological intervention. And as one member after the other was going down with influenza, the wheels naturally stopped turning.

If possible, I shall write to Rank and Reik today. I add in haste, also from my wife, cordial greetings to you and all yours!

Yours,

Karl Abraham

1. Ernst, an architect, had designed the interior of the clinic.
2. The unsuccessful attempt to overthrow the government by extreme rightist Wolfgang Kapp [1858–1922] between 13 and 17 March. It forced the government to flee to Dresden and Stuttgart temporarily, but the putsch collapsed after a general strike.
3. On "Selected chapters of psychoanalysis: 1. Historical development of psychoanalytic therapy; 2. Basic lines of psychoanalytic drive theory; 3. The role of sexuality in the aetiology of neuroses; 4. The dream and the unconscious; 5. Psychopathology of anxiety; 6. Hysteria; 7. Obsessional states; 8. Psychoses" (Zeitschrift, 1920, 6: 100).
4. Freud, 1919a [1918].
5. Paper read at the meeting of 11 March 1920 and published as the first of four "Contributions to the Psychology of Homosexuality" (Böhm, 1920, 1922, 1926, 1933).

372A

Berlin-Grünewald, Bismarckallee 14
4 April 1920

Dear Professor,

That was really a disappointment![1] I could now have been with you and all our closest friends, had it not been for the countless difficulties of travelling! I must at least send a few lines to follow up my telegram.[2] Unfortunately, the telegraphic invitation arrived too late! First I had to get my photograph taken on Monday and use the four days at my disposal for all the different things I had to do until I had everything needed from the local authorities. But unfortunately one must also have Austrian and Czech visas. There was such an enormous crowd before Easter at both consulates that I went away with my business not done. I was really dependent on the only train going via Prague on Saturday morning. If that had been a daily train, I should have been able to travel today (Sunday), but it does not run again until Tuesday. And the trains via Bavaria were quite impossible, because you would have got stuck either in Regensburg or in Passau. If your invitation had only come a few days earlier, or if I had already had a passport and only needed a visa from the consulate, everything would have gone smoothly! Now we shall probably not meet until the autumn.

I have done a great deal of writing during recent weeks. While it lasted, the general strike cut my practice down to half, and so I had sufficient free time. The article for the *Neue Rundschau*, amounting to some 20 pages, has now been sent off and will be published in June or July; its title is "Ψα as a Source of Knowledge for the Humanities".[3] The memorandum for the Ministry of Education and Arts is completed and will go off after Easter.

My course for doctors is nearing its end. Attendance was not good because it was advertised too late (10 participants). I have, however, made two valuable acquisitions for us, which are, in effect, more important than large numbers. One young colleague, Dr Alfred Gross,[4] an assistant of Bonhoeffer's, has become an enthusiastic follower of our cause and will probably soon start his training at the polyclinic. Another colleague attending the course, a woman just about to take her final exam, who was already well informed before she started, wants to take up Ψα with the particular aim of treating *children*. It is imperative for me to enlist younger colleagues, and I hope the next course will be more successful in this respect.

Now I must give you and all your family my wife's congratulations and mine on Ernst's engagement![5] We have not yet seen E. since his return, but we hope we shall soon, and we should also like to make the acquaintance of his fiancée.

With cordial greetings, also to those members of the Committee who may have stayed on in Vienna,

Yours,

*Karl Abraham*

1. At the beginning of April, four members of the Committee (Ferenczi, Jones, Rank, and Sachs) met with Freud in Vienna; Abraham and Eitingon were unable to come.
2. Missing.
3. Abraham, 1920[69].
4. Dr Alfred Gross emigrated to England and settled in Manchester; he later accepted a position at the Menninger Clinic (Topeka, Kansas) and finally at Yale University. He died in 1957.
5. With Lucie ("Lux") Brasch [1896–1989]. The wedding took place on 18 May 1920 in Berlin. The couple were to have three children: Stephan Gabriel [b. 1921], now known as Stephen, a businessman, Lucian Michael [b. 1922], now known as Lucien, artist, and Clemens Raphael [b. 1924], now Sir Clement, writer and broadcaster and, from 1973 to 1987, member of Parliament.

### 373F

Vienna IX, Berggasse 19
22 April 1920

Dear Friend,

I answer your letter of the 4th inst. only today because in these last weeks my pleasure for work and writing has been unusually disturbed. I too cannot get over the disappointment about Easter. It would have been so delightful to see you all together for once and to reinforce the harmony between you that guarantees the future of our cause.

My wife came through Berlin on 19 April. If she did not see you, she must surely have been very much in demand. She will probably stay in Berlin longer for Ernst's wedding.

The holidays, for which I have a large work project in mind, will probably be in Gastein to begin with.[1] There are still nearly three months to go, and already I do not like to work any more.

All the difficulties of life here make one feel very blunted. But even in Vienna interest in Ψα has grown livelier. I have reopened communication with Havelock Ellis.[2] There would be a great many things of interest to discuss, let us hope we shall be able to catch up.

I send my cordial greetings to you and yours, and my lively regrets that I hear from you so seldom, certainly partly through my own fault.

Your faithfully devoted,

*Freud*

1. On 30 July, Freud and Minna Bernays went to Gastein, where Freud finished *Group Psychology and the Analysis of the Ego* (1921c). After a month there, Freud and Anna travelled to Hamburg to visit the widowed Max Halberstadt and the two grandsons. There they were met by Eitingon, and on 6/7 September the three of them went to the congress in The Hague.
2. Freud and Ellis (see letter 91F, 3 July 1910, n. 5) had lost touch during the war; publication of Ellis's "Psycho-Analysis in Relation to Sex" (in Ellis, 1919) had revived communication between them and inspired Freud to write "A Note on the Prehistory of the Technique of Analysis" (1920b). (Cf. Freud & Jones, 12 February 1920, 1993: p. 370; Grosskurth, 1980: pp. 291–293.)

374A
Berlin-Grünewald, Bismarckallee 14
1 May 1920

Dear Professor,

This time I will not keep you waiting long for a reply. There is a holiday today and therefore less work, and, having finished the reviews for the Annual Report, I want to resume nerve-contact[1] with you and to begin by wishing you as much happiness for the 7th[2] as can be expected in these difficult times. The burden of my other duties made it impossible for me to present you with a ψα contribution this year, but I want at least to give you some news about which I now feel *reasonably* optimistic. Four months ago I was asked by the privy councillor in charge in the Ministry of Education to submit a memorandum drawn up by our Society on the introduction of Ψα as a subject to be taught at the University. He advised me to use our first experiences at the polyclinic concerning the number of patients attending for treatment and the lecture courses. I did this, but, just when the document was completed, the military revolt[3] and the ensuing chaos made conditions unfavourable for consideration of our case. Therefore I only visited the Ministry yesterday to deliver the memorandum and to discuss the matter once again with the same official. I was very pleasantly received, which you will only be able to understand when I tell you that we have now, since the revolution, some privy councillors aged 30–40 working alongside the older ones. The head of the department will hand the document directly on to the Minister. In the middle of next week, after the latter has read it, I shall ask for an interview with him. The Minister (Haenisch[4]) is very interested in all innovations. He will pass the matter on to the Faculty for their assessment. I shall personally meet the relevant men there— Bonhoeffer, Kraus, and His. The Ministry will only turn our application down if the Faculty puts forward irrefutable objections. The assurance I was given leaves room for hope that a merely unfriendly and negative attitude on the part of the Faculty will not have an effect on the decision; and there is a certain probability that the outcome might be favourable. The question to be decided is not my personal admission for *Habilitation* but the setting up of a Chair in $\Psi\alpha$, that is to say of a professorship.[5] Almost too good to be true!*

I too deplore the bad luck that prevented me from travelling at Easter. You are now making me curious to hear about your work project for the holidays! There is probably no hope of a meeting before the autumn, that is, at the Congress. Until then one must be content with correspondence, which nowadays is so slow.

I must thank you for your recommendation in two cases that were to come under treatment from me. The practice continues to be very lively, and as salaries have risen it appears quite lucrative, but whatever you earn slips away through your hands.

In the meantime we have made the acquaintance of Ernst's fiancée. She is a sensitive, intelligent person who greatly appeals to us. We hope to see your wife when she comes back from Hamburg. We have now learnt to admire Ernst's competence privately too. He is seeing to the redecoration of my waiting-room with great skill and taste.

We are not thinking of going on holiday this year. We can do without going away better than many other people as we live outside the town and in green surroundings. But I shall relax for a few weeks in July.

Tomorrow I am sending the reviews to Rank.

With cordial greetings, also from my wife,

Yours,

*Karl Abraham*

* It is possible, dear Herr Professor, that the Ministry might send an official enquiry to you concerning the person suitable for the Professorship. I hope I shall not founder on this rock!

1920 May

1. See letter 96F, 24 October 1910, & n. 2.
2. A repeated error of Abraham's regarding the date of Freud's birthday (see letter 354A, 5 May 1919)—so close to his own [3 May].
3. See letter 371A, 13 March 1920, & n. 2.
4. Konrad Haenisch [1876–1925], Minister of Education in the post-war Weimar Republic [1919–1933].
5. *Außerordentliche Professur*: There is no exact equivalent to this in British or American academia, the rights of an "extraordinary" professor being slightly less than those of an "ordinary" one. Abraham's hopes never materialized, however.

375F
Vienna IX, Berggasse 19
14 May 1920

Dear Friend,

Must I then play the part of the pampered old man to whom everybody brings a fine present for his birthday (6th inst.)? Eitingon the magnificent American donation for the Fund,[1] and you the wonderful news of the imminent adoption of $\Psi\alpha$ at the University of Berlin. If only the second gift were as assured as the first! I am impatient to answer the Ministry's enquiry. Can you not press the privy councillors there to write to me at last?

You already know enough about my family now; and you will see some of its members before I do. The fact that you like my new daughter agrees with everything I have heard about her up to now. I myself am not coming to the wedding; my daughter Anna is leaving here on the 17th inst. so as to arrive in time.

All that is fixed about the summer is Gastein until the middle of August. Then a gap until the Congress, which this time we wish to arrange comfortably.

In Gastein I want to compose my intention on mass psychology[2] into a short book. With nine hours of analysis that is impossible.

With cordial greetings to you and your dear wife,
Yours,

*Freud*

1. On Eitingon's initiative, American relatives of his had donated a considerable sum (cf. Freud to Eitingon, 16 May 1920, SFC).
2. *Massenpsychologie* has been rendered as "Group Psychology" in the *Standard Edition* (Freud, 1921c).

## 376A

Berlin-Grünewald
25 May 1920

Dear Professor,

What a pity we had to do without you at Ernst's wedding! I want at least to tell you that the young couple made so pleasant an impression on that day that one felt justified in giving a favourable prognosis for this marriage. Once more, all best wishes!

Unfortunately we saw your wife and daughter only briefly. The latter will bring you my collection.[1] Many thanks for thinking of me. I shall send a preface on later. I have not found time to write it down today. Some days ago I wrote to Rank that I should like to add a few non-medical papers too, but I have since decided to omit them as they would be out of tune with the rest.

My matter with the Ministry is still pending. I hope to hear tomorrow at what stage it is. I have reason to assume that the opinion of the Faculty, that is to say of Bonhoeffer, will not be completely negative. As soon as I hear more, I shall let you know.

What about the programme for The Hague? Do you intend to speak there about mass psychology? I am considering the female castration complex as a possible subject.[2]

With cordial greetings,
Yours,

*Karl Abraham*

1. That is, Abraham's manuscript (1921[75]), to appear in the Verlag.
2. Abraham carried out his intention to speak on this topic.

## 377F

Vienna IX, Berggasse 19
4 June 1920

Dear Friend,

My wife and daughter have told me a great deal about you, most of it pleasing, although not yet what we are waiting for. Today's letter from me serves for one single question.

Urban & Schwarzenberg have sent me a letter and a reply card on which I am supposed to commit myself to sending in the contribution, "Psychoanalytical Theory of the Neuroses" to the Kraus–Brugsch handbook in autumn of this year. I intend not to do this, *I* could only copy my lectures, and I cannot maintain my interest in an independent new version at present. So I should like you to take over from me, and I think it will be a stimulus for a holiday task, no trouble, and in a certain sense a furtherance. You could certainly have a postponement, size 3–4 sheets. I am only waiting for your "yes", perhaps by telegram, in order to put this change strongly before the Editorial Board.

Lack of paper and money have again damped our creative pleasure which had been kindled by the new fund. More about this next time.

With kindest regards to you and your dear wife,
Yours,
*Freud*

## 378A

Berlin-Grünewald
10 June 1920

Dear Professor,

In spite of certain reservations, I answered positively to your question about Urban and Schwarzenberg. As far as our cause is concerned, it makes a difference whether you yourself or someone else contributes to a comprehensive work of this kind, and it may even happen that the editors will decide to omit any presentation of our view on the theory of neuroses. On the other hand, I should be glad to relieve you of this burden. It is better for all of us if you are free to do your own work. It will definitely not be a holiday task for me. Because my holidays will only last for three weeks (15 July to 5 August) and I very much need this short spell—which, incidentally, I shall spend at home—for a rest. But if the editors commission me for the work, I shall spread it over some time and shall postpone other plans. To conclude, I want to assure you that I do not simply regard it as a burden but am pleased that I should be the one whom you entrust with the task of standing in for you!

Our memorandum is now with the Medical Faculty. Some days ago I had a longish discussion with Bonhoeffer, who is the most influential person concerned. B. is no friend of $\Psi\alpha$; but he is not an enemy on principle either, especially not an unfair one. He openly admitted to me that his reasons against are of an emotional nature, "quite unscientific"! But he says he acknowledges much of it. He has no factual objection to a Chair in Psycho-Analysis, only a technical one, which does need discussing. There is a tendency in Berlin to convert all Professorships in the special subjects into Chairs, thereby making the subjects in question obligatory for students and also examination subjects. In his opinion, $\Psi\alpha$ is not yet mature enough for this. But he says he has no objection to my being personally entrusted with lecturing. I replied that, in our view, $\Psi\alpha$ would gradually establish itself and that for the time being we were not concerned with making it a compulsory subject but only with the possibility of teaching it to such students who were interested, of whom there were many. The latter he acknowledged without further ado. He promised to ask me to come and see him again after having had a look through the memorandum, which had not yet been in his hands. I believe therefore that his opinion will not be entirely unfavourable, especially as his personal attitude to me is very friendly. *With* the Faculty the matter would naturally be much easier than *without* it or opposing it. Above all, we would then be independent of political hazards, since the socialist Prussian Minister of Education may be overthrown overnight, and a great deal would then become problematic. Therefore, Coraggio, Casimiro!

Yesterday we had a business meeting of our Society in order to draw up an autumn and winter programme. We are very enterprising and have planned the following:

1. August–September, a pedagogical course by Frau Hug-Hellmuth. It has been decided to pay for her travelling expenses and her stay here. Frau Dr Horney will welcome her into her home and act as hostess, which will be very pleasant for Frau H.-H. as the Horneys live in a villa in the suburbs.[1] She will then have as absolute profit any income the course brings in. The polyclinic has put the venue at her disposal.

2. Following the Congress, there will be lectures in Berlin, which, in addition to you and me, will include Jones, Ferenczi, Ophuijsen, and possibly Rank and Sachs. Liebermann will give you and the others all necessary information in the next few days and ask you for your collaboration. We are thinking of having three hours of lectures on each of two evenings. We shall give you unlimited time to speak and allot half an hour to each of the others.

3. A course for doctors each quarter-year.

4. Individual lectures for doctors.

5. Lectures for laymen (Sachs).

6. Analyses of doctors for the purpose of learning $\Psi\alpha$ (Sachs). I hope you agree with these plans, especially with item 2!

Tomorrow I am being visited by a local publisher (Reuss & Pollak), who wants to have contact with our publishing house somehow or other.[2] He has already corresponded with Rank. Eitingon and I hope to manoeuvre Sachs into it in some position or other.

Did you know that I have been treating Frau Dr Nacht[3] for several weeks? The analysis is progressing wonderfully, but one cannot tell yet what the final therapeutic result will be. There is much to be learned from her. She is as great an authority on obsessional neurosis as Schreber on paranoia.

I am enclosing a general review on all the Spanish literature I have received.[4] It is meant for the Annual Report. I hope Rank will find room for this small contribution. I am prepared to review for the *Zeitschrift* the new Spanish and Portuguese publications mentioned in Number 2 of the *Zeitschrift*, of which I have the proofs.

I am still undecided what to talk about in The Hague—either about "The Female Castration Complex" or about "Contributions to the Theory of the Anal Character." There is still ample to be said on both subjects. Which would you prefer?

With kindest regards to you and your family, also in my wife's name, I remain your

Karl Abraham

1. Karen and Oskar Horney, a Ph.D. in political science, had settled in Berlin in 1909 as newlyweds. Oskar made a successful career within the empire of coal baron Hugo Stinnes—who built up the biggest industrial trust in Europe after the war—enabling them to buy an impressive villa in a new suburb, Zehlendorf, in 1918 (Quinn, 1987).
2. These plans did not materialize. In November, however, Reuss & Pollak hosted a series of lectures on psychoanalysis (circular letter of 20 November 1920, BL).
3. A patient previously treated by Freud and Eitingon (Eitingon to Freud, 13 January 1920, SFC); evidently not related to the French psychoanalyst Sacha Nacht.
4. See letter 368F, 6 January 1920, n. 3.

379F
Vienna IX, Berggasse 19
21 June 1920

Dear Friend,

This is the true Berlin energy again. Phew, what a programme, and how many flies you intend to hit with these repeated swipes! Well, I am tremendously pleased that so much is going on in Berlin, and that you too are beginning to be convinced of the impossibility of restricting $\Psi\alpha$ to the doctors (cf. Reuss-Pollak). Best of all is the installation of Sachs. If he retains his health, you will have a great and lasting gain in him. We could do nothing for him.

Now comes the snag! I shall not be able to take on the excellent role that you destined for me. I shall probably not be present at the Berlin week at all. The first and external reason for this is as follows. Between Gastein (the end of August) and the Congress (8 September) there is one week left, with which I can do nothing except travel to The Hague via Berlin–Hamburg. After the Congress I shall either stay in Holland and meet a friend from London (Loë Jones, now Mrs Herbert Jones),[1] who has announced herself, or leave there quickly to catch Ernst and his Lucie somewhere in the south. The deeper context is this: I am growing old and undeniably idle and indolent. Also I am spoilt rotten by the many gifts of food, cigars, and money that are made to me, and that I have to accept because otherwise I could not live. But for the time being I am still working harder than is good for me. This year I have prolonged my working season by two weeks and am taking with me to Gastein a difficult germinating piece of work (mass psychology). Another week of the thus shortened holiday period has to go to the Congress, and for the remaining time I shall have to rest from Ψα, otherwise I will not be able to get down to the hard work again in October. If at all possible, I do not propose to read a paper at the Congress either. I think I have talked enough. Do you know the story of the doctor and the patient full of the joys of life, which ends in the doctor's saying: "Pissed enough"? Things were near enough to that with me, except that in that respect I am unexpectedly well.

Also it will do no harm if all of you slowly get used to the situation of my not being present. What is the Committee for, but to make me more and more dispensable? You, I think, should choose the subject of the female castration complex as the richer. I shall follow your excellent expositions with tranquil enjoyment.

I hear you have summoned Rank to Berlin. That, I fear, will be shattered on his over-determination to remain here. But the applicant is welcome in Vienna, and especially when Sachs is already here, everything else can be settled by letter or at the Congress. I have still had no reply from Urban & Schw.[arzenberg], I hope they are sensible enough to agree to the change. Otherwise they will simply get nothing at all. I am still sceptical about your matter with the Ministry; it is going too slowly for my liking, and you certainly have reason to fear that political and personal changes are a serious threat to your chances. Even then it will be no great misfortune, Ψα will go ahead all the same. The only thing is that I wish it for your sake. Ferenczi has now been excluded from the Budapest Medical Society as a punishment for his Bolshevik professorship. As a consequence of the still existing letter censorship I could only congratulate him on the honour.[2]

I cordially bid you farewell and do grant yourself some holiday peace with your dear family.

Your faithfully devoted

*Freud*

1. Louise ("Loë") Dorothea Kann [?–1945], of Dutch extraction, Ernest Jones's former common-law wife (Kann and Jones had not been married but presented themselves as a married couple). In 1912 and around the turn of the years 1913/14 she had been analysed by Freud. She had married Herbert Jones, a writer, in 1914.
2. Letter of 17 June 1920.

## 380A

Berlin-Grünewald
27 June 1920

Dear Professor,

You misinterpret the purpose of the Committee! It is not meant to put you out of action but to make your work easier, particularly within the ψα circle. Even though I cannot speak for all the C. members, I am certain that none of them would agree to your staying away from our event. That would really make it pointless. Because no one in local medical circles knows anything about Jones, Ophuijsen or Ferenczi. You, however, are the focus of positive interest as of the refusal. Therefore, to make the whole matter acceptable to you, I suggest the following changes. We arrange the lectures, which incidentally will not take a week but only two evenings with three papers on each, not *after* the Congress but *before* it. That way your time before The Hague is best organized. So please do agree! We shall then try to get the other speakers for the earlier dates as well. I am hoping for your "yes"!

My views about bringing in laymen have not changed. The lectures planned by Sachs deal with *non-medical* matters, and I have always been in agreement with extending this part of our science to lay circles and have indeed furthered it with my own writings.

About the business of Reuss & Pollak, Rank wrote to me exhaustively. I agree with him in everything and am writing to him about it today.

As regards the question of a Professorship, the delays are due to the fact that the Faculty must first ask the holder of the Chair of Psychiatry to give his assessment, and they then have to decide about the matter at a subsequent meeting. Without being too optimistic, I do not view the matter as hopeless. I should also like to give you some further news, which may not be of much importance in itself but is a pleasant sign of the times. I am going to Halle at the end of the week to read a paper to the doctors at the Clinic for Internal Medicine of the University. The director of the clinic, Professor Volkhardt, has invited me, through a colleague who is a mutual acquaintance, to read a ψα paper. I have chosen as my subject the neurotic disturbances of the digestive tract. The doctors of the Psychiatric Clinic are to be invited.

In our group we have a new guest, Dr Zutt, who wants to learn Ψα. He will first go to Bonhoeffer for six months from 1 October to learn general diagnosis etc., then for a time to Bleuler, then to our polyclinic. Our conditions for working at the latter are: (1.) sufficient previous neurological and psychiatric experience; (2.) sufficient knowledge of ψα literature; (3.) personal analysis of the candidate, which Sachs will undertake. I am very much looking forward to S.[1] For it is not pleasant always to be the one to stimulate others without receiving any stimulation in return.—I have not yet heard from Urban and Schwarzenberg. I have registered my paper (female castr.-c.).

With cordial greetings from house to house,
Yours,

*Karl Abraham*

---

1. Sachs moved to Berlin in early October.

## 381F

Vienna IX, Berggasse 19
4 July 1920

Dear Friend,

We have now known each other for about 13 years and have always got on excellently. It will be the same this time, but for this purpose you must give in and admit that what you are asking is no small thing. When you come to be 64 years old and have behind you ten months of a working year such as this one has been, the claim to an undisturbed break will no longer seem to you an unwarranted act of stubbornness, and the possible effect on Berlin medical circles will seem rather like a matter of indifference in comparison. So leave me out; I shall speak in Berlin neither *before* nor *after* the Congress. You need not alter your programme because of that. My rest will be by no means complete in any case. In August I have a difficult subject to write on, which will require full concentration, and in September there is the Congress, which leads back to analysis again. But more than that is impossible.

You say your event is pointless unless I co-operate. That is precisely the attitude that I want to work against. Only try, and you will see that it will work out fine. Tomorrow or the day after tomorrow you will have to make do without me in any case, so you had better begin today.

Your summons to Halle seems to me to be very gratifying. In Germany and England there is indeed plenty going on. Even with us interest in $\Psi\alpha$ is growing, probably through the influence of the foreigners. The Society is at present applying to obtain a $\psi\alpha$ department in an extension of the general hospital. Getting it would be quite unwelcome for me, because it would have to be in my name; I cannot devote any time to it, and there is no one in the Society to whom I could entrust its management.[1]

Yesterday Stekel wrote me a funny, cheekily silly, affectionate letter to woo for a renewal of our relationship. That is to do with the new journal *Eros and Psyche*, which he is bringing out with Tannenbaum[2] and Silberer.[3] Naturally I am not replying. Frau Hug is very much looking forward to Berlin; she is bright and intelligent, but unfortunately petty, over-sensitive, and quarrelsome as well.

You will all have great pleasure from Sachs if only his health stands up. My son Oliver is taking up his post in a Berlin company this week.

Cordial greetings to you and to your dear wife,
Your faithfully devoted

*Freud*

---

1. These plans did not materialize; instead, the "ambulatorium" of the Vienna Society would be opened on 22 May 1922.
2. Samuel Tannenbaum [1874–1948], M.D., 1898, Columbia, of New York; charter member

1920 July 431

of the New York Society [1911]. During the war, he had already approached Jones to start an Anglo–American psychoanalytical periodical. After the war, when the *International Journal of Psycho-Analysis* was being planned, however, he was not accepted as co-editor and joined Stekel and Herbert Silberer in issuing a periodical entitled *Eros & Psyche*. In 1922, Stekel and Silberer resigned from the editorial board (cf. Jones, 1957: pp. 35–36; Mühlleitner, 1992: pp. 301–303). (See letter 142F, 21 November 1912, & n. 4.)
3. Herbert Silberer, see letter 142F, 21 November 1912, & n. 4.

382A

Berlin-Grünewald
16 July 1920

Dear Professor,

Naturally I obey your arguments. I would definitely not have made the *second* proposal—that you should speak in Berlin *before* the Congress—had you given *that* reason for declining the *first*. You wrote at the time that the dates we had originally proposed were not convenient. Your first letter did not contain a refusal in principle. Therefore I am not quite so much at fault. We have, incidentally, given up the whole plan. In the form we planned it, it would have involved considerable expense, and this could only have been met with your name to arouse interest in medical circles.—But surely you will be speaking in The Hague?

Now I want to tell you about Halle. The paper was read only on 10 July, and was very successful. I spoke before 30 doctors, most of them from the Clinic for Internal Medicine. The psychiatrists stayed away with all kinds of excuses. Only one doctor from the municipal mental hospital turned up. My listeners were at first sceptical and negative. In the course of the paper, their supercilious smiles gave way to the utmost attention. The discussion yielded far more agreement than disagreement. One *Privatdozent* spoke very definitely in favour of $\Psi\alpha$; a second followed. Others put factual questions, including some concerning the possibility of learning $\Psi\alpha$. One of the senior physicians of the clinic told me afterwards that he had up to now completely rejected $\Psi\alpha$ but through my paper he had come to see that there was something in it after all. One young assistant definitely declared that he wanted to get to know $\Psi\alpha$ and that he would come to Berlin for this purpose. The only psychiatrist present, whom I mentioned above, said that the youngest generation of psychiatrists "inclined strongly towards Freud". I left well satisfied. I may possibly speak in the autumn before the Medical Association of Halle, which has about 200 members. Such invitations are in general becoming more frequent. Today, for instance, I was asked whether I would speak this winter to the *Monistenbund*. I did not refuse, hoping to keep a possibility open for Sachs.

There are already about 30 applications for Frau Hug-Hellmuth's course.

Today Ignotus from Budapest,[1] who has been living in Berlin for some months, came to see me to get some news about Ferenczi. I could not tell him anything. Please do give me some information about him! If F's position in Budapest is in so much danger, we should perhaps try to bring him to Vienna. *He* would be the suitable man for the planned polyclinic, which Schmiedeberg was telling me about yesterday. The question "Who?" would in that way be brilliantly solved. But I do not know whether this plan can be carried out.

I have not yet heard anything from Oliver, and Ernst too is silent. I hope you are all well. We are staying at home for the holidays, I am only going away for a few days with my wife at the end of the month, to celebrate my brother's engagement.

With the most cordial greetings to you and your family,
Yours,

*Abraham*[2]

1. Hugó Ignotus (pseudonym for Veigelsberg) [1859–1949], chief editor of the periodical *Nyugat* [West], founded in 1908, which played a major role in Hungarian cultural life as a radical organ of modernity and renewal, and in which many articles about psychoanalysis were also published. Ignotus was a founding member of the Hungarian Psychoanalytic Society and a translator of Freud. In 1919, after the fall of the Soviet republic, Ignotus went to Austria and Germany, but he was again active in Budapest during the 1930s. In 1938 he emigrated to New York, to return to Budapest in 1948.
2. In the following interval in the correspondence, the Sixth International Psychoanalytical Congress took place from 8 to 11 September in The Hague, made possible by the Dutch analysts who paid for the travelling expenses of colleagues from Central Europe and housed 20 of them. Freud talked about "Supplements to the Theory of Dreams" (1920f), Abraham about the female castration complex (1920[67]). Ernest Jones was elected president of the IPA, John Flügel secretary. The *International Journal of Psycho-Analysis* was made the official organ of the Anglo-Saxon societies (see the minutes in the *Zeitschrift*; 1920, 6: 376–402). In The Hague it was also decided to start regular *Rundbriefe* (circular letters) among the members of the Committee.

After the congress Freud and Anna, instead of going to England, as originally planned, toured Holland with van Emden and van Ophuijsen. On 28 September Anna went to Hamburg to visit her nephews, while Freud went to Vienna via Berlin, getting home on 30 September (Jones, 1957: pp. 26–28).

## 383F

Vienna IX, Berggasse 19
31 October 1920

Dear Friend,

I never had in mind that the circular letters should put an end to our private correspondence, only I am afraid that my writing will have to be restricted to Sundays. Nine analytic sessions daily have become a greater strain because of the shift to English (5 sessions). I note with surprise how greatly the effort of listening and inwardly translating uses up one's free energy. Yet by no means have I ever learned English as well as your wife has, and my earnings are still only two-thirds of what they were in times of peace. But one has to be satisfied with that too.

I got excellently over the fact that the distribution of the Nobel Prize passed me over twice and have also realized that any such official recognition would not fit into my style of life at all. On an occasion when I had to appear as an expert witness before a committee investigating a breach of military duties arising out of a charge against Wagner,[1] I could once more see the mendacious spitefulness of the psychiatrists here. But naturally they dared to come out only after I had left. In my presence they were *scheißfreundlich*[2] as one says in the language of the erogenous zones.

I have indeed read your article in the *Rundschau*,[3] it is very clear and correct and for us particularly worth reading. The public will miss phrases and decorations, it may be that it will not have an affective impact.

We are all proud of the upswing in Berlin. Nothing similar is to be expected here. Nunberg will not get a passport, at least that is the rationalized explanation.[4] But here he will probably get no patients. Conditions here are quite dreadful, and nobody knows what will happen.

We are well and lonesome.

With cordial greetings to you and your whole family,

Your faithfully devoted

*Freud*

1. Julius von Wagner-Jauregg [1857–1940], eminent Austrian psychiatrist, director of the First Psychiatric Clinic in Vienna, winner of the Nobel Prize [1927] for the malaria therapy of general paralysis, and discoverer of the role of the thyroid in cretinism and its prevention by the use of iodine (cf. Whitrow, 1993). In December 1918 a committee had been founded to investigate cases in which "electrotherapy" with war neurotics had led to suicides and deaths. Wagner-Jauregg, originally a member of the committee, was himself accused of mistreatment, and his case was brought before the commission on 14 and 16 October. Freud, the chief expert on the first day, confined himself to outlining the differences between his and Wagner's theoretical and clinical views and defending "friend Wagner" (Eissler, 1979: p. 55), with whom he was acquainted from their student days. Wagner was acquitted and fully rehabilitated.
2. Literally, friendly as shit. Austrian expression for being "friendly" in an exaggerated and hypocritical way. [Trans.]
3. Abraham, 1920[69].
4. Nunberg had wanted to move to Berlin (Rank's circular letter, 14 October 1920, BL) but actually stayed in Vienna. Hermann (later Herman) Nunberg [1884–1970] came from Galicia; he studied medicine in Cracow and Zurich, where he worked at the Burghölzli with Jung on the latter's association studies. At the outbreak of the First World War he went to Vienna, where he underwent an analysis with Paul Federn. In 1925 he was a training analyst, and in 1930 a member of the training committee of the Vienna Society.

In 1929 he married Margarethe Rie, the daughter of Freud's friend Oskar Rie. He emigrated in 1932, first to Pennsylvania, in 1934 to New York. He was president of the New York Psychoanalytic Society from 1950 to 1952. Along with Ernst Federn, Nunberg was an editor of the *Minutes of the Vienna Psychoanalytic Society*.

## 384F

Vienna IX, Berggasse 19
28 November 1920

Dear Friend,

On the basis of your agreeing assessment I have spoken to Reik and offered him the position of a literary director, with responsibility for reviews and the annual report.[1] I did not conceal the criticism of his work in the Verlag, and referring to his psychology expressed the hope of a better performance by him in an independent position. He agreed to accept the post with effect from 1 January 1921 and understood that personal considerations will not prevent his being removed if it turns out that he does not measure up to the job. His salary remains the same as before, that is to say very modest, but he has four analyses, which will enable him to keep his head above water.

Now another point arises. He is also willing, even keen, to move to Berlin, where his task would be facilitated in all sorts of ways by association with the polyclinic. The position of the polyclinic itself as the headquarters of the $\psi\alpha$ movement would be only strengthened thereby. The question I now want to ask you is whether in addition to Sachs, whose activities must not be reduced, you also have room for Reik analysing doctors and giving lectures. If that is the case, he can move very quickly, the Verlag will take over his flat here, and we shall have extricated one more of our people from the Vienna quagmire. As Reik has a small family, he has to be found a roof over his head in Berlin. I ask you for an answer to all this.

I am as usual very busy, but the special feature now is that I have to speak and listen to a foreign language for four to six hours a day. To that I attribute my complete lack of productivity. It is an exhausting business. You will receive the "Beyond"[2] in a few days; when my daughter returns I shall be able to devote myself to the mass psychology again. Your book[3] will be ready very soon, you will have heard of other plans from the circular letters, which, though a nuisance, are certainly very useful.

I send my cordial greetings to you and to your dear wife, and I hope the children enjoy "life in the country" also in winter.

Yours,

*Freud*

1. In the *Zeitschrift*.
2. Freud, 1920g.
3. Abraham, 1921[75].

385A

Berlin-Grünewald
6 December 1920

Dear Professor,

Eitingon, Sachs, and I are in full agreement regarding your enquiry on Reik's behalf—that *for the time being* the answer must be negative. We prepared for Sachs for months in advance, that is to say saved up for him all the doctors who were eager for analysis. At the moment there are no cases or, at most, one appropriate one. As the colleague in question is in a bad financial position, it is as good as if he were nonexistent—speaking in Reik's own financial interest. Sachs is fully occupied. If *new* analysands turn up, we could keep them for Reik, but that will take rather a long time. With regard to lectures, there is sufficient scope for one, but *at present* there is not enough for *two*.

We feel that all of you in Vienna have a mistaken idea about conditions in Berlin. You write about R. that he is "keeping his head above water" in Vienna. He could not expect more here, for it is no different for *any of us*. Expenditure on necessities completely runs through even a "large" income. We are very pleased that Sachs, for instance, has *sufficient* income to live comfortably. Reik, who would naturally for some time earn less than Sachs, has a wife and child to feed and would have great difficulties. You must consider also that I, for instance, can only just earn enough for our needs. The only thing that Reik might find better here is that food is easier to get. But I shall keep the whole matter in mind. The gratifying progress of our cause in Berlin may present better prospects at a later date! Incidentally, it is not clear to us how the person responsible for the literature could work at such a distance from the journals. Correspondence is too difficult at present.

We have decided to include something about conditions in Berlin in our next Committee letter, so that, for instance, Ferenczi and his colleagues are informed and are preserved from having too great hopes.

I have very good news to report about my introductory course. The participants remain as keen as ever, and there is already pressure for an advanced course.

You, dear Professor, will be interested to hear that your gift of 100 guilders has found its use.[1] With the help of a patient I shall get bicycles for *both* children, and there will soon be double rejoicing.

At yesterday's charity evening for the polyclinic Oliver and Anna were also present. It went off very satisfactorily.

I hope you and your family are well; that is the case with *my* family too. I still suffer often from the consequences of the intestinal infection, and today I again had the pleasure of an evacuation of the stomach. I must soon have a break for at least 14 days.

With best regards, as always,

Yours,

*Abraham*

1. Because of inflation in Austria and Germany, Freud had received Dutch currency for his congress expenses. He gave the remainder to Abraham to buy presents for his children.

# 1921

386F
[to Mrs Abraham]
Vienna IX, Berggasse 19
3 January 1921

Dear Mrs Abraham,

Your children's letters were too charming—I hope they did not cost them too much trouble or even tears, were not rewritten several times, etc. I should have answered the little ones directly, but I was afraid of undermining their morals, because I should certainly have thought of confessing that the finest gifts are spoilt by having to say thank you for them. It would also have embarrassed me either to go on playing the part of the great patron or having to admit that I had made them happy by means of the resources of others. When the opportunity arises, please tell them the true state of affairs, to which the moral can be attached that also by work like the practice of psychoanalysis it is possible to acquire a few Dutch guilders sometime late in life.

From your news I pick out the one that your husband is now at last well again. We were already quite annoyed about his illness. Here too we are haunted by more illness than is actually indispensable.

Wishing you all a Happy New Year, richer in fulfilment and entirely devoid of anything disagreeable,
Your faithfully devoted
*Freud*

387F
Vienna[1]
4 February 1921

Dear Friend,

My hearty congratulations on the appearance of your book, which is generally appreciated by the analysts as a collection of classical, model papers. Incidentally, Deuticke is willing to publish a second edition of *Dreams and Myths*, if you would get in touch with him.

With warmest greetings
from your
   *Freud*

C.[orragio] C.[asimiro]!

1. Postcard.


## 388A

Berlin-Grünewald
9 February 1921

Dear Professor,

My most sincere thanks for letting me know with such warm congratulations about the publication of my book. You know best how much of the book stems from ideas that you had started working on. I may say that, as I wrote each separate paper over all these years, I wanted to make my readers aware of my gratitude and devotion towards you. And because I thought that these sentiments were clearly enough recognizable, I omitted dedicating the book as a whole to you. Rank will present you with a copy on my behalf for, due to the trouble with exporting, I would not be able to send it from here in any case. I know no better way to heed the encouraging "CC" on your card than by unadulterated loyal participation in our common work.

I shall get in touch with Deuticke about *Dreams and Myths* as soon as I have a more precise idea about the amount of revision it will require.

My wife was particularly pleased with the letter she received from you some time ago and sends her belated thanks. It is virtually impossible to separate the children from their bicycles; if you have ever made anyone happy, dear Professor, you definitely have succeeded here!

With kindest regards from house to house,
Yours,
   *Karl Abraham*


## 389A

Berlin-Grünewald
27 February 1921

Dear Professor,

A few days ago I was visited by a lady from Warsaw whose brother, Julius Hering, was treated by you at the end of 1919. Apparently he had a psychosis, which improved under Ψα. It seems that on the way home he had an acute relapse. H. has been in a lunatic asylum in Warsaw for a year. The family would like to bring him to Berlin, to let him continue his treatment with me. There has evidently been a remission, but he still has a fixed persecution mania.

In such circumstances I naturally have great misgivings, especially as H. would have to be in a sanatorium here and would need someone to accompany him in order to come to me. I have asked for a report from the doctor treating him at present, which is to be sent to me to Merano, and I would be very grateful to you, dear Professor, for a *very short* expression of opinion (to Merano).

I am leaving with my wife on the evening of 2 March; we shall be in M. (Park Hotel) on the 4th. Should you by any chance be travelling southwards over Easter . . . but that would be too lovely. We should like then to go to Verona—Venice for a few days. With kindest regards from house to house.

Yours,

*Karl Abraham*

## 390F

Vienna IX, Berggasse 19
6 March 1921

Dear Friend,

Ungrudging congratulations on your well-earned convalescence leave! I hope your "hand luggage" (the two Glovers[1]) will not disturb you too much. Unfortunately I cannot think of coming to see you in the beautiful south. I am glad to be tolerably well, and able to mint money and work on the Mass Psychology.

Jul. Hering is a real persecution fanatic, whose chances are not good. He suffers from uncontrollable sexual excitement during the night, which is probably directed towards men. For me the beginnings of influencing him broke down when the money with which he should have paid me did not materialize. A bad case!

Recently I have quite frequently given your address to people who applied to me for treatment, including on one occasion, after a suggestion from America, to a lady in Königsberg. In this respect your absence from Berlin is an embarrassment to me. Otherwise I count on your handing on to others the cases you cannot deal with yourself.

With best wishes for weather and well being (alliteration!),

Yours,

*Freud*

1. The brothers James and Edward Glover, both in analysis with Abraham since the beginning of the year (circular letter of 10 January 1921, BL); they became full members of the British Society in 1922.
   James Glover [1882–1926], M.B., CH.B. 1903 Glasgow, at the Medico-Psychological Clinic, Brunswick Square. Of delicate health, he left the London climate for Spain; he returned from there with dysentery and malaria and died at the age of 44. "He had galvanized the British Psycho-Analytic Society with his personality" (Meisel & Kendrick, 1986: p. 307).
   Edward Glover [1888–1972], M.D. 1915 Glasgow. He later played an important role in the British Society, especially in the "Freud/Klein controversies" in the 1940s, being on all the main committees of the Society and Institute and chairing many of the Special Meetings. Originally a supporter of Klein, he later joined her daughter (and his analysand) Melitta Schmideberg in her criticism of her mother. Chairman of the Training Committee until his resignation from the Society in January 1944, whereupon, in 1949, he joined the Swiss Society. (Cf. Roazen, 2000.)

## 391A

Berlin-Grünewald
2 May 1921

Dear Professor,

Our good wishes were expressed in the Committee letter which has just gone off, and Eitingon will certainly repeat what we wanted to say when he presents you with the bust.[1] This does not prevent me, however, from sending my personal and special good wishes in this letter, naturally on behalf of my wife as well. I very much regret that I do not have Eitingon's freedom of movement; otherwise, nothing would have stopped me from visiting you on the occasion of your birthday and expressing my good wishes to you personally. I hope we shall spend some harmonious time together in the autumn.

I take this opportunity of thanking you, dear Professor, for the various recommendations that were recently delivered to me by patients (including Dr Sternberg, and Lewin-Epstein).

With the "Corragio, Casimiro!" so appropriate nowadays and with kindest regards,
Yours,

*Karl Abraham*

1. A bust of Freud by the Viennese sculptor David Paul Königsberger, which was presented to Freud as a gift for his 65th birthday. Jones gave a copy to the University of Vienna, where it was unveiled in 1955 (Jones, 1957: p. 25). "Evidently, I was taken in after all; I really thought Eitingon wanted to have it for himself, otherwise I wouldn't have sat for it last year" (Freud to Ferenczi, 8 May 1921).

1921 June

## 392F

Vienna IX, Berggasse 19
8 May 1921

Dear Friend,

Be satisfied with this short letter of thanks and Eitingon's report. I am short of sleep, and am trying to clear a mountain of correspondence.

With so many good wishes one is reminded how old one is, and presents make one infantile, which indeed goes well together.

We Viennese agree to your suggestion for the Committee meeting.[1] With best wishes for you and yours,
Yours,

*Freud*

1. Abraham's suggestion, in a circular letter of 21 April 1921 (BL), for a meeting of the Committee in September in the Harz mountains.

## 393A

Berlin-Grünewald
12 June 1921

Dear Professor,

As I sent off the Committee letter only yesterday, there is not much to tell you, but I come as a petitioner in a cause that, for me and other members of our Society, is very urgent.

In one of the latest Committee reports I mentioned a woman student called Hubermann,[1] who has established herself very well in our circle through splendid work and an extraordinary understanding of Ψα. It has now come to light that she has pulmonary tuberculosis in a relatively benign form, i.e. dry pleurisy taking a very chronic course, but recently with daily fever. An excellent specialist predicts that three months of bed rest would have *lasting* success. By acting quickly, we could save a really valuable worker for Ψα quite apart from the humanitarian side of the matter. Apart from the patient's own small means, 5–6,000 M are necessary for the cure. I spoke with Eitingon, who was also of the opinion that I should ask you, dear Professor, for a contribution out of one of the funds, especially as *this* source would make it much easier for the patient to accept support, whereas she resists private help. Eitingon thinks the American fund could perhaps be called upon. 100 dollars would correspond exactly with the sum needed. It would be wonderful if the matter could be settled in this way. I am asking only for a very brief decision as to whether we can expect the money. I enclose the address of my bank; naturally the contribution can just as well go to

**PROF. DR. FREUD**      16. 6. 21.
WIEN, IX., BERGGASSE 19.

Lieber Freund

Die Sache ist einfach. Sie stehen für die Personen die Eitingon bekräftigt nicht auf jeden sonst. Bleibt aber nur übrig, der Leipziger Firma den Auftrag für Überweisung von $100 an die neue Ihnen bekannten Adresse zu geben was auch bereits geschehen ist.

Herzlich
Ihr Freud

1921   June

Eitingon, if that is perhaps more convenient, as he is always dealing with American money.
Heartfelt thanks in advance! And best wishes from
Your
*Karl Abraham*

1. Circular letter of 21 May 1921 (BL).


## 394F

Vienna IX, Berggasse 19
16 June 1921

Dear Friend,

It is a simple matter. You vouch for the person, Eitingon approves the expenditure. So all there is for me to do is to give instructions to the Leipzig firm to transfer $100 to the address you have enclosed. Which has already been done.

Cordially,
Yours,
*Freud*


## 395A

Grünewald[1]
26 June 1921

Dear Professor,

Soon after you wrote to me, I received the transfer from Leipzig. As 100 dollars come to almost 7,000 M. at present, the whole cost of the cure for three months is covered by it, and I believe we are doing an extraordinarily good deed with this money. I am very grateful to you for dealing with it so promptly. Frau H. is already going into the sanatorium on 1 July. She will write to you personally.

At the moment I am alone. My wife has gone to the Harz for two to three weeks with the children. I suppose you are soon getting ready to leave too. Yesterday evening Sachs was here, and we rejoiced in advance in the pleasure of the meeting in September.

With cordial greetings,
Yours,
*Abraham*

1. Postcard.

## 396A

Berlin-Grünewald
21 July 1921

Dear Professor,

The Comm. letters have just been finished. Rank will send you the Vienna copy,[1] so that I do not have to report a great deal from here. Anyhow I want to mention to you, before I come to the point of this letter, that a publishing house here wants to translate a selection of your writings into Yiddish.—

I have to ask you today for some information I need for a quotation. I am busy writing a short paper on rescue phantasies.[2] It deals particularly with the phantasy in which the neurotic sees a carriage approaching along the road, with the emperor or some other father-substitute in it, and the horses bolting. He seizes the horses' reins and thus rescues the emperor.—I think you have mentioned this particular phantasy somewhere. In "Contributions to the Psychology of Love, I" I can only find a general reference to the rescue of a high-ranking father substitute.[3] Even Eitingon, with his almost unfailing knowledge of the literature, cannot help me. I therefore ask for a hint on your part! I have come across this phantasy in several analyses, but feel that I first heard about it from *you*. Many thanks in anticipation!

Secondly, could you let me know now *approximately*[4] when and for how long you think we shall be meeting in September? I must know this as soon as possible because of other arrangements. An *approximate* date would naturally be sufficient!

I hope, dear Professor, that things are going well with you there and you will fully recuperate, so that in September we shall find you as fit as you were last year. With cordial greetings, also from my wife,

Yours,

*Abraham*

1. To Gastein, where Freud had gone on holiday with his sister-in-law Minna Bernays on 15 July. His wife Martha, who was in poor health, had joined Anna and Ernstl Halberstadt in the Salzkammergut. On 14 August the whole family went via Innsbruck to Seefeld in the Tyrol. On 14 September Freud went to Berlin, then to Hamburg, from where he travelled, on 21 September, to the Committee meeting in the Harz.
2. Abraham, 1922[76].
3. Freud, 1910h: pp. 172–173.
4. Doubly underlined in original.

## 397F

Vienna IX, Berggasse 19
24 July 1921
Bad Gastein

Dear Friend,

You are right, the phantasy stems from me, even though it refers only to an imago, a man of importance, not to father or emperor. But where is it? It is difficult to trace it here, as I do not take all my works with me on my travels. But I think you will find it in the Everyday Life, among the paramnesias, where I try to explain why I call the day-dreamer in *Le Nabab*[1] Mr Jocelyn, though his real name is Joyeuse. If that is not where it is, this hint will be sufficient to guide your or Eitingon's memory to the right place. (*Interpretation of Dreams?*)[2]

It will incidentally interest you to hear that a few months ago a young woman student sent me a Hof[f]mann booklet in which such a rescue is described; because of the verbal correspondence it must have been the cryptomnesic source of my Paris phantasy.[3] Surely you know these pearls of a high school library? I naturally read and forgot many of these booklets, because whenever one boastfully applied for a serious book, one was always thrown back into one's childhood by one of these Hofmann booklets, which were innumerable.

Here I am enjoying rest and idleness, and send my cordial greetings.
Yours,

*Freud*

1. Novel by Alphonse Daudet [1840–1897], whom Freud "more than once met . . . in Charcot's house" (Freud, 1901b: p. 149).
2. In *The Psychopathology of Everyday Life* (1901b: pp. 149–150), Freud discussed his slip of remembering "Jocelyn" instead of "Joyeuse" (French for Freud) when writing *The Interpretation of Dreams* (cf. 1900a: pp. 491 and 535).
3. Referring to a popular series, Franz Hoffmann's *Jugendbibliothek* [Library for Young People]. In 1924, Freud added a footnote to the pertinent passage in *Everyday Life*, tracing his rescue phantasy to his having read such a scene between the ages of 11 and 13 (1901b: p. 150).

## 398A

Grünewald
6 August 1921

Dear Professor,

Just as I was about to write to you, the Mass Psychology arrived. I am looking forward to reading it for the second time during the next few days and for now only want to thank you very much indeed!

At the same time I am sending you the short manuscript on rescue phantasies. Rank has already received a copy. I prefer to send you a copy before it goes to print, firstly, because I do not wish to introduce something as *new* when it may already have been said; and secondly, because I should like to know whether you agree with the contents. And since the paper is only a short one, I hope you will not be angry with me for sending it to you during your holidays. If anything that I assumed to be new is already contained in one of your papers, I would ask you to return the manuscript with a short remark. Otherwise, I should be grateful if you would briefly let me know that you agree!*

Furthermore, I have to thank you for the hint you gave me. I am sure the section in the *Interpretation of Dreams* that you mentioned is the one I had been looking for without success.

But I must remind you of the other question contained in my earlier letter, because you have not yet answered it. I asked you for a rough idea of when our meeting shall take place. Because of another journey I want to make beforehand, I ought to have the rough information in my hands already. If you could give me the approximate date of the rendezvous on the same postcard on which you reply to me about the article, I shall be very happy.

After having had patients only in the mornings for two to three weeks, I have recently reopened the whole business. Not very easy in this heat! But after the almost five-week-long journey to Merano in March, I cannot very well have another longish interruption at present, yet I am thinking of using the second half of September for it. In any case, the practice is very lucrative, and recently it has at the same time been particularly successful from a therapeutic point of view.

With cordial greetings, also from my wife,
Yours,

*Abraham*

* The manuscript can then be destroyed.

## 399A

Grünewald[1]
7 August 1921

Dear Professor,

I have just heard that as long as a week ago you became a grandfather in Berlin as well.[2] So I am hastening to send this card after my letter; it is laden with good wishes for you and your wife, naturally also from my wife.

With cordial greetings,
Yours,

*Abraham*

1921 August

1. Postcard.
2. Stephan Gabriel, son of Ernst and Lucie Freud, was born on 31 July.

## 400F

Vienna IX, Berggasse 19
8 August 1921
Bad Gastein

Dear Friend,

I have nothing to lay my claim on and no objections to make, I fully agree with your deeper interpretation of the rescue phantasy, and I wish only to draw your attention to an awkward feature of the Oedipus passage which has already caused me a great deal of trouble.

You write of a "hollow way" as a place where they met, which is just as suitable to us as a symbol of the genital as for the incident about giving way. L. *Frank*, who has retold the story of the ψα patricide in the "Ursache",[1] also makes his hero engage in phantasies about a "hollow way" that he cannot properly remember. But the Greek texts known to me speak of a ὁδος σχίστη, which means, not "hollow way" but "crossroads", at which, one would suppose, giving way would not be difficult. Would it not be as well to consult a scholar before you publish?

I cannot decide the date of our congress[2] alone. I was thinking of the last week in September, so that I could be in Vienna on the 30th. The question of the beginning should soon be settled. A great deal depends on Jones's arrangements.

My cordial greetings to you and yours,
Yours,

*Freud*

1. Frank, 1915. Leonhard Frank [1882–1961], German writer and pacifist.
2. That is, the meeting of the Committee.

## 401A

Grünewald
10 August 1921

Dear Professor,

I owe you thanks for the prompt answer to my request, and I am glad that you agree with the results of the short work. I would have liked to get some information about the "hollow way", but as I have no expert available immediately, I preferred to leave this detail out completely.

I hope you will be able to enjoy the next few weeks in Seefeld with your family. In the meantime I shall go on working up to our meeting. I have seldom had such scientifically satisfying material. It seems that a supplement to the problem of melancholy is taking shape[1]; perhaps I can talk about it in the autumn, as well as about a few other new discoveries.

Your Ernst, who is a very proud and happy father, recently spent an evening with us. He is designing a re-furbishing of my study for me, which promises to be very fine.

Now I have two more questions, but there is absolutely no hurry for the answers. Perhaps in the course of the next few weeks you would give me a brief opinion. (1.) Would it be all right if, for our meeting, I were to pick you up from Hamburg, so that we could travel together to the general meeting-place in *Hanover*?[2] (More details about that in the circular letter, which will reach you via Rank in the next few days). In that case I should like to ask Herr Halberstadt to take a photograph of me while I am there. (2.) It was mentioned in an earlier circular letter that the expenses of our meeting would be paid through a fund. As I should like to make arrangements for lodgings etc. in several places some time in advance, it would be convenient for me to know whether I must keep to certain limits in the choice of hotels, rooms, etc. In my view it would not be a bad thing at all if everybody were to contribute to the costs; but as in first-class hotels prices have now risen greatly, I should prefer not to have to act entirely off my own bat.

Sachs came back yesterday and was our guest in the evening. He has become considerably slimmer, but is in good health.

Nothing else new from here. My wife and I greet you and yours with all our hearts!

Yours,

*Abraham*

1. About which Abraham would speak at the next Psychoanalytic Congress [Berlin, 1922]; he incorporated it into his classic *Study of the Development of the Libido* (1917[105]).
2. Actually, Freud, Eitingon, and Sachs would travel together from Berlin to the meeting-place in Hildesheim. Abraham, who visited relatives in Bremen, arrived via Hamburg (Grosskurth, 1991: p. 19).

## 402F

Vienna IX, Berggasse 19
19 August 1921
Seefeld

Dear Friend,

A reply to both your questions: I shall be very glad if you pick me up from Hamburg, but I may come to Berlin from there. Two purposes intersect in me; one is to bring my grandson Ernst[1] home without a long delay, the other is to make the acquaintance of my new Gabriel.

The second point is much easier to deal with. As Eitingon is the dispenser of the Fund and has access to it, I have asked him to bring the money for the Congress with him. I have [asked him] to bring 3,000 marks for each participant (6, not including myself); have had no reply to tell me whether that seems to him to be enough. You could therefore discuss it with him and get the money needed directly from him.

It is very fine here, and I am very inactive.

Cordially yours,

*Freud*

1. Who stayed with the Freuds in Seefeld.

## 403A

Grünewald[1]
25 August 1921

Dear Professor,

Many thanks for your prompt information! In the meantime Jones has declared himself in agreement with 21 September, which can now be considered as decided. But as Jones may be going to Nuremberg *beforehand*, and you yourself may be travelling from Berlin, Hanover can perhaps no longer be considered as a meeting-place, and we could meet directly in Hildesheim. We in Berlin ask you to let us know up to 7 September *from where* you are coming to join the others. If we know this about everybody, we will fix the place and the exact time and let you know. Therefore I ask you, dear Professor, also to let us know where you can be reached by post between 10 and 15 September. (Should Ferenczi be near you, please inform him about everything. As he has not replied to a letter to Partenkirchen,[2] I am uncertain whether my card of today will reach him.[)]

Accept, together with your family, the most cordial greetings, also from my wife!

Yours,

*Abraham*[3]

1. Postcard.
2. Ferenczi followed a course of treatment in Garmisch-Partenkirchen in southern Germany, from where he visited Freud in Seefeld on 30 August (telegram to Freud, 29 August 1930).
3. The meeting in the Harz took place as planned. For this occasion, Freud had prepared a talk on "Psychoanalysis and Telepathy", published posthumously in abbreviated form (Freud, 1941d [1921]; cf. Falzeder, 1994).

## 404A

Berlin-Grünewald
4 December 1921

Dear Professor,

This is the first letter I have written to you directly since our meeting. Our circular letters fulfil so completely the purpose of giving new information and asking questions that only occasionally are a few private things left over.

You surely remember the talk we had on that rainy day on the way to Schierke. To my delight I can tell you today that I have recently had a more favourable impression of Sachs. Offences like those that attracted our attention on the way, and all the other changes that I mentioned at the time, are scarcely evident now. On the contrary, I found that on certain occasions a good, firm sense of tact appears. I am beginning to hope that the worries we had are thus becoming without substance; but naturally we still have to wait for the near future. I shall report to you again in a short time. I know that this news will please you, and so I did not want to keep it from you any longer.

Now for something else. Recently my wife and I spent an evening in Ernst's charming home in the Regentenstrasse. On this occasion I was again convinced of the splendid progress of your little grandson. I cannot remember having seen, in a child of this age, such a calmly observant expression, as though he were scanning all about him systematically (heritage from the grandfather?).

Last Sunday we had Oliver with us; before this he had not come out of his work at all. He is always particularly kind to our children; our little boy is his special friend and feels very honoured by the project of a mutual exchange of bicycle handlebars.

I do not expect any answer to this letter, dear Professor. If you want to acknowledge that you have received it, you can do that in the next circular letter.

With cordial greetings to you and yours, also from my wife.

Yours,

*Karl Abraham*

## 405F

Vienna IX, Berggasse 19
9 December 1921

Dear Friend,

I am very pleased at your news about Sachs, as happens every time I have reason to assume that the gloominess of old age makes me see things from too unfavourable a point of view. Unfortunately Sachs

1921 December

has become somewhat estranged from me in the last few years, and knows that himself.

In the name of my lady of the house I invite you to be our guest when you come here at the New Year for your lecture. We have arranged a room as a guest-room, which is at present occupied by Frau Lou Andreas.[1] She praises it highly, we know it not to be ideal, but still it is as good as a hotel-room—hotels are now terribly dear—and it is well heated.

With cordial greetings to you and to your wife and children,
Yours,

*Freud*

1. Lou Andreas-Salomé stayed until 20 December. "In the room in which Frau Lou stayed, we will house early in January, one after the other, Abraham and Ferenczi, who shall lecture to our Americans" (Freud to Ernst and Lucie Freud, 20 December 1921, LOC). Abraham eventually postponed his trip to late January (see letter 407A, 18 January 1922).

## 406A

Grünewald[1]
25 December 1921

Dear Professor,

This card brings you my most sincere thanks for your delightful Christmas gift![2] You yourself know best how beautiful the lectures look in this binding, and so I do not need to say any more about it.— If no *vis maior* (strike?!) intervenes, I hope to be with you on 3 January. For your wife's information I would like to mention that I shall be having dinner on the train. There is therefore no need for even the smallest preparations for my arrival. Also I would expressly ask that no one should take the trouble to meet me at the station. A car will take me to Berggasse in a few minutes.

Oliver, who has just left us, has told me everything a foreigner needs to know. I am very much looking forward to seeing all of you *in Vienna* once again after such a long interval and hope to find you well. With kind regards to you and your whole house,
Yours,

*Karl Abraham*

1. Postcard.
2. A special leather-bound pocket edition of Freud's *Introductory Lectures*, published by the Verlag.

# 1922

### 407A

Grünewald[1]
18 January 1922

Dear Professor,

You will have heard from Rank that I am prepared to leave on Sunday the 22nd, thus to reach Vienna on Monday afternoon. I hope to find you and your family in the best of health. But I must make it very clear that my journey is again threatened. Today's morning papers report that a railway strike is imminent in Saxony. Since the lines via both Passau and Prague go through Saxony, you must be prepared for my calling it off at the last minute. If necessary, I can leave a little earlier and try to go a roundabout way to catch the connection in Passau.

Meanwhile I hope everything will go well.

With the most cordial greetings from house to house.

Yours,

*Abraham*

1. Postcard.

### 408A

Berlin-Grünewald
13 March 1922

Dear Professor,

It is a long time since I was in Vienna, and you have not had any direct news since then. I only wrote to your wife after my return home to thank you all for the pleasant days in Vienna. Everything that has happened since has found room in the circular letter, and, since in Vienna I again had the opportunity of seeing how your correspondence keeps you busy far into the night, I feel even more reluctant than before to add to your burden. At other times, however, my wish to report to you gains the upper hand, and today I am giving in to this for a change.

My load of work is frequently so overwhelming that it prevents me from ploughing my way, as I would like to, through certain problems in my spare time. Particularly the problems of manic-depressive states. Nevertheless, my two analyses in this field give me a great deal of

1922 March

*The "Secret Committee" in Vienna—front row, left to right: Sigmund Freud, Sándor Ferenczi, Hanns Sachs; back row, left to right: Otto Rank, Karl Abraham, Max Eitingon, Ernest Jones (1922).*

information in their daily sessions, and some of the questions we discussed in the autumn are beginning to take more definite shape. I think the parallels to kleptomania, which also stems from the oral phase and represents the biting-off of penis or breast, are quite interesting. The regression of the melancholic has the same aim, only in a different form.[1]

The taking in of the love-object is very striking in my cases. I can produce very nice material for this concept of yours, revealing the process in all its detail. In this connection I have a small request—for an offprint of "Mourning and Melancholia", which would be extremely helpful to me in my work. Many thanks in anticipation.

One brief comment on this piece of work! You, dear Professor, state that you miss in the course of normal mourning a process that would correspond to the swing-over from melancholia to mania. I think, however, that I could identify such a process, without knowing whether this reaction is regularly found. My impression is that a fair number of people show an increase in libido some time after a bereavement. It shows itself in heightened sexual need and appears quite often to lead, e.g., to conception shortly after a bereavement.[2] Sometime at your convenience I should like to know what you think about this and whether you can confirm this observation. The increase in libido some time after "object-loss" would seem to be a good addition to the parallel between mourning and melancholia.—

What you told me about *pseudologia phantastica* has been fully confirmed for me. My female patient's quite fantastic lies do in fact correspond to a *psychological* truth.[3]

I should like to mention briefly that I shall in the near future speak in our Society on a special form of parapraxis. I shall soon be dictating this short paper[4] and shall send it off to Rank. It is about those slips that, like obsessional actions, do not permit the repressed tendency to break through but overcompensate for it.

About our doings here I can tell you that my wife and I went to see Oliver once, when he was still in bed, and recently we had him with us for an evening. The knee injury appears to be healing.

In analytic circles here there is nothing new apart from what was reported in the circular letter.

I hope you are all well. I can say the same of us. At present we are already making plans for the summer (St Anton on the Arlberg?). Before that, however, my wife will have to go to a thermal bath for her sciatica.

Another small comment. At a recent meeting, one of our members drew our attention to an interesting misprint. In your *Kleine Schriften IV*, "History of the Ψα Movement", in the footnote on p. 74—"discredition" instead of "discretion". This misprint does *not* occur in the original (*Jahrbuch der Ψα*). How the type-setter made the error is less interesting than the fact that it was overlooked in proof-reading. The intention of discrediting Jung comes to the fore in a most amusing way.[5]

With many cordial greetings to your whole house, also in my wife's name!

Yours,

*Karl Abraham*

1. Cf. Abraham, 1917c: pp. 483, 485, 498.
2. Cf. Abraham, 1917c: 472–473.
3. Cf. Abraham, 1917c: 483–484.
4. Abraham, 1922[78].
5. Freud had used the report of a patient of Jung's to criticize the latter's technique, by adding "that I cannot allow that a psycho-analytic technique has any right to claim the protection of medical discre[di]tion" (1914d: p. 64).

1922 March

## 409F

Vienna IX, Berggasse 19
30 March 1922

Dear Friend,

After more than a fortnight I decide to reread your kind private letter and discover your request for a reprint, which for some reason made no impact on me when I received it.

I plunge with pleasure into the abundance of your scientific insights and intentions, only I wonder why you do not take into account at all my last suggestion about the nature of mania after melancholia (in the Mass Psychology).[1] Might that be the motivation for my forgetting about the "Mourning and Melancholia"? For analysis, no absurdity is impossible. I would still have felt like discussing all these things—particularly with you—but no possibility of writing about them. In the evening I am lazy, and above all there is the urgent "business" correspondence, cancelling lectures, journeys, collaborations, and the like, which stands in the way of a decent exchange of ideas with one's friends. I am now doubly glad that we instituted the circular letters. With eight and soon nine hours' work, I do not manage to achieve the composure required for scientific work. At Gastein, between 1 July and 1 August, I hope to be able to commit to paper some little things that I told you about in the Harz.[2]

The rest of the summer, from 1 August until the middle of September, is still as blank as the map of Central Africa was in my schooldays.[3] The Austrian summer is going to be a difficult problem. Meanwhile the spring is also appalling.

You will see my daughter before I do,[4] and you are no doubt in contact with my two sons as well. Our house is quite lonely, enlivened at present only by the semi-young American niece.[5] Of your American audience only one is still here, Dr Polon.[6] But Dr Frink[7] is to come back on 26 April. Mrs Strachey was dangerously ill, so that both she and her husband have broken off the analysis.[8] Substitutes always move in on time; at present I have three Swiss people: Sarasin,[9] the Kempner woman[10] and a young Dr Blum from Zurich,[11] three English, Rickman,[12] that proud woman Riviere,[13] whom you will surely remember from The Hague, and a Prof. Tansley from Cambridge,[14] who is starting tomorrow, and two Americans, including the only full patient. At Easter a Dutch *dottoressa*[15] who has just received her doctorate is to take over from Dr Polon. I find character analyses with pupils more difficult in many respects than with professional neurotics, but admittedly I have not yet worked out the new technique.

My cordial greetings to your dear wife and the two rapidly growing children. I did not know your wife had acquired such an obstinate sciatica.

Do let yourself be carried away into writing a private letter again to your faithful

*Freud*

1. Freud, 1921c: pp. 132–133.
2. "Psycho-analysis and Telepathy" (Freud, 1941d [1921]). "The MS. bears at its beginning the date '2 Aug. 21' and at its end 'Gastein, 6 Aug. 21'" (editor's note in *S.E. 18*: p. 175).
3. On 30 June, Freud and Minna Bernays went to Gastein; on 1 August they went on to Berchtesgaden, where they were joined by Martha, Anna, Oliver, the Hollitschers, and Ernst and Lucie. In Berchtesgaden Freud wrote *The Ego and the Id* (1923b), was visited by Eitingon, and analysed Frink. On 14 September Freud and Anna went to Hamburg, from where they arrived in Berlin on the 21st, where the VIIth International Psychoanalytic Congress was held from 25 to 27 September 1922.
4. Anna had left Vienna on 2 March for Hamburg via Berlin for a stay with her nephews and brother-in-law. On 19 April she went to Berlin and on 25 April to Lou Andreas-Salomé in Göttingen, returning home on 5 May (Freud/Anna Freud correspondence, LOC).
5. Judith ("Ditha") Bernays [1885–1977], daughter of Freud's brother-in-law Eli Bernays [1860–1923] and his sister Anna [1858–1955].
6. Albert Polon [1881–1926], neurologist, M.D. 1910 Cornell University Medical College.
7. Horace Westlake Frink [1883–1935], professor of neurology at Cornell University Medical College [1914], founding member of the New York Psychoanalytic Society, its first secretary [1911], and president in 1913 and 1923. During a previous analysis, in 1921, "Freud advised Frink . . . to divorce his wife and marry a former patient . . . The prospect set off a series of manic depressive episodes, and Frink returned twice to Freud for more analysis. . . . As Frink's state deteriorated, he sought treatment with Adolf Meyer, was divorced by his second wife" (Hale, 1995: p. 29), but "never fully recovered" (Hale, 1971a: p. 387; cf. Edmunds, 1988).
8. Alix, née Sargant-Florence [1892–1973], and James Strachey [1887–1967], best known today for their work on what became known as the *Standard Edition*. Prominent members of the "Bloomsbury" group, including James's brother Lytton, Virginia and Leonard Woolf, analysts Karin and Adrian Stephen (Virginia's brother), John Maynard Keynes, Clive Bell, Saxon Sydney-Turner, and Roger Fry, among others. Both had started analysis with Freud in October 1920. Although Alix's analysis soon had to be interrupted because of illness, she and James were declared fit to practice analysis by Freud. Associate Members [1922] and Members [1923] of the British Society. In 1924/25, Alix continued analysis with Abraham. (Cf. Meisel & Kendrick, 1986; Roazen, 1995; and the vast "Bloomsbury" literature.)
9. Philipp Sarasin [1888–1968], M.D., from Basel. He had worked at the Burghölzli [1915] —where he had had analysis with Franz Riklin—and at the psychiatric clinic in Rheinau, Switzerland [1916–1921]. After his analysis with Freud, he settled in Basel in private practice. Long-term president of the Swiss Society [1928–1960]. (See Walser, 1976/77: p. 473.)
10. Salomea Kempner [1880–194?], from Plock, Poland, formerly assistant doctor at the clinic in Rheinau. In 1921 she had moved to Vienna and in 1923 to Berlin, where she worked at the polyclinic. Member of the Swiss, Vienna, and Berlin Societies, consecutively. She disappeared in the Warsaw ghetto. (Cf. Mühlleitner, 1992: pp. 181–182.)
11. Ernst Blum [1892–1981]. After his analysis with Freud, in 1924 he settled as a neurologist, psychiatrist, and psychoanalyst in Bern (Weber, 1991). "He had a wide range of interests and assumed an independent point of view within Swiss psychoanalysis" (Moser, 1992: p. 295).
12. John Rickman [1891–1951], M.D., associate member [1920], member [1922], and

president [1948] of the British Society. Also analysand of Ferenczi's [1928–31] and Melanie Klein's (prior to the Second World War). Rickman "played a key role in the early administration of the Society and Institute, in its publications activities and its link with allied professions" (King & Steiner, 1991: p. xviii). Having belonged first to Melanie Klein's group, he was later considered part of the "Middle Group" and took an active part in the compromise with Anna Freud.

13. Joan Riviere [1883–1962], in analysis with Freud since February 27 (Freud to Riviere, 5 February 1922, LOC). She had already been in analysis with Ernest Jones [1915]. Riviere was a founding member of the British Society [1919], an important translator of Freud's, translation editor of the *International Journal of Psycho-Analysis*, and member of the Glossary Committee. Riviere later supported Melanie Klein. There are numerous references to her sharp intellect and tongue.

14. Sir Arthur George Tansley [1871–1955], British botanist and plant ecologist, a friend of James Strachey's. Founder of the science of ecology (Payne, 1956). Member of the British Society.

15. Adriana (Jeanne) de Groot [1895–1987], M.D., in analysis with Freud from 1922 to 1925, and again in 1931. In 1925 she moved to Berlin and married analyst Hans Lampl. Between 1933 and 1938 again in Vienna, then in the Netherlands. Member of the Dutch [1925], German [1926], and Vienna [1933] Societies. (Cf. Mühlleitner, 1992: pp. 202–204.)

## 410A

Berlin-Grünewald
2 May 1922

Dear Professor,

Your forthcoming birthday gives me a welcome excuse to write to you once again outside the framework of the circular letters. Thus this letter is filled with best wishes. As far as I am aware, I have no need to overcompensate for *bad* wishes, and a few words will therefore suffice to assure you once again of the cordiality of my affection.

As on several former occasions, I am once again enclosing a small contribution[1] for the *Zeitschrift* as a birthday present, in the hope that it will interest you and meet with your approval.

Your letter of 30 March is still waiting for a reply, while I have already thanked you for the reprint of "Mourning and Melancholia". I fully understand your forgetting it. Your failure in sending the paper I asked for was meant to indicate that I should first of all study the other source (Mass Psychology). Now, I am quite familiar with its contents concerning the subject of mania and melancholia, but, in spite of going through it once again, I cannot see where I went wrong. I can find no mention anywhere of a parallel in *normal* cases, i.e. the onset of a reaction state after mourning that can be compared to mania (after melancholia). I only know from your remark in "Mourning and M". that you *miss* something of that kind. And I referred to this in my comment. The increase in libido *after* mourning would be fully analogous to the "feast" of the manic. But I have not found this parallel from normal life in that section of "Mass Ψ" where the feast is discussed. Or have I been so struck by blindness that I am unable to see the actual reference?

So you are setting off on your travels already on 1 July. I shall start my holidays on about 10 July. First of all I am going to Bremen for a few days for my mother's 75th birthday, then we want to go to St Anton on the Arlberg. I am trying to compensate for the quite high prices by the fact that I have a patient there.

Many thanks for your news from there. At present I am analysing Mrs Powers,[2] Blumgart's[3] friend.

My family joins me in sending cordial greetings to you and your whole house,

Yours,

*Karl Abraham*

1. Abraham, 1922[79] or 1922[80].
2. Margaret Powers, American psychoanalyst, in analysis with Abraham since early April (circular letter, 15 April 1922, BL).
3. Leonard Blumgart [1880–?], M.D. 1903 Columbia, psychiatrist, in analysis with Freud until the middle of February 1922 (5 February 1922, Freud & Jones, 1993: p. 458).

## 411F

Vienna
28 May 1922[1]

Dear Friend,

Still with Eitingon's assistance, I have realized to my amusement that I completely misunderstood you through no fault of yours. You were looking for a normal example of the transition mel.[ancholia]/mania, and I was thinking of the explanation of the mechanism! Many apologies!

Cordially yours,

*Freud*

1. Postcard.

## 412A

St Anton am Arlberg, Hotel Post[1]
3 August 1922

Dear Professor, we have been here for a fortnight and are thoroughly enjoying our stay in the mountains, in spite of very uncertain weather. Mountaineering, a passion that I had long ago been weaned from, has

1922 October

taken hold of me again, and my son is proving a good companion on these excursions. I have not heard from you for a long time but hope you and yours are well. I am in lively contact with Jones and Eitingon, and yesterday revised the programme for the Congress. Could you not let me know what the "undisclosed" subject of your paper is going to be? I am starting to prepare my own paper[2] today. With cordial greetings and good wishes for your holiday to all of you from all of us,
Yours,

*Karl Abraham*

1. Picture postcard, addressed to Bad Gastein, forwarded to Berchtesgaden.
2. In Berlin, at the last Psychoanalytic Congress Freud ever attended, he gave a short paper on *Some Remarks on the Unconscious* (1922f), foreshadowing the contents of *The Ego and the Id*. Abraham spoke about manic-depressive states (1922[81]). Ernest Jones was re-elected president of the IPA.

413A

Berlin-Grünewald
22 October 1922

Dear Professor,

Since the Congress I have given no sign of life, and as I now have various reasons for writing, I am breaking my silence today. I hope you and yours are all well. Last Sunday Oliver accompanied us on an excursion. I am glad to be able to say that I find him definitely changed for the better.[1] All is well with us, only my daughter is struggling a little with the transference at the beginning of her analysis with van Ophuijsen. But I have the impression that Ophuijsen is handling the matter in a very nice and sensitive way. The circular letter reports on everything else that is going on here, so I can restrict myself to personal news, i.e. I can report to you about a few patients.

Almost a year ago your relative Gustav Brecher consulted me on your advice. The $\Psi\alpha$ had to be postponed for various reasons. I wrote to him recently that I now had time for him. I received the reply that he has to deny himself the $\Psi\alpha$ for financial reasons. Well, there is nothing to be done.

The American Dr Bibby has arrived. Intellectually, and in other ways too, he is better than most of his fellow countrymen, but dubious with regard to staying power and prognosis.

A former patient of yours, Cyrill Strauss from Frankfurt, whom you recommended to come to me or, if I could not take him, to Alexander, was here eight days ago. I had to put him off for a little. He wrote to me yesterday that he was not well; he wanted to start treatment at once, and was ready to go to Alexander if necessary. That is how we shall have to do it.

Today I had a letter from a Dr Tauss from Wittenberg, to whom you had also given my address. He is coming here soon for a consultation. Another similar enquiry came recently, which I cannot remember at the moment. So, many thanks for kindly thinking of me!

Róheim's lectures,[2] which finish this week, were very stimulating for me. It is sad that nothing can be done for him to make his existence stable.

In a few days I am sending Rank the promised manuscript (anal character)[3]; I hope it contains a few useful new things. Then the paper for the Congress in an extended form will follow as soon as possible. In addition I have made a few more new discoveries on the subject of man.[ia]-depr.[ession].

Our circle here has been pleasantly enriched this winter with Ophuijsen and Radó.[4] The latter has stayed here after the Congress and in the meantime is doing a few teaching analyses and waiting until I have an hour free for him. This afternoon we had a very pleasant circle in our house, including Delgado. He will also come to Vienna in a short time, and would like to join the group there, so as to be able, as a member of the International Association, to set up the South American group. He is well-instructed, very modest and likeable.

With the most cordial greetings to you, dear Professor, and yours.

Yours,

*Karl Abraham*

So as not to add to your correspondence, I should like to emphasize that this letter needs no answer.

1. Oliver was in analysis with Franz Alexander.
    Franz Alexander [1891–1964], M.D., of Budapest. After studying medicine in Göttingen, he went to Berlin [1920–1930], where he was the first to complete a standardized psychoanalytic training. In 1930, he was invited to Chicago (professor at the University of Chicago Department of Medicine, founder of the Chicago Institute of Psychoanalysis); 1938 professor at the University of Illinois, 1956 director of the psychiatric research department at the Mount Sinai Hospital in Los Angeles. Alexander was a key figure of American psychoanalysis—particularly noted for his interest in a rapprochement between psychoanalysis, academia, and the sciences, and for his works on criminology, cultural phenomena, psychosomatics, and psychotherapeutic technique.
2. "In the month of October, Dr G. *Róheim* of Budapest gave six talks on 'Psychoanalysis and Ethnology' at the polyclinic" (*Zeitschrift*, 1922, 8: 528).
    Géza Róheim [1891–1953], founder of psychoanalytic anthropology, creator of the ontogenetic culture theory. After analyses with Ferenczi and Vilma Kovács he became a training analyst in the Hungarian Society. In 1921 he received the Freud Prize (see Freud 1919c) for applied psychoanalysis. In 1928, with financial support from Marie Bonaparte, he undertook a research trip to central Australia and Melanesia in order to gather data there which would counter Malinowski's objections to the universality of the

Oedipus complex. In 1938 Róheim fled to the United States and became active as an analyst in New York.
3. Abraham, 1921[70].
4. Sándor Radó [1890–1972], lawyer and physician; first secretary of the Hungarian Society [1913]. In Berlin he underwent analysis with Abraham and became a member of the Education Committee of the Institute. In 1924 he became chief editor of the *Zeitschrift*, and in 1927 of *Imago*. In 1931 he was invited by Brill to set up an institute in New York modelled on the one in Berlin. He went more and more his own way, left the New York Society, and organized his own analytic institute at Columbia University, which was finally recognized by the American Psychoanalytic Association. Radó represented a behaviourist view within psychoanalysis; he is especially well known for his works on toxicomania. (See Roazen & Swerdloff, 1995.)

## 414F

Vienna[1]
11 December 1922

Dear Friend,

Thank you very much for the newspaper cutting.[2] Naturally I am following this piece of news with eager interest. But it will be months before we hear any more about it. A pity we can have nothing of it, not even see it. Such important things and so tangible, no ass may dare to contest such discoveries.

Cordially yours,

*Freud*

1. Postcard.
2. Missing; about the discovery, by the British archaeologist Howard Carter [1873–1939], of the tomb of Pharaoh Tutankhamen (see letter 417A, 21 February 1923).

## 415F

Vienna IX, Berggasse 19
26 December 1922

Dear Friend,

I have received the drawing[1] that is supposed to show your head. It is hideous.

I know what an excellent person you are. It shocks me all the more that such an insignificant shadow on your character as your tolerance or sympathy for modern "art" should have to be punished so cruelly. I hear from Lampl[2] that the artist has said that that is how he sees you! People like him should have the smallest possible access to analytic circles, for they are illustrations, only too undesirable, of Adler's thesis that it is precisely people with severe innate defects of vision who become painters and draughtsmen.

Let me forget this portrait, when I wish you and your dear family the finest and best for 1923.

Cordially yours,

*Freud*

1. A lithograph by the Hungarian deaf-mute artist Lajos Tihanyi.
2. Hans Lampl [1889–1958], M.D., a schoolmate and friend of Martin Freud's. From 1921 on in Berlin, where he underwent analytic training with Hanns Sachs and later with Helene Deutsch. Associate Member [1926] and Member [1930] of the German Society. In 1933 he and his wife returned to Vienna, and in 1938 they emigrated to Holland. (Cf. Mühlleitner, 1992: pp. 188–201.)

# 1923

## 416A

Berlin-Grünewald
7 January 1923

Dear Professor,

It is wonderful to be able to start the first letter of the New Year with congratulations. Today at midday my wife and I congratulated Oliver and his fiancée,[1] and brief though our meeting was, we had a pleasant impression of her. I have known her father, Dr F.[uchs], for many years from the practice. We also send you and yours our best wishes. I should like to take the opportunity to remark that for quite a long time I have found Oliver distinctly changed for the better, more cheerful and much less restless.

I have to thank you, dear Professor, for your amusing lines about my picture. Naturally I cannot agree with you completely. The painter is without doubt very gifted. I had seen a number of sketches of portrait drawings in his studio, which were of such brilliant nature that I decided to ask him to sketch me. I did not know that these drawings dated from an earlier period and that he had in the meantime changed over to the most modern school. I am in no way inclined toward this abstract school. However, since the picture was finished, I did not wish to withhold it from our circle. If one looks at it often over a period of time, more and more characteristics become apparent. In order to make good the wrong I have done you, I intend to give myself over to another artist sometime soon. At the end of February, I am to read a paper in Hamburg[2] and intend to consult an artist there of whom you too will approve.[3]

I am glad that the differences of opinion that had been expressed in the circular letters have been settled with the Old Year.[4] Sachs told me about the discussions in Vienna[5] and passed on to me your wish that the Berlin letters should be based on discussions between us three, so that they should give an extract of our combined views. You expressed exactly what I feel! But you cannot have any idea with what difficulties I have to struggle. You know yourself how careless Sachs has become in many things, and that Eitingon's domestic fixation cannot be broken through. I have asked *both* of them repeatedly to give me at least a marginal note on the letters coming in from outside. What I received was once a trivial note from E., and once from S. the request to inform the Comm. that he has recovered from the influenza! When we get together, then everything is talked through in detail, but that occurs too rarely, and so it happens that most of the time I have to do all the correspondence on my own. But I should like to believe that there has never been anything of primary importance in it that had not been approved by the others.

In the next few days I shall write to Rank more fully about the *Kindersammlung* [*Collection about children*].[6] The day's work leaves little time for other matters. At present I am writing a short essay containing some contributions on the vicissitudes of the Oedipus complex.[7] If possible, I shall enclose it in my letter to Rank. In that case, dear Professor, I should like to have your opinion, whether you agree with the conclusions. Reading this essay will not take up more than ten minutes of your time, and no special letter is necessary. A comment in the circular letter will be sufficient!—The subject I spoke on at the Congress is growing more and more into a longer work,[8] which I intend to write in the next few months. Perhaps it can appear as a supplementary issue.

To my delight I heard yesterday from Storfer[9] that suitable accommodation has been found for the Verlag; a good beginning, at least, in such difficult conditions!

Our polyclinic received from Fräulein van der Linden, who is here with Ophuijsen, a present of 100 guilders, now = 330,000 marks, which is useful even in present times. We shall have to expand somehow in the course of the year. The consulting-rooms are no longer sufficient, and it is the same with the courses in the old rooms.

There is good news about developments here. Yesterday a young doctor from Leipzig came to see me. He has taken a house appointment in Berlin so as to undergo an analysis in order to learn it. Such cases are becoming increasingly frequent.

With cordial greetings from house to house,
Yours,

*Abraham*

1. Henny Fuchs [1892–1971]; she and Oliver married in Berlin on 10 April 1923.
2. On 3 March Abraham gave a paper before the Oriental Seminar of the University of Hamburg (Abraham, 1923[84]).
3. That is, Freud's son-in-law, the photographer Max Halberstadt.
4. For months, there had been considerable personal tension between the members of the Committee, particularly between Jones (supported by Abraham) and Rank (supported by Ferenczi), who quarrelled over competencies of and relations between the *Verlag* in Vienna and the *Press* in London. Freud had intervened with a circular letter (26 November 1922, BL), in which he had stood up for Rank and interpreted Jones's and Abraham's behaviour as being governed by ambivalent feelings towards himself, directing their hostile side towards Rank.
5. Sachs had come to Vienna on 23 December 1922 (Abraham's circular letter, 16 December 1922, BL).
6. A project to publish a book on the subject in the *Verlag*, which did not materialize.

7. Abraham gave a talk on the subject before the Berlin Society on 29 March 1924 (Abraham, 1924[98]) but did not publish it.
8. Another reference to Abraham's work on his classic *Study of the Development of the Libido* (1917[105]).
9. See letter 98F, 18 December 1910, & n. 2.

## 417A

Berlin-Grünewald
21 February 1923

Dear Professor,

A relative in England has sent me the enclosed pictures of the Egyptian discoveries. They show the contents of the antechamber of the tomb. Later I hope to receive some of the actual burial chamber, which has been opened in the meantime.

May I ask you to send me back the pictures by registered post in about eight days? They do not belong to me, and I am supposed to send them back to London in good time.

With cordial greetings from house to house,
Yours,

*Abraham*

### Addendum[1]
#### New Discoveries in Egypt

As reported from Cairo, the English researchers succeeded on 16 February in opening the burial chamber of the Pharaoh Tutankhamen. We reported in detail the earlier discoveries, which caused an immense sensation in the scientific world. The new discoveries appear, according to the reports to hand, of even greater historical importance. Besides artistic and historical objects in fairy-tale abundance, the gigantic sarcophagus, "covered over and over with gold", was brought out into the light of day. It has not yet been possible to open the sarcophagus, which has now lain in the earth for about 3,000 years. It is thought that great treasures of papyrus are contained in the shrines that stand around the chamber. A second chamber contains another golden shrine, and beside it a statue of Anubis, a huge bull's head, black boxes of all sizes, small cabinets, the golden portrait of the king, a series of ivory and ebony caskets and a state carriage. After these discoveries, the report speaks of 16 February as a "day of the greatest importance in the history of Egyptian archaeology".

1. A newspaper cutting glued to the letter.

## 418F

Vienna IX, Berggasse 19
4 March 1923

Dear Friend,

I return the newspaper cuttings with thanks. Some of them I had received already from another side. Chief feeling—annoyance at not being able to be there, and above all of descending to the Styx[1] without having sailed on the Nile.

It now seems indubitable that they will soon find the mummy of the king and perhaps also that of his consort, a daughter of our analytic Pharaoh.[2] According to a rumour spread by the Swiss here, Jung's Mrs McCormick[3] has announced that she knows she was this queen. Personally I hope Tutankhamen had better taste. A mad hussy!

In Vienna things are pretty quiet, as Berlin has taken the wind out of our sails. Also the times are too wretched. A charming letter from Romain Rolland[4] arrived here recently like a breath of spring; he mentions in passing that he was already interested in analysis 20 years ago.

I hope that things are well with you and your wife and children and send my regards to you as well as the Ophuijsens.

Cordially yours,

*Freud*

1. In Greek mythology, the river of the underworld.
2. Referring to Abraham, 1912[34].
3. Edith Rockefeller McCormick [1872–1932], a patient of Jung's, married to Harold Fowler McCormick [1872–1941], Chicago industrialist. Both were liberal benefactors of analytical psychology. (Cf. McGuire, 1995.)
4. Romain Rolland [1866–1944], the noted French writer, biographer, musicologist, and dramaturge. Nobel Prize for literature in 1915. He and Freud subsequently had friendly relations. (See Freud's reply, 1960a: pp. 341–342; Freud's discussion of Rolland's "oceanic feeling", 1930a; Vermorel & Vermorel, 1993.)

## 419A

Berlin-Grünewald
1 April 1923

Dear Professor,

The Berlin circular letter has just been sent off but, as it is no substitute for personal contact with you, I am using the free time of the Easter days to send you a direct sign of life once again. I have received the newspaper cuttings about Egypt and your letter. I will not have it that a trip to Egypt is quite out of the question for you. It would naturally be expensive and time-consuming, but if you cut your summer holiday by a month, you could surely be absent for a few months at the beginning of next year and enjoy Egypt. I do not consider it right that you should simply resign yourself. I had an uncle who, at the age of 75, celebrated his golden wedding by travelling to Egypt with his wife, and he even took camel rides in the desert. And you say *you* cannot take a boat up the Nile!

The subject of travel brings me to summer. Some time ago, dear Professor, you suggested that we six should meet without you. At that time I made the complementary suggestion that a meeting with you should follow it. If a meeting is to take place in one way or another, it would be a good thing to decide the approximate time now. I should therefore like to ask you to make a suggestion in the next circular letter. I feel that a meeting this year is urgently needed, for I see from all kinds of signs that there is still tension between Jones and Rank, and it should be removed as soon as possible!

A further question concerns your plans for the summer. Mine are strongly determined by the invitation to Oxford.[1] But afterwards (in August) I should perhaps like to go somewhere not too far from where you are based, so that we could meet. I should be grateful if you could give me a hint sometime.

In the circular letter I mentioned my recent talk on the history of the development of object-love.[2] It has brought me an unusual amount of appreciation from our circle, and I myself feel that it is an important addition to the theory of sexuality and, at the same time, my best work up to now. I shall try to write it up soon. At the same time I feel that this whole idea accords with your own views and will also meet with your approval. Apart from the main result (enlightenment of the developmental process from narcissism towards object-love), the paper makes a not unimportant contribution to the understanding of paranoia and other forms of neurosis, such as pseudologia, etc., which have so far not been exhausted. If travelling were not so very difficult, I would come to Vienna in the near future in order to hear your views.

I hope you and your family are well. I can give a good account of us as well. Our children are staying in various places with friends over Easter, so that my wife and I are spending the holiday alone for the first time.

With cordial greetings from both of us to you, dear Professor, and your family,

Yours,

*Karl Abraham*

---

1. The Seventh International Congress of Psychology, Oxford, 25 July to 1 August 1923, where Abraham gave a paper (1923[93]; see Jones's Congress report in the *Zeitschrift*, 1923, 9: 540). Among the speakers were also Alfred Adler, Morton Prince, and Pierre Janet.
2. Abraham, 1923[87], read at the meeting of 27 March (*Zeitschrift*, 1923, 9: 242; in Abraham, 1917[105]).

420F

Vienna IX, Berggasse 19
8 April[1] 1923

Dear Friend,

Every letter of yours bears the mark of the lively and successful Berlin constellation and moreover of your own optimism. May you retain it. Only yesterday my wife went to Berlin with Martin for the wedding,[2] and I can hope that she will also see you and your wife.

It is strange how much you still overrate me, both materially and physically! Though I am still eight years short of your uncle's age at the time of his ride in the desert, I cannot imitate, but only envy him. I am neither rich nor well enough. You will gradually have to get used to the idea of my mortality and frailty.

I shall be glad to tell you what I know about the summer.[3] Little is certain, Minna and I should be in Gastein in July—if the condition of her heart does not prevent it. This is the only definite point, apart from that there are only tendencies. We should prefer to spend August together in the Dolomites: Prags? Madonna di Campiglio? But then little Ernst from Hamburg cannot come with us there. Therefore my wife thinks of going with Anna and him to Lake Ossiach[4] in July, where we came to know Annenheim before the war as a really satisfying place to stay, with, unfortunately, very bad accommodation. If it is better there this time, I shall perhaps go there during August as well. September is less difficult. Then my wife and sister-in-law feel most comfortable in Reichenhall; Anna is urging for Rome, and I too am thinking that ten terrible years have passed since I was last there.

These are the dates: Now can you do anything with them? We can always discuss them further.

You are right that the former situation in the Committee has not been established, but Jones has behaved too badly, which you could not possibly know in detail.

I am very glad to note that my paladins, you, Ferenczi, and Rank, always tackle fundamentals in your writings instead of playing around with foothill decorations of any kind. That is the case now with your object-love. I am very curious to read it, but cannot tell how far you have got with it.

With the most cordial greetings to you and your wife and children,
Yours,

*Freud*

P.S.: I am very interested in what is now developing with Oph.

1. In the handwriting: "March", but evidently a mistake of Freud's for "April". Clearly this letter is a reply to Abraham's of 1 April, the date of which is confirmed by the mention of Easter and of the Berlin *Rundbrief* of the same date (BL).

1923  May

2. See letter 416A, 7 January 1923, n. 1.
3. Only shortly afterwards, at the end of April, Freud underwent the first operation on his jaw. The excised growth was found to be cancerous, but Freud was not told this. On 19 June his beloved grandchild Heinerle died. On 30 June he and Minna went to Gastein, while Martha, Anna, and Ernst were on Lake Ossiach. Freud joined them on 30 July, and then the whole family (except Minna, who stayed on in Gastein) spent the month of August in Lavarone in the South Tyrol. Knowing that there would be another major operation on his return to Vienna, he and Anna went to Rome [31 August to 21 September].
4. In Carinthia, in today's southern Austria.


421A

Berlin-Grünewald
3 May 1923

Dear Professor,

I am combining my reply to your letter with my most cordial wishes for your new year of life. But please do not be angry if straightaway I draw your attention to a contradiction in your letter! You express the hope that I will retain my optimism, and you advise me in the next sentence to get accustomed to the idea that *your* vitality is limited. How am I to manage these two things at once? Well, since for both at the same time are impossible, I shall choose the former, and without further ado I take my standpoint on the omnipotence of wishes and express my conviction that the new year will give you all possible brightness and health compatible with your years. If you are a psychoanalyst (as Stekel would say), you will have to permit me to point out the over-determination of my conviction. I am just reading your book.[1] I still have to thank you for sending it to me. I think it shows evidence of such an unchanged sprightliness that can only delight all of us who are attached to you. The second reason stems from myself, since, as in many previous years, *my* own birthday is the day when I write to you to congratulate you on yours. Thus, I fill this letter with the maximum amount of confidence and only ask you to introject it for suitable use!

We too are thinking of the Southern Tyrol for August and particularly of the Gröden valley (St Ulrich or Wolkenstein). I am curious what our meeting at the end of August will be like.

I have still had no news of Ophuijsen since he went away a month ago. Sachs will be able to tell you more exactly at Whitsuntide about what has gone on. I myself am indeed grateful to Oph., as Ψα with him has really helped my daughter immensely.

Only good news today from here. Our courses have started and are very well attended. Our young members and the guests of our circle are extremely keen; among them, Lampl is coming along very well too! My analysand from Vienna (Frau Dr D.[eutsch][2]) presents no easy task, but

I expect good results. The same is true of Radó, who has some excellent characteristics that only need to be released from the neurotic accessories. Neither analysis is easy, but it is a question not only of getting rid of two neuroses, but of freeing, for our cause's sake, two unusual talents from their inhibitions. I hope it will work out.

It is not possible for me to write about recent scientific results today. I am now formulating the manic depressives (my Congress paper) and might wish to publish this, possibly together with the history of the development of object-love, as a supplement of the *Zeitschrift*. I should like to put the basic ideas about the latter subject before our small circle in August.—In Oxford I shall probably speak about something on the psychology of early childhood.

To conclude for today, dear Professor—my thanks for all your kind and appreciative words in your last letter!

*E tanti buoni auguri*[3]—for a new year of life that will bring you, your family, and all of us—the growing analytic family—the best with you, not forgetting another draught for you from the Fontana di Trevi![4]

Yours,

*Karl Abraham*

1. Freud, 1923b, which had appeared at the end of April (Rank's circular letter, 1 May 1923, BL).
2. Helene Deutsch, née Rosenbach [1884–1982], M.D., the well-known psychoanalyst. She was one of the first women to study medicine in Vienna. From 1912 to 1918 she worked at Wagner-Jauregg's clinic, directing the women's ward during the war. Analysis with Freud, member of the Vienna Society [1918]. After her analysis with Abraham and her stay in Berlin [1923], she returned to Vienna, where she organized and directed the Teaching Institute [1925] and the Technical Seminar [1932]. In 1935 she emigrated to Boston, working in private practice and as a training analyst at the Institute there. She is especially known for her works on female psychology. (Cf. Roazen, 1985, 1991, 1992.)
3. Italian: "and many cordial wishes".
4. Fountain in Rome. The traveller who throws a coin into it will, according to tradition, return.

## 422F

Vienna[1]
10 May 1923

Dear Friend,

I must shamefacedly ask you to accept this wretched card in payment for your long, warm letter. Because of the visits and celebrations of the last week I am behind with the fulfilment of all my duties. I can again chew, work, and smoke, and I shall try your optimistic formula: *many happy returns of the day and none of the new growth!*[2]

Cordially yours,

*Freud*[3]

1. Postcard.
2. Italicized words in English in original.
3. In August, while Freud spent his holidays in Lavarone, the members of the Committee met, without him, in the nearby San Cristoforo. The meeting was marked by a heated controversy between Rank and Jones. Rank was infuriated by an allegedly anti-Semitic remark Jones had made about him to Brill and demanded Jones's expulsion from the Committee, while Abraham defended Jones. The Committee was not dissolved for the moment but would collapse shortly afterwards. (Cf. Freud & Jones, 1993: p. 527; Gay, 1988: p. 424; Grosskurth, 1991: p. 134; Lieberman, 1985: pp. 188–191.)

## 423A

Berlin-Grünewald
7 October 1923

Dear Professor,

During the last few weeks I have been in continuous and lively contact with you in my thoughts, which were certainly charged with affect though not expressed in a letter. I knew you would not interpret my reserve in any other way than it was intended. After having heard, however, about your own attitude to the illness and operation, I cannot hold out any longer and am therefore writing to you. But I promise beforehand that this letter will not say anything further about your condition and will not even contain any good wishes apart from those that you read between the lines.—

I think there is only one thing I can do for the time being to give you pleasure. That is to let you have good reports about our position in Berlin. And, always providing that very bad political conditions do not paralyse our work, I hope to be able to carry out my intentions. Some days ago I reported in the circular letter on our first two meetings. Since then more good news is to be noted. In the next few days we are starting our lending library, which will have to give our younger members access to $\psi\alpha$ literature. Apart from the courses already announced, a further one will be arranged—by Frau Dr Klein[1]—for kindergarten teachers on the sexuality of the child.

I have something pleasant to report in the scientific field. In my work on melancholia etc., of which Rank has the manuscript, I have assumed the presence of a basic irritation[2] in infancy as a prototype for later melancholia. In the last few months Frau Dr Klein has skilfully conducted the $\Psi\alpha$ of a three-year-old boy with good therapeutic results. This child faithfully presented the basic melancholia that I had assumed and in close combination with oral erotism. The case offers in general amazing insight into the infantile instinctual life.

I am pleased to see that my assumptions about the two stages in the anal-sadistic phase are confirmed by new material. I had a remarkable experience with one of my melancholics, who is still in treatment with me. On my return from the journey, I found him at the beginning of a new depression triggered by a disappointment connected with his fiancée. The depression had not set in with the same intensity as on previous occasions, but the rejection of the love-object was visible in its characteristic form. Quick intervention resulted in the melancholia changing within a fortnight, and more clearly on each subsequent day, into an obsessional neurosis with ~~the main symptom of the fear~~ the main obsessional idea of having to strangle the mother (fiancée). In contrast to previous times, no cannibalistic-oral sadism, but manual sadism. The patient has already resumed working, and my impression is that it has been possible to divert a melancholia *in statu nascendi* into a relatively more favourable form of illness.

May I go on gossiping a little more about my work? What I said in Lavarone about the stages of object-love, and particularly about partial incorporation, is being very nicely confirmed at present. I had assumed that in paranoid and related psychoses regression to this phase could be demonstrated. The analysis of a psychosis that Loofs presented at our first meeting[3] supplied excellent confirmatory material. Among other things, the patient had the delusional idea that a monkey was sitting inside her. This monkey could be shown with absolute clarity to be the father's penis.

This shall be enough for today. But I would just like to add a word about the general impression made by our first two meetings. The keenness of the slowly growing circle has increased, and I feel as never before that I am keeping our members firmly together. Registrations of papers for the Congress are already coming in to the extent that one will have to try to subdue them.

Now only one more remark, and that is that I naturally do *not* expect any reply. I do have my own sources, from which I get the news I want. Perhaps I shall come myself in November or December to see that things are going well. I conclude in haste in order not to break the promise I gave at the beginning of this letter, and am, with cordial greetings to you and your family,

Yours, as ever,

*Karl Abraham*

1. Melanie Klein [1882–1960], née Reizes (she had no academic degree). Having spent her childhood in Vienna, she moved to Budapest in 1910, where she became acquainted with Freud's writings and underwent analysis with Ferenczi, who encouraged her to work with children; in July 1919 she became a member of the Hungarian Society. In 1921 she moved to Berlin, where in 1923 she became a member of the Society there and had further analysis with Abraham [1924]. After Abraham's death she moved to London, where she was supported primarily by Jones, whose children she analysed. She became a member of the British Society in 1927.

Klein brought influential innovations to the theory of early development and to the practice of child analysis. Her views on the prominent role of the very early development of an extremely differentiated fantasy life of the infant and small child, as well as her technique of direct, "deep" interpretations, found positive resonance in the London group but led, after the emigration there of many Viennese analysts, to considerable conflict with the group around Anna Freud; these "controversial discussions" were settled in 1946 with the introduction of two parallel training programs. (See Grosskurth, 1986; King & Steiner, 1991.)

2. *Urverstimmung*; in the translation of Abraham's work this is rendered as "primal parathymia" (1925[105]: p. 469). [Trans.]

3. Paper by Dr F. A. Loofs about "A Case of Schizophrenia" on 25 September 1923, followed by further discussion on 2 October (*Zeitschrift*, 1924, *10*: 106). Loofs is not listed as a member of the Berlin Society; he might be identical with Friedrich O. A. Loofs [1886–?], author of a thesis on kidney diseases.

## 424A

Berlin-Grünewald
16 October 1923

Dear Professor,

During the last few days Rank, Lampl, and Deutsch[1] have virtually vied with each other in keeping me informed about your state of health.[2] Lampl came back today and gave me a full report. This is indeed a day of joy, and now that I know that there is every cause for optimism, I want to wish you and your family wholeheartedly the best of luck. I do not tend towards pessimism, as you know, and I was therefore able during these anxious days to hold on to the impression of undiminished vitality that I had so recently observed in you. And the confidence I felt did not deceive me. But I breathe more freely again now that I know that it my hope has become a reality. From the reports it appears that you are not suffering too much from the direct consequences of the operation. Thus all of us who are attached to you may permit ourselves to enjoy the great gift that fate has granted us! I have been asked by my wife, my daughter, and my son to convey all their good wishes to you.

It is customary to send convalescents of all ages pictures to look at and pleasant things to read. That is why I am sending as "printed matter" a number of new Egyptian photographs, which may give you pleasure already now or at any rate later on, and I should also like to tell you about some pleasant things.

Last night—I could not report any more about this in the circular letter—Sachs began his course on psychoanalytic technique; the rest of us do not start for another fortnight. He had an audience of about 40, a very satisfactory number for a course of this kind. My own course of introductory lectures, which had 80 to 90 participants last autumn, will no longer be held in the limited accommodation of the polyclinic, but across the road in the *Zentralinstitut für Erziehung und Unterricht* [Central Institute for Education and Instruction].

October 1923

You will be pleased to hear that Frau Dr Deutsch has now got far enough to be able to do efficient theoretical work and that she is working on her investigation into the psychology of women.[3] She has also completed a short article, which will probably go off to the *Zeitschrift* soon.[4]

We shall have our meeting on Saturday. Sachs and Radó will give a review of Ego and Id.[5] There is no better proof of the keenness in our Society than the fact that members from outside Berlin—Foerster from Hamburg, Frau Dr Happel from Frankfurt,[6] and possibly also Frau Dr Benedek from Leipzig[7]—will come to Berlin especially for the occasion.

I shall continue to get news from Deutsch about your health, dear Professor, and shall write again myself as soon as there is anything to tell you.

In glad confidence,
Yours,

*Karl Abraham*

1. Felix Deutsch [1884–1964], M.D., general practitioner, then Freud's personal physician; husband of Helene Deutsch. Analysed by Bernfeld, he had become a member of the Vienna Society in 1922. In 1936 he followed his wife to Boston, where he became a training analyst and president of the Society there [1951–1954]. He was a pioneer of psychosomatic medicine, having already in 1919 established a clinic for "organic neuroses" and becoming the first Professor for Psychosomatic Medicine at Washington University, St. Louis, Missouri. (Cf. Mühlleitner, 1992: pp. 72–74; Roazen, 1985.)
2. After extensive preparations, Professor Hans Pichler [1877–1949] had performed preparatory surgery on 4 October and, on 11 October, the resection designed to remove the cancerous growth. Freud's convalescence followed a rather uncomplicated course over the next four weeks, but he had to be operated on again on 12 November—the third operation in the long series to come. (For details of Freud's medical record, see Jones, 1957; Romm, 1983; Schur, 1972.)
3. Deutsch, 1925a (in Deutsch, 1992), her paper for the psychoanalytic congress to be held in Salzburg.
4. Deutsch, 1925b (in Deutsch, 1992).
5. Meeting of 30 October (*Zeitschrift*, 1924, *10*: 106).
6. Dr Clara Happel-Pinkus [1889–1945], analysand of Hanns Sachs. Together with Frieda Fromm-Reichmann, Erich Fromm, Karl Landauer, and Heinrich Meng, she founded the "Frankfurt Psychoanalytic Working Group" (1926). She emigrated to Detroit. In 1941, she was denounced by a psychotic ex-patient as an "enemy of the American people" and was imprisoned for six weeks. Unable to resume her analytical work, she eventually committed suicide.
7. Dr Therese Benedek [1892–1977], from Leipzig, where she presided over the "Society for Psychoanalytic Research". On 24 November she was admitted as an associate member of the Berlin Society (see letter 426A, 26 November 1923). She emigrated to Chicago, where she became a training analyst. She is noted for her work on female sexuality and psychosomatic medicine.
   Caricatures and photographs of Benedek and Happel, taken at the congresses in Salzburg [1924] and Lucerne [1934], in Székely-Kovács & Berény, 1954 [1924]and in Gidal & Friedrich, 1990.

## 425F

Vienna[1]
19 October 1923

Dear Incurable Optimist,

Tampon renewed today, got up, put what is left into clothes. Thanks for all news, letters, greetings, newspaper cuttings. If I can sleep without injection, I go home soon.

Cordially yours,

*Freud*

1. In touchingly shaky handwriting.


## 426A

Berlin-Grünewald
26 November 1923

Dear Professor,

It was very painful for me to hear that you had to undergo a post-operation and have therefore still some way to go to final recovery. The last reports sound reassuring, and I therefore hope that this episodes will soon be over and well behind you.

I must now thank you most sincerely for giving time and trouble to going through my paper in spite of your suffering condition. I had wanted to ask your critique for a long time, but did not wish to burden you with such matters. With the right *Kück*,[1] you have immediately found the weak point—the chapter on mania. I have revised it in the meantime, and I think that the whole work has gained by this. During this revision I came to understand the reasons for the initial failure. I am glad, however, that you had no criticism of other large sections of my manuscript, and I was indeed touched that you tried to make your criticism of some parts more acceptable by quite a few appreciative remarks at the end. The day before yesterday I sent Rank a short addendum to the problem of mania, which I had just met with. It strikingly confirms your concept of the "feast"-character of mania and at the same time the ceremony of the liberation of the ego by an act of cannibalism. My patient told me, after a hypomanic episode of barely three days had subsided, that during that time he had felt the wish "to sate himself silly on meat";[2] so a euphoria of consuming meat.

A short paper on an infantile sexual theory[3] will go off to Rank soon. A paper on a pathological impostor[4] is to follow. It is always the case that a few small matters accumulate, which one has to write down.

Frau Dr Benedek of Leipzig was admitted as a member after she had given a paper on the development of the organization of society,[5] which revealed very good comprehension.

The training courses are going well. Sachs and Radó have about 40 students each, I have about 80 in the introductory course, so that I have had to emigrate from the polyclinic. I now have a very nice lecture-room in the *Centralinstitut für Erziehung und Unterricht*, which is exactly opposite the polyclinic.

At the moment there are six new registrations for training analyses; so Ψα is alive in Berlin, despite the dreadful outside circumstances.

With many cordial greetings and all good wishes!

Yours,

*Abraham*

1. Yiddish: from the German *gucken* [look, peer into the distance] and alluding to a joke told by Freud: "In the temple at Cracow the Great Rabbi N. was sitting and praying with his disciples. Suddenly he uttered a cry, and, in reply to his disciples' anxious enquiries, exclaimed: 'At this very moment the Great Rabbi L. has died in Lemberg.' The community put on mourning for the dead man. In the course of the next few days people arriving from Lemberg were asked how the Rabbi had died and what had been wrong with him; but they knew nothing about it, and had left him in the best of health. At last it was established with certainty that the Rabbi L. in Lemberg had not died at the moment at which the Rabbi N. had observed his death by telepathy, since he was still alive. A stranger took the opportunity of jeering at one of the Cracow Rabbi's disciples about this occurrence: 'Your Rabbi made a great fool of himself that time, when he saw the Rabbi L. die in Lemberg. The man's alive to this day.' 'That makes no difference', replied the disciple. 'Whatever you may say, the *Kück* from Cracow to Lemberg was a magnificent one'" (Freud, 1905c: p. 63).
2. Abraham, 1917[105]: p. 473–474.
3. Abraham, 1925[110].
4. Abraham, 1923[95]; cf. letter 294A, 16 July 1916.
5. Meeting of 24 November (*Zeitschrift*, 1924, *10*: 106).

## 427A

Berlin-Grünewald
26 December 1923

Dear Professor,

The Old Year shall not come to an end without your receiving once more a direct sign of life from me. For on such an occasion one does feel that our circular letters do not make personal correspondence entirely superfluous. This letter takes a whole load of good wishes with it, and also the sincere offer to put at your disposal, dear Professor, all my tried and tested optimism for 1924!

1923  December

There are scarcely four months left before the Congress.¹ If I had followed my own sentiments, I should have loved to have come to Vienna for a short visit during these holidays, in order to see for myself how you are doing. You will surely not think that it was out of indifference that I have not done so. As I know that you are not yet free from symptoms, and that visitors will be many at Christmas time, I preferred to refrain and am waiting for a more favourable moment.

I am making a short journey on 5 January to Hamburg, to give a lecture there,² which could not take place a short time ago because of the political situation. Interest is increasing in H., and I also hear favourable reports of the small circle in Leipzig.

I recently heard from Dr Weiss in Trieste³ that a distinguished psychologist, Prof. Benussi in Padua,⁴ who specializes in hypnosis and suggestion, would like to come into closer contact with us. He would like to be invited to the Congress. I am writing to him today in order first of all to make nerve-contact.⁵ I have in the background similar plans to those I mentioned in the circular letter with regard to Spain.⁶

Now yet another question! We have in our psychoanalytic circle a woman colleague who works in the polyclinic and is liked by everyone. She is, with her child, in a very difficult situation, and after a long struggle has agreed to accept financial support. As once before in a similar case you gave us money from a fund, I suggested to the lady in question that I would write to you about it. That was only to make it easier for her to accept it. In actual fact I will send her what is immediately necessary from my own resources. But I can do that only within certain limits, as at present I too have many other commitments. Now my question is whether I could, *if necessary*, in the near future ask for a financial contribution from the fund. I would approach Eitingon, but—discreet as he is—he has once more disappeared without breathing a word to me or Sachs about how long he was staying away and where he was going. As I have absolutely no wish to burden you, dear Professor, with correspondence, I am only asking you for a Yes or No on a postcard. I am not expecting any further reply to this letter!

In the meantime my *Study of the Development of the Libido* will presumably be in your hands. I am planning something new, and will perhaps bring it up at the Congress, if it is mature by then.

And now, once again, all good wishes for you and yours, and the most cordial greetings from your

*Karl Abraham*

1. Eighth International Psychoanalytic Congress, 21–23 April 1924, Salzburg. Minutes in the *Zeitschrift* (1924, *10*: pp. 211–228).
2. Abraham, 1924[97].

3. Edoardo Weiss [1889–1970], M.D., pioneer of psychoanalysis in Italy, analysand of Paul Federn. Founding member of the first Italian Psychoanalytical Society [1925], which he re-founded in 1932 with members who had all been analysed. Founder, in the same year, of the *Rivista Italiena di Psicoanalisi*, the official organ of the Society. He emigrated to the United States, first to the Menninger Clinic in Topeka, Kansas; he then became a Visiting Professor in Psychiatry at Marquette University (Milwaukee, Wisconsin) and a prominent member of the Chicago Institute for Psychoanalysis. (For his correspondence with Freud, see Weiss, 1970.)
4. Vittorio Benussi, psychologist, analysed by Otto Gross, and himself analyst of Cesare Musatti [1908–1989], a central figure in post-war psychoanalysis in Italy.
5. *Nervenanhang*, Schreberism; see letter 96F, 24 October 1910, & n. 2.
6. That is, to give introductory papers there (circular letter of 17 December 1923, BL).

# 1924

## 428F

Vienna IX, Berggasse 19[1]
4 January 1924

Dear Friend,

I have left so many of your friendly letters unanswered that today I am virtually delighted to have to write you about a factual matter. Though there is nothing pleasing about the fact itself.

For the psychoanalytic fund cannot be counted on at the moment. Apart from the devalued Marks, it contains a little over 20 pounds, which I beg to keep strictly secret. I would gladly have stepped into the breach myself, but for half a year I have had only expenditure and no income.

Because of the numerous Christmas visitors from Berlin, I have heard and talked a great deal about you recently. I was delighted to hear only good things about you, so your optimism is at least not unfounded. I declined all Christmas visits that were meant for me personally with the motivation that you yourself give; only my son Oliver was with us here with his young wife. I did not wish to postpone further making the acquaintance of my new dear daughter.

I am by no means without any symptoms or released from treatment, but I resumed my analytic work on the 2nd of this month and hope to be able to manage.

With cordial greetings and New Year wishes to you and your dear family,

Yours,

*Freud*

---

1. Typewritten and hand-signed letter, evidently dictated to Anna, who used a more modern orthography than the one Freud was accustomed to using (e.g. *zahlreich* and *Motivierung* instead of *zalreich* and *Motivirung*). The typewriter could not reproduce the German double-s ("ß") and the *Umlaute*; the dots on the latter were inserted by hand.

## 429F

# INTERNATIONAL PSYCHO-ANALYTICAL ASSOCIATION[1]
## CENTRAL EXECUTIVE

Vienna
15 February 1924

Dear Friends,

It is not without astonishment that I have heard from various sides that the recent publications of our Ferenczi and Rank, I mean their joint work[2] and that on birth trauma,[3] have evoked unpleasant agitation in Berlin. Apart from that, I was directly asked, by someone in our midst,[4] to express among you my opinion of the undecided matter in which he sees the germination of a split. Thus I am complying with his wish, do not interpret it as obtrusiveness; my purpose being rather to exercise as much restraint as possible and to let each of you to follow his way freely.

When Sachs was last here, we exchanged a few comments on the birth trauma and perhaps the impression that I discern in the publication of this work an oppositional movement or do not at all agree with its content stems from that. I think, however, that the fact that I have accepted its dedication should make this interpretation impossible.

The fact of the matter is this: The harmony among us, the respect you have so often shown me, should not disturb any of you in the free exercise of his productivity. I do not ask that in your writings you orientate yourself more towards whether I will like them rather than whether they have turned out in accordance with observation and your views. Complete agreement on all questions of detail of the science and on all newly broached themes among half a dozen people of different natures is not at all possible nor even desirable. The sole condition for our working together fruitfully is that no one leaves the common ground of psychoanalytic prerequisites, and of this we may be certain in the case of every individual member of the Committee. On top of this there is another circumstance that is not unknown to you and that makes me particularly unsuited for the role of a despotic and ever-vigilant censor. It is not easy for me to feel my way into unfamiliar trains of thought, and I have as a rule to wait until I have found the connection with them by way of my own winding paths. So if you wanted to wait with every new idea until I can approve it, it would run the risk of growing quite old in the meantime.

My attitude towards the two books concerned, then, is the following. The joint work I value as a correction of my view of the role of repetition or acting out[5] in analysis. I had still been afraid of them, and had regarded these incidents, you now call them experiences, as undesired failures. R.[ank] and F.[erenczi] draw attention to the inevitability of this experiencing and the good use that can be made of it. Otherwise the work can be recognized as a refreshing and subversive intervention into our present analytic habits. In my opinion it has the fault of not being complete, i.e. it does not set out in detail the changes of technique that are dear to the two authors, but only hints at them. There are no doubt various dangers involved with this deviation from our "classical technique", as Ferenczi called it in Vienna, but that is not to say that they cannot be avoided. Insofar as questions of technique are concerned here, I think that both authors' attempt to find out whether it can be done otherwise for practical purposes is absolutely justified. Time will tell, after all, what will come out of it. In any case we must take care not to condemn such an undertaking as heretical from the start. However, certain doubts need not be repressed. Ferenczi's active therapy is a dangerous temptation for ambitious beginners, and there is scarcely any way to keep them away from such experiments. I will also make no secret of another impression or prejudice. In my illness I learned that a shaved beard takes six weeks to grow again. Three months have now passed since my last operation, and I am still suffering from changes in the scars. So I find it hard to believe that it is possible in a slightly longer time, 4-5 months, to penetrate even into the deep layers of the unconscious and bring about lasting changes in the psyche. Naturally, however, I shall bow to experience. Personally I will probably continue making "classical" analyses, because firstly I take hardly any patients, only pupils, with whom it is important that they should experience as much as possible of the inner processes—training analyses cannot be dealt with in quite the same way as therapeutic analyses—and secondly I am of the opinion that we still have a great many new things to discover and cannot yet allow ourselves to rely solely on our prerequisites, as is necessary with shortened analyses.

Now to the second, and incomparably more interesting, book, Rank's birth trauma. I do not hesitate to say that I regard this book to be very significant, that it has given me a great deal to think about, and that I have not yet formed my final opinion about it. What I clearly recognize is as follows: We have indeed long known and appreciated the womb phantasy, but in the position that Rank gives it, it takes on a much higher meaning and shows us all at once the biological background of the Oedipus complex. To recapitulate in my language: An instinct that desires to re-establish the former existence must be attached to the birth trauma. One could call this the instinct to seek happiness,[6] understanding there that the concept "happiness" is mostly used in an erotic sense.

Rank now goes beyond psychopathology into the general human field and shows how people in the service of this instinct alter the outside world, while the neurotic in his phantasy spares himself this labour by going back via the shortest route to the mother's womb. If we add to Rank's view Ferenczi's idea that a man is represented by his genitals,[7] one can for the first time get a derivation of the normal sexual instinct that fits in with our concept of the world.

Now comes the point at which, for me, the difficulties begin. The phantasized return to the mother's womb is beset by obstacles that cause anxiety; the incest barrier, where does that come from? Its representative is apparently the father, the reality, the authority, which does not allow incest. Why did they erect the barriers to incest? My explanation[8] was a historical-social, phylogenetic one. I deduced the incest barrier from the prehistory of the human family and thus saw in the current father the real obstacle that erects incest barriers in the new individual too. Here Rank differs from me. He refuses to go into phylogenesis and lets the anxiety, which opposes incest, directly repeat the birth anxiety, so that, he says, the neurotic regression into oneself is inhibited by the nature of the birth process. This birth anxiety, he says, is transferred to the father, but he is only a pretext for it. Basically the attitude to the mother's body or genital is assumed to be *a priori* an ambivalent one. This the contradiction. I find it very difficult to decide here, nor do I see how one can easily succeed from experience, for in analysis we shall always come upon the father as the bearer of the prohibition. But that is naturally no argument. I must for the time being leave the question open. I can bring forward as a counter-argument also that it is not in the nature of an instinct to be associatively inhibited, as here the instinct to return to the mother would be by association with the fright of birth. Actually every instinct as a drive to re-establish a former state presupposes a trauma as the cause of the change, and so there could be no other than ambivalent instincts, i.e. instincts accompanied by anxiety. There is naturally a great deal more that could be said about this in detail, and I hope that the idea evoked by Rank will be the subject of numerous and fruitful discussions. But we are not faced with a coup d'état, a revolution, a contradiction of our certain knowledge, but an interesting complement the value of which should be recognized by us and by those outside our circle.

When I add that it is not clear to me how the premature making conscious of the transference to the doctor as a bond to the mother can contribute to the shortening of the analysis, I have given you a true picture of my position with regard to both the works in question.

So, I value them highly, in part acknowledge them already now, have my doubts and reservations to some parts of their contents, am expecting clarification to emerge from further consideration and experience, and would like to recommend all analysts not to make too hasty a judgement on the questions raised, least of all a negative one.

Forgive my prolixity, perhaps it will prevent you from rousing me to express my opinion on matters that you could judge just as well for yourselves.

FREUD m.p.

1. Circular letter to the members of the Secret Committee; typewritten on IPA stationery.

1924 February

2. Ferenczi & Rank, 1924. The authors put forward that, instead of remembering, the repetition of infantile material should play "*the chief rôle in analytic technique*" (p. 4), although the repeated material should then gradually be transformed into remembering. This material should be consistently interpreted in its relation to the "analytic situation". They also introduced the systematic method of setting "a definite period of time for completing the last part of the treatment" (p. 13).
3. Rank, 1924a. For Rank, the trauma of birth, experienced by the infant as separation from the mother, was the foundation and the core of the unconscious. Therapy thus consisted in subsequently bringing to a close the incompletely mastered birth trauma. The transference libido, to be analytically dissolved for both sexes, was in his view the maternal transference libido. Birth anxiety was seen as the root of any anxiety, intrauterine pleasure as the origin of any later pleasure.
4. Eitingon had written that these books had "acted like a bomb in the Committee", particularly with Abraham, who would be "especially angered at the fact that nothing of [their] contents had been revealed in advance to the Committee". Eitingon had asked Freud to intervene with a statement on the new theories (letter to Freud, 31 January 1924, SFC).
5. *Agieren.*
6. *Glückstrieb.*
7. Ferenczi, 1924[268].
8. In Freud, 1912–13a.

## 430A

Berlin-Grünewald[1]
21 February 1924

Dear Professor,

You hardly need to be assured that your letter made a deep impression on me too. It was, as everything else you write, a document that leaves an impression. I too owe you a debt of gratitude for it. *What* you say and *the way* you say it has made me revise once again my statement on the three books by Sándor and Otto.

The objections that Hanns raises in his letter[2] accord with yours on the important points, dear Professor. Now Ernest's letter[3] has arrived too and contains similar comments. I agree with all these objections; also with those that go beyond your criticism. But I am worried with regard to the implications of certain phenomena in the new books, and my concern has increased in weeks of constantly renewed self-examination. Your letter and the discussion I had yesterday with Hanns have reassured me somewhat on certain points. In advance: there is no question of an inquisition! Results of whatever kind obtained in a legitimate analytic manner would never give me cause for such grave doubts. Here we are faced with something different. I see signs of a disastrous development concerning vital matters of $\Psi\alpha$. They force me, to my deepest sorrow, and not for the first time in the 20 years of my $\psi\alpha$ career, to take on the role of the one who issues a warning. When I add that these facts in question have robbed me of a good deal of my optimism with which

I face the progress of our cause, you will be able to gauge the depth of my disquiet.

I have one request to make, dear Professor, which you must not refuse. Call a meeting of the Committee just before the Congress and give me the possibility of a free discussion. The time allowed for the necessary exchange of opinions should however not be too short. The confirmation of your agreeing to this plan would reassure me greatly.

Faithfully as ever,
Yours,

*Abraham*

1. There exist two hand-written versions of this letter, the one actually sent to Freud and an identical copy in which most of the words were abbreviated. Abraham probably kept a copy of this important letter for himself.
2. In his letter to Freud of 20 February, Sachs had criticized the lack of a clinical basis of Rank's theory, reducing the whole exposition to "an analogy" and the book to "a torso" (in Jones, 1957: p. 66).
3. In his circular letter of February 18, Jones had raised "the question of the ulterior tendencies of the work, particularly in the hands of either ambitious or reactionary readers", and put forward the criticism "that many ideas ... were expressed in too dogmatic and even dictatorial manner, with sweeping condemnation of every other possibility. ... Such passages could easily have been softened, if they had been seen beforehand by any other member of the Committee" (BL).

431F

Vienna, Berggasse 19
25 February 1924

Dear Friends,

I am delighted that my circular letter reassured you on some points. But obviously it did not reassure you on all of them. I am ready to do anything to bring about further clarification. Perhaps you will come earlier to Vienna, so that we can travel to Salzburg together and so use this travelling time also to continue the exchange of ideas. Jones has asked for a day of discussion in Salzburg to avoid having to come to Vienna. This must be taken into account. The day for further discussion can only be Easter Sunday.

Rank has been confined to bed, I have not seen him for a fortnight and have not been able to discuss anything with him.

As my letter showed you, I am still far from having a definite opinion, and am myself not free from an inclination towards a critical standpoint. But I should like to be told what the impending danger is that I do not see. The matter may be further clarified in the interval until we meet.

1924 February

I am very sorry to think that your organization would disintegrate immediately after my disappearance, but in any case I am selfish enough to wish to prevent this as long as I am still here.
With cordial greetings,
Yours,

*Freud*

432A

Berlin-Grünewald
26 February 1924

Dear Professor,

I can scarcely tell you how much gratification your second letter gave me. Since I see that you are prepared to listen to criticisms even though they go beyond your own and concern persons who are particularly close to you, I begin once again to hope for a solution of the difficulties. Your words regarding the preservation of the Committee accord fully with my own ideas and intentions, and I therefore await further developments with somewhat greater confidence.

You, dear Professor, would like to know what dangers I mean. If I tell you, you may well shake your head and refuse to listen further to me. But it is no longer possible for me to keep them back, and I shall therefore state briefly what I intend to put before our meeting, giving full and detailed *reasons* for my opinion.

—After very careful study, I must see in the *Entwicklungsziele* as well as in the *Trauma der Geburt* manifestations of a scientific regression that correspond, down to the smallest detail, with the symptoms of Jung's renunciation of $\Psi\alpha$.

This was not easy to say. All the more glad I am to be able to add that I am not blind to the differences in personality: Sándor and Otto, with all their pleasant qualities, on the *one* side; Jung's deceitfulness and brutality on the *other*—I have by no means overlooked these. This must not prevent me, however, from stating that their new publications are a repetition of the Jung case, which I was initially loath to believe myself. This is the one great danger I can see! Two of our best members are in danger of straying from $\Psi\alpha$ and will therefore be lost to $\Psi\alpha$. However, their turning away from what we have up to now called $\psi\alpha$ method is closely connected with the signs of disintegration in the Committee, and this disintegration represents the *second* danger. The *third one* is the damaging effect on the $\psi\alpha$ movement to be expected from the new books.

Before I continue, I must ask your forgiveness, dear Professor, if I have caused you pain just now when you are so much in need of friendly and encouraging impressions. How much I should like to be able to give you these today too! But I have no choice if I wish to protect you from worse to come. The discussion I intend for our meeting appears to me the only means of preventing what you yourself see coming: the disintegration of our most intimate circle. Already last autumn it nearly fell apart. I may say it was I in the first place who prevented this at the time. I now would like to use all my influence once again to avert these dangers I referred to, as far as is still possible. I promise you, dear Professor, in advance that it will be done on my part in a non-polemic and purely factual manner and only with the wish to serve you and our cause, which is identical with your person.

Do you remember that after the first Congress in Salzburg I warned you about Jung? At the time you rejected my fears and assumed that my motive was jealousy. Another Salzburg Congress is just around the corner, and once more I come to you in the same role—a role that I would far rather do without. If, on this occasion, I find you ready to listen to me despite the fact that I have so much to say that is painful, then I shall come to the meeting with a hope of success.

Another word on practical procedure! As I see it, we must put at the top of our agenda a question that involves the very existence of the Committee itself. So Ernest ought to be there from the very beginning. We should therefore be in S. somewhat earlier. As there has to be a meeting of the heads of groups on Sunday, *we* should reserve *at least* Saturday for our purpose. Thus I propose that we should meet on Friday, so as to be able perhaps to discuss already in the afternoon or evening of that day. If, dear Professor, that is not convenient to you for any reason, we should all come to Vienna; in this case Ernest too is prepared to make a detour via Vienna. We should then have to be in Vienna for noon on Friday at the latest, and Thursday evening would probably be better.

With cordial greetings,
Yours,

*Karl Abraham*

## 433F

Vienna, Berggasse 19[1]
4 March 1924

Dear Friend,

You certainly made my heart heavy by the reawakening of old Salzburg memories. I reluctantly discern from your letter the opinion that it is not easy to discuss certain personal as well as factual differences with me. I know that that is what my opponents proclaim to the world, but my nearest friends should know better. Nor is there any reason for you to make any such assumption, because, though my personal intimacy with Rank and Ferenczi has increased because of geographical factors, you ought to have complete confidence that you stand no lower than they in my friendship and esteem.

I want to let you know that an apprehension of the kind that you expressed is not so far from my mind. When Rank first told me about his finding, I said jokingly: "With an idea like that, anyone else would set up on his own." I think that the emphasis is on the "anyone else", as you yourself admit too. When Jung used his first independent experiences to free himself from analysis, we both know that he had strong neurotic and selfish motives that took advantage of this discovery. I could then say with justification that his crooked character did not compensate me for his lopsided theories. Incidentally, I learn from a case that came to me from him that he has been tempted into tracing back a severe obsessional neurosis to the conflict between individualism and collectivism.

In the case of our two friends, the situation is different. We are, after all, confident that they have no bad motives other than those secondary tendencies involved with scientific work, the tendencies to make new and surprising discoveries. The only danger arising out of this is of falling into error, which is difficult to avoid in scientific work after all. Let us assume the most extreme case: if Ferenczi and Rank were to come right out with the claim that we were wrong to stop at the Oedipus complex. The real decision was with the trauma of birth, and one who has not overcome this will later also fail at the Oedipus complex. Then, instead of our sexual aetiology of neurosis, we should have an aetiology determined by physiological chance, because those who became neurotic would either have experienced an unusually severe birth trauma or would have brought an unusually "sensitive" organization to that trauma. Further, a number of analysts would make certain modifications in technique on the basis of this theory. What further damage would ensue? We could remain under the same roof with the greatest calmness, and after a few years' work it would become evident whether one side had exaggerated a valuable finding or the other had underrated it. That is how it seems to me. Naturally I cannot in advance refute the ideas and arguments that you want to put forward, and therefore I am in full agreement with the proposed discussion.

Now to the practical procedure, as you write. You want us to begin the discussion already on the Friday before Easter, for which there would be time until Sunday evening. Here I must try an objection. Two or two and a half days' discussion would be practically equivalent to a doubling of the time of the congress, and that is too much for my weakened capabilities. I must once again contradict your incurable optimism and point out that I really am no longer the glutton for work that I used to be. Efforts I should not have noticed before my illness are now clearly too much for me. I even doubt whether I shall be able to listen to all the 15 papers to be read at the Congress, and in a corner of my heart, to quote our Nestroy,[2] there actually lurks a desire to be spared the whole bother of the Congress. I hope that by then my state of health will have extinguished this impulse, but it is quite certain that I shall not be able to read a paper or attend the meal. These two injured functions do not permit any exhibition.

I therefore think that all the free hours of Saturday will have to be sufficient to settle the matter. Our all meeting in Vienna is out of the question at Jones's urgent request to be spared the journey to Vienna.

Please be so good as to let our friend Sachs have a look at this letter, which is intended for him too, and let me conclude with the hope by the time of our date at Easter much of this business will have been cleared up and quietened.

With cordial greetings to you and your whole house,
Yours,
*Freud*

1. Typewritten.
2. Johann Nepomuk Nestroy [1801–1862], famous Austrian dramatist and actor.

### 434A

Berlin-Grünewald
8 March 1924

Dear Professor,

I knew that with my last letter I would cause you pain. I shall not try to describe how difficult it was for me to write all this. My doubts on how you would receive my revelations referred really *only* to the fact that I had once again confronted you with the necessity of having to listen to very serious criticisms of two who stand so close to you. Neither in my letter nor at any time previously have I suggested that it is difficult to discuss *factual* differences with you. My opinion is exactly the opposite.—I can only admire over and over again your readiness in this respect. Just as little have I ever felt myself slighted by you. On the contrary, at our meetings in the Harz and in Lavarone, I felt that you deemed me worthy of your very special confidence. It is 17 years, dear Professor, since I first met you, and in all these years I have always felt happy that I could count myself among those closest to you; and nothing has changed about this even today. I do not wish the slightest doubt about this to arise.

Concerning the factual aspect, I find it satisfying that my opinion and yours are not incompatible. When I speak in more detail in Salzburg, I hope we shall come to a *full* understanding. Wherever I see a possibility of convergence, I shall, as always, be glad to seize on it! I do not want to bother you any further today. There is only one point I wish to stress once again: I have *no* difficulty in assimilating a new finding if it has been arrived at along a legitimate psychoanalytic path. My doubts are not directed at the results achieved by Sándor and Otto but against the *paths* they took. These seem to me to lead away from $\Psi\alpha$, and my criticisms will refer *solely* to this.

I gladly agree that we should meet at noon on Saturday in Salzburg. My suggestion that we should meet a day earlier was not intended to prolong our debates by another day but, *on the contrary*, to have more time for *rest* in-between!

This letter will go first to Hanns, who will probably add a few lines. In unaltered (and unalterable!) devotion,
Yours,

*Abraham*

## 435F

Vienna, Berggasse 19[1]
14 March 1924

Dear Friend,

Please send me a visitor's ticket for the Congress in the name of A. G. Tansley.

Tansley is or was Lecturer of Botany at Cambridge, resigned his post, and is thinking of devoting himself entirely to psychoanalysis. A book of his, *The New Psychology*,[2] which has also appeared in German translation, has done a great deal for the spread of psychoanalysis, although it shows him still in a phase of development prior to being completely an adherent. He is now in analysis with me for the second time, and I hope to make considerable progress with his convictions. He is a distinguished, correct person, a clear, critical mind, well-meaning and highly educated. Naturally I should also be glad if you would notice and honour him at the Congress.

With cordial greetings,
Yours,

*Freud*

1. Typewritten.
2. Tansley, 1920.

## 436A

Berlin-Grünewald
17 March 1924

Dear Professor,

A few quick words in reply to your letter which arrived today. Why so much fuss about a guest ticket for someone whom *you* recommend? It would really have been enough to give the name. I cannot send any tickets, because there are none as yet. One of these days a circular is going to the groups to say that the admittance of guests shall be regulated by the groups. Those admitted by them will simply come to Salzburg and receive there their guest ticket on the recommendation of the relevant group. This way we shall spare ourselves endless letter-writing. If, then, you want to introduce further guests, the way is very easy. The main thing is that Frau Dr Rank knows about it, for she has to see to accommodation!

I take the opportunity of assuring you, dear Professor, that this time the Congress will be much less tiring. The number of papers is much smaller, and some of them are *very* short. I believe that the morning sessions will last scarcely three hours. Do not worry, I am taking care that it will not be a bother to you, but a real satisfaction as regards scientific achievements!

Cordial greetings from house to house,
Yours,

*Abraham*

## 437F

Vienna, Berggasse 19[1]
31 March 1924

Dear Friend,

This letter is to inform you of a possibility that you have perhaps not yet taken into account.

Since a possibly influenzal nasal catarrh at the beginning of this month, my health has progressively deteriorated so much that last Saturday and Sunday, for the first time in my whole medical career, I had to stop working over the weekend. The short visit to the *Kurhaus* in Semmering has done me conspicuous good, but precisely because of that there is a possibility that I foresee. Unless my general condition improves in a quite extraordinary way by Easter—your tried and tested optimism will immediately assume that it will, but I remain doubtful—then I shall not come to the Congress to Salzburg but will again go to that sanatorium, where I can obtain some recuperation to continue the most essential part of my work.

1924 April

Thus in that case neither the meeting of the former Committee and myself nor the lecture in which you wanted to warn me of the impending dangers of the new movement would take place. I think you should get used to the idea of such a possible course of events, and I take it that there would be no way about it other than you communicating person to person with each other as it should really have happened in the first place. For to whatever extent your reaction to F.[erenczi] and R.[ank] may have been justified, quite apart from that, the way you set about things was certainly not friendly, and it has become completely clear on this occasion that the committee no longer exists, because the ethos that would make a committee of this handful of people is no longer there. I think that it is now up to you to prevent a further disintegration, and I hope that Eitingon, whom I expect here on the 13th, will help in this. It cannot be your intention by reason of this apprehension of yours to cause the tearing down of the *Internationale Vereinigung* and everything connected with it.

I am selfish enough to feel it an advantage that because of my frailty I am at least spared having to listen to and to form an opinion on everything connected with the new squabble. I am neither very pleased about this advantage nor about the situation from which it derives. As a cautious question-mark still hangs over my decision, I shall wait until the week before the Congress before letting you know definitely.

With cordial greetings,
Yours,

*Freud*

1. Typewritten.

## 438F

Vienna, Berggasse 19
3 April 1924

Dear Friend,

I promised to write to you again as soon as I had made up my mind. I am therefore now writing to let you know that I shall not be attending the Congress, but shall be on the Semmering also at Easter, seeking out the peace and the pleasure of good air that I have needed so urgently since my influenza. I am simultaneously informing Jones and Eitingon, who is expected in Merano.

With cordial greetings,
Yours,

*Freud*

## 439A

Berlin-Grünewald
4 April 1924

Dear Professor,

My first reaction to your letter which I received yesterday was deep regret that your health is troubling you again. I was particularly sorry—both for your sake and for the sake of us all—to hear that you think you may have to stay away from the Congress. My next thought was that the discussion *before* the Congress could be held among *ourselves* and, on your arrival, we could just report the result to you. You would thus be spared anything that might be detrimental to your health. If you agree to this suggestion, everyone else will as well. In the meantime, I shall not stop hoping that your indisposition will soon pass, so that we may after all expect you for the Congress itself.

Subsequently your letter expresses a distrust of me that I find extremely painful and, at the same time, strange. I had believed that the correspondence we had some time ago had been concluded in a satisfactory manner, and suddenly I must hear the most serious reproaches! I must however admit that your letter has not evoked even a shadow of guilt in me. It is easy for me, dear Professor, to show you that I am the victim of a lapse of your memory and that all your accusations rest on a displacement of facts in my disfavour.

Your main reproach is that I should have tried to obtain a communication person to person. By avoiding this, I had acted in an unfriendly way towards Sándor and Otto. This reproach would have been justified if I had written *spontaneously* to you, dear Professor, to tell you of my doubts. *But the facts are exactly the reverse*. You yourself on 15 February directed a long circular letter at us all, and each of us replied *in his own way* to it; I in *my way*, which I had after all the right to do. At your express desire, I then wrote more extensively. There was, therefore, no behaviour on my part that could give the impression of evading the others or of insinuation, but only a legitimate reaction to your circular letter! Therefore this "guilt" is already without basis.

The further lapse of memory on your part concerns the purpose of our meeting before the Congress. You write that I want to give a "lecture" in order to "warn" you. It is true that in two of my letters I expressed a warning; but the purpose of the *meeting* was, as I explained in detail in my letter, to have a free discussion among all of us in order to re-establish the unity of the Committee! You understood me correctly at the time and replied: "therefore I am in full agreement with the proposed discussion". Only afterwards did a misinterpretation of my intention creep in, and now I appear as the disturber of the peace and even as the destroyer of the Committee.

So, now to this third point! Last year in San Cristoforo the Committee would certainly have fallen apart had *I* not kept it together. During those days I worked with all my devotion to preserve this institution, which is so important to me, and to save you, dear Professor, from seeing the disintegration of the Committee. You must also remember that in Lavarone I tried hard to clear up the differences and to mediate. We said good-bye to each other on the *Postplatz* in Lavarone, glad to have achieved that much at least; and now you say that *I* want to destroy the Committee? This again can only have been due to a blotting out in your memory of all that speaks in my favour. Your reminder that it is up to *me* to prevent the disintegration of the Committee does in fact perfectly correspond with what I considered my foremost task when I wrote my recent letters.

And finally: It cannot be my intention to cause the tearing down of the *Internationale Vereinigung*! I can truly say of myself, dear Professor, that in my 20 years' adherence to our cause there has never been one day of vacillation in my attitude towards it. I do not exaggerate if I state that I have devotedly worked on the organization of the Berlin Society as well as the overall Association. During the last few months I have borne practically the whole burden of preparation for the Congress, in the hope of making it particularly harmonious and giving you a particularly pleasant and encouraging impression. And I was quietly occupied with plans for the *Vereinigung* with which I wanted to please you at the Congress—and now you suspect me of wanting to dissolve the *Vereinigung*.

I am very well aware of what I have done! I have plainly put before you the existing dangers to $\Psi\alpha$, to the harmony among the closest circle, and to the whole cause. I knew how painful all this would be for you. But you also know from my letters *how hard* I found it to do this. And I added that I was exposing myself to a similar reaction from you as in the past, when I first drew your attention to unwelcome facts. You, dear Professor, vigorously dismissed that I should expect any kind of affective reaction, admitted that my doubts were not too far removed from your own, and agreed to my proposal for discussion. But now, four weeks later, the reaction is there after all!

I feel with all certainty: talking with you, dear Professor, would disperse your suspicions within a few moments. This solution is impossible at present. But I know well enough; you cannot misjudge my ethos and intentions indefinitely in this way. On the contrary, I am certain that one day you will change your opinion. For the moment, just the assurance once again that I shall approach a meeting, also if you do not take part in it, without any polemic intent. I reckon with the fact that at the meeting some of the Committee members will treat me with the same distrust as you. Disquiet stemming from very certain sources is readily directed

against the man who honestly indicates these sources. But just because I am fully aware and conscious of having behaved with loyalty towards everyone, I can calmly face these reactions too. I continue to go along with my friend Casimiro and am therefore also now,
faithfully as ever,
Yours,

*Abraham*

440A

Berlin-Grünewald
5 April 1924

Dear Professor,

I hasten to send you the programme, which has just come from the press, with the most sincere wish that your health may allow you to take part in the proceedings. The limitation of the number of papers seems to me a fortunate circumstance from this point of view; this time there can scarcely be any question of a strain. I believe that by far the greater part of the papers will gratify by their quality. I consider that too as *bonum felix faustumque*[1]; may it mobilize in you all the psychic forces that may serve to overcome the indisposition!
Yours,

*Abraham*

1. After the Latin saying: "*Quod bonum faustum felix fortunatumque sit*" ["what should be good and favourable, lucky and salutary"].

441A

INTERNATIONAL PSYCHO-ANALYTICAL ASSOCIATION
CENTRAL EXECUTIVE

Munich
26 April 1924

Dear Professor,

Even before I am back in Berlin, I want to report to you about the Congress.[1] If the report becomes somewhat extensive, I will tell you in advance, to encourage you, that in the essentials it is entirely favourable.

I will tell you first of all that the closer contact between the group presidents, which you suggested, has been decided; we must wait and see how it develops in practice. Apart from the official quarterly reports (for the *Korrespondenz-Blatt*), a more intimate report is to be exchanged

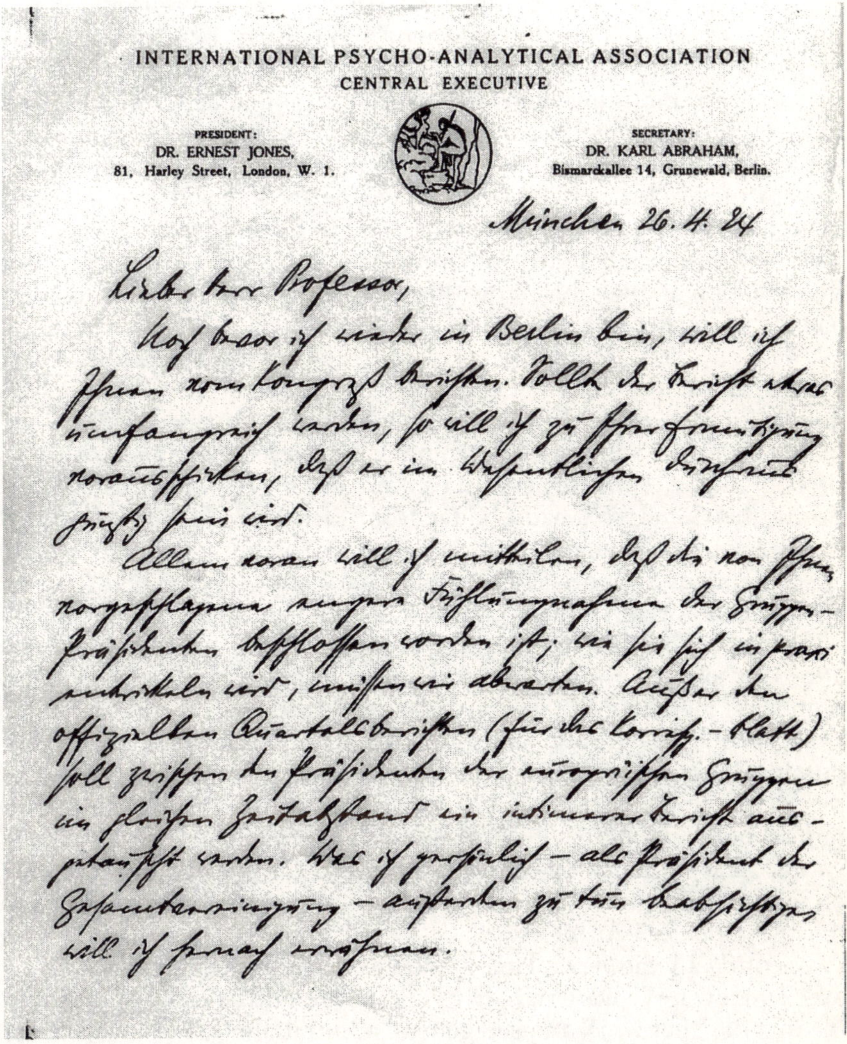

INTERNATIONAL PSYCHO-ANALYTICAL ASSOCIATION
CENTRAL EXECUTIVE

PRESIDENT:
DR. ERNEST JONES,
81, Harley Street, London, W. 1.

SECRETARY:
DR. KARL ABRAHAM,
Bismarckallee 14, Grunewald, Berlin.

München 26. 4. 24

Lieber Herr Professor,

Noch bevor ich wieder in Berlin bin, will ich Ihnen vom Kongreß berichten. Sollte der Bericht etwas umfangreich werden, so will ich zu Ihrer Beruhigung vorausschicken, daß er im Wesentlichen durchaus günstig sein wird.

Allem voran will ich mitteilen, daß die von Ihnen vorgeschlagene engere Fühlungnahme der Gruppen-Präsidenten beschlossen worden ist; wie sie sich in praxi entwickeln wird, müssen wir abwarten. Außer den offiziellen Quartalberichten (für das Korresp.-Blatt) soll zwischen den Präsidenten der europäischen Gruppen in gleichem Zeitabstand ein intimerer Bericht ausgetauscht werden. Was ich persönlich – als Präsident der Gesamtvereinigung – außerdem zu tun beabsichtige, will ich hernach erwähnen.

at the same intervals between the Presidents of the European groups. What I also intend to do personally—as President of the General Association—I will mention later on.

Our more intimate circle agreed not to reinstate the Committee artificially. A repeated, thorough discussion took place between Sándor and me, after which we parted in old friendship with the agreement to send each other—calling in Max and Hanns—informal reports, and in every way to keep communication alive by exchanging letters. I should have liked to find a similar *modus vivendi* with Otto. Although that has not succeeded, I am still not giving up hope. The rather long separation because of his journey[2] will perhaps level the ground, and if he sees after his return what—as I hope—will be there to be seen: that between the rest of us, especially between Sándor and me, there is no longer any disgruntlement, then this impression will surely convince Otto too that a new rapprochement is possible.

(continued, Berlin, 27 April)

The general harmony between the participants at the Congress was good. Criticism of the new literary publications remained within very moderate limits and was free from any polemical sharpness. As you probably know, America and India were not represented. Just shortly before the Congress I had a letter from Ermakov.[3] Nobody, he said, could afford the journey from Moscow to Salzburg; perhaps Wulff[4] might get State support. This must not have happened; at any rate, W. did not come. From Holland there was only van Emden; according to what he said, our Dutch colleagues are so badly off that they could not afford the journey. Switzerland was not represented in proportion to the number of members, but the most competent members were there: Frau Oberholzer,[5] Pfister, Kielholz,[6] Fräulein Fürst,[7] Zulliger.[8] Blum was missing; I would have been glad to make his acquaintance, as he seems the most promising to me. The English were well represented. The mutual understanding with them as well as among the Austrians, Hungarians, and Germans was very good indeed. The business session went off without a hitch. No sign of any danger for the continued existence of the *Internationale Vereinigung*.

Scientifically the general impression was that the Congress was on an excellent level. We were right to put Frau Dr Deutsch in the forefront of the first day; her work aroused general admiration. (In her $\Psi\alpha$ with me she has come a great deal further; her work inhibition in particular has disappeared). James Glover was equally outstanding, then very competent were Hárnik[9] and Dr F. Deutsch; only Liebermann dropped off badly. This first morning ended with *my* paper, which I will soon get ready for printing so as to send it to you.[10]

The symposium in the afternoon was of a similarly high standard. After Ernest's short introduction there followed the three detailed re-

1924 April

views,[11] each in itself an excellent accomplishment, and after that a few brief words from Otto and Sándor.

On the 2nd day Frau Klein's paper on the technique of child analysis was an original achievement, and the rest was without exception good, as was also the 3rd day, on which Reik's paper was especially praiseworthy.[12]

I would much rather have told you all this personally, dear Professor. I would have been so glad to come to Vienna from Salzburg. But I heard from Fräulein Bernays that you were going home on Thursday evening. According to the strict travel restrictions I was absolutely bound to have crossed the Austrian–German border by Friday evening. That would have meant that I could *only* have seen you on Friday morning. And as I knew from you about your state of health, it would have been to put pressure on you if I had demanded to see you on the morning after your return. But to have waited longer in Vienna would have exposed me to a very high fine, i.e. at least 1,000 Goldmarks. It became easier for me to give up the visit to Vienna when I heard from various sides that you prefer at present to be left undisturbed. But you know, dear Professor, that at a sign from you I would come to Vienna. In the present circumstances I believe it is better to wait until I have a positive indication of that sort.

I would now like to tell you a few more things that, as I hope, will give you pleasure. While the Congress was still on, I managed to arrange a discussion with all German analysts present and with those who wished to become analysts, in order to bind to our organization interested persons living scattered over central and southern Germany. Around 1 October of this year a first meeting of German analysts will take place in Würzburg or another centrally situated town; this will bring about a collegial rapprochement and at the same time serve scientific purposes, giving temporary preference to questions of practical importance. In the course of time a second German Society is to develop from this. I have asked Landauer[13] to undertake the preparations for this first meeting. He is the only one whose interest in the cause coincides with an unqualified personal devotion to you, dear Professor. I have also taken the opportunity, immediately after the Congress, of spending another day with Landauer and our wives on the Königsee, and I believe that in that way I have made our personal relationships much firmer.

The only group whose attitude to the *Internationale Psychoanalytische Vereinigung* seems to me to be somewhat disquieting is the Swiss one. Oberholzer, as chairman, stayed away, and his example must have affected others. I have now spoken to his wife about the situation. The resistances of the Swiss, which we have known about for a long time and believe we understand, are recently being rationalized through their rejection of the speculative direction of the *last* Congress and of everything that is not entirely free from the suspicion of being speculative. Now, apart from Frau Oberholzer's information, I can see other signs that the Swiss are sympathetic to my choice as President. As I shall be in Switzerland in the summer with my family—if they have not in the meantime put a death penalty on visits abroad—I plan to do something then to improve relations. You can see from this that I am not limiting my presidential activity to chairing the next Congress, but that I want to support the cause from the first day onwards.

Everything up to now, dear Professor, needs no reply. I need information from you on only one point, which is coming now, but a few dictated words on a card will be sufficient. Shortly before the Congress I received an invitation from New York, which, because it was inadequately addressed, wandered around for about six weeks. It comes from Dr Asch[14] in New York, who is acquainted with one of my analysands. He refers to the immobilization of scientific activity and the need to attract younger forces following the Brill/Frink conflict. He says that there is a host of good young people who are being held back by this. If I were to come, I could be profitably occupied for about half a year with their analysis and other treatments and consultations. I heard only afterwards that Otto went directly from the Congress to America. My answer to Asch was a postponing one. I said I did not want to increase the difficulties by coming and would therefore like to know first what the others in N.Y. thought of this; in addition I must naturally be certain about the circumstances. It is not out of the question that I might make use of the invitation perhaps in November. I must now wait for information from N.Y. But in the meantime I would like to know, dear Professor, what you think of Asch, who, I believe, has been with you. Can one entrust to him a business like this, with its not inconsiderable risks? Do you know what the colleagues in N.Y. think of him? Do you see any contraindication to my visit, or do you even have positive reasons for it? Perhaps particularly as President I could do some good there. For the time being the whole thing is a *perhaps* for me. The possibility of getting to know America is a very great attraction indeed, but the whole plan is not definite yet, so we had better not talk about it. However, advice from you regarding the above questions would be useful. Many thanks in advance for it!

Another quick piece of information: in addition to the subject of my paper to Congress I am preparing something else, a study of the significance of the number seven in myths, customs, etc. I believe I have found something nice there.[15]

With all good wishes and the kindest regards from house to house
Yours,

*Abraham*

## 1924 April

1. The Eighth International Psychoanalytic Congress took place in Salzburg, 21–23 April. Abraham was elected president and Eitingon secretary of the IPA. (See Abraham's report in the *Zeitschrift*, 1924, *10*: 211–228.)
2. Rank left for New York immediately after the Congress. There, he lectured with great success on his new theories, i.e. before the Academy of Medicine, at Columbia University, at the New School for Social Research, and at the New York Psychoanalytic Society. On 3 June he was elected an honorary member of the American Psychoanalytic Association. Moreover, many leading New York analysts came to Rank for analysis or supervision.
3. Ivan Dmitrievitch Ermakov, M.D., director of the psychiatric clinic in Moscow. "The activity of Professor *Serbsky* at the University Clinic in Moscow led to the foundation of the 'Little Friday Society' in 1912. The war intervened, but in 1921 the movement took a new shape, namely, in the foundation of an institute for children under the age of three years under Professor *Ermakov*. This became the State Institute for Psychoanalysis. In 1921 the Russian Psychoanalytic Association was founded, Professor *Ermakov* was President and Dr *Luria* Secretary. The activity of the Institute was expanded and now includes lectures, seminars, the psychoanalytic child guidance clinic and laboratory, the psychoanalytic polyclinic and a specific ambulatorium for children" (Jones's report in *Zeitschrift*, 1924, *10*: 226). The Russian Association had been acknowledged as a member society before the Salzburg Congress.
4. See letter 64A, 14 February 1909, & n. 2.
5. See letter 183A, 7 November 1913, n. 1.
6. Arthur Kielholz [1897–1962], M.D., long-term director of the Cantonal Psychiatric Clinic of Königsfelden, founding member of the Swiss Psychoanalytical Society [1919].
7. Emma Fürst, M.D., neurologist in Zurich, member of the Swiss Society.
8. Hans Zulliger [1893–1965], teacher at a primary school, a pioneer in psychoanalytic pedagogy, and a popular author and lecturer. He developed a form of child analysis centred on play therapy, using as few verbal interpretations as possible. He also developed two modified Rorschach tests.
9. Jenö Hárnik, M.D., of Budapest. In 1919 he had taken part in the psychiatric reform in public hospitals under the short-lived Hungarian "Council Republic". In 1922 he emigrated to Berlin, became a member of the Society there, and, from 1926 on, was a teacher at the Berlin Institute. According to Charlotte Balkányi, Hárnik died in an insane asylum in Budapest.
10. The titles of the presentations: Helene Deutsch, "The Psychology of Woman in Relation to the Functions of Reproduction"; James Glover, "Notes on an Unusual Form of Perversion"; Jenö Hárnik, "The Compulsion to Count and Its Significance for the Psychology of the Representation of Numbers"; Felix Deutsch, "Psychoanalysis at the Patient's Bedside"; Hans Liebermann, "On Monosymptomatic Neuroses"; Karl Abraham, "Contributions of Oral Eroticism to Character Formation". Abstracts in the *Zeitschrift*, 1924, *10*: 212–214.
11. A discussion on "The Relationship between Psychoanalytic Theory and Practice", with papers by Sachs, Radó, and Alexander (*Zeitschrift*, 1924, *10*: 215–217).
12. Melanie Klein, "On the Technique of Early Child Analysis"; Theodor Reik, "The Creation of Woman. Analysis of the Account in the Genesis and in Related Scripts" (*Zeitschrift*, 1924, *10*: 217, 223–224).
13. See letter 256F, 25 November 1914, n. 6.
14. Joseph J. Asch [b. 1880], M.D., member of the New York Society; in analysis with Freud in 1922 (9 December 1921, Freud & Jones, 1993: p. 446).
15. This project is discussed several times in the following letters but did not lead to publication.

## 442F

Vienna, Berggasse 19[1]
28 April 1924

Dear Friend,

This letter, which is to congratulate you on the presidency, would have gone off several days earlier had not the "waves of the steamer" of the Congress thrown up on my shores so many visitors who could not be refused. I think with regret that you let yourself to be deterred from coming to Vienna and yet I must be selfish enough to regard it as a relief for which I thank you. The good Casimiro will have understood that this time it is not a matter of a passing indisposition on my part but of a new and badly reduced level of life and work.

I have heard with pleasure that the Congress passed off without any disturbing clashes, and I am very glad to acknowledge your services in this matter. As for the affair itself, I am, as you know, in an uncomfortable position. As regards the scientific aspect, I am in fact very close to your standpoint, or rather I am growing closer and closer to it, but in the personal aspect I still cannot take your side. Though I am fully convinced of the correctness of your behaviour, I still think you might have done things differently. On the question of nuance of attitude I agree with Eitingon.

Now let me wish you an active and successful period of office, and I send my greetings to you and yours with unruffled cordiality.

Yours,

*Freud*

1. Typewritten.

## 443A

### INTERNATIONAL PSYCHO-ANALYTICAL ASSOCIATION
### CENTRAL EXECUTIVE

Berlin-Grünewald
29 April 1924

Dear Professor,

Our hotel in Salzburg has sent on to me all the letters for the participants in the Congress that arrived after our departure. Would you give the enclosed card to Prof. Tansley? Miss Newton[1] is presumably staying in Vienna again. I am therefore also enclosing a letter to her. I would send it to Frau Dr Rank, but I know that she is not in Vienna.

With kind regards,
Yours,

*Abraham*

1924  May  501

1. Caroline Newton [1893–1975], a social worker from Philadelphia. She had gone to Vienna in 1922, where she had analysis with Otto Rank (Ferenczi to Rank, 25 May 1924, Archives Judith Dupont) and became a member of the Vienna Society in 1924 [until 1938]. Participant at the Salzburg Congress, shortly after which she returned to the States. (Cf. Lieberman, 1985: pp. 254, 273, 275; Mühlleitner, 1992: pp. 234–235.)

## 444F

Vienna, Berggasse 19
4 May 1924

Dear Friend,

Your very conscientious report has completed my knowledge of events at the Congress in the most desirable manner. My heartfelt thanks for that. Also it did me a great deal of good to hear that real difficulties stood in the way of your coming to Vienna, so that its prevention did not depend on my will alone. It is very painful to me to think that of all people it was you, my *rocher de bronce* [sic],[1] whom I kept away, while I had to see and speak to Emden, Jones, Laforgue,[2] and Lévy.[3]

You must make a real effort to put yourself in my position if you are not to bear some ill-will towards me. Though apparently on the way to recovery, there is deep inside me a pessimistic conviction of the closeness of the end of my life, nourished by the never-ceasing petty torments and discomforts of the scar, a kind of senile depression centred around the conflict between irrational pleasure in life and sensible resignation. Accompanying this there is a need for rest and a disinclination for human contact, neither of which is satisfied because I cannot avoid working for six or even seven hours a day. If I am mistaken and this is only a passing phase, I shall be the first to confirm the fact and again put my shoulder to the wheel. If my forebodings are correct, I shall not fail, if sufficient time remains, to ask you quickly to come to see me.

The idea that my 68th birthday the day after tomorrow might be my last must have occurred to others too, for the city of Vienna, which usually waits until the 70th, has hastened to grant me the *Bürgerrecht* on that day.[4] I have been informed that at midday on the 6th Professor Tandler,[5] representing the mayor, and Dr Friedjung,[6] a paediatrician and a district councillor, who is one of our people, are to pay me a ceremonial visit. This recognition is the work of the Social Democrats, who now rule the City Hall. Dr Friedjung shares my birthday but not, naturally, the year of birth.

The answer to your question is not difficult. Dr Asch was with me for a whole season, and I know him quite well. He is not an analyst at all, but a urologist. What standing he has with the analysts is easily told. None at all, it is only too clear that he is a pathological fool. His analysis with me was the most miserable you can imagine, without any trace of understanding, either analytic or simple (common sense).[7] I did not want to hurt or expose him by sending him away, so I kept him on and waited, waited in vain to see whether the penny would drop. I have to say in his favour that he is a very kind-hearted, helpful person—because of inhibited sexual aggression—and therefore much loved. He wants to make everybody happy, meddles with everything, takes all kinds of things on in which he does not shrink from certain sacrifices; naturally he bites off more than he can chew and has to be set aside as utterly unreliable. Certainly he is not the man by whom you can let yourself be invited to America.

I would in any case be only sorry if you left the Association in the lurch in the autumn so as to make the journey[8] to America. The prospects there are poor, the human material unusable. We took it amiss that Brill did not make more of the Association, but we owe him an apology, it is not possible to do anything more. Since Frink's misdemeanour[9] I have given up all hope. I think I also know the young people who are waiting for the saviour: they are few and not worth much.

I have no doubt that you could get something done in New York if you could work there for two years, but nothing can be organized there in a few months, and as you are not prepared to do instantly boiling analysis, you could not do anything for the treatment of the sick either. Luckily the motive of improving your income, which could be the only excuse for going to America, is not necessary for you; you have too much you would have to give up in Berlin. You are not losing the chance to see America as an object of study; I have no doubt that sometime you will get to know the country on the basis of a more honourable invitation.—

After having been able to write during the worst period a few small things that you will see in the *Zeitschrift*,[10] I am at present quite inactive and without ideas. I am moving further and further away from the birth trauma. I believe it will "fall flat"[11] if it is not criticized too sharply, and Rank, whom I value because of his gifts, his great service to our cause, and also for personal reasons, will have learned a valuable lesson. Your reconciliation with Ferenczi seems to me to be particularly valuable as a guarantee for the future. The whole episode has had an unfavourable effect on my spirits in these difficult times too.

And now I send you my very cordial greetings and wish you and your wife and children a happy time that will justify your optimism.

Yours,

*Freud*

1. *Rocher de bronze* [rock of bronze]; after a dictum of the Prussian King Friedrich Wilhelm I.

1924 May

2. René Laforgue [1894–1962], M.D., from Alsace, a central though controversial figure in the history of psychoanalysis in France (see de Mijolla, 1992; Roudinesco, 1982, 1986). Analysed by Eugenia Sokolnicka [1923], he was himself analyst of many influential figures in French psychoanalysis and mediated Marie Bonaparte's analysis with Freud. Cofounder of the Psychoanalytic Society of Paris [1926]. During the Nazi occupation he attempted to organize a psychotherapy group close to the "Aryan" Göring Institute in Germany.
3. See letter 339F, 29 May 1918, n. 5.
4. *Bürger der Stadt Wien*—freedom of the city of Vienna.
5. Julius Tandler [1869–1936], M.D., 1910 Professor of Anatomy, 1914–1917 Dean of the Medical Faculty. After the war Tandler was the Social Democratic City councillor for Health and Welfare. His name stands, with others such as Breitner, Glöckel, Seitz, and Speiser, for the social reforms in "Red Vienna". After the civil war in February 1934 he was removed from office and spent his last years in the United States, China, and the Soviet Union.
6. Josef Karl Friedjung [1871–1946], M.D., paediatrician, *Dozent* for paediatrics at the University of Vienna, and social-democratic politician. Member of the Vienna Psychoanalytic Society since 1909; he was the only adherent of Adler's to stay in Freud's group after the break. Like Tandler, he was removed from office in 1934. In 1938 he emigrated to Haifa/Palestine. (Cf. Mühlleitner, 1992: pp. 1871–111; Handlbauer, 1992.)
7. Words in parentheses in English in original.
8. This word in English in original.
9. This word in English in original.
10. Probably Freud, 1924c, 1924e, and 1924d, the latter being a reaction to Rank's *Trauma of Birth*, although Freud eventually did not include some critical passages.
11. These words in English in original.

## 445A

Berlin-Grünewald
7 May 1924

Dear Professor,

Our letters crossed. In order to prevent this happening a second time, I postponed writing until I received your reply concerning America and only sent you a congratulatory telegram yesterday. Now you have rewarded me so generously with your two letters, particularly with the second, which actually arrived yesterday, making me feel as if it were my own birthday. I find it difficult to put into words my thanks for all the warmth and cordiality expressed in your letter. I feel infinitely relieved since I know that there is no factual discrepancy. For the last six months I have been very seriously worried. I cannot, naturally, in principle refute the possibility of having made an error in *form*. If I were to try to give a fuller explanation of my behaviour, I would have to go into many things that I have so far intentionally left untouched in our correspondence. I believe it is better to leave them unsaid; instead, I promise in future to show every consideration necessary in this far from simple situation.

I was glad, dear Professor, to receive your good wishes for my Presidency. If I on my part repeat my good wishes for your new year, I feel I am justified in being far more confident about the wishes than you are yourself. I can well imagine how the constant discomfort from the scar keeps painful thoughts alive. Even the necessity of having to think about one's health is a burden, and I never doubted the gravity of last year's illness. But on the other hand, six months have now passed since the operation without any new objective reasons for concern, and the latest news from my various informants—the most recent being Jones and Hitschmann—is that they found you better and more capable than expected. If my informants are correct and the discomfort from the scar is also gradually receding, I look forward to the immense pleasure of visiting you fairly soon and of congratulating you on your recovery. I am not to be easily put off from seeing the future in this light. As far as the Viennese are concerned, I give them two years to think of something even better for your 70th birthday than the honours of yesterday.

I am most especially grateful to you for the very detailed information on America; I was very touched by the exactitude with which you considered every detail. In the circumstances you describe—which up to now I did not know quite so exactly—I am no longer considering the project seriously. So I am staying at home, but I shall occasionally carry on the correspondence with your translator in Madrid,[1] so that if possible I can give lectures in Madrid next spring. Another plan is to make contact now with internal medicine. I enclose a newspaper report[2] that shows that soon a time will come when we can make an entry into these circles for our cause.

As the journals have not yet reached me, I have not yet read your latest article[3]; but I already knew about the various articles announced, and hope to read it soon. The first two volumes of the *Collected Works*,[4] in full leather, stand resplendent in my room; they are a joy to look at.

I have already written about my work plans. At Deuticke's suggestion, I am preparing the 2nd edition of the *Segantini*.[5] It makes me uneasy to think that this small booklet was not taken over by the Verlag along with so many others.

Tomorrow I am giving the first lecture in my course; after that I have a meeting with Max and Hanns. We want to meet regularly now.

Some time ago we rented a small flat for the summer months in Sils-Maria (Engadine), where we shall do our own housekeeping—that is, if we are allowed out of this country. Travelling difficulties are still very considerable.

I do not expect a reply to this letter, dear Professor!! Neither visits to your house nor correspondence should become a burden to you. I shall write again soon if there is anything to report.

1924  May

Wishing you again all the best I can think of and with the most cordial greetings from house to house I am,
Yours,

*Karl Abraham*

1. Luis López-Ballesteros y de Torres.
2. Missing.
3. Freud, 1924e.
4. Volumes 4 and 5 of the 12-volume *Gesammelte Schriften von Sigm. Freud*, ed. Anna Freud, Otto Rank, and Adolf Storfer, in the Verlag.
5. Abraham, 1911[30], second, enlarged edition, 1925.

## 446A

Berlin-Grünewald
25 May 1924

Dear Professor,

This letter needs no reply. It is itself a reaction, one of joy to the good news I have heard through Lampl: that you will soon be released from surgical trusteeship and can enjoy your holiday in the mountains. I believe that you too feel heartened by this decree, and so I hope that this summer will for you and yours take place against a background of decreasing worries about health!

I am taking the opportunity to give you some good news from here. Especially our courses are making gratifying progress. Sachs has about 40 students for the "Kings' Dramas"; I have announced four lectures on "The $\Psi\alpha$ of Mental Disturbances" and was amazed to get an audience of 50. The other courses too are—for summertime—well attended. The Society's activity is satisfactory. The consultation practice has equalled zero for some time, as nobody here has any money and the influx of foreigners is very much smaller since Berlin is no longer cheap. However we dare hope that this crisis will be over in time.

Yesterday I sent Reik a review of a work that appeared in Buenos Aires.[1] In a prison the author has analysed quite deeply and, with much understanding, a man sentenced for murder! This sort of thing has to come to us from South America!

I have still heard nothing more from Asch in New York. Perhaps the best and simplest thing is if it is left at that.

I have read the short article on neurosis and psychosis with the greatest pleasure. Apart from all the other excellent points, which I do not need to mention, it was a delight to read something that has come from living experience and gives the reader such a unique feeling of security. And best of all, something is soon going to appear again—the pleasures of holidays!

Holidays—yes, if the authorities will allow it. I do not get the journey out to Sils-Maria free of charge for us. The *"Gebühr"* or rather *"Ungebühr"*[2] would come to 2,000 Goldmarks and mean the failure of the whole plan, including appointments with patients. Apart from the fact that dogs have to be kept permanently on a leash; now human beings have to be tied up as well. There is a charming apartment waiting for us in Sils; the living-room is furnished entirely with antique carved built-in pieces, and there is also a garden, forest, water, and mountains. It would be a cruel sacrifice. But I am not giving up hope, and I shall insist to the limit.

Cordial greetings from house to house!
Yours,

*Abraham*

1. Beltrán, 1923; see Abraham, 1917[105b].
2. German play on words: *Gebühr* [fee], *Ungebühr* [impropriety]. [Trans.]

## 447A

Berlin-Grünewald
1 June 1924

Dear Professor,

This letter calls rather more for an answer than the previous one, but only when the opportunity arises, and you also need not give it *yourself*.

I have just heard from Sachs that you too are thinking of going to Switzerland, and also to Graubünden; he said that you are negotiating with Waldhaus-Flims. That would really be an ideal place, with the most beautiful forests and walks and, in addition, a lake that can certainly be deemed the equal of that of Lavarone. Should you not be able to decide on Waldhaus, I should like to offer to put at your disposal my special knowledge of Graubünden. I only mention at the moment that you might consider *Klosters* and *Churwalden*, both at the same elevation as Flims, and perhaps also *Lenzerheide*, which is 1300 m above sea level.

All these places can easily be reached from Sils-Maria, where we hope to go on 22 June. (But you know, dear Professor, that I shall not come if I have not been called for!). So prospects are opening to me that I welcome with great joy.

I should be very glad to know whether you will be in Switzerland, and where, and whether I can be of use to you in any way. Perhaps Fräulein Anna would tell me on a card what you have decided.

I am sure you will like it in Graubünden. The Flims region is particularly interesting from the point of view of nature and cultural history. Graubünden is my old love, and I hope it will meet with your approval.

With cordial greetings and many good wishes,
Yours,

*Abraham*


448F

Vienna, Berggasse 19[1]
4 June 1924

Dear Friend,

It was very opportune for me that you produced such appreciative words for Waldhaus Flims. We booked there yesterday and want to arrive on 8 July. This time I am also taking with me a well-capitalized negro[2] who will certainly not bother me more than that one hour in the day.

Being so near the Engadine, I count with certainty on seeing you and your family. You write that you hope to arrive in Sils-Maria on 20 June. If this were to be a slip of the pen, it would at least not be difficult to explain.

For good Casimiro the news that I am at least beginning to feel stronger and to be content with my defects. Perhaps my unsociability is also subsiding.

Cordially yours,

*Freud*

1. Typewritten.
2. When Freud began to practise, "[t]he consultation hour was at noon, and for some time patients were referred to as 'negroes.' This strange appellation came from a cartoon in the *Fliegende Blätter* depicting a yawning lion muttering 'Twelve o'clock and no negro'" (Jones, 1953: p. 151).


449A

Sils-Maria, Engadine, Haus Gilly
30 June 1924

Dear Professor,

I was distressed to hear that you gave up your journey to Switzerland.[1] I have no idea where you will spend your holidays now, but must naturally agree with you that it is better not to be too far away from Vienna. Since travel restrictions in Germany have been lifted, I could perhaps come at the end of my vacation to wherever you are staying. I therefore hope to hear sometime where you will be spending the first half of August.

It is 18 years since I was in the Engadine and I am again as enchanted with it as on all previous occasions. Especially now in the spring there are more flowers in bloom here than anywhere else in the Alps. It is well before the season and therefore everything is rather empty, enabling us to enjoy to the full all the splendours of the alpine mountains. This time we have rented a small flat and brought our tried and trusted "mainstay" from Berlin, and we are looking after ourselves. Our flat is completely self-contained. The living-room is a typical Engadine room with a three-cornered bay window, panelled walls and ceiling, built-in furniture, etc., more comfortable than any hotel would ever have been; the bedrooms are large, light, and immaculately arranged.

Some daily analytic work—for the time being only one patient is here—keeps me in contact with my customary activity. Apart from that I am writing on the new edition of Segantini for Deuticke and am going over my Congress paper.[2] If you, dear Professor, should wish to read it, I could send you the manuscript sometime (but you are not to say yes just to please *me*!).

I hope you are getting on quite well on the whole, despite your rather frequent difficulties, and I would be very, very happy to hear it confirmed by you yourself once more. Your last letter sounded so much more hopeful and positive and showed clearly that you had even got your sense of humour back. It is pleasant to hear news like that more often.

The new volume of the *Collected Works* reached Berlin after I had left, so that I shall not be able to read the two new articles[3] until after I get back.

There is nothing else to report from the quietness of Sils-Maria. I wish you and your family very restful holidays and am, with cordial greetings from house to house,

Yours,

*Karl Abraham*

1. A communication of Freud's is evidently missing.
2. Abraham, 1924[99].
3. Freud, 1924e, 1925a [1924], in Volume 6 of the *Gesammelte Schriften*.

## 450F

Vienna, Berggasse 19[1]
4 July 1924

Dear Friend,

There are circumstances in which one can be altruistic even in old age. So I take pleasure with you in the Engadine, although I myself cannot be there. I have too clearly recognized my dependence on my doctor's studio to put such a distance between him and me, and have rented the *Villa Schüler*, near the southern railway station in *Semmering*, from where I can comfortably get to Vienna and back in a day. The rent is so high that I need not think of a second sojourn anywhere else. So, if you want to come and see me in August, you need make no other journey. This time I too have brought a patient with me as hand-luggage who shall keep me in practice. My state of health has recently been showing ups and downs,[2] according to whether the prosthesis, the nose or the ear chose to torment me more or less. I hope we shall now find a *modus vivendi* with each other.

If you wish to send me your Congress paper, it is *exceedingly probable* that I shall read it with the greatest interest. We intend to move on 8 July.

With cordial greetings to you and your house and best wishes for the summer,

Yours,

*Freud*

1. Typewritten.
2. These three words in English in original.

## 451A

Sils-Maria, Engadine, Haus Gilly
22 July 1924

Dear Professor,

If everything has gone according to your plan, you have now been enjoying your summer holidays for a fortnight, and I wish with all my heart that this time has been marred by as few troubles as possible. Thank you very much for your letter; I am sending you my manuscript today. I did not want to bother you with it *earlier*. Fortunately it is short, as the lecture lasted only half an hour, and so it will take up at the most half an hour of your time.

After our stay in Sils I shall arrange, dear Professor, to visit you there. But I ask you most earnestly to put me off honestly if my coming is not convenient for you. I shall let you know again nearer the time, probably somewhere around 10 August.

I recently had a few lines from Mrs Strachey, whom you kindly referred to me. I think she will probably come to me on 1 October.

We are very well here. Even after four weeks' stay Sils is still as splendid as it was on the first day. Wishing you very healthful and restful holidays, I am, with best regards from all of us,

Yours,

*Karl Abraham*

## 452F

Semmering[1]
31 July 1924

Dear Friend,

It is nice to hear that you can so thoroughly enjoy Sils-Maria. There is no question of my saying no to your coming to see me, if the small extra journey does not put you off. I am having a good rest here, I am no longer so withdrawn, and I am looking forward greatly to seeing you again. I have read your manuscript with the interest it deserves. Forgive me one small comment of secondary importance. You charge Adler with the responsibility for the connection between ambition and urethral erotism. Well, I have always believed that that was my discovery.[2]

Until we meet again, then! With cordial greetings to you and your wife and children,

Yours,

*Freud*

1. Typewritten.
2. This was corrected by Abraham in the printed version (1924[99]: p. 404).

## 453F

Semmering
22 August 1924

Dear Friend,

Ad vocem[1]: 7.

I am putting at your disposal an idea the value of which I cannot judge myself because of ignorance.

I should like to take a historical view and believe that the significance of the number 7 originated in a period when people had a system of counting in sixes. (Here ignorance sets in.) Then 7 was not the last of a series as it is now, in the week, but the first of a second series and, like all beginnings, subject to taboo. The fact that the initial number of the third series, that is to say 13, is one of the most eerie of all numbers would fit in with this.

The origin of my idea was a remark in a history of Assyria that 19 was also one of the suspect numbers, which was explained there with reference to the month that had passed by the equation 30 + 19 = 49, thus 7 × 7. However, 19 = 13 + 6, the beginning of a 4th series of sixes.

This system of sixes would thus be pre-astronomical. One should now investigate what is known of such a system, of which enough traces remain (dozen, three score, division of the circle into 360 degrees).

Moreover, it is strange how many prime numbers appear in this series:

1
7
13
19
25 is an exception, but then
31
37
43
49, which is again 7 × 7.

Mad things can be got up to with numbers. Be careful!
Cordially yours,

*Freud*

1. Latin: "as to the word (there is to remark)"—equivalent to the English use of re.

## 454A

Berlin-Grünewald
23 August 1924

Dear Professor,

I have been home for just a week[1] and cannot wait any longer to send you at least a sign of life to express certain feelings. First of all, the great and incomparable pleasure of finding you, dear Professor, in spite of all you have gone through, *so* well, so sympathetic and capable, as I had scarcely dared hope from all written accounts. I left you expecting that the comfortable days spent on the Semmering would further contribute to your recuperation. And then I must thank you and all your family for all the kindnesses shown me! The days I spent with you made a particularly pleasant end to my holidays. I very much hope that your health will permit me to repeat my visit fairly soon.

I spent a day and a half in Vienna. At the Verlag I spoke to Storfer about the printing of my paper. You already know that he intends to combine it with an earlier paper and make one issue out of them. It is just possible that I may quickly add a short supplementary chapter about character formation at the genital level.[2]

Further, I had an opportunity in Vienna of speaking with Dr Deutsch. Although the objections you express against him cannot be entirely invalidated, it was important to me to be able to convince myself that his behaviour is more excusable than I had to assume from your description.[3] I avoid going into details, because such things are unedifying in a letter and because I do not want to interfere. I will say just one thing: that there were still *other* motives for Dr Deutsch's policy of keeping you in the dark, apart from those that we were recently discussing.—I have not seen Frau Dr D., but I have written to her that you, dear Professor, would ask her to come and see you in Vienna.

It is somewhat comical that I am becoming the mouthpiece of the most assorted kinds of people. When I came home, I found a letter from Reik that had been forwarded to me, in which he asked me to give you his regards if I saw you, and to tell you that he was thinking of you with unchanged devotion and was very busy with scientific work. In this way he wanted to give you a hint that he was thinking about you, without your being obligated in any way.—

25 August 1924

I had got to this point the day before yesterday when your letter arrived. In the meantime I have studied your suggestions and want first of all to thank you for your stimulation. I was so pleased that you immediately took up the problem of the number seven and made it yours! I have meanwhile studied the ethnological and other relevant literature, but with very meagre results. Either the "7 planets" or the "quarter of the lunar month"—that is all people know.

The idea about the system of the sixes is very interesting and undoubtedly an important contribution, especially in connection with 13, 19, etc. and with the taboo of the beginning. But this on its own is not enough, apart from the fact that I have so far only found some confirmation of a primitive system of *fives, not* of *sixes*. Here is one of the many arguments: not only are the *seventh* day, the 7th month, etc. taboo with the Jews, Babylonians, etc., but all dangerous things representing a taboo, such as evil spirits etc., are seven in number. Most important, there are strong psychological reasons that make a connection between the number 7 and the *Ucs* irrefutable. But I am convinced that these psychological sources are linked with others, among which the one you suggest may well be of great importance. One must once again ask oneself why none of the orientalists had this *Kück*.[4]

Your communication encourages me to report to you as soon as I have any new results in this matter. But I cannot promise anything as the literature has let me down and I am still waiting for analytic material.

Perhaps something soon about another project. For now, only many thanks and the most cordial greetings from house to house!

Yours,

*Abraham*

1. Abraham had come to the Semmering on 10 August (Freud to Rank, 6 August 1924, Archives Judith Dupont).
2. This plan was carried out (Abraham, 1925[106]).
3. Felix Deutsch had not told Freud about the malignant nature of the tumour, fearing that Freud would commit suicide (cf. Jones, 1957: p. 90).
4. See letter 426A, 26 November 1923, n. 1.

## 455A

Berlin-Grünewald
9 September 1924

Dear Professor,

We already know that we cannot expect you at the meeting in Würzburg. But I will at least inform you of what goes on, so that you can see that our cause is not dormant.

At the same time I send hearty congratulations to you and all your family on the second granddaughter.[1] Also on behalf of my wife! *Vivant sequentes!*[2]

As my latest feat, I will tell you about a parapraxis. I read in the paper about the League of Nations Congress in Geneva. The disarmament proposals of the Great Powers, bristling as they are with arms, aroused my mistrust, so that in the review of a speech, instead of "the League of Nations must see to the necessary *guarantees* [*Garantien*]" I read "the necessary *grenades* [*Granaten*]". The transposition of letters is quite amusing.

Cordial greetings from
Your

*Abraham*

1. Eva, daughter of Henny and Oliver, born in Berlin on 3 September 1924. Shortly before, on 8 August 1924, Sophie, daughter of Esti and Martin, had been born.
2. Latin blessing: "Long live the ones that follow!"

## 456A

Berlin-Grünewald
17 September 1924

Dear Professor,

You have not heard from me for some time even though I promised to report everything that might be of interest to you.

At present, the projected meeting in Würzburg is of prime importance for us. It promises to be quite satisfactory, and I am very pleased that the participation of a number of non-Germans will dispel the suspicion of our wishing to isolate ourselves. We already have a good selection of papers. Moreover, the question of training will be discussed in detail, as Simmel will report on the organization of our Institute with special reference to the teaching syllabus, and Sachs will talk on didactic analyses in particular. You will have heard that the latter will be giving a course on technique in London.[1] We had, incidentally, to move our meeting to 11 and 12 October.

The courses for our winter term will be similar to those of last year. The only change is that Radó will give the introductory course in my place and I shall probably speak on character development to an audience of doctors and teachers.

The following little story will amuse you. A few days ago I found this announcement in an antiquarian's catalogue: "Freud, S., *Entwicklung der Spinalganglien bei Petromyzon*, 1878."[2] I did not know this paper but remembered that I had recently come across an allusion to it in your manuscript (*An Autobiographical Study*).[3] I have now obtained the booklet—it has the name of a Dr Langerhans in it, who died here some time ago and to whose work on a similar theme your paper refers. I found it very interesting to recognize your later style in this, your earliest paper. After I had been the only one in ψα circles to own a copy of your dissertation on the coca plant,[4] I am now, in that I possess your two earliest papers, *hors de concours*.

Mrs Strachey has been with me for a week. Up to now the analysis has been going well. The husband came with her for a time but will soon return to England.

I am at present dictating a third paper for the "Character"-issue (genital level of character formation). There is a good essay on the stereotypical posture of catatonic patients in the Peruvian *Revista de Psiquiatria*. I am having it translated and will then send it to Ferenczi for inclusion in the *Zeitschrift*.[5]

Wishing you and your family pleasant autumn days on the Semmering, I am, with cordial greetings,

Yours,

Karl Abraham

1. Sachs spent the months of August and September in London (cf. Freud & Jones, 1993: p. 556).
2. Freud, 1878a.
3. Freud, 1925d [1924]: p. 10.
4. Freud, 1884e.
5. Caravedo, 1924, reviewed by Abraham, 1917[105b], but not published in the *Zeitschrift*.

## 457F

Semmering
21 September 1924

Dear Friend,

Thank you for so conscientiously keeping your promise. But in what are you not conscientious?

There is little to report from here. I am waiting with eager expectation for the return of Rank, who will probably not be in Vienna before the end of next month. I have been in lively correspondence with Ferenczi and would like you also not to lose contact with him. His behaviour in the "affair" was vacillating, but he is now retreating from his partisanship for R[ank].

I am thinking of breaking off my stay here in a week's time. Not without great regret, because the last few days have been magnificent. I, that is to say my prosthesis, is again under treatment to adapt it to changed conditions.

It is making severe demands on the unity of the personality to try to make me identify myself with the author of the paper on the spinal ganglia of the petromyzon. Nevertheless, it does seem to be the case, and I think I was happier about that discovery than about others since then.

In the autumn I shall have to give up the leadership of the Vienna group, because I am too tired in the evening to be able to follow a meeting lasting several hours, and my hearing works on one side only. I do not yet know what the group will do.

My best wishes for the German meeting!
With cordial greetings to you and your house,
Yours,
   *Freud*

## 458A

Berlin-Grünewald
15 October 1924

Dear Professor,

Your telegram[1] arrived at the end of the Würzburg meeting, and I want to begin by thanking you for it. I had planned to send you a detailed report about the proceedings but I think you will already have heard personally from van Emden and perhaps from others as well, so I can be briefer.

Attendance was quite satisfactory; the list shows 48 names. Most of the papers were of a remarkably high standard. We were glad to see also a number of non-Germans (Van Emden, from Vienna the Deutschs and Reik, from Basle Sarasin[2] and Christoffel[3]). Above all the atmosphere was excellent, so that in general people wanted another meeting very soon. This will take place in Weimar between Easter and Whitsuntide. I think that even more really interested people who are still outside the Association will be attracted to it. These smaller meetings are certainly useful to our movement as a whole and to our organization. It was also important for me to gain a little more contact with the Swiss. I think all the participants were pleased with the way the meeting went. Besides, those two sunny autumn days on the Main were delightful, and it was a great pleasure to visit the lovely old town.

I heard from the Viennese that you, dear Professor, will continue to be officially President of the Society. It is really the only way out of this difficult situation. The good reports on your state of health lead me to hope that you will go to the meetings now and again.

In the Spanish language, which I like so very much, one puts the question-mark at the *beginning* of the sentence. I shall therefore precede a piece of news received today with a question mark: ?Are you, dear Professor, really coming to Berlin quite soon, and is it true that you will read a paper? This interests me, first of all because I would see in it an extraordinary sign of objective improvement and subjective well-being; and besides . . . but I do not need to say this!

—I have just now received the final proofs of my booklet on character-formation.—The investigation into the number seven has come altogether to a standstill—that is to say, I could not read anything relevant. But I come to believe more and more that in the idea I put forward to you on the Semmering there is a kernel of truth. I see that one cannot attack the problem either from the angle of astronomical significance or from that of numerical systems etc. The basic *psychological* phenomenon seems to me to lie in the *ambivalent attitude* of mankind to the number seven. This must represent the thing towards which one is most ambivalent, and I thus always come back to the Oedipus complex. Seven is the number of abstinence (Sabbath, etc.) everywhere, it expresses the taboo and is at the same time the number of many rites compulsively performed. I see in this double significance the justification for assuming a fusion of two other numbers in this one and believe that the significance of the 3 = father and the 4 = mother (the 3 arch-fathers and 4 arch-mothers in the Bible, etc.) will have to be retained. I hope I shall soon be able to look for further material. (The above requires *no* reply!) Another

1924 October

thing that has occupied me recently is the subject of *anxiety in an enclosed space*, a phenomenon that, as far as I know, has not yet been dealt with in detail. A few observations made recently have provided me with some interesting information and, at the same time, demonstrated the *slight* significance of the birth process in the formation of this neurotic symptom.

Sachs has naturally told me in detail what you discussed about Otto and further collaboration with him. I am deliberately not going into this, as we shall first have to wait and see.

With cordial greetings from house to house,
Yours,

*Abraham*

1. Missing.
2. See letter 409F, 30 March 1922, n. 9.
3. Hans Christoffel, M.D., neurologist from Basel, member of the Swiss Society.

## 459F

Vienna, Berggasse 19
17 October 1924

Dear Friend,

How ambivalent can rumour be! In Vienna I am declared dead about once a fortnight and in Berlin my visit, in order to deliver a lecture, is expected! Well, neither is true, the truth lies in-between. I am still alive, as you see, but I have no desire to lecture and will be able to think of travelling again only if Pichler succeeds in making a good and stable fastening for my prosthesis, which so far is not the case. My condition, that is to say, my capacity to speak and chew, is still so variable that there is ample room for the optimism of all the Casimiros.

I have heard only good things about Würzburg, but you are surely the most competent reporter about that. The whole thing is very gratifying.

Emden is here, as you know. He wanted to have an hour's analysis daily for four weeks, but I had to decline. I am now stingy with my work, alien as that may be to my previous nature, and am unwilling to do more than five hours. Nevertheless a 6th is almost invariably added, because of consultations and having to see people. Apart from that, I am correcting proofs, beginning the revision of the *Interpretation of Dreams* for the complete edition, and the like. The *Autobiographical Study*, which you have read, has already been set and corrected. I shall turn the fee into reprints and distribute them generously.

Rank is expected at the end of the month. You are right, we too must wait, but I think that nothing good lies ahead. I should like to separate his personality from the birth trauma and would like to have grounds for an opinion as to what of it may be valuable. The $\Psi\alpha$ *Review* announces a paper of his on the significance of the birth trauma for analysis[1]; I have not received it.

I am sending a proposal in writing to the next meeting of the Society that I should retain the presidency for a time and be represented by a deputy at the meetings. It would be a semi-miracle if I were ever able to resume my functions, and I do not believe in it. So it is only putting it off.

The prospect of getting a house for a out-patient clinic has evaporated. The wealthy lady who wished to build it is now acting as if she were offended and is withdrawing. I was thinking of arranging a flat in the house for Ferenczi, who would then have moved to Vienna as the head of the institute. But now nothing has come of it, and I have one more confirmation that nothing will grow on Viennese soil.[2]

In the issue of the Hirsch Archives that arrived today I found a priceless criticism of your stages of development of a fool, Placzek,[3] whom you must know better than I do. I only know that I have had in hands all sorts of rubbish by him.

These comments are often very interesting. The American critics, for example, show a unique mixture of ignorance and irreverence,[4] and the French a swaggering arrogance combined with the greatest possible naiveté, and such-like.

I send my cordial greetings to you and your house,
Yours,

*Freud*

1. Rank, 1924b. The *Review* was published by Jelliffe and White, an analysand of Rank's.
2. "I convey to you the sad news that Frau Kraus, who wanted to build the ambulatorium, has made a written declaration that she gives up her plan because of the generally bad economical situation.... Gone with it is my last hope that something good would come out of $\psi\alpha$ in Vienna. I had set all my hopes on your move here" (Freud to Ferenczi, 12 October 1924).
3. See letter 302F, 26 September 1916, & n. 3.
4. These three words in English in original.

## 460A

Berlin-Grünewald
20 October 1924

Dear Professor,

The resistance of a patient who presents me with an hour of undisturbed peace gives me the chance of replying to you at once. I had not expected such a detailed letter and was therefore doubly pleased to find you, if not keen to talk, at least keen to write. But to reassure you straight away—*this* letter requires no reply. It merely contains some news that I could have sent you a fortnight later, but it gives me pleasure to report to you a little.

The "rumour" had already been dispelled before your letter arrived. The speaker, who is to talk to a Zionist organization here, is a school-teacher from Vienna who bears your name. However, the invitation to the lecture went out with the name "Professor Fr. from V". Probably a slip on the part of the president of the organization, which will have the effect of providing your namesake with a larger audience than anticipated.

Recently I had a visit from a young teacher from my son's grammar school to ask me questions about $\psi\alpha$ literature. He told me that he had to produce, for the State examination, a treatise on "Freud's Concept of the Erotic". There are signs and wonders even in Prussia! A few days ago I read through the little work, which is charming and quite a success.

I have started to read the book by Lévy-Bruhl (Sorbonne) on thought in primitive people,[1] the first work that will be useful in my investigation into the number seven. More about this later!

Perhaps, dear Professor, you may be interested in hearing something about $\Psi\alpha$ from Mrs Str.[achey] from London. It struck me from the very beginning that the long period of work with you has been, as it were, obliterated. We have to discover everything afresh, as all the facts elicited by the first analysis have disappeared, while the general knowledge of $\Psi\alpha$ is intact. You will remember that the patient lost her father in the first weeks of her life and has no memories of her own of him. Apart from other motives for the amnesia, there is a complete identification of your person with the father—she has no memory of either. On the other hand she has directed towards you the same rescue phantasies as towards her father.

I have already read the criticism of Placzek; I found nothing new in it. But Pl. is not without danger through the spitefulness of his attacks. Recently in a discussion he knowingly made a false statement that was intended generally to discredit $\Psi\alpha$. He was made to retract his untrue assertion. Pl.'s personality may be characterized by the fact that he is a baptized Jew who, as such, had the effrontery to take over the management of a kosher sanatorium and write about the ritual diet as a "curative factor" but at the same time to sit on the church council of the Kaiser Wilhelm Memorial Church. In these circumstances it is hardly necessary to say any more.

I am immensely sorry, dear Professor, that you may experience further agitation because of Rank's return and that nothing can be done to spare you this sort of thing. I also do not foresee anything good and can scarcely imagine the possibility of collaboration. The other question—how we are to replace such an exceptionally capable worker—is, by comparison, less important; for after a detailed discussion with Hanns and Max, I think that all difficulties can be overcome. We have also discussed the future of the Verlag; it looks as though this too may be put on a firmer basis. So if we definitely have to do without Otto, this situation will not find us at a loss. The practical consequences, then, do not worry me as much as the personal effects that meeting Otto might have. I hope that Max's presence in Vienna at the end of this month[2] will contribute something towards easing the situation.

In spite of everything there is a small hope in connection with the coming events. If a complete separation should come about between Otto and yourself, then there would hardly be anything to prevent the rest of us from re-establishing the Committee. One can say today that in S. Cristoforo and Lavarone Otto's efforts were directed towards blasting the Committee apart. We sat then in judgement over Ernest's incorrect behaviour, because the continued existence of the Committee seemed in danger due to this behaviour. The much graver danger lay in quite another quarter.

With hindsight, I would like to say that the neurotic process in Otto has been in the making over the course of several years. At the same time as he tried to compensate for his negative tendencies by over-conscientious work, his need for friendly togetherness with us others lessened and his arbitrary and tyrannical behaviour became more striking in many ways. Added to this, there has been an increased emphasis on money interests and, simultaneously, increased irritability and hostility. Thus, an undeniable regression to anal sadism. The disappearance of all friendly feelings towards you has recently become very clear. When I consider all this, I can also now only take an analytic point of view; I do not feel a trace of hostility towards Otto. My reaction is one of infinite regret that you have to suffer this trial, and particularly with Otto, and that Otto himself seems to have come—apparently unstoppably—onto a pathological track. I noticed together with Hanns and Max at our meeting that they were both strongly involved emotionally and for that reason reject any further getting together with Otto, whereas I finished with the emotional side long ago and can now only stress the psychological hopelessness.—

Last week I wrote a detailed letter to Sándor, and I hope to hear from him soon.

With the most cordial greetings from house to house and all good wishes for your health,

Yours,

*Karl Abraham*

1. Lévy-Bruhl, 1910. Lucien Lévy-Bruhl [1857–1939], the well-known French philosopher and ethnologist. Professor of History of Philosophy at the Sorbonne since 1889.

2. "Eitingon and Ferenczi were here on 31 October and 1 November in order to confer with me and Rank, who has returned at last . . . It was decided that Rank will resign from his post as editor of the *Zeitschrift* and director of the Verlag. Together with Sachs, he is to retain his editorship of *Imago*. Storfer has been appointed head of the Verlag . . . The editorial office itself will be moved to Berlin and entrusted to Radó" (Freud to Jones, 5 November 1924, Freud & Jones, 1993: p. 559).

## 461A

Berlin-Grünewald
12 November 1924

Dear Professor,

The evening paper reports that rail traffic in Austria is to be resumed tonight. I take this as a signal for writing to you at last. But the letter will need no reply!

After Max's return, we three had a discussion and consulted Radó. We are all of the opinion that the solution is as favourable as it could possibly be under the given circumstances. The sad feeling remains that at the end of nearly two years of first latent and then open conflict we have to be satisfied to have brought off the divorce from Rank in a definite form and yet made it appear as unobtrusive as possible.

We have lost one of our best, but he is, after all, only one of us. During that same time we were threatened by another loss[1] from which we were fortunately spared. We of the old guard who remained round you, dear Professor, shall certainly not slacken in our endeavours to provide you after a great deal of trouble with some gratifying experiences. In a short while I will take steps to start the circular letters again. I envisage that Berlin, Budapest, and London should write once a month and that a 4th copy should go off each time to you, dear Professor, without your needing to take any part in the correspondence, just to keep you up to date. If you should on any occasion want to express your opinion we should welcome it, but it must not become an obligation.—I believe that the most important outcome of the discussion in Vienna will be that the harmony with Ferenczi will be re-established.

We thought with regard to the editing in Berlin that Radó would do the actual current work, in constant contact with Max, but Hanns and I would meet them when necessary to discuss any important matters.

A few days ago Pfister was with me; he had a lecture to give here. I believe by spending quite a great deal of time with him to have achieved something of a kind of a somewhat warmer relationship with the Swiss.

In Berlin things are going smoothly. The courses have begun, and all seem to be going well. My course (character development) has an audience of about 40, which is quite a great deal for a specialized subject.

Radó will probably leave for Vienna at noon on Saturday and arrive there early Sunday morning. He will telephone you when he arrives to ask when you can see him at your home.

My wife and I were looking forward to having your wife here one of these evenings with Ernst and his wife, van Emdens, Sachs, and Lampl. Unfortunately the strike got in the way of this plan, and we do not yet know whether it can be carried out at least in part.

I shall today also follow my old custom of raising in my letters theoretical matters that occupy me. You, dear Professor, will certainly remember the idea you told me about on the Semmering on the way home from the strawberry hunt. It referred to the origin of predicting the future from entrails. I was recently reminded of your theory in an analysis. Certain cannibalistic phantasies of my patient led to the presumed roots of the Jewish prohibition against eating milk and meat together. In this analysis the milk proved to be an allusion to the mother, the meat an allusion to the typical biting castration phantasy against the father. This made me reflect about this prohibition; its origin is the biblical law, repeated several times and enigmatic in meaning: Thou shalt not seethe a kid in his mother's milk.[2] This law prohibits the killing and eating of even an *animal* shortly *after* its birth, obviously with the intention of preventing the same action in the case of a *human* child, and even *before* birth. This would make it a direct prohibitory law against the primitive customs you suggest!

With cordial greetings,
Yours, faithfully as ever,

*Karl Abraham*

1. Ferenczi.
2. *Exodus* 23, 19.


## 462F

Vienna[1]
21 November 1924

H[err] Dr K. Abraham
D. Friend!

I urgently recommend to you the lady bringing you this, whom you also know,[2] and I hope that you will be successful in rescuing "mankind's noble part".

Cordially yours,

*Freud*

1. Written on the back of a visiting-card; date at the end of the note.
2. Evidently Frau Orska; see letter 465A, 3 December 1924.

## 463
[by Abraham, Eitingon, Sachs]

INTERNATIONAL PSYCHO-ANALYTICAL ASSOCIATION
Berlin
26 November 1924

Dear Friends,

We are glad to take the opportunity to take up again the correspondence that was broken off quite a long time ago very much against our wishes. We are most particularly pleased that the encouragement to do so came from your side, dear *Sándor*.[1] We hope that the revived Committee will work together in the future without internal difficulties, and we will be glad to contribute our bit.

We are especially delighted to welcome the Professor's readiness to take part in our correspondence in the old way. We had expected that Fräulein *Anna* would carry on the correspondence. But we do not approve of her taking part merely as her father's secretary; we would like to welcome her into our circle as a member with equal rights, so that she can take part in our discussions and meetings as they occur. We are incidentally of the opinion that the fact of our correspondence does not need to be kept a strict secret, although naturally no outsiders may look at it.

We have heard with satisfaction that you, dear *Sándor*, completely share our view of *Rank*'s behaviour. But we should be also glad to know your attitude towards his scientific innovations. In Salzburg you seemed to be tending towards these views, which we took to be the case from a few passages in your last book[2] and particularly from *Róheim*'s paper.[3] We are far from seeing, in a different point of view on your side, a reason for alienation, but it seems important to us to make the new beginning of the correspondence an occasion to express ourselves frankly so that the road will be clear for further scientific discussions.

This letter had reached this point when we had further news from Vienna, Budapest, and London almost all at the same time. We therefore arranged another meeting yesterday to answer all these letters at once.

In your letter to *Max*, dear Professor,[4] you suggest taking *Brill* into our circle. Our general opinion is that our close circle should be consolidated first of all, and that we should only then think about widening it. As far as *Brill* is concerned, we do not think he is very suitable to take part in the correspondence. We think on the other hand that he should know of the existence of our circle, and we think we should ask him to take part in our next deliberation before the Congress, if he comes to Europe.

In the letter from London, which arrived with the usual speed, we find a proposal to accept even more new members.[5] We suggest that we should refrain from this first of all and discuss this question at our next meeting. Discussion of each isolated case in letters would be very complicated. For the rest, we are completely in agreement with *Ernest*'s general remarks.

As we are only asked to express our opinions first of all, we are not reporting in detail today. We propose to send the next letter on 15 December, and we believe that we should limit ourselves at first to one letter a month.

With friendly greetings,

    *Sachs   Eitingon   Abraham*

1. Shortly before the Salzburg Congress Rank had announced the dissolution of the Committee (circular letter of 10 April 1924, SFC). On 16 November Ferenczi had suggested re-establishing it—without Rank, to be sure—and the *Rundbriefe* (Archives Judith Dupont).
2. Ferenczi, 1924[268].
3. "Totemism and Dragon-Fight", Róheim's paper at the Salzburg Congress, in which he maintained that "Australian totemism revolves around the trauma of birth" and that "the dragon-fight is a repetition of the birth trauma, and the dragon a personification of the dangerous vagina" (*Zeitschrift*, 1924, *10*: 224–225).
4. Letter of 19 November 1924 (SFC).
5. In his letter of 20 November 1924 (SFC), Jones suggested Anna Freud, Sándor Radó, Franz Alexander, James Glover, and Joan Riviere as possible members.

## 464F

Vienna, Berggasse 19
28 November 1924

Dear Friend,

I had your presidential letter[1] read aloud in the Society, which was, as I take it, your intention. Today I would like, as the president here, to begin my monthly report in an informal way. But do say if you think that another form is more effective.

There is little to report. As a result of my writing, the Society has elected me again in its general meeting.[2] Federn is vice-president, Bernfeld and Rank secretaries, Reik librarian. At the audit of the guests we withdrew the right of a guest from Dr Urbantschitsch.[3] The majority of the younger elements disapproved of the noiseless [sic] and tasteless advertisement for his praxis in Vienna, which he displays. Some of the older ones are on his side, Federn was deeply hurt by this treatment of his analysand, although he could not contradict the judgement of the latter's poor intellectual suitability nor of his unreliability and lack of love of truth.

Frau Deutsch held at the last meeting, on 26 November, a generally praised talk on the woman's menopause. I saw her today and she presented a plan to form a new Training Committee and to organize the ψα teaching following the Berlin pattern closely. I am in agreement and hope that she will get it through. It is an attempt to get rid of Hitschmann's mismanagement.[4]

Not within the scope of the life of the Society is an experience of mine that could turn out to be important. The physiologist Durig, who is the top senior medical official and as such highly official, has asked me for an expert opinion on lay analysis.[5] I have delivered it to him in written form, then held a discussion on it, and there was far-reaching agreement between us. I hope to be listened to by the authorities in all such questions.

---

You will already have read my letter to Eitingon with the description of Rank's farewell visit.[6] I hope Ferenczi has also passed on to you the important letter by Brill,[7] which had been first sent to him. I may now perhaps expect Berlin's statement on the establishment of the Committee, which had last been suggested by Jones and Ferenczi.

A short while ago I have revised my recent contribution to the *Zeitschrift*, the Note upon the Mystic Writing-Pad,[8] since then I have not worked. My prosthesis still torments me a great deal. At your mentioning the biblical cooking prohibition in your last letter, I had a still unexplained déjà vu, as if the connection had already been emphasized at some time, although I cannot easily recall it.

With cordial greetings to you and yours,

Yours,

*Freud*

1. The regular reports of the presidents of the local Societies, as agreed upon at the Salzburg Congress (see letter 441A, 26–27 April 1924).
2. On 28 October 1924 (*Zeitschrift*, 1925, *11*: 137).
3. Rudolf von Urbantschitsch (after 1943, Urban) [1879–1964], M.D., from Vienna. In 1908 he had founded the Cottage-Sanatorium in Vienna and had also become member of the Wednesday Society. In 1922 he had analysis with Federn in Vienna and in 1924 with Ferenczi in Budapest, but afterwards he gradually distanced himself from psychoanalysis. (Cf. Urban, 1958.)
4. Hitschmann had been the head of the psychoanalytic outpatient clinic in Vienna since 1922.
5. It was evidently Arnold Durig (and not Julius Tandler, as is sometimes proclaimed) who served as a model for the "impartial person" in *The Question of Lay Analysis* (Freud, 1926e; cf. Freud, 1926i).
6. Letter of 19 November 1924 (SFC).
7. A letter that threw "a clear light on Rank's activity in America" (Freud to Ferenczi, 17 November 1924).
8. Freud, 1925a [1924].

## 465A

Berlin-Grünewald
3 December 1924

Dear Professor,

The day before yesterday I received your reply to the circular letter to the presidents. Up to now you are the only one to reply! I am sorry that you gave yourself so much trouble, although I was delighted to have your letter. The presidential correspondence was to be a substitute for the Committee's circular letter, and when the latter is functioning again, the first can safely be abandoned. It was important to me, before beginning the intimate correspondence again, to get the official correspondence going at least once, as there had been a decision to this effect after all.

Our statement on the question of the Committee has obviously crossed with your letter, and I hope it was gratifying for you. The delay happened because the letter had to be written twice and then circulated for signature. We shall write again about the middle of the month, if we are not instructed otherwise.

All your news interested me greatly, particularly the expert opinion you were asked to give. I received Brill's letter from Ferenczi, and I am enclosing it today. Br. is basically a decent fellow who does not have an easy time with the others in New York, but as an analyst he is not first-class and as a person he is too vacillating. What he says about Rank's destructive activity in New York is very sad! But I believe this wave will soon wear itself off.

I saw your handwriting quite unexpectedly today. Frau Orska brought me your recommendation, and I shall try to fit her into my day. A difficult case, like all poison-addictions, but probably one from which something new can be learned.

I cannot remember where the kid and the mother's milk could have been mentioned. But I must naturally not rely on my memory, which is always dangerous when one thinks one has found something new.

I have at last got hold of some clinical material for the investigation into the number *seven*. First of all—something that had also been forgotten!—in the dream about the wolves in the "Infantile Neurosis"[1]; and then in the analysis of a new patient. I think I shall soon have collected sufficient material.—Despite careful searching, I have not been able to find any proof for the numerical system with the six that you, dear Professor, suggest, and especially not among the Babylonians. Did you know, incidentally, that the Babylonians had a five-day week? The taboo on the seventh day seems to be completely independent of this. I hope to have time for further research at Christmas.

I have another scientific question but there is *no* urgency for a reply, and you should under no circumstances write or dictate a letter for this

1924 December

purpose! The question concerns a point in the theory of sexuality. Your concept of a change of leading zones in the woman at puberty[2] has always proved correct *in praxi*. But I have recently wondered whether in early infancy there may be an early *vaginal* blossoming of the female libido, which is destined to be repressed and which is subsequently followed by clitoral primacy as the expression of the phallic phase. A number of observations seem to bear this out. If the assumption is correct, it would have one advantage for us: we would be better able to understand the *female Oedipus complex* as the result of an early vaginal reaction to the father's penis* and the change of the leading zone in puberty would then be a resumption of the original state of affairs. Perhaps it is legitimate to follow up this assumption, which is based on a number of observations. It could be fitted into our existing theory, to which it is not opposed in any case and to which it might make a small addition. If it seems worth the while to you, I could report some of my observations that gave me the idea. It has not yet been clarified and the relationship to the phallic phase in particular is so far unclear.

Yesterday we had a meeting (short comments) and among others heard an excellent short (clinical) contribution by Frau Dr Benedek from Leipzig on erythrophobia.† This lady is of great value in her ability to attract young people as well as in her excellent practical work. I shall save up any other news from Berlin for the next circular letter. Thus for now, only many good wishes for your health and the most cordial greetings from house to house from your,

*Karl Abraham*

\* possibly in the form of spontaneous contractions.
† this has already been accepted for the *Zeitschrift*.[3]

1. The Wolf Man's dream of "six or seven" wolves (Freud, 1918b [1914]: p. 29).
2. Cf., e.g., Freud, 1905d: pp. 220–221.
3. Benedek, 1925.

## 466F

Vienna, Berggasse 19[1]
8 December 1924

Dear Friend,

On 15 December the two Viennese members will enter the correspondence with the first circular letter and will give their opinion on various questions.

My dark memory with regard to the subject of the lamb and its mother's milk cannot refer to you. I have the impression that this dietary ban was pointed out by someone else too, to whom I mentioned my idea. It may have been Rank. In any case, your memory is not at fault.

The problem of the seven still arouses a lively interest in me. I have not got any further with it either, and not got any closer to the opinion at which you hinted.

Finally, your last theme, the assumed vaginal share in the early infantile blossoming of the libido, interests me greatly. I do not know anything about it. As I will altogether gladly admit, the female side of the problem is extraordinarily dark to me. If your ideas and observations already permit communication, I should very much like to hear about them, but I can wait. According to my prejudice, the vaginal share would more be likely to be replaced by anal expressions. The vagina, as we know, is a later acquisition through separation from the cloaca.

With cordial greetings to you and your family,
Yours,
*Freud*

1. Typewritten.

## 467F

Vienna, Berggasse 19
15 December 1924

Circular letter Nr. I

Dear Friends,

We inaugurate the correspondence today, the interruption of which I deeply regretted. The newly entered member, my daughter and secretary, appreciates the recognition.

We want to inform you that the Society has at its last meeting decided for Lucerne and prefers the first half of the month of September as the time for the Congress to all other settings. Probably the other Societies will express similar opinions. Frau Dr Deutsch, who is still under the after-effects of her Berlin impressions, has come forward with the plan to found a Training Institute, which is independent of the management of the polyclinic. It shall set up the teaching curriculum, take on the referral of patients to their analysts, and carry out the control-analyses of the trainees. It shall consist in its organization of three members, representative, deputy, and secretary, and the people lecturing shall be affiliated as the teaching staff. Frau Dr Deutsch has suggested herself as head of the training institute, Dr Bernfeld as deputy, and as secretary Anna Freud. The names of the lecturers are known. This proposal was approved of in a meeting of the committee of the Society and is negotiated today, the 15th, at a business meeting. It is expected that despite

1924 December

anticipated opposition from some sides it will go through. The management of the out-patients' clinic shall remain as up to now with Dr Hitschmann.

The point of this innovation is that it will be a gentle attempt to reduce Hitschmann's activity, against whom serious objections have been raised. It is not a secret among us that Dr Hitschmann has not been nearly as good intellectually and has developed character traits that are not desirable in a manager of such an enterprise.

The life of the Society, in which I can unfortunately not take part, seems to me to be quite lively. The old members are mostly in a state of ossification, but the younger ones get together in groups, meet privately, and show lively interest.

Concerning the question of taking new members into the Committee, we would also like to vote for a conservative restraint, at least for some time, until the present Committee has sorted itself out and is certain of its position. Jones is quite right when he wants to put the emphasis this time more on a group of people who share interests than forced personal intimacy. But the latter exists already and there is certainly nothing to be done against it.

Another matter of the Society. We are thinking of introducing a subdivision between full and associate members in Vienna too. But this will not happen until we have heard from Berlin and London what they are going to do in their circles. So we ask Berlin and London to give us helpful information as soon as possible and to send it to us outside the circular letters.

Last not least,[1] in the Rank affair a surprising, for each of us pleasing innovation turn has taken place, about which the individual members will be informed directly.[2]

With cordial greetings,

*Freud*

*Anna Freud*

1. In English in original.
2. After "analytical interviews" with Freud, Rank sent a letter to the former members of the Committee on 20 December (BL), in which he wrote that his previous "neurotic" state had been triggered by Freud's illness and could be traced to the "Oedipus and brother complex". He begged the others to "forgive" him and to let him be once again part of the "working community".

468A

Berlin-Grünewald
26 December 1924

Dear Professor,

I owe you a reply to your letter of the 8th inst. and to an enquiry in the circular letter. I am glad to take advantage of the quiet of the Christmas days to tell you the necessary things and some others.

So first of all to the question of the membership of our Society! I enclose two copies of the latest edition of our statutes; § 5 and 6 contain the relevant regulations. I should like to emphasize that we have fairly strict conditions for the admission of extraordinary members; however, the paragraphs are couched in such a way as to allow exceptions everywhere, if special cases really arise. If someone has proved his worth as an extraordinary member, there are absolutely no difficulties in the way of his election as an *ordinary* member. At the general meeting in January we shall, for example, elect several extraordinary members as ordinary members without them, themselves, having made an application. Election as an extraordinary member will usually have taken place after taking part in the meetings as a guest for quite a long time. As §12 shows, we are already careful about admitting permanent guests. On the whole the regulations have proved themselves to be quite good.

At the end of the circular letter we found a remark about Rank that seemed at first mysterious to us. In the meantime we all three heard from him directly, and in the next few days we are answering him together, but each of us will add a few personal remarks.[1] You, dear Professor, will have a copy, so that you know our statement. In general I can already say now that we shall express ourselves in a completely conciliatory way, but with a certain reticence that the circumstances appear to demand. I may add personally that from the bottom of my heart I wish for you to have a satisfactory solution to the whole business for the New Year.

The question of the female leading zones that I hinted on in my last letter is far from ready to be incorporated into our theory of sexuality as it stands. Lately I have felt that several things in the view about the leading zones appeared incomplete. I have for a long time questioned whether the displacement from the clitoris to the vagina could happen in a way different from the one it had taken *earlier*—though in an inverse direction. We have had to convince ourselves in so many other contexts that the psycho-sexual processes of puberty are repetitions. This assumed pre-stage would have to have as a sexual aim the reception of the penis. The opening intended for this seems to me, too, to have cloacal characteristics; that is to say, one has to assume that vaginal sensations arise that are transferred from the anal zone as well as that pleasurable contractions of the vagina must somehow be linked with

1924 December

contractions of the anal sphincter. The ease with which little girls can be seduced to coitus-like actions, as well as the tendency to vaginal masturbation and, in particular, the introduction of foreign bodies, must probably all rest on such processes. Two neurotic symptoms have forced me to assume a—let us say, vaginal–anal—pre-stage: frigidity and vaginism. In the light of all my $\psi\alpha$ experience, I cannot believe that frigidity is merely based on the *failure to appear* of the transition of the libido from the clitoris to the vagina. There must be a prohibition that has an immediate local basis; this is even more valid for vaginismus. Why should the vagina react so negatively to the first attempt at coitus unless something positive has preceded this? Hysterical vomiting also requires a positive and pleasurable experience to have taken place in the same part in primeval times.

As I mentioned last time, such an assumption would also throw light on the obscure origins of the female Oedipus complex.

My investigation into the number seven is progressing, though a great deal still remains unclear. The *significance* of seven has already become comprehensible to a great extent. The second problem—why *seven* is suitable for expressing certain things in the human inner life—proves to be more difficult, but here too *a few* points have become clearer. I may shortly be able to tell you something about it. To return once again to your assumption of a numerical system with the *six*; there seems to be nothing of that kind, though you are right in one sense. The mysterious series does not, however, start with 6 but with 3. If 1 is added, we have 4 (which dominates American mythology), 7 (for which I know several other determinants but am looking for more), 10, 13, and 19 (Babylonian).

So much for today! *Perhaps* I may soon be able to let you have some news of importance to the $\psi\alpha$ movement. But today it is still too uncertain. May it come true in 1925, just as everything else I wish for you, dear Professor, your house, and for all of us!

With the most cordial greetings from my family and myself to you all, Yours,

*Karl Abraham*

1. Letter of 25 December 1924 (LOC).

### 469F

Vienna, Berggasse 19[1]
29 December 1924

Dear Friend,

Thank you for sending me the statutes, which will be very useful to us in the question of the extraordinary members.

That you would be conciliatory in the Rank affair was something that I only expected from your kindness and correctness. I cannot be surprised by your reserve in the matter. It can be explained by the fact that you do not know all the circumstances of the case and cannot have got from the letter a detailed impression of the individual concerned and his transformation. I know everything connected with it, know the whole sad story, and can say that I am sure that he has been cured of his neurosis by this experience, just as if he had gone through a proper analysis. He is, incidentally, still very depressed, understands the whole difficulty of his position, wants to go to America in the next few weeks and make good there the harm he has done, but he has no illusions about how much greater his difficulties will be than on the occasion of his first visit.

In the letter to Eitingon, which is going off at the same time, I expressed myself in rather greater detail over the whole thing.

As for the two scientific questions on which your letter touches, my attitude is different towards each. Concerning the first, the question of the female leading zone, I am quite eager to learn, look forward to your novelties in the matter, and have no preconceived ideas. With regard to the 7, I cannot suppress my sceptical expectation. I am very ready to believe that my idea will lead to nothing. But I doubt whether you are on the right track. *Vederemo!*[2]

It will only make our letters richer and livelier.

The date reminds me to express my heartfelt good wishes for the next year 1925 to you, your wife and children, though the change of year only plays the role of a commonplace *agent provocateur*.

Cordially yours,

*Freud*

1. Typewritten.
2. Italian: "We will see!"

# 1925

### 470F

Vienna, Berggasse 19[1]
27 January 1925

Dear Friend,

Today I received a letter from Pfister[2] about the Congress difficulty, in which he says he is bringing the same information to your attention at the same time. The decision is now yours, but I think that in such circumstances we cannot do anything else but accept Pfister's hint and do without Switzerland. Concessions on your part are excluded, as I was glad to hear from Eitingon. But perhaps, just when you show yourself inclined to renunciation, you may find the way to an agreement with the stubborn mules, in which none of the valuable features of our Congress will be sacrificed. If it does not happen, we will get over it.

Personal news will be brought to you by Eitingon, who left us yesterday.

With cordial greetings to all of you,
Yours,

*Freud*

1. Typewritten.
2. Letter of 24 January 1925, missing from Freud/Pfister correspondence. In preparation for its publication, Anna Freud compiled a list (SFC) of Pfister's letters to Freud, in which she wrote "No" (i.e. not to be printed) after the date of this letter.

### 471A

Berlin-Grünewald
6 February 1925

Dear Professor,

When your lines about the Congress arrived, I had already received from Pfister a copy of the letter he sent you. Of course I immediately informed both Pfister and Oberholzer that I agreed that the Congress should be moved to Germany. Immediately after that I discussed the remaining points with Max. The Congress will now take place from 3 to 5 September in Bad Homburg, near Frankfurt. In a few days you will learn everything necessary from a circular letter. The administrators of the spa in H. are very interested in the Congress. Landauer and Frau Dr Happel in Frankfurt have taken on the local arrangements, and we have already been informed about the venues for the meetings, lodgings, etc. This was done in three days, whereas the fruitless dealings with the Swiss took two months; a convolution of letters developed, which cannot be read without a shake of the head[1] and a smile. So everything is going beautifully. Very soon the preparations for the 2nd *German* meeting in Weimar (2nd half of April) shall also begin.

I should like to let you have some good news without waiting for the circular letter. In all my 17 years of work in Berlin, no medical society has ever asked me to speak on $\Psi\alpha$. I have now been invited, and have accepted the invitation, to speak to the Berlin Society for Gynaecology and Obstetrics on 13 March. Subject: "$\Psi\alpha$ and Gynaecology".[2] If the paper meets with a favourable reception, this will have a very positive effect, since other specialist medical societies will follow suit, and then a first official recognition of $\Psi\alpha$ in Germany will have been achieved.

Various other good news shall be told in the *circular letter*.

Now I want to say a few frank words about another matter. Sándor's article on sexual habits[3] is to be the first in the new volume of the *Zeitschrift*. As far as wealth of ideas is concerned, this is perhaps his most mature and best work, but I have grave doubts about its technical content. At the end of 1923 the *Entwicklungsziele*[4] appeared, with the technical rule of setting a time limit and altogether with a strong active tendency. After one year, the time-limit rule is greatly cut back, but a *new* activity is now recommended in its stead, which can hardly have been tested for more than a year in this form and the rules of which are somewhat vague and aphoristic. Perhaps it might have been better not to have been in such a hurry with a new set of technical innovations and with their publication. Max has already suggested to you that it would be preferable if it were to follow *after* your essay on the mystic writing-pad (which I read with the greatest pleasure, since one feels so secure in the clear and unassailable structuring of your thoughts!). Max's suggestion has my full approval. If Sándor's paper were placed *before* yours, this would give it an official character; otherwise it is, like any other paper, the author's own responsibility.

This leads to another question. We cannot in the long run avoid discussing technical problems. What would you, dear Professor, prefer: to arrange a symposium at the Congress or to have an exchange of opinions in several issues of the *Zeitschrift*? And, in the latter case, would you yourself wish to participate?

1925 February

I am very glad to have continued good news about your health.
With the most cordial greetings from house to house,
Yours,

*Abraham*

1. Allusion to an expression in Wilhelm Busch's [1832–1908] *Jobsiade*.
2. Abraham, 1925[111].
3. Ferenczi, 1925[269].
4. Ferenczi & Rank, 1924.


472F

Vienna, Berggasse 19[1]
11 February 1925

Dear Friend,

Naturally in complete agreement with the settlement of the Congress question. If I continue to be well, I too shall be there. My wife and sister-in-law do not want to miss the chance to be in Germany again, and people are already used to Anna as my companion. What is more, I am ready to set a bad example and go for a drive instead of listening to talks. So actually you should not invite me at all.

Your invitation to speak at the Berlin Gynaecological Society is really a good sign. You are right to expect that others will follow.

I have just written to Eitingon that I submit to the editorial decision with regard to the precedence of the "Mystic Writing-Pad" over Ferenczi's work. But I find your judgement of this note too kind. Despite the probable short-livedness of some stimuli, I would rather have perpetrated Ferenczi's work.

Your proposal to open a discussion on technical questions in the *Zeitschrift* seems to me very useful and preferable to postponing it until the Congress. Very many contributions will surely come in. I too am prepared to do something. But do not make me say the first and the last word, let me come somewhere in the middle. Indeed I often have occasion to note that my utterances have a kind of living paralysing effect on the liveliness of the others', and I think I must be careful.

With cordial greetings to you and your house,
Yours,

*Freud*

1. Typewritten.

## 473A
[by Abraham and Eitingon][1]
## INTERNATIONAL PSYCHO-ANALYTICAL ASSOCIATION

Berlin
11 February 1925

Dear President,

At last year's Congress in Salzburg it was decided to hold the next assembly in Autumn 1925 in England or Switzerland. Particularly in consideration of our American colleagues, it was necessary to change the date of the Congress to the first week in September. It will therefore take place from 3 to 5 September.

Special circumstances make it impossible to meet in England or in Switzerland. In agreement with the Berlin Psychoanalytical Association, we have therefore decided to hold the Congress in Germany. We looked for a place situated as conveniently as possible for colleagues from the Western countries, as they had had to travel a particularly long way to Salzburg. As a large part of West Germany is occupied, the most suitable place seemed to us to be *Bad Homburg*. This place, situated near Frankfurt am Main, has particularly favourable connections on all sides and enjoys special popularity in England. We hope that the choice we have made will meet with general agreement. For participants from eastern countries the distance is no greater than to Switzerland.

We should like to ask you to decide within your groups already whether a definite subject for discussion (symposium) should be fixed; we are asking for suggestions in this respect. Also, we ask you to let us know approximately how many participants there will be from your Society.

You are asked kindly to let us have the answers to both questions by 15 April.

With collegial regards,
devotedly,

*Dr K. Abraham*   *Dr M. Eitingon*
*President*       *Secretary*

1. Typewritten and hand-signed circular letter, with a note on top ("Herrn Prof. Dr S. Freud, Wien") in Abraham's handwriting.

## 474A

Berlin-Grünewald
26 February 1925

Dear Professor,

First of all very hearty thanks for the *Autobiographical Study*[1]; I read it again at once with the same enjoyment as I did half a year ago on the Semmering. And then I must express my great joy about your intention of coming to the Congress! To me that is proof of your good state of health, that you are making plans again and regard your attendance at the Congress as self-evident.

In the meantime you have probably received from London my correspondence with the Swiss. I gave it to Ernest first, because he had raised objections in the circular letter to the change in venue for the Congress. Already today I received a letter from him in which he withdraws his objections.

With regard to the date of the Congress, I convinced myself later on that it was decided in Salzburg to meet at the end of August *or* the beginning of September. The change in the date already fixed (3–5 September) would thus be no obstacle to us, except for the general objection that such alterations always have something awkward about them. Landauer inquired in Homburg and found out that the last week in August is still part of the "season", and that we would not find such good and comfortable accommodation. I should now like to ask your opinion of a suggestion by Ernest, naturally taking into account *your* comfort with regard to the journey. Would you agree to meet the wishes of the English at least by a few days, that is to say from 31 August to 2 September instead of 3–5 September? In that case we would fix the change and make it known at once by means of a circular.—

I shall come back very soon to the question of the discussion on technique in the *Zeitschrift*!

With cordial greetings to you and yours from my wife and me,
Yours,

*Abraham*

1. Freud, 1925d [1924].

## 475F

Vienna, Berggasse 19[1]
3 March 1925

Dear Friend,

The correspondence on the Congress is already with Ferenczi, who fetched it himself the day before yesterday, Sunday. There is no doubt that you could not have done or said anything else.

With regard to the date of the Congress, I do not dare to emphasize consideration for me. You are right to remark that I am making plans again, but when it comes to it I often lose the courage to carry them out. For example, if at the time of the Congress I was not doing better with my prosthesis than in the past weeks, I should certainly not make the journey. So you decide, without taking me into account. Unofficially I can tell you that the early date, whether 31 August or 3 September, does not appeal to me much at all. But that does not matter much.

Rank is back and says that he did his best in America to make good the damage caused, and a letter from Brill that arrived today confirms it completely. This letter will come to you from Budapest and should then be sent to Jones. Rank himself is weakened and hardly capable of scientific work. I again have complete trust in him and was glad to learn that Ferenczi, who has just seen him again, has reached the same conclusion.

I had a letter today from Miss Newton, telling me of her recovery and thanking you very much for your tactful intervention.[2]

With cordial greetings to you and your house,
Yours,

*Freud*

1. Typewritten.
2. The New York Society had refused to accept lay analyst Newton as its member, and the correctness of her having previously been accepted a member of the Vienna Society had been questioned (cf. Berlin circular letter, 11 February 1925, LOC; Freud & Jones, 1993: pp. 570, 571, and 582).

## 476A

Berlin-Grünewald
15 March 1925

Dear Professor,

I have just written the circular letter, which contains most of the information worth giving. So today I will tell you only a few personal things. I very much hope that the troubles of which you complained in your last letter are over, and will gradually occur more rarely.

I entirely agree that it would have been nicer to meet in Geneva than in Homburg. You know that for me there is nothing better than Switzerland, and I shall probably spend a few weeks' holiday there before the Congress. If you should feel lively and ready for anything, would you perhaps do the same thing this year? But I know well enough that for the time being these plans can only be uncertain. So I will at once come out with the confession that I should like to be in Vienna for a few days during Easter week. So many subjects for discussion are accumulating, and I should also like to convince myself personally of how you are

1925 March

getting on. So I ask you, dear Professor, to get Fräulein Anna to send me a short but frank note as to whether my visit—which I should naturally arrange entirely in accordance with times suitable to you—is convenient to you or not. I should like to bring my wife, who does not yet know Vienna at all.

Something else to tell you from my house—my daughter recently had to write a school essay on the psychology of dreams, and was especially requested by her teacher to describe Freudian doctrines without restriction. Yet another sign of progress, which only a few years ago would have been impossible!

I was very glad to hear of Rank's safe return and the satisfactory result of his journey!

Finally, one more little piece of information! I hear a Dr Frensdorff gave you notice of a visit. I should say in connection with this that he is one of my manic-depressive patients. Unfortunately he was coerced by his family to marry before the end of his analysis, very much against my will and advice. Since then he has occasionally been in a really bad way. There is a possibility that his wish to speak to you was prompted by a hypomanic frame of mind. He is, incidentally, an absolutely reliable, decent man. Naturally he must not know anything of what I have told you.

With the most cordial greetings to you and yours from my wife and me!

Yours,

*Karl Abraham*

477F

Vienna, Berggasse 19[1]
20 March 1925

Dear Friend,

Your offer pleased me very much at first, but later on upset me somewhat, which is not your fault but mine. I find it very bitter to turn you down, and I do not dare to accept your visit because it would probably only be a disappointment to you. Without wanting to offend your ~~famo~~ famous optimism, I must confess that I am not really of much use. Witness to my great inclination to meet you, so hard to overcome, is the fact that I am leaving the reply to my daughter, as you asked.

With the most cordial greetings,
Yours,

*Freud*

Dear Doctor,[2]

Papa says that to spare him you asked that I should reply, but he has written the beginning himself in any case. When your letter came, he was particularly happy about your request, and his doubts about whether he would really be able to be visited in the four free days of Easter did not come until later. He wanted to use those days for a complete rest without any obligations, because he has had a great deal to bother him in the last few weeks and could never rest. Pichler wants finally to "sanitize" the prosthesis, as he puts it, and now he is suffering from it, as Austria is from its sanitation. Naturally he does not like to tell you all this, and that is very understandable. But I believe he would get much more out of a summer visit from you, if you could make it possible again. Or is it a great sacrifice for you to come from your beautiful Switzerland to our Semmering, for which we have already arranged again?

Papa hopes you will not be angry about his reply, which is really very candid. I too would have been very pleased to help to show your wife Vienna. The other members of the family say the same.

With cordial greetings, and I hope to be able to take you instead to the Sonnwendstein again.

Yours,

*Anna Freud*

1. Typewritten.
2. The rest of the letter in Anna Freud's handwriting.

## 478A

Berlin-Grünewald
5 April 1925

Dear Professor,

Certainly your reply was a disappointment for me, but much less so than if I had come to Vienna and then found you in a state in which you were in need of care. So we are postponing our meeting! Whether I come to the Semmering in the summer will have to remain undecided for the present. For I am hoping, provisionally, that you will come to *Homburg*, and then, perhaps, it would be possible to meet without too many complications. However, to encourage you to come to Homburg, I will tell you—in case you have not heard it direct from Landauer—that the directors of the Spa will put at your disposal and that of your family part of a peacefully situated villa. We shall all have great reductions, for example free accommodation for 25–30 participants and very moderate prices for the rest. H. is an excellently equipped spa with beautiful, convenient paths through the forest and the opportunity for excursions of all kinds.—

We are now staying in Berlin over Easter. Today I received from Ophuijsen the official request to give a few lectures in Holland at the end of May. As I am going to write and accept,[1] it is probable that we shall be in Holland for Whitsuntide.

Talking of Holland brings me to Lampl, whose engagement[2] has surprised all of us. He has given us in the Society a second surprise by his first lecture,[3] which was quite excellent.

I shall now publish the lecture that I gave recently to the gynaecologists in the *Archiv für Gynäkologie*. Not so long ago such an invitation could scarcely have been conceivable.

And now I will express the hope that the alterations to the prosthesis will finally meet with your entire satisfaction, and that you will have a trouble-free summer! With this wish and cordial greetings to you and all your family,
Yours,

*Karl Abraham*

Recently I had a visit from Prof. Kayserling,[4] whom you kindly referred to me. I will see if I can give him a little help. A neurosis existing from childhood, with organic brain disease in addition, is not very encouraging, but perhaps one can be of some use to him in any case.—

This letter needs no reply!!

1. Abraham held three talks (1925[113], 1925[114]; see letter 479A, 4 May 1925).
2. To Jeanne de Groot.
3. On "A Case of Borrowed [*entlehnt*] Guilt Feeling", at the meeting of 28 March (*Zeitschrift*, 1925, *11*: 250).
4. Perhaps Hermann Graf von Keyserling [1880–1946], German philosopher (cf. Freud & Groddeck, 1974, letters of 28 and 21 December 1924).

## 479A

Grünewald
4 May 1925

Dear Professor,

Your birthday is just around the corner and, as it is not possible for me to bring you my good wishes in person this year either, it has once again to be done by letter (and with the waiver of a written answer!). Even though your state of health often leaves much to be desired, I firmly believe you have made good progress since your last birthday. May this progress be accelerated in the new year!

So that you hear also on your birthday that ψα matters have not come to a standstill in Berlin (about which Eitingon will also inform you), I wish to tell you that, apart from three lectures on "Crime" in Berlin,[1] I have to give three further lectures in Holland this month: one in The Hague to the Medical Association on the "Hysterical Symptom", and two in Leyden to psychiatrists on the "Ψα Treatment of Schizophrenic States".

In the Berlin Medical Society Moll launched a very nasty, spiteful attack on Ψα. We did not react at all and are pleased with that. Kraus, who was chairman, very loyally clamped down on M's behaviour, and the audience in general was painfully affected by M's tactless action. Indirectly he helped us instead of harming us. The behaviour of the chairman and of the assembly is also a sign of the times.

Our news is that my daughter has started her last year at grammar school. In the summer she will spend the holidays with a friend in western Switzerland. Gerd is already as tall as his sister and his mother. Both his intellectual and his physical development please us greatly. In the summer I am thinking of taking him on a high-mountain tour through the Berner Oberland and Wallis. My wife wants to accompany me to Paris for a short time after the Congress, and then to spend a few weeks in Italy.

If all goes according to plan, I hope to see you, dear Professor, and yours in exactly four weeks' time in Homburg. Please accept the most cordial greetings to all of you from all of us!

With many good wishes,
Yours,

*Abraham*

1. During the second quarter-term of the year, Abraham gave a course on "Psychoanalytic Theory of Crime. (For jurists, medical doctors and pedagogues)" (*Zeitschrift*, 1925, *11*: 503) at the Institute.

## 480F

Vienna, Berggasse 19[1]
20 May 1925

Dear Friend,

In spite of your waiver of a reply, herewith my heartfelt thanks! And the request to pass them on also to the Society. It was splendid, though rather tiring, in fact it was a test to which I did not stand up very well. As the annual general meeting happened to have been arranged for the same afternoon, apart from Eitingon, Ferenczi was present too.

1925 June

The good news about your family and work gave me great pleasure. If one is a hopeless (I mean incurable) optimist, one should at least have good reason to be so.

In contrast to your travel plans, we propose to spend the summer quietly on the Semmering at the villa that you know.

With cordial greetings to you, your wife and children,
Yours,

*Freud*

1. Typewritten.

## 481A

Wassenaar[1]
29 May 1925

Dear Professor,

On the 3rd day of my lecture tour in Holland we are enjoying a splendid afternoon in the Wassenaar Park and thinking of you and all your family. With cordial greetings,
Yours,

*Karl Abraham*[2]

1. Picture postcard "Den Haag", stamped in Leyden.
2. And several other signatures, of which only van Ophuijsen's is legible.

## 482A

Grünewald
7 June 1925

Dear Professor,

This time I am writing from my bed; I brought back a feverish bronchial catarrh from Holland, which appears persistent.[1] Just before I went to bed, the day before yesterday, an unexpected question was put to me about which I must tell you.

The owner of an important film company came to see me and told me of his decision to produce a popular scientific $\psi\alpha$ film[2] with your authorization and with the collaboration and supervision of your recognized scholars. With regard to the latter, I am to have the right to make suggestions.

I need hardly mention that this kind of thing is really *not* up my street; nor that this type of project is typical of our times and that it is *sure* to be carried out, if not *with us* then with people who know nothing about it. We have so many "wild" analysts in Berlin—if only to mention

Kronfeld,[3] Schultz,[4] and Hattingberg,[5] who would be only too keen to grasp at such an offer should we decline. In that event, they would have the financial gain and our cause would be damaged.

From the enclosed writing, which I should like back as soon as possible, you can see the provisional proposition. I also enclose a sheet of paper, which you might sign if you agree with it.

In the final agreement, in which my brother-in-law, who is a lawyer, will support me, it must be expressly emphasized that the 10% profit-sharing refers to the gross income, as was agreed verbally. *Your* share of the profits, dear Professor, remains as in the agreement between *us*; there will surely not be any difficulties there.

The difference between this correct offer compared with that of the American Goldwyn[6] is obvious. The actual plan for the film is as follows: the first part is to serve as an introduction and will give impressive single examples illustrating repression, the unconscious, the dream, parapraxis, anxiety, etc. The manager of this company, who knows some of your writings, is, for instance, very enthusiastic about the analogy of the invader used in the five lectures to illustrate repression and resistance.[7] The 2nd part will present a life history from the viewpoint of $\Psi\alpha$ and will show the cure of neurotic symptoms.

Furthermore, Herr Neumann suggests the drafting of an easily comprehensible popular pamphlet on $\Psi\alpha$. My idea is not to describe $\Psi\alpha$ systematically but to give examples from life and to develop the theory around them. N. would like to publish this pamphlet, which should be sold at 2–3 marks, either through a large publishing firm, which would ensure the widest circulation, or through *our* Verlag. This may present an opportunity of helping the fortunes of the Verlag.

I assume, dear Professor, that you will have no great sympathy for the plan as a whole, but that you will come to acknowledge the force of the practical argument. Our influence should extend into every detail in order to avoid anything that seems to us to discredit the cause in any way.

Tomorrow I shall discuss the whole matter with Hanns if my voice has returned by then. I shall, with his and Max's help, choose some suitable young colleagues from our circle. It goes without saying that I am grateful to *you* for any kind of advice.

I am limiting myself today to this one subject; writing in bed is rather uncomfortable. I shall tell you about Holland and other matters in the circular letter on the 15th.

In the hope that your reply will also bring very, very good news about your health,

I remain, with cordial greetings,
Yours,

*Karl Abraham*

## Addendum 1
## NEUMANN PRODUKTION[8]
FERNSPRUCH: AMT ZENTRUM 11471 9834 / TELEGRAMM-ADRESSE:
NEUPRODUKT BERLIN
Berlin SW 19; Leipziger Strasse 77

5 June 1925

DIREKTION
Herrn Dr Karl A b r a h a m,
*Berlin/Grünewald,*
Bismarck Allee 14.

Dear Dr Abraham,

With reference to our consultation today, I am repeating to you once again the business part of it in writing as follows:

Our Company wishes to make a popular-scientific film on the doctrines of Freud's psychoanalysis and to seek official authority for this from Herr *Geheimrat* S. Freud.

The manuscript and the other necessary work for this film will be carried out by our gentlemen, together with a psychoanalyst to be proposed by you, who will be paid an honorarium by us.

We should like to ask you to act as scientific adviser and also to help us with the elaboration of the manuscript.

We would pay you and Herr *Geheimrat* Freud together 10% (ten per cent) of the proceeds from the film, and guarantee for 10,000 M (ten thousand marks); part of this would be paid on the conclusion of the contract and the rest on the completion of the film.

Our condition is that Herr *Geheimrat* Freud and you, for a period of three years, do not authorize the making of a film on Freudian theory, or take part in any way in the making of a film of this type

In accordance with your wishes we are sending you at the same time a few leaflets about our principal films in recent years, from which you can see that we are no novices in the field of this type of cultural film.

We should be greatly obliged to you if you would take this matter in hand at your earliest convenience, and hoping to hear from you very soon, we remain,

Yours sincerely,

*NEUMANN PRODUKTION*

*L. T. D.*

## Addendum 2

Vienna[9]
June 1925

To
Neumann Produktion Ltd,
Berlin, S.W. 19

On condition that I agree with the proposed contract between you and Dr Karl Abraham, I am prepared to give my authorization to a popular-scientific film on the doctrine of psychoanalysis to be made by you, and, for a period of three years, neither to take part in any way in the making of a film of this type, nor to authorize its making.

Yours sincerely,

1. According to the editors of Freud & Abraham, 1965, "[t]his apparent bronchitis was the first manifestation of Abraham's fatal illness. It in fact started with an injury to the pharynx from a fish-bone and was followed by septic broncho-pneumonia, lung abscess, and terminal subphrenic abscess. The illness took the typical course of septicaemia, prior to the introduction of antibiotics, with swinging temperatures, remissions, and euphoria. Abraham's previous emphysema had doubtless made him susceptible to such infection" (p. 382). It is possible, however, that Abraham suffered from an undiagnosed lung cancer.
2. *Geheimnisse einer Seele* [Secrets of the Soul], directed by G. W. Pabst, was eventually produced by Neumann. Shooting began in September and lasted 12 weeks. The "film affair" would overshadow the remaining months of this correspondence. (For details, see Fallend & Reichmayr, 1992; Ries, 1995.)
3. See letter 121F, 14 January 1912, & n. 1.
4. See letter 275A, 26 April 1915, & n. 6.
5. Hans Ritter von Hattingberg [1879–1944], L.L.D., M.D., of Munich. Hattingberg later became a member of the Aryanized German General Medical Society for Psychotherapy and the German Institute for Psychological Research and Psychotherapy in Berlin. He was editor, with Niels Kampmann, of the *Zeitschrift für Menschenkunde*.
6. "Samuel Goldwyn, the well-known film director, [had approached] Freud with an offer of $100,000.00 if he would cooperate in making a film depicting scenes from the famous love stories of history, beginning with Antony and Cleopatra" (Jones, 1957: p. 114).
7. Freud, 1910a [1909]: p. 25.
8. Typewritten letter with pre-printed letterhead.
9. Typewritten.

## 483F

Vienna, Berggasse 19[1]
9 June 1925

Dear Friend,

First of all let me express the hope that by the time you receive this letter—written an hour after receiving yours—you will be out of bed and have the use of your voice again. My news is not bad, I have my usual small complaints to put up with, but on the whole I am better. I stop work on the 27th inst.

I do not feel comfortable about the magnificent project. Your argument that if we do not do it, it will be done by others seemed at first irresistible. But then it struck me that what these people are willing to pay for is obviously the authorization. That they can get only from us. If they do something completely wild because we refuse, we cannot stop them and are not implicated. After all, we cannot stop anyone from making such a film without obtaining our consent.

After settling this argument, the matter can at least be discussed. My chief objection is still that I do not believe that satisfactory plastic representation of our abstractions is at all possible. We do not want to give our consent to anything insipid. Mr Goldwyn was at any rate clever enough to stick to the aspect of our subject that can be plastically represented very well, that is to say, love. The small example that you mentioned, the representation of repression by means of my Worcester simile, would have an absurd rather than an instructive impact.

I am naturally completely confident that you yourself would never approve of anything susceptible to such or similar objections. As you seem not disinclined to engage in the matter, I suggest that you do the following. Tell them that I do not believe in the possibility that anything good can be produced and therefore for the time being cannot give my authorization. But if examination of the script should satisfy you, and me also, of the opposite, I shall be willing to give it afterwards. I do not deny that I should prefer my name not to come into it at all.

If, contrary to expectations, everything were to turn out satisfactorily, we should need no judge, as they say in Vienna, with regard to the 10%. If anything came of it, I should gladly give my share to the Verlag.

I am retaining the letter to the company.

With cordial greetings and in the expectation of a rapid wish-fulfilment

Yours,

*Freud*

1. Typewritten.

## 484F

Vienna, Berggasse 19[1]
21 June 1925

Dear Friend,

I hear from Sachs, to my surprise and also to my dismay, that your illness is still not a thing of the past. That does not fit in with my picture of you. I like to think of you only as a man continually and unfailingly at work. I feel your illness to be a kind of unfair competition and appeal to you to stop it as quickly as possible. I expect news about your condition from someone very close to you and meanwhile send you my cordial good wishes.

Yours,

*Freud*

1. Typewritten.

## 485A

[25 June 1925][1]

IMPROVEMENT CONTINUING THANKS—GREETINGS ABRAHAM

1. Telegram.

## 486A

Berlin-Grünewald[1]
26 June 1925

Dear Professor,

Your letter with the inquiry arrived some days ago, and almost simultaneously Dr Deutsch telephoned to enquire about my health. My wife gave him detailed information and asked him afterwards by letter to pass this on to you, dear Professor. This morning an unsigned telegram arrived from Vienna; my wife assumed that it was from you and telegraphed the reply to your address. I am however dictating this to her in order to give you detailed news.

The actual illness had run its course by the beginning of this week—the bronchial pneumonic foci have healed, but part of the pleura is still sensitive, so that I shall have to stay in bed for the time being. In about a fortnight I am to go to the mountains to recuperate, do feel quite exhausted from my illness, though I hope everything will clear up satisfactorily.

Thanking you very much for your sympathy and wishing you and your family an extremely restful summer, I am, with kind regards, in which the writer of these lines joins me,

Yours,

*Karl Abraham*

1. In Frau Abraham's handwriting.

## 487F

Semmering, Villa Schüler
1 July 1925

Dear Friend,

It was not I who sent you the telegram, at the time I had already been reassured by Deutsch by telephone, but I was glad to have received your telegram. I was delighted to hear that you see yourself as convalescent again—but be conscientious in that as well, for your own sake as well as ours.

We arrived here yesterday; overjoyed to be here in spite of the gales and the modesty of the natural surroundings. Everything is so comfortable and quiet, as is only appropriate to the old, it is a kind of *Austragstüberl*,[1] if you know that Alpine expression.

My own state of health, which unfortunately is still a matter of interest to my friends, promises well. With truly angelic—or asinine—patience, my worthy physician dealt with all the complaints that disturbed the peace of my prosthesis until he got a tolerable result. Finally he paid me the parting compliment of saying that, considering my age and the troubles that I had been through, I was in "pretty smart condition". I notice above all a reluctance to work and a need of rest.

The foundation in Teramo (Abruzzi)[2] has surely been reported to you. Bianchini[3] is asking for it to be publicized.

I have written a memorial for J. Breuer, which will appear in No. 2 of the *Zeitschrift*.[4] I exchanged cordial letters with the family and so brought my fateful relations with Breuer to a dignified conclusion.

Do not fail to keep me informed of the progress of your recovery. With good wishes to you and your family,

Yours,

*Freud*,

who has been worrying.

1. Room set aside in a peasant's house for parents who have retired from work.
2. The foundation of the Italian Psychoanalytical Society (cf. letter 427A, 26 December 1923, n. 3).
3. See letter 254F, 31 October 1914, & n. 7.
4. Freud, 1925g.

## 488A

Berlin-Grünewald
6 July 1925

Dear Professor,

This is to show you that I am making good progress; at the same time I want to tell you how pleased I was with your warm and fatherly letter.

I was glad to hear that your health continues to improve. Although I am 21 years younger than you, I shall have to spend just as quiet a holiday. We have decided on Wengen in the Bernese Oberland. It is at an altitude of 1,270 metres and has the advantage of mountain railways for *riding* up if one cannot climb much. Address from 17 July: Hotel Victoria.

Max came to see me yesterday. He has, during my illness, made excellent preparations for the Congress. The programmes are already in print.

If you, dear Professor, are not coming to Homburg, I am afraid that I shall not see you for the time being, as I cannot do very much for a while. It is only now I realize how much strength this month has cost me. I shall therefore not be able to help you with raspberry picking.

With the most cordial greetings from my family and myself to you all,

Yours,

*Karl Abraham*

## 489F

Semmering, Villa Schüler
9 July 1925

Dear Friend,

Anna, with her telepathic sensitivity, remarked yesterday that it was time we had news of A. We lacked confirmation that on the occasion of your recent exertions you had coughed up all the noxious substances.

Now I am delighted to have that confirmation. Precisely because of the 21 years' difference in our ages, your illness means more to our cause than mine. But the quiet holidays must be doing you good, I myself am feeling the good effect. If I did not have a capriciously sensitive spot—Pichler seriously assures me that there is no disease of the tissue and that it is only hyper-aesthesia—I should feel very well, and the bits of writing I have started would go ahead quickly. Before he left, the good man attacked the bad spot with a galvano-caustic "horse-cure", as he called it, and so I now have the burn to complain about instead of the spontaneous sore. Strangely enough, however, this is a gain.

For your amusement, let me tell you that a copy of the *Matin* arrived today with a leader[1] on psychoanalysis. Nothing remarkable about that, you may say, but this *Matin* is published in Port-au-Prince in Haiti, with which one does not have correspondence every day.

It is at present the strawberry season on the Semmering; with the raspberries I shall certainly remember your help.

1925 July

Accept my warmest and most genuine—because fundamentally rather selfish—wishes for a quick and complete recovery, and give my kindest regards to your certainly delighted wife and children.

Cordially yours,

*Freud*

1. In English in original.

## 490A

Wengen, Hotel Victoria
18 July 1925

Dear Professor,

Here are my first greetings from Wengen, where I am conscientiously resting in a deck-chair to recover my health. I have weathered the long journey well and am pleased with the choice of place and hotel. The situation of Wengen, exactly opposite the Jungfrau, is extraordinarily beautiful; besides, the peace here is unique considering present conditions. Wengen can be reached from Lauterbrunnen only by funicular or on a path. There is no road, therefore no cars or dust. We are also very lucky with the weather. Thus all prerequisites for my recovery are fulfilled. But for the time being the patient's egocentric mode of thinking remains with me, owing to the unaccustomed necessity of having to consider myself at every step. Until now I did not even know that one could walk *so* slowly or that a lift could become one of the necessities of life. In other words, my breathing is not yet freed, but I confidently hope that the high mountain air will have a good effect.

So much about myself! My wife, who nursed me until it became impossible to go on without an outside nurse, is also rather exhausted, but I hope she too will benefit from our stay here.

I should like to know what became of the discomforts you mentioned in your last letter. I hope to hear about it soon. If writing is a nuisance for you, dear Professor, I shall be well content with a few lines from Fräulein Anna.

Before my departure there were negotiations about the question of the film. Today I only want to say that Sachs and I believe that we have every guarantee that the matter will be carried out with genuine seriousness. In particular, we think we have succeeded in principle in presenting even the most abstract concepts. Each of us had an idea concerning these, and they complemented each other in the most fortunate way. More about this another time!

Otherwise, I am completely inactive scientifically and intend to remain so for some time. Instead, I am reading, since I can read again, I am enjoying my old favourites, Aristophanes[1] and Heine, and as a semi-invalid have learned really to value the game of solitaire.

With the most cordial greetings from my wife and myself to you and all your family,

Yours,

*Karl Abraham*

### Addendum[2]

#### Lapsus linguae

In the fifth act of the "Pfefferrösel" of Birch-Pfeiffer,[3] at the banquet of the Emperor "Adolph von Nassau", the representatives of the nobility have to offer him their congratulations. The first speaker among them (Herr P., choral singer and player of small parts) has to speak as follows: "God keep Your Majesty always with an open ear and a healthy body." Unfortunately, however, he turns the sentence round and says: "God keep Your Majesty always with a healthy ear and an open body."—The Emperor's thanks, which followed, went on amid cheerful murmuring from a surprised audience.

---

1. Whom Abraham read in Greek, according to Hilda Abraham.
2. Newspaper cutting pasted to the original letter; "Frankfurter Ztg." and "15.7.1925" added in Abraham's handwriting.
3. Charlotte Birch-Pfeiffer [1800–1868], German actress and writer.

### 491F

Villa Schüler, Semmering
21 July 1925

Dear Friend,

No, writing is really no burden to me. I was delighted to have news of you so soon, because my thoughts often stray from an ego the claims of which have become a nuisance to other objects of love. When you describe how much you are occupied with the unaccustomed needs of your own "poor Conrad,"[1] I am consoled, being experienced in the matter, by the certainty that you are having to practise this adaptation only for a short time. A permanent re-adaptation is far more difficult.

The unexpected situation has occurred that on looking through the list of Congress papers I was glad to see that your name is *not* among the speakers. With such a task ahead it would be difficult to rest the intellectual faculties. But we all hope that by the first week of September our president will have re-acquired his freedom of respiration and of action.

1925 July

We are very comfortable this year in the Semmering surroundings that you know. This summer has a different, friendlier character, and with prolonged familiarity the modest charms of the neighbourhood make a strong impact. The women find the housekeeping very convenient, and living in this well-equipped house can be called almost ideal.

The day goes by without one's really noticing it. If one thinks about it in the evening, its content has been little. Giving some free play to one's phantasy at the writing desk, an hour with the crazy American who is supposed to pay the high rent, some adventures with Wolf,[2] whom you do not know yet—with his passionate affection and jealousy, his mistrust of strangers, and his mixture of wildness and quickness to learn he is an object of the most general interest. A few letters, some proof-correcting, family visitors from America, etc. The firm intervention with which my doctor took leave of me three weeks ago has changed the character of my complaints thoroughly for the better. All the paraesthesias that tyrannically forced themselves upon my attention have disappeared and have left behind an individual free to complain, if he feels like it, about his awkward speech and never-ending nasal catarrh. So life is admittedly tolerable, but after this spoiling and weaning process what will regular work taste like in October?

I have written a few short papers, but they are not meant very seriously. Perhaps, if I am willing to admit their parentage, I shall tell you about them later. Their titles I can reveal to you: "Negation",[3] "Inhibition and Symptom",[4] and "Some Psychological Consequences of the Anatomical Distinction between the Sexes".[5]

Now get well quickly, and may you find in Wengen whatever you need to bring your period of illness to an end. Our heartfelt thanks are due to your wife for her nice contribution to your recovery. I can remember something similar.

Heartfelt greetings to you all!
Yours,

*Freud*

P.S.: The slip of the ~~print~~ tongue was very impressive!

1. The character Viktor in Carl Spitteler's novel *Imago* (1906) "was accustomed ... to calling his body Konrad in a comradely way, because he got along so well with it" (p. 21). Freud borrowed the expression, which became a standard in psychoanalytic circles, and certainly talked frequently about "poor" Konrad. Carl Spitteler [1845–1924]; Swiss writer, won Nobel Prize in 1919.
2. Anna's Alsatian.
3. Freud, 1925h.
4. Freud, 1926d [1925].
5. Freud, 1925j.

## 492F

Semmering[1]
10 August 1925

Dear Friend,

My nephew Edward Bernays from New York,[2] who has been especially active in the processing of public relations—a profession still unknown in Europe—was recently here in my home and declared himself ready to undertake an appeal for the Psychoanalytic Fund in his rich and crazy native country. Success may be doubtful, but nothing can be lost either.

Asked by him to propose the European section of a Committee to share with me in the administration of the Fund, I proposed our personalities charged with the most official functions, that is, you, Eitingon, Storfer, and in continuation of the former Committee, Ferenczi. He will provide the Americans, among whom there are to be a financier and a banker. I am now asking you for your written agreement to the use of your name.

I am corresponding with Sachs today about an incorrect procedure of your film people.[3] One should not, after all, get mixed up with such people.

We are doing splendidly in this lovely summer. I hope your recovery is making great progress, and I expect that your family will prevent you from exceeding your strength at the Congress.

With cordial greetings to all of you.

Yours,

*Freud*

1. Typewritten.
2. Edward Louis Bernays [1891–1995], son of Anna Freud and Eli Bernays.
3. The UFA had advertised: "In 'Ufa's' Neumann-Film *Geheimnisse einer Seele* . . . everything worth knowing about Psycho-analysis will be disclosed by means of an interesting story." *The New York Times* (26 July 1925) had even reported that Freud himself was going to direct the film, and *The Times* (4 August 1925) had claimed that the film would be "supervised by Professor Freud" (all in Ries, 1995: pp. 765, 771). "The company which turned the heads of Sachs and Abraham, have of course not been able to refrain from proclaiming my 'agreement' to all the world. I have protested vehemently to Sachs. The N[eue] F[reie] Presse has brought out a correction already today" (Freud to Ferenczi, 14 August 1925).

1925 August

## 493A

Sils-Maria, Hotel Edelweiss[1]
14 August 1925

Dear Professor,

Naturally I fully and gladly agree with the use of my name!

I am very glad to hear that you and yours feel so well and happy. In the circumstances I am not yielding to the temptation to ask you to come to Homburg. But we can surely count on Fräulein Anna, if only because of the Committee meeting!

I am improving from week to week, but certain residues of my illness remain—for instance, my breathing, which is not yet quite freed. But the results of the examination are very favourable and promise a complete restitution of the status quo. My wife has just left for home; I shall stay until the 31st of the month in this, my favourite spot, which is unequalled by anything else in the Alps.—

I am sorry to hear that there has been some upset to do with the film (incidentally, I do not know what), but the work is progressing well and I feel sure that one day you will come round to agreeing with Sachs and myself.

Cordially yours,

*Abraham*

1. Postcard.

## 494A

Sils-Maria, Hotel Edelweiss
20 August 1925

Dear Professor,

When you wrote to me recently about the American affair, I hastened to assure you of my agreement, but I postponed answering the rest of the letter until a later date.

I am so glad to hear continuing good reports of you. Ferenczi too found you well and energetic.[1] However it is painful for me that I see no chance of coming to convince myself in person of this for some time. A year has passed since I had the last "*Kück*" of you on the Semmering.

Of myself, I can give increasingly good news. Yesterday I had a particularly good day and walked for several hours—very slowly of course and with breaks—and climbed about 400 metres. Certainly a good sign. Other days leave much to be desired, and, particularly for the first hour after getting up, I cough and have difficulty in breathing. I still feel all the time how weakening my illness has been. I hope with confidence that the Engadine air will have helped me even further by the end of this month.

My stay in Sils suits me far better than the first stay in the Bernese Oberland. The level woodland paths along the shores of the lakes, the valleys and slopes have greater variety than I have ever found anywhere else. My wife and I are toying with the phantasy of building a holiday cottage here. This dream will probably be shattered by lack of money, especially as these months of my illness have not done anything to help me financially.

The work on the film is progressing well. Sachs is devoting himself to it and is proving very competent, and I am also trying to do my share. All the same, I agree with you, in view of their advertisement, that one should not have anything to do with these people. Our attitude in the matter is very far removed from theirs. But one thing you will admit, dear Professor: the advertisement is much more harmless than what has happened in our own circle. Storfer's behaviour can really not be judged in any other way than Sachs judged it, to you as well. It seems to me that there is only one way out of the situation: the Verlag must repudiate that notice, if you like, because it was based on inadequate information, and it must be guaranteed that this repudiation is sent faithfully to every place that has received the first notice. As perhaps they may not all wish to print it, the Verlag will have to state toward the respective journals that it is ready to bear the cost of this second notice.[2]

It can be most clearly seen how little the Verlag was hurt from *our* side by the fact that already in my *first* letter on the question of the film I mentioned that the proposed explanatory brochure might well be very lucrative for the Verlag. If it handles the matter sensibly, this income could be ensured for the Verlag even now. At any rate, the firm with which we are working must not be treated with such discourtesy any more.

This letter needs *no* reply. Whatever you, dear Professor, may think or intend to do about the latter matter, would you please inform Sachs *only*, so that you are spared the trouble of writing twice.

I shall try to follow your advice not to tire myself too much at the Congress but should like to know, too, how to do this successfully.[3]

With the most cordial greetings to you and yours,

Yours,

*Abraham*

1. Ferenczi had visited Freud on 3 August (Ferenczi to Freud, 27 July 1925).
2. Bernfeld and Storfer planned to make a rival film, with Bernfeld as script author, and the Verlag had issued a press release in August to the effect that "the Verlag ... has itself decided to provide for the production of a psycho-analytic film, so that the danger of a misleading representation or an objectionable or nonsensical bowdlerization may be

1925 September

eliminated" (in Fallend & Reichmayr, 1992: p. 137; translation in Ries, 1995: p. 773)—a barely disguised attack on Abraham and Sachs. Nothing came of this project, however.
3. The Ninth International Psychoanalytic Congress took place in Bad Homburg, 3–5 September. Presided over by Abraham (who did not give a talk himself), it was opened with Freud's paper on "Some Psychical Consequences of the Anatomical Distinction between the Sexes" (Freud, 1925j), read by Anna. Abraham was re-elected president. Furthermore, an International Training Committee [*Internationale Unterrichtskommission*] was constituted to deal with the problems of analytic education. (See the Congress report in the *Zeitschrift*, 1926, *12*: 506–528.) Behind the scenes, the conflict raged between Abraham/Sachs and Bernfeld/Storfer about their rival film projects.

495A

Berlin-Grünewald
8 September 1925

Dear Professor,

I started writing a report in Homburg about my impression of the Congress which I intended to send to you. But hundreds of things claimed my attention, and I could not finish it. Meanwhile you have already received first-hand reports about all that happened, and the photograph, which turned out well, is also in your hands. So I prefer to start anew and only to emphasize what I may see somewhat differently from your other informants. To begin with, the assurance that the Congress was scientifically of a satisfying standard and that what I have to report is mainly favourable. It was better attended than Salzburg and more international. America was strongly represented and—to my delight—some of the American colleagues proved more capable and better informed than we had expected. Coriat[1] made the soundest impression on me. Papers given by the others were less good, though Pierce Clark's,[2] at least, had an interesting core. Among the other papers, there was only one that was really bad, and that was Groddeck's,[3] who, at his first talk, seemed full of brilliant ideas but this time was incredibly platitudinous and monotonous. Reik, Ophuijsen, Reich, Alexander, and Róheim all spoke splendidly.[4] Ferenczi's new statement regarding the problem of therapy[5] implies a rapprochement that gave me much pleasure, but this time his paper was not as rich as usual in original ideas. Rank tried in a commendable way to come closer to us and we, on our part, have—I believe—helped him in this. On the evening of the banquet I had a lengthy discussion with him which should certainly have a good effect on our future relationship. One thing, however, I could not say to him—that even now he seems really ill to me. He read his paper[6] at a furious speed, so that no one could follow, and once again all his statements were without foundation and completely unproven. Added to this, the euphoric mood and another journey to America. For me all this means a new manic phase, this time however with more euphoric than irritable colouring. That is why I could not really get any pleasure from our meeting.

His new journey to America is very unwelcome to the Americans, and it would have been better for him not to go. One of my main efforts at the Congress was to establish good personal relations with the Americans, not only in order to provide a counterbalance to the painful incidents of the past year (Rank's appearance, the Newton case, etc.), but also to counteract all ideas about secession. I think the business meeting greatly contributed to this. As regards the "lay analysts",[7] a rapprochement has been reached. The appeal that *training* should be as uniform as possible in the various countries was sympathetically received, and it would be far more effective to lay down strict demands about this rather than issue printed rules about the acceptance of candidates. Federn's open admission of the mistakes made in Vienna had a favourable effect, as did my own plea for considering the different circumstances in other Societies. The question of discussions at future Congresses was also settled in a satisfactory manner. My re-election took place in a form that I can certainly regard as a vote of confidence. The replacement of the Council, consisting of all the Presidents of Societies by only two representatives, gave me the welcome opportunity of getting Hitschmann nominated to the Executive.

But now I come to the best part of the whole Congress. The news that Fräulein Anna would read a paper of yours evoked spontaneous *Freundäusserung* [friend-expression][8] at the beginning of the Congress, which I wish you could have heard for yourself! Her extremely clear way of speaking did full justice to the contents. But it was not only its scientific content that gave the Congress its brilliant send-off; the personal note in certain trains of thought aroused strong emotions in all of us. The impression that, in the one and a half years since the last Congress, there has been immense improvement in your health and vitality was intensified by the distribution of the latest issue of *Imago*, containing three of your papers.[9]

Immediately before the Congress, the *Frankfurter Zeitung* published an article by Drill, who was highly appreciative of Ψα, provided it left religion undisturbed.

On the whole, therefore, I am satisfied with the Congress. I quite understand, incidentally, why you kept away. I really had some exhausting days. All the people who only wanted to speak to me for "half a minute" exacted such an amount of talking from me that I found it a very great strain, and I shall need several days to rest my breathing organs again. I will in any case have to undergo some treatment for my nose and throat from Fliess. If this letter were not already unduly long, I would tell you how my illness has most strikingly confirmed all Fliess's views on periodicity.

I have still to go into the matter in dispute with Storfer and Bernfeld. I have tried every way I could to keep the peace and, not least, exerted myself more than was good for me in these hour-long discussions. But the result was negative. Storfer took an attitude of harsh refusal. Bernfeld openly admitted the mistakes made by him and Storfer, but for the rest I had a really bad impression of him. He tried with the promise of fantastic amounts of dollars to induce me to ignore the agreement I had signed in July, in order to take part in his project. When I showed him that that was inadmissible both legally and morally, he began to make proposals to me that I can only describe as dirty tricks.[10] As I hear, he appears subsequently to have taken a different attitude. But my judgement of him, which has never been very favourable, has been confirmed. As little as I would entrust a child's education to him, would I expect anything else good from him. Fortunately we seem to have been able to *avoid* a controversy in the press. In a discussion about our film this evening I shall try again to do something about it. In addition I want to emphasize once more that Sachs has put too much emotion into this affair, which has perhaps made many things more difficult. But I think this is nothing in comparison with the completely unfair activities of the other side. As you will have heard from Eitingon, Storfer has resigned. But he has flung himself into all questions concerning the Verlag as though he were remaining in office for all time. It is very doubtful whether one should want him to go or stay. It will be hard to match him in enthusiasm and good ideas. On the other hand, he is certainly to blame for the repeated financial crises of the Verlag; he is obviously no good at mathematics. And it is also not very pleasant that everybody dealing with him has always to watch out for his morbid sensitivity.

I am gradually resuming my work, starting with a few hours each day. After these months of scientific sterility, I want first of all to write a short paper on a criminal psychological theme (history of an impostor).[11]

In the *Berliner Tageblatt* I found the little story enclosed, which is interesting as a demonstration of the nature of "forebodings" as wishes. Only we would like to know whether it is authentic.

And now, only all good wishes for the remainder of your stay on the Semmering to you and your family, and most cordial greetings!

Yours,

*Karl Abraham*

## Addendum[12]

### The dream

The wife of a miner had a terrible dream one night. She dreamt that the walls of the mine-tunnel in which her husband worked caved in, so that all miners were buried. In her dream she saw the dreadfully mutilated bodies being unearthed, and her husband whom she loved was among them.

When she awoke in the morning she hurried to tell her husband the dream and then she implored him not to go down to the depths, for she knew that disaster was imminent. Her husband laughed at first and tried to chase away his wife's forebodings, but then when she did not stop pleading with him, he agreed not to work on that day and asked his wife to report his illness at the office.

He enjoyed the light of the day, which he had to miss most of the time, looked from his lonely room longingly at the countryside, and when it got dark he sat down at the oven-bench and blew blue clouds of tobacco, which he drew from his pipe, in the air. His wife then stepped to him and said gravely:

"The disaster I had seen in my dream came true."

"No", he said, "you are joking!"

"By God, I am not joking. A tunnel has caved in; luckily no one is seriously injured. Your comrades have all been brought up, they are well, only a few have small injuries. How good that you gave in to my plea and stayed at home—who knows whether fate would have been as kind to you as to the others."

He leaned back against the oven, full of amazement and filled with emotions of gratitude.

Then a smoothing iron, which his wife had leaned against the edge of the oven, fell down with its tip exactly onto the most sensitive part of his scull, so that he sank down with a soft scream and died on the spot.

Hans Bethge.

1. Isador Henry Coriat [1875–1943], M.D., founding member and first secretary of the Boston Psychoanalytic Society [1914]. He talked about "The Oral-Erotic Components of Stammering" (Coriat, 1927). Abstracts of this and of the other papers in the *Zeitschrift*, l.c.
2. L. Pierce Clark [1870–1933], M.D., neurologist and psychoanalyst in New York, consulting neurologist at Manhattan State Hospital, specialist in epilepsy. He gave a paper on "The Phantasy Method of Analysing Narcissistic Neuroses" (Clark, 1926).
3. "Psychoanalysis and the It".
4. Reik, "The Origin of Psychology" (1925); Ophuijsen, "Some Observations on the Origin of Sadism" (1926); Reich, "On the Structure and Aetiology of 'Hypochondriacal Neurasthenia'" (not published); Alexander, "Neurosis and the Whole Personality [*Gesamtpersönlichkeit*]" (1926); Róheim, "The Scapegoat" (not published).
5. Ferenczi, 1925[269].
6. "On the Genesis of Genitality" (Rank, 1925).
7. These words in English in original.
8. A slip for *Freudenäußerung* [rejoicing].

9. In fact, the number in question contained two articles by Freud (1925e [1924], 1925h).
10. These two words in English in original.
11. Abraham, 1923[95].
12. Newspaper cutting pasted to the original letter.

## 496F

Semmering
11 September 1925

Dear Friend,

So what I feared has happened. The Congress was a great strain on you, and I can only hope that your youth will soon get the better of the disturbance.

Many thanks for the trouble you took in compensating me for my absence by your detailed report. To me the only fully enjoyable thing was your pleasure at the appearance of my paper on the programme. I had not thought of it myself, it was a last-minute idea of my daughter's.

There are many other things I should rather have liked to discuss with you; in writing, differences stand out too luridly. For example, I think the Americans are quite worthless. Coriat is likeable and is, incidentally, not close to the New Yorkers, Jelliffe is very clever and capable, and not very scrupulous. I know P. Clark least well, and the others are not worth consideration. Their resistance against Rank's return is based on the pettiest motives, exactly like their attitude to lay analysis. Rank's latest visit to America is not a manic symptom; there are several important real reasons for it, and I had advised him very definitely to go. Whether I was right will only appear later.

The business of the film, now happily solved, has left me with an unpleasant aftertaste. Imagine what sort of impression it makes when first one, then another, resigns over such a worthless affair. I judge Sachs much more strictly and Bernfeld and Storfer much more mildly than you, and would like to seek the protection of those two against your harshness. Storfer has withdrawn his resignation, he would have been irreplaceable. You cannot maintain that he is to blame for the embarrassments of the Verlag. Like everyone else, he has his foibles, and they call for tolerance. In all these years I have never heard anything bad about Bernfeld.

I do not want to be a Cato, but I do not like the *victrix causa*[1] of the Ufa. I only hope that Sachs, who is pleading its cause more and more, does not try again to enlist me for it. I should have preferred you too not to have got involved. Our circle has not stood up well to this test. Let us rather turn our attention to worthier causes.

I am staying here until the end of September. The weather is unfortunately very bad, but I hear that you are just as cold in Berlin.

Let me hear of your complete recovery and with cordial greetings from

Your

*Freud*

1. After the Latin *"Victrix causa diis placuit, sed victa Catoni"*: the victorious cause pleased the Gods, but the inferior one pleased Cato (Lucanus [39–65 AD], *Pharsalia*)—referring to Cato Uticensis, who committed suicide when the cause of the Roman Republic was lost in the wake of Caesar's victories.

## 497F

Vienna, Berggasse 19[1]
16 October 1925

Dear Friend,

Your direct letter[2] gave me more pleasure, of course, and was more reassuring than all the indirect news. I hope you will soon be able to write and say that in this respect you have become completely uninteresting again.

Your short paper[3] is enchanting. I think you should not wait for your turn in *Imago*, but that it should be used as the introductory article in the next annual series of the *Zeitschrift*. The subject is interesting enough for physicians too. In one respect I should have stated the train of thought rather differently, I should have emphasized not the deprivation of pleasure but the fact that he could form no superego because he had been unable to achieve an Oedipus complex. The fact that in these circumstances he was able to establish an unconscious need of punishment instead of a normal conscience could be the point of departure for further reflections.

We have almost forgotten the summer, though the weather is now more summer-like than it was at the end on the Semmering. I have interesting work and not too much of it, and am still struggling with my usual minor complaints.

With cordial greetings to you and your family,

Yours,

*Freud*

1. Typewritten.
2. Missing.
3. Abraham, 1923[95].

## 498A

Berlin-Grünewald
19 October 1925

Dear Professor,

Your letter has just arrived. You probably already know from the circular letter[1] that I am very much better. The process in the lung appears to be healing: I did not completely get over the infection when it occurred the first time in June. The very disagreeable addition of gallbladder colic has also disappeared and, according to the last examination, the liver enlargement seems to have gone down. I still need to be careful and shall probably resume work at the end of the month, provided no further trouble occurs.

I am so sorry to hear that you are continuously troubled by certain discomforts. As far as I know these are due to a disturbing amount of secretion, and I have been wondering whether a stay in a very dry climate might be beneficial. But I do not know whether you still need to be near your surgeon. You may be interested to hear that Fliess, who heard about your illness two years ago, has repeatedly asked after your health with the warmest interest. As far as *I* am concerned, I must repeat here once again that I owe him the utmost gratitude.

I gladly accept your hint about the one point in my manuscript on the Impostor. I have, after all, mentioned elsewhere the failure to form an ego-ideal and need only put it more precisely in the place you mention. As far as publication is concerned, Radó had already accepted the manuscript for No. 1 of the *Zeitschrift*. I heard from Sachs that *Imago* was short of material and said I agreed to having it published there if necessary. Then Storfer was here and complained to Radó that the next issue of *Imago* could not be published because it could not be completed. So R. gave him the manuscript, and I think it is already being printed. If I take it back now, I shall cause an awkward situation, so I do not know what to do. Under these circumstances I would like to lay the decision into your hands. Perhaps Fräulein Anna would discuss the matter on the telephone with Storfer, and a way out might be found. I should be very grateful for that. Naturally it is perfectly all right by me for it to appear in the *Zeitschrift*.

With the most cordial greetings from house to house,
Yours,

*Abraham*

1. Letter of 17 October (LOC).

## 499A

Berlin-Grünewald
27 October 1925

Dear Professor,

Our last correspondence referring to the publication of my short paper (The Impostor) was overtaken by events. I received the proofs for correction some days ago, so that in any case nothing could be done about its publication in *Imago*. It seems it was needed to fill a gap there. I am now writing an essay of similar length—"Psycho-Analytical Notes on Coué's System of Self-Mastery"[1]—which leans on your group psychology. Radó wants to include it in Number 1 of 1926, and I shall therefore appear in that issue in a different way.

You know, dear Professor, that I am very unwilling to enter once again into a discussion of the Bernfeld and Storfer affair. But because of your reproach of harshness (in your circular letter), I find myself in the same position again as on several previous occasions. In almost 20 years, we have had no differences of opinion except where personalities were concerned whom I, very much to my regret, had to criticize. The same sequence of events repeated itself each time; you indulgently overlooked everything that could be challenged in the behaviour of the persons concerned, while all the blame—which you subsequently recognized as unjustified—was directed against me. In Jung's case your criticism was that of "jealousy"; in the case of Rank "unfriendly behaviour", and this time "harshness". Could the sequence of events not be the same once again? I advanced an opinion that is basically yours as well, but which you did not admit into consciousness. All the unpleasure linked to the relevant facts is then turned against the person who has drawn attention to them.

What has actually happened—I mean on the part of Sachs and myself—that could leave you with so unpleasant an "after-taste"? Neither of us ever thought to plan a $\psi\alpha$ film and to seek a company to make it. *We* were approached by "Neumann Productions" to work with them because they wanted competent analysts. If we had refused, all the "wild" analysts in Berlin would eagerly have rushed in. The "Ufa" already had "$\psi\alpha$" film outlines of the most minor sort waiting to be tried. Besides, I told you about the situation immediately, even though I was already ill in bed. In addition, Sachs and I have not done the slightest thing that would have been open to ethical objections.

I know that Sachs got very worked up about the notice issued by Storfer, but that is simply a matter of temperament. But I must say that in the last few months he has worked with more enthusiasm and spirit of self-sacrifice than anyone else would have done.

On the other side there are the following facts: (1.) the nasty notice about the "bowdlerization" directed against Sachs and me. (2.) the offering of Bernfeld's draft to various firms, *none* of which had spontaneously approached St. and B. (3.) the underhandedness of the letter to Sachs and me, dripping with loyalty while *at the same* time they sent the notice to the press that I have mentioned. Thus an unfair competitive manoeuvre under the cloak of friendship. (4.) Storfer wrote to Eitingon that he would comply with his instructions. When Eitingon gave him some, he did not follow them. (5.) The "resignation" was an empty gesture. Immediately after announcing his resignation in Homburg, Storfer took part in a meeting about matters of the Verlag (Fräulein Anna was present as well) and let nobody get a word in, but went on developing his plans for the future of the Verlag. The "resignation" was thus as untrue as everything else. I saw this at once but did not protest because I wanted to keep the peace. (Harshness?) (6.) Bernfeld tried to get me to break my word or my contract with regard to the Neumann Company, always juggling with promises of gigantic sums in dollars. After that, he spread it about in Homburg that I wanted to eliminate his film out of greed for money. He knew that Sachs and I had only had a moderate fixed amount for our work, and because of it had accused the Ufa of deceiving us, whereas *he* had assured us of enormous profits. He left the Congress prematurely because—according to his own statement—he could not bear to be there when I was elected President again. A strange repetition; Rank had said and done exactly the same in Salzburg. (7.) The news that you doubted, dear Professor, certainly did not come from the Ufa. It is as such that the head of the only company that could make such a film in Vienna (Pan-company), Dr Robert Wiene, gave Sachs the verbal explanation that St. and B. had approached "Pan" with the statement that they had an offer from the Ufa but were waiting in Homburg for an even higher one from the American side. Negotiations came to a swift and negative end.

These are a *few* main points that show that on that side an underhanded and untruthful game was being played from the very beginning.

And where is the harshness I am accused of? Sachs and I demanded that the notice in the press should be withdrawn; that did *not* happen. The "satisfaction" given to us was St.'s resignation, which—as I have said—was only a manner of speaking. We gave in and did everything to keep the "Ufa" out of all proceedings, and we did it successfully. As I have recently mentioned, I am corresponding with Storfer as though nothing had happened. Thus *we* gave in all along the line, and when some time ago you wrote about the "causa victrix of the Ufa", it was a great mistake. So what is there left that could be called harshness on our part? *Only* a few open statements in the circular letters (and in other correspondence), which is actually intended for free utterances. In addition, as far as my means of voice allowed, I mediated and smoothed things over in Homburg at every turn, and the whole of my behaviour within the Society makes it improbable that I would be so hard and harsh towards a few people.

Much as I regret it, I cannot alter my opinion of Bernfeld and Storfer. The former is a talented person, but one for whom the boundaries between reality and phantasy, between idealistic love of truth and instinctive compulsive pseudologia are completely blurred. I have always had a personal sympathy for Storfer; I have always patiently put up with his peculiarities in respect to his earlier illness, and have come to terms with him in all earlier cases. I also value his enthusiasm for the Verlag and his good ideas; only a few days before that notice appeared in the press I had written to him in a friendly way, most warmly recognizing the excellence of the idea of the *Almanach*[2] and how it was carried out in detail. But I have absolutely no doubt that this pitiable person is in his ambivalence helping the Verlag with one hand and harming it with the other. You know better than I into what constantly renewed difficulties the Verlag has fallen through his bad management, and it is to be wondered whether the harm does not greatly outweigh the good. I cannot decide this question.

This whole affair is to me a bagatelle that I should have liked to pass over long ago to return to the order of the day. But it gives me pain to have aroused your displeasure once again, although I am certain that this time, as on previous occasions, you will one day reconsider your judgement of me; but I on my part wanted to do everything to get the facts clear. I am, with kindest regards to you and your family, in unaltered and unalterable cordiality!

Yours,

*Karl Abraham*

1. Abraham, 1926[115], published posthumously.
2. The *Almanach* (first issue 1926; from 1930 on *Almanach der Psychoanalyse*), ed. Storfer, a yearly periodical containing reprints and original works of a more popular character.

## 500F

Vienna, Berggasse 19
5 November 1925

Dear Friend,

I note with pleasure that your illness has not changed you in any way, and I am willing to regard you as having again recovered. That takes a great load off my mind.

It does not make a deep impression on me that I cannot be converted to your point of view in the affair B-St film. There are things that I see differently and things that I know differently. The ready admission that B. and St. were in the wrong gives me a right to point out the errors of the other side. I do not find Sachs's threat to resign any more praiseworthy than Storfer's; the behaviour of the Ufa towards me was so incorrect that I lost patience and made my own denial instead of waiting for the promised denial. Because of your complaint that St. did not comply after Eitingon had reached his decision, I turned directly to Eitingon, and from him I learned the *contrary*.[1]

Let us also not give too much play to repetition compulsion. You were certainly right about Jung, and not quite so right about Rank. That matter took a different course and would have passed more easily if it had not been taken so very seriously in Berlin. It is still quite possible that you may be even less right in the matter with which we are concerned now. It does not have to be the case that you are always right. But should you turn out to be right this time too, nothing would prevent me from once again admitting it.

With that, let us close the argument about something that you yourself describe as a bagatelle. Such differences of opinion can never be avoided, but only quickly overcome.

What matters more to me is to hear whether you intend to stay in Berlin or spend the winter in a milder climate. I am not quite sure in my mind what to wish for you, but in any case let the outcome be that you cause us no more worry.

With cordial greetings to you and your wife and children.

Yours,

*Freud*

1. On 30 October 1925 Freud had sent Abraham's letter of 27 October to Eitingon with the request "to hear from you, who witnessed everything, if I really do A. an injustice and if I am misled by sympathy for those who live nearer to me" (SFC). Eitingon's answer of 3 November sharply criticized Abraham, his "harshness", "lack of humour", "love for himself", "intellectual self-righteousness" and "moral contentedness" (ibid.).

# 1926

501F
[to Frau Abraham]

Vienna, Berggasse 19
17 January 1926

Dear Frau,

Since my telegram on receiving the news of your husband's death I have put off writing to you. It was too difficult, and I hoped it would become easier. Then I fell ill myself, became feverish, and have not yet recovered. But already I see that putting it off was pointless, it is just as difficult now as it was then. I have no substitute for him, and no consolatory words for you that would tell you anything new. That we have to submit with resignation to the blows of fate you know already; and you will have guessed that to me his loss is particularly painful because I think, with the selfishness of old age, that the loss could easily have been spared for the probable short duration of my own life.

The only consolation is the news that in your brother you have found a helper who will enable you to watch over the development of your daughter and son, free from crippling cares. May you find a new and rich meaning in life from your motherhood!

I have no prospect of travelling, so I do not know whether I shall see you again. Do keep me too in your memory.

With heartfelt sympathy,
Your devoted

*Freud*

# REFERENCES

The works of Abraham have been cited according to the bibliography in *Selected Papers of Karl Abraham, M.D.* (London: Hogarth, 1927 [reprinted London: Karnac, 1988]), those of Ferenczi according to the bibliography in *Schriften zur Psychoanalyse II* (Frankfurt/M.: S. Fischer, 1972), and those of Freud according to the *The Standard Edition of the Complete Psychological Works of Sigmund* Freud (ed. James Strachey, with Anna Freud, Alix Strachey, and Alan Tyson) (London: Hogarth).

Abraham, Hilda (1974). Karl Abraham: An unfinished biography. *International Review of Psycho-Analysis*, 1: 17–72.

Abraham, Karl (1907[9]). Über die Bedeutung sexueller Jugendtraumen für die Symptomatologie der Dementia praecox. *Centralblatt für Nervenheilkunde und Psychiatrie, Neue Folge, 18*: 409–416. On the significance of sexual trauma in childhood for the symptomatology of dementia praecox. In: *Clinical Papers and Essays on Psycho-Analysis* (pp. 13–21), 1955.

Abraham, Karl (1907[10]). Das Erleiden sexueller Traumen als Form infantiler Sexualbetätigung. *Centralblatt für Nervenheilkunde und Psychiatrie, Neue Folge, 18*: 855–866. The experiencing of sexual traumas as a form of sexual activity. In: *Selected Papers of Karl Abraham, M.D.* (pp. 47–63), 1927.

Abraham, Karl (1908[11]). Die psychosexuellen Differenzen der Hysterie und der Dementia praecox. *Centralblatt für Nervenheilkunde und Psychiatrie, Neue Folge, 19*: 521–533. The psycho-sexual differences between hysteria and dementia praecox. In: *Selected Papers of Karl Abraham, M.D.* (pp. 64–79), 1927.

Abraham, Karl (1908[12]). Die psychologischen Beziehungen zwischen Sexualität und Alkoholismus. *Zeitschrift für Sexualwissenschaft, 8* (Aug.): 449–458. The psychological relations between sexuality and alcoholism. In: *Selected Papers of Karl Abraham, M.D.* (pp. 80–89), 1927.

Abraham, Karl (1909[13]). Die Stellung der Verwandtenehe in der Psychologie der Neurosen. *Jahrbuch für psychoanalytische und psychopathologische Forschungen*, 1 (1): 110–118. The significance of intermarriage between close relatives in the psychology of the neuroses. In: *Clinical Papers and Essays on Psycho-Analysis* (pp. 21–28), 1955.

Abraham, Karl (1909[14]). *Traum und Mythus: Eine Studie zur Völkerpsychologie* (*Schriften zur angewandten Seelenkunde* 4). Leipzig, Vienna: Deuticke. Dreams and myths: A study in folk-psychology. In: *Clinical Papers and Essays on Psycho-Analysis* (pp. 153–209), 1955.

Abraham, Karl (1909[15]). Freuds Schriften aus den Jahren 1893–1909 [Freud's writings from the years 1893–1909]. *Jahrbuch für psychoanalytische und psychopathologische Forschungen*, 1 (2): 546–574.

Abraham, Karl (1909[16]). Bericht über die österreichische und deutsche psychoanalytische Literatur bis zum Jahre 1909 [Report on the Austrian and German psychoanalytic literature to the year 1909]. *Jahrbuch für psychoanalytische und psychopathologische Forschungen*, 1 (2): 575–594.

Abraham, Karl (1910[17]). Über hysterische Traumzustände. *Jahrbuch für psychoanalytische und psychopathologische Forschungen*, 2 (1): 1–32. Hysterical dream states. In: *Selected Papers of Karl Abraham, M.D.* (pp. 90–124), 1927.

Abraham, Karl (1910[18]). Bemerkungen zur Psychoanalyse eines Falles von Fuß- und Korsettfetischismus. *Jahrbuch für psychoanalytische und psychopathologische Forschungen*, 3 (2) (1911/12): 557–567. Remarks on the psycho-analysis of a case of foot and corset fetishism. In: *Selected Papers of Karl Abraham, M.D.* (pp. 125–136), 1927.

Abraham, Karl (1911[26]). Ansätze zur psychoanalytischen Erforschung und Behandlung des manisch-depressiven Irreseins und verwandter Zustände. *Internationale Zeitschrift für ärztliche Psychoanalyse*, 2 (1912): 302–315. Notes on the psycho-analytical treatment of manic depressive insanity and allied conditions. In: *Selected Papers of Karl Abraham, M.D.* (pp. 137–156), 1927.

Abraham, Karl (1911[28]). Über die determinierende Kraft des Namens. *Zentralblatt für Psychoanalyse: Medizinische Monatsschrift für Seelenkunde*, 2 (1911/12): 133–134. On the determining power of names. In: *Clinical Papers and Essays on Psycho-Analysis* (pp. 31–32), 1955.

Abraham, Karl (1911[29]). Eine Traumanalyse bei Ovid [A dream analysis in Ovid]. *Zentralblatt für Psychoanalyse: Medizinische Monatsschrift für Seelenkunde*, 2 (1911/12): 159–160.

Abraham, Karl (1911[30]). *Giovanni Segantini: Ein psychoanalytischer Versuch.* (*Schriften zur angewandten Seelenkunde* 11). Leipzig, Vienna: Deuticke. Giovanni Segantini: A psycho-analytical study. In: *Clinical Papers and Essays on Psycho-Analysis* (pp. 210–261), 1955.

Abraham, Karl (1912[32]). Über ein kompliziertes Zeremoniell neurotischer Frauen. *Zentralblatt für Psychoanalyse: Medizinische Monatsschrift für Seelenkunde*, 2 (1911/12): 421–425. A complicated ceremonial found in neurotic women. In: *Selected Papers of Karl Abraham, M.D.* (pp. 157–163), 1927.

Abraham, Karl (1912[34]). Amenhotep IV. (Echnaton). Psychoanalytische Beiträge zum Verständnis seiner Persönlichkeit und des monotheistischen Aton-Kultes. *Imago, Zeitschrift für Anwendung der Psychoanalyse auf die Geisteswissenschaften*, 1: 334–360. Amenhotep IV. Psycho-analytical contributions towards the understanding of his personality and of the monotheistic cult of Aton. In: *Clinical Papers and Essays on Psycho-Analysis* (pp. 262–291), 1955.

Abraham, Karl (1913[38]). Eine Deckerinnerung, betreffend ein Kindheitserlebnis von scheinbar ätiologischer Bedeutung. *Internationale Zeitschrift für ärztliche Psychoanalyse*, 1: 247–251. A screen memory concerning a childhood event of apparently aetiological significance. In: *Clinical Papers and Essays on Psycho-Analysis* (pp. 36–41), 1955.

Abraham, Karl (1913[39]). Zur Psychogenese der Straßenangst im Kindesalter. *Internationale Zeitschrift für ärztliche Psychoanalyse*, 1: 256–257. On the psychogenesis of agoraphobia in childhood. In: *Clinical Papers and Essays on Psycho-Analysis* (pp. 42–43), 1955.

Abraham, Karl (1913[40]). Einige Bemerkungen über die Rolle der Großeltern in der Psychologie der Neurosen. *Internationale Zeitschrift für ärztliche Psychoanalyse*, 1: 224–227. Some remarks on the role of grandparents in the psychology of neuroses. In: *Clinical Papers and Essays on Psycho-Analysis* (pp. 36–41), 1955.

Abraham, Karl (1913[42]). Psychische Nachwirkungen der Beobachtung des elterlichen Geschlechtsverkehrs bei einem neunjährigen Kinde. *Internationale Zeitschrift für ärztliche Psychoanalyse*, 1: 364–366. Mental after-effects produced in a nine-year-old child by the observation of sexual intercourse between its parents. In: *Selected Papers of Karl Abraham, M.D.* (pp. 164–168), 1927.

Abraham, Karl (1914[43]). Über Einschränkungen und Umwandlungen der Schaulust bei den Psychoneurotikern nebst Bemerkungen über analoge Erscheinungen in der Völkerpsychologie. *Jahrbuch der Psychoanalyse, Neue Folge des Jahrbuchs für psychoanalytische und psychopathologische Forschungen*, 6: 25–88. Restrictions and transformations of scoptophilia in psychoneurotics; with remarks on analogous phenomena in folk-psychology. In: *Selected Papers of Karl Abraham, M.D.* (pp. 169–234), 1927.

Abraham, Karl (1914[44]). Über eine konstitutionelle Grundlage der lokomotorischen Angst. *Internationale Zeitschrift für ärztliche Psychoanalyse*, 2: 143–150. A constitutional basis of locomotor anxiety. In: *Selected Papers of Karl Abraham, M.D.* (pp. 235–243), 1927.

Abraham, Karl (1914[45]). Über neurotische Exogamie. Ein Beitrag zu den Übereinstimmungen im Seelenleben der Neurotiker und der Wilden. *Imago, Zeitschrift für Anwendung der Psychoanalyse auf die Geisteswissenschaften*, 3 (6): 499–501. On neurotic exogamy: A contribution to the similarities in the psychic life of neurotics and of primitive man. In: *Clinical Papers and Essays on Psycho-Analysis* (pp. 48–50), 1955.

Abraham, Karl (1914[46]). Ohrmuschel und Gehörgang als erogene Zone. *Internationale Zeitschrift für ärztliche Psychoanalyse*, 2: 27–29. The ear and auditory passage as erotogenic zones. In: *Selected Papers of Karl Abraham, M.D.* (pp. 244–247), 1927.

Abraham, Karl (1914[47]). Kritik zu C. G. Jung, "Versuch einer Darstellung der psychoanalytischen Theorie". *Internationale Zeitschrift für ärztliche Psychoanalyse, 2*: 72–82. Review of C. G. Jung's "Versuch einer Darstellung der psychoanalytischen Theorie" (Attempt at a representation of psychoanalytical theory). In: *Clinical Papers and Essays on Psycho-Analysis* (pp. 101–115), 1955.

Abraham, Karl (1914[51]). Spezielle Pathologie und Therapie der nervösen Zustände und der Geistesstörungen (Sammelreferat Bleuler, Eugen, Lehrbuch der Psychiatrie) [Special pathology and therapy of nervous conditions and mental disorders (Collective review of Bleuler, Eugen, Textbook of psychiatry)]. *Jahrbuch der Psychoanalyse, Neue Folge des Jahrbuchs für psychoanalytische und psychopathologische Forschungen, 6*: 343–363.

Abraham, Karl (1916[52]). Untersuchungen über die früheste prägenitale Entwicklungsstufe der Libido. *Internationale Zeitschrift für ärztliche Psychoanalyse, 4* (1916/17): 71–97. The first pregenital stage of the libido. In: *Selected Papers of Karl Abraham, M.D.* (pp. 248–279), 1927.

Abraham, Karl (1917[53]). Einige Belege zur Gefühlseinstellung weiblicher Kinder gegenüber den Eltern. *Internationale Zeitschrift für ärztliche Psychoanalyse, 4* (1916/17): 154–155. Some illustrations on the emotional relationship of little girls towards their parents. In: *Clinical Papers and Essays on Psycho-Analysis* (pp. 52–54), 1955.

Abraham, Karl (1917[54]). Über Ejaculatio praecox. *Internationale Zeitschrift für ärztliche Psychoanalyse, 4* (1916/17): 171–186. Ejaculatio præcox. In: *Selected Papers of Karl Abraham, M.D.* (pp. 280–298), 1927.

Abraham, Karl (1917[55]). Das Geldausgaben im Angstzustand. *Internationale Zeitschrift für ärztliche Psychoanalyse, 4* (1916/17): 252–253. The spending of money in anxiety states. In: *Selected Papers of Karl Abraham, M.D.* (pp. 299–302), 1927.

Abraham, Karl (1918[57]). Erstes Korreferat. In: *Zur Psychoanalyse der Kriegsneurosen* (Internationale Psychoanalytische Bibliothek, No. 1) (pp. 31–41), Leipzig: Internationaler Psychoanalytischer Verlag, 1919. Psycho-analysis and the war neuroses. In: *Clinical Papers and Essays on Psycho-Analysis* (pp. 59–67), 1955.

Abraham, Karl (1919[58]). Über eine besondere Form des neurotischen Widerstandes gegen die psychoanalytische Methodik. *Internationale Zeitschrift für ärztliche Psychoanalyse, 5*: 173–180. A particular form of neurotic resistance against the psycho-analytic method. In: *Selected Papers of Karl Abraham, M.D.* (pp. 303–311), 1927.

Abraham, Karl (1919[59]). "Tiertotemismus" [Animal totemism]. Paper presented to the Berlin Psychoanalytic Society, 16 Mar.

Abraham, Karl (1919[61]). Bemerkungen zu Ferenczis Mitteilungen über "Sonntagsneurosen". *Internationale Zeitschrift für ärztliche Psychoanalyse, 5*: 203–204. Observations on Ferenczi's paper on "Sunday neuroses". In:

Robert Fließ (Ed.), *The Psychoanalytic Reader I* (pp. 349–352). New York: International Universities Press, 1948.

Abraham, Karl (1919[63]). Zur narzißtischen Bewertung der Exkretionsvorgänge in Traum und Neurose. *Internationale Zeitschrift für Psychoanalyse*, 6 (1920): 64–67. The narcissistic evaluation of excretory processes in dreams and neurosis. In: *Selected Papers of Karl Abraham, M.D.* (pp. 318–322), 1927.

Abraham, Karl (1919[63a]). Pötzl, Otto. Über einige Wechselwirkungen hysterieformer und organisch zerebraler Störungsmechanismen [Review of: Pötzl, Otto. On the interrelationship of hysteria-like and organic cerebral mechanisms of disorder]. *Internationale Zeitschrift für ärztliche Psychoanalyse*, 5: 222–224.

Abraham, Karl (1919[63b]). Pötzl, Otto. Experimentell erregte Traumbilder in ihren Beziehungen zum indirekten Sehen [Review of: Pötzl, Otto. Experimentally induced dream images and their relationship to indirect vision]. *Internationale Zeitschrift für ärztliche Psychoanalyse*, 5: 129.

Abraham, Karl (1920[67]). Äußerungsformen des weiblichen Kastrationskomplexes. *Internationale Zeitschrift für Psychoanalyse*, 7 (1921): 422–452. Manifestations of the female castration complex. In: *Selected Papers of Karl Abraham, M.D.* (pp. 338–369), 1927.

Abraham, Karl (1920[69]). Die Psychoanalyse als Erkenntnisquelle für die Geisteswissenschaften. *Die neue Rundschau, Vol. 31 der Freien Bühne*, No 10 (Oct.): 1154–1174. The cultural significance of psycho-analysis. In: *Clinical Papers and Essays on Psycho-Analysis* (pp. 116–136), 1955.

Abraham, Karl (1921[70]). Ergänzungen zur Lehre vom Analcharakter. *Internationale Zeitschrift für Psychoanalyse*, 9 (1923): 27–47. Contributions to the theory of the anal character. In: *Selected Papers of Karl Abraham, M.D.* (pp. 370–392), 1927.

Abraham, Karl (1921[74]). Literatur in spanischer Sprache. In: *Bericht über die Fortschritte der Psychoanalyse in den Jahren 1914–1919* (pp. 366–367). Leipzig: Internationaler Psychoanalytischer Verlag. The literature in Spanish. *International Journal of Psychoanalysis*, 1 (1920): 457–458.

Abraham, Karl (1921[75]). *Klinische Beiträge zur Psychoanalyse aus den Jahren 1907–1920* [Clinical contributions to psychoanalysis, 1907–1920] (Internationale Psychoanalytische Bibliothek, No. 10). Leipzig: Internationaler Psychoanalytischer Verlag.

Abraham, Karl (1922[76]). Vaterrettung und Vatermord in den neurotischen Phantasiegebilden. *Internationale Zeitschrift für Psychoanalyse*, 8: 71–77. The rescue and murder of the father in neurotic phantasy-formations. In: *Clinical Papers and Essays on Psycho-Analysis* (pp. 68–75), 1955.

Abraham, Karl (1922[78]). Über Fehlleistungen mit überkompensierender Tendenz. *Internationale Zeitschrift für Psychoanalyse*, 8: 345–348. Mistakes with an overcompensating tendency. In: *Clinical Papers and Essays on Psycho-Analysis* (pp. 76–79), 1955.

Abraham, Karl (1922[79]). Die Fehlleistung eines Achtzigjährigen. *Internationale Zeitschrift für Psychoanalyse*, 8: 350. An octogenarian's mistake. In: *Clinical Papers and Essays on Psycho-Analysis* (p. 80), 1955.

Abraham, Karl (1922[80]). Die Spinne als Traumsymbol. *Internationale Zeitschrift für Psychoanalyse, 8*: 470–475. The spider as a dream symbol. In: *Selected Papers of Karl Abraham, M.D.* (pp. 326–332), 1927.

Abraham, Karl (1922[81]). Neue Untersuchungen zur Psychologie der manisch-depressiven Zustände [New investigations in the psychology of manic-depressive states]. Abstract in *Internationale Zeitschrift für Psychoanalyse, 8*: 492–493; in Abraham, 1924[105].

Abraham, Karl (1923[84]). "Die Wiederkehr primitiver religiöser Vorstellungen im Phantasieleben des Kindes." Orientalisches Seminar der Universität Hamburg, 3. März [The return of primitive religious ideas in the child's phantasy life. Paper presented to the Oriental Seminar of the University of Hamburg, 3 March].

Abraham, Karl (1923[87]). "Anfänge und Entwicklung der Objektliebe" [The beginnings and the development of object love]. Paper presented to the Berlin Psychoanalytic Society, 27 Mar. In: *Versuch einer Entwicklungsgeschichte der Libido auf Grund der Psychoanalyse seelischer Störungen*, 1924[105].

Abraham, Karl (1923[93]). "Psycho-analytic views on some characters of early infantile thinking." Paper given at the Seventh International Congress of Psychology, Oxford, 31 Jul. In: *Clinical Papers and Essays on Psycho-Analysis* (pp. 86–90), 1955.

Abraham, Karl (1923[95]). Die Geschichte eines Hochstaplers im Lichte psychoanalytischer Erkenntnis. *Imago, Zeitschrift für Anwendung der Psychoanalyse auf die Geisteswissenschaften, 11* (1925): 355–370. The history of an impostor in the light of psycho-analytical knowledge. In: *Clinical Papers and Essays on Psycho-Analysis* (pp. 291–305), 1955.

Abraham, Karl (1924[97]). "Über unbewußte Strömungen im Verhältnis der Eltern zum Kind" [On unconscious currents in the parents' relation to the child]. Paper given in Hamburg, 5 Jan.

Abraham, Karl (1924[98]). "Umwandlungsvorgänge am Ödipuskomplex im Laufe einer Psychoanalyse" [Transformations of the Oedipus complex in the course of a psychoanalysis]. Paper presented to the Berlin Psychoanalytic Society, 29 Mar.

Abraham, Karl (1924[99]). "Beiträge der Oralerotik zur Charakterbildung." Paper given at the Eighth International Psychoanalytic Congress, Salzburg, 21 Apr. In: *Selected Papers of Karl Abraham, M.D.* (pp. 393–406), 1927.

Abraham, Karl (1924[105]). *Versuch einer Entwicklungsgeschichte der Libido auf Grund der Psychoanalyse seelischer Störungen*. Leipzig: Internationaler Psychoanalytischer Verlag. *A Short Study of the Development of the Libido, Viewed in the Light of Mental Disorders.* In: *Selected Papers of Karl Abraham, M.D.* (pp. 418–501), 1927.

Abraham, Karl (1924[105b]). Aus der südamerikanischen Literatur [From the literature of South America]. *Internationale Zeitschrift für Psychoanalyse, 10*: 308–309.

Abraham, Karl (1924[105d]). † Dr. Rudolf Foerster [obit.]. *Internationale Zeitschrift für Psychoanalyse, 10*: 103–104.

# REFERENCES

Abraham, Karl (1925[106]). *Psychoanalytische Studien zur Charakterbildung* [Psychoanalytic studies on character formation]. Leipzig: Internationaler Psychoanalytischer Verlag (Internationale Psychoanalytische Bibliothek No. 16).

Abraham, Karl (1925[110]). Eine unbeachtete kindliche Sexualtheorie. *Internationale Zeitschrift für Psychoanalyse, 11*: 85–87. An infantile sexual theory not hitherto noted. In: *Selected Papers of Karl Abraham, M.D.* (pp. 334–337), 1927.

Abraham, Karl (1925[111]). "Psychoanalyse und Gynäkologie." Paper presented to the *Berliner Gesellschaft für Gynäkologie und Geburtshilfe*, 13 Mar. *Zeitschrift für Geburtshilfe und Gynäkologie, 89*: 451–458. Psycho-analysis and gynaecology. In: *Clinical Papers and Essays on Psycho-Analysis* (pp. 91–97), 1955.

Abraham, Karl (1925[113]). "Die Psychoanalyse schizophrener Zustände" [The psychoanalysis of schizophrenic states]. Paper presented to the *Leidsche Vereeniging voor Psychopathologie en Psychoanalyse*. Leyden, 27 and 29 May.

Abraham, Karl (1925[114]). "Das hysterische Symptom" [The hysterical symptom]. Paper presented to the *Nederlandsche Maatschappij ter Bevordering der Geneeskunst*. The Hague, 28 May.

Abraham, Karl (1926[115]). Psychoanalytische Bemerkungen zu Coués Verfahren der Selbstbemeisterung. *Internationale Zeitschrift für Psychoanalyse, 12*: 131–154. Psycho-analytical notes on Coué's system of self-mastery. In: *Clinical Papers and Essays on Psycho-Analysis* (pp. 306–327), 1955.

Abraham, Karl (1927). *Selected Papers of Karl Abraham, M.D.* London: Hogarth [reprinted London: Karnac, 1988].

Abraham, Karl (1955). *Clinical Papers and Essays on Psycho-Analysis*. London: Hogarth [reprinted London: Karnac, 1979].

Abraham, Karl (1969). *Psychoanalytische Studien I* [Psychoanalytic Studies I] (ed. Johannes Cremerius). Frankfurt/Main: S. Fischer.

Abraham, Karl (1976). Klein Hilda: Tagträume und ein Symptom bei einem siebenjährigen Mädchen [Little Hilda: Day dreams and a symptom of a seven-year-old girl.] In: Hilda Abraham, *Karl Abraham: Sein Leben für die Psychoanalyse* (pp. 173–182). Munich: Kindler.

Abraham, Karl (1991). Six lettres inédites de K. Abraham à W. Fließ [Six hitherto unpublished letters of K. Abraham to W. Fließ]. *Littoral*, No. 31–32 (Mar): 247–257.

Abraham, Karl, & Keibel, Franz (1900[1]). Normentafel zur Entwicklungsgeschichte des Huhnes [Standardization table of the development of the fowl]. *Normentafeln zur Entwicklungsgeschichte der Wirbeltiere*, No. 2, Jena.

Adler, Alfred (1910). Der psychische Hermaphroditismus im Leben und in der Neurose [On psychic hermaphroditism in life and in neurosis]. *Fortschritte der Medizin, 28*: 486–493. In: Alfred Adler & Carl Furtmüller, *Heilen und Bilden: Ein Buch der Erziehungskunst für Ärzte und Pädagogen* (pp. 85–93). Frankfurt/Main: Fischer, 1973.

Adler, Alfred (1912). *Über den nervösen Charakter: Grundzüge einer vergleichenden Individual-Psychologie und Psychotherapie*. Frankfurt/Main: Fischer Taschenbuch Verlag, 1972. *The Neurotic Constitution*. New York, 1917. *The Neurotic Character: Fundamentals of a Comparative Individual Psychology and Psychotherapy*. San Francisco, CA: Classical Adlerian Translation Project–Alfred Adler Institute of San Francisco, 2002.

Adler, Alfred, & Furtmüller, Carl (Eds.) (1973 [1914]). *Heilen und Bilden: Ein Buch der Erziehungskunst für Ärzte und Pädagogen*. Frankfurt/Main: Fischer.

Alexander, Franz (1926). Neurose und Gesamtpersönlichkeit. *Internationale Zeitschrift für Psychoanalyse*, 12: 334–347. Neurosis and the whole personality. *International Journal of Psycho-Analysis*, 7: 340–352.

Alexander, Franz, & Selesnick, Sheldon T. (1965). Freud–Bleuler correspondence. *Archives of General Psychiatry*, 12: 1–9.

Alexander, Franz; Eisenstein, Samuel, & Grotjahn, Martin (Eds.) (1966). *Psychoanalytic Pioneers*. New York: Basic Books.

Andreas-Salomé, Lou (1913). Vom frühen Gottesdienst [Early religion]. *Imago, Zeitschrift für Anwendung der Psychoanalyse auf die Geisteswissenschaften*, 2: 457–467.

Andreas-Salomé, Lou (1914). Zum Typus Weib [The feminine type]. *Imago, Zeitschrift für Anwendung der Psychoanalyse auf die Geisteswissenschaften*, 3: 1–14.

Andreas-Salomé, Lou (1916). "Anal" und "sexual" [Anal and sexual]. *Imago, Zeitschrift für Anwendung der Psychoanalyse auf die Geisteswissenschaften*, 4: 249–273.

Andreas-Salomé, Lou (1917). Psychosexualität [Psychosexuality]. *Zeitschrift für Sexualwissenschaft*, 4: 1–12, 49–57.

Andreas-Salomé, Lou (1958). *In der Schule bei Freud, Tagebuch eines Jahres (1912/13)*. Frankfurt/Main: Ullstein, 1983. *The Freud Journal of Lou Andreas-Salomé*. London: Hogarth, 1965. New York: Basic Books, 1964.

Baroncini, Luigi (1908). Il fondamento e il meccanismo della psicoanalisi. *Rivista di Psicologia Applicata*, 4 (3): 211–213.

Beltrán, Juan Ramon (1923). *La Psicoanalisis al servicio de la crimilogia*. Buenos Aires: Talleres graficos de la penitenciaria nacional.

Benedek, Therese (1925). Aus der Analyse eines Falles von Erythrophobie. *Internationale Zeitschrift für Psychoanalyse*, 11: 88–95. Notes from the analysis of a case of ereuthophobia. *International Journal of Psycho-Analysis*, 6: 430–439.

Benedek, Therese (1973). *Psychoanalytic Investigations: Selected Papers by Therese Benedek*. New York: Quadrangle.

*Bericht über die Fortschritte der Psychoanalyse in den Jahren 1914–1919* [Report on the progress of psychoanalysis, 1914–1919] (1921). Leipzig: Internationaler Psychoanalytischer Verlag.

Binion, Rudolph (1968). *Frau Lou: Nietzsche's Wayward Disciple*. Princeton, NJ: Princeton University Press.

Binswanger, Ludwig (1909). Versuch einer Hysterieanalyse (1. Teil) [An at-

tempt of the analysis of a case of hysteria, part 1]. *Jahrbuch für psychoanalytische und psychopathologische Forschungen, 1* (1): 174–318.
Binswanger, Ludwig (1922). *Einführung in die Probleme der allgemeinen Psychologie* [Introduction to the problems of general psychology]. Berlin: Springer.
Binswanger, Ludwig (1956). *Erinnerungen an Sigmund Freud*. Bern: Francke. *Sigmund Freud: Reminiscences of a Friendship*. New York: Grune & Stratton, 1957.
Bleuler, Eugen (1909). Zurechnungsfähigkeit und Krankheit [Accountability and illness]. *Centralblatt für Nervenheilkunde und Psychiatrie, 20*: 241–246.
Bleuler, Eugen (1910). Die Psychoanalyse Freuds: Verteidigung und kritische Bemerkungen [Freud's psychoanalysis: Defense and critical remarks]. *Jahrbuch für psychoanalytische und psychopathologische Forschungen, 2* (2): 623–730.
Bleuler, Eugen (1911). *Dementia Praecox, oder die Gruppe der Schizophrenien*. In: G. Aschaffenburg (Ed.), *Handbuch der Psychiatrie*. Leipzig, Vienna: Deuticke. *Dementia Praecox, or The Group of Schizophrenias*. New York: International Universities Press, 1950.
Bleuler, Eugen (1912). Das autistische Denken [Autistic thinking]. *Jahrbuch für psychoanalytische und psychopathologische Forschungen, 4* (1): 1–39.
Bleuler, Eugen (1913a). Kritik der Freudschen Theorien [Criticism of Freud's theories]. *Allgemeine Zeitschrift für Psychiatrie, 70*: 665–719.
Bleuler, Eugen (1913b). Das Unbewußte [The unconscious]. *Journal für Psychologie und Neurologie, 20*: E89–E92.
Bleuler, Eugen (1916). Physisch und Psychisch in der Pathologie, nach einem Vortrag gehalten in der Gesellschaft der Ärzte in Zürich in der Sitzung vom 30. Jan. 1915 [The physical and psychic in pathology according to a lecture given at the meeting of the Society of Physicians in Zurich on 30 Jan. 1915]. *Zeitschrift für die gesamte Neurologie und Psychiatrie, 30* (4, 5). In book form: Berlin: Springer.
Bleuler, Eugen (1916). *Lehrbuch der Psychiatrie*. Berlin: Springer. *Textbook of Psychiatry*. London: Allen & Unwin, 1923. New York: Arno Press, 1976.
Bleuler, Eugen, & Jung, Carl Gustav (1908). Komplexe und Krankheitsursache bei Dementia praecox [Complexes and aetiology in dementia praecox]. *Zentralblatt für Nervenheilkunde und Psychiatrie, 31* (Mar.): 220–226.
Boehm, Felix (1920). Beiträge zur Psychologie der Homosexualität [Contributions to the psychology of homosexuality]. I. Homosexualität und Polygamie [Homosexuality and polygamy]. *Internationale Zeitschrift für Psychoanalyse, 6*: 297–319.
Boehm, Felix (1922). Beiträge zur Psychologie der Homosexualität. II. Ein Traum eines Homosexuellen [A dream of a homosexual]. *Internationale Zeitschrift für Psychoanalyse, 8*: 313–320.
Boehm, Felix (1926). Beiträge zur Psychologie der Homosexualität. III. Homosexualität und Ödipuskomplex [Homosexuality and Oedipus complex]. *Internationale Zeitschrift für Psychoanalyse, 12*: 66–79.
Boehm, Felix (1933). Beiträge zur Psychologie der Homosexualität. IV. Über

zwei Typen von männlichen Homosexuellen [Concerning two types of male homosexuals]. *Internationale Zeitschrift für Psychoanalyse, 19*: 499–506.

Bonomi, Carlo (1996). Der Traum von Irma: der Körper, das Wort, die Schuld [The dream of Irma: the body, the word, the guilt]. *texte; psychoanalyse, ästhetik, kulturkritik, 4*: 7–34.

Breasted, James Henry (1905). *A History of Egypt, from the Earliest Times to the Persian Conquest: With Two Hundred Illustrations and Maps.* New York: Charles Scribner's Sons.

Brecht, Karen (n.d.). *"Here Life Goes On in a Most Peculiar Way": Psychoanalysis before and after 1933.* London: Goethe Institute.

Breuer, Josef, & Freud, Sigmund (1895d). *Studien über Hysterie. G.W. I* (pp. 75–312), *G.W., Nachtr.* (pp. 217–218, 221–310). *Studies on Hysteria. S.E., 2* (pp. 1–305).

Brill, Abraham A. (1936). Introduction. In: Carl Gustav Jung, *The Psychology of Dementia Praecox* (pp. vii–ix). New York, Washington: Nervous and Mental Diseases Publishing Company.

Burnham, John C. (1983). *Jelliffe: American Psychoanalyst and Physician and His Correspondence with Sigmund Freud and C. G. Jung* (ed. William McGuire). Chicago, IL: The University of Chicago Press.

Burns, Robert (1986). *The Complete Works of Robert Burns* (ed. James A. Mackay). Ayrshire: Alloway.

Burrow, Trigant (1958). *A Search for Man's Sanity: Selected Letters of Trigant Burrow.* New York: Oxford University Press.

Cameron, Laura, & Forrester, John (1999). "A nice type of the English scientist": Tansley and Freud. *History Workshop Journal, 48*: 65–100.

Cameron, Laura, & Forrester, John (2000). Tansley's psychoanalytic network: An episode out of the early history of psychoanalysis in England. *Psychoanalysis and History, 2* (2): 189–256.

Caravedo, Baltazar (1924). Actitudes regresivas en los esquizofrenicos [Regressive attitudes in schizophrenics]. *Revista de Psiquiatria, 5(2)*.

Carotenuto, Aldo (Ed.) (1980). *Diario di una segreta simmetria: Sabina Spielrein tra Jung e Freud.* Rome: Ubaldina. *A Secret Symmetry: Sabina Spielrein between Jung and Freud.* New York: Pantheon, 1982.

Chalewsky, Fanny (1909). Heilung eines hysterischen Bellens durch Psychoanalyse [A cure of hysterical barking through psychoanalysis]. *Zentralblatt für Nervenheilkunde und Psychiatrie*, n.s., *20*.

Clark, L. Pierce (1926). Über die Phantasie-Methode bei der Analyse narzisstischer Neurosen. *Internationale Zeitschrift für Psychoanalyse, 12*: 457–465. The phantasy method of analyzing narcissistic neuroses. *Archives of Psychoanalysis, 1*: 226.

Clark, Ronald W. (1980). *Freud: The Man and the Cause.* New York: Random House.

Coles, Robert (1992). *Anna Freud: The Dream of Psychoanalysis.* Reading, MA: Adddison-Wesley.

Coriat, Isador H. (1927). The oral-erotic components of stammering. *International Journal of Psycho-Analysis*, 8: 56–62.
Delgado, Honorio F. (1919). *El Psicoanálisis*. Lima: Sammarti.
De Mijolla, Alain (1992). France 1893–1965. In: Peter Kutter (Ed.), *Psychoanalysis International, Vol. 2* (pp. 66–113). Stuttgart: frommann-holzboog.
Deutsch, Helene (1925a). Psychologie des Weibes in den Funktionen der Fortpflanzung. *Internationale Zeitschrift für Psychoanalyse*, 11: 40–53. The psychology of women in relation to the functions of reproduction. *International Journal of Psycho-Analysis*, 6: 430–439. In: *The Therapeutic Process, the Self, and Female Psychology: Collected Psychoanalytic Papers of Helene Deutsch* (ed. Paul Roazen) (pp. 3–16), 1992.
Deutsch, Helene (1925b). Beitrag zur Psychologie des Sports. *Internationale Zeitschrift für Psychoanalyse*, 11: 222–226. A contribution to the psychology of sports. *International Journal of Psycho-Analysis*, 7 (1926): 223–227.
Deutsch, Helene (1991). *Psychoanalysis of the Sexual Functions of Women* (ed. Paul Roazen). London: Karnac.
Deutsch, Helene (1992). *The Therapeutic Process, the Self, and Female Psychology: Collected Psychoanalytic Papers of Helene Deutsch* (ed. Paul Roazen). New Brunswick, NJ: Transaction Publishers.
Edmunds, Lavinia (1988). His master's choice. *Johns Hopkins Magazine* (Apr.): 40–49.
Eissler, Kurt R. (1971). *Talent and Genius*. New York: Grove.
Eissler, Kurt R. (1979). *Freud und Wagner-Jauregg vor der Kommission zur Erhebung militärischer Pflichtverletzungen*. Vienna: Löcker. *Freud as an Expert Witness: The Discussion of War Neuroses Between Freud and Wagner-Jauregg*. Madison, CT: International Universities Press, 1986.
Eissler, Kurt R. (1983). *Victor Tausk's Suicide*. New York: International Universities Press.
Eissler, Kurt R. (1995). Ärztliche Schweigepflicht und wissenschaftliche Forschung. Bemerkungen zur Glosse Gerhard Fichtners [Medical confidentiality and scientific research. Comments on Gerhard Fichtner's Glossary] *Psyche*, 49: 182–183.
Eitingon, Max (1931). Dr. Hans Liebermann, Berlin † [obit.]. *Internationale Zeitschrift für Psychoanalyse*, 17: 296–927.
Ellenberger, Henri F. (1970). *The Discovery of the Unconscious: The History of the Evolution of Dynamic Psychiatry*. New York: Basic Books.
Ellis, Havelock (1910). Review of Freud, Leonardo da Vinci and a memory of his childhood. *Journal of Mental Science*, 56: 522–523.
Ellis, Havelock (1919). *The Philosophy of Conflict, and Other Essays in War-Time* (second series). London: Constable.
Engelbrecht, Hilke, & Castro, Alvaro Rey de (1995). Peru. In: Peter Kutter (Ed.), *Pschoanalysis International, Vol. 2* (pp. 160–173). Stuttgart: frommann-holzboog.
Erikson, Erik H. (1950). *Childhood and Society*. New York: Norton [second, enlarged edition, 1963].

Eulenburg, Albert (1916). *Moralität und Sexualität* [Morality and sexuality]. Bonn: Marcus & Weber.
Fallend, Karl, & Reichmayr, Johannes (Eds.) (1992). *Siegfried Bernfeld oder die Grenzen der Psychoanalyse: Materialien zu Leben und Werk* [Siegfried Bernfeld, or The limits of psychoanalysis. Materials on life and work]. Basel: Stroemfeld/Nexus.
Falzeder, Ernst (1992). 1924—le trauma de naissance de nouvelles perspectives en psychanalyse [1924—The trauma of birth of new perspecives in psychoanalysis]. *Psychothérapies, 12:* 241–250.
Falzeder, Ernst (1993). Einleitung [Introduction]. In: Sigmund Freud & Sándor Ferenczi, *Briefwechsel, Vol. 1/2: 1912–1914* (pp. 7–25). Vienna: Böhlau.
Falzeder, Ernst (1994a). My grand-patient, my chief tormentor. A hitherto unnoticed case of Freud's and the consequences. *Psychoanalytic Quarterly, 63:* 297–331.
Falzeder, Ernst (1994b). The threads of psychoanalytic filiations or Psychoanalysis taking effect. In: A. Haynal & E. Falzeder (Eds.), *100 Years of Psychoanalysis, Contributions to the History of Psychoanalysis* (pp. 169–194). Geneva, Switzerland: Cahiers Psychiatriques Genevois, Special Issue.
Ferenczi, Sándor (1909[66]). Az álom psychoanalysise és annak kórtani jelentösége. *Orvosi Hetilap, 44–45.* On the psychological analysis of dreams. *American Journal of Psychology, 21* (1910): 309–328.
Ferenczi, Sandor (1909[67]). Introjektion und Übertragung. In: Michael Balint (Ed.), *Schriften zur Psychoanalyse I.* Frankfurt/Main: S. Fischer, 1970. Introjection and Transference. *First Contributions to Psychoanalysis.* London: Hogarth Press, 1952.
Ferenczi, Sándor (1910[69]). Referat über die Notwendigkeit eines engeren Zusammenschlusses der Anhänger der Freudschen Lehre und Vorschläge zur Gründung einer ständigen internationalen Organisation [Report on the necessity of a closer amalgamation of the adherents to Freudian doctrine and suggestions for founding a permanent international organization]. Abstract in *Zentralblatt für Psychoanalyse: Medizinische Monatsschrift für Seelenkunde, 1* (1910–11): 131.
Ferenczi, Sándor (1911[79]). A psychoanalytikusok szervezkedése. *Gyógyászat, 31.* On the organization of the psycho-analytic movement. *Final Contributions to the Problems and Methods of Psychoanalysis* (pp. 299–307), 1955.
Ferenczi, Sándor (1913[109]). Glaube, Unglaube und Überzeugung. *Schriften zur Psychoanalyse I* (pp. 135–147). Frankfurt/Main: S. Fischer, 1970. Belief, disbelief and conviction. *Further Contributions to the Theory and Technique of Psycho-Analysis* (pp. 437–450), 1926.
Ferenczi, Sándor (1913[124]). C. G. Jung, *Wandlungen und Symbole der Libido* [Review of C. G. Jung, Transformations and symbolisms of the libido]. *Internationale Zeitschrift für ärztliche Psychoanalyse, 1:* 391–403.
Ferenczi, Sándor (1914[148]). Allgemeine Neurosenlehre (Sammelreferat) [General theory of the neuroses (collective review)]. *Jahrbuch der Psychoanalyse, Neue Folge des Jahrbuchs für psychoanalytische und psychopathologische Forschungen, 6:* 317–328.

Ferenczi, Sándor (1915[175]). Die psychiatrische Schule von Bordeaux über die Psychoanalyse [The psychiatric school of Bordeaux on psychoanalysis]. *Internationale Zeitschrift für ärztliche Psychoanalyse*, 3: 352–369.

Ferenczi, Sándor (1916[186]). *Contributions to Psychoanalysis*. Boston: R. G. Badger.

Ferenczi, Sándor (1916[189]). Über zwei Typen der Kriegsneurose. *Internationale Zeitschrift für ärztliche Psychoanalyse*, 4 (1916/17): 131–145. Two types of war neuroses. *Further Contributions to the Theory and Technique of Psycho-Analysis* (pp. 124–141), 1926.

Ferenczi, Sándor (1916[190]). Mischgebilde von erotischen und Charakterzügen. *Internationale Zeitschrift für ärztliche Psychoanalyse*, 4 (1916/17): 146–147. Composite forms of erotic and character traits. *Further Contributions to the Theory and Technique of Psycho-Analysis* (pp. 257–259). London: Hogarth Press, 1926.

Ferenczi, Sándor (1916[191]). Schweigen ist Gold. *Internationale Zeitschrift für ärztliche Psychoanalyse*, 4 (1916/17): 155–156. Silence is golden. *Further Contributions to the Theory and Technique of Psycho-Analysis* (pp. 250–251), 1926.

Ferenczi, Sándor (1917[195]). Von Krankheits- oder Pathoneurosen. *Internationale Zeitschrift für ärztliche Psychoanalyse*, 4 (1916/17): 219–228. Disease- or patho-neuroses. *Further Contributions to the Theory and Technique of Psycho-Analysis* (pp. 78–94), 1926.

Ferenczi, Sándor (1917[204]). Putnam, J. J. The work of Alfred Adler, considered with especial reference to that of Freud. *Internationale Zeitschrift für ärztliche Psychoanalyse*, 4 (1916–17): 161–163.

Ferenczi, Sándor (1917[205]). Schultz, J. H. S. Freud's Sexualpsychoanalyse [Review of J. H. Schultz, S. Freud's sexual psychoanalysis]. *Internationale Zeitschrift für ärztliche Psychoanalyse*, 4 (1916–17): 270–272.

Ferenczi, Sándor (1919[210]). Technische Schwierigkeiten einer Hysterieanalyse (Zugleich Beobachtungen über larvierte Onanie und "Onanie-Äquivalente"). *Internationale Zeitschrift für ärztliche Psychoanalyse*, 5: 34–40. Technical difficulties in an analysis of hysteria (including observations on larval forms of onanism and "onanistic equivalents". *Further Contributions to the Theory and Technique of Psycho-Analysis* (pp. 189–197), 1926.

Ferenczi, Sándor (1919[223]). *Hysterie und Pathoneurosen* [Hysteria and pathoneuroses]. Internationale Psychoanalytische Bibliothek, No. 2. Leipzig: Internationaler Psychoanalytischer Verlag.

Ferenczi, Sándor (1924[268]). *Versuch einer Genitaltheorie*. Leipzig: Internationaler Psychoanalytischer Verlag. *Thalassa; Theory of Genitality*. Albany, NY: The Psychoanalytic Quarterly Inc., 1938.

Ferenczi, Sándor (1925[269]). Zur Psychoanalyse von Sexualgewohnheiten (mit Beiträgen zur therapeutischen Technik). *Internationale Zeitschrift für ärztliche Psychoanalyse*, 11: 6–39. In book form: Leipzig: Internationaler Psychoanalytischer Verlag. Psychoanalysis of sexual habits (with contributions about therapeutic technique). *Further Contributions to the Theory and Technique of Psycho-Analysis* (pp. 259–297), 1926.

Ferenczi, Sándor (1926). *Further Contributions to the Theory and Technique of Psychoanalysis*. London: Hogarth Press [reprinted London: Karnac, 1980].

Ferenczi, Sándor (1955). *Final Contributions to the Problems and Methods of Psychoanalysis*. New York: Basic Books [reprinted London: Karnac, 1980].

Ferenczi, Sándor, & Rank, Otto (1924). *Entwicklungsziele der Psychoanalyse: Zur Wechselbeziehung von Theorie und Praxis* (Neue Arbeiten zur ärztlichen Psychoanalyse No. 1). Leipzig: Internationaler Psychoanalytischer Verlag. *The Development of Psychoanalysis*. New York: Nervous and Mental Disease Publishing Co., 1925. Madison, CT: International Universities Press, 1986.

Fichtner, Gerhard (1992). Einleitung [Introduction]. In: Sigmund Freud & Ludwig Binswanger, *Briefwechsel 1908–1938* (pp. ix–xxxi), 1992.

Fichtner, Gerhard (1994). Die ärztliche Schweigepflicht, der Analytiker und der Historiker [Medical confidentiality, the analyst, and the historian]. *Psyche, 48*: 738ff.

Fliess, Wilhelm (1914). Männlich und Weiblich [Male and female]. *Zeitschrift für Sexualwissenschaft, 1* (1).

Flugel, John Carl (1921). *The Psychoanalytic Study of the Family*. London: Hogarth Press.

Frank, Leonhard (1915). *Die Ursache: Erzählung*. Leipzig: Insel Verlag. *The Cause of the Crime*. London: P. Davis, 1928.

Frank, Ludwig (1908). Zur Psychanalyse (Festschrift für Forel) [On psychoanalysis. Festschrift in honor of Forel]. *Journal für Psychologie und Neurologie, 13*: 126–135.

Freud, Ernst, Freud, Lucie, & Grubrich-Simitis, Ilse (1974). *Sigmund Freud: Sein Leben in Bildern und Texten*. Frankfurt/Main: Insel Verlag, 1989. *Sigmund Freud: His Life in Pictures and Words*. New York: Harcourt Brace Jovanovich, 1978. London: André Deutsch, 1978.

Freud, Martin (1958). *Sigmund Freud: Man and Father*. New York: Aronson, 1983.

Freud, Sigmund (1878a). Über Spinalganglien und Rückenmark des Petromyzon. *Sitzungsberichte der Akademie der Wissenschaften in Wien* (Math.-Naturwiss. Kl.), 78 (3): 81–167.

Freud, Sigmund (1884e). Über Coca. *Centralblatt für die gesamte Therapie*, 2: 289–314. Coca. *The Saint Louis Medical and Surgical Journal*, 47 (6): 502–505. In: Sigmund Freud, *The Cocaine Papers*. Vienna: Dunquin Press, 1963.

Freud, Sigmund (1891b). *Zur Auffassung der Aphasien*. Leipzig, Vienna: Deuticke. [Partly in *S.E., 14* (pp. 206–215).] Reprint Frankfurt/Main: Fischer, 1992.

Freud, Sigmund (1895b). Über die Berechtigung, von der Neurasthenie einen bestimmten Symptomenkomplex als "Angst-Neurose" abzutrennen. *G.W. I* (pp. 315–342). On the grounds for detaching a particular syndrome from neurasthenia under the description "anxiety neurosis". *S.E., 3* (pp. 90–115).

Freud, Sigmund (1896b). Weitere Bemerkungen über die Abwehr-Neuropsychosen. *G.W. I* (pp. 379–403). Further remarks on the neuro-psychoses of defence. *S.E., 3* (pp. 162–185).

Freud, Sigmund (1896c). Zur Ätiologie der Hysterie. *G.W. I* (pp. 425–459). The aetiology of hysteria. *S.E., 3* (pp. 191–221).

Freud, Sigmund (1900a). *Die Traumdeutung. G.W. II/III. The Interpretation of Dreams. S.E.,* 4 and 5.

Freud, Sigmund (1901a). Über den Traum. *G.W. II/III* (pp. 643–700). On Dreams. *S.E., 5* (pp. 633–686).

Freud, Sigmund (1901b). *Zur Psychopathologie des Alltagslebens (Über Vergessen, Versprechen, Vergreifen, Aberglaube und Irrtum). G.W. IV. The Psychopathology of Everyday Life. S.E., 6.*

Freud, Sigmund (1904f). Rezension von [Book review of]: Löwenfeld, Leopold, *Die psychischen Zwangserscheinungen. G.W. Nachtr.* (pp. 496–499).

Freud, Sigmund (1905c). *Der Witz und seine Beziehung zum Unbewußten. G.W. VI. Jokes and Their Relation to the Unconscious. S.E., 8.*

Freud, Sigmund (1905d). Drei Abhandlungen zur Sexualtheorie. *G.W. V* (pp. 27, 33–145). Three Essays on the Theory of Sexuality. *S.E., 7* (pp. 135–243).

Freud, Sigmund (1905e [1901]). Bruchstück einer Hysterie-Analyse. *G.W. V* (pp. 161–286). Fragment of an analysis of a case of hysteria. *S.E., 7* (pp. 7–122).

Freud, Sigmund (1906a [1905]). Meine Ansichten über die Rolle der Sexualität in der Ätiologie der Neurosen. *G.W. V* (pp. 149–159). My views on the part played by sexuality in the aetiology of the neuroses. *S.E., 7* (pp. 271–279).

Freud, Sigmund (1907a [1906]). Der Wahn und die Träume in W. Jensens "Gradiva". *G.W. VII* (pp. 29–122). Delusions and Dreams in Jensen's "Gradiva". *S.E., 9* (pp. 7–93).

Freud, Sigmund (1908a). Hysterische Phantasien und ihre Beziehung zur Bisexualität. *G.W. VII* (pp. 191–199). Hysterical phantasies and their relation to bisexuality. *S.E., 9* (pp. 159–166).

Freud, Sigmund (1908b). Charakter und Analerotik. *G.W. VII* (pp. 203–209). Character and anal erotism. *S.E., 9* (pp. 169–175).

Freud, Sigmund (1908c). Über infantile Sexualtheorien. *G.W. VII* (pp. 171–188). On the sexual theories of children. *S.E., 9* (pp. 209–226).

Freud, Sigmund (1908d). Die "kulturelle" Sexualmoral und die moderne Nervosität. *G.W. VII* (pp. 143–167). "Civilized" sexual morality and modern nervous illness. *S.E., 9* (pp. 181–204).

Freud, Sigmund (1908e [1907]). Der Dichter und das Phantasieren. *G.W. VII* (pp. 213–223). Creative writers and day-dreaming. *S.E., 9* (pp. 143–153).

Freud, Sigmund (1908f). "Vorwort" zu Stekel, W., *Nervöse Angstzustände und ihre Behandlung. G.W. VII* (pp. 467–468). Preface to Wilhelm Stekel's *Nervous Anxiety-States and Their Treatment. S.E., 9* (pp. 250–251).

Freud, Sigmund (1909a [1908]). Allgemeines über den hysterischen Anfall. *G.W. VII* (pp. 235–240). Some general remarks on hysterical attacks. *S.E., 9* (pp. 229–234).

Freud, Sigmund (1909b). Analyse der Phobie eines fünfjährigen Knaben. *G.W. VII* (pp. 241–377). Analysis of a phobia in a five-year-old boy. *S.E., 10* (pp. 5–147).
Freud, Sigmund (1909d). Bemerkungen über einen Fall von Zwangsneurose. *G.W. VII* (pp. 379–463). Notes upon a case of obsessional neurosis. *S.E., 10* (pp. 155–249).
Freud, Sigmund (1910a [1909]). *Über Psychoanalyse. G.W. VIII* (pp. 1–60). The origin and development of psychoanalysis. *American Journal of Psychology, 21:* 181–218. Five Lectures on Psycho-Analysis, *S.E., 11* (pp. 7–55). On Psychoanalysis. Five Lectures. In: Saul Rosenzweig, *Freud, Jung, and Hall the King-Maker. The Historic Expedition to America with G. Stanley Hall as Host and William James as Guest* (pp. 395–438), 1992.
Freud, Sigmund (1910c). *Eine Kindheitserinnerung des Leonardo da Vinci. G.W. VIII* (pp. 127–211). Leonardo Da Vinci and a Memory of His Childhood. *S.E., 11* (pp. 63–137).
Freud, Sigmund (1910d). Die zukünftigen Chancen der psychoanalytischen Therapie. *G.W. VIII* (pp. 104–115). The future prospects of psycho-analytic therapy. *S.E., 11* (pp. 141–151).
Freud, Sigmund (1910e). Über den Gegensinn der Urworte. *G.W. VIII* (pp. 214–221). The antithetical meaning of primal words. *S.E., 11* (pp. 155–161).
Freud, Sigmund (1910f). Brief an Dr. Friedrich S. Krauss (26.6.1910) über die *Anthropophyteia. G.W. VIII* (pp. 224–225). Letter to Dr. Friedrich S. Krauss on *Anthropophyteia. S.E., 11* (pp. 233–235).
Freud, Sigmund (1910h). Über einen besonderen Typus der Objektwahl beim Manne (Beiträge zur Psychologie des Liebeslebens I). *G.W. VIII* (pp. 66–77). A special type of choice of object made by men (Contributions to the psychology of love I). *S.E., 11* (pp. 165–175).
Freud, Sigmund (1910k). Über "wilde" Psychoanalyse. *G.W. VIII* (pp. 118–125). "Wild" psycho-analysis. *S.E., 11* (pp. 221–227).
Freud, Sigmund (1911b). Formulierungen über die zwei Prinzipien des psychischen Geschehens. *G.W. VIII* (pp. 230–238). Formulations on the two principles of mental functioning. *S.E., 12* (pp. 218–226).
Freud, Sigmund (1911e). Die Handhabung der Traumdeutung in der Psychoanalyse. *G.W. VIII* (pp. 350–357). The handling of dream-interpretation in psycho-analysis. *S.E., 12* (pp. 89–96).
Freud, Sigmund (1911c [1910]). Psychoanalytische Bemerkungen über einen autobiographisch beschriebenen Fall von Paranoia (Dementia paranoides). *G.W. VIII* (pp. 239–316). Psycho-analytic notes on an autobiographical account of a case of paranoia (dementia paranoides). *S.E., 12* (pp. 9–79).
Freud, Sigmund (1911j). Übersetzung mit zusätzlicher Fußnote von Putnam, J.J., On the etiology and treatment of the psychoneuroses. Footnote in *G.W., Nachtr.* (p. 766) and *S.E., 17* (pp. 271–272).
Freud, Sigmund (1912a [1911]). Nachtrag zu dem autobiographisch beschrie-

## REFERENCES

benen Fall von Paranoia (Dementia paranoides). *G.W. VIII* (pp. 317–320). Postscript. *S.E., 12* (pp. 80–82).

Freud, Sigmund (1912b). Zur Dynamik der Übertragung. *G.W. VIII* (pp. 364–374). The dynamics of transference. *S.E., 12* (pp. 97–108).

Freud, Sigmund (1912c). Über neurotische Erkrankungstypen. *G.W. VIII* (pp. 322–330). Types of onset of neurosis. *S.E., 12* (pp. 231–238).

Freud, Sigmund (1912d). Über die allgemeinste Erniedrigung des Liebeslebens (Beiträge zur Psychologie des Liebeslebens II). *G.W. VIII* (pp. 78–91). On the universal tendency to debasement in the sphere of love. *S.E., 11* (pp. 179–190).

Freud, Sigmund (1912e). Ratschläge für den Arzt bei der psychoanalytischen Behandlung. *G.W. VIII* (pp. 376–387). Recommendations to physicians practising psycho-analysis. *S.E., 12* (pp. 109–120).

Freud, Sigmund (1912g). A note on the unconscious in psycho-analysis. *S.E., 12* (pp. 260–266). [First published in English.]

Freud, Sigmund (1912h). Nachfrage über Kindheitsträume. *G.W. Nachtr.* (p. 612). [Quoted in Editor's Note, *S.E., 17* (p. 4).]

Freud, Sigmund (1912–13). *Totem und Tabu. G.W. IX. Totem and Taboo. S.E., 13* (pp. vii, xiii–xiv, 1–161).

Freud, Sigmund (1913a). Ein Traum als Beweismittel. *G.W. X* (pp. 12–22). An evidential dream. *S.E., 12* (pp. 269–277).

Freud, Sigmund (1913c). Zur Einleitung der Behandlung (Weitere Ratschläge zur Technik der Psychoanalyse, I). *G.W. VIII* (pp. 454–478). On beginning the treatment (Further recommendations on the technique of psychoanalysis I). *S.E., 12* (pp. 121–144).

Freud, Sigmund (1913f). Das Motiv der Kästchenwahl. *G.W. X* (pp. 24–37). The theme of the three caskets. *S.E., 12* (pp. 291–301).

Freud, Sigmund (1913g). Zwei Kinderlügen. *G.W. VIII* (pp. 422–427). Two lies told by children. *S.E., 12* (pp. 305–309).

Freud, Sigmund (1913i). Die Disposition zur Zwangsneurose. Ein Beitrag zum Problem der Neurosenwahl. *G.W. VIII* (pp. 442–452). The disposition to obsessional neurosis (A contribution to the problem of choice of neurosis). *S.E., 12* (pp. 317–326).

Freud, Sigmund (1913j). Das Interesse an der Psychoanalyse. *G.W. VIII* (pp. 389–420). The claims of psycho-analysis to scientific interest. *S.E., 13* (pp. 165–190).

Freud, Sigmund (1914b). Der Moses des Michelangelo. *G.W. X* (pp. 172–201). The Moses of Michelangelo. *S.E., 13* (pp. 211–236).

Freud, Sigmund (1914c). Zur Einführung des Narzißmus. *G.W. X* (pp. 137–170). On narcissism. An introduction. *S.E., 14* (pp. 73–102).

Freud, Sigmund (1914d). Zur Geschichte der psychoanalytischen Bewegung. *G.W. X* (pp. 43–113). On the history of the psycho-analytic movement. *S.E., 14* (pp. 7–66).

Freud, Sigmund (1914g). Erinnern, Wiederholen und Durcharbeiten (Weitere Ratschläge zur Technik der Psychoanalyse, II). *G.W. X* (pp. 126–136).

Remembering, repeating and working-through (Further recommendations on the technique of psycho-analysis II). *S.E.*, *12* (pp. 145–156).
Freud, Sigmund (1915a [1914]). Bemerkungen über die Übertragungsliebe (Weitere Ratschläge zur Technik der Psychoanalyse, III). *G.W. X* (pp. 306–321). Observations on transference love (Further recommendations on the technique of psycho-analysis III). *S.E.*, *12* (pp. 157–171).
Freud, Sigmund (1915b). Zeitgemäßes über Krieg und Tod. *G.W. X* (pp. 324–355). Thoughts for the times on war and death. *S.E.*, *14* (pp. 275–300).
Freud, Sigmund (1915c). Triebe und Triebschicksale. *G.W. X* (pp. 210–232). Instincts and their vicissitudes. *S.E.*, *14* (pp. 117–140).
Freud, Sigmund (1915d). Die Verdrängung. *G.W. X* (pp. 248–261). Repression. *S.E.*, *14* (pp. 146–158).
Freud, Sigmund (1915e). Das Unbewußte. *G.W. X* (pp. 264–303). The unconscious. *S.E.*, *14* (pp. 166–204).
Freud, Sigmund (1915f). Mitteilung eines der psychoanalytischen Theorie widersprechenden Falles von Paranoia. *G.W. X* (pp. 234–246). A case of paranoia running counter to the psycho-analytic theory of the disease. *S.E.*, *14* (pp. 263–272).
Freud, Sigmund (1915g). Brief an Dr. Frederik van Eeden (28.12.1914). *Uit de Groene*, 17 Jan. (p. 3). *G.W. Nachtr.* (pp. 697–698). Letter to Dr. F. van Eeden. *S.E.*, *14* (pp. 301–302).
Freud, Sigmund (1916c). Eine Beziehung zwischen einem Symbol und einem Symptom. *G.W. X* (pp. 394–395). A connection between a symbol and a symptom. *S.E.*, *14* (pp. 339–340).
Freud, Sigmund (1916d). Einige Charaktertypen aus der psychoanalytischen Arbeit. *G.W. X* (pp. 364–391). Some character-types met with in psycho-analytic work. *S.E.*, *14* (pp. 311–333).
Freud, Sigmund (1916–17 [1915–17]). *Vorlesungen zur Einführung in die Psychoanalyse*. *G.W. XI*. *Introductory Lectures on Psycho-Analysis*. *S.E.*, *15*.
Freud, Sigmund (1917a). Eine Schwierigkeit der Psychoanalyse. *G.W. XII* (pp. 3–12). A difficulty in the path of psycho-analysis. *S.E.*, *17* (pp. 137–144).
Freud, Sigmund (1917c). Über Triebumsetzungen, insbesondere der Analerotik. *G.W. X* (pp. 402–410). On transformations of instincts as exemplified in anal erotism. *S.E.*, *17* (pp. 127–133).
Freud, Sigmund (1917d [1915]). Metapsychologische Ergänzung zur Traumlehre. *G.W. X* (pp. 412–426). A metapsychological supplement to the theory of dreams. *S.E.*, *14* (pp. 222–235).
Freud, Sigmund (1917e [1915]). Trauer und Melancholie. *G.W. X* (pp. 428–446). Mourning and melancholia. *S.E.*, *14* (pp. 243–258).
Freud, Sigmund (1918a [1917]). Das Tabu der Virginität (Beiträge zur Psychologie des Liebeslebens III). *G.W. XII* (pp. 159–180). The taboo of virginity (Contributions to the psychology of love III). *S.E.*, *11* (pp. 193–208).
Freud, Sigmund (1918b [1914]). Aus der Geschichte einer infantilen Neurose. *G.W. VIII* (pp. 437–567). From the history of an infantile neurosis. *S.E.*, *17* (pp. 7–122).

Freud, Sigmund (1919a [1918]). Wege der psychoanalytischen Therapie. *G.W. XII* (pp. 183–194). Lines of advance in psycho-analytic therapy. *S.E., 17* (pp. 159–168).
Freud, Sigmund (1919b). James J. Putnam † [obit.]. *G.W. XII* (p. 315). James J. Putnam. *S.E., 17* (p. 271).
Freud, Sigmund (1919c). Internationaler psychoanalytischer Verlag und Preiszuteilungen für psychoanalytische Arbeiten. *G.W. XII* (pp. 333–336). A note on psycho-analytic publications and prizes. *S.E., 17* (pp. 267–269).
Freud, Sigmund (1919f). Victor Tausk † [obit.]. *G.W. XII* (pp. 316–318). Victor Tausk. *S.E., 17* (pp. 273–275).
Freud, Sigmund (1919g). Vorrede zu: Reik, Theodor, *Probleme der Religionspsychologie*, I. Teil: *Das Ritual*. *G.W. XII* (pp. 325–329). Preface to Reik's *Ritual: Psycho-Analytic Studies*. *S.E., 17* (pp. 259–263).
Freud, Sigmund (1919h). Das Unheimliche. *G.W. XII* (pp. 229–268). The uncanny. *S.E., 17* (pp. 219–256).
Freud, Sigmund (1920b). Zur Vorgeschichte der analytischen Technik. *G.W. XII* (pp. 309–312). A note on the prehistory of the technique of analysis. *S.E., 18* (pp. 263–265).
Freud, Sigmund (1920c). Anton von Freund † [obit.]. *G.W. XIII* (p. 435). Anton von Freund. *S.E., 18* (p. 267).
Freud, Sigmund (1920f). Ergänzungen zur Traumlehre. *G.W. Nachtr.* (pp. 622–623). Supplements to the theory of dreams. *S.E., 18* (pp. 4–5).
Freud, Sigmund (1920g). *Jenseits des Lustprinzips*. *G.W. XIII* (pp. 1–69). *Beyond the Pleasure Principle*. *S.E., 18* (pp. 7–64).
Freud, Sigmund (1921c). *Massenpsychologie und Ich-Analyse*. *G.W. XIII* (pp. 71–161). *Group Psychology and the Analysis of the Ego*. *S.E., 18* (pp. 69–143).
Freud, Sigmund (1922f). Etwas vom Unbewußten. *G.W. Nachtr.* (p. 730). Some remarks on the unconscious. *S.E., 19* (pp. 3–4).
Freud, Sigmund (1923b). *Das Ich und das Es*. *G.W. XIII* (pp. 237–289). *The Ego and the Id*. *S.E., 19* (pp. 12–59).
Freud, Sigmund (1924c). Das ökonomische Problem des Masochismus. *G.W. XIII* (pp. 371–383). The economic problem of masochism. *S.E., 19* (pp. 159–170).
Freud, Sigmund (1924d). Der Untergang des Ödipuskomplexes. *G.W. XIII* (pp. 395–402). The dissolution of the Oedipus complex. *S.E., 19* (pp. 173–179).
Freud, Sigmund (1924e). Der Realitätsverlust bei Neurose und Psychose. *G.W. XIII* (pp. 363–368). The loss of reality in neurosis and psychosis. *S.E., 19* (pp. 183–187).
Freud, Sigmund (1925a [1924]). Notiz über den "Wunderblock". *G.W. XIV* (pp. 3–8). A note upon the "mystic writing-pad". *S.E., 19* (pp. 227–232).
Freud, Sigmund (1925d [1924]). *Selbstdarstellung*. *G.W. 14* (pp. 31–96). *An Autobiographical Study*. *S.E., 20* (pp. 7–70).
Freud, Sigmund (1925e [1924]). Die Widerstände gegen die Psychoanalyse. *G.W. XIV* (pp. 99–110). The resistances to psycho-analysis. *S.E., 19* (pp. 213–224).

Freud, Sigmund (1925g). Josef Breuer † [obit.]. *G.W. XIV* (pp. 562–563). Josef Breuer. *S.E., 19* (pp. 279–280).
Freud, Sigmund (1925h). Die Verneinung. *G.W. XIV* (pp. 11–15). Negation. *S.E., 19* (pp. 235–239).
Freud, Sigmund (1925i). Einige Nachträge zum Ganzen der Traumdeutung. *G.W. I* (pp. 561–573). Some additional notes on dream-interpretation as a whole. *S.E., 19* (pp. 127–138).
Freud, Sigmund (1925j). Einige psychische Folgen des anatomischen Geschlechtsunterschieds. *G.W. XIV* (pp. 19–30). Some psychical consequences of the anatomical distinction between the sexes. *S.E., 19* (pp. 248–258).
Freud, Sigmund (1926d [1925]). *Hemmung, Symptom und Angst. G.W. XIV* (pp. 111–205). *Inhibitions, Symptoms and Anxiety. S.E.,* 20 (pp. 77–175).
Freud, Sigmund (1926e). *Die Frage der Laienanalyse. Unterredungen mit einem Unparteiischen. G.W. XIV* (pp. 207–286). *The Question of Lay Analysis. Conversations with an Impartial Person. S.E.,* 20 (pp. 183–250).
Freud, Sigmund (1926i). Dr. Reik und die Kurpfuscherfrage. Brief an die *Neue Freie Presse. G.W. Nachtr.* (pp. 715–717). Dr. Reik and the problem of quackery. A letter to the *Neue Freie Presse. S.E., 21* (pp. 247–248).
Freud, Sigmund (1930a [1929]). *Das Unbehagen in der Kultur. G.W. XIV* (pp. 419–506). *Civilization and Its Discontents. S.E., 21* (pp. 64–145).
Freud, Sigmund (1933a [1932]). *Neue Folge der Vorlesungen zur Einführung in die Psychoanalyse. G.W. XV. New Introductory Lectures on Psycho-Analysis. S.E., 22* (pp. 5–182).
Freud, Sigmund (1939a [1934–38]). *Moses and Monotheism: Three Essays. S.E., 23* (pp. 7–137).
Freud, Sigmund (1941d [1921]). Psychoanalyse und Telepathie. *G.W. XVII* (pp. 25, 27–44). Psycho-analysis and telepathy. *S.E., 18* (pp. 177–193).
Freud, Sigmund (1945a [1939]). Foreword [in English] to J. Hobman's *David Eder* (1945) (p. 9).
Freud, Sigmund (1950a [1887–1902]). *Aus den Anfängen der Psychoanalyse. Briefe an Wilhelm Fließ, Abhandlungen und Notizen aus den Jahren 1887–1902* (ed. Marie Bonaparte, Anna Freud and Ernst Kris). *The Origins of Psycho-Analysis. Letters to Wilhelm Fliess* (ed. Ernst Kris). London: Imago.
Freud, Sigmund (1950c [1895]). Entwurf einer Psychologie. *G.W., Nachtr.* (pp. 387–477). A Project for a Scientific Psychology. *S.E., 1* (pp. 295–397).
Freud, Sigmund (1955a [1907–08]). Originalnotizen zu einem Fall von Zwangsneurose. *G.W., Nachtr.* (pp. 509–569). Original record of the case. *S.E., 10* (pp. 254–255, 259–318).] New transcription in *G.W., Nachtr.* (pp. 509–569).
Freud, Sigmund (1956j [1913]). Letter to Alfons Maeder (21 September 1913). In: Alfons Maeder, Persönliche Erinnerungen an Freud und retrospektive Besinnung Personal recollections of Freud and retrospective evaluation]. *Schweizerische Zeitschrift für Psychologie, 15*: 114–122.
Freud, Sigmund (1960a). *Briefe 1873–1939* (ed. Ernst Freud & Lucie Freud).

Frankfurt/Main: S. Fischer [second enlarged edition, 1968; third revised edition, 1980]. *The Letters of Sigmund Freud* (ed. Ernst Freud). New York: Basic Books, 1975.

Freud, Sigmund (1966b [1938]). Introduction. In: Sigmund Freud & William Christian Bullitt (1966). *Thomas Woodrow Wilson, Twenty-Eighth President of the United States: A Psychological Study.* Boston: Riverside Press, 1967 (pp. xi–xvii).

Freud, Sigmund (1985a [1915]). *Übersicht der Übertragungsneurosen: Ein bisher unbekanntes Manuskript* (ed. Ilse Grubrich-Simitis). Frankfurt/Main: S. Fischer. Also in *G.W. Nachtr.* (pp. 634–651). *A Phylogenetic Fantasy: Overview of the Transference Neuroses.* Trans. Axel and Peter Hoffer. Cambridge, MA: Harvard University Press, 1987.

Freud, Sigmund (1985c [1887–1904]). *Briefe an Wilhelm Fließ 1887–1904*, ungekürzte Ausgabe (ed. Jeffrey M. Masson [German edition, Michael Schröter]. Frankfurt/Main: S. Fischer. *The Complete Letters of Sigmund Freud to Wilhelm Fliess 1887–1904* (ed. Jeffrey M. Masson). Cambridge, MA: Harvard University Press.

Freud, Sigmund (1988k [1909]). Freud and fetishism: Previously unpublished minutes of the Vienna Psychoanalytic Society (ed. and trans. Louis Rose). *Psychoanalytic Quarterly, 57*: 147–166. Zur Genese des Fetischismus. In: Ernst Federn & Gerhard Wittenberger, *Aus dem Kreis um Sigmund Freud: Zu den Protokollen der Wiener Psychoanalytischen Vereinigung* (pp. 10–22). Frankfurt/Main: Fischer, 1992.

Freud, Sigmund (1989a). *Jugendbriefe an Eduard Silberstein 1871–1881* (ed. Walther Boehlich). Frankfurt/Main: S. Fischer. *The Letters of Sigmund Freud to Eduard Silberstein 1871–1881.* Cambridge, MA: Belknap Press, 1990.

Freud, Sigmund, & Abraham, Karl (1965). *Briefe 1907–1926* (ed. Hilda C. Abraham & Ernst L. Freud). Frankfurt/Main: S. Fischer [second edition, 1980]. *A Psycho-Analytic Dialogue: The Letters of Sigmund Freud and Karl Abraham 1907–1926* (ed. Hilda C. Abraham & Ernst Freud). London: Hogarth & Institute of Psycho-Analysis.

Freud, Sigmund, & Andreas-Salomé, Lou (1966). *Briefwechsel* (ed. Ernst Pfeiffer). Frankfurt/Main: S. Fischer. *Letters* (ed. Ernst Pfeiffer). London: Hogarth & Institute of Psycho-Analysis, 1972.

Freud, Sigmund, & Binswanger, Ludwig (1992). *Briefwechsel 1908–1938* (ed. Gerhard Fichtner). Frankfurt/Main: S. Fischer. *The Freud–Binswanger Correspondence 1908–1938* (ed. Gerhard Fichtner, trans. Arnold J. Pomerans; editorial notes and additional letters trans. Tom Roberts). New York: Other Press, 2001.

Freud, Sigmund, & Bullitt, William Christian (1966). *Thomas Woodrow Wilson, Twenty-Eighth President of the United States; A Psychological Study.* Boston: Houghton Mifflin, 1967.

Freud, Sigmund, & Ferenczi, Sándor (1992). *Sigmund Freud–Sándor Ferenczi, Briefwechsel, Band I/1 (1908–1911), Band I/2 (1912–1914)* (ed. Eva Brabant,

Ernst Falzeder, & Patrizia Giampieri-Deutsch). Vienna: Böhlau, 1993, 1994. *The Correspondence of Sigmund Freud and Sándor Ferenczi, Vol. 1: 1908–1914*. Cambridge, MA: Harvard University Press, 1994.

Freud, Sigmund, & Ferenczi, Sándor (1996). *Sigmund Freud—Sándor Ferenczi, Briefwechsel, Band II/1 (1914–1916), Band II/2 (1917–1919)* (ed. Ernst Falzeder & Eva Brabant). Vienna: Böhlau. *The Correspondence of Sigmund Freud and Sándor Ferenczi, Vol. 2: 1914–1919*. Cambridge, MA: Harvard University Press.

Freud, Sigmund, & Ferenczi, Sándor (2000). *The Correspondence of Sigmund Freud and Sándor Ferenczi, Vol. 3: 1920–1933*. Cambridge, MA: Harvard University Press, 2000. *Sigmund Freud–Sándor Ferenczi, Briefwechsel, Band III/1 (1920–1924), Band III/2 (1925–1933)* (ed. Ernst Falzeder & Eva Brabant). Vienna: Böhlau [forthcoming].

Freud, Sigmund, & Groddeck, Georg (1974). *Briefe über das Es*. Munich: Kindler. Georg Groddeck, *The Meaning of Illness: Selected Psychoanalytic Writings by Georg Groddeck, Including His Correspondence with Sigmund Freud*. New York: International Universities Press, 1977.

Freud, Sigmund, & Jones, Ernest (1993). *The Complete Correspondence of Sigmund Freud and Ernest Jones 1908–1939* (ed. R. Andrew Paskauskas). Cambridge, MA: Harvard University Press.

Freud, Sigmund, & Jung, Carl Gustav (1974 [1906–13]). *Briefwechsel* (ed. William McGuire & Wolfgang Sauerländer). Frankfurt/Main: S. Fischer. *The Freud/Jung Letters: The Correspondence between Sigmund Freud and C. G. Jung* (ed. William McGuire). Cambridge, MA: Harvard University Press, 1988.

Freud, Sigmund, & Oppenheim, David Ernst (1957a [1911]). Träume im Folklore. *G.W., Nachtr.* (pp. 573, 576–600). Dreams in folklore. *S.E.*, 12 (pp. 180–203).

Freud, Sigmund & Pfister, Oskar (1963). *Briefe 1909–1939* (ed. Ernst L. Freud & Heinrich Meng). Frankfurt/Main: Fischer. *Psychoanalysis and Faith: The Letters of Sigmund Freud and Oskar Pfister*. New York: Basic Books.

Freud, Sigmund, & Weiss, Edoardo (1970). *Briefe zur psychoanalytischen Praxis: Mit den Erinnerungen eines Pioniers der Psychoanalyse* (Vorbemerkung und Einleitung von Martin Grotjahn; mit Kommentaren von Edoardo Weiss). Frankfurt/Main: Fischer. *Sigmund Freud as a Consultant: Recollections of a Pioneer in Psychoanalysis* (ed. Martin Grotjahn, commentaries by Edoardo Weiss). New York: Intercontinental Medical Book Corporation [reprinted, with a new foreword by Emilio Weiss and a new introduction by Paul Roazen, New Brunswick, NJ: Transaction Publishers, 1991].

Freud, Sigmund, & Zweig, Arnold (1968). *Briefwechsel* (ed. Ernst L. Freud). Frankfurt/Main: S. Fischer. *The Letters of Sigmuund Freud and Arnold Zweig*. London: Hogarth & Institute of Psycho-Analysis, 1970.

Friedländer, Adolf A. (1907–08). Sammelreferat. S. Freuds neuere Abhandlungen zur Neurosenfrage [Collective review. S. Freud's newer papers on the question of neurosis]. *Journal für Psychologie und Neurologie*, 10 (4–5): 201–206.

Friedländer, Adolf A. (1911 [1910]). Hysteria and modern psycho-analysis. *Journal of Abnormal Psychology*, 5 (Feb.–Mar.): 297–319.
Gay, Peter (1988). *Freud, A Life for Our Time*. New York: Anchor Books, 1989.
Gidal, Tim N., & Volker, Friedrich (1990). *Die Freudianer: Auf dem 13. Internationalen Psychoanalytischen Kongreß 1934 in Luzern*. Munich: Verlag Internationale Psychoanalyse.
Goggin, James E., & Goggin, Eileen Brockman (2001). *Death of a "Jewish Science": Psychoanalysis in the Third Reich*. West Lafayette, IN: Purdue University Press.
Green, Martin (1999). *Otto Gross, Freudian Psychoanalyst 1877–1920: Literature and Ideas*. Lewiston, NY: Edwin Mellen Press.
Groddeck, Georg (1917). *Die psychische Bedingtheit und psychoanalytische Behandlung organischer Leiden* [The psychic determination and psychoanalytic treatment of organic diseases]. Berlin: Hirzel.
Groddeck, Georg (1923). *Das Buch vom Es: Psychoanalytische Briefe an eine Freundin*. Leipzig: Internationaler Psychoanalytischer Verlag. *The Book of the It: Psychoanalytic Letters to a Friend*. New York: Nervous and Mental Diseases Publishing Company, 1928.
Grosskurth, Phyllis (1980). *Havelock Ellis: A Biography*. London: Quartet Books, 1981.
Grosskurth, Phyllis (1986). *Melanie Klein, Her World and Her Work*. New York: Alfred A. Knopf.
Grosskurth, Phyllis (1991). *The Secret Ring, Freud's Inner Circle and the Politics of Psychoanalysis*. Reading, MA: Addison-Wesley.
Grossman, Carl M., & Grossman, Sylvia (1965). *The Wild Analyst, The Life and Work of Georg Groddeck*. New York: G. Braziller.
Häberlin, Paul, & Binswanger, Ludwig (1997). *Paul Häberlin–Ludwig Binswanger Briefwechsel 1908–1960: mit Briefen von Sigmund Freud, Carl Gustav Jung, Karl Jaspers, Martin Heidegger, Ludwig Frank und Eugen Bleuler* (ed. Jeannine Luczak). Basel: Schwabe.
Hale, Nathan G., Jr. (1971a). *Freud and the Americans: The Beginnings of Psychoanalysis in the United States, 1876–1917*. New York: Oxford University Press, 1995.
Hale, Nathan G., Jr. (Ed.) (1971b). *James Jackson Putnam and Psychoanalysis: Letters between Putnam and Sigmund Freud, Ernest Jones, William James, Sandor Ferenczi, and Morton Prince, 1877–1917*. Cambridge, MA: Harvard University Press.
Hale, Nathan G., Jr. (1995). *The Rise and Crisis of Psychoanalysis in the United States*. Oxford: Oxford University Press.
Handlbauer, Bernhard (1992). *Die Adler–Freud-Kontroverse*. Frankfurt/Main: Fischer. *The Freud–Adler Controversy*. Oxford: Oneworld, 1997.
Harmat, Paul (1986). *Freud, Ferenczi und die ungarische Psychoanalyse* [Freud, Ferenczi, and Hungarian psychoanalysis]. Tübingen: edition diskord.
Haynal, André (1992). Introduction. In: Sigmund Freud & Sándor Ferenczi, *The Correspondence of Sigmund Freud and Sándor Ferenczi, Vol. 1: 1908–1914* (pp. xvii–xxxv). Cambridge, MA: Harvard University Press, 1994.

Haynal, André (1995). Entgegnung auf Gerhard Fichtners "notwendige Stellungnahme" und Anmerkungen zu Michael Schröters Buchbesprechung [Reply to Gerhard Fichtner's "necessary comment" and remarks on Michael Schröter's book review]. *Psyche, 49*: 174–181.

Herzer, Manfred (1992). *Magnus Hirschfeld: Leben und Werk eines jüdischen, schwulen und sozialistischen Sexologen* [Magnus Hirschfeld. Life and work of a Jewish, gay and socialist sexologist]. Frankfurt/Main: Campus.

Hirschmüller, Albrecht (1978). *Physiologie und Psychoanalyse in Leben und Werk Josef Breuers*. Bern: Hans Huber. *The Life and Work of Josef Breuer: Physiology and Psychoanalysis*. New York: International Universities Press, 1989.

Hitschmann, Eduard (1913). Schopenhauer. Versuch einer Psychoanalyse des Philosophen [Schopenhauer. An attempted psychoanalysis of the philosopher]. *Imago, Zeitschrift für Anwendung der Psychoanalyse auf die Geisteswissenschaften, 2*: 101–174. *Great Men, Psychoanalytic Studies* (ed. Sydney G. Margolin). New York: International Universities Press, 1956.

Hitschmann, Eduard (1914). Trieblehre [Drive theory]. *Jahrbuch der Psychoanalyse, Neue Folge des Jahrbuchs für psychoanalytische und psychopathologische Forschungen, 6*: 283–295.

Hobman, Joseph Burton (Ed.) (1945). *David Eder: Memoirs of a Modern Pioneer*. London: Victor Gollancz.

Hoche, Alfred E. (1910). Eine psychische Epidemie unter Ärzten [An epidemic of insanity among doctors]. *Medizinische Klinik, 6* (26 Jun.): 1007–1010.

Hoffer, Axel (1996). Introduction. In: Sigmund Freud & Sándor Ferenczi, *The Correspondence of Sigmund Freud and Sándor Ferenczi, Vol. 2: 1914–1919* (pp. xvii–xlvi). Cambridge, MA: Harvard University Press.

Hoffman, Edward (1994). *The Drive for Self: Alfred Adler and the Founding of Individual Psychology*. Reading, MA: Adddison-Wesley.

Horney, Karen (1912). "Ergebnisse der Psychoanalyse für die Sexualpädagogik des frühen Kindesalters" [Psychoanalytic results for the sexual pedagogy in early childhood]. Paper presented to the Berlin Psychoanalytic Society, 18 Jan.

Horney, Karen (1937). *The Neurotic Personality of Our Time*. New York: Norton.

Horney, Karen (1939). *New Ways in Psychoanalysis*. New York: Norton.

Huber, Wolfgang (1980). Die erste Kinderanalytikerin [The first child analyst]. In: Heimo Gastager et al. (Eds.), *Psychoanalyse als Herausforderung* (pp. 125–134). Vienna: Verlag Verband der wissenschaftlichen Gesellschaften Österreichs.

Hug-Hellmuth, Hermine (1912). Über Farbenhören. Ein Versuch, das Phänomen auf Grund der psychoanalytischen Methode zu erklären [Colored audition. An attempt to explain the phenomenon with the psychoanalytic method]. *Imago, Zeitschrift für Anwendung der Psychoanalyse auf die Geisteswissenschaften, 1*: 228–264.

Hug-Hellmuth, Hermine (1914). Kinderpsychologie, Pädagogik. *Jahrbuch der Psychoanalyse, Neue Folge des Jahrbuchs für psychoanalytische und psycho-*

*pathologische Forschungen*, 6: 393–404. Child psychology and education. *International Journal of Psycho-Analysis*, 1 (1920): 316–323.

Hug-Hellmuth, Hermine (Ed.) (1919). *Tagebuch eines halbwüchsigen Mädchens*. Leipzig, Vienna: Internationaler Psychoanalytischer Verlag. *A Young Girl's Diary*. London: Allen & Unwin, 1921.

Hurwitz, Emanuel (1979). *Otto Gross, Paradies-Sucher zwischen Freud und Jung* [Otto Gross, seeker of paradise between Freud and Jung]. Frankfurt/Main: Suhrkamp.

Jackson, [John] Hughlings (1884). On the evolution and dissolution of the nervous system. *The Lancet*: 555–558, 649–652, 739–744.

Jackson, [John] Hughlings (1887a). Remarks on evolution and dissolution of the nervous system. In: James Taylor (Ed.), *Selected Writings of John Hughlings Jackson, Vol. 2* (pp. 76–91). London: Hodder & Stoughton, 1932.

Jackson, [John] Hughlings (1887b). Remarks on evolution and dissolution of the nervous system. In: James Taylor (Ed.), *Selected Writings of John Hughlings Jackson, Vol. 2* (pp. 92–118). London: Hodder & Stoughton, 1932.

Jelgersma, Gerbrandus (1914). Ongeweten Geestesleven [Unconscious mental life]. Leiden: V. Doesburgh. *Unbewußtes Geistesleben. Erstes Beiheft zur Internationalen Zeitschrift für ärztliche Psychoanalyse*. Leizig, Vienna: Heller.

Jensen, Wilhelm (1903). *Gradiva: ein pompejanisches Phantasiestück*. Dresden and Leipzig. *Gradiva, A Pompeiian Fancy*. New York: Moffat, Yard & Co., 1918.

Jeremias, Alfred (1904). *Das alte Testament im Lichte des alten Orients*. Leipzig. *The Old Testament in the Light of the Ancient East*. London: Williams & Norgate, 1911.

Jones, Ernest (1910a). Bericht über die neuere englische und amerikanische Literatur zur klinischen Psychologie und Psychopathologie. *Jahrbuch für psychoanalytische und psychopathologische Forschungen*, 2 (1): 316–346. Review of the recent English and American literature on clinical psychology and psychopathology. *Archives of Neurology and Psychiatry*, 5 (1911): 120–147.

Jones, Ernest (1910b). "Freud's theory of dreams." Paper presented to the American Psychological Association, Boston, 29 Dec. 1909. *Review of Neurology and Psychiatry*, 8: 135–143. *American Journal of Psychology*, 21: 283–308.

Jones, Ernest (1910c). The Oedipus complex as an explanation of Hamlet's mystery: A study in motive. *American Journal of Psychology*, 21: 72–113. *Das Problem des Hamlet und der Ödipus-Komplex* (*Schriften zur angewandten Seelenkunde 10*). Leipzig, Vienna: Deuticke, 1911.

Jones, Ernest (1911). Remarks on Dr. Morton Prince's article "The mechanism and interpretation of dreams". *Journal of Abnormal Psychology*, 5 (Feb.–Mar.): 328–336.

Jones, Ernest (1914a). Die Stellungnahme des psychoanalytischen Arztes zu den aktuellen Konflikten. *Internationale Zeitschrift für ärztliche Psychoanalyse*, 2: 6–10. The attitude of the psycho-analytic physician towards current conflicts. *Papers on Psycho-Analysis* (pp. 334–339). London: Baillière, Tindall & Cox [third edition 1925].

Jones, Ernest (1914b). Psychoanalytische Therapie (Sammelreferat) [Psychoanalytic therapy (Collective review)]. *Jahrbuch der Psychoanalyse, Neue Folge des Jahrbuchs für psychoanalytische und psychopathologische Forschungen, 6*: 329–342.

Jones, Ernest (1918). War shock and Freud's theory of the neuroses. *Proceedings of the Royal Society of Medicine, 11*: 21–36.

Jones, Ernest (1926). Karl Abraham 1877–1925. *International Journal of Psycho-Analysis, 7*: 155–181.

Jones, Ernest (1953). *The Life and Work of Sigmund Freud, Vol. 1: The Formative Years and the Great Discoveries 1856–1900.* New York: Basic Books.

Jones, Ernest (1955). *The Life and Work of Sigmund Freud, Vol. 2: Years of Maturity 1901–1919.* New York: Basic Books.

Jones, Ernest (1957). *The Life and Work of Sigmund Freud, Vol. 3: The Last Phase 1919–1939.* New York: Basic Books.

Juliusburger, Otto (1909a). Beitrag zur Lehre von der Psychoanalyse [Contribution to the theory of psychoanalysis]. *Allgemeine Zeitschrift für Psychiatrie, 64*.

Juliusburger, Otto (1909b). Zur Psychotherapie und Psychoanalyse [On psychotherapy and psychoanalysis]. *Berliner Klinische Wochenschrift, 46*: 248–250.

Juliusburger, Otto (1911). Weiteres von Schopenhauer [More about Schopenhauer]. *Zentralblatt für Psychoanalyse: Medizinische Monatsschrift für Seelenkunde, 1* (1910/11): 173–174.

Jung, Carl Gustav (1902). *Zur Psychologie und Pathologie sogenannter okkulter Phänomene.* Leipzig. On the psychology and pathology of so-called occult phenomena. *Collected Works, 1.*

Jung, Carl Gustav (Ed.) (1906). *Diagnostische Assoziationsstudien: Beiträge zur experimentellen Psychopathologie, Vol. 1.* Leipzig: Barth. *Studies in Word-Association; Experiments in the Diagnosis of Psychopathological Conditions Carried out at the Psychiatric Clinic of the University of Zurich, under the Direction of C. G. Jung.* London: W. Heinemann, 1918.

Jung, Carl Gustav (1907a). Die Freud'sche Hysterietheorie. *Monatsschrift für Psychiatrie und Neurologie, 23* (4) (Mar., 1908): 310. The Freudian theory of hysteria. *Collected Works, 4.*

Jung, Carl Gustav (1907b). *Über die Psychologie der Dementia praecox: Ein Versuch.* Halle a. S.: Marhold. *The Psychology of Dementia Praecox.* New York: The Journal of Nervous and Mental Disease Publishing Company, 1909, 1936. *The Psychology of Dementia Praecox. Collected Works, 3.*

Jung, Carl Gustav (1908). Der Inhalt der Psychose (*Schriften zur angewandten Seelenkunde 3*). Leipzig, Vienna: Deuticke. *The Content of the Psychoses. Collected Works, 3.*

Jung, Carl Gustav (1909a). Die Bedeutung des Vaters für das Schicksal des Einzelnen [The significance of the father for the fate of the individual]. *Jahrbuch für psychoanalytische und psychopathologische Forschungen, 1* (1): 155–173.

Jung, Carl Gustav (Ed.) (1909b). *Diagnostische Assoziationsstudien: Beiträge zur experimentellen Psychopathologie, Vol. 2.* Leipzig: Barth. *Studies in Word-Association; Experiments in the Diagnosis of Psychopathological Conditions Carried out at the Psychiatric Clinic of the University of Zurich, under the Direction of C. G. Jung.* London: W. Heinemann, 1918.

Jung, Carl Gustav (1910a). Referate über psychologische Arbeiten schweizerischer Autoren (bis Ende 1909) [Abstracts of the psychological works of Swiss authors (to the end of 1909)]. *Jahrbuch für psychoanalytische und psychopathologische Forschungen*, 2 (1): 356–388.

Jung, Carl Gustav (1910b). The association method. *American Journal of Psychology*, 21: 219–282.

Jung, Carl Gustav (1910c). Bericht über Amerika [Report on America]. Abstract in *Jahrbuch für psychoanalytische und psychopathologische Forschungen*, 2 (2): 737.

Jung, Carl Gustav (1910d). Abstract of paper presented to Congress in Salzburg. *Zentralblatt für Psychoanalyse*, 1: 128.

Jung, Carl Gustav (1911–12). Wandlungen und Symbole der Libido [Transformations and symbols of the libido]. I. *Jahrbuch für psychoanalytische und psychopathologische Forschungen*, 3 (1) (1911): 120–227. II. *Jahrbuch für psychoanalytische und psychopathologische Forschungen*, 4 (1) (1912): 162–464. In book form: Vienna, Deuticke, 1912 [reprinted Munich: Deutscher Taschenbuch Verlag, 1991].

Jung, Carl Gustav (1913). "Versuch einer Darstellung der psychoanalytischen Theorie." Neun Vorlesungen, gehalten in New York im September 1912. [An attempt at a presentation of the psychoanalytical theory. Nine lectures held in New York in September 1912.] *Jahrbuch für psychoanalytische und psychopathologische Forschungen*, 5: 307–441. In book form: Vienna, Deuticke, 1913.

Jung, Carl Gustav (1917). *Die Psychologie der unbewussten Prozesse; ein Überblick über die moderne Theorie und Methode der analytischen Psychologie*. Zurich: Rascher. The psychology of the unconscious processes. *Collected Papers on Analytical Psychology* (pp. 354–444). London: Baillière, Tindall & Cox [second edition 1917].

Kaplan, Leo (1914). *Grundzüge der Psychoanalyse* [Principles of psychoanalysis]. Vienna: Deuticke.

Kerr, John (1993). *A Most Dangerous Method: The Story of Jung, Freud, and Sabina Spielrein*. New York: Alfred A. Knopf.

King, Pearl, & Steiner, Riccardo (Eds.) (1991). *The Freud–Klein Controversies 1941–45*. London, New York: Tavistock/Routledge.

Kleinpaul, Rudolf Alexander (1898). *Die Lebendigen und die Toten in Volksglauben, Religion und Sage* [The living and the dead in popular belief, religion, and myth]. Leipzig.

Kraepelin, Emil (1883). *Psychiatrie: Ein Lehrbuch für Studierende und Ärzte: Clinical Psychiatry*. Delmar, NY: Scholars' Facsimiles & Reprints, 1981. *Psychiatry: A Textbook for Students and Physicians* (ed. & intro. Jacques M. Quen). Canton, MA: Science History Publications, 1990.

Kraus, Friedrich, & Brugsch, Theodor (Eds.) (1919–1927). *Spezielle Pathologie und Therapie innerer Krankheiten* [Special pathology and therapy of internal diseases], 11 vols. Berlin.

Kronfeld, Arthur (1911). Über die psychologischen Theorien Freuds und verwandte Anschauungen. Systematik und kritische Erörertung [On the psychological theories of Freud and on related views. Systematic description and critical discussion]. *Archiv für die gesamte Psychologie, 22* (Dec.): 130–248 [in book form: Leipzig: Engelmann, 1912].

Kuhn, Adalbert (1859). *Die Herabkunft des Feuers und des Göttertranks*. Berlin [second edition Gütersloh, 1886].

Kutzinski, Arnold (1910). Book review of Freud, *Sammlung kleiner Schriften zur Neurosenlehre*, second volume. *Monatsschrift für Psychiatrie und Neurologie, 27*: 185.

Leitner, M. (1998). *Freud, Otto Rank und die Folgen: Ein Schlüsselkonflikt für die Psychoanalyse* [Freud, Otto Rank, and the consequences. A key conflict for psychoanalysis]. Vienna: Turia & Kant.

Lévy-Bruhl, Lucien (1910). *How Natives Think*. London: Allen & Unwin, 1926. Princeton: Princeton University Press, 1985.

Lieberman, James E. (1985). *Acts of Will: The Life and Work of Otto Rank*. New York: The Free Press.

Lobner, Hans (1909). "Zur Genese des Fetischismus". Ein wiederentdeckter Vortrag Sigmund Freuds ["On the genesis of fetishism". A rediscovered talk by Sigmund Freud]. In: Ernst Federn & Gerhard Wittenberger, *Aus dem Kreis um Sigmund Freud: Zu den Protokollen der Wiener Psychoanalytischen Vereinigung* (pp. 23–33). Frankfurt/Main: Fischer, 1992.

MacLean, George, & Rappen, Ulrich (1991). *Hermine Hug-Hellmuth: Her Life and Work*. New York: Routledge.

Maeder, Alphonse E. (1906–07). Contributions à la psychopathologie de la vie quotidienne; oublis, confusions, lapsus. I. [Contributions to the psychopathology of everyday life; forgetfulness, confusion, slips of the tongue. I.] *Archives de Psychologie de la Suisse Romande, 6*: 148–152. Nouvelles contributions à la psychopathologie. II. [New contributions to psychopathology. II.] *Archives de Psychologie de la Suisse Romande, 7* (1907).

Maeder, Alphonse E. (1909a). Une voie nouvelle en psychologie (Freud et son école) [A new path in psychology (Freud and his school)]. *Coenobium*.

Maeder, Alphonse E. (1909b). Sexualität und Epilepsie [Sexuality and epilepsy]. *Jahrbuch für psychoanalytische und psychopathologische Forschungen, 1* (1): 119–154.

Maeder, Alphonse E. (1988 [1912–1913]). Lettres à Sigmund Freud [Letters to Sigmund Freud]. *Le Bloc-Notes de la psychanalyse, 8*: 219–226.

Maetze, Gerhard (1976–77). Psychoanalyse in Deutschland [Psychoanalysis in Germany]. In Dieter Eicke (Ed.), *Tiefenpsychologie, Vol. 2: Neue Wege der Psychoanalyse: Psychoanalyse der Gesellschaft: Die psychoanalytische Bewegung* (pp. 408–437). Weinheim: Beltz, 1982.

Mahony, P. (1986). *Freud and the Rat Man*. New Haven, CT, London: Yale University Press.

Marcinowski, Jaroslaw (1912). Kurze Bemerkungen zu dem Abraham'schen

Aufsatz über die psychoanalytische Erforschung der manisch-depressiven Zustände [Brief remarks on Abraham's paper on the psychoanalytic investigation of manic-depressive states]. *Zentralblatt für Psychoanalyse: Medizinische Monatsschrift für Seelenkunde,* 2 (1911/12): 541–542.

Martynkewicz, Wolfgang (1997). *Georg Groddeck: Eine Biographie.* Frankfurt/ Main: Fischer.

*Max Eitingon, in memoriam* (1950). Jerusalem: Israel Psycho-Analytical Society.

McGuire, William (1995). Firm affinities. Jung's relations with Britain and the United States. *Journal of Analytical Psychology,* 40: 301–326.

Meghnagi, David (Ed.) (1993). *Freud and Judaism.* London: Karnac.

Meisel, Perry, & Kendrick, Walter (Eds.) (1986). *Bloomsbury/Freud: The Letters of James and Alix Strachey 1924–1925.* London: Chatto & Windus; New York: Basic Books.

Meisel-Hess, Grete (1911). *Die Intellectuellen* [The intellectuals]. Berlin: Österheld.

Meisel-Hess, Grete (1911–12). Neomalthusianismus, Mutterschutz und Sexualreform [Neomalthusianism, protection of mothers, and sexual reform]. *Zentralblatt für Psychoanalyse: Medizinische Monatsschrift für Seelenkunde,* 2: 149–157.

Meyer, Adolf F. (1917). "Jung's laatste boek: 'Die Psychologie der unbewußten Prozesse'" [Jung's last book: *The Psychology of the Unconscious Processes*]. Paper presented to the Dutch Psychoanalytic Society, 16 Dec. In Dutch: *Nederlandsch Tijdschrift voor Geneeskunde,* 1 (10) (1919). In German: Dr. C. G. Jungs Psychologie der unbewußten Prozesse. *Internationale Zeitschrift für ärztliche Psychoanalyse,* 4 (1916/17): 302–314.

Michaëlis, Karin (1910). *Das gefährliche Alter: Tagebuch-Aufzeichnungen und Briefe.* Berlin: Concordia Deutsche Verlags-Anstalt. *The Dangerous Age, Letters and Fragments from a Woman's Diary.* New York: J. Lane, 1911.

Moellenhoff, Fritz (1966). Hanns Sachs: The creative unconscious. In: Franz Alexander et al. (Eds.), *Psychoanalytic Pioneers* (pp. 180–199). New York: Basic Books.

Moll, Albert (1908). *Das Sexualleben des Kindes.* Leipzig: Vogel. *The Sexual Life of the Child.* New York: Macmillan, 1912, 1924.

Morichau-Beauchant, Pierre Ernest René (1911). Le "rapport affectif" dans la cure des psychonévroses [The "affective rapport" in the cure of psychoneuroses]. *Gazette des Hôpitaux,* 84 (129) (14 Nov.): 1845–1849.

Moser, Alexander (1992). Switzerland. In: Peter Kutter (Ed.), *Psychoanalysis International: A Guide to Psychoanalysis Throughout the World, Vol. 1: Europe* (pp. 278–313). Stuttgart: frommann-holzboog.

Mühlleitner, Elke (1992). *Biographisches Lexikon der Psychoanalyse: Die Mitglieder der Psychologischen Mittwoch-Gesellschaft und der Wiener Psychoanalytischen Vereinigung 1902–1938* [Biographical dictionary of psychoanalysis. The members of the Psychological Wednesday-Society and of the Vienna Psychoanalytic Society 1902–1938]. Tübingen: edition diskord.

Nachmannsohn, Max (1915). Freuds Libidotheorie verglichen mit der Eros-

lehre Platos [Freud's theory of the libido compared with Plato's teachings concerning Eros]. *Internationale Zeitschrift für ärztliche Psychoanalyse, 3*: 65–83.
Näcke, Paul (1901). Review of Freud, The Interpretation of Dreams. *Archiv für Kriminal-Anthropologie und Kriminalistik, 70*: 168.
Näcke, Paul (1906). Review of Freud, Three Essays on the Theory of Sexuality. *Archiv für Kriminal-Anthropologie und Kriminalistik, 24*: 166.
Nunberg, Herman, & Federn, Ernst (Eds.) (1962). *Minutes of the Vienna Psychoanalytic Society, Vol. 1.* New York: International Universities Press.
Nunberg, Herman, & Federn, Ernst (Eds.) (1967). *Minutes of the Vienna Psychoanalytic Society, Vol. 2.* New York: International Universities Press.
Nunberg, Herman, & Federn, Ernst (Eds.) (1974). *Minutes of the Vienna Psychoanalytic Society, Vol. 3.* New York: International Universities Press.
Nunberg, Herman, & Federn, Ernst (Eds.) (1975). *Minutes of the Vienna Psychoanalytic Society, Vol. 4.* New York: International Universities Press.
Ophuijsen, Johan H. W. van (1917). Beiträge zum Männlichkeitskomplex der Frau [Contributions to the masculinity complex of women]. *Internationale Zeitschrift für ärztliche Psychoanalyse, 4* (1916/17): 241–251.
Ophuijsen, Johan H. W. van (1926). De oorsprong van het sadisme [The origin of sadism]. *Nederlandsch Tijdschrift voor Geneeskunde,* 1854.
Payne, Sylvia (1956). Sir Arthur George Tansley, F.R.S. *International Journal of Psycho-Analysis, 37*: 197.
Peters, Heinz Frederick (1962). *My Sister, My Spouse: A Biography of Lou Andreas-Salomé.* New York: Norton, 1974.
Pfister, Oskar (1910). *Die Frömmigkeit des Grafen Ludwig von Zinzendorf; ein psychoanalytischer Beitrag zur Kenntnis der religiösen Sublimierungs-Prozesse und zur Erklärung des Pietismus* [The piety of Count Ludwig von Zinzendorf; a psychoanalytic contribution to the study of religious sublimation processes and to the explanation of pietism] (*Schriften zur angewandten Seelenkunde 8*). Leipzig, Vienna: Deuticke.
Pfister, Oskar (1912). Die Ursache der Farbenbegleitung bei akustischen Wahrnehmungen und das Wesen anderer Synästhesien [The cause of chromosthesias associated with acoustic impressions and the meaning of other synaesthesias]. *Imago, Zeitschrift für Anwendung der Psychoanalyse auf die Geisteswissenschaften, 1*: 265–275.
Pfister, Oskar (1913). Kryptolalie, Kryptographie und unbewußtes Vexierbild bei Normalen [Cryptophasia, cryptography, and the unconscious puzzle-picture]. *Jahrbuch für psychoanalytische und psychopathologische Forschungen, 5* (1): 117–156.
Pfister, Oskar (1914a). Echnaton. *Wissen und Leben* (Apr.–May).
Pfister, Oskar (1914b). Psychoanalyse und Theologie [Psychoanalysis and theology]. *Theologische Literaturzeitung* (6 Jun.).
Pfister, Oskar (1914c). Die Pädagogik der Adler'schen Schule [The pedagogics of Adler's school]. *Berner Seminarblätter* (No. 8).
Pfister, Oskar (1915). Ist die Brandstiftung ein archaischer Sublimierungs-

versuch? [Is arson an archaic attempt at sublimation?] *Internationale Zeitschrift für ärztliche Psychoanalyse*, 3: 139–153.

Pfister, Oskar (1917). *Die Psychoanalyse im Dienste der Erziehung*. Leipzig: Klinkhardt. *Psycho-Analysis in the Service of Education. Being an Introduction to Psycho-Analysis*. London: Kimpton, 1922.

Pick, Arnold (1901). Review of Freud, *Über den Traum. Prager medizinische Wochenschrift*, 26 (12): 145.

Placzek, Siegfried (1907). Review of Freud, *Sammlung kleiner Schriften zur Neurosenlehre. Berliner klinische Wochenschrift*, 31: 1000.

Placzek, Siegfried (1915). Freundschaft und Sexualität [Friendship and sexuality]. *Zeitschrift für Sexualwissenschaft*, 2: 265–283 [in book form: Bonn: Marcus & Weber].

Pomer, Sydney L. (1966). Max Eitingon: The organization of psychoanalytic training. In: Franz Alexander et al. (Eds.), *Psychoanalytic Pioneers* (pp. 51–62). New York: Basic Books.

Prince, Morton (1911). The mechanism and interpretation of dreams. A reply to Dr. Jones. *Journal of Abnormal Psychology*, 5 (Feb.–Mar.): 337–353.

Protze, H. (1917). Der Baum als totemistisches Symbol in der Dichtung [The tree as totemistic symbol in poetry]. *Imago, Zeitschrift für Anwendung der Psychoanalyse auf die Geisteswissenschaften*, 5: 58–62.

Putnam, James Jackson (1909–10). Personal impressions of Sigmund Freud and his work, with special reference to his recent lectures at Clark University. *Journal of Abnormal Psychology*, 4 (Dec. 1909–Jan. 1910): 293–310; 4 (Feb.–Mar. 1910): 372–379.

Putnam, James Jackson (1910a). Introduction to Brill's translation of Freud's *Drei Abhandlungen zur Sexualtheorie*. In: *Nervous and Mental Diseases Monograph Series No. 7*. New York: Nervous and Mental Diseases Publishing Company.

Putnam, James Jackson (1910b). On the etiology and treatment of the psychoneuroses. *Boston Medical and Surgical Journal*, 163: 75–82. Über Ätiologie und Behandlung der Psychoneurosen. *Zentralblatt für Psychoanalyse: Medizinische Monatsschrift für Seelenkunde*, 1 (1910/11): 137–154.

Putnam, James Jackson (1914). Dream interpretation and the theory of psychoanalysis. *Journal of Abnormal Psychology*, 9 (Apr.–May): 36–60.

Putnam, James Jackson (1915). *Human Motives*. Boston, MA: Little, Brown.

Putnam, James Jackson (1916): The work of Alfred Adler considered with especial reference to that of Freud. *Psychoanalytic Review*, 3: 121–240.

Quinn, Susan (1987). *A Mind of Her Own: The Life of Karen Horney*. New York: Summit Books.

Raimann, Emil (1916). Book review of *Jahrbuch für Psychoanalyse (1916)*. *Wiener klinische Wochenschrift*, 28: 127.

Rank, Otto (1907). *Der Künstler: Ansätze zu einer Sexualpsychologie*. Vienna: Heller. *The Artist. Journal of the Otto Rank Association*, 15 (1980): 1.

Rank, Otto (1909). *Der Mythus von der Geburt des Helden: Versuch einer psychologischen Mythendeutung (Schriften zur angewandten Seelenkunde 5)*. Leipzig,

Vienna: Deuticke. *The Myth of the Birth of the Hero: A Psychological Interpretation of Mythology. Nervous and Mental Diseases Monograph Series No. 18.* New York: Nervous and Mental Diseases Publishing Company, 1914. New York: Brunner, 1952.

Rank, Otto (1912). *Das Inzest-Motiv in Dichtung und Sage.* Vienne: Deuticke. *The Incest Theme in Literature and Legend: Fundamentals of a Psychology of Literary Creation.* Baltimore: Johns Hopkins Press, 1992.

Rank, Otto (1917a). Homer, Psychologische Beiträge zur Entstehungsgeschichte des Volksepos. I. [Homer, Psychological contributions to the history of the origin of the folk epic. I.] *Imago, Zeitschrift für Anwendung der Psychoanalyse auf die Geisteswissenschaften,* 5: 133–169.

Rank, Otto (1917b). Das Volksepos. II: Die dichterische Phantasiebildung [The folk epic II: The formation of poetic fantasies.] *Imago, Zeitschrift für Anwendung der Psychoanalyse auf die Geisteswissenschaften,* 5: 372–393.

Rank, Otto (1919). *Psychoanalytische Beiträge zur Mythenforschung: Gesammelte Studien aus den Jahren 1912 bis 1914* [Psychoanalytic contributions to the research on myths. Collected works from the years 1912 to 1914]. Leipzig, Vienna: Internationaler Psychoanalytischer Verlag (Internationale Psychoanalytische Bibliothek No. 4).

Rank, Otto (1924a). *Das Trauma der Geburt und seine Bedeutung für die Psychoanalyse.* Leipzig, Vienna: Internationaler Psychoanalytischer Verlag. *The Trauma of Birth.* London: Paul, Trench, Trubner, 1929. New York: Dover, 1993.

Rank, Otto (1924b). The trauma of birth and its importance for psychoanalytic therapy. *Psychoanalytic Review,* 11: 241–245.

Rank, Otto (1925). Zur Genese der Genitalität [On the genesis of genitality]. *Internationale Zeitschrift für Psychoanalyse,* 11: 411–428.

Rank, Otto, & Sachs, Hanns (1912). Entwicklung und Ansprüche der Psychoanalyse [The development and claims of psychoanalysis]. *Imago, Zeitschrift für Anwendung der Psychoanalyse auf die Geisteswissenschaften,* 1: 1–16.

Rank, Otto, & Sachs, Hanns (1916). *The Significance of Psychoanalysis for the Mental Sciences.* New York: The Nervous and Mental Disease Publishing Company. New York: Johnson Reprint, 1970.

Régis, Emmanuel, & Hesnard, Angelo Louis Marie (1913). La doctrine de Freud et de son école [The theory of Freud and of his school]. *Encéphale, Journal de Psychiatrie,* 8: 356–378, 446–481, 537–564.

Régis, Emmanuel & Hesnard, Angelo Louis Marie (1914). *La Psychoanalyse des névroses et des psychoses, ses applications médicales et extra-médicales* [The psychoanalysis of neuroses and psychoses, its medical and non-medical applications]. Paris: Alcan.

Reik, Theodor (1911). Flauberts Jugendregungen. Der liebende Flaubert. [Emotional impulses of young Flaubert. Flaubert as a lover.] *Pan,* 2 (3, 4) (Nov.).

Reik, Theodor (1912). *Flaubert und seine "Versuchung des Heiligen Antonius": ein Beitrag zur Künstlerpsychologie* [Flaubert and his "Temptations of St. Anthony": A contribution to the psychology of artists]. Minden: Bruns.

Reik, Theodor (1914). Die Couvade und die Psychogenese der Vergeltungsfurcht. *Imago, Zeitschrift für Anwendung der Psychoanalyse auf die Geisteswissenschaften*, 3: 409–455. The couvade and the psychogenesis of the fear of retaliation. *Ritual: Psycho-Analytic Studies* (pp. 27–89). London: Hogarth and Institute of Psycho-Analysis, 1931.

Reik, Theodor (1915a). Zur Auffassung der Wiedergeburtsphantasie [On the conception of the phantasy of rebirth]. *Internationale Zeitschrift für ärztliche Psychoanalyse*, 3: 181.

Reik, Theodor (1915b). Die Pubertätsriten der Wilden. Über einige Übereinstimmungen im Seelenleben der Wilden und der Neurotiker [The puberty rites of savages. On some parallels in the mental lives of savages and neurotics]. *Imago, Zeitschrift für Anwendung der Psychoanalyse auf die Geisteswissenschaften*, 4 (1915/16): 125–144, 189–222.

Reik, Theodor (1917). Vom Seelenleben eines zweijährigen Knaben [The mental life of a two-year-old boy]. *Internationale Zeitschrift für ärztliche Psychoanalyse*, 4 (1916/17): 329.

Reik, Theodor (1919). *Probleme der Religionspsychologie, 1. Teil: Das Ritual* (Internationale Psychoanalytische Bibliothek No. 5). Mit einer Vorrede von Sigmund Freud. Leipzig, Vienna: Internationaler Psychoanalytischer Verlag. *Psycho-Analytic Studies*. Preface Sigmund Freud. New York: International Universities Press, 1958.

Reik, Theodor (1925). Der Ursprung der Psychologie [The origin of psychology]. *Internationale Zeitschrift für Psychoanalyse*, 11: 513.

Reik, Theodor (1940). *From Thirty Years with Freud*. New York, Toronto: Farrar & Rinehart. Westport, CT: Greenwood Press, 1975.

Reik, Theodor (1951). *Dogma and Compulsion. Psychoanalytic Studies of Religion and Myths*. New York: International Universities Press.

Reik, Theodor (1956). *The Search Within, The Inner Experiences of a Psychoanalyst*. New York: Grove Press. New York: J. Aronson, 1974.

Rey de Castro, Alvaro (1990). Las cartas de Sigmund Freud a Honorio Delgado [Freud's letters to Honorio Delgado]. In: J. Mariátegui (Ed.), *Freud y el psicoanálisis: Escritos y testimonio*. Lima: Universidad Peruana Cayetano Heredia, Fondo Editorial.

Ries, Paul (1995). Popularise and/or be damned: Psychoanalysis and film at the crossroads in 1925. *International Journal of Psycho-Analysis*, 76: 759–791.

Riklin, Franz (1907). Psychologie und Sexualsymbolik der Märchen [Psychology and sexual symbolism of fairy tales]. *Psychiatrisch-neurologische Wochenschrift*, 9: 22–24.

Riklin, Franz (1908). *Wunscherfüllung und Symbolik im Märchen* (*Schriften zur angewandten Seelenkunde 2*). Vienna, Leipzig: Hugo Heller. Wishfulfillment and symbolism in fairy tales. *Nervous and Mental Diseases Monograph Series*. New York: Nervous and Mental Diseases Publishing Company, 1915.

Riklin, Franz (1912a). Ödipus und Psychoanalyse [Oedipus and psychoanalysis]. *Wissen und Leben*, 5: 20.

Riklin, Franz (1912b). Über Psychoanalyse [On psychoanalysis]. *Korrespondenzblatt schweizerischer Ärzte*, 42: 1015–1026.

Roazen, Paul (1968). *Freud: Political and Social Thought*. New York: Knopf. New York: Da Capo Press, 1986. With a new introduction by the author, New Brunswick, NJ: Transaction Publishers, 1999.
Roazen, Paul (1969). *Brother Animal: The Story of Freud and Tausk*. New York: Knopf. With a new introduction by the author. New Brunswick, NJ: Transaction Publishers, 1990.
Roazen, Paul (1975). *Freud and His Followers*. New York: Knopf. New York: Da Capo, 1992.
Roazen, Paul (1985). *Helene Deutsch: A Psychoanalyst's Life*. New Brunswick, NJ: Transaction Publishers, 1992.
Roazen, Paul (1990). *Encountering Freud: The Politics and Histories of Psychoanalysis*. New Brunswick, NJ: Transaction Publishers.
Roazen, Paul (Ed.) (1991). Tausk, Victor. *Collected Psychoanalytic Papers*. See Tausk (1991).
Roazen, Paul (Ed.) (1992). *Collected Psychoanalytic Papers of Helene Deutsch*. See Deutsch (1992).
Roazen, Paul (1993). *Meeting Freud's Family*. Amherst, MA: University of Massachusetts Press.
Roazen, Paul (1995). *How Freud Worked: First-Hand Accounts of Patients*. Northvale, NJ: Jason Aronson.
Roazen, Paul (2000). *Oedipus in Britain: Edward Glover and the Struggle over Klein*. New York: Other Press.
Roazen, Paul (2001a). *The Historiography of Psychoanalysis*. New Brunswick, NJ: Transaction Publications.
Roazen, Paul (2001b). Using oral history about Freud: A case in his "Secret essay". *American Imago*, 58 (4): 793–812.
Roazen, Paul (2001c). The exclusion of Erich Fromm from the IPA. *Contemporary Psychoanalysis*, 37 (1): 5–42.
Roazen, Paul, & Swerdloff, Bluma (Eds.) (1995). *Heresy: Sandor Rado and the Psychoanalytic Movement*. Northvale, NJ: Jason Aronson.
Rohleder, Hermann (1912). *Die Masturbation. Eine Monographie für Ärzte, Pädagogen und gebildete Eltern* [Masturbation. A monograph for physicians, pedagogues, and educated parents]. Berlin: H. Kornfeld.
Romm, May (1966). Abraham Arden Brill: First American translator of Freud. In: Franz Alexander et al. (Eds.), *Psychoanalytic Pioneers* (pp. 210–223). New York: Basic Books.
Romm, Sharon (1983). *The Unwelcome Intruder: Freud's Struggle with Cancer*. New York: Praeger.
Rosenstein, Gaston (1912). Eine Kritik [A criticism]. *Jahrbuch für psychoanalytische und psychopathologische Forschungen*, 4 (2): 741–799.
Rosenthal, Tatiana (1911). Karin Michaelis: "Das gefährliche Alter" im Lichte der Psychoanalyse [Karin Michaelis: "The dangerous age" in the light of psychoanalysis]. *Zentralblatt für Psychoanalyse: Medizinische Monatsschrift für Seelenkunde*, 1 (1910/11): 277–294.
Rosenzweig, Saul (1992). *Freud, Jung, and Hall the King-Maker: The Historic*

*Expedition to America with G. Stanley Hall as Host and William James as Guest. Including the Complete Correspondence of Sigmund Freud and G. Stanley Hall and a New Translation of Freud's Lectures at Clark University on the Origin and Development of Psychoanalysis.* St. Louis, MO, Seattle, WA: Rana House, Hogrefe & Huber.

Rothe, Hans-Joachim (Ed.) (1991). *Karl Landauer: Theorie der Affekte und andere Schriften zur Ich-Organisation* [Karl Landauer. A theory of affects and other writings on the organization of the ego]. Frankfurt/Main: Fischer.

Roudinesco, Elisabeth (1982, 1986). *La Bataille de Cent Ans: Histoire de la Psychanalyse en France* [The battle of 100 years. The history of psychoanalysis in France], *Vol. 1: 1885–1939*. Paris: Seuil.

Roudinesco, Elisabeth (1986). *La Bataille de Cent Ans: Histoire de la Psychanalyse en France, Vol. 2: 1925–1985*. Paris: Seuil. *Jacques Lacan & Co.: A History of Psychoanalysis in France, 1925–1985*. Chicago: University of Chicago Press, 1990.

Sachs, Hanns (1914). Völkerpsychologie (Sammelreferat) [Ethnopsychology (Collective review)]. *Jahrbuch der Psychoanalyse, Neue Folge des Jahrbuchs für psychoanalytische und psychopathologische Forschungen*, 6: 374–382.

Sachs, Hanns (1944). *Freud, Master and Friend*. Cambridge, MA: Harvard University Press.

Sadger, Isidor (1908). *Konrad Ferdinand Meyer: Eine pathographisch-psychologische Studie* [Konrad Ferdinand Meyer. A pathographic–psychological study] *(Grenzfragen des Nerven- und Seelenlebens, Bd. 59)*. Wiesbaden: Bergmann.

Sadger, Isidor (1914). Perversionen [Perversions]. *Jahrbuch der Psychoanalyse, Neue Folge des Jahrbuchs für psychoanalytische und psychopathologische Forschungen*, 6: 296–313.

Schilder, Paul (1918). *Wahn und Erkenntnis, eine psychopathologische Studie* [Delusion and insight, a psychopathological study]. Berlin: J. Springer. Heft 15 der Monographien aus dem Gesamtgebiete der Neurologie und Psychiatrie.

Schmid, Hans (1914). Zur Psychologie der Brandstifter [On the psychology of arsonists]. *Psychologische Abhandlungen*, 1: 80–179.

Schreber, Daniel Paul (1903). *Denkwürdigkeiten eines Nervenkranken, nebst Nachträgen und einem Anhang über die Frage: "Unter welchen Voraussetzungen darf eine für geisteskrank erachtete Person gegen ihren erklärten Willen in einer Heilanstalt festgehalten werden?"* Leipzig: Oswald Mutze. *Memoirs of My Nervous Illness*. London: W. Dawson, 1955. Cambridge, MA: Harvard University Press, 1988. New York: New York Review of Books, 2000.

Schur, Max (1972). *Freud: Living and Dying*. New York: International Universities Press.

Servaes, Franz (1907). *Giovanni Segantini: Sein Leben und Werk* [Giovanni Segantini. His life and work]. Leipzig: Klinkhardt & Biermann.

Shamdasani, Sonu (1997). "Should this remain?" Anna Freud's misgivings concerning the Freud–Jung letters. *International Forum of Psychoanalysis*, 5, 227–232. In: P. Mahony, C. Bonomi & J. Stensson (Eds.), *Behind the Scenes, Freud in Correspondence* (pp. 357–367). Stockholm: Scandinavian University Press.

Simmel, Ernst (1918). *Kriegsneurosen und psychisches Trauma, Ihre gegenseitigen Beziehungen, dargestellt auf Grund psychoanalytischer, hypnotischer Studien* [War neuroses and psychic trauma. Their mutual relations, presented on the basis of studies in psychoanalysis and hypnosis]. Munich, Leipzig: Nemnich.

Simmel, Ernst (1919a). Zweites Korreferat [Second discussion]. In: *Zur Psychoanalyse der Kriegsneurosen* (pp. 42–60). Internationale Psychoanalytische Bibliothek, No. 1. Leipzig: Internationaler Psychoanalytischer Verlag.

Simmel, Ernst (1919b). Psychoanalyse der Massen [Psychology of the masses]. Zweite Beilage [second insert], *Vossische Zeitung* (24 Aug.).

Simmel, Ernst (1920). "Zur Psychoanalyse des Spielers." Paper presented to the Berlin Psychoanalytic Society, (14 Oct. 1919) and at the Sixth International Psychoanalytic Congress (The Hague, 1920). *Internationale Zeitschrift für Psychoanalyse*, 6: 397. Psycho-analysis of the gambler. *International Journal of Psycho-Analysis*, 1: 352–353.

Skliar, N. (1904). *Über Gefängnispsychosen* [On prison psychoses]. Berlin: S. Karger.

Spitteler, Carl (1906). *Imago*. Frankfurt/Main: Suhrkamp, 1979.

Stegmann, Arnold Georg (1908). Zur Ätiologie des Asthmas bei Kindern [On the aetiology of asthma in children]. *Medizinische Klinik*, 29.

Stekel, Wilhelm (1908). *Nervöse Angstzustände und ihre Behandlung*. Berlin, Vienna: Urban & Schwarzenberg. *Conditions of Nervous Anxiety and Their Treatment*. London: Paul, Trench, Trubner, 1923.

Stekel, Wilhelm (1911). *Die Sprache des Traumes: Eine Darstellung der Symbolik und Deutung des Traumes in ihren Beziehungen zur kranken und gesunden Seele*. Munich, Wiesbaden: Bergmann. *Sex and Dreams; the Language of Dreams* (a translation of first part of above). Boston: Badger, 1922.

Stekel, Wilhelm (1917). *Onanie und Homosexualität (Die homosexuelle Neurose)*. Berlin: Urban & Schwarzenberg. *Auto-Erotism, a Psychiatric Study of Onanism and Neurosis*. New York: Liveright, 1950.

Stekel, Wilhelm (1950). *The Autobiography of Wilhelm Stekel: The Life Story of a Pioneer Psychoanalyst* (ed. Emil A. Gutheil). New York: Liveright.

Stepansky, Paul E. (1983). *In Freud's Shadow: Adler in Context*. Hillside, NJ: Analytic Press. Distributed by L. Erlbaum.

Stockmayer, Wolf (1909). Review of Freud, S., Die Traumdeutung. *Zentralblatt für Nervenheilkunde und Psychiatrie*, 32: 364–368.

Storfer, Adolf Josef (1911). *Zur Sonderstellung des Vatermordes; eine rechtsgeschichtliche und völkerpsychologische Studie* [On the exceptional position of patricide. A lego-historical and folk-psychological study] (*Schriften zur angewandten Seelenkunde 12*). Leipzig, Vienna: Deuticke.

Strohmayer, Wilhelm (1908). Über die ursächlichen Beziehungen der Sexualität zu Angst- und Zwangszuständen [On the causal relations of sexuality to anxiety- and compulsive states]. *Journal für Psychologie und Neurologie*, 12: 69–95.
Stucken, Eduard (1907). *Astralmythen der Hebräer, Babylonier und Ägypter* [Astral myths of the Hebrews, Babylonians, and Egyptians] (5 parts). Leipzig: E. Pfeiffer.
Swales, Peter J. (1983). Freud, Martha Bernays & the language of flowers. Privately published by the author.
Székely-Kovács, Olga, &, Berény, Robert (1954 [1924]). *Caricatures of 88 Pioneers in Psychoanalysis: Drawn from Life at the Eighth International Psychoanalytic Congress*. New York: Basic Books.
Tansley, Arthur G. (1920). *The New Psychology and Its Relation to Life*. London: Allen & Unwin.
Tausk, Victor (1914). Philosophie [Philosophy]. *Jahrbuch der Psychoanalyse, Neue Folge des Jahrbuchs für psychoanalytische und psychopathologische Forschungen*, 6: 405–412.
Tausk, Victor (1916–17). Zur Psychologie des Deserteurs. *Internationale Zeitschrift für ärztliche Psychoanalyse*, 4: 193–204, 229–240. On the psychology of the war deserter. *Psychoanalytic Quarterly*, 38 (1969): 354–381.
Tausk, Victor (1917). Bemerkungen zu Abrahams Aufsatz "Über Ejaculatio praecox" [Remarks on Abraham's paper "On ejaculatio praecox"]. *Internationale Zeitschrift für ärztliche Psychoanalyse*, 4 (1916/17): 315–327.
Tausk, Victor (1919). Über die Entstehung des "Beeinflussungsapparates" in der Schizophrenie. *Internationale Zeitschrift für ärztliche Psychoanalyse*, 5: 1–33. On the origin of the "influencing machine" in schizophrenia. *Psychoanalytic Quarterly*, 2 (1933): 519–556.
Tausk, Victor (1991). *Sexuality, War and Schizophrenia: Collected Psychoanalytic Papers* (ed. Paul Roazen). New Brunswick, NJ: Transaction Publishers.
Timms, Edward (Ed.) (1995). *Freud and the Child Woman: The Memoirs of Fritz Wittels*. New Haven, CT: Yale University Press.
Tuchman, Barbara W. (1962). *The Guns of August*. New York: Bantam Books, 1989.
Urban, Rudolf von (1958). *Myself not Least: A Confessional Autobiography of a Psychoanalyst and Some Explanatory History Cases*. London: Jarrolds.
Veneziani Svevo, Livia (1989). *Memoir of Italo Svevo*. London: Libris. Marlboro, VT: Marlboro Press, 1990. Evanston: Northwestern University Press, 2001.
Vermorel, Henri, & Vermorel, Madelaine (1993). *Sigmund Freud et Romain Rolland, Correspondance 1923–1936* [Sigmund Freud and Romain Rolland, Correspondence 1923–1936]. Paris: Calmann-Lévy.
Walser, Hans H. (1976–77). Psychoanalyse in der Schweiz [Psychoanalysis in Switzerland]. In: Dieter Eicke (Ed.), *Tiefenpsychologie, Band 2: Neue Wege der Psychoanalyse, Psychoanalyse der Gesellschaft, Die psychoanalytische Bewegung* (pp. 455–481). Weinheim: Beltz, 1982.

Warda, Wolfgang (1909). Zur Geschichte und Kritik der sogenannten psychischen Zwangszustände [On the history and critique of so-called psychic obsessional states]. *Archiv für Psychiatrie, 39*.
Weber, Kaspar (1991). Aus den Anfängen der Psychoanalyse in Bern [On the beginnings of psychoanalysis in Berlin]. *Bulletin, Schweizerische Gesellschaft für Psychoanalyse, 32*: 67–72.
Weiss, Edoardo (1970). *Briefe zur psychoanalytischen Praxis. Mit den Erinnerungen eines Pioniers der Psychoanalyse* (Vorbemerkung und Einleitung von Martin Grotjahn; mit Kommentaren von Edoardo Weiss). Frankfurt/Main: Fischer. *Sigmund Freud as a Consultant: Recollections of a Pioneer in Psychoanalysis* (ed. Martin Grotjahn, commentaries by Edoardo Weiss). New York: Intercontinental Medical Book Corporation [reprinted, with a new Foreword by Emilio Weiss and a new Introduction by Paul Roazen. New Brunswick, NJ: Transaction Publishers, 1991].
Welsch, Ursula, & Wiesner, Michaela (1988). *Lou Andreas-Salomé: Vom "Lebensurgrund" zur Psychoanalyse*. Munich: Internationaler Psychoanalytischer Verlag.
Whitrow, Magda (1993). *Julius Wagner-Jauregg (1857–1940)*. London: Smith-Gordon.
Will, Herbert (1984). *Georg Groddeck: Die Geburt der Psychosomatik* [Georg Groddeck. The birth of psychosomatics]. Munich: Deutscher Taschenbuch Verlag.
Winckler, Hugo (1901). *Himmels- und Weltenbild der Babylonier als Grundlage der Weltanschauung und Mythologie aller Völker* [The Babylonians' view of heaven and earth as the basis of the Weltanschauung and mythology of all peoples]. Leipzig: J. C. Hinrichs.
Wittels, Fritz (1907). *Die Sexuelle Not* [The sexual need]. Vienna, Leipzig: C. W. Stern.
Wittels, Fritz (1910). *Ezechiel der Zugereiste* [Ezekiel the newcomer]. Berlin: E. Fleischel.
Wittels, Fritz (1924). *Sigmund Freud: Der Mann–die Lehre–die Schule*. Leipzig. *Sigmund Freud, His Personality, His Teaching, and His School*. New York: Dodd, Mead & Co. Freeport, NY: Books for Libraries Press, 1971.
Wittenberger, Gerhard (1995). *Das "Geheime Komitee" Sigmund Freuds, Institutionalisierungsprozesse in der "Psychoanalytischen Bewegung" zwischen 1912 und 1927* [Sigmund Freud's "Secret Committee". Processes of institutionalisation within the "Psychoanalytic Movement" between 1912 and 1927]. Tübingen: edition diskord.
Wittenberger, Gerhard, & Tögel, Christfried (Eds.) (1999). *Die Rundbriefe des "Geheimen Komitees"* [The circular letters of the "Secret Committee"], *Vol. 1*. Tübingen: edition diskord.
Wulff, Mosche (1909). Beitrag zur Psychologie der Dementia Praecox [Contribution to the psychology of dementia praecox]. *Zeitschrift für die gesamte Neurologie und Psychiatrie*.
Wulff, Mosche (1910–11). Die russische psychoanalytische Literatur bis zum

Jahre 1911 [The Russian psychoanalytic literature until the year 1911]. *Zentralblatt für Psychoanalyse: Medizinische Monatsschrift für Seelenkunde*, 1: 364–371.

Zulliger, Hans (1966). Oskar Pfister: Psychoanalysis and faith. In: Franz Alexander et al. (Eds.), *Psychoanalytic Pioneers* (pp. 169–179). New York: Basic Books.

# INDEX

Abraham, Karl (*passim*):
   Amenhotep IV, 146, 147, 149, 152, 154, 164
   *Dreams and Myths*, 29, 30, 34, 40, 54, 58, 62, 63, 66, 83, 85, 86, 150, 162, 179, 194, 253, 438
   editor of *Jahrbuch*, 204, 209, 210
   editor of *Zeitschrift*, 389
   *Giovanni Segantini*, 81, 82*bn*,* 83–86, 97, 98, 101, 103, 104, 108, 112, 113, 116, 117, 120, 122, 124–126, 129, 132, 136–138, 143, 147, 155, 504, 508
   president of IPA, 234, 235, 239, 498, 499
   *Study of the Development of the Libido*, 376, 386, 448, 465, 477, 478
Abraham, August, 109
Abraham, Gerd, 117, 307–308, 315, 321, 328, 338, 345, 542
Abraham, Hedwig Marie, *née* Bürgner (*passim*), 10*bn*
Abraham, Hilda C., xxix, 88*bn*, 542
   editor of Freud–Abraham correspondence, ix, x
Abraham, Johanne, 293
accident neurosis, 53
acting out, role of in analysis, 480

active therapy, 481
Adler, Alfred (*passim*), 107*bn*
   and Abraham, conflict with, 132, 160, 254
   on aggression, 131
   chairman, Vienna Society, 109
   editor of *Zentralblatt*, 28, 109, 115
   resignation, 142, 169
   and Freud, conflict with, 131, 133, 141, 142, 181, 242, 246, 283, 330, 358
   and Jung, 109
   on organ inferiority, 180
   president of Vienna Society, resignation from, 129–132
   and Rank, 31
Adler, Friedrich, 350
Adler, Otto, 198
Adler, Victor, 350
Adorno, Theodor W., 286
aggression, role of, 107
agoraphobia, 91, 92, 210
Alcan, F., 261
Alexander, Franz, 120, 143, 459, 460*bn*, 499, 524, 557, 560
Alexander, Tsar, 35
Altenberg, Peter, 47
Alzheimer, Alois, 276*bn*
ambivalence, xxviii, 7, 247, 248, 250

---

*\*bn* indicates that the page includes a biographical note.

American Psychoanalytic Association, 130, 139, 292, 461, 499
  foundation of, 116, 130
  Hoch president of, 234
  Putnam president of, 102
  recognition of as branch society of IPA, 139
American Psychological Association, 102
anal erotism, 3, 29, 31, 34, 77–80, 299, 303–305, 309, 356
anal-sadistic aetiology, 368
Andreas-Salomé, Lou, 125, 150*bn*, 151, 166, 173, 189, 253–255, 263, 316, 362, 451, 456
  Freud correspondence, ix
  "six" (actually five) brothers of, 287–290
animal totemism, 187
anorexia, hysterical, 324
anxiety, 286
  in enclosed space, 517
  neurosis(es), 25–27, 87
aphasia–abasia, 297
Archimedes, 33
Aristophanes, 552
Ärztliche Gesellschaft für Sexualwissenschaft und Eugenie [Medical Society for Sexology and Eugenics], 176, 188, 196, 197, 198, 230, 252
Asch, Joseph J., xii, 498, 499*bn*, 501, 505
Aschaffenburg, Gustav, 118, 119*bn*, 120, 129
Assagioli, Roberto Greco, xx
Association for Sexual Science, 175, 178
auto-eroticism, xxiv, 2, 4, 5, 26, 29, 132
  infantile, 2

Bach, David, 142
Bahr, Hermann, 47
Balfour, Arthur James, 364
Balkányi, Charlotte, 499
Bárány, Robert, 339*bn*
Bárczy, István, 387*bn*
  fund, 385
Baroncini, Luigi, 62
Beer-Hofmann, Richard, 47
Behrmann, Ida, 110

Bell, Clive, 456
Beltran, Juan Ramon, 506
Benedek, Therese, 474*bn*, 476, 527
Benussi, Vittorio, 477, 478*bn*
Berény, Robert, 474
Bergmann, J. F., 142, 168, 169, 219, 244
Berlin Central Institute for Psychotherapy and Depth Psychology, 263
Berlin Psychoanalytic Institute, 110, 142, 143, 391
Berlin Psychoanalytic Polyclinic, 50, 403, 404, 410, 418
Berlin Psychoanalytic Society, *passim*
  Abraham president of, xxiii
Bernays, Anna, *née* Freud, 456
Bernays, Edward Louis, 554
Bernays, Eli, 456
Bernays, Emmeline, 115
Bernays, Judith ("Ditha"), 456*bn*
Bernays, Minna, 61, 115, 126*bn*, 189, 193, 194, 318, 421, 444, 456, 468, 469, 497
Bernfeld, Siegfried, 528, 556, 557, 559, 561, 564, 565, 566
  "film affair", xiii
  secretary of Vienna Society, 524
Bibby, Dr, 459
Binswanger, Hertha, *née* Buchberger, 102
Binswanger, Ludwig, xx, 20, 58, 59*bn*, 60, 65, 83, 87, 101, 102, 155, 208, 262, 280, 283, 307, 337, 355, 356, 402
  –Freud correspondence, x
  president of Zurich Psychoanalytic Society, 59, 114, 118
Binswanger, Otto, 20*bn*, 59
Birch-Pfeiffer, Charlotte, 552*bn*
Birstein, J., 196
birth trauma, 480–484, 502
Bjerre, Poul Carl, 125*bn*, 188, 339
Bleuler, Eugen (*passim*), 7*bn*
  on dementia praecox, 20
  director of *Jahrbuch*, 37
  "dynamic psychiatry", 7
  editor of *Jahrbuch*, 44
  and Freud x, 52, 54, 114
  and Freud/Jung controversy, x, xxi–xxvii, xxx, 114

# INDEX

and IPA, 112, 118
and Jung, x, 37
reservations on psychoanalysis, 37, 38, 55, 60, 113, 55
on schizophrenia, xxiii, 1, 7
Bloch, Iwan, 56, 57*bn*, 80, 176, 252
Bloomsbury group, 456
Blum, Ernst, 455, 456*bn*, 496
Blumgart, Leonard, 458
Böcklin, Arnold, 126, 127*bn*
Böhm, Felix, 110, 262, 263, 391*bn*, 392, 396, 405, 406, 407, 410, 418, 419
Bonaparte, Marie, 128, 460, 503
    Fliess–Freud correspondence, x
Bondy (Fliess), Ida, 128*bn*
Bonhoeffer, Dietrich, 169
Bonhoeffer, Karl, 168, 169*bn*, 173, 174, 178, 200, 203, 365, 366, 371, 420, 422, 424, 425, 429
Bonomi, Carlo, 21
Boston Psychoanalytic Institute, 387
Boston Psychoanalytic Society, 244, 560
Braatz, Emil, 64, 65*bn*
Brasch (Freud), Lucie ("Lux"), 98, 420, 421, 422, 424, 427, 447
Braun, Heinrich, 350
Braun-Vogelstein, Julie, 350
Breasted, James Henry, 152, 153
Brecher, Guido, 148, 149*bn*
Brecher, Gustav, 459
Brecht, Karen, 110
Breitner, Hugo, 503
Bresler, Johannes, 27, 28*bn*
Breuer, Josef, 21, 45, 59, 79, 202*bn*, 383, 395, 396, 397, 549
    on "complex", 8
Breuer, Mathilde, 21*bn*
Brill, Abraham Arden, xx, xxiv, xxx, 71, 72*bn*, 75, 122, 123, 130, 131, 159, 234, 330, 461, 471, 498, 502, 523, 525, 526, 538
British Psycho-Analytical Society, 205, 457
    establishment of, 299
Brugsch, Theodor, 170, 199–201, 203, 207, 209, 210, 398, 424
Bryan, Douglas, 197
Buchberger (Binswanger), Hertha, 102

Budapest Society, 204
Bullitt, William Christian, 392*bn*
Bürgner, Hedwig Marie (*passim*), 10*bn*
Burnham, John C., 162, 285
Burns, Robert, 301
Burrow, Trigant, xx, 292*bn*, 293
Busch, Wilhelm, 35*bn*, 535
Byron, George Gordon, Lord, 241, 315

Campbell, Charles Macfie, xx
Campbell, Thomas, 315
cannibalistic-oral sadism, 472, 522
Caravedo, Baltazar, 515
Carotenuto, Aldo, 35, 177, 248, 294
Carter, Howard, 461
Cassian, P., 397
castration, 254
    anxiety, 214, 252, 254
    complex, 309
    female, 396, 399, 408, 424, 428, 432
    phantasy
        biting, against father, 522
Cato Uticensis, 561, 562
censorship, 29
Chalewsky, Fanny, 93, 94*bn*, 129
character formation, genital level of, 512, 514
Charcot, Jean-Martin, 35, 36, 445
Chicago Institute of Psychoanalysis, 460
child analysis, 181
childhood sexual trauma, 2–4
Christoffel, Hans, 516, 517*bn*
circular psychosis, 127
Clark, L. Pierce, 557, 560*bn*, 561
Clark, Ronald W., 96, 166
Clarke, C. K., 76
Clark University, Worcester, Mass., 76, 77, 86, 95, 101, 102, 384
    Freud's lectures at, 111
classical technique, deviation from, 481
coitus interruptus, 25, 26, 28
condensation, 29, 291
consciousness, 286
Controversial Discussions, 473
conversion hysteria, 286
Copernicus, 345, 346
coprophilia, 105
Coriat, Isador Henry, 244, 557, 560*bn*, 561

countertransference, negative, 362
cryptomnesia, 445
*Cs.* (Conscious), 291
cyclothymia, 152, 154

Danielsen (Horney), Karen, 143*bn*, 144, 148, 149, 237, 358, 362, 392, 396, 418, 426, 110, 427
Darwin, Charles, 345, 346
Darwinism, 369
Daudet, Alphonse, 445
de Bruine Groeneveldt, Jan Rudolf, 246
Decke, Bettina, 293
Décsi, Imre, xx
de Groot (Lampl), Adriana (Jeanne), 457, 541
Delgado, Honorio F., 416*bn*, 460
delusion:
   of being watched, 226
   of grandeur, 6, 376
      unconscious, fear of light as, 153
   of inferiority, 376
dementia, 5, 6–7, 10–12
dementia praecox, xxiii, xxiv, 1–7, 11, 14, 16, 18, 20, 29, 37, 41, 46, 56, 59, 64, 85, 107, 131, 132, 162, 300, 301
de Mijolla, Alain, 503
depression, xxviii, xxix, 152
Deuticke, Franz (*passim*), 28*bn*
   publisher of Jahrbuch, 28, 41, 44, 111, 206, 209, 220, 250, 294, 409
Deutsch, Felix, 474*bn*, 496, 499, 512, 513, 516, 548, 549
Deutsch, Helene, *née* Rosenbach, xix, 181, 462, 470*bn*, 473, 474, 496, 499, 516, 524, 528
Deutscher Verein für Psychiatrie, 1
discharge, 291
displacement, 291
Doesburgh, S. C. von, 194
"Dora", Freud's case, 22
dream(s):
   flying, 19–22
   Godiva, 23, 24
   Seal, 24
Dreyfuss, Daniel K., 108, 109
drives, 300

Drucker (Freud), Ernestine ("Esti"), 404
Dubois, Paul Charles, 263*bn*
Durig, Arnold, 525
Dutch Society for Psychoanalysis, founding of, 343, 344

Eckermann, Johann Peter, 72*bn*
Eder, David Montague, 197, 202*bn*, 229, 266, 286, 298
Eder, Edith, 266*bn*, 286
Edmunds, Lavinia, 456
ego:
   -cathexes, localization of mourning in, 305
   -ideal, 226
      failure to form, 563
   -psychology, 152
Eibenschütz, Miss, 136
Einstein, Albert, xx
Eisner, Kurt, 385
Eissler, Kurt R., xvii, 166, 433
Eitingon, Max, 50*bn*, 55–567 (*passim*)
   American donation, 423
   analysed by Freud, 98, 104
   and Berlin Society, 50
   criticism of Jung, 221, 222
   director, psychoanalytic polyclinic, Berlin, 372, 402, 403, 407, 410, 418
   "film affair", xiii
   Freud correspondence, xvii
   military service in World War I, 270, 283, 294, 297, 330, 334, 349, 358
   president of IPA, 50
   secretary of IPA, 499
   and Secret Committee, 50, 404, 405, 411, 412, 420, 453
      conflict within, xii
Eitingon, Mirra Jacovleina, *née* Raigorodsky, 356
ejaculatio praecox, 252, 290, 374
Ellenberger, Henri F., 56, 242
Ellerman, Winifred (Bryher), 412
Ellis, Havelock, 114, 115*bn*, 220, 421
Emerson, Louville E., 234
Emmich, General von, 270
Engelbrecht, Hilke, 416

# INDEX

Ephron, Harmon, 144
Erikson, Erik H., xxix
*Erinnerungsunlust*, 3
Ermakov, Ivan Dmitrievitch, 496, 499*bn*
erotism, anal, 3
erythrophobia, 527
ethnopsychology, 29
Eulenburg, Albert, 176, 197, 198*bn*, 229, 232, 336, 337
exhibitionism, 215
  and fetishism, 83
  as perversion, 214

Fallend, Karl, 546, 557
Falzeder, Ernst, ix–xvii, xix–xxx, xxxi, 184, 237, 255, 449
fear of light, 153
Federn, Ernst, 434
Federn, Paul, 151, 152*bn*, 166, 272, 275, 353, 405, 406, 433, 478, 525, 558
  vice-president, Vienna Society, 524
female castration complex, 399
female leading zones, 530, 532
Fenichel, Otto, 373
Ferenczi, Sándor (*passim*), 63*bn*
  active therapy, 481
  analysands:
    Klein, 472
    Rickman, 457
    Róheim, 460
    Sokolnicka, 370
    Urbantschitsch, 525
  analysed by Freud, 281, 337
  Basedow's disease of, 346, 347, 348, 349, 351
  criticism of Bleuler, 202
  criticism of Jung, 221, 222, 247
  director, University Psychoanalytic Clinic, Budapest, 403
  Eder's analysis with, 202
  editor of *Zeitschrift*, 166, 167, 175
  Freud correspondence, x, xvi
  interest in clairvoyance, 158
  Jones's analysis with, 186, 187
  Jones's translation of works of, 350
  marriage to Gizella Pálos, 350, 358, 360
  military service in World War I, 272, 283, 285, 291, 292
  president, IPA, 384, 404
  Professor of Psychoanalysis, 398, 403, 415, 416, 428
  and Rank, collaboration between, 480, 483
  Secret Committee, 184, 290, 327, 406, 420, 453, 524, 525, 554
    conflict within, xii, 464, 502, 515, 521
  trauma of birth, 487
  University Psychoanalytic Clinic, Budapest, 403
  war neuroses, 351
fetishism, 105–107, 148
  *see also* foot fetishism
Feuerbach, Ludwig, 108
Fichtner, Gerhard, xvii, 102
"film affair", xiii, xxiii, 543, 554, 556, 564, 566
Flaubert, Gustave, 143
Flechsig, Paul Emil, 276*bn*
  Flechsig Clinic, 276
Fliess, Ida, *née* Bondy, 128*bn*
Fliess, Wilhelm, xxix, xxx, 9*bn*, 12, 127, 128, 130, 131, 132, 134, 229, 230, 325, 360, 361, 390, 558, 563
  Freud correspondence, ix, x
Flugel (Flügel), John Carl, 413, 414*bn*, 416
  secretary of IPA, 432
Foerster, Friedrich Wilhelm, 242*bn*
Foerster, Rudolf, 110*bn*, 242, 474
foot fetishism, 81, 83, 93, 105
Forel, Auguste Henri, xx, 79, 81, 82*bn*, 129, 242
Forsyth, David, 406, 407*bn*
Frank, Leonhard, 447*bn*
Frank, Ludwig, 78, 79*bn*, 81, 82
Frankfurt Psychoanalytic Working Group, 474
Franz Ferdinand, Archduke, assassination of, 252
free association, 392
Frenkel, Henri, 83, 84*bn*
Frensdorff, Dr, 539

Freud, Alexander, 86*bn*, 313, 314, 332
Freud, Amalie, 379
Freud, Anna (*passim*), 181*bn*
  Controversial Discussions, 473
  Freud's correspondences, x
  journey to England at start of World War I, 235, 272, 273, 275
Freud, Anton Walter, 404*bn*
Freud, Clemens Raphael (Clement), 420*bn*
Freud, Ella, *née* Haim, 321
Freud, Emanuel, 59, 91, 92
Freud, Ernestine ("Esti"), *née* Drucker, 404
Freud, Ernst, 98, 115*bn*, 197, 198, 199, 227, 268, 272, 279, 395, 401, 409, 412, 419, 420, 432, 448
  editor of Freud–Abraham correspondence, ix, x
  marriage to Lucie ("Lux") Brasch, 420, 421, 422, 424, 427
  military service in World War I, 265, 275, 280, 283, 291, 294, 295, 298, 300, 309, 313, 316, 322, 330, 332, 334, 340, 342, 349, 358, 361, 369, 371, 372, 374, 386
Freud, Eva, 513
Freud, Gabriel, 449
Freud, Henny, *née* Fuchs, 463*bn*, 464
Freud/Klein controversies, 440
Freud, Lucian Michael ("Lucien"), 420*bn*
Freud, Lucie ("Lux"), *née* Brasch, 98, 420, 421, 422, 424, 427, 447
Freud, M. Sophie, 404*bn*
Freud, Marie ("Mitzi"), 61*bn*, 213
Freud, Martha (*passim*)
Freud, Martin, 268, 276, 277, 279, 291, 302, 309, 340, 395, 404, 409, 462, 513
  marriage to Ernestine Drucker, 404, 405, 409, 468
  military service in World War I, 126, 265, 272–275, 280, 281, 283, 296, 297, 300, 313, 316, 322, 330, 332, 342, 346, 349, 358, 359, 361, 371, 372, 387, 389–391, 394, 401
Freud, Mathilde, 24, 25, 28, 30, 31, 79, 89, 163

Freud, Maurice (Moritz), 61, 213
Freud, Oliver ("Oli"), 115*bn*, 271, 321, 430, 432, 435, 450, 454, 459, 460, 479, 513
  analysed by Franz Alexander, 460
  engagement and marriage to Ella Haim, 321, 463, 464
  military service in World War I, 265, 280, 298, 300, 313, 340, 343, 346, 349, 358, 361, 371, 372, 386
Freud (Graf), Rosa, 353
Freud, Sigmund (*passim*)
  *An Autobiographical Study*, 514, 517, 537
  *Beyond the Pleasure Principle*, 434
  *Delusions and Dreams in Jensen's "Gradiva"*, 28, 71
  *On Dreams*, 350, 370
  *The Ego and the Id*, 456, 459
  *Group Psychology and the Analysis of the Ego*, 421, 423
  *Inhibitions, Symptoms and Anxiety*, 286
  *The Interpretation of Dreams*, 3, 401
  *Introductory Lectures on Psycho-Analysis*, 68, 329, 334, 417, 451
  *Jokes and Their Relation to the Unconscious*, 40, 41, 158, 476
  *Leonardo da Vinci and a Memory of His Childhood*, 97, 98, 101, 103, 106, 111, 114, 129, 130, 143, 391, 401
  president of Vienna Society, 130
  Prize, 460
  *The Psychopathology of Everyday Life*, 46, 68, 350, 401, 460
  *The Question of Lay Analysis*, 21, 525
  *Three Essays on the Theory of Sexuality*, 66, 67, 121, 133, 136, 140, 211, 297, 299, 306, 324
  *Totem and Taboo*, 141, 146, 152, 155, 165, 179, 184, 195, 210, 329, 357
Freud (Halberstadt), Sophie, 159*bn*, 176, 181, 218, 266, 273, 280, 332, 339, 344, 398, 403, 417
Freud, Stephan Gabriel (Stephen), 420*bn*, 447
Freund von Tószeghi, Anton, 273, 379*bn*,

# INDEX

382, 384, 386, 387, 389, 396, 400, 404, 406, 407, 409–412, 416, 417
Secret Committee, 406
Friedjung, Josef Karl, 142, 501, 503*bn*
Friedländer, Adolf Albrecht, 29, 30*bn*, 56, 57, 58, 111, 117, 119, 132, 398
Friedmann, F. F., 414
Friedrich the Great, 255
Friedrich Wilhelm I, 502
frigidity, 531
Frink, Horace Westlake, 455, 456*bn*, 498, 502
Fromm, Erich, 144, 286, 362, 474
Fromm-Reichmann, Frieda, 286, 362, 474
Frud, Amalie, 379*bn*
Fry, Roger, 456
Fuchs (Freud), Henny, 463*bn*, 464
Fürst, Emma, 496, 499
Furtmüller, Karl, 142

Garbai, Sándor, 396
Gaupp, Robert Eugen, 37*bn*, 47, 81, 82, 94, 118
Gay, Peter, 166, 384, 471
Gebsattel, Victor Emil Freiherr von, 262, 263*bn*
German Psychoanalytical Society, 391, 462
German Society for Psychiatry, 20
Gidal, Tim N., 474
Gildemeister, O., 241
Gincburg, Mira, 208, 209*bn*, 392
Glöckel, Hans, 503
Glover, Edward, xix, 439, 440*bn*
Glover, James, xix, 439, 440*bn*, 496, 499, 524
Goethe, Johann Wolfgang von, xxx, 20, 35, 106, 107, 223, 313
Goggin, Eileen Brockman, 110
Goggin, James E., 110
Goldwyn, Samuel, 544, 546
Göring Institute, 503
Grabbe, Christian Dietrich, 269
"Gradiva" study, Freud's, 27, 28, 70, 71
Graf, Cäcilie ("Mausi"), 353
Graf, Heinrich, 353*bn*
Graf, Herbert ["Little Hans"], 46
Graf, Hermann, 353*bn*

Graf, Max, 46*bn*
Graf, Rosa, *née* Freud, 353
Green, Martin, 47
Griesinger, Wilhelm, xx
Grimm, Jacob, 344*bn*
Grimm, Wilhelm, 344*bn*
Groddeck, Walter Georg, 362*bn*, 557
  Freud correspondence, ix
Gross, Alfred, 420*bn*
Gross, Otto, 73, 74*bn*, 478
Grosskurth, Phyllis, 184, 327, 421, 448, 471, 473
Grossman, Carl M., 362
Grossman, Sylvia, 362
group therapy, 292
Grubrich-Simitis, Ilse, 98
Grüner, Franz, 142
Grüner, Gustav, 142
Gudden, Bernhard Aloys von, xx

Haas, Miss, 380, 382, 383, 390
Häberlin, Paul, 86*bn*
Haeckel, Ernst, 57
Haenisch, Konrad, 422, 423
Haim (Freud), Ella, 321
Halberstadt, Ernst Wolfgang ("Ernstl"), 159*bn*, 339, 343, 403, 444, 449, 468
Halberstadt, Heinz Rudolph ("Heinerle"), 159, 403, 469
Halberstadt, Max, 98, 159*bn*, 176, 266, 273, 276, 403, 421, 448, 464
Halberstadt, Sophie, *née* Freud, 159*bn*, 176, 181, 218, 266, 273, 280, 332, 339, 344, 398, 403, 417
Hale, Nathan G., Jr., 96, 116, 241, 261, 456
Hall, Granville Stanley, 77*bn*
Hall, Stanley, 106, 219
Hampstead Clinic, 181
Hampstead Nurseries, 181
Handlbauer, Bernhard, 107, 142, 503
Happel-Pinkus, Clara, 474*bn*, 534
Harmat, Paul, 384
Hárnik, Jenö, 496, 499*bn*
Hattingberg, Hans Ritter von, 544, 546*bn*
hay fever, psychoanalysis of, 249
Haynal, André, xvii, xix–xxx
hebephrenia, 179
Heine, Heinrich, 364*bn*, 552

Heller, Hugo, 28*bn*, 45, 141, 146, 152, 166, 167, 206, 218, 288, 289, 294, 296, 323, 329, 342, 355, 363, 372, 374, 375
Hellpach, Willy, 113*bn*, 114
Henschel, Mrs, 112
Hering, Julius, 438, 439
Herzer, Manfred, 28, 230
Hesnard, Angelo Louis Marie, 146, 261
Hilferding, Margarete, 142, 281, 282, 287
Hiller, Eric, 401, 406
Hindenburg, Paul von Beneckendorff und von, 278*bn*
Hirsch Archives, 518
Hirschfeld, Elfriede, 255*bn*, 259, 262, 282
Hirschfeld, Magnus, 28*bn*, 36, 40, 41, 42, 47, 56, 75, 76, 78, 80, 93, 108, 109, 110, 113, 139, 140, 141, 154, 176, 230
Hirschmüller, Albrecht, 202
His, Wilhelm, 34, 35*bn*, 413, 422
Hitschmann, Eduard, 130, 185, 186*bn*, 194, 204, 205, 209, 213, 224, 225, 228, 229, 232, 234, 243, 247, 250, 256, 274, 275, 287, 289, 327, 389, 390, 504, 525, 529, 558
    editor of *Jahrbuch*, 205
    editor of *Zeitschrift*, 389
Hitzig, Eduard, xx
Hobman, Joseph Burton, 202
Hoch, August, 234
Hoche, Alfred E., 114*bn*, 116, 117, 180, 184, 220, 228, 413
Hoffer, Axel, 321
Hoffer, Peter, 4
Hoffman, Edward, 107
Hoffmann, Franz, 445
Hoffmann, Heinrich, xx
Hofmannsthal, Hugo von, 47
Hollerung, Edwin, 53*bn*
Hollitscher, Mathilde, 332, 456
Hollitscher, Robert, 31*bn*, 67, 79, 332, 456
Homer, 292
homosexuality, 20, 40, 43, 53, 64, 76, 78, 79, 85, 130, 141, 158, 404
    legalization of, 28
Honegger, Johann Jakob, xx
Horace, 112, 266

Horkheimer, Max, 286
Horney, Karen, *née* Danielsen, 143*bn*, 144, 148, 149, 237, 358, 362, 392, 396, 418, 426, 110, 427
Horney, Oskar, 427*bn*
Huber, Wolfgang, 187
Hubermann, Mrs, 441, 443
Hug-Hellmuth, Hermine [orig. Hug von Hugenstein], 186, 187*bn*, 247, 279, 344, 426, 430, 432
Huguenin, Gustav, xx
Hungarian Psychoanalytic Society, 379, 432
Hungarian Society, 461
Hurwitz, Emanuel, 47
Hye, Baron Franz von, 142
hypochondria, 232, 243
hysteria, xxiv, 1–5, 16, 20, 27, 34, 48, 53, 56, 58, 84, 85, 87, 98, 118, 122, 143, 207, 210, 223, 292, 299, 304, 330, 354, 408, 469
    case of "Dora", 22
hysterical anorexia, 324
hysterical phantasies, 29
hysterical vomiting, 531

Ibsen, Henryk, 344
"Ictus laryngis", 35, 36
identification, 29, 304
idiopathics [*Originäre*], 5
Ignotus (pseudonym for Veigelsberg), Hugó, 432*bn*
Ilm, Grete, 356
*Imago*, 141, 147, 148, 151, 156, 157
    foundation of, 141, 146
    Heller publisher of, 28, 141, 167, 288
    prize, 386
    problems of, in World War I, 296, 316, 349, 363
    Rank editor of, 31, 141, 521
    Sachs editor of, 141, 142, 521
impotence, 163
incest:
    barrier, 482
    taboo, 157
incestuous phantasies, 82
incorporation phantasy, 375
infantile auto-erotism, 2

infantile neurosis, 396
infantile sexuality, 1, 4, 64, 65, 66, 259, 262
infantile transference, 88
infantilism, 29
inhibition of the personality, 11
inner reality, 4
instinct(s):
　as drive, 482
　vicissitudes of, 291
Institute for Psychoanalysis, Chicago, 143
Internationale Gesellschaft für Sexualforschung [International Society for Sexual Research], 196
*International Journal of Psycho-Analysis*, 432
International Psychoanalytic Association [IPA]:
　Abraham president of, 234, 235, 239, 498, 499
　dissolution of, 205–206
　education committee of, 143
　Eitingon president of, 50
　Eitingon secretary of, 499
　Ferenczi founder of, 63
　Ferenczi president of, 63, 384
　Flügel secretary of, 414, 416, 450
　foundation of, 109
　*Internationale Zeitschrift für ärztliche Psychoanalyse*, 166, 167
　Jones president of, 41, 239, 432, 459
　Jung president of, 109, 112, 139
　Riklin secretary of, 28, 109, 142, 168, 238
　and Swiss Society for Psychoanalysis, 392
　von Freund secretary of, 384
International Psychoanalytic Congresses:
　First (Salzburg), xxiii, 20, 26, 29, 31, 36, 37, 38, 41, 50, 54, 55
　Second (Nuremberg), 101, 103, 104, 108, 109, 111
　Third (Weimar), 125, 134, 137, 138, 139, 141, 150, 170, 180
　Fourth (Munich), 183, 186, 187, 190, 191, 193, 238
　Fifth:
　　(Dresden—abandoned), 214, 215, 226, 236, 243, 254, 267
　　(Budapest), 379, 381, 383, 384, 385, 387, 403
　Sixth (The Hague), 404, 406–407, 415, 416, 421, 424, 427–429, 431, 432
　Seventh (Berlin), 456, 459
　Eighth (Salzburg), 477, 486, 490, 491, 492, 493, 494–498, 499, 500, 524, 525
　Ninth (Bad Homburg), 534, 536, 537, 557–559
International Society for Sexual Research, 196
International Training Committee, foundation of, 557
introjection, xxix
IPA, *see* International Psychoanalytic Association
"Irma's injection", 19
Isserlin, Max, 118, 119, 377, 378*bn*
Italian Psychoanalytical Society, 478

Jacobsen, Jens Peter, 381, 382*bn*
*Jahrbuch* (*passim*):
　under direction of
　　Bleuler, 37
　　Freud, 37
　discontinued in World War I, 294, 302, 328, 408
　edited by Abraham, 204, 209, 210
　edited by Hitschmann, 204
　edited by Jung, 37, 54, 58, 70, 71, 232
　resignation of, 194, 203–207
　first edition of, 80
　foundation of, 37, 41
　and Freud–Jung break, 194, 208, 209, 221, 222, 237, 239, 250
　last issue, 249, 287
　published by Deuticke, 28, 41, 409
　renaming of, 250
James, William, 102
Janet, Pierre, xxiv, 467
Jaspers, Karl, 283*bn*
Jelgersma, Gerbrandus, 217*bn*, 220, 235
Jelliffe, Smith Ely, xx, 162*bn*, 163, 234, 285, 518, 561

Jensen, Wilhelm, 70, 71*bn*
Jeremias, Alfred, 30, 31*bn*
Jones, Ernest (*passim*), 41*bn*
  on action against Jung, 223, 224
  American Psychoanalytic Society, 41
  analysed by Ferenczi, 187
  analyst of Joan Riviere, 457
  British Psycho-Analytical Society, foundation of, 299
  conflict within Secret Committee, xii
  criticism of Jones, 221
  criticism of Jung, 221, 222
  editor of *Zeitschrift*, 166
  and Freud, x, 276
  and Loë Kann, 155
  London Psychoanalytic Society, 41, 202
    dissolution of, 299
    president of, 197
  and Melanie Klein, 472
  marriage with Morfydd Owen, 347, 349, 386, 387
  president of IPA, 41, 404, 432, 459
  Secret Committee, 184, 290, 327, 420, 453, 525
    conflict within, 464, 467, 468, 471
Jones, Herbert, 187, 428
Jones, Morfydd, *née* Owen, 347, 387
*Jugendstil* [art nouveau], 138
Juliusburger, Otto, 26*bn*, 56, 58, 64, 80, 82, 83, 87, 93, 95–99, 108, 121, 125, 126, 140, 142, 167, 174, 196
Jung, Carl Gustav (*passim*), 7*bn*
  and Abraham, conflict with, x, 37–40, 48–50, 52–56, 60, 70–72
  action against, 221–223, 233, 264
  analyst of Burrow, 292
  analyst of Gross, 47
  analyst of Spielrein, 35, 216, 247
  association studies of, 28
  and Bleuler, conflict with, 37, 60, 123
  complex theory of, 8
  dementia praecox, 55
  on dream interpretation, 412
  discrediting, 454
  editor of *Jahrbuch*, 37, 58, 194, 204–206, 232, 287
    resignation, 194, 203–206, 287
  editor of *Korrespondenzblatt*, 28
  estrangement from Abraham, 37, 38, 40, 46, 49, 53, 54, 70, 71, 160
  estrangement from Freud, 20, 155, 160, 162, 167, 168, 181, 182, 186, 207, 208, 262, 358, 485
  and Hirschfeld, 141
  on Jena, 20
  on "life task", 226, 227
  president of IPA, 109, 112, 139, 193
    resignation, 232, 233
  secession of, from IPA, 258
  Secret Committee, 184
*Jung-Wien* or *Junges Wien* [Young Vienna], 47

Kahlbaum, Karl Ludwig, 65
Kampmann, Niels, 546
Kann, Louise ("Loë"), Dorothea, 116, 155, 187, 427, 428*bn*
Kaplan, Leo, 245, 246*bn*
Kapp, Wolfgang, 419
Károlyi, Count Mihály, 396
Karpas, Morris J., 102, 103, 104*bn*
Kayserling, Count Hermannvon, 541
Keibel, Franz Karl, 174, 175*bn*
Kelman, Sarah, 144
Kempner, Salomea, 455, 456*bn*
Kendrick, Walter, 440, 456
Keplerbund, 242
Kerr, John, 35
Kesselring, Max, 242
Keynes, John Maynard, 456
Keyserling, Hermann Graf von, 541
Kielholz, Arthur, 496, 499*bn*
King, Pearl, 412, 457, 473
*King Lear*, 156
King Ludwig II of Bavaria, xxix
Klein, Melanie, *née* Reizes, xix, xxvii, 181, 412, 440, 457, 471, 472–473*bn*, 497, 499
Klein (Schmideberg), Melitta, 412*bn*, 440
Kleinpaul, Rudolf Alexander, 151*bn*
Klemperer, Paul, 142
kleptomania, 453
Knapp, Alfred, 102
Koerber, Heinrich, 56, 57*bn*, 109, 113, 118,

## INDEX

121, 126, 140, 143, 188, 196, 198, 199, 203, 410
Kohnstamm, Oskar Felix, 153, 154*bn*
   Kohnstamm phenomenon, 154
*Korrespondenzblatt* [Bulletin], 109, 206, 207, 234, 236, 238, 242, 243, 245, 260, 261, 280
   foundation at Second IPA congress, 109
   incorporated into *Zentralblatt*, 139
   Jung, editor of, 28, 109, 168
Kovács, Vilma, 460
Kraepelin, Emil, xx, 1, 94, 118, 119*bn*, 378
Kraus, Friedrich, 134, 135, 143, 201–203, 209, 210, 254, 258, 398, 413, 415, 422, 424, 542
   Abraham's *Habilitation*, 169, 170, 173, 174, 177, 178, 181, 199, 200, 365–369
   head of Charité, 134, 135
   intern clinic, 143
Kraus, Karl, 47, 94
Kraus, Mrs, 518
Krauss, Friedrich Salomon, 188
Kriser, Rudolf, 379
Kronfeld, Arthur, 147*bn*, 157, 544
Kubie, Lawrence, 144
Kuhn, Adalbert, 29, 30*bn*, 31, 42
Kun, Béla, 396
Kunfi, Zsigmond, 398
Kurella, Hans, 196
Kutner (Sokolnicka), Eugenia, 370*bn*
Kutzinski, Arnold, 199, 200*bn*, 203

Laforgue, René, 501, 503*bn*
Lamarck, Jean-Baptiste de, 359*bn*, 360, 361, 363, 364
Lampl, Hans, 457, 461, 462*bn*, 469, 473, 505, 522, 541
Lampl de Groot, Adriana (Jeanne), 457, 541
Landauer, Karl, 285, 286, 362, 474, 497, 534, 537, 540
Langerhans, Paul, 514
Lanzer, Ernst ("Rat Man"), xv, 25, 37, 42, 98, 104, 200, 303, 357
latency period, 3
Lauritzen, Ellen, 274

lay analysis, 525, 558, 561
Leitner, M., xii
Lenz, E., 263
Leonardo (da Vinci), 117
   see also Freud, *Leonardo da Vinci*
Levi-Bianchini, Marco, 283*bn*, 549
Lévy, Kata F., 379*bn*
Lévy, Lajos, 379*bn*, 501
Lévy-Bruhl, Lucien, 519, 520*bn*
Lewandowsky, Felix, 374
Leyden, Ernst von, 34, 35*bn*
libidinal cathexis, 247
libidinal organization, stages of, xxviii
libido:
   concept of, 247
   development of, 136, 386
      pregenital stages of, 300
   oral-cannibalistic organization of, 306
   oral phase of, in melancholia, 308
   pre-genital stages of development of, 386
   regression of, in melancholia, 308
   theory, xxiii
   transference, 483
   withdrawal of, 5, 6, 14, 18, 248, 291
Lichtheim, Anna, 21*bn*
Lieberman, James E., 31, 471, 501
Liebermann, Hans, 197, 198*bn*, 206, 249, 253, 262, 284–288, 333, 334, 338, 342, 344, 356, 376, 381, 386, 388, 392, 396, 418, 426, 496, 499
   analysed by Abraham, 198
   military service in World War I, 296, 391
Liebknecht, Karl, 385
Liepmann, Hugo Karl, 35, 36*bn*, 64, 169, 178
"Little Hans" [Herbert Graf], 42, 45, 46, 76, 200
Lobner, Hans, 84
London Society, 407
Long, Constance, 286
Loofs, F. A., 472, 473*bn*
López-Ballesteros y de Torres, Luis, 504, 505
love-object, identification with, of melancholic, 305
Low, Barbara, 266*bn*

Löwenfeld, Leopold, 196, 197*bn*
Ludendorff, Erich, 278
Ludwig, A., 262, 263*bn*
Luther, Martin, 195
lycanthropy, 305

MacCurdy, John, 234
MacLean, George, 187
Maday, Stefan von, 142
Maeder, Alphonse E., 20*bn*, 41, 50, 83, 87, 94, 168, 195, 205, 227, 234, 242, 245, 248, 251, 259–262
  psychopathology of everyday life, 19
Maetze, Gerhard, 110
Mahler, Gustav, 246
Maier, Hans Wolfgang, 128, 129*bn*, 132, 133, 249
Malinowski, Bronislaw, 460
mania, problem of, 475
manic-depressive states, xxviii, 452
Mann, Heinrich, 398*bn*
Marcinowski, Jaroslaw, 92*bn*, 93, 106, 107, 155, 156, 330
Marcuse, Herbert, 286
Marhold, Carl, 41
"Marsh, Bernard" (Eric Mosbacher), xvii
Martynkewicz, Wolfgang, 362
masculine protest, 133, 177
  and theory of repression, 130
masochism, 3, 20, 54, 78, 80, 157, 214, 215, 304
  genesis of, 214
masturbation, 188
McCormick, Edith Rockefeller, 466*bn*
McCormick, Harold Fowler, 466*bn*
McGuire, Martin, 246, 466
McGuire, William, x, xvii, xxx
Meghnagi, David, 308
Meier, E., 55
Meisel, Perry, 440, 456
Meisel-Hess, Grete, 150*bn*
melancholia, xxix, 152, 302, 308–312, 453, 454, 471
  Freud's theory of, 303–305
  mania after, 455, 457
melancholic delusions, 68
melancholic depression, 303
melancholic regression, 453

Mendel, Kurt, 128, 129*bn*
Meng, Heinrich, xv, 286, 362, 474
Mensendieck, Otto, 264*bn*
metapsychology, 12
Meyer, Adolf F., 370, 456
Meyer, Konrad Ferdinand, 64, 66
Michaëlis, Karin, 124, 125*bn*
Middle Group, British, 457
Moellenhoff, Fritz, 142
Moll, Albert, 46*bn*, 47, 53, 65, 66, 77, 84, 89, 90, 92, 93, 103, 196, 197, 542
Monistenbund, 242, 431
Morel, A., 1
Morgenstern, Christian, 147*bn*
Morichau-Beauchant, Pierre Ernest René, 145, 146
Mosbacher, Eric ("Bernard Marsh"), ix, xvii
Moser, Alexander, 456
mourning, xxviii, 303, 454
mouth eroticism, 179
Mühlleitner, Elke, 53, 84, 94, 125, 286, 369, 375, 412, 431, 456, 457, 462, 474, 501, 503
Müller-Braunschweig, Carl, 110*bn*
Munich Psychoanalytic Society, *passim*
Murray, Henry A., 70
Musatti, Cesare, 478
myth, 29, 34, 36, 42, 45, 51
  birth of the hero, 30, 63, 72
  Descent of Fire, 29
  flood, 49, 62, 63, 90
  Prometheus, 42
  Rank on, 408
  significance of 7, 498, 531
  Soma, 42

Nachmannsohn, Max, 298
Nacht, Sacha, 427
*Nachträglichkeit*, 3, 4
Näcke, Paul, 121*bn*
narcissism, 121, 195, 197, 198, 218, 467
narcissistic identification, dissolving of object-cathexes in, 305
narcissistic neuroses, repression in, 291
National Psychological Association for Psychoanalysis, 144
neo-analysis, 144
Nestroy, Johann Nepomuk, 488*bn*

# INDEX

Neumann Company, and "film affair", 565
neurosis(es), 18, 107, 118, 128, 148, 156, 160, 174, 179, 187, 192, 193, 207, 217, 467, 534, 544
  accident, 53
  aetiology of, 2, 4
  anxiety, 25–27, 87
  infantile, 396
  obsessional, xxviii, 5, 16–18, 24, 81, 126, 127, 262, 286, 306, 309, 310, 362, 382, 383, 399, 420, 432, 477, 496
  vs. psychosis, xxiv
  sexual, 81
    aetiology of, 487
  in sexual latency period, 3
  symptomatology of, 2
  theory of, 291, 425
  traumatic, 56, 81, 82, 85, 297, 322, 327, 336
neurotic exogamy, 198
neurotic regression, 482
neurotic symptoms, cure of, film on, 544
Newton, Caroline, 500, 501bn, 538, 558
New York Psychoanalytic Society, 104, 130, 135, 139, 144, 152, 434, 461
Nietzsche, Friedrich, 150, 362
number seven, symbolic meaning of, xii, 510–512, 516, 519, 526, 528, 531, 532
Nunberg, Hermann (later Herman), xx, 401, 433bn, 434

Oberholzer, Emil, 208, 209bn, 392, 497, 533
Oberholzer, Mira, 392, 496, 498
object:
  cathexis(es)
    dissolution of, in narcissistic identification, 305
    unconscious, abandonment of, 309
  -love:
    development of, 467
    stages of, 472
obsession, xxviii, xxix, 21, 24–25
obsessional brooding, 368
obsessional counting, 383
obsessional neurosis(es), xxviii, 5, 16, 17, 18, 24, 81, 126, 127, 262, 286, 306, 309, 310, 362, 382, 383, 399, 420, 432, 477, 496
obsessional symptoms, 22
obsessional thinking, 17
Oedipus complex, 146, 217, 219, 374, 461, 464, 481, 487, 516
  female, 527, 531
Oedipus dreams, 176
Oedipus phenomena in infancy, 232
omnipotence:
  of excreta, 411
  of thought, 304, 361
Ophuijsen, Johan H. W. van, xx, 167, 168bn, 263, 334, 339, 343, 344, 349, 350, 358, 409, 426, 429, 432, 459, 460, 464, 466, 469, 541, 543, 557, 560
Oppenheim, David Ernst, 97, 98bn, 142
Oppenheim, Hermann, 17, 20bn, 22, 26, 35, 46–49, 52, 64, 65, 69, 75, 81–85, 87, 90, 93, 95, 108, 116–119, 148, 162, 337
Oppenheim, Martha, 20
"organ inferiority" [*Organminderwertigkeit*], 180
*Originäre* [idiopathics], 5
Orska, Frau, 522, 526
Ossipow, Nikolai Jewgrafowitsch, xx, 111bn
Owen (Jones), Morfydd, 347, 387
Oxford Movement, 20

Pálos, Gizella, 350, 356
paranoia, 1, 7, 120–123, 131, 135, 136, 157, 176, 247, 286, 348, 426, 474
paranoia querulans, 42, 43, 396, 404
Paris, judgement of, 156
Payne, Sylvia, 457
persecution mania, 148
perversion, 128
Pfister, Oskar, 89bn, 114, 115, 117, 186, 208, 249, 256, 257, 258, 259, 260, 261, 263, 283, 298, 322, 347, 392, 496, 521, 533, 534
  Freud correspondence, ix, xiv
phantasies:
  hysterical, 29
  rescue, 444

phobia, railway, 211
Piaget, Jean, 35
Pichler, Hans, 474*bn*, 517, 540, 550
Pick, Arnold, 369, 370*bn*
Pick, Yerta, 94
Placzek, Siegfried, 336, 337*bn*, 518, 519
Plato, 266, 298
Plautus, 35
pleasure principle, 132
poison-addiction, 526
Polgar, Alfred, 46*bn*, 47
Pollak, Max, 226, 227*bn*
Polon, Albert, 455, 456*bn*
Pomer, Sydney L., 50
Pötzl, Otto, 368, 369*bn*, 370, 376, 377, 394, 395
Powers, Margaret, 458*bn*
premature ejaculation, 164
Prince, Morton, 70*bn*, 71, 75, 102, 132, 467
Princip, Gavrilo, 252
projection, 286
Protze, H., 345, 348, 350
pseudologia, 467
 phantastica, 454
psychic apparatus, models of, 12
*Psychoanalytic Review*, 285
Psychoanalytic Society, 142
Psychoanalytic Society of Paris, 503
psychosexual development, xxix
psychosis:
 circular, 127
 vs. neurosis, xxiv
Putnam, James Jackson, 95, 101, 102*bn*, 115, 116, 122, 123, 129, 130–132, 139, 151, 179, 181, 241, 243, 244, 260, 261, 313, 314, 330, 331, 333, 393
Pythagoras, 179

Quinn, Susan, 110, 144, 427

Radó, Sándor, xix, 460, 461*bn*, 470, 474, 476, 521, 522, 563, 564
 editor of Verlag, 521
Raigorodsky (Eitingon), Mirra Jacovleina, 356
railway phobia, 211

Raimann, Emil, 117, 119*bn*
Rank, Beata ("Tola"), *née* Mincer (Münzer), 387
Rank, Helene, 401*bn*
Rank, Otto (*passim*), 31*bn*
 analyst of Caroline Newton, 501
 controversy, xiv
 editor of *Imago*, 31, 141, 146
 director of Verlag, resignation, 521
 editor of Verlag, 391, 404
 editor of *Zeitschrift*, 31, 166, 167
 resignation from, 521
 and Freud:
  correspondence, xvii
  estrangement from, 387, 517
 military service in World War I, 313
 on myths, 30, 36, 408
 secretary of Vienna Society, 524
 Secret Committee, 184, 290, 327, 406, 420, 453, 471
  conflict within, xii, 464
 trauma of birth, 481, 487
  foundation and core of unconscious, 483
Rappen, Ulrich, 187
"Rat Man" (Ernst Lanzer), xv, 25, 37, 42, 98, 104, 200, 303, 357
reaction formations, 146
Régis, Emmanuel, 145, 146, 261
regression, neurotic, and birth process, 482
Reich, G., 557, 560
Reichmayr, Johannes, 546, 557
Reik, Theodor (*passim*), 144*bn*
 *Imago* prize, 386
 librarian, Vienna Society, 524
 military service in World War I, 330, 340, 345, 348, 349, 358, 370
Reiss, Erich, 168*bn*
Reitler, Rudolf, 283*bn*
Reizes (Klein), Melanie, xix, xxvii, 181, 412, 440, 457, 471, 472–473*bn*, 497, 499
Renterghem, Albert Willem van, 217*bn*, 356, 358, 392
repetition:
 compulsion, 567
 role of in analysis, 480

repression, 3, 29, 83, 291, 300
  film on, 544
  theory of, 130
    and masculine protest, 130
rescue phantasies, 444, 447
resistance(s), 11, 17, 104, 155, 186, 380
  film on, 544
Rey de Castro, Alvaro, 416
Rickman, John, 455, 456*bn*
Rie, Margarethe, 401, 434
Rie, Oskar, 401, 434
Ries, Paul, xiii, 546, 554, 557
Riklin, Franz, xx, 27, 28*bn*, 29, 32, 34, 50, 106, 107, 139, 168, 170, 240–243, 260–264, 343, 456
  editor of *Korrespondenzblatt*, 28
  secretary of IPA, 109, 238
Rilke, Rainer Maria, 150
Rioch, Janet, 144
Riviere, Joan, 455, 457*bn*, 524
Roazen, Paul, 166, 202, 282, 369, 371, 375, 379, 387, 404, 440, 456, 461, 470, 474
Robbins, Bernard, 144
Róheim, Géza, 460*bn*, 524, 557, 560
Rohleder, Hermann, 188*bn*
Rolland, Romain, 466
Romm, May, xvii, 73, 474
Rorschach, Hermann, xx
  Rorschach tests, 499
Rosenbach (Deutsch), Helene, xix, 181, 462, 470*bn*, 473, 474, 496, 499, 516, 524, 528, 181, 462, 473, 474, 496, 499, 516, 524, 528
Rosenstein, Gaston, 147
Rosenthal, Tatiana, xx, 124, 125, 126, 129
Rosenzweig, Saul, 77, 96, 102
Rothe, Hans-Joachim, 286
Roudinesco, Elisabeth, 503
Russian Association, 499

Saaler, Bruno, 229, 230*bn*
Sachs, Hanns (*passim*), 142*bn*
  alienation from Freud, 450, 480
  analyst of Clara Happel-Pincus, 474
  analyst of Hans Lampl, 462
  analyst of Karen Horney, 143
  criticism of Rank's theory, 484
  editor of *Imago*, 141, 146, 346, 349, 351, 355, 521, 563
  editor of *Zeitschrift*, 346, 363
  estrangement from Freud, 450
  "film affair", xiii, 554–561, 564, 565, 567
  military service in World War I, 286, 288, 313, 318, 319, 330
  Secret Committee, 184, 290, 327, 420, 453
    conflict within, xii
Sadger, Isidor, 53*bn*, 64, 66, 106, 147, 216, 217, 225, 228, 232, 234, 246, 247, 249, 250, 283, 287, 290
sadism, 303–305, 356, 472
Salten, Felix, 47
Sarasin, Philipp, 455, 456*bn*, 516
Sargant-Florence (Strachey), Alix, 455, 456*bn*, 510, 514, 519
Schächter, Miksa, 182
Schilder, Paul, 374, 375*bn*
Schiller, Friedrich von, 189, 200, 273
schizophrenia, xxiv, xxviii, 1, 7
  and paranoia, xxx
Schmid, Hans, 298
Schmid, Z., 298
Schmideberg, Melitta, *née* Klein, 412*bn*, 440
Schmideberg, Walter, 411, 412*bn*, 415, 432
Schnee, Adolf, 372, 373, 397
Schnitzler, Arthur, 47
Schönberg, Ignaz, 126
Schopenhauer, Arthur, 126, 346
Schreber, Daniel Paul, xx, 120, 122, 123*bn*, 153, 276, 426
  case, Freud's, 123, 136, 139, 148, 154, 176, 200, 247, 399
Schubert, Franz, 314
Schultz, Johannes Heinrich, 307, 308*bn*, 370, 544
Schur, Max, xvii, 474
Schwab-Paneth, Sophie, 21*bn*
Schwarzacher, Caroline, xxxiii
scoptophilia, 77, 179, 182, 198, 214, 216, 220, 248
screen memory, 17, 171

Secret Committee, 50, 142, 184, 212, 267, 290, 405, 406, 420, 428, 432, 435, 440, 441, 444, 447
  conflict within, xii, 464, 467, 468, 471, 480–484, 485–486, 494, 520
  dissolution of, 524
  membership of, 290, 327, 524
  photograph of, 453
  revival of, 523–524, 525, 526, 528
  ring of members, 412
seduction theory, Freud's, 4
Segantini, Giovanni, 81, 82*bn*, 83, 85, 86, 97, 98, 101, 103, 104, 108, 112, 113, 116, 117, 120, 122, 124–126, 129, 132, 136–138, 143, 147, 155, 504, 508
Segantini, Mario, 129
Seidler, Frau, 158
Seif, Leonhard, xxi, 168*bn*, 234, 245, 248, 251, 260–262
Seitz, Karl, 503
Selesnick, Sheldon T., 120
senile dementia, 178, 182
Servaes, Franz Theodor Hubert, 137, 138*bn*
sexual aetiology, 372
"sexual displacement" [*Sexualverlegung*], 24
sexuality, theory of, 527
sexual neurosis, 81
sexual trauma, 2, 3, 4, 8, 10, 57, 70, 216
  childhood, 2–4, 13
  and unconscious intention, 3
*Sexualverlegung* ["sexual displacement"], 24
Shakespeare, William, 344
  *The Merchant of Venice*, 156
Shamdasani, Sonu, xvi, xxx
sibling rivalry, 107
*Sicherung*, 213
Sidis, Boris, 101, 102*bn*
  Sidis Institute for Nervous and Mental Disorders, Portsmouth, New Hampshire, 102
Silberer, Herbert, 168*bn*, 430, 431
Silberstein, Eduard, x
Silverberg, William V., 144
Simmel, Ernst, 362, 372*bn*, 373–377, 383, 386, 387, 391–397, 403, 405, 410–415
  analysed by Abraham, 396, 402, 410
Skliar, N., 81, 82*bn*
Società Psicoanalitica Italiana, 283
Société Psychanalytique de Paris, 370
Society for Free Psychoanalytic Investigation, 142
Society for Psychoanalytic Research, Leipzig, 474
Sokolnicka, Eugenia, *née* Kutner, xxi, 370, 503
Soma, 58
  myth, 42, 43
  potion, 46
Spielrein, Sabina, xxi, 35*bn*, 177, 216, 247, 294
Spitteler, Carl, 146, 553*bn*
Stärcke, August, 194*bn*, 237, 330, 331, 350, 370
Stärcke, Johan, 349, 350
starvation, fear of, 305
Stegmann, Arnold Georg, 78, 79*bn*, 81, 82, 112, 113, 124, 126, 134, 143, 184, 186, 284, 296
  killed in action in World War I, 318
Stegmann, Margarete, 185, 186, 262
Stein, Philipp (Fülöp), xxi, 72, 73*bn*, 75
Steiner, Riccardo, 412, 457, 473
Steinthal, Hajim (Heymann), 34, 35*bn*
Stekel, Wilhelm (*passim*), 28*bn*
  on anxiety hysteria, 27
  editor of *Eros and Psyche*, 430
  editor of *Zentralblatt*, 153, 166, 167, 175
  and Freud, 28
    alienation from, 165–170
  and Tausk, 166
  vice-president of Vienna Society, resignation from, 130, 131
Stephen, Adrian, 456
Stephen, Karin, 456
Stephen (Woolf), Virginia, 456
Stern, William, 85*bn*
Stevens, Miss, 179, 181
Stinnes, Hugo, 427
Stöcker, Helene, 173*bn*, 174, 175
Stockmayer, Wolf, xxi, 93, 94*bn*, 184, 203, 206, 216, 249, 262, 281

INDEX

Storfer, Adolf (after 1938, Albert) Josef, 122*bn*, 129, 464, 505, 512, 521, 554–567
 "film affair", xiii
Strachey, Alix, *née* Sargant-Florence, Alix, 455, 456*bn*, 510, 514, 519
Strachey, James, xv, 4, 456*bn*, 457
 –Alix Strachey correspondence, xv
Strachey, Lytton, 456
Strasser, Artur, 110
Strauss, Cyrill, 459
Strohmayer, Wilhelm, 76, 77*bn*, 78, 142
Stromme, Johannes Irgens, xxi
structural model, xxix
Stuchlík, Jaroslaw, xxi
Stucken, Eduard, 30, 31*bn*
Stürgkh, Karl Graf, 350
sublimation, 146, 226, 286
Sullivan, Harry Stack, 144
Svevo, Italo, 282
Swales, Peter J., 21
Swerdloff, Bluma, 461
Swiss Psychoanalytical Society, 499
Swoboda, Hermann, 135
Sydney-Turner, Saxon, 456
synaesthesias, 186
system *Cs.*, 291
system *Ucs.*, 291
Székely-Kovács, Olga, 474

Tandler, Julius, 501, 503*bn*, 525
Tannenbaum, Samuel, 430*bn*
Tansley, Sir Arthur George, 455, 457, 489, 500
Tausk, Victor, 166*bn*, 189, 202, 247, 283, 336, 358–360, 371, 374–376, 394, 395, 400, 402, 413, 416
Tauss, Dr, 460
Thomas, Ambroise, 314
Thompson, Clara, 144
Tihanyi, Lajos, 462
time–space problem, 247, 286
Timms, Edward, 94
Titus Flavius Vespasianus, 194
totem animals, 140
transference, 103, 152, 266, 362, 459, 482
 infantile, 88, 99
 libido, 483
 maternal, 483
 love, 266
 negative, 362
 premature making conscious of, 482
 onto mother, 78
 onto non-human objects, 81
 neuroses, 286, 291
 repression in, 291
transformations of libido, 161
trauma(s):
 birth, 487
 multiplicity of, 2
traumatic neurosis(es), 56, 81, 82, 85, 297, 322, 327, 336
Tuchman, Barbara W., 270
Tutankhamen, Pharaoh, 461, 465, 466

*Ucs.* (Unconscious), 291, 300, 324
 psychology of, 353
University Psychoanalytic Clinic, Budapest, 403
unpleasure released by memories [*Erinnerungsunlust*], 3
Urbantschitsch (after 1943, Urban), Rudolf von, 94, 425, 428, 429, 524, 525*bn*,
urethral erotism, and ambition, 510
*Urverstimmung*, 473

vaginism, 531
van der Linden, Miss, 464
van Eeden, Frederik Willem, 267*bn*, 296
van Emden, Jan E. G., 189*bn*, 272, 273, 276, 280, 285, 290, 293, 318, 330, 343, 358, 384, 398, 409, 432, 496, 501, 516, 517, 522
Veneziani Svevo, Livia, 281, 282*bn*, 283, 284
Verlag:
 Anna Freud working in, 406
 editorial office moved to Berlin, 521
 film controversy, 556
 financing of, 404, 409, 464, 520, 544, 559, 561
 foundation of, 390, 391
  financed by von Freund, 379
 Radó's work in, 521

Verlag (*continued*):
  Rank director of, 31, 464
    resignation of, 521
  Reik's work in, 434
  Storfer director of, 521
    resignation of, 559, 565, 566
Vermorel, Henri, 466
Vermorel, Madelaine, 466
Vienna Psychoanalytic Outpatient
    Clinic, 187
Vienna Psychoanalytic Society (*passim*)
  Adler chairman of, 109
    resignation of, 130, 132
  ambulatorium, 430
  decline of, 405
  Federn vice-president of, 152
  Freud president of, 131, 515
  Reik secretary of, 144
  Stekel vice-president of, resignation
    of, 130
  training committee of, 433
  Training Institute of, 181
Vierkandt, Alfred, 90, 91*bn*, 92
Virgil, 273
Volkhardt, Professor, 429

Wagner-Jauregg, Julius von, 369, 375,
    433*bn*, 470
Waldeyer, Heinrich Wilhelm Gottfried
    von, 174, 175*bn*, 337
Walser, Hans H., 456
Wanke, Georg, 182, 183*bn*
Warda, Wolfgang, 48, 49*bn*, 50, 112, 118,
    142
war neurosis(es), 351, 372, 379, 391, 392,
    405, 406
Weber, Kaspar, 456
Wednesday (Psychological) Society, 13,
    15, 28, 31, 41, 50, 53, 98, 104, 152,
    186, 283, 525
Weiss, Edoardo, 282, 283, 477, 478*bn*
  Freud correspondence, ix
Weiss, Karl, 83, 84*bn*, 336, 337
White, William A., 150, 162, 234, 285,
    518
  William White Institute, New York
    City, 144
Whitrow, Magda, 433

Wiene, Robert, 565
Wilhelm II Hohenzollern, 385, 398
Will, Herbert, 362
William White Institute, New York City,
    144
Wilmanns, Karl, 118, 119*bn*
Wilmers, Mary-Kay, 397
Wilson, Thomas Woodrow, 391, 392*bn*
Winckler, Hugo, 30, 31*bn*, 33
wish-fulfilment, 29, 108, 341
withdrawal of libido, 5, 18, 248, 291
Wittels, Fritz, 53, 93, 94*bn*
Wittenberger, Gerhard, 184, 327
"Wolf Man", 177, 280, 287, 375, 397, 527
Wolter, Charlotte, 47*bn*
Woolf, Leonard, 456
Woolf, Virginia, *née* Stephen, 456
Wulff, Mosche, 80, 82*bn*, 85, 95, 96, 103,
    112, 496

Young, G. Alexander, xxi

*Zeitschrift*, 207, 280, 404
  edited by Abraham, 389
  edited by Hitschmann, 389
  edited by Rank, 31
  Heller publisher of, 28
*Zeitschrift für Sexualwissenschaft*, 230
*Zentralblatt*, 151, 152
Ziehen, Theodor, 64, 65*bn*, 68, 69, 96, 99,
    103, 115, 127, 128, 131, 132, 143,
    162, 168, 337
  editor of *Monatsschrift*, 153
Zilboorg, Gregory, 144
Zinzendorf, Graf Ludwig von, 114,
    115*bn*
Zulliger, Hans, 89, 496, 499*bn*
Zurich Psychoanalytic Society, 20
  Binswanger president of, 59, 114, 118
  conflict with Freud and Vienna
    Society, 49–50, 53–56, 113, 114,
    159, 160, 168–169, 183, 184, 192,
    204, 206, 208, 232, 241, 242, 245,
    256, 260–262, 264, 279
Zutt, Dr, 429
Zweig, Arnold, –Freud correspondence,
    ix
Zweig, Walter, 239*bn*